East Asia,

The Great Tradition

Edwin O. Reischauer · *John K. Fairbank*

HARVARD UNIVERSITY

HOUGHTON MIFFLIN COMPANY · BOSTON

26461

To

Haru and Wilma

Acknowledgments

THIS BOOK HAS GROWN out of our collaboration in a lecture course initiated in 1939 and offered since 1947 under the auspices of the Harvard Program in General Education. During these years we have profited from each other's stimulus and criticism and from the reactions of our students. The responsibility for chapters in this volume reflects the division of lecturing assignments in the course. Chapters 2 through 6 and 10 through 13 are largely the work of E. O. Reischauer, Chapters 7 through 9 that of J. K. Fairbank. Each of us, however, owes the other a heavy debt for aid in his own chapters. This volume therefore is much more a joint undertaking than the division of responsibility for the chapters might suggest.

Even with this division of responsibility, the subject covered is so broad that we have had to depend heavily on the advice and aid of others. Our greatest debt of course is the usually unacknowledged one to the host of scholars and writers who have preceded us in discovering the facts and interpreting the meaning of the various aspects of East Asian history. We hope that our colleagues in all parts of the world who recognize in this volume facts or interpretations they themselves have brought to public attention will forgive the lack of footnote references.

We are especially indebted to Mrs. Wilma C. Fairbank for helping to organize the illustrative materials in this volume and to the three men whose work made possible the writing of Chapter 10 on Korea. Because of the lack of adequate general studies of this phase of East Asian history, we were unusually dependent on the book by Hatada Takashi entitled *Chōsen shi* and on the very careful revision of our draft by Professor Yi Pyeng-do of Seoul National University and Dr. Edward W. Wagner of Harvard University.

Portions of the rest of the volume were read by various colleagues and friends, each of whom provided valuable corrections and comments. Although it would be impossible to cite the particular sections of the manuscript each one covered and the specific corrections he made, we are deeply grateful to all of these persons for their generous and painstaking aid, which has given to the volume a much higher degree of accuracy and a much sounder balance than it otherwise would have had. Among those

Acknowledgments

who gave the greatest help are: Professor Derk Bodde of the University of Pennsylvania, Mr. Peter Chen, Dr. Kee-il Choi, Professor Francis W. Cleaves of Harvard University, Professor Albert Craig of Harvard University, Professor Herrlee Glessner Creel of the University of Chicago, Mr. Lloyd Eastman, Dr. David Farquhar of the University of Maryland, Professor L. Carrington Goodrich of Columbia University, Professor John W. Hall of the University of Michigan, Professor David Hawkes of Oxford University, Professor Arnold Herstand of Colgate University, Professor Howard S. Hibbett of Harvard University, Professor Charles O. Hucker of the University of Arizona, Professor Mitsusada Inouye of Tokyo University, Professor Edward A. Kracke, Jr., of the University of Chicago, Professor Frederick W. Mote of Princeton University, Professor John C. Pelzel of Harvard University, Dr. A. K. Reischauer, Professor H. F. Schurmann of the University of California, Professor Thomas C. Smith of Stanford University, and Professor Lien-sheng Yang of Harvard University. We are also deeply indebted to Mrs. Norma Farquhar for the many helpful suggestions she made in the course of typing and retyping the manuscript and for the painstaking care with which she has compiled the index.

E. O. R.
J. K. F.

Cambridge, Massachusetts

Contents

ix

CHAPTER FOUR

The First Chinese Empire:
The Ch'in and Han Dynasties 85

Ch'in Creates the Empire · Han Receives the Mandate · The
Consolidation of Han Rule · The Apogee of Han Power · The
Triumph of Confucianism · Cultural Growth During the Han ·
Ssu-ma Ch'ien and Historical Scholarship · The Dynastic Cycle:
Personal Factors · The Dynastic Cycle: Economic and Adminis-
trative Factors · The Later Han Dynasty · The End of the
First Chinese Empire

CHAPTER FIVE

The "Barbarian" Challenge
and the Regeneration of the Empire 134

The Nature of the Challenge · The Upsurge of Taoism · Indian
Buddhism · The Coming of Buddhism to China · The "Barbarians" and the Chinese Imperial Ideal · Sui and T'ang Reconstitute the Empire · The Revival of Centralized Government:
Finances · The Revival of Centralized Government: The Bureaucracy · T'ang Government · The Absorption of Buddhism
· The Growth of Chinese Culture

CHAPTER SIX

The Late T'ang and Sung:
The Golden Age of Chinese Culture 183

The Nature of the Period · Collapse and Reform in the Middle
T'ang · The Political Transition from the T'ang to the Sung ·
Sung Government · Decline and Reform in the Middle Sung ·
The Southern Sung · The "Commercial Revolution" · The
Growth of Foreign Trade · The Development of an Advanced

Money Economy · The Early Modern Society of China · The Development of the Arts · Printing and Scholarship · The Development of Literature · Neo-Confucianism · Cultural Stability

"Barbarian" Participation in the Chinese State · The Society of the Steppe · The Khitan Empire · The Liao Dynasty · The Chin Dynasty of the Jürched · The Mongols · The Career of Chinggis Khan · The Mongol Empire · Mongol Rule in China · Life under the Yüan Dynasty · The First Direct Contact with the West · Chinese Culture under the Mongols

Chinese "Culturalism" · The Founding of the Ming · The Ming Administration · The Examination System and Scholarship · The "Gentry" Class · The Ming Despotism · The Tribute System and Japan · The Maritime Expeditions · The Mongol Problem · Troubles with Japan · Economic Growth: The Single Whip Reform · The Collapse of the Ming Government

The Rise of the Manchu Tribes · The Creation of a Sinicized Manchu State · The Manchu Conquest · The Ch'ing Empire in Central Asia · The Incorporation of Tibet in the Empire · The

Contents

Preservation of Manchu Power · Ch'ing Rule in China · The Unity of State and Culture · Intellectual Development: The School of "Empirical Research" · The Official Domination of Learning · Chinese Culture in the Ming and Ch'ing Periods · The Beginning of Dynastic Decline

CHAPTER TEN

Traditional Korea:
A Variant of the Chinese Cultural Pattern   394

The Place of Korea in East Asian Civilization · The Beginnings of Korean History · The Three Kingdoms · Silla Rules a Unified Korea · The Koryŏ Dynasty · Internal Decline and Foreign Pressures in the Later Koryŏ Period · The Social and Political Organization of the Yi Dynasty · The Culture of Yi-Dynasty Korea · Factionalism Disrupts the Yi Government · Foreign Invasions · The Later Years of Yi Rule

CHAPTER ELEVEN

Early Japan:
The Absorption of Chinese Civilization   450

The Geographical Foundations of Japanese History · The Origins of the Japanese and Their Culture · The Formation of the Japanese State · The *Uji* System · The Adoption of the Chinese Pattern · The Government of the Nara Period · Buddhist Art and Philosophy · Chinese Writing and Scholarship · The Modification of Chinese Institutions · The Fujiwara Period · The Naturalization of Buddhism and Art · The Development of a Japanese Writing System and Literature

Contents

CHAPTER TWELVE

Feudal Japan:
A Departure from the Chinese Pattern 519

The Rise of a Semi-Feudal Society · The Triumph of the Provincial Military Class · The Early Feudal System · The Kamakura Shogunate · Early Feudal Culture · The Buddhist Revival of the Kamakura Period · The Collapse of the Kamakura System · The Ashikaga Shogunate · Economic Growth in Feudal Japan · The Zen Culture of the Ashikaga Period · Art, Literature and Thought · The Late Ashikaga Period · Signs of Disintegration of the Feudal System

CHAPTER THIRTEEN

Tokugawa Japan:
A Centralized Feudal State 579

Political Centralization and Foreign Stimuli · Nobunaga and Hideyoshi Reunify the Country · Ieyasu Founds the Tokugawa Shogunate · The Return to Isolation · The Samurai and Daimyo System · Tokugawa Government · The Ethical System · The Dynastic Cycle in Tokugawa Japan · Economic Growth: Agriculture and the Peasantry · Economic Growth: Urbanization and a Money Economy · Economic Growth: Trade and Industry · The New Urban Culture · Tokugawa Literature · Tokugawa Art · Confucian Philosophy · Other Intellectual Trends

CHAPTER FOURTEEN

East Asia on the Eve of Modernization 669

Maps and Charts

East Asia

The Great Tradition

1

The Setting of East Asian History

THE OBJECTIVES OF THIS STUDY

When Europeans traveled far to the east to reach Cathay, Japan and the Indies, they naturally gave those distant regions the general name "Far East." Americans who reached China, Japan and Southeast Asia by sail and steam across the Pacific could, with equal logic, have called that area the "Far West." For the people who live in that part of the world, however, it is neither "East" nor "West" and certainly not "Far." A more generally acceptable term for the area is "East Asia," which is geographically more precise and does not imply the outdated notion that Europe is the center of the civilized world.

The Extent of East Asia. East Asia can be defined in three ways: in geographical terms as the area east of the great mountain and desert barrier that bisects Asia; in racial terms as the habitat of Mongoloid man (except for the Eskimo and American Indian branches of that race); and in cultural terms as the domain of what we call East Asian civilization. In this book the last definition is naturally the most important. We concentrate on the histories of China, Japan, Korea and, to a lesser extent, Vietnam, the areas that derived much of their higher culture and their primary system of writing from ancient China.

Two other large areas that are, for the most part, east of the great barrier and basically Mongoloid in population also enter the story in a secondary way. One is Central Asia, particularly Mongolia, Sinkiang (Chinese Turkestan) and Tibet. The nomadic inhabitants of these

3

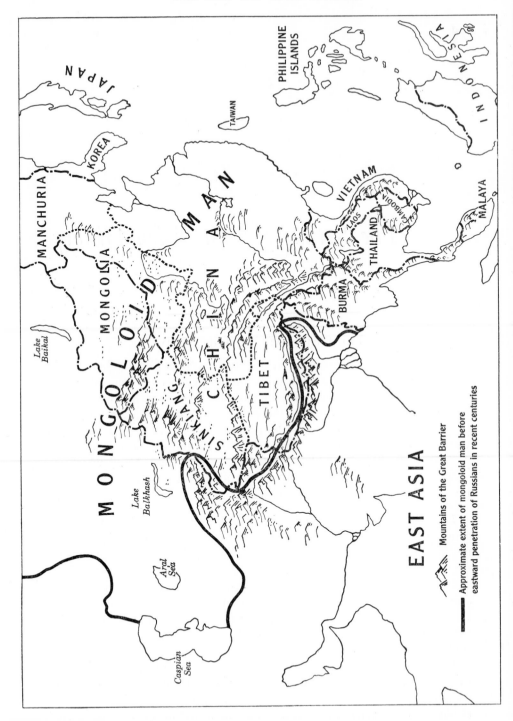

EAST ASIA

〜〜〜〜 Mountains of the Great Barrier

▬▬▬▬ Approximate extent of mongoloid man before
eastward penetration of Russians in recent centuries

regions have had their histories interwoven with that of China through commerce, war and conquest. The other area is Southeast Asia, comprising in addition to Vietnam the lands of Burma, Siam (Thailand), Cambodia, Laos, Malaya, Indonesia and the Philippines. The higher cultures of much of Southeast Asia stemmed more from India than from China, and Islam and Christianity later helped make this area still more distinctive from the countries to the north. In recent centuries, however, this region too has become increasingly linked with the rest of East Asia, economically, culturally and strategically.

For Americans the most important facts about East Asia are, first, its vast size, particularly in population; second, its growing power; and third, the cultural gap that lies between East and West.

In population, ancient China was at least the equal of the Roman Empire. Today China holds almost one quarter of the human race — more than 600 million people. The single Indonesian island of Java, roughly the size of New York State, has over 40 millions. There are more than 90 million Japanese living in a country that is smaller than California. The people of East Asia together constitute almost a third of mankind.

Until recent times these dense populations were of little immediate importance to the West. It is true that trade with East Asia has had a steadily growing significance for the European economy ever since the Roman era, and a slow trickle of inventions from China has also influenced Europe's development. Only in the last few decades, however, have we come to realize that in a rapidly shrinking world the third of humanity that lives in East Asia directly affects our own lives and the future of our civilization. Two wars, the first against the Japanese, the second against the North Koreans and Chinese, made the point quite clear to the American public.

These wars revealed a disquieting fact. The peoples of East Asia had risen more rapidly in power during the past century than had we or the other Western nations. In 1854 a small squadron of American warships was able to force the Japanese against their will to open their ports; ninety years later it took the fully mobilized power of the whole American nation to make Japan give up its imperialistic course. In the nineteenth century Western troops and gunboats could occupy any port in China with impunity; in 1950 the Chinese were able to fight the best of American ground forces to a bloody standstill in Korea. In a world that is deeply divided by conflicting ideologies and precariously balanced between hostile military camps the rising power of the massed populations of East Asia may some day be decisive.

The Need for Understanding. Without understanding between ourselves and the peoples of East Asia we cannot hope for harmonious relations and fruitful cooperation; in fact, we may face ultimate disaster. But understanding can be based only on knowledge, and a sound knowledge of East Asia is not easily achieved. The cultural gap is too great.

Until recent times we and the East Asians lived virtually in different worlds. Even within Asia the contacts between China and the Hindu civilization of India and the Islamic civilization of West Asia and North Africa were not great. Languages, social customs, ethical values and historical traditions varied greatly between East Asia, India, the Islamic world and the West.

Rapidly growing contacts during the past century among all these areas have tended to lessen the cultural gap, but other factors have widened the gulf between us and the non-Western world. There has been a great upsurge of national consciousness and patriotic pride among the masses of people in the countries of Asia. A more critical attitude and sometimes animosity toward the West have been the natural result, and rapid changes in relations between the West and Asia have inevitably followed.

The gap between East and West has also been widened by a growing discrepancy in material standards of living. Nowhere is the contrast sharper than between Americans and the peoples of Asia. In part because of accidents of history and geography, we enjoy a far more favorable balance between population and natural resources than do they. As a result we live on an economic plane that appears unattainable by them under existing conditions. This economic gap perpetuates and sometimes heightens the difference between our respective attitudes and ways of life.

On the other hand, there are many signs in East Asia, as elsewhere in the world, of the growth of what may be called a common world culture. In every phase of life, whether it be transportation facilities, political systems, or even ethical ideas and family relations, we and the peoples of East Asia today have much more in common than we did a century ago.

Ultimately the growth of this common world culture and of mutual interests may greatly facilitate harmonious understanding among the various parts of the world. In the meantime, however, the process has probably made understanding more difficult. A mixing of things that are familiar to us with things that are quite foreign tends to confuse rather than enlighten. Moreover, cultural changes in East Asia, as in the rest of the world, have been accompanied by violent upheavals of all sorts. If China had actually been "unchanging," we would find it much easier to understand, no matter how different its culture from that of the West. Instead, China has been changing rapidly and explosively. Our task of focusing clearly on this alien culture is compounded by its rapid motion.

The wars we have fought in East Asia illustrate the rapidity of change and also the complexity of the problem we face. In World War II we fought Japan partly in defense of China; five years later in Korea we fought China partly to defend Japan. It is scarcely surprising that these changes are confusing.

This situation, however, makes it all the more imperative for us to come to understand East Asia better than we do. This is a difficult and never-ending task which calls for hard work and clear thinking. As a minimum, we must achieve between ourselves and the peoples of East Asia mutual respect, a willingness to cooperate, and a certain meeting of minds.

Power politics and the quest for peace are by no means the only considerations prompting us to learn more about East Asia. There are other important dimensions to our study in the fields of the humanities and the social sciences. For the humanist interested in art, literature, philosophy and religion, the ancient societies of China, Japan and Korea hold the mirror up to our own Western culture. They show us our own peculiarities by demonstrating alternative systems of value and belief, different traditions of aesthetic experience, and different forms of literary expression. Already we have received important influences from the literature and philosophy of China and Japan and still more from their arts. The latter are evident not only in our museums, but also in American architecture, landscape gardening, and interior decoration. The possibilities for further cultural stimulation from East Asian civilization are almost unlimited.

For the social scientist, whether in anthropology, sociology, economics, political science or history, the human record in East Asia is a rich source that can no longer be disregarded. In certain periods and in certain fields it is a far fuller record than we have in the West. The family system of China, the economic development of Japan, the institutions of bureaucratic government in Korea, and the interactions of peoples and cultures in Southeast and Central Asia are important chapters of the human story. The concepts of the social scientist will be much sounder when they have been measured against the relevant data from East Asia and retailored accordingly.

The need for more knowledge about East Asia is obvious, but the best way to achieve an understanding of so vast and diverse an area is less certain. The richest experience for most people would be to live for a time in East Asia. Such a stimulus, however, is not possible for everyone and would in any case only point up the need for deeper study.

The Approach to East Asia Through its History. The historical approach seems to us the best for a number of reasons. One is that the peoples of East Asia, more than those of the rest of the world, see themselves in historical perspective. They are strongly aware of their heritage from the past and also conscious of the historical judgment of the future. To approach them through their history is to look at them as they see themselves, which is the first requisite for understanding.

The historical approach is also necessary for a clear understanding of the major aspects of our subject. We are interested first in the distinctive aesthetic, intellectual and institutional achievements of the peoples of East Asia during their long period of semi-isolation from the rest of the world. These cultural achievements can best be studied genetically as they evolved. They should be looked at separately from the rapidly changing, hybrid cultures of the contemporary East Asian countries.

A clear understanding of the traditional cultures of these countries, finally, is essential to any comprehension of what is happening in East Asia today. The past is the unseen hand that molds the present; it would be futile to describe a situation of flux in static terms. Only as we look at the long flow of East Asian history can we understand what is happening there now and perceive the direction of motion, which is often more important than the momentary situation itself.

The essence of the present turmoil in East Asia is the interaction between new forces, many of which were derived from the West, and traditional habits and modes of thinking. Our story divides naturally into two major phases: the evolution of traditional East Asian civilization in relative isolation over three thousand years, and the upheavals and modernization of that civilization in recent times under the impact of the modern Western world. This is the reason for dividing the history into two volumes under separate titles.

Certain elements in the picture, however, do not readily lend themselves to historical presentation. There are, for example, the geographical factors and the racial and linguistic groups that constitute the dramatis personae. The major outlines of the Chinese economy and society as they have functioned over the past millennium also deserve more than piecemeal treatment, period by period. These various facets of our subject are presented together in the following sections of this chapter as a setting for the historical study, which will then begin with Chapter 2.

THE NATURAL ENVIRONMENT

A determining influence on East Asian civilization has been its relative isolation from the other great civilizations of mankind. Growing up at the eastern extremity of the Old World and separated from the other major centers of early civilization by great distances and formidable mountains and deserts, it developed distinctive cultural patterns which have been retained in large part until today. For example, the modern writing systems of all the rest of the world derived ultimately from a single series of inventions made in West Asia. Only in East Asia is there a writing system — the Chinese — which does not clearly derive from this source and which, in fact, is based on entirely different principles.

Western civilization grew up around the eastern end of the Mediterranean in a number of closely connected areas such as Mesopotamia, Egypt and Greece. Only after it had spread to include most of Europe, North Africa and Western Asia did it divide into its two present halves, Western Christian civilization and Islamic civilization. The Indus Valley in Northwest India (now a part of Pakistan) is the second great center of early civilization. It had relatively easy land and coastal communications with the whole zone of early Western civilization. Alexander's invasion of the Indus Valley in 327 B.C. is but one example of the close contact between the ancient West and India.

The home of early East Asian civilization in North China was very much more isolated than were these other early centers. On one side stretched the seemingly boundless Pacific, which until recent times was simply the end of the map. On the other side rose the tremendous central massif of Asia. The Himalayas, the Tibetan Plateau standing more than ten thousand feet high, and the huge mountain chains that radiate from this roof of the world constitute even today an almost uncrossable barrier. North of this massif lie the vast deserts and steppes of Central Asia — cold, inhospitable, and all but impassable for early man until he domesticated the horse and camel. South of the massif the rugged mountains and jungles of Southwest China and Southeast Asia form an even more formidable barrier than the deserts of the north. The southward-trailing arm of Malaya separated East Asian waters from the Indian Ocean and greatly lengthened the early routes of coastal navigation. Within the Old World this tremendous barrier of terrain and climate stretching from the arctic wastes of Siberia to the jungles of Malaya constituted the greatest single obstacle to the free movement of men. Even today this barrier is crossed by only two railway lines and only a very few roads that a jeep can negotiate.

Climatic differences between East Asia and the other early centers of settled life also contributed to its cultural distinctiveness. Unlike the Indian area, which is largely tropical, the main area of East Asian civilization has the more invigorating climate of the temperate zone, with cold winters and hot summers. The climatic contrast with Europe and West Asia, however, is even more significant. These areas, which have their weather determined largely by the Atlantic Ocean, receive the bulk of their rainfall in the cooler months. North Europe, because of its location, has relatively little sunshine, while the Mediterranean areas and West Asia receive relatively little rainfall. As a result the soils in Europe and West Asia are for the most part not cultivated very intensively, and usually only one crop can be grown each year.

9

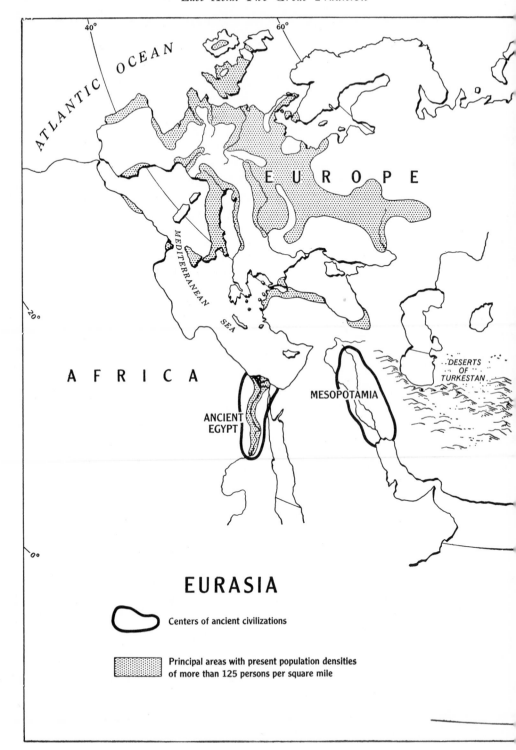

ATLANTIC OCEAN

EUROPE

MEDITERRANEAN SEA

AFRICA

DESERTS OF TURKESTAN

MESOPOTAMIA

ANCIENT EGYPT

EURASIA

Centers of ancient civilizations

Principal areas with present population densities
of more than 125 persons per square mile

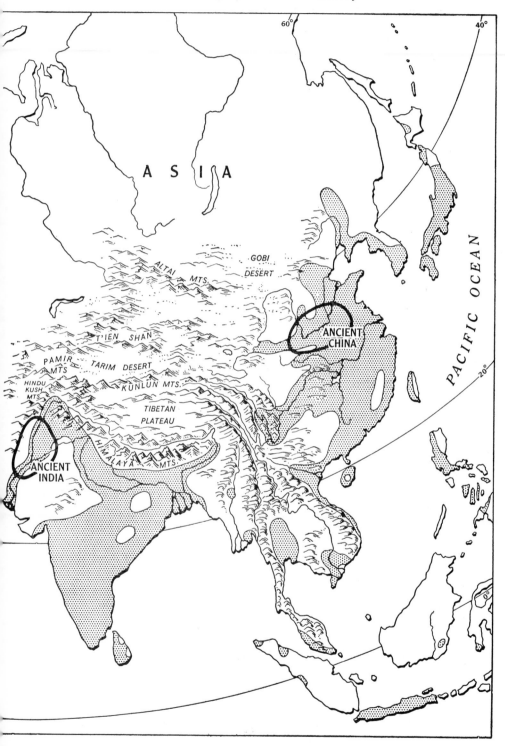

ASIA

ALTAI MTS.

GOBI DESERT

T'IEN SHAN

PAMIR MTS

TARIM DESERT

HINDU KUSH MTS.

KUNLUN MTS.

TIBETAN PLATEAU

HIMALAYA MTS.

ANCIENT INDIA

ANCIENT CHINA

PACIFIC OCEAN

60°

40°

20°

0°

The climate of East Asia, like that of India, is largely determined by the great land mass of Asia. In winter the air over Central Asia, far removed from the ameliorating influence of water, becomes very cold and heavy, flowing outward and bringing with it cool, dry weather to the southern and eastern fringes of the continent. In the summer the reverse takes place. The air over Central Asia warms up and rises, and moist oceanic air rushes in to take its place, dropping a heavy load of water on the continental fringes. As a result of these monsoon winds, most of East Asia and much of India have ample rainfall during the best growing months. This abundant water supply combined with the hot sunshine to be expected at their respective latitudes, which are far south of Europe and even south of much of West Asia, permit an intensive cultivation of the soil and in many places two crops per year.

This distinctive climate together with isolation gave to East Asia even in ancient times an agricultural pattern that was quite different from that of the West. The crops and domesticated animals of early Western civilization came largely from the temperate dry areas between the Mediterranean and the Caspian Sea; but many of the principal crops and animals of East Asia, notably rice, the soy bean, the chicken, the water buffalo and the pig, seem to have come from hot and humid Southeast Asia. In the West, cattle raising and sheep herding became a fundamental part of the economy, but in the more intensive agriculture of East Asia domesticated animals were used primarily as scavengers or beasts of burden.

Most important of all, the chief cereal of the West has always been wheat, while that of most of East Asia and much of India has been rice. Rice, which grows best in flooded fields, is well adapted to the hot and wet summers of this area. Producing a much larger yield per acre than wheat, it supports a heavier population on the land than most of Europe or West Asia can maintain. Thus, right from the start of agriculture, there seems to have been a significant difference in the ratio between people and land in East Asia and India on the one hand, and West Asia and Europe on the other. Demographic maps reveal that even today, when industrialization has added so heavily to the population of Europe, largely pre-industrial East Asia and India still have greater densities of population.

Naturally a vast area like East Asia does not have a uniform climate. As we shall see, even within China proper there is a tremendous difference between the cold, arid northwest and the humid, subtropical south coast. The chief climatic distinctions, however, are to be drawn between the three major cultural areas within East Asia already mentioned — Central Asia, Southeast Asia, and East Asia proper. In fact, the cultural differences between these areas in large part reflect their varying climates.

Most of the true area of East Asian civilization, that is, Japan, Korea and China (except the northwest and extreme south coast), is the well-watered temperate region we have been discussing above. The closest parallel to the climate of this area is that of the eastern half of the United States, which has the same relative position in the North American continent as this area has in the Eurasian land mass. To the south is tropical Southeast Asia, which for the most part is as distinct in culture as it is in climate from its northern neighbors. To the north and west of the central zone lie Mongolia, Tibet and Sinkiang. Arid and cold, these lands support agriculture only in the lower valleys of Tibet, the southern fringes of Mongolia, and a few irrigated oases in Sinkiang. These vast regions have been inhabited primarily by sheep-herding nomads, living a life which throughout history has contrasted sharply with that of their Chinese neighbors.

THE PEOPLES

The area from the great Asian barrier eastward is for the most part the domain of Mongoloid man, while the area west of the barrier, including the greater part of India, most of the area of Islamic civilization, and the full zone of Western civilization, is the home of white or Caucasoid man. Negroid man, the third major racial type, occupies a discontinuous band of southerly areas in Africa, in spots along the southern edges of Asia, and on out into the islands of Melanesia.

The origin of the races of mankind is still an unknown story. Some scholars have sought to trace present racial differences back to various earlier forms of man that antedate the appearance of *homo sapiens,* or modern man. One early type, with a brain capacity intermediate between that of the great apes and *homo sapiens,* is *Pithecanthropus erectus,* or Java Man, found on the island of Java. Solo Man was a full-brained successor to *Pithecanthropus* in the same area.

The most interesting of the predecessors of *homo sapiens* in East Asia is *Sinanthropus pekinensis,* or Peking Man, discovered in 1927 in a cave at Chou-k'ou-tien about thirty miles southwest of the Chinese capital. *Sinanthropus,* who may have lived around 400,000 B.C., was already in possession of fire, though he had only about the same brain capacity as Java Man. He also had certain features, notably shovel-shaped incisor teeth, that are more characteristic of Mongoloid man than of the other modern races. From this fact it has been inferred by some that the Mongoloid race derives in part from this early inhabitant of North China.

A more generally accepted theory is that the modern races of mankind developed after modern man had either replaced or absorbed all his near relatives. The rather late persistence of variant human types, such as Solo Man in East Asia, may have been the result of the isolation of their habitats, which permitted these variant forms to maintain themselves longer against the rising tide of *homo sapiens*. This general conclusion has been borne out by the discovery in 1933 in a second or "upper" cave at Chou-k'ou-tien of a group of skeletons, dating from around 20,000 to 10,000 B.C., which show proto-Negroid and proto-Caucasoid as well as proto-Mongoloid characteristics.

When the curtain rises on the first act of recorded history in East Asia, however, we find the Mongoloids already in a solid block covering almost the whole area. The assumption is that they had originally evolved in that part of the world. Their relative shortness of limb, which facilitates the retention of body heat, and their fleshy, narrow eyelids, which protect the eyes from snow glare, are thought by some to be the result of a cold original habitat in Northeast Asia. The range of skin color among Mongoloids, from very light in the north to dark brown in southern areas such as Indonesia, is clearly a product of environment, as is the comparable color range in the so-called white race. The other distinctive features of Mongoloid man — straight, coarse, black hair, relatively flat faces, and dark eyes — seem less obviously attributable to environment.

Mongoloids are not limited to East Asia, nor are they the only inhabitants of that part of the world. Some Mongoloids spilled westward north of the great barrier just as in recent times the Russians have pushed a thin column of settlement eastward across Siberia. The earliest known inhabitants of Siberia and northeastern Russia proper were all Mongoloids, and in historic times other Mongoloid peoples, though often with considerable Caucasoid admixtures, have come to occupy the vast territories of Russian Turkestan and some adjoining regions. The Eskimos represent a relatively recent incursion of the Mongoloid race into North America, while the American Indians themselves, who are thought to have come originally from Siberia by way of Alaska, form a branch of Mongoloid man that presumably diverged from the East Asian stock before the distinctive attributes of the race had fully developed.

On the other hand, the peripheral areas of East Asia, and particularly the islands that lie to the south and east, contain many survivals of non-Mongoloid races. There are Negroids in various southern areas — in the Andaman Islands off Burma, the forest fastnesses of the Malay Peninsula, the mountains of the Philippines, in New Guinea, and in the Melanesian Islands to the north and east of it. Presumably these Negroid peoples were pushed down and confined in their present habitats by the expansion of the Mongoloids. Archaeology suggests the spread of the Mongoloids from the north and central parts of East Asia southward and outward to the offshore islands. Some of this expansion has continued into historic times. The movement of the Thai people some seven centuries ago from Southwest China to their present home in Siam and the large-scale emigration of Chinese in recent centuries to Southeast Asia can be regarded as parts of this same great movement.

The most interesting racial survivals in East Asia are the Ainu, at present restricted to the northern extremities of Japan. Like some of the Australian aborigines, the Ainu show certain traits of Caucasoid man. For example, they have considerable facial and body hair, a feature notably lacking in most Mongoloids. Very probably the Ainu and the Australian aborigines represent primitive, undifferentiated types of *homo sapiens*, stemming from a time before the modern races had fully evolved.

THE LANGUAGES

The significant human divisions within East Asia are primarily linguistic, as in the West, where language rather than physical type usually marks off the culturally and politically significant sub-units within Europe. In both East Asia and the West there is a common misconception that these linguistic differences correspond to racial divisions, but there is no more a Chinese or Japanese race than there is a French or German race. In other words, the physical differences within these linguistic groups are as great as the differences between them and their neighbors.

The Sinitic Languages. The largest linguistic division in East Asia is the Sinitic (or Sino-Tibetan) family of languages, which is comparable to the great Indo-European family that spreads over most of Europe and much of the Islamic and Indian zones of civilization. The Sinitic family of languages occupies a very solid block in the center of East Asia, covering all of China proper, Tibet, Vietnam, Siam, Laos, and most of Burma. With the exception of the Tibetans, who occupy a land that is too cold for much agriculture, all the members of this language group appear to have been farmers since the Neolithic period. There is every evidence that for a very long time they have been sedentary occupants of their part of the world, contrasting with the early Indo-Europeans, who often were nomadic, herding peoples and therefore wandered far afield.

Within the Sinitic group, Chinese is by far the largest and historically the most important linguistic subdivision. Chinese-speaking people have been in possession of North China, the original home of East Asian civilization, since the earliest recorded times. In the course of history they have spread by emigration and also by the assimilation of culturally and linguistically allied groups. In time they came to occupy almost the whole of China proper and more recently Manchuria, much of

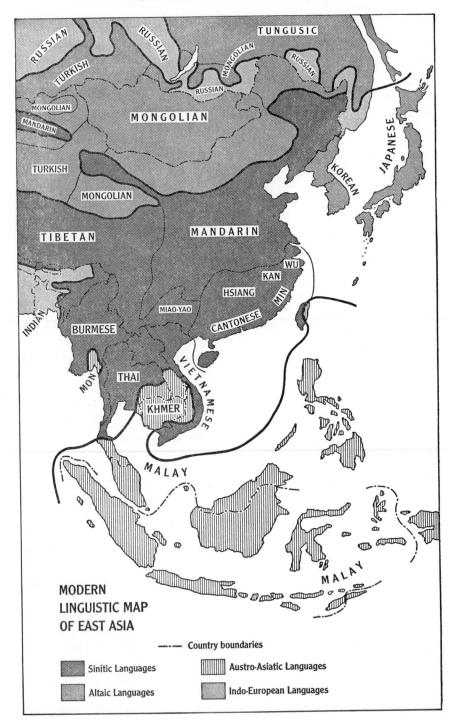

MODERN
LINGUISTIC MAP
OF EAST ASIA

----- Country boundaries

Sinitic Languages

Altaic Languages

Austro-Asiatic Languages

Indo-European Languages

Inner Mongolia, parts of Sinkiang, most of Taiwan (Formosa), as well as Chinese sectors in the cities and towns of all Southeast Asia and particularly Malaya, where Chinese now constitute more than a third of the population.

In the course of this expansion the Chinese language divided into several mutually unintelligible languages, as distinct from each other as Spanish is from Italian, or Swedish from German. Chinese proper, which is called Mandarin, *kuan-hua* ("the language of the officials"), or *kuo-yü* ("the national language"), is spoken as a mother tongue by more people than any other language in the world. Its various dialects cover all North China, the northern peripheral areas, and most of Central and Southwest China. In the south central provinces of Hunan and Kiangsi, respectively, the Hsiang and Kan dialects have diverged far enough from Mandarin to be considered virtually independent languages. Along the coast from Shanghai southward to the Vietnam border, the Chinese-type tongues, usually miscalled "the Chinese dialects," are even more distinct from Mandarin. There are, in sequence from north to south, the Wu "dialect" of the Shanghai area; the Min "dialect" of Fukien, which has further subdivided into Fukienese and the Amoy "dialect"; Hakka, which occurs in several widely scattered areas; and finally, Cantonese. These various coastal "dialects" are also the languages of Taiwan and the Chinese communities in Southeast Asia, and Cantonese is the language of most Chinese communities in the United States.

In addition to the Chinese languages, there are several other groups of Sinitic tongues spoken by peoples in Southwest China and contiguous areas. These languages are related to Chinese in much the same way that the Germanic and Slavic branches of Indo-European are related to Latin and its derivatives. Among these other Sinitic languages are the Miao-Yao group of Southwest China and the Tibeto-Burmese group, which includes the Tibetan dialects, Burmese, and several other languages spoken in Burma and Southwest China. In addition, the Thai group of Siam and Laos as well as Southwest China, and Vietnamese, the language of modern Vietnam, are often included among the Sinitic languages. The non-Chinese languages of Southwest China listed above are spoken by a number of small tribal groupings which represent the unassimilated survivors of the original inhabitants of South China.

The Altaic Languages. North of the Sinitic bloc are a large group of Mongoloid peoples who speak languages of a family that is as distinct from the Sinitic tongues as from the Indo-European. This linguistic family has been named Altaic after the Altai Mountains in Mongolia. These peoples, like many of the early Indo-Europeans but in sharp contrast with their sedentary neighbors to the south, were nomadic, horse-riding sheepherders. As a result, they have moved about a great deal; indeed, some have wandered right out of East Asia.

Turkish is the westernmost of the Altaic languages. Turkish-speaking groups now inhabit Turkey, the greater part of Central Asia, and scattered communities throughout West Asia. In the course of their wide wanderings, however, they absorbed a sometimes preponderant quantity of Caucasoid blood, and the Turks of Turkey now show little sign of their Mongoloid ancestry. Next to the east are the Mongols, who occupy much of the original home of the Altaic peoples in Mongolia and are found also in many isolated pockets in Central and West Asia. Further east are Tungusic-speaking tribes, such as the Manchus, who once constituted the chief population of Manchuria and the Siberian areas to the north but are now overshadowed in their homelands by Chinese from the south and Russians from the west.

Turkish, Mongolian and Tungusic are usually considered to be the three major Altaic language groups. Korean and Japanese, however, show close structural resemblances to the definitely Altaic languages, and the Koreans and Japanese may, therefore, be two eastern extensions of Altaic-speaking peoples into predominately agricultural areas.

Other East Asian Language Groups. The third great linguistic family of East Asia is the Austronesian, which occupies a far-flung zone south of the Sinitic bloc. Included in this family are the Malay languages of Malaya and Indonesia, the closely related languages of the Philippines, and the tongues of the aborigines of Taiwan. Distant outposts of this family of languages are also to be found in Madagascar to the west and in Melanesia and the remote islands of Polynesia to the east.

In addition to these three major linguistic families of East Asia, there are a few scattered representatives of other types of languages. The Mon language of southern Burma and the Khmer of Cambodia, usually grouped together as Austro-Asiatic languages, may be related to the Munda language of India. There are also the tongues of the Negroid inhabitants of the southern fringes of East Asia and the Ainu language of North Japan. Indo-European languages were also to be found in ancient times in some of the pastoral northwestern areas of East Asia. Kansu, the northwestern province of China proper, may have had an Indo-European population in early historic times. Until the ninth century Sinkiang was inhabited by blondish peoples, speaking Iranian or now extinct Indo-European languages, such as Sogdian (which was closely related to Iranian) and Tokharian (which had many close parallels to Latin). Westward-moving waves of Turkish-speaking peoples, however, eventually blotted out these languages and absorbed their speakers racially into the Turkish groups. Thus, an Indo-European element disappeared from East Asia a millennium ago and was reintroduced only in the last few centuries by Russian colonization in Siberia.

CHINA'S GEOGRAPHICAL SETTING

East Asian civilization was born, and developed most of its major features, in China. We shall therefore examine more closely the geographical setting of China and some of the fundamental characteristics of the society that grew up there.

China is geographically a less united area than either India or the traditional zone of Western civilization. It lacks the easy communications made possible by the Mediterranean or by the geographical unity of the great plains of the other regions. The North China Plain, the largest stretch of level terrain in the whole area, is very much smaller than the plain that extends across North India, to say nothing of the still greater North European Plain or the American Middle West.

China is broken up into a sort of checkerboard by two intersecting sets of parallel mountain chains. One major inland chain may be traced from southwestern China northeastward through Shansi and western Manchuria. A parallel range extends from Canton northward along the coast to the lower reaches of the Yangtze and then reappears in the Shantung Peninsula and again in the mountains along the Korean and Manchurian border. Intersecting these two southwest-to-northeast ranges, three parallel mountain chains spaced at roughly equal intervals protrude from west to east toward the Pacific. Across the center of South China, the southernmost chain creates the watershed dividing the Hsi or West River system of the Canton region from the Yangtze Valley. In the extreme north another east-west range divides North China from the Mongolian plateau. Between these two the important Tsinling range, the eastward extension of the massive Kunlun of northern Tibet, creates the watershed between the Yangtze and the Yellow rivers and (together with the Huai River) marks the boundary between North and South China.[1] This cross-hatching of mountain ranges has created a number of distinct geographical regions. It has inevitably given rise to problems of economic and political unity and has determined military strategy.

River Systems. The great rivers of China water the central cores of habitation which lie within the mountain ranges. All the rivers flow eastward from the Central Asian massif. Within historic times all have extended the good earth of China many miles into the sea.

---

[1] "South China" commonly denotes the Yangtze Valley and areas south of it, but sometimes the Yangtze Valley is differentiated from the rest of the South by the term "Central China."

The Yellow River (Hwang Ho) in the north is some 2700 miles in length. After it enters the North China Plain about 500 miles from the sea, it crosses a broad flood plain built up over the ages by its own silt. The river bed here slopes only about one foot per mile. In the summer flood season the waters from the great treeless mountain ranges to the west bring with them a heavy deposit of yellow silt (sometimes as much as 46 per cent by weight), which gives the river its name. As a result, the Yellow River constantly builds up its own bed, and from earliest times Chinese administrators in this most ancient part of China have had to construct dikes to keep it within its channel. Ordinarily the waters of "China's Sorrow" move across the plain within these dikes between ten and forty feet above the level of the surrounding land. A single breach in the dikes may spread a few inches or feet of water over hundreds of square miles and cut millions of farmers off from their sustenance. In the flood of 1935 the Yellow River left silt deposits up to six feet thick. Years may elapse before flood-ravaged lands can be cultivated again. Meanwhile famine will have followed upon the flood.

The vastness of the Yellow River problem has been graphically demonstrated by the historic shifts of its bed from the north to the south of the Shantung promontory and back again. From 1191 to 1852 its waters for the most part entered the ocean south of the peninsula; from 1852 to 1938 on the north; and from 1938 to 1947 again to the south. Dikes blasted in 1938 to check the Japanese invasion were repaired with American assistance only in 1947, putting the river back in its present channel, which again enters the ocean north of the peninsula near Tientsin. More than the Mississippi or any other great river, the Yellow River presents mankind with a seemingly insoluble problem. Rulers of China have always faced but never conquered it.

The Yangtze, however, is a larger river than the Yellow. It is 3200 miles in length, with a catchment basin twice as large and receiving

PROFILE OF THE YELLOW RIVER

This diagram is a cross section with the vertical aspect greatly exaggerated. It shows how the river rises between its dikes above the level of the countryside during the flood season. The dikes are far apart to provide space for flood waters when they come.

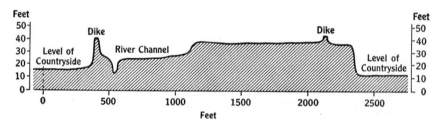

twice as much rainfall. It is also navigable, as the Yellow River is not. Steamers as large as 10,000 tons can in season ascend 630 miles to Hankow and smaller vessels another 1000 miles, almost to the borders of Tibet. In flood season the river rushes through the famous Yangtze gorges above Hankow at fourteen knots, and special steamers are required to make the ascent. Joined by a great network of tributaries, the Yangtze itself carries an enormous volume of silt (some 400 million tons a year) into the China Sea, extending the rich Shanghai delta region at the rate of about one mile in seventy years. The Tungting and Poyang lakes serve as water catchment and storage basins for the lower Yangtze. Even so, the rainy season raises the water level in places as much as forty or fifty feet between the dikes, and disastrous floods are not infrequent.

Climate. China embraces a wide range of climate. The southernmost parts are subtropical and parallel in latitude to North India, but the bulk of China is in the temperate zone. It suffers in winter from continental cold of a type unknown to India because of the mountain ramparts that protect India on the north. On the other hand, China lies far south of most of Europe. Peking in the extreme north is south of both Naples and Madrid; Canton in the south is in the same latitude as the Sahara Desert. Despite these latitudes, however, China's position between the sea and the Asian land mass gives it for the most part more rainfall than most of Western Eurasia and a far greater temperature range than the Mediterranean countries and Western Europe. Peking in July can be as hot as Cairo and in January as cold as Stockholm.

The eastern half of the United States offers a closer parallel to this range of climate, though with notable differences. China is somewhat further south, with Peking corresponding to Philadelphia, Shanghai to Mobile, and Canton to Havana, Cuba. The greater land mass to which China belongs gives it an even more markedly continental climate, with much lower winter temperatures and somewhat higher summer temperatures than are to be found at corresponding latitudes in the United States.

The seasonal monsoon winds of China are supplemented by cyclonic storms, such as determine much of our American weather, and by typhoons, comparable to our hurricanes. An average of eight or nine typhoons originate in the region of the Philippines during the latter part of each summer and slam into China with wind velocities up to 150 miles an hour.

China is a battleground between cold, dry, continental air and warm, humid, oceanic air which brings it most of its rainfall. During the summer this sea air reaches further into the continent, sometimes as far as Mongolia. Naturally a great deal more rain falls on South

China than on the North. Most of the South receives more than sixty inches a year and some coastal mountains receive as much as a hundred inches. This rainfall, together with the run-off from the Central Asian massif, gives South China an ample water supply, which can be used not only for irrigating rice fields but also for transportation. The network of navigable streams and canals, which covers most of the central and lower Yangtze basin and the less mountainous regions south of it, has been a great economic resource throughout history. In marked contrast, the Northwest receives less than the twenty inches minimum rainfall necessary for farming unirrigated lands and has little or no water transportation.

The most important climatic dividing line in China thus is formed by the Tsinling Mountains. South of the Tsinling rainfall for the most part is over forty inches, making possible the irrigated rice economy that supports two-thirds of the Chinese people. North of the Tsinling agriculture is largely confined to dry field farming. South of the dividing line one finds green and humid areas crisscrossed by waterways; north of it stretch brown, parched lands traversed by cart or wheelbarrow tracks. (See Plates 1 and 2.)

An equally significant climatic boundary is that between the farming areas of China proper and the steppe lands to the north that are too lightly watered to support any sort of agriculture. This climatic boundary has usually corresponded with the linguistic and cultural border between the agricultural Chinese and the pastoral, Altaic-speaking nomads. It has been sharply demarcated by the Great Wall, which the Chinese erected to defend themselves from their northern neighbors.

Soils and Agriculture. The winds blowing outward from the continent are not only cold and dry but also dust-laden. These winds produce veritable dust storms today and in the remote past deposited the fine loess soil that covers about 100,000 square miles of northwest China south of the Great Wall. The loess is often 100 and sometimes 300 feet thick. Geologists speculate that in the last Ice Age the frozen interior of Asia sent forth tremendous winds, greater than anything modern man experiences, which moved this enormous deposit of earth to its present resting place, whence the Yellow River has spread some of it over the North China Plain as alluvium. The loess region appears never to have been forested, except on mountains above the level of the loess itself, and there is no certain prospect that afforestation can hold back the steady process of erosion by the Yellow River and its tributaries, although an effort is now being made. Fortunately the loess makes a fertile soil. In a region of light rainfall, it has remained unleached; that is, its mineral substances have not been percolated out by the constant passage of water through it. It also has the peculiar characteristic of vertical cleavage, which has produced deeply sunken roads but has also permitted the making of convenient cave-like dwellings.

South China has an ideal climate for agriculture, but its soils have been leached by the heavy rainfall and exhausted by millenniums of intensive farming. South of the Yangtze, moreover, only 15 per cent of the uplands are flat enough for cultivation. Most of the area, however, produces two crops a year (for example, winter wheat or vegetables in the cooler months and rice in the summer), and around Canton two rice crops can be grown each year. As a result, South China has a denser population than the North and higher standards of nutrition.

North China, despite its fertile loess, balances dangerously on the edge of famine. The northern peasant faces the constant threat of drought. The growing season is short, precipitation is light, and rainfall varies from year to year about 25 per cent. It is not surprising that in the last 1800 years more than 1800 famines affecting one or more areas in China have been recorded. The North China Plain, the richest and most populous part of the region, faces the additional threat of floods by the Yellow River. As an alluvial plain, moreover, it has a high water table, often not far below the surface. Soluble salts, brought to the surface through capillary action and deposited there when the water evaporates, may not be washed away in the rainy season, thus making the land unusable.

THE TRADITIONAL CHINESE ECONOMY

Features of terrain and climate have had a constant influence upon human life in China, setting certain limits and creating special problems, which in turn have molded economic and social institutions. Both the farm economy and the family system, for example, have borne a distinctive "Chinese" imprint throughout history. While China most certainly has not been "unchanging," it has shown strong cultural continuity and Chinese history has been characterized by "change within tradition." Since the historical records of China, as do those of most countries, generally neglect the life of the common people, we shall try to sketch here certain traditional features which have usually been typical of the life of the Chinese masses. Although our picture is clearest for the recent century of direct contact, the essential outlines are visible in earlier times also.

The Agriculture Base. China's greatest natural resource has always been her agricultural land. Yet her vast population, now almost four times that of the United States, must get its food supply from a cultivated area about one-half the size of that of the United States. The country is so mountainous that only about one-seventh of the total area has been under cultivation, and the amount of arable land cannot be greatly increased.

Despite the prodigious use of labor, the four-fifths of the populace who live upon the soil and till it have been barely able to produce a surplus adequate to maintain the other 20 per cent. Some nine-tenths of their crops have had to be food crops. Aside from the scavengers, pigs and chickens, they have not been able to afford the raising of animals for food, and since ancient times they have had a strong prejudice against dairy products. Limited to an almost completely cereal diet, the Chinese have suffered a widespread calcium deficiency from lack of leafy vegetables, even when their caloric intake has been adequate. Thus, at best, Chinese agriculture has been a precarious business and is today an increasingly insecure base for China's huge and growing population.

China's economic life has been distinguished by its dependence upon human backs and muscles. The peasant four-fifths of the population have had to grub a hard and often precarious living from the niggardly soil. The fields of the hillier regions have had to be carved out by the hand of man. In many places earlier generations have laboriously constructed terraced rice paddies or wheat fields up one side of the mountain and down the other. The farmer today makes use of this accumulated investment of earlier labor.

Because of the pressure of the population on the land, the farmer has to make every effort to maximize the fertility of his fields. In South China, mud containing decomposed organic matter of value as fertilizer is scooped from ponds and canals and applied to the land. Elsewhere, the Chinese peasant is largely dependent on human excrement, or "night soil," for his fertilizer. This he painstakingly collects from his own farm and from any near-by town and carefully applies by ladle or in dried form to his growing plants. Animal manures are not plentiful in an economy poor in domestic animals, and the cellulose of straw and plant stalks is devoted to purposes such as cooking and heating, which seem more essential than compost.

The Use of Manpower. The whole agricultural cycle illustrates the lavish use of human energy. In growing rice, for example, seed is thickly scattered in nursery beds (about twenty bushels to an acre). Meanwhile the winter crops are harvested in the main fields, and the latter are cultivated and flooded in preparation for the rice. When the rice seedlings are about eight inches high after a month's growth, they are transplanted by hand to the main paddy fields. This annual transplanting of the rice seedlings would be roughly equivalent to the planting of the American wheat and corn crops by hand. It conserves seed

挿秧

晨雨麥秋潤午風槐
夏凉溪南與溪北笠
歌挿新秧擲不傳
千左右無亂行我教
挿種馬人勞民莫忘

TRANSPLANTING RICE

With their bundles of rice seedlings, which have already been grown in a seed bed, these farmers wade backward ankle-deep in the flooded fields to transplant the seedlings by hand in orderly rows. Communication paths are on top of the field dikes. The bridge crosses the irrigation canal. The inscription is a poem about planting rice. From P'ei-wen-chai keng-chih t'u, an early-eighteenth-century work extolling the imperial patronage of agriculture.

rice and permits the longer use of the main fields for other crops, but it requires a tremendous amount of back-breaking labor.

Similarly, the famous silk industry of China requires almost endless work. A pound of silkworms at hatching may number about 700,000 individual worms. Fed mulberry leaves by hand and carefully tended for five weeks until their maturity, the pound of worms will grow to a weight of some five tons, consuming about twelve tons of mulberry leaves in the process, but producing in the end only about 150 pounds of silk. The semi-mechanized reeling of silk cocoons to get their thread is only the last step after an enormous application of hand labor. (See page 335.) The other traditional household industry of South China, tea production, involves a comparable use of hands to pick, sort, roast, pick over, re-sort, re-roast, and package the tea leaves.

Silk and tea are but two of the handicraft products which can be derived from the labor resources of the farm household, particularly in the off-season when work is slack in the fields. Other important household handicraft products are straw sandals and cloth shoes, which respectively take the place of leather in the damp South and colder North, and cotton yarn and textiles in the cotton-growing areas of Central and North China.

The labor-intensive nature of the economy is typified by the moving of irrigation water by human muscle, customarily with a simple foot treadle or even more simply by a bucket on ropes held by two persons. While non-mechanized labor has been the norm in all pre-modern societies, the Chinese economy seems to have become peculiarly adjusted to heavy applications of manpower with little use of metal or other capital equipment.

Transportation also has customarily been labor-intensive. Porters with carrying poles on mountain paths, men pushing wheelbarrows over the plains, boatmen sculling sampans on the waterways, chair-bearers with their palanquins in the cities (supplanted in recent decades by ricksha coolies and later by pedicab drivers), all illustrate this motif.

While the pressure of numbers has not always been so great, Chinese farming from ancient times has applied large amounts of labor and, when possible, water to small plots of land. Land has generally been valued over labor, landowning has been the main goal of economic endeavor and investment, and landlords have usually been the dominant element in the countryside. Problems of landlordism and agricultural taxation have therefore occupied the attention of both populace and officialdom in every generation. An increasingly serious problem in recent centuries has been the size of Chinese farms. Even in the unirrigated region of North China, a farming family has had on the average little more than five acres, and in the irrigated South as little as two and a half. Millions of Chinese peasant families have attempted to live on an acre or less of land. Until recently, even such small farms might be broken up into several widely scattered holdings, requiring the farmer to waste much time and effort plodding back and forth between them.

The farmer's relations with the market have also been inefficient. His traditional lack of capital and storage facilities kept him at the mercy of the middleman, who bought cheaply in the harvest season and lent capital in the off-season to the impoverished cultivator at rates of two per cent or more a month. Tenancy, which has been common in many periods, led to further exploitation of the farmer, who might be obliged to pay as much as half his crop to the landlord.

Economic Decentralization. Transportation of produce to market has similarly been a problem. Transport by sampan and junk on the interlacing network of waterways in Central and South China has been reasonably efficient, but villages in the North and in the remoter areas of the South have commonly been connected only by footpaths. Transport by means of a carrying pole over the shoulder of a coolie, powered by his own grain consumption, is costly. If he goes very far, the coolie will have to consume a large proportion of what he can carry.

The typical market pattern has therefore been decentralized, each village community remaining largely self-sufficient in its own locality, exchanging produce by barter at the local town or at periodic markets (held, typically, every ten days). There has been no need for the farmer to travel to the city, no opportunity for seasonal migration in search of work elsewhere, and little national market for which a peasant could produce. Peddlers and traveling merchants distributed specialized products of other regions and a few manufactured wares such as ceramics, lacquer ware, or metal goods. Government monopolies licensed the distributors of salt and sometimes other necessities such as iron. But beyond the level of the copper cash used for everyday transactions, the use of money and credit remained limited. A locality could live almost by itself as long as nature was kind and, conversely, could be nearly wiped out by natural calamities such as flood or drought.

The fragmented and cellular nature of the traditional village economy enabled it to survive with a high degree of inertia, or persistence, in established channels, in spite of wars, invasions, and great social changes in the cities and administrative centers where history was recorded. The written record has naturally depicted mainly the upper stratum of Chinese life above the village level. In reading of emperors and poets, conquerors and bureaucrats, we must keep in mind as a background the stable rural scene — the myriad villages and hamlets that have formed the economic foundation of China's long history and contributed to its unusual continuity.

CHINA'S SOCIAL HERITAGE

The crowding of people upon the land and in tight-walled villages is not new in China's history. The Han Empire, which was contemporary with the Roman Empire, had a population of sixty million people, most of it concentrated in North China. Throughout their history the Chinese have habitually lived close-packed in their social and family relationships.

The Family Pattern. Since ancient times the family, rather than the individual, state or church, has formed the most significant unit in Chinese society. For each individual, the family was the chief source of economic sustenance, security, education, social contact and recreation. Through ancestor worship, it was even his religious focus. The family was also the foundation for political organization. Through the system of mutual responsibility (the so-called *pao-chia* system), individuals were responsible for each other's actions within each household, and families were responsible for one another within a community, much as in Communist China today.

Of the five famous Confucian relationships — between ruler and subject, father and son, husband and wife, elder brother and younger brother, and friend and friend — it is noteworthy that three were determined by kinship. As we shall see, the Confucian virtue of "love" (*jen*) was equivalent to "graded love" — that is, love for others according to one's relationship to them. China's whole ethical system thus tended to be family-centered and particularistic, not universalistic and oriented toward God or the state, as in the West.

The Chinese kinship group was extensive in scope and was conceived as reaching out in each direction to the fifth generation. This meant that an individual's ancestors back to his great-great-grandparents, his descendants down to his great-great-grandchildren, and his contemporaries to his third cousins (descendants of his great-great-grandparents) were all acknowledged members of his family nexus.

The ideal was to have all the living generations reside in one great household, divided among the various courtyards of a big compound. Actually this was seldom achieved except by the rich. Because of economic necessity and the smallness of farms, most Chinese households seem to have averaged around five persons and were usually limited to close relatives: parents, their unmarried children, their eldest son and his wife, and the latter's children. The typical household was in fact a stem family of a type familiar in the West, rather than the ideal Chinese extended family.

By its very nature the family system was both hierarchic and authoritarian. The status of each person depended on his position by birth or marriage in the family. The gradations of kinship were carefully spelled out. A complex terminology differentiated between paternal and maternal uncles, aunts, cousins, and in-laws, and expressed fine distinctions in seniority. In general, authority went by generation and within each generation by sex and by age. Age was respected as a thing worthy in itself and as a source of wisdom. The patriarchal father was the center of authority. He could be autocratic and on occasion even tyrannical. At least in theory he controlled the family property and production of goods. He arranged his children's and grandchildren's marriages. An insubordinate child might be severely punished. In times of stress, parents might even sell their children.

The Subordination of the Individual. Because of the subordination of the individual to the family, the highest virtues and greatest social satisfactions naturally attached to family life. Filial piety was the most admired of virtues. (See Plates 3, 4, and 5.) The greatest satisfaction could be derived from the worship of the ancestors and from the birth of a son or grandson to carry on the family line. Few experiences can have been more satisfying than that of the old man whose successful career as head of an extended family was crowned by the affection of his many descendants and the esteem of the community.

The arrangement of marriages, for which a good deal can no doubt be said when wise matchmakers were used, symbolized more clearly than anything else the individual's subordination to his family. Marriage was in fact more a union of families than of individuals, and family considerations predominated. A family might find it most economical to buy a child bride and rear her within the family for eventual marriage to a son. Such a girl might even be brought into the family before her prospective husband was born, as a "daughter-in-law in anticipation." A rich family might even acquire a bride who would "marry the spirit" of a dead husband.

Women in general were subordinate to men. Traditionally they obeyed their fathers in youth, their husbands in middle life, and their sons in old age. Relationship through the male line took precedence over kinship through the female line. Only sons could carry on the family name and line. As a consequence, baby girls were sacrificed in times of famine, and boys were preserved. Women were expected to be faithful to their husbands and not to remarry if widowed; men on the contrary could take secondary wives and concubines into the household. Except for a dowry, women had no property rights and on marriage entered their husband's families as humble newcomers, often treated little better than servants. Only with age and after she had become a mother-in-law because of her son's marriage did a woman typically become a dominating or autocratic figure.

The traditional family pattern seems to have made the individual even more inclined to seek security through conformity than was the case in the less family-bound society of the West. A high premium was placed on acceptance of a fixed position in the family hierarchy and on observing the proper relationships demanded by each specific tie of kinship. In effect, this authoritarian family pattern was applied to the whole of society, providing a basis for authority and social order in political as well as in domestic life. The role of the emperor and his officials was merely that of the father writ large. A district magistrate was called the "father and mother" of the people within his area of jurisdiction. Similarly, the non-official associations of Chinese life, such as the secret societies and the guilds of artisans and merchants, were fraternal organizations. Each member undertook to assist his "brothers." Both family and society thus were organized by the same ethic, which applied equally to the moral life on the personal level and in politics.

The Ethical and Political Systems. The Chinese family pattern provided little basis for a pluralistic type of society, like that of the West, in which the many forces of church and state, capital and labor, government and private enterprise are balanced under a rule of law. Instead, in Chinese life the personal virtues of probity and loyalty, sincerity and benevolence, inculcated by the family system, provided the norms for social conduct. Law was a convenient tool of administration; but personal morality was the foundation of society. Far from being anarchic because of the weakness of the legal concept, Chinese society was firmly knit together by Confucianism. This great ethical institution, which in a sense occupied in China much of the place filled by both law and religion in the West, produced strong social cohesion and extraordinary equilibrium.

Unchecked by the forces of church or law, and supported by the father image, the exercisers of political power in China have tended to be absolute within their own interpretation of the ethical code. As in most peasant societies, there was a wide gulf in power and prestige between ruler and ruled. Society was traditionally divided into four classes, which in descending order were the scholar-administrator (or warrior-aristocrat in ancient times), the farmer, the artisan and the merchant. Whatever the actual relationship between the last three classes, no one disputed the supremacy of the scholar-administrator, who as an educated man was presumed to be morally superior. Exercising the supreme authority of the emperor, the paterfamilias of all Chinese society, the scholar-administrator came to dominate all aspects of public life.

It can be readily seen that traditional Chinese society was very different from the present pluralistic and individualistic society of the West. That does not necessarily mean that it was inferior. The modern urbanized West, where individuals often suffer from a lack of kinship ties and community status, might learn much from the old Chinese family system, which was not plagued by juvenile delinquency. On the other hand, there can be no doubt that the traditional system has crumbled in China. Communism represents only the latest of a series of assaults on old concepts and social institutions. Some aspects of traditional society may survive better than others — for example, the authoritarian nature of political leadership, the domination of society by the educated man, and the emphasis on ethics rather than law. In any case, the Chinese social tradition, while less limiting than the natural environment, will help determine China's future.

2

Early China: The Birth

of a Civilization

THE ARCHAEOLOGICAL RECORD

Early Chinese civilization grew up along the Yellow River on the North China Plain and in contiguous smaller river valleys. This area, despite its severely cold winters, was well suited to agriculture. In fact, it closely resembled the other ancient centers of civilization — the valleys of the Nile in Egypt, the Tigris and Euphrates in Mesopotamia, and the Indus in modern Pakistan — which were all flood plains of great rivers. Because of the light rainfall, there was no forest cover to be removed before crops could be planted. The great rivers provided abundant water and in their annual floods replenished the fertility of the soil.

Early Contacts With West Asia. Since Chinese archaeologists are making extensive discoveries from year to year, our picture of China's prehistory may be greatly modified, but thus far the evidence suggests that cultural influences from West Asia were important stimuli to the rise of civilization in North China. It is significant that the ancient home of Chinese civilization on the North China Plain is the part of agricultural East Asia that is most accessible by land from the West. The ancient civilizations of West Asia and the Indus Valley seem to have been older than that of North China, and, according to archaeological data, many of the basic elements of civilization appear to have been developed first in these regions and to have spread from there to East

Asia. The steppes and deserts of Central Asia constituted a passable even if long and difficult way between West and East, and human discoveries and inventions flowed slowly across this trail. Important grains like wheat; domesticated animals such as sheep, cattle, and horses; bronze and iron, which are the metals that made higher civilization possible; and such basic inventions as the wheel and the war chariot — all seem to have spread in this way from West to East. Even complicated cultural developments like writing may have been passed along as general ideas.

One should not imagine, however, that such cultural elements were brought to China from outside by invaders or migrants. There is no evidence for such an idea, and the Neolithic peoples of North China appear to have been the direct ancestors of the modern Chinese. Nor should one think of ancient Chinese civilization as a Western transplant in a new environment. Cultural importations and stimuli from the West undoubtedly contributed in some measure to the development of the early civilization of North China; but even in prehistoric times this area showed strong cultural distinctiveness.

The most characteristic Paleolithic remains of West Asia, India, Europe, and Africa are carefully chipped stone axes; east of the great barrier this implement is replaced by a distinctive stone chopper. When man took to agriculture in the Neolithic age, the plow became the principal agricultural tool in both India and the West, but in East Asia the long-bladed hoe served in its place. Silk was produced in prehistoric China and spread to the West only much later. As we have seen, rice and other crops, as well as several domestic animals, probably came to China from a Southeast Asian zone of early agriculture. Thus, the ancient culture of China was no mere geographical extension of the civilization of the West but an independent civilization showing apparently native East Asian traits as well as elements borrowed from the West.

The blending of different influences is well illustrated by the Late Neolithic and Early Bronze cultures of North China. The archaeological record in East Asia is still tantalizingly incomplete, but certain salient features can be roughly discerned. Most of East Asia from Siberia to Malaya was characterized in Neolithic times by grey pottery with mat and cord markings and by a stone knife, shaped like a half-moon, that is quite different from anything found in Western Eurasia. In North China the people lived in sunken-pit dwellings and raised pigs and dogs for food (dogs are still considered edible in parts of China). One of their characteristic pottery forms was a hollow-legged tripod called a *li* (possibly evolved from three pots leaning together over a fire) which was the stylistic ancestor of the famous bronze tripods of historic times.

PREHISTORIC PAINTED POT FOUND IN KANSU

The Painted Pottery Culture. Within this general East Asian Neolithic culture, two distinctive variant cultures appeared in North China near the end of the Neolithic period — perhaps somewhat before 2000 B.C. One was the Red or Painted Pottery culture, known from a type site in northwest Honan as the Yang-shao culture. The greatest concentration of Painted Pottery sites and the oldest ones are found along the Yellow River in the general vicinity of Yang-shao, but this culture extended from Manchuria in the northeast all the way to the borders of Sinkiang in the northwest. It never spread eastward, however, into Shantung or the coastal parts of China proper, and it seems to have lingered longest, probably into the historical era, in Kansu in the northwest.

The Painted Pottery culture was typified by large, bulbous red pots painted with bold geometric designs, usually in black. This pottery bears a marked resemblance to the painted pottery of West Asia and Southeastern Europe. A few scattered finds of similar types of pottery in Russian Turkestan and Sinkiang suggest the route by which these cultural influences may have penetrated to China.

The Black Pottery Culture. A second Late Neolithic culture grew up on the North China Plain and in coastal regions as far south as Hangchow. It is named for a characteristic shiny black pottery and is also called the Lung-shan or Ch'eng-tzu-yai culture after a type site in Shantung. This Black Pottery culture shared many elements with the general Neolithic culture of East Asia, and it seems to have been a close ancestor of the Shang (or Yin), the first historic culture of China.

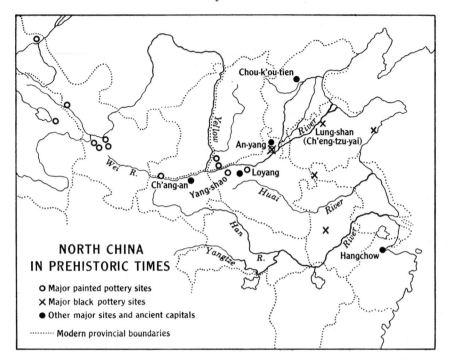

NORTH CHINA
IN PREHISTORIC TIMES

O Major painted pottery sites
X Major black pottery sites
● Other major sites and ancient capitals
········ Modern provincial boundaries

Many of the animals and crops of the Black Pottery people were the same as those of the Shang; they shared a common system of divination; the Black Pottery people even had pounded earth walls, thirty feet thick and a mile long in the case of Ch'eng-tzu-yai, much like the walls that still surround the towns of North China. It is possible, however, that some of these similarities do not indicate cultural descent from the Black Pottery people to the Shang but cultural diffusion from the Shang to them, since the Black Pottery culture may have lingered on in the extreme east into historic times.

While the Black Pottery culture was in many ways more purely East Asian than was the Painted Pottery culture, it too showed apparent borrowings from the West. Some of these may have come by way of the Painted Pottery culture; in fact, the Black Pottery culture may be more of a direct descendant of the Painted Pottery culture than was at first assumed. Moreover, there are parallels to the black pottery itself in the West, and bones of domesticated sheep and horses and the potter's wheel, all apparently of Western origin, are first encountered in China in Black Pottery sites.

The Shang. The historic Bronze culture of the Shang, which centered around An-yang from about 1400 to 1100 B.C., was obviously a composite of many influences. Near An-yang, Shang sites overlay

35

Black Pottery sites and the latter overlay Painted Pottery sites. This part of North China thus seems to have been a cultural crossroads. Into it poured influences from the nomadic sheep-herding peoples to the north and west, from the agricultural peoples to the east, and from the forest dwellers to the south; and inter-stimulation among these contrasting cultures probably contributed to the more rapid development of civilization in this area than in other parts of East Asia.

Shang culture shows several traits not encountered in the earlier archaeological cultures of this region. Some of these seem to have been borrowings from West Asia. Bronze metallurgy, which was the glory of the Shang, perhaps came originally from West Asia. The same seems to be true of the cultivation of wheat and the utilization of horse-drawn chariots and certain types of bronze weapons, pottery shapes, and artistic designs. On the other hand, the major design concepts of the Shang people, as we shall see, were characteristically East Asian. Moreover, the wood-carving background for much of the artistic work that has been preserved in bronze, stone, and bone, and the strong emphasis in their culture on hunting, particularly of forest animals, suggest an original forest home for the Shang people, presumably in the wooded areas of South China.

The earliest historic culture of China thus was clearly a mixture of East Asian, with some West Asian, elements. But before entering on the more fully lighted stage of recorded history, let us take another look back into primitive times from a second vantage point, that afforded by Chinese mythology and historical tradition.

Early Chinese Traditions

The oldest remaining Chinese books, which date from the early centuries of the first millennium before Christ, tell us very little about previous ages. In the next few centuries, however, the Chinese wrote a great deal about the beginnings of their civilization and its early history. In fact, as one comes down in history and approaches the time of Christ, the Chinese writers have more and more to tell about earlier and earlier periods.

These later accounts of more ancient times are not the products of historical research. Yet one should not dismiss them as mere fantasy, because they undoubtedly contain some bits of authentic history. Even the later accretions were not created out of whole cloth. As serious attempts to reconstruct antiquity out of old traditions, established ethical principles, and current cosmological concepts and mythology, they do throw light on the thought of the period in which they were composed, besides being a rich mine of information on the social organization and beliefs of the earlier, more primitive Chinese.

From these sources emerges a shadowy picture of a patriarchal, tribal or clan-like society. From the clan name the *hsing* or family name had already developed in very ancient times. Then, as now, it always preceded a man's personal name, instead of following the personal name as does the Western surname. Succession was often from brother to brother rather than from father to son. There was also a strong emphasis on exogamy, which has persisted throughout Chinese history, so that even today the Chinese feel that persons of the same surname, even though they are not related by blood, should not marry.

In a clan-centered society religious ideas tended to focus around the clan, and the ancestor worship of later ages traces back to this ancient period. Animistic beliefs were widespread, and these have persisted among the common people of China until the present day. As was natural in an agricultural society, there was strong emphasis on cosmological and calendrical theories, on grain gods and the fertility of the soil, and on heaven (and later on earth also) as the controlling factors in agriculture. Authority in this society was strongly religious, and the ruler was in a sense the chief priest as well as the calendar-maker.

The Chinese early developed a strong sense of history and the ideal of political unity. Unaware of the great civilizations to the west, they considered China the unique land of civilization, surrounded on all sides by the "four barbarians." They therefore called it the "Central Country," or *Chung-kuo*. This name, which is often translated "The Middle Kingdom," is still the Chinese name for China. The term *t'ien-hsia*, meaning "all under heaven," was also applied by the early Chinese to the civilized world known to them, and in time it came to mean "the empire."

It was natural for the ancient Chinese to organize their information and speculation about earlier times into a strict historical sequence of events attributed to a politically and culturally unified state. This pseudo-history eventually became standardized in sober historical works, with the result that until recent decades Chinese scholars accepted this reconstructed history and chronology as established fact, and the more credible portions of it were not seriously doubted in the West.

The Culture Heroes. There are several versions of this early pseudo-history, all differing considerably as to the earlier stages but following this general pattern: In the beginning there was the creator, P'an-ku. Then followed three series of brothers — twelve Celestial Sovereigns, eleven Terrestrial Sovereigns, and nine Human Sovereigns — representing collectively the triad of Chinese thought: heaven, earth, and man. These three groups were either themselves known as the Three Huang or, in other accounts, they were followed by three individual sovereigns so designated. These in turn were followed by the Five Ti, who included the Yellow Emperor (Huang Ti) and the model rulers, Yao and Shun.

These mythical sovereigns, together with some lesser figures, were culture heroes, that is, the magical individuals who were credited with having provided the basic elements of civilization known to the ancient Chinese. Among them were the first builder of houses; the hero who first made fire; the originators of fishing, hunting, and agriculture; the inventor of the calendar; the developer of medicine; and the hero who invented Chinese characters to replace knot writing, a system of communication that the early Chinese may once have shared with other primitive peoples. The Yellow Emperor's wife developed sericulture, for silk production is typically the work of women. Yao introduced a new political ideal by choosing the unrelated but virtuous Shun to be his successor in place of his own less worthy son. Shun did the same in selecting his minister Yü to be his own successor, and he also established unified weights and measures and conquered barbarian tribes.

The Hsia, Shang, and Chou Dynasties. Though Yü was the culture hero who drained off the flood waters and opened up the waterways, he also represents a new and somewhat more credible aspect of the tradition. He founded a dynasty named Hsia, which has been assigned the dates 2205–1766 B.C. in the most traditional chronology, though another source gives the dates 1994–1523 B.C. The Hsia rulers also were credited with reigns of reasonable length, in contrast with the Methuselah-like spans of the earlier culture heroes.

The last of the Hsia rulers was so depraved that the people revolted under the leadership of a man called T'ang, who founded the second dynasty, named the Shang but called by its successors the Yin (1766–1122 B.C. or 1523–1027 B.C.). Its rulers were known by names based on the cyclic symbols of the calendar. Succession from brother to brother was almost as common among them as from father to son, and they frequently moved their capital from one place to another.

The last Shang ruler, like the last of the Hsia, was a very evil man, debauched in his personal life and tyrannical as a ruler. One of those who suffered most from him was his subject, King Wen (Wen Wang) of the principality of Chou. The long-suffering King Wen refused to revolt, but his son and successor, King Wu (Wu Wang), eventually overthrew the Shang, in either 1122 or 1027 B.C., and founded the Chou, the third Chinese dynasty. King Wu was greatly aided in his rule by his brother, the Duke of Chou (Chou Kung), who after the succession of King Wu's young son refrained from seizing the throne and instead became the wise and saintly consolidator of the dynasty.

The story of the founding of the Chou bears all the marks of later idealization, but there has never been any doubt about the full historical authenticity of the dynasty. The earliest surviving Chinese books date from the early era of Chou rule. After 841 the traditional dating seems quite reliable, and in the next century we begin to encounter our first fully verifiable events — eclipses of the sun that did occur just when the Chinese records date them.

The question remains as to how much of the pre-Chou tradition should be accepted as having any historical basis. For a while, modern skepticism relegated even the Shang dynasty to the realm of pure fancy. Then, in the late 1920's, all this was reversed. For some time, so-called "dragon bones," some with writing incised on them, had been appearing on the Peking market, usually to be ground up for medicinal purposes. These were traced to the vicinity of the modern city of An-yang (or Changteh) on the North China Plain in northern Honan. This place, known as the Waste of Yin, was traditionally said to be the site of the Shang capital during the latter part of the dynasty. Now from deep in the ground of this capital emerged inscribed bones on which were found the names of practically all of the traditional Shang rulers. Study revealed that these were clearly Shang remains, dating approximately from 1400 to 1100 B.C. The modern archaeological records, moving backward in time, down through successive archaeological levels and the traditions of the ancient Chinese, leading into the past through successive dynasties, were seen to coincide perfectly in the late Shang.

Perhaps the Hsia too will in time be removed from the realm of unfounded tradition by further archaeological finds. The Black Pottery culture or the Painted Pottery culture, or perhaps some still undiscovered culture, may some day be identified with the Hsia. For the time being, however, true Chinese history must be regarded as commencing with the Shang.

THE CHINESE WRITING SYSTEM

The outstanding feature of the Shang finds at An-yang was the writing they contained; the most remarkable thing about the writing was that it was unmistakably in the Chinese language and represented an early form of the writing system that still dominates East Asian civilization. Some characters were recognizable even to the untutored eye as identical with characters appearing in newspapers today. It was very much as if the Arabic-speaking inhabitants of Egypt and Iraq were able to recognize in hieroglyphics or cuneiform the same language they now use and could point out occasional words that any schoolboy could read. The Chinese have always felt a complete cultural and racial identity with the ancient inhabitants of their land, and here was striking proof that they were justified in doing so. They have good reason to feel a greater degree of affinity with the people of Shang than we feel for the ancient Romans and Greeks, to say nothing of the early Egyptians and Mesopotamians.

Characteristics of the Sinitic Languages. One of the chief features of the Sinitic languages, to which Chinese belongs, is their tonal structure. This means that syllables which otherwise sound alike are distinguished from one another by the tone in which they are spoken. In modern Mandarin there are four tones, which may be classified roughly as "even," "rising," "falling-rising," and "falling." For example, *ma* pronounced in the first of these tones is, as with us, an informal word for "mother"; in the second tone *ma* means "hemp"; in the third, "horse"; and in the fourth, "to curse." Other Chinese and Sinitic languages are characterized by similar tonal distinctions.

Another characteristic of the Sinitic languages is that a relatively high percentage of their words consists of uninflected monosyllables. Chinese was once considered to be entirely monosyllabic — an idea fostered by the system of writing each syllable as a separate unit — but this is not true. Nevertheless, one-syllable words are more the rule in Chinese and most other Sinitic languages than in the Indo-European tongues of the West.

Still another characteristic of Chinese and most other Sinitic languages is the absence of inflection. The Chinese monosyllable *shan*, for instance, can mean "mountains" as well as "mountain." In the case of verbs, the difference from the languages of the West is even more marked. The Chinese can use the single word *hsing* where we must use "go," "went," "gone," or still more complex forms derived from "go." Writing in the ancient West, as in China, developed originally from pictures, but, partly because of the inflected nature of the languages of the West, a shift to phonetic principles took place quite early. In China no such change was necessary.

Chinese Characters. By Shang times the Chinese writing system had progressed far beyond simple pictographs and was in fact highly developed and sophisticated. Undoubtedly it had already undergone a long evolution. The Shang people had more than 2000 different characters, or individual symbols for words. The later Chinese were to develop 50,000 or more characters and variants, but all the principles for character formation were present in the Shang writing system. The Shang characters for the most part look very different from the modern forms into which they have evolved, yet most have been positively identified as prototypes of characters still used or at least known from later literature. Writing usually ran from top to bottom, as it does today. Probably much of it was done with a brush on slips of wood and bamboo, though these materials have not been preserved.

There were, of course, many pictographs in Shang writing, but these were often very stylized, even if more recognizable as pictures than are their modern forms. For example, the character for "sun" (now 日) originally was a circle with a line in it; that for "moon" (now 月) was still quite recognizably a crescent moon; and "tree" 木 was written in Shang times 义 , a sketch representing both the branches and the roots of a tree. Some pictographs were quite complicated, as, for example, one of the words for "sacrifice," which showed two hands holding a bird upside down over a symbol that meant "the spirits."

There were, in addition, a large number of ideographs, that is, sketches of ideas rather than actual pictures. Perhaps the numbers "one" 一 , "two" 二 , and "three" 三 should be put in this category. "Above" 上 , originally a shorter line above a longer line, and "below" 下 , analogously formed, certainly belong to this group. So also do more complex characters, like those for "grove" or "forest" 林 , which is made up of two trees, and "bright" 明 , composed of the characters for "sun" and "moon." Many of the ideographs are very picturesque: a woman under a roof 安 means "peace," a woman beside a child 好 means "good" or "to like," and a woman beside the character for "to give birth to" 姓 means "surname." Ideographs of this type are so characteristic of the Chinese writing system that it is better described as ideographic rather than pictographic in nature.

A third category of characters was derived at least in part according to phonetic principles. Already by the Shang period many words were written with pictographs that actually represented some more easily depictable homophone, or word of identical pronunciation. Thus 來 , which originally was a picture of some sort of grain, presumably pronounced *lai*, is the character used for the word *lai*, meaning "come." Several other characters whose meanings are well known but whose origins are obscure may also have developed in this way.

Phonetics, Significs, and Radicals. A large subdivision of the phonetic category consists of compound characters made up of so-called phonetics and significs. The phonetics are characters used to indicate the approximate pronunciation of these compound characters; the significs are characters added to indicate the category of meaning to which each belongs. Thus, hundreds of characters for words in some way associated with trees or wood are made up of the character for "tree" combined with some other character which is used purely for its phonetic value. For example, 柿 means "persimmon," 枝 "branch," 植 "to plant," and 棟 "ridgepole." These characters represent four different types of words that could all be construed as coming under the "tree" category: that is, a type of tree, a part of a tree, an act associated with trees, and an object made from the wood of a tree. Similarly, the character for "peace," which is pronounced *an,* acts as the phonetic in several characters all pronounced *an:* for example, with the "hand" signific in the word for "to press down" 按 , with the "tree" signific in the word "table" 案 , and with the "leather" signific in the word "saddle" 鞍 . In the case of the "tree" signific, "tree" is usually written on the left, but some significs are written above and a few below, around, or on the right of the phonetic.

Most characters created in later times were compound phono-pictographs made up of phonetics and significs, and as a result the vast majority of the present-day characters belong to this type. These significs, in fact, became the basis for a system of classifying all the characters. Two hundred and fourteen characters, largely made up of those commonly used as significs, were selected as "radicals," or classifiers, under which all the other characters could be listed, since at least one of these radicals could be identified in each Chinese character. Thus "ridgepole" 棟 is listed as belonging under "tree" (radical 75) plus eight additional strokes. This makes a far more cumbersome system of classification than our alphabet, and hundreds of characters fit into it only very poorly, but at least it achieves some order in what is otherwise an ocean of unique symbols.

Advantages and Disadvantages of the Writing System. The Chinese writing system has certain drawbacks when compared with the simpler phonetic systems of the West. It obviously takes a great deal more time and effort to master. Many characters are extremely complex, some being made up of more than twenty-five strokes. At least two or three thousand characters must be memorized before one can read even simple texts. The writing system thus has been an increasing handicap in modern times, when the need for widespread literacy has sharply risen. The emphasis on rote memory work to learn all these characters may also have had a limiting influence in Chinese education, putting a premium on memorizing abilities but giving less scope for creative talents. Moreover, even though the Chinese invented printing, their writing system has made printing a much more complicated technique than in the West. In the modern age, a system of code numbers has proved necessary in order to send telegraphic messages in Chinese; that is, each character must be encoded, transmitted by number, and then decoded. Chinese characters have so far defied all efforts to construct a Chinese typewriter that is anything less than a small printing press or electronic brain.

On the other hand, the Chinese writing system has certain values that our Western systems lack. The very complexity of the characters and their graphic qualities give them a vitality that is entirely absent in the Latin alphabet. Once the characters are learned, who can forget that "peace" is a woman under a roof or that "bright" is made up of "sun" and "moon"? By comparison, our written words for "peace" and "bright" (despite the latter's curious spelling) are as dull as numbers in a phone book. No one who has learned Chinese characters can ever free himself of the notion that somehow the written word has richer substance and more subtle overtones than the spoken word it was originally designed to represent. Chinese characters thus lend themselves to a terse vividness in both prose and poetry that is quite unattainable in our phonetically-bound writing systems.

In ancient times the Chinese characters undoubtedly had magical values, and these have by no means been entirely lost in the modern world. Prayers in Chinese were not spoken to the gods but were written. All writing was considered to be of value, and until recently there was a strong feeling that paper with writing on it might be burned but should not be simply thrown away. In East Asian civilization the written word has always taken precedence over the spoken; Chinese history is full of famous documents — memorials, essays, and poems — but lacks the great speeches of the West. The magic quality of writing is perhaps one of the reasons why the peoples of East Asia have tended to place a higher premium on book learning and on formal education than have the peoples of any other civilization. It is no mere accident that, despite their extremely difficult systems of writing, literacy rates in East Asia run far higher on the whole than in the rest of the non-Western world (and in the case of Japan even surpass those of the West).

The Chinese writing system also has far greater aesthetic interest than our simple scripts. Until recently good penmanship was considered a desirable skill for scribes and clerks in the West, but in East Asia a distinguished hand has been the mark of all educated men since antiquity. Calligraphy is a great art and the direct ancestor of all the graphic arts of East Asia, for the writing brush has also been the brush of the artist. Whatever the drawbacks of the characters for mass education, people in East Asia still appreciate their aesthetic, if not their magical, values.

Another tremendous advantage of the Chinese writing system is that it easily surmounts differences of dialect or even more fundamental linguistic barriers. All literate Chinese, even if they speak mutually unintelligible "dialects," can read the same books and feel that classical written Chinese is their own language. If they had had a phonetic system of writing they might have broken up into separate national groups, as did the Italians, French, Spanish, and Portuguese. The stature of China as the largest national grouping in the world is to be explained at least in part by the writing system. It may also explain the extraordinary cultural cohesiveness of the Chinese abroad. The millions of Chinese who have migrated to Southeast Asia are actually divided from one another and from the mass of the Chinese at home by the different languages they speak; yet even after generations abroad they have not, for the most part, lost a sense of identity with the homeland. The same is often true of the smaller communities which have migrated to the cities of the West.

The larger unity of East Asian civilization has also depended greatly on the writing system. A love and veneration for Chinese characters has been a binding link between the various countries. Until the last century, virtually all books written in Korea and Vietnam and many of those written in Japan were in Chinese, not in the national languages. Even today any educated Japanese or Korean and until recently any educated Vietnamese could pick up a Chinese book and read its title at a glance. In fact, it is impossible to tell from the titles of many contemporary books, as printed in Chinese characters, whether these books are actually written in Chinese, Japanese, or Korean. If the Chinese had had a phonetic system of writing, East Asia would certainly not have been so distinct a unit in world civilization.

SHANG CULTURE

The Bronzes. Next to writing, the most remarkable find at An-yang was the bronzes. For many centuries Chinese connoisseurs had attributed to the Shang dynasty certain types of bronze vessels inherited from antiquity. Now bronze vessels of these very types were dug up by archaeologists from tombs indubitably of that period. Like the writing, the bronzes present a puzzle. Bronze metallurgy may have been learned from West Asia, but the bronzework of the Shang was so highly developed and perfect that it must have had a long and complex development in Chinese hands. So far only a very few examples of earlier phases of bronze metallurgy have been found in China.

The Shang bronzes (see Plates 6 and 8) are largely of two types: weapons, and elaborate vessels used in religious sacrifices and ceremonies. The vessels are often of imposing size and are extremely handsome. Their beauty is enhanced by their present patination of varied shades of green, given them by the chemical action of the soil in which they rested for 3000 years. Both the ceremonial vessels and the weapons are frequently covered with elaborate designs in incised lines or sometimes in high relief. The angular shapes of many of the vessels and the sharp lines of the designs on them suggest wooden prototypes.

The Shang technique of bronze casting was superior even to that of the famed craftsmen of the Renaissance and it has never been surpassed anywhere in the world. The incised lines in the patterns, for instance, are not just grooves but perfect miniature trenches, with perpendicular sides and flat bottoms that meet at sharp ninety-degree angles.

The designs on the bronzes and the shapes of the vessels appear to be entirely East Asian. The bronze tripods, for example, hark back to the hollow-legged *li* tripod of Neolithic times. Some vessels were cast in the shape of animals such as the elephant, which still inhabited North China at this time, when the climate was slightly warmer and wetter than it is today. The chief design element has come to be known as the *t'ao-t'ieh* or animal mask. (See Plates 7 and 8, and page 32.) It is a frontal view of an animal head, centered on the nose, with eyes (frequently embossed) and prominent horns and ears and other elements spreading outward symmetrically on either side. The mask is portrayed with angular lines in a highly conventionalized manner, and the subsidiary elements, such as horns and ears, often turn out to be equally conventional portrayals of dragons and birds, tigers, and other animals. Similar designs are found on the bone artifacts and marble sculptures excavated at An-yang.

The whole Shang approach to the problem of design is quite distinct from anything known in the prehistoric or ancient West. There are, however, certain parallels in other East Asian areas, and also in the South Seas and among the Indians of our Pacific Northwest, who similarly portrayed an animal as if they had skinned it and laid out the divided pelt on either side of the nose. Other similarities are the superimposed figures, as in a totem pole, and the rigid bilateral balance of design. These striking points of identity have given rise to the concept of a Pacific Basin type of design, of which the Shang offers the earliest example, in contrast to the Western approach, in which animals are portrayed in profile.

"Oracle Bones," Divination, and Sacrifice. Inscriptions have been found on some Shang bronzes, but most of the Shang writing has been discovered incised on the plastrons or under-shells of tortoises, the scapulae or shoulder bones of cattle, and other flattish bones. The An-yang site abounds in bones of this sort, and as many as 17,800 have been found in a single pit. These bones were used in divination. Hence, they are commonly called "oracle bones," and this method of divination, scapulimancy. A small groove was carved on one side of the bone and heat was then applied near this thin spot, producing cracks from which the diviner somehow derived "yes" or "no" answers to his questions. Perhaps, like all good oracles, he controlled the prophecy by making the cracks appear where he wished.

Similar methods of divination were used by the Black Pottery people and, more recently, by other primitive peoples in East Asia. What

ORACLE BONE TEXT   MODERN CHINESE   LITERAL TRANSLATION

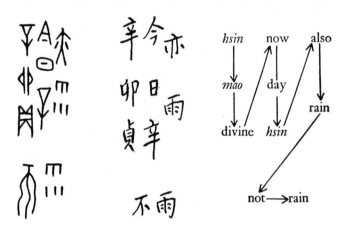

ORACLE BONE INSCRIPTION

The characters are to be read from top to bottom, as in modern Chinese, but the lines in this particular case read from left to right, the reverse of modern Chinese. The two characters at the bottom, which are to be read from left to right, follow the rest of the text. The meaning of the text is: "[On the day] hsin-mao, it is divined whether on this hsin day it will rain — or not rain." Most of the characters in this text are clearly identifiable from their modern forms. The second character in the second column is a picture of the sun with a spot in it, while the second character in the third column as well as the lower right-hand character show rain falling from a cloud. The upper right-hand character, showing a man's armpits (the two spots under the arms), was at this time a homophone for the undepictable word "also."

makes the Shang oracle bones unique is that about a tenth of them have the question asked by the diviner inscribed on them, and a few also have the answer and sometimes even the eventual outcome. The questions concern such matters as sacrifices and other relations with the spirits, crops and the weather, war, hunting and fishing, travel, illness, and the luck of the next ten-day period (which by Shang times had been established as the East Asian "week"). From these inscriptions, as well as from the other remains found at An-yang, a great deal can be learned about Shang society.

The Shang made frequent sacrifices to the spirits. Usually animals were used, but sometimes liquor, probably a sort of beer, was poured on the ground in libation. Sacrifices were made to the earth and the wind and to various rather vague nature deities, as well as to the cardinal points. One deity was called Ti or Shang Ti (Supreme Ti). As we have seen, one series of the mythical early sovereigns of China was known as the Five Ti. Probably we have in Shang Ti merely a "first ancestor." In any case, the ancestors were of great importance. In fact, traditional Chinese ancestor worship seems to date back to these early times. Many of the inquiries on the oracle bones concern the aid or harm of an ancestor to his living descendants.

The Shang State and Society. The Shang economy was mainly agricultural, though the aristocrats, at least, did a great deal of hunting. The Shang had sheep and cattle but already seem to have acquired the traditional Chinese abhorrence for milk and milk products. Since bronze was rare and costly, agricultural tools were made of wood or stone. Even arrowheads were usually made of bone or stone, and they were fitted into shafts of bamboo. This plant of many uses, though no longer native to North China because of the more rigorous climate of recent millenniums, has remained a characteristic and invaluable resource for all East Asia. Jade was highly prized by the Shang, as it has been throughout Chinese history, and cowrie shells were used as a sort of primitive money. These shells from southern waters have been valued in many parts of the world, in part because their vague resemblance to the female sex organ was thought to give them magical qualities. In China they have left their mark on the writing system; many characters having to do with wealth and trade have the "shell" signific.

Shang appears to have been a kind of city-state with a few outlying settlements close by. It may also have exercised a degree of authority over some of the similar but smaller communities scattered over much of the North China Plain and in the lower reaches of the Wei River in Shensi and the Fen River in Shansi. Recent finds of smaller numbers of inscribed bones in this general area may represent more distant parts of the political unit, or they may indicate rival states of like culture or earlier sites of the Shang capital, which tradition says was moved several times. Shang culture obviously was spread over a wide area but we know that the effective political unit was relatively small, because the Shang were frequently at war with nearby neighbors and trespassing herdsmen. On the other hand, the unit was large enough to put in the field armies of 3000 or even 5000 men.

Shang was ruled over by a line of hereditary kings. The tombs of these kings were huge pits (one was forty-three feet deep and sixty-five feet square), subsequently filled in with hard beaten earth. It was customary to bury with the corpse articles of use and value, presumably for the benefit of the deceased in some afterlife. The kings and the aristocrats fought in war chariots not unlike those of Homeric Greece. These chariots were drawn at first by two and later by four horses. Judging from the practice in the following Chou period, we may suppose that each chariot carried a charioteer and a spearman in addition to the king or aristocrat.

The palace buildings of the city of Shang were large and imposing, one measuring twenty-six by ninety-two feet. The style of architecture was essentially the same as that of modern China, contrasting with the stone architecture of the ancient West. The roof was carried by rows of wooden pillars, and the walls, at first made of pounded earth but in later times usually of brick, were merely non-structural screens. The pillars rested on individual foundation stones set on a platform of pounded earth. As is still the custom in North China, buildings were carefully oriented to face south.

Unlike the palace buildings, the houses of the common people appear to have been crude pit dwellings, as in Neolithic times. The gap between ruler and ruled is further illustrated by the seemingly casual manner in which the Shang sacrificed human beings, usually in multiples of ten. Most such human sacrifices were described as captives or, more specifically, as having belonged to sheep-herding tribes to the west. Human sacrifices and the burial of the living with the dead persisted sporadically well into the Chou period. Many historians have concluded that Shang was a slave society. There is no real evidence for this, but there can be little doubt that there were sharp social and economic cleavages within Shang society. Originally the kings may have been little more than chief shamans mediating between the people and the spirits of ancestors and natural phenomena, but by the late Shang period their authority appears to have been very great.

Origins of the Authoritarian Pattern. Whatever the nature of Shang political rule, the tendency of the Chinese throughout their history to establish and accept a unified, absolutist state has given rise to some interesting theories. A virtual monopoly of bronze metallurgy, bronze weapons, and costly chariots may have given the ruling class great power over the other members of the state in Shang times. Certain broader factors may also have been operative. As we have seen, the family pattern of China lends itself to authoritarianism. The development of an absolute, centralized state may also have been fostered by the constant need that the Chinese have felt since ancient times for a unified defense against their nomadic neighbors. The Great Wall is a dramatic illustration from a later period of this desire for large-scale, coordinated defense efforts.

Another source for the authoritarian state in China may have been the need for huge cooperative efforts to keep the Yellow River within bounds and to provide for necessary drainage and irrigation. A few men had to direct the work of a great many people in order to complete these great undertakings. Wherever such water-control efforts were necessary on a large scale, it is argued, a despotic or "Oriental" type of society developed, with absolutist monarchs supported by a bureaucratic official class and ruling over dense peasant populations. Proponents of this water-control or "hydraulic" theory point to ancient Egypt and

Mesopotamia as well as North China as typical examples of such "Oriental" societies, in contrast to the freer, more diversified societies of Europe, where large-scale water control was not necessary.

This particular theory fits in neatly with the myths about the culture hero Yü, original controller of the flood waters of China. The use of conscripted labor gangs for great public works, moreover, seems to date far back into Chinese history, and great efforts at water control and wall-building did take place at much the same time that the first great Chinese empire was being created. But it should be pointed out that this happened almost a thousand years after the Shang. Since the Shang people depended on rainfall rather than irrigation for agriculture, the water-control theory does not apply to them very well, however valid it may be for later ages.

THE EARLY CHOU

The Chou people, who conquered the Shang, came from the Wei Valley west of the great bend of the Yellow River. At first they seem to have lived on the northern edges of the valley, but even before their conquest of Shang they had moved to the center of the valley and had established their capital at Hao, not far from the modern city of Sian, or Ch'ang-an, as it was known during its heyday as the capital of the Chinese Empire. This area was on the fringes of Shang civilization, and the Chou seem to have shared the language and basic culture of the Shang. At the same time, their proximity to the sheep-herding "barbarians" of the west and north no doubt strengthened their martial spirit and skills. Some historians even believe that the Chou themselves were at least partly of such "barbarian" origin.

The Chou conquest of the Shang, traditionally dated as 1122 B.C. or 1027 B.C., did not mark any sharp break in the emerging culture of China. The writing system continued its uninterrupted evolution. Scapulimancy was still practiced, though other methods of divination gradually took its place. Unlike the Shang, succession under the Chou was from father to son, not from brother to brother. The Chou kings, who took the old Shang title of *Wang*, were buried under massive, square earthen pyramids, but out on the North China Plain people still followed the Shang practice of pit burials.

Under the Chou, imposing bronze sacrificial vessels continued to be cast, many with lengthy inscriptions. (See Plate 7.) The early Chou bronzes, however, were sometimes cruder in design than those of the Shang, and as the period progressed the elaborate decoration of the bronzes became weaker and plainer, perhaps because these details had lost their original religious significance and had become merely traditional.

The chief Chou deity, identified by them with the Shang Ti of their predecessors, was T'ien. *T'ien* came to mean "Heaven," but it was obviously anthropomorphic in origin, being written with a character that was originally a rough sketch of a man. The Chou kings called themselves "Son of Heaven," and they justified their conquest of the Shang on the grounds that they had received the "Mandate of Heaven" (*T'ien-ming*). They were thus the mediators between man and nature.

The chief ceremonial activities of the state centered around the ancestral temple of the kings. Sacrifices were also made to the supposed founder of the ruling house, Hou Chi, or "Millet Ruler," who was obviously an agricultural deity, millet having been the chief North Chinese grain since prehistoric times. Each community also had its earthen mound where sacrifices were made to the life-giving soil. It is interesting to note that the later Chinese dynasties maintained these ancient sacrifices up into the twentieth century. A square Altar of Earth and a round Altar of Heaven, both imposing structures, still stand in Peking. (See Plate 9.)

The Individual States. The empire that King Wu conquered and the Duke of Chou consolidated covered most of the North China Plain. But the primitive communications of the time made it impossible to rule this extensive area as a unified political and economic state. Instead, the Chou kings, while maintaining their direct control over the Wei Valley, delegated authority over the eastern territories to a large number of vassals. These vassals were for the most part their own descendants and relatives, but they also included unrelated henchmen and local aristocrats who acknowledged the kings' suzerainty. For example, the state of Lu in southern Shantung, which proudly traced the ancestry of its ruling house to the Duke of Chou himself, may have been in origin one of the many Chou garrisons in the newly conquered eastland. On the other hand, the rulers of the state of Sung in eastern Honan traced their origin to a scion of the Shang royal line who had been established in Sung to maintain the ancestral cult after a revolt by the Shang remnants had been crushed in the early years of Chou rule. This Chou system of rule through vassal lords was probably no more than a geographical extension and systematization of what had been the Shang method of controlling subject territories.

The usual unit of local rule, as in earlier times, was the walled town and its surrounding countryside. How many such units there were is uncertain. Tradition tells of the Chou destroying more than fifty states and setting up seventy; one source even says 1773. In the eighth century, by which time extensive consolidation into larger units had already occurred, there were still perhaps as many as 170 states in the area of the original Chou conquests, and more than 200 if newer peripheral states are included.

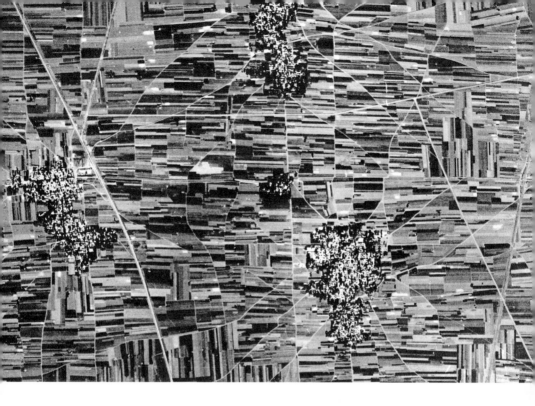

PATTERNS OF LAND USE, NORTH AND SOUTH

PLATE 1. Aerial view of villages, fields and footpaths on the densely populated North China Plain. Curved route on left, a railroad, avoids the villages.

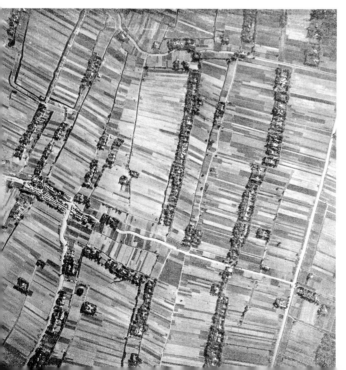

PLATE 2. Aerial view of long, narrow, irrigated rice fields in Kiangsu, north of Yangtze River. Village houses and trees are in strips on dikes along major canals. Transportation is by water.

STORIES OF FILIAL PIETY

PLATE 3.   This primary Confucian virtue is celebrated in three pictures of the same story, from the Han, Sung and Ch'ing periods. Above: In this Han stone engraving (second century A.D.), "Old Lai-tzu" (right caption), in order to show his seventy-year-old parents (left caption) that seventy is not old, amuses them by dressing and playing like a small child.

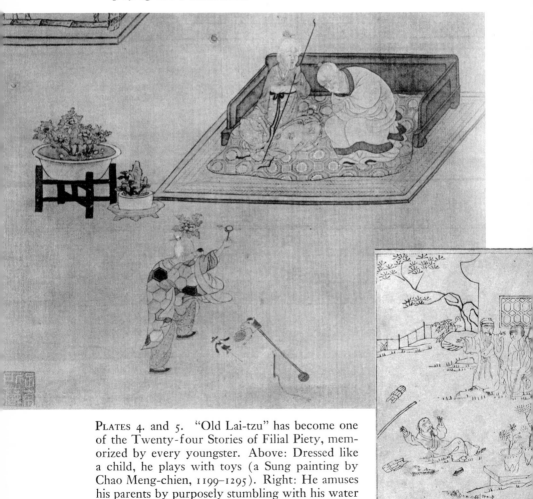

PLATES 4. and 5.   "Old Lai-tzu" has become one of the Twenty-four Stories of Filial Piety, memorized by every youngster. Above: Dressed like a child, he plays with toys (a Sung painting by Chao Meng-chien, 1199–1295). Right: He amuses his parents by purposely stumbling with his water buckets (from a Shanghai wood block of 1873).

PLATE 6. A bronze ritual vessel of the shape known as *ku*, dating from the Shang dynasty.

PLATE 7. A bronze of *yu* shape dating from the early Chou period. The upward-curving horns on the central *t'ao-t'ieh* (animal mask) resemble those of a water buffalo.

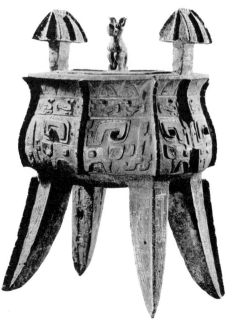

PLATE 8. A bronze of *chia* shape from the Shang or early Chou dynasty. The incurving horns on the central *t'ao-t'ieh* suggest a ram-like creature.

PLATE 9. The round Altar of Heaven on its triple terrace, where the emperor performed rites. Beyond it is the "Temple of Heaven." At the far end of the axis stands the three-storied, round "Temple for Praying for a Good Harvest," which is popularly known as the "Temple of Heaven." To the north of the temple compound lies the city of Peking.

At first the various lords seem to have gone periodically to the Chou court for elaborate ceremonies of investiture which confirmed them in their respective principalities. By the eighth century, however, such investiture had become rare, and few bothered to go to the Chou court for any purpose. In theory, only the Chou ruler could be called *wang*, or king, but there were various other traditional titles loosely applied to the different lords. In time these titles became graded in a strict hierarchy — *kung, hou, po, tzu,* and *nan,* usually translated duke, marquis, earl (or count), viscount, and baron — but the title no longer indicated the actual power or prestige of its holder.

With the passing of time, too, the individual states grew larger and more complex in organization. Some walled towns won control over others; bureaucratic divisions of functions developed among a lord's military followers; cadet branches of the lordly house and hereditary functionaries came to possess large private holdings; and a complicated tax and administrative structure began to evolve.

Chou Society. The Chou, like the Shang, had a sharply divided society in which aristocratic warriors ruled over the peasant masses and the outright slaves, who were used largely as domestic labor. Much later this social cleavage was to be described by the axiom, "The ritual does not extend down to the common people; punishments do not extend up to the great officers." [1]

Within his domain each lord apparently had unlimited power. At first the organization of society was probably quite simple. Under the hereditary lord were his hereditary aristocratic fighting men, and below them the mass of peasants, whose labors supported the whole community. Later writers say that in this period eight peasant families, each with its own field, would cultivate among them a central field for the support of the lord. This system has been called the "well field" (*ching-t'ien*) system, because the character for "well" 井 indicates the pattern of nine fields that would make a unit. This is obviously a later idealization, but it may reflect a period when agricultural property and its produce were communally shared, and a fixed portion went to the lord.

The term "feudal" has usually been used to describe the decentralized rule of the Chou dynasty, particularly in reference to this early period. It is hard to say how well it applies. There undoubtedly were some points of comparison with the feudal age of Europe two thousand years later. On the other hand, our knowledge of the first three centuries of the Chou is very sketchy. Much of the traditional view of this period is based on later writers, who, reading their own desires for political unity and organization back into this supposedly golden age,

[1] From the *Record of Rituals* (see page 66).

built up a complicated picture of close political coordination and elaborate ritual that may never have existed. At any rate, by the eighth century B.C. the various independent states and the organization within these states showed only occasional semi-feudal elements.

The word "feudal" has been much misused in recent years, and it is sometimes applied to almost any system that is felt to be outmoded and therefore bad. The confusion has been compounded by the Chinese use of the single term *feng-chien* for the constantly evolving political system of the eight hundred years of the Chou period and also for Western feudalism. It would probably be a mistake to consider any part of the Chou period as having had a fully developed feudal system, with complex contractual and legal concepts such as we know from Western history or such as the Japanese experienced in their own Middle Ages. In some ways it might be better to consider the early Chou system as simply an extension of a tribal type of organization, in which effective control, both in the Chou realm as a whole and in its component states, depended more on bonds of blood relationship than on feudal legal principles. In any case, the early Chou system was at most only proto-feudal, and the feudal elements decreased rather than grew in the later centuries of the Chou era.

Up through the ninth century B.C. our knowledge of China is somewhat shadowy. Then, in the eighth century, we begin to have fairly detailed and reliable historical records. We find already at that time a China with a highly developed, distinctive civilization, full of vigor and growing rapidly. China stands, in fact, on the threshold of its most dynamic and creative age — the time of its great classic literature and the philosophers who were to set the pattern, and to some extent the limits, for all later thought, not only for China but for the whole of East Asia.

3

Classic China: The Golden Age
of Chinese Thought

ECONOMIC AND CULTURAL GROWTH
IN THE EASTERN CHOU

We do not know how long the early Chou maintained effective control over their wide conquests — perhaps not for long or only sporadically. In any case, Chou power was snuffed out permanently in 771 B.C., when "barbarians" in alliance with rebel Chinese states destroyed Hao, the Chou capital. Tradition says that the king, by lighting a series of beacon fires, had repeatedly summoned his vassals' armies merely to amuse a favorite concubine. Now, when help was really needed, the fires were lighted again, but no one responded.

After this disaster the royal line was re-established at Loyang, which had been a subsidiary Chou capital from the early years of the dynasty. Situated in Honan near the center of population, it was safer from "barbarian" attack than the old capital in the Wei Valley. The Chou kings, however, never again exercised any real political or military power. Until the extinction of the state in 256 B.C., they were accorded certain religious functions and some ceremonial respect, but their domain was smaller and weaker than those of many of their so-called vassals, and they survived as long as they did only because of the tolerance and mutual jealousies of the greater lords.

Counting Time by Dynasties and Periods. The dynastic period before 771 B.C. is known to the Chinese as the Western Chou, because of the location of the capital; thereafter the dynasty is called the Eastern Chou. The Chinese, despite a strong emphasis on the decimal system in counting (they had little use for dozens, the seven-day week, and the like), have not traditionally counted time by centuries, as we have in the modern West. Instead they have used the dynasty as the major unit of historical time, and within that unit various subdivisions, such as Western Chou and Eastern Chou. Actually, two other sub-units are commonly used within the period of the Eastern Chou. One is the "Spring and Autumn" period, 722–481 B.C., the epoch covered by a famous historical work which we shall discuss later, and the "Warring States" period, 403–221 B.C., which, though named for another book, is an apt description of the political conditions of these last two centuries of the Chou era.

Even Occidental scholars fall into the habit of dating events in Chinese history by dynastic and other traditionally named periods, much as they use terms like Carolingian France or Tudor England to describe periods in European history. It is for this reason that we have included as the back end paper of this volume a chronological chart of East Asian history, which will help the reader to coordinate the East Asian system of counting time with his own notion of centuries.

The Eastern Chou is an exciting and romantic phase of Chinese history. Later historians, inbued with the ideal of a unified Chinese empire, have looked back to this period as one of hopeless division. It is true that there was only a shadow of central authority during these five centuries. But the histories of the individual states and the stories of the hundreds of heroes, wise men, and scoundrels they produced make fascinating reading as presented by the gifted literary craftsmen of the late Chou period. More important, this was an age of dynamic growth, bursting energy, and tremendous creativeness, unparalleled by any later stage in Chinese history. Possibly the multiplicity of states and their rivalries served as stimuli.

Technological and Cultural Development. In the eighth century B.C. China was technologically still far behind Western Asia and the lands of the Mediterranean. Iron, for example, was still unknown, though it had already been in use for six or seven centuries in West Asia. By the third century, however, China had probably drawn technologically abreast of the rest of the civilized world. Iron had been introduced around the sixth century and had come into general use before the end of the period. Not only had iron weapons replaced those made of bronze, but the iron-tipped, ox-drawn plow had wrought an agricultural revolution in the broad fields of North China. Agricultural yields were also greatly expanded by large-scale irrigation and other water-control projects in the latter centuries of the Chou, and great effort was devoted to the construction of transport canals, indicating the growth of the economic unit and the rising need to move large quantities of tax grains and other commodities over long distances. By the third century B.C. the Chinese people may already have been the greatest aggregation of human beings in the world, as they are today.

Growth in population was accompanied by a rapid development of trade and a tremendous growth of wealth. As the Chou period progresses one hears more and more of wealthy traders and merchants of all types. This newly risen class proved disruptive to the old aristocratic order, which, perhaps in self-defense, propagated a theory that society consists of four classes: the warrior-administrator at the top, the peasants or primary producers next, the artisans or secondary producers third, and last of all the merchants, whose economic value seemed dubious to the aristocrats. However unrealistic this theory was even in late Chou times, it remained East Asian dogma for the next two millenniums.

With the growth of trade, towns developed into busy commercial centers. Cowrie shells, which had been imitated for a time in bone and metal, were replaced by more intrinsically valuable media of exchange. Bolts of silk and ingots of precious metals came into early use as exchange media, continuing to be used for this purpose until modern times. Later, copper coinage was developed. The earliest coins were rough imitations of metal objects of value, such as spades and knives, but before the end of the Chou era the copper cash, a small round coin with a square hole for stringing purposes, had come into use, and it remained the standard Chinese coin until late in the nineteenth century.

The late Chou saw also the appearance of other characteristic features of Chinese civilization. Chopsticks, for example, had come into use by the third century B.C. Almost as much a symbol of East Asian civilization as the Chinese writing system, chopsticks are the simplest but perhaps the most convenient of all the eating and cooking tools man has devised for himself. Similarly, lacquer, another symbol of East Asian civilization, was being used by the Chinese at least as early as the fourth century B.C.

The Influence of Horseback Riding. The development of horseback riding by the pastoral peoples of Central and Western Eurasia seems to have had several profound effects on Chinese civilization. The greater mobility that this innovation gave to these peoples meant the speeding up of communication between the agricultural civilizations of West and East Asia. In the late Chou the inventions and ideas of the Mediterranean and Indian areas apparently flowed with ease and rapidity into China, eliminating the technological gap that had once existed.

MOUNTED ARCHER

This design stamped on a tile, from the late-Chou-dynasty site of Chin-ts'un in Honan, shows a horseman making a Parthian shot over the horse's rump, turning backward in the saddle to draw his compound bow while at full gallop. He carries a bow case at his side, and a quiver on his back.

Even in the field of the visual arts, for example, the Western emphasis on portrayal in silhouette, as transmitted by the intermediary nomads, came to replace the old Shang approach to design.

The use of the horse made the pastoral northern neighbors of China a greater military threat than they had been before. Since prehistoric times there had been continuous strife between farmers and herdsmen along the ill-defined ecological border of North China, but now the scale of conflict was much increased. This menace called forth more heroic defense efforts, and during the late Chou the states of North China began erecting great walls along their northern frontiers. These, when unified a short time later, became the Great Wall of China.

At about the same time the Chinese themselves took to horseback. Cavalry, introduced first by the states of the northwestern borderland, soon replaced the chariot in Chinese armies. The change was perhaps hastened by the introduction of the crossbow, probably a local invention, which, together with the old native composite bow, made the cavalry a formidable striking force. Horseback riding also sped communications within China, probably hastening the process of political centralization, which, as we shall see, was already well under way. It also brought trousers to the Chinese. During the Chou and for many centuries thereafter flowing robes with long dangling sleeves, not unlike the kimono of modern Japan, remained standard ceremonial dress, ʰut the Chinese were already on their way to becoming the first great agricultural people to clothe both men and women in trousers.

THE GROWTH OF THE POLITICAL AND CULTURAL UNIT

Hand in hand with technological and economic progress in the Eastern Chou period went a steady growth of the effective political unit and of the whole Chinese cultural area. The great wall-building and water-control activity of the latter centuries of the era was clear evidence of political as well as technological and economic advances.

Among the welter of petty states that covered the North China Plain, the old heartland of Chinese civilization, some ten by the eighth century already stood out as larger and more efficient units, dominating the others. These states, however, gradually lost their leadership in later centuries. One reason for this was their proximity to one another; they had less room for growth than the states located on the periphery of the Chinese cultural area. Another reason was perhaps their bondage to tradition. Innovations in political, military, and economic techniques were for the most part carried out by the peripheral states, which were freer of the past and were also stimulated by the challenge of rapidly expanding territorial control. Chou, the embodiment of tradition, gradually shriveled into a political figment. The dukes of Lu and Sung, despite their descent from, respectively, the heroic Duke of Chou and the Sung royal line, failed to consolidate their power and achieve effective control over their hereditary chief officers. It is not surprising, then, that their principalities, like the other central states, gradually degenerated to the status of semi-satellites of the peripheral powers.

The State of Ch'i. Ch'i typified the growth of the peripheral states. As a political unit, it probably antedated the Chou conquest, though it spuriously claimed descent from an officer of the early Chou rulers. More important was its location on the eastern edge of the North China Plain. Here it had ample opportunity for growth, primarily through the incorporation of hitherto unassimilated "barbarians" in the Shantung Peninsula. In the seventh and sixth centuries B.C. it increased its territory at least sixfold, winning control over an area comparable in size to a modern Chinese province. In fact, all of Shantung is still today sometimes called Ch'i.

At much the same time, Ch'i started to modernize its governmental structure. The chief innovations are attributed to Duke Huan and his great advisor Kuan Chung, who lived in the middle of the seventh century. The latter is better known to history as Kuan-tzu, or Master Kuan, and a later book known as the *Kuan-tzu* is attributed to this worthy.

Political modernization meant centralization. Ch'i is said to have divided its population into geographical and functional units, all controlled by the central governmental apparatus. It instituted a uniform tax system and reorganized its military forces by requiring that the various sub-units provide levies for a central army, instead of relying on such household units as the hereditary aristocracy might bring into the field. Ch'i also had an active economic policy, attempting to control prices, regulate weights and measures, and encourage trade. The first state monopolies of salt and iron production, which were to become major economic supports of centralized government in China, are also traditionally attributed to Kuan-tzu.

It is hard to say how many of these innovations actually date back to the seventh century B.C. or took place first in Ch'i. An iron monopoly seems most improbable at this time, when the knowledge of iron perhaps had not yet reached China. A rudimentary monopoly of salt production from sea water is more plausible for this first of the great coastal states. In any case, the reforms attributed to Duke Huan and Kuan-tzu, whenever and wherever they occurred, did represent an early step toward more centralized government.

Unquestionably a major aspect of this centralization of power was the development of a clear system of agricultural taxes, at first in terms of percentages of yields but later in fixed amounts. At the same time private ownership began to replace the old communal use of land, and many peasants thus became landowners. On the other hand, other peasants degenerated to the status of serfs or even fell into slavery.

Centralization of power was accompanied by the development of written law codes and the appearance of bureaucratic administrators, who began to supplement the old aristocracy as aides of the ruler. Kuan-tzu himself is our first clear example of the bureaucratic type. This change in leadership was probably associated with a spread of literacy and education. More and more men appeared who, though lacking high hereditary status themselves, were useful in the increasingly complex administration of the principalities. Many of these men wandered from state to state seeking employment. Others became teachers and thinkers — the philosophers of the golden age of Chinese thought. While such professional bureaucrats and teachers appeared in largest numbers in the central area of Chinese culture, they achieved their greatest practical roles as administrators in the peripheral states.

The Other Peripheral States. Other states, in much the same way as Ch'i, expanded and grew powerful on the edges of the Chinese cultural area. Ch'in appeared in the Wei Valley after the flight of the Chou and became the great power of the extreme west. Chin (often spelled Tsin) came to control roughly what we know as Shansi Province

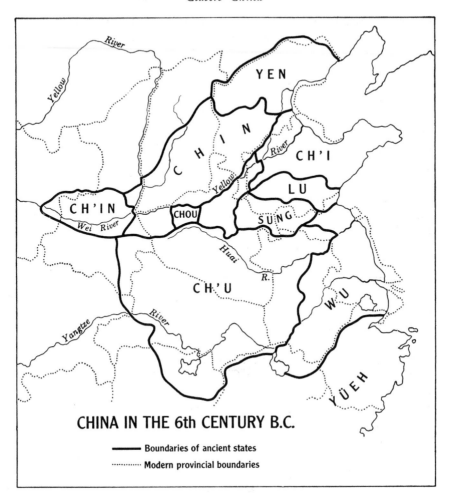

CHINA IN THE 6th CENTURY B.C.

——— Boundaries of ancient states

·············· Modern provincial boundaries

today. It did not succeed, however, in consolidating its power so fully as Ch'i and in 453 B.C. was partitioned by three of its princely families: Han in western Honan, Wei in southern Shansi, and Chao in northern Shansi. The legitimacy of these three rebel succession states was recognized by the Chou house in 403 B.C., a date usually taken as the beginning of the Warring States period.

In the far north around modern Peking and in southern Manchuria appeared the state of Yen, which probably was of "barbarian" origin though it claimed descent from the Chou line. From it has been derived the literary name for Peking: Yen-ching, or "the Yen capital."

Similarly, states of obviously "barbarian" origin, though claiming descent from Chou kings or from earlier Chinese heroes, arose in the Yangtze Valley to the south. Ch'u, occupying the middle Yangtze area and the valley of its large northwesterly tributary, the Han River, was already a great power by the eighth century. Significantly, the Ch'u rulers from the start called themselves *wang*, or kings, thus indicating their rejection of the empty theory of Chou supremacy.

By the sixth century B.C. two other southern "barbarian" states had become major powers: Wu in the lower Yangtze area around modern Nanking and Shanghai, and Yüeh in the modern province of Chekiang. Both followed Ch'u's lead in calling their rulers *wang*. These southern states, situated in an area of great lakes and navigable rivers, were water powers, with fleets as well as armies. Wu has given us the name "Wu dialect" for the language of the Shanghai area. In Yüeh we have the first appearance of a geographical name that clung to the edge of the advancing southern boundary of the Chinese cultural area and has its current metamorphosis in Vietnam, or "Yüeh South."

The tremendous expansion of the Chinese cultural area during the Eastern Chou period thus was achieved primarily through the incorporation of previously "barbarian" elements, in part by conquest but more significantly by the voluntary adherence of political units once considered beyond the pale of civilization. This raises the question: who were these so-called "barbarians"? In the west and north they presumably were pastoral peoples, some perhaps already Chinese-speaking, who now became part of the Chinese agricultural civilization — a transition perhaps made by the Chou and Ch'in peoples themselves at an earlier time. Along the east coast the incorporated peoples probably were already closely allied in culture and language to the civilized Chinese group. The "barbarians" of the Yangtze Valley, however, are said to have had unintelligible languages, and clearly they had many other distinctive cultural features. They presumably were non-Chinese in the sense that they originally spoke other Sinitic languages, like those that still survive in the mountains of Southwest China. Their incorporation into the Chinese cultural area was the start of that great process of acculturation whereby the non-Chinese peoples of Central and South China, except for a few still unassimilated remnants, were gradually drawn into the main stream of Chinese culture and politics.

THE SEARCH FOR POLITICAL STABILITY

In the early years of the Eastern Chou, the small states of the cultural heartland placed great emphasis on legitimacy and the observation of *li*, or the proprieties, that is, the established customs of civilized life. Although warfare was incessant, strict rules of conduct were observed, even in battle. The comparison is often made to the medieval chivalry of the West. A closer parallel might be the rules of warfare observed in modern Europe before the twentieth century. There was a particularly strong feeling that noble lines, which had the responsibility of maintaining ancestral sacrifices, should not be extinguished. Through this emphasis on legitimacy, the weaker central states may have sought to check the menace of the peripheral powers.

As the period progressed, however, proper conduct in warfare became more and more honored in the breach, and legitimacy became a fiction like that of Chou rule. Whereas conquered states had once been made into satellites, they were now annexed as new provinces of the centrally controlled victor state. In the fourth and third centuries B.C., all the principal states followed Ch'u's lead in assuming the title of *wang* for their rulers, indicating that they no longer recognized even the legitimacy of Chou. Battles were fought to the finish; enemy armies were sometimes exterminated and princely lines extinguished.

The scale of battle also grew. Some states could put several thousand chariots into the field. Each chariot was probably supported by a score or more of peasant foot soldiers. Gradually these peasant armies came to number in the tens of thousands, and the newly developed cavalry became vast hosts. Thus they were comparable to the armies of ancient Persia or of Rome.

Naturally, efforts were made to stabilize the political situation and to minimize warfare. Bilateral or multilateral interstate conferences were held with considerable frequency; disarmament proposals were discussed; treaties were signed and alliances formed. Marriages between princely lines were an important means of strengthening alliances, while hostages were widely used to insure the loyalty of a satellite state.

The chief problem of the older but smaller Chinese states in the early Eastern Chou period was to preserve themselves from the rising power of the southern state of Ch'u, which betrayed its "barbarian" origin by its disrespect for accepted custom and its readiness to destroy and swallow up old principalities. There was, therefore, a tendency for the states of the North China Plain to league together against Ch'u in an effort to maintain the principle of legitimacy against this "barbarian" encroachment. This league first took effective form in 651 B.C., when at a great conference the representatives of Chou and the other central states recognized Duke Huan, the great ruler of Ch'i, as hegemon (*pa*) of the Chinese confederation.

The system of hegemony, however, gave China very brief and sporadic stability which lasted only during the lifetime of each strong man who was able to establish himself as hegemon. After Duke Huan, the next to achieve this status was Duke Wen of Chin in 632. The original purpose of the system was completely lost when King Chuang of Ch'u became the third hegemon before the turn of the century.

At times during the sixth century B.C. some real stability was achieved through a formalized balance of power between Chin in the north and

Ch'u in the south, but Wu had meanwhile been rising rapidly on Ch'u's eastern frontier and in 482 won recognition as the paramount military power of China, only to be crushed and annexed by Yüeh in 473. With the extermination of the great state of Wu and the assumption of the role of hegemon by Yüeh, the southernmost and most "barbarian" of the Chinese states, the attempt to prevent radical change and halt "barbarian" domination through the system of hegemony was reduced to its ultimate futility.

There were no further attempts to organize an interstate order in ancient China. Brute conquest had become the rule of the day. Chin eliminated itself as a major power by breaking up in 453, leaving Ch'i in the east, Ch'in in the west, and Ch'u in the south as the chief contenders for supremacy. Ch'u exterminated Yüeh in 334 and the small central state of Lu in 249. Ch'i, surviving a usurpation of the throne, annexed the central state of Sung in 286. Ch'in, after greatly expanding its territory in the late fourth century by incorporating the semi-"barbarian" states of Shu and Pa in what is now Szechwan Province, calmly exterminated Chou itself in 256. Finally, in a series of great campaigns between 230 and 221 B.C., Ch'in conquered all the remaining independent states, unifying China for the first time and opening a new phase in its history.

The Age of the Philosophers
and the Classics

Despite the political instability of the middle and late Chou, this was the greatest age of Chinese thought. Rapid geographical, cultural, and institutional growth stirred men's curiosity and imagination. The failure of the old order — of the old authority, both temporal and spiritual — presented a challenge. Innovations in political and social organization demanded new guiding ideals. Traditions could be safely disregarded. Men's minds could wander at will and did range more freely than ever again in East Asian history.

One cannot but be struck by the parallel in time between this intellectual outburst in China and the heyday of the Greek philosophers, the Hebraic prophets, and the historical Buddha and other early religious leaders in India. Throughout the whole civilized world it was a time of prodigious philosophical activity. One reason for this may have been the intellectual stimulation among the great centers of civilization. Mention has already been made of the acceleration of communications at this time. Certainly the similarity between the paradoxes which interested both the Greeks and the Chinese during the fourth and third centuries B.C. is probably no mere accident. A more fundamental explanation, however, may be the stage of civilization which all these areas had achieved by this time. They had become wealthy enough to support large numbers of thinkers. Moreover, the increased pace of human invention was shattering traditional points of view, and therefore men everywhere were beginning consciously to grapple with the fundamental problems of the meaning and purpose of human life and society.

The challenge was the same, but the answers varied greatly, setting the civilizations of the Mediterranean, South Asia, and East Asia off in decidedly different directions. The contrasting philosophical attitudes developed during this great age of intellectual ferment still stand out among the factors that differentiate these major cultural zones.

Chinese philosophical interest from this time on centered primarily on man as a social and political animal. In these terms it was overwhelmingly "humanistic," in sharp contrast to the emphasis on the divine and the otherworldly in the philosophies of India and of much of the Mediterranean world. The Chou Chinese had Shang Ti and T'ien as supreme deities; they were very conscious of a great variety of spirits and supernatural beings, but for the most part they focused their attention on man and his adjustment to his social environment. Needless to say, this Chinese attitude was not an exact counterpart of the humanism of Renaissance Europe. Rather than stressing the individual, it stressed man in society.

It is difficult to determine why Chinese thought took this particular direction. Possibly political and social problems posed themselves more vividly to Chinese minds because the interstate anarchy of the Chou period existed within a single large cultural and linguistic unit. Or possibly Chinese culture already had this penchant, though what we know of the Shang and the early Chou does not suggest that they were any less inclined to believe in the divine than were their contemporaries in the West.

There can be no doubt, however, that the distinctive role of the philosopher in Chou times was both a product of and a contributing factor in this humanistic or this-worldly tendency. The philosophers were first of all practical politicians. The growing complexity of government required the services of educated men, and changing conditions put a premium on bold, penetrating minds. Great thinkers were the cream of the rising bureaucracy of talent and naturally set themselves up as the mentors of the hereditary rulers.

Whether successful or not as practical politicians, the philosophers attracted followers and thus became teachers. The disciples of the great thinkers gradually formed into schools of philosophy, and from these schools the sayings of the original masters, as reworked and supplemented by many later hands, eventually emerged as the philosophical books of Chou times.

Although the philosophers were often daring innovators, many of them looked back for inspiration toward supposedly golden ages in the past. This has been a common tendency in most periods of history, but interest in the past as a model for the present has been particularly marked in China. This strong consciousness of history may already have been a distinctive feature of Chinese culture in the early Chou period. In any case, the historical-mindedness of East Asian civilization ever since the time of the Chou philosophers has never been equaled in the rest of the world. History, as the repository of human experience, not unnaturally became the chief subject of study in a civilization primarily concerned with the problems of society.

This interest in the past, together with the peculiar Chinese respect for the written word, discussed in the preceding chapter, produced a tremendous veneration for the writings of earlier times. Such an attitude was common to all ancient civilizations but, again, it seems to have been particularly strong among the Chinese. Confucius and other ancient Chinese philosophers looked upon the writings of earlier ages as classics from which they drew their own teachings, and this idea persisted in East Asia until recent times. For over two thousand years Chinese scholars reinterpreted the ancient writings in an effort to wring from them the ideas required by each new age. Up until the very end of the nineteenth century major political innovations in China were justified or attacked on the basis of varying texts of ancient works. As a consequence, those of the early writings that came to be considered classics have had a tremendous influence throughout Chinese history.

The Chinese Classics

One cannot enumerate the Chinese classics without first mentioning another characteristic of Chinese thought which had already become quite evident by late Chou times. This is a love of order and balance. To the Chinese "the classics" is not just a vague term for ancient literature in general but means a clearly specified set of books associated with the dominant Confucian tradition. Works clearly recognized as belonging to other traditions were naturally excluded from the classical canon. The classics, together with the vast body of commentaries that has grown up around them, constitute the first of the traditional four divisions of Chinese literature. The various listings of the classics were all made after Chou times and consequently contain works of diverse epochs, but the Five Classics, the earliest and most important listing, dating from the second century B.C., contain the most ancient and most venerated works.

The Five Classics. The first of the Five Classics is the *Shih ching* or *Classic of Songs* (also known as the *Book of Poetry*). *Ching*, it should be noted, literally means "warp," a graphic term for the classic literature that has helped set the pattern and limits of Chinese thought. The *Classic of Songs* consists of 305 songs dating from about the tenth to the seventh century B.C. Many are simple love poems; others are political poems and ritual hymns of greater length. All are characterized by such a strict pattern of meter, rhythm, and rhyme that they clearly are not just folk songs but the products of a sophisticated literary tradition. Poetry was obviously an important part of Chinese culture even at this early time, and the ability to recite and also to compose poetry has remained ever since the mark of the educated man in East Asia. An excerpt from one of the simpler pieces in the *Classic of Songs* will give an idea of the charm of this first Chinese work of literature:

> Chung-tzu, please
> Don't jump my fence,
> Don't break my willow;
> Not that I grudge them,
> I fear my parents.
> Chung-tzu is dear
> But what my parents would say
> Makes me afraid.[1]

The *Shu ching* or *Classic of Documents* (also known as the *Shang shu* and as the *Book of History*) may be listed next. It contains semi-historical documents and speeches dating from the early centuries of the Chou period, but a large part of the text is now known to consist of later forgeries. Forging, or, as it has often appeared to the forgers themselves, the imaginative reconstruction of lost texts, has always been one form of scholarly activity in China. The development of two differing versions of the *Shu ching* in the second century B.C. and the problem of the forged portions of the work have led to endless philosophical and philological controversy during the past 2000 years.

The *I ching* or *Classic of Changes* (also known as the *Book of Divination*) is another work of mixed age. It is built up around the eight trigrams and sixty-four hexagrams which developed as a system of divination alternative to scapulimancy. The eight trigrams, which are frequently portrayed in East Asian art, are all the possible permutations of three-line combinations of complete or broken lines, as follows: ☰ ☱ ☲ ☳ ☴ ☵ ☶ ☷. If six lines are used instead of three, the possible combinations number sixty-four. Probably by drawing odd or even numbers of stalks of the milfoil plant, a specific trigram or hexagram could be selected, and the *Classic of Changes* would then be consulted on this hexagram. It was, in other words, a diviner's handbook.

---

[1] Translated by James R. Hightower in a forthcoming book on Chinese literature.

Under the various hexagrams, the *Classic of Changes* contains some popular omen lore and a great number of other auguries, some quite specific ("advantageous to cross a large river") and others enigmatic ("a young fox wets his tail crossing a stream"). While some of the work derives from the early Chou, there have been later accretions, and the more philosophical appendices probably date from the end of the Chou or even later.

The *Ch'un ch'iu* or *Spring and Autumn Annals* is a very different sort of work. It is a brief chronological record of major events as they occurred at the court of the state of Lu, or were reported there, between the years 722 and 481 B.C. As we have seen, this text gave rise to the name by which this period is known. The text is terse and entirely factual, but Confucius, according to tradition, and certainly later thinkers read great philosophical significance into the choice of words used to describe each event.

The last of the Five Classics, the *Li chi* or *Record of Rituals* (also known as the *Book of Rites*), is a later work, being a compilation made in the second century B.C. of a miscellany of earlier materials dealing with rites and rituals.[2] These rituals, as we shall see, were a key element in the whole Confucian concept of social order.

The *Record of Rituals* thus is a work that definitely stems from the Confucian tradition. The other Five Classics, too, in time became so closely identified with this main stream of Chinese thought that the group as a whole is commonly called the Confucian Classics. There is some justification for this term. The tradition that Confucius composed or at least edited all five works is undoubtedly false, but he seems to have used the *Classic of Songs* and possibly also the *Spring and Autumn Annals* and the *Classic of Documents* as sources of instruction. Even the *Classic of Changes* came to have a valid connection with Confucianism, for the later philosophical appendices show Confucian inspiration.

The Thirteen Classics. Before leaving the subject of the classics, some mention should be made of two other popular systems of classifying these works. Next to the Five Classics, one hears most frequently of the Thirteen Classics, a grouping that was made well over a millennium after the Chou. These include the Five Classics, but with the *Spring and Autumn Annals* counting as three separate classics because of the three so-called commentaries that usually accompany the main text. Two of these commentaries, the *Kung-yang chuan* (*Tradition of Kung-yang*) and the *Ku-liang chuan* (*Tradition of Ku-liang*) are simple exegetical works dating from the last century of the Chou. The third,

---

[2] During the Han dynasty, a *Classic of Rituals*, possibly the *I li* discussed below, was considered the fifth of the Five Classics, but in later times the *Li chi* took its place.

the *Tso chuan* (*Tradition of Tso*), is actually an entirely independent work which has been cut up to fit under the brief entries of the *Spring and Autumn Annals*. The *Tso chuan* is an elaborate account of the political history of these years, containing, of course, much imaginative reconstruction of detail but constituting, nevertheless, the chief historical source for the period. It is variously dated by modern scholars between the late fourth and early second centuries B.C. The inclusion of the *Tso chuan* as well as the *Classic of Documents* and the *Spring and Autumn Annals* among the classics indicates the importance of historical records to the early Chinese thinkers.

The Thirteen Classics also include, in addition to the *Record of Rituals,* two other works on the same subject and of similar date though somewhat more systematic in composition. These are the *I li* (*Ceremonies and Rituals*) and the *Chou li* (*Rituals of Chou*). The latter is a somewhat fanciful reconstruction in the Confucian tradition of the governmental structure of Chou times and a source of much misinformation as well as information on that period.

Four other works round out the Thirteen Classics. The *Lun yü* or *Conversations* (usually translated *Analects*) of Confucius himself and the comparable work of his greatest successor, the *Meng-tzu* or *Mencius,* will be discussed more fully later. The *Hsiao ching* or *Classic of Filial Piety,* dating from the third or second century B.C., was a reworking of elements found in the *Record of Rituals* and became a prime text for elementary instruction in East Asia. Finally, the *Erh ya,* of the third century B.C., is a collection of glosses to literary texts and marks the beginning of the great Chinese tradition of dictionary-making, which naturally became a very important part of the scholarship of a civilization whose system of writing was so complicated and esoteric.

The Four Books. More than a thousand years after the end of the Chou, four relatively short texts were also selected from this vast mass of classical literature as the supreme embodiment of Confucian teachings. These, known as the Four Books, were the *Analects* or *Conversations* of Confucius, the *Mencius,* and two chapters from the *Record of Rituals:* the *Ta hsüeh* (*Great Learning*) and the *Chung yung* (*Doctrine of the Mean*). The chart on page 68 will help to clarify these three overlapping listings of the Chinese classics.

In addition to the writings of non-Confucian philosophers, several other Chou works of literature failed of inclusion among the classics. Among these were certain historical works comparable to the *Spring and Autumn Annals* and the *Tso chuan.* The *Kuo yü* or *Conversations of the States* is a voluminous account which in scope and time parallels the *Tso chuan* and is even fuller in imaginative details. A similar work, the *Chan kuo ts'e* or *Intrigues of the Warring States,* gave its name to

FIVE CLASSICS	THIRTEEN CLASSICS	FOUR BOOKS
Shih ching *(Classic of Songs)*	*Shih ching*	

Shu ching
  (Classic of
    Documents)
	Shu ching	

I ching *(Classic of Changes)*	*I ching*	

Ch'un ch'iu
  (Spring and Autumn
    Annals)
	Ch'un ch'iu
	
	  :Kung-yang chuan
	    (Tradition of
	      Kung-yang)
	
	  :Ku-liang chuan
	    (Tradition of
	      Ku-liang)
	
	  :Tso chuan
	    (Tradition of Tso)	

Li chi
  (Record of Rituals)
	Li chi	*Li chi*
		
		  :Ta hsüeh
		    (Great Learning)
		
		  :Chung yung
		    (Doctrine of
		      the Mean)

	I li
	  (Ceremonies and
	    Rituals)	

	Chou li *(Rituals of Chou)*	
	Lun yü *(Analects)*	*Lun yü*
	Meng-tzu *(Mencius)*	*Meng-tzu*
	Hsiao ching *(Classic of Filial Piety)*	
	Erh ya	

the last period of the Chou dynasty. Finally, the *Chu-shu chi-nien* or *Bamboo Annals* was a set of records of the Chin state, comparable to the Lu records preserved in the *Spring and Autumn Annals*, and containing also one of the variant chronologies for earlier ages. It was buried in a grave in 295 B.C. and rediscovered in 279 A.D., by which time the bamboo slips on which it, like most other Chou books, was written were such an oddity as to give rise to the name by which it is now known. The *Bamboo Annals* was subsequently lost, and the text that later circulated under that name was a forgery.

Besides the *Classic of Songs*, the only other important poetic work of Chou times is the *Ch'u tz'u* or *Elegies of Ch'u*, which is made up to a large extent of poems by Ch'ü Yüan. An aristocrat of Ch'u living at the beginning of the third century, Ch'ü Yüan fell out of royal favor and, after some wandering, drowned himself in despair. According to tradition the great dragon-boat festival of South China originated from the search for his body. During his wanderings Ch'ü Yüan composed the *Li sao*, which is an allegorical description of the author's search for an understanding ruler. More than half of it is devoted to a fanciful flight through time and space. Ch'ü Yüan's poems represent a very sophisticated and technically advanced development which strongly influenced the exuberant, word-manipulating poetry of the next several centuries.

CONFUCIANISM

It is fitting that the first man we know to have been a professional teacher and philosopher in China should always have been recognized in East Asia as the greatest of all teachers and philosophers. This was Confucius, the Latinized form of K'ung-fu-tzu, or Master K'ung. His traditional dates, 551–479 B.C., are probably not far wrong.

The life and teachings of Confucius have naturally attracted a vast quantity of hagiographic writing, most of it highly fanciful. What little we know of the original man must be drawn from the *Analects (Lun yü)*. This work consists largely of Confucius' answers to questions, prefaced by the phrase, "The Master said." Written by disciples or perhaps by the disciples of disciples, with many later additions, the *Analects* are a weak reed to support so heroic a figure.

Confucius, a native of the state of Lu, was not born to hereditary power, but he was a man of education and, therefore, probably came from the lower aristocracy. Throughout his life he aspired to high political office but never achieved it. As a young man he probably held petty posts and in later life, possibly because of the influence of some of his disciples who did achieve political prominence, he seems to have been given an honorable sinecure. Dissatisfied with this, he wandered from state to state for about a decade, seeking in vain for a post worthy of his talents. Eventually he returned to Lu to die. Thus, in his chosen role as a practical politician, he was a complete failure; in his incidental occupation as a teacher, however, time proved him an unparalleled success.

At first glance the concepts Confucius taught seem unexciting and flat to those accustomed to a more rarefied philosophical atmosphere. He does not have the intellectual appeal of a Socrates or a Plato; nor does he fit the pattern of the great religious leaders of India and the Mediterranean world. For that matter, the system that he taught was not a religion in the Western sense. He fully recognized the spirits and Heaven (T'ien), sometimes showing a sense of mission derived from the latter, but he was obviously not much interested in the supra-human realm. To an inquiry about death, he replied, "Not yet understanding life, how can you understand death?" He advised respect for the spirits but keeping them at a proper distance. This lack of concern for the otherworldly, as one might expect, led in time to a strong agnostic strain in the Confucian tradition, which contrasts sharply with the dominant interest in the divine in India and the West.

Confucius showed the bias of his day by a paramount interest in political problems. But here too his ideas at first seem unimpressive. He proclaimed himself to be above all else a devoted student of antiquity, a transmitter of the wisdom of the past. He looked back in particular to the early days of Chou rule as a golden age of peace. The anarchy of his own day, he felt, could be corrected if men would return to the political and social order supposedly created by the founders of the dynasty, King Wen and the Duke of Chou, who were his chief heroes. In this connection, it is significant that Lu was known as a conservative state which had preserved many of the early Chou traditions, and that its rulers were descended from the Duke of Chou.

To return to the ancient Way, Confucius felt, men must play their proper assigned roles in a fixed society of authority. The idea is succinctly expressed in the famous statement: "Let the ruler be a ruler and the subject a subject; let the father be a father and the son a son." Later this concept was expressed by the term "the rectification of names" (*cheng ming*), implying that theory should correspond to reality or, as the Confucians really meant it, that reality should be made to conform with theory.

If this were all there was to the teachings of Confucius, he would be nothing more than an arch-conservative or even a reactionary — a man who hoped to turn back the clock of history. Where he innovated, though apparently quite unconsciously, was in his concept that government is basically an ethical problem. He did not question the hereditary right of the lords to govern, but he insisted that their first duty was to set a proper example of sound ethical conduct. In a day when might was right, he argued that the ruler's virtue and the contentment of the people, rather than power, should be the true measures of political success. Chinese thought before Confucius might be characterized as largely pre-moral; it centered primarily around auguries and sacrifices. Confucius was China's first great moralist, the founder of a great ethical tradition in a civilization which above all others came to concentrate on ethical values.

Confucius' chief aim in life was to convince rulers of his ethical principles; his chief immediate accomplishment was the instruction of his disciples in these principles, so that they could be virtuous officials. He devoted himself to the training of their characters. His ideal was the *chün-tzu*, literally "ruler's son" or "aristocrat," a term which at his hand changed its meaning from "a noble" to "a man of nobility." The term is perhaps best translated as "gentleman" in the sense of a "culti-vated man" or "superior man."

The Confucian Virtues. Confucius had much to say of the virtues which the *chün-tzu* or "gentleman" should possess. There were *chih* (uprightness or inner integrity), *i* (righteousness), *chung* (conscien-tiousness toward others, or loyalty), *shu* (altruism or reciprocity), and, above all, *jen* (love or human-heartedness). The second translation for *jen* is derived from the fact that it is a cognate for the word for "man" and is written with the character for "two" beside the "man" signific, thus 仁. The concept of *shu* or "reciprocity" is neatly summed up in the *Analects* as "not doing to others what you do not like yourself," a close parallel to the Golden Rule of Christianity.

The necessary qualities of the "gentleman," Confucius felt, were not limited to these inner virtues. The "gentleman" must also have *wen*, meaning "culture" or possibly "polish," and *li*, literally "ritual," that is, an understanding of proper decorum and etiquette. Confucius was not interested in producing "diamonds in the rough." As he says, "Upright-ness uncontrolled by etiquette becomes rudeness." (In this connection it should be pointed out that Confucius, like Aristotle, was also much in-terested in music, not as a simple pleasure, but as a force helping to produce the proper ethical attitudes.) Confucius' emphasis on the *li* of antiquity contributed to the tremendous importance of ritual and eti-quette in later Confucianism and the reliance in East Asia on inculcating inner attitudes through the practice of external forms — a sound peda-gogical principle that is too little honored in the contemporary Occident.

The judicious balancing of inner virtues and external polish is charac-teristic of the moderation of Confucius in all his ideas. Great philoso-phers and religious leaders in India and in the West have commonly dealt in absolutes; or perhaps one might say they have tended to think in logico-mathematical terms. Confucius was a relativist, thinking in socio-human terms. He set the East Asian pattern of compromise, of always seeking the middle path. He was flexible. He hated obstinacy and distrusted clever talkers. As the *Mencius* so aptly says, "Confucius did not go to extremes."

The Triumph of Confucianism. Moderation and balance are perhaps the major reasons for the eventual triumph of Confucianism in China. The products of the balanced Confucian training, which stressed both inner virtues and outer polish, were men unquestionably valuable in government. At a more fundamental level, we can perceive the fine balance between the basic political conservatism of Confucianism, which naturally made it popular with most subsequent rulers in East Asia, and its high ethical principles, which gave political authority a stronger foundation than mere hereditary right and served as a constant stimulus for the improvement of government.

Another basic reason for the eventual triumph of Confucianism was its timeliness. A bureaucracy of education was slowly growing up in China in response to political needs, and this functional group needed a philosophy, which Confucius admirably supplied. While never questioning the legitimacy of hereditary power, Confucius assumed that he, as a man of superior learning, had the right to tell the rulers how they should conduct themselves and their government. In this sense he was an unconscious revolutionary and his whole life a challenge to hereditary power.

Significantly, there is no word corresponding to Confucianism in East Asia. The Confucianists have always been known as the *ju*, or "literati," as the term is usually translated, and Confucianism is known as "the learning of the *ju*." *Ju* literally meant "the weaklings," that is, men of the pen rather than the sword; but with the eventual triumph of the civil bureaucrats, Confucianism triumphed too, because it justified their rule and gave it a strong philosophical foundation.

TAOISM

Next to Confucianism, the most important stream in Chinese thought is Taoism (pronounced *dowism*). Although not a unified and homogeneous school of thought, the Taoism of the late Chou period stood out in sharp contrast to Confucianism. In fact, it was in large part a philosophy of protest — the rebellion of the common man against the growing despotism of his rulers, and the rebellion of the very uncommon man of intellect or sensitivity against the growing rigidity of the moralists, who were following in the footsteps of Confucius.

Where both the moralists and the rulers sought to bring men into conformity with social patterns, the Taoists stoutly championed the independence of the individual, whose only concern, they maintained, should be to fit into the great pattern of nature, not that of man-made society. This pattern of nature was the *Tao*, literally the "Road" or "Way," a term used by Confucius to describe the social system he advocated but given a metaphysical interpretation in Taoism. Quite appropriately, the Taoists derived their name from their favorite word.

Some scholars have associated early Taoism with the state of Ch'u in the Yangtze Valley, suggesting that it may thus represent an enrichment of Chinese thought derived in part from "barbarian" sources. It is also thought to represent the survival or, rather, the metamorphosis of religious concepts of the pre-Confucian period. Thus, the concern of the Shang and early Chou peoples to placate the spirits of nature through sacrifices may have found a more sophisticated expression in the Taoist attempt to merge the individual in the great *Tao* of the universe. The interest of the Chinese farmer in his natural environment, the fertility cults of the ancient Chinese rulers, and the role of the rulers as mediators between nature and man may all have found philosophical expression in the Taoist attempt to fit human life smoothly into nature's rhythms.

The mysticism of the Taoists, which was an important element and possibly the core of their whole point of view, may also have been derived from the primitive shamans or medicine men of earlier days. The latter, through self-induced trances, had communicated directly with the spirits; the Taoists, through "sitting and forgetting" and "fasts of the mind," experienced trance-like ecstasies in which they achieved the state of the "true man" and directly apprehended the oneness of the universe. Such practices may conceivably have been influenced by the Indian concepts of yoga; the Taoists, like the Indians, stressed breathing exercises for achieving their trances. Taoist mysticism, however, remained strictly within the bounds of Chinese thought. Whereas Western mysticism has tended to express itself in terms of direct contact or identification with a personal deity, the Taoists stressed the union of the individual with an impersonal natural order.

The first representatives of this second great stream of Chinese thought may have been the antisocial recluses who figured in the Confucian *Analects*. Yang Chu, a fourth-century philosopher, seems also to have been an early figure in this tradition. He was not a mystic, but his hedonistic Stoicism represents one aspect of later Taoist thought.

Our chief knowledge of Chou Taoism is derived from three books of unknown authorship and somewhat doubtful date. The most venerated of these is the *Lao-tzu* or *Tao te ching* (*The Way and Power Classic*). It is a composite text, probably dating from the third century B.C., though attributed to a presumably mythical sage known as Lao-tzu, or the "Old Master," whose traditional dates have been fixed to give him a slight edge in seniority over Confucius. Terse and cryptic in style, the

Tao te ching has given itself to diverse interpretations by later Chinese thinkers and a startling variety of translations into Western languages.

The second text is the *Chuang-tzu*, also probably of the third century but attributed to a man of the late fourth century. The *Chuang-tzu*, which consists of delightful parables, metaphors, and poetic passages, is a work of high literary merit and represents the most important formulation of early Taoist thought. The third work, the *Lieh-tzu*, which in content and style is much like the *Chuang-tzu*, is variously attributed to the same period or to the third century A.D.

Tao and Wu-wei. Like all other mystics, the ancient Taoists found it difficult to express their basic ideas. As they said, "The one who knows does not speak, and the one who speaks does not know." The *Tao* is founded on a nameless, formless "Non-being"; it "cannot be heard," "cannot be seen," and "cannot be spoken." But it is, in essence, the totality of the natural processes to which man must conform. Despite constant flux, the *Tao* is unitary, having no distinctions of big or little, high or low, life or death, good or bad. The relativity of all things and the dependence of any quality on its opposite are constant Taoist themes. As they say, "Water, which is life to fish, is death to man," and "It is only because everyone recognizes beauty as beauty that we have the idea of ugliness."

The man who can transcend mundane human distinctions and become one with the *Tao* is "beyond all harm" and achieves "tranquillity in the midst of strife." Merging with the *Tao*, he derives from it his individual *Te* or mystical "Power." This word later came to have the moralistic meaning of "virtue," having followed a semantic development similar to that of the Latin *virtus*.

The key to merging with the Way of nature is the doctrine of *wu-wei*, or "doing nothing." By this the Taoists did not mean complete inaction but rather doing what is natural: "Do nothing and nothing will be not done" — that is, everything will be spontaneously achieved. The favorite figure of the Taoists is water, which, though the softest of all things, wears away the hardest. If left to itself, the universe proceeds smoothly according to its own harmonies. Man's efforts to change or improve nature only destroy these harmonies and produce chaos. There is a spontaneous knack to all accomplishment which conscious effort only mars.

The sage knows no ambition and therefore experiences no failure. He refuses all honors and responsibilities. Chuang-tzu, when invited to manage the realm of the King of Ch'u (the story is, of course, apocryphal), compared himself to a holy tortoise, to whom the veneration of others could bring no satisfaction, and indignantly concluded, "Be off and leave me to drag my tail in the mud." The true sage does not even attempt to teach others. By this criterion, our Taoist authors are themselves admittedly imperfect.

The Ideal of Primitivity. The Taoists, despite their nature mysticism and their antisocial beliefs, were sufficiently in tune with the prevailing interests of the day to draw their own picture of a perfect society. Like other contemporary Chinese philosophers, they looked back to a golden age, but for them this past was a time of perfect knowledge, before the ancients even realized that "things had come into existence," much less had recognized the "distinction" between things or reached the consequent expression of "approval and disapproval." The concept of good and bad and the embodiment of this concept in rituals, they felt, were the real sources of human misery. The Confucian sages thus became the unwitting villains of history. The virtues they had invented were the reasons for the existence of vice. Law was the source of crime; without wealth there could be no stealing.

Primitivity was the ideal of the Taoists, and their expressive term for it was *p'u*, meaning literally an uncarved block of wood. Knowledge can only corrupt; it creates desires that cannot be fulfilled. The Taoists even advocated the abandonment of writing and the return to a supposedly earlier stage of communication by knotted strings. For them the symbol of perfection was the infant and, later, the unborn child in the womb. In the *Chuang-tzu* we find the parable of Primitivity, whose two friends, Change and Uncertainty, decided to give him the usual seven apertures that are needed for seeing, hearing, breathing, and eating; this they did with success, boring one a day, but Primitivity died in the process. The Taoists laud the peasant who, though he knew of the water wheel, chose to carry water up from a well on his back, realizing that ingenious devices would lead to a devious mind.

The political ideal of the Taoists was a small state from which the cocks and dogs of a nearby state could be heard, but whose people were so contented that none had ever bothered to visit this neighboring village. Their recipe for rule was to empty the people's minds and fill their bellies. And over such a primitive, passive society the Taoist sage would rule, without effort and without benevolence, accomplishing everything by doing nothing.

The Taoist Balance to Confucianism. Needless to say, the primitive anarchy which the Taoists advocated usually had less appeal for the actual rulers of China than did Confucianism. As a school of philosophy, moreover, it suffered serious debasement in later centuries. Taoistic attitudes, however, remained fresh and strong throughout Chinese history.

The chief reason for Taoism's continuing vitality seems to have been that it supplied things which otherwise were weak or lacking in Chinese society. Growing political conformity and heavy Confucian morality were not conducive to aesthetic expression. But the Chinese have always had a strong aesthetic urge, which the individual freedom of Taoism and its mystical union with nature encouraged. Chinese artists and poets, however closely identified with the Confucian tradition, have usually been Taoists at heart.

Taoism, in fact, has always served as an admirable balance wheel to the dominant concepts of Chinese culture. The centralization of power placed sharp limits on human freedom; Confucian morality and insistence on social conformity were even more restrictive. But in Taoism the individual could achieve full self-expression; his intellect was free to wander at will. Since neither Confucianism nor Taoism were jealously exclusive religions in the Western sense, the individual and even the whole society could be Confucian and Taoist at the same time, achieving perhaps a healthier psychological balance on these two bases than could have been achieved on only one.

The man in power was usually a Confucian positivist, seeking to save society. The same man out of power became a Taoist quietist, intent on blending with nature around him. The active bureaucrat of the morning becomes the dreamy poet or nature lover of the evening. This balanced dualism in philosophy and in personality has persisted until the modern day. No one is surprised to find the defeated general turn into a hermit philosopher, and it is still assumed that the cabinet minister may also be a poet or painter.

The Hundred Schools

Confucianism and Taoism were by no means the only philosophies that flourished in late Chou times. With a characteristic love of categorizing and of round numbers, the Chinese have dubbed the proliferation of philosophical teachings in this period The Hundred Schools. Some of these "hundred" deserve mention because of their contemporary prominence or subsequent influence.

The Naturalists. One school, which might be called Naturalism, consisted of men who attempted to explain nature's working on the basis of certain cosmic principles. The greatest name of this school is Tsou Yen, who lived around the year 300 B.C. in Ch'i. It is worth noting that this whole school was in its early days associated with the peripheral coastal states of Ch'i and Yen, a region famed for its magicians. Thus it may represent another survival of non-moralistic, shamanistic attitudes or a "barbarian" accretion to Chinese culture.

One of the chief concepts of the Naturalists is the basic dualism of nature: *yang* is male, light, hot, positive; *yin* is female, dark, cold, negative. Unlike the dualism of the Mediterranean world, in which good

and bad are in perpetual conflict, *yin* and *yang* are mutually complementary and balancing. The greater *yang* grows, the sooner it will yield
to *yin;* the sun at noon is starting to give way to night. The inter-
dependence of the two principles was well symbolized by an interlock-
ing figure (see page 53), which today, for example, is used as the central
element in the flag of the Republic of Korea.

Actually, the *yin-yang* concept often seems more useful than Western dualism for analyzing nature and also human affairs. It fits so neatly
the rhythms of day and night, summer and winter, and the balancing
roles of male and female. To apply it to the subject matter of this chapter, one might say that Confucianism is the *yang* of Chinese thought
and Taoism the *yin*. This would explain their complementary roles in
Chinese society, which according to Western dualism would be incom-
prehensible.

Another basic concept of the Naturalists is that all nature is made up
of varying combinations of the "five elements" or "five powers" (*wu
hsing*): wood, metal, fire, water and earth. The parallel to the four
elements of the Greeks (earth, fire, air and water) is striking. The exact
sequence of elements varies in different texts, but, however arranged, the
sequence was felt to have a strictly causal and magical significance.
Thus, metal was said to cut wood, fire to melt metal, water to quench
fire, earth to overcome water, and wood to triumph over earth.

The "five elements" concept led in time to the development of an
extensive pseudo-science that persisted through later ages. Cosmic cor-
relations were worked out between the five elements and other categories of five: colors, tastes, sounds, planets, directions (including the
center), and so on. History is explained on the basis of the succession of
the elements, each one representing a dynasty. Medicine is analyzed
in the same terms: water quenches a fever (fire), and the like. With
the addition of numerology and astrology, the possibilities became infinite. The ancient calendar signs were also incorporated into the system. These were the ten "heavenly stems" and twelve "earthly
branches" (associated with the signs of the zodiac). When combined
together in a sequence of pairs of characters, these formed the traditional cycle of sixty, which was used for counting time in periods of
sixty days and sixty years. As applied to the lay of the land and the proper
situations for houses, graves, and the like, this pseudo-science became
geomancy (*feng-shui*, literally meaning "wind and water"), which still
has its hold among China's rural population.

The Dialecticians. Another group of philosophers, also known as
the School of Names (*Ming chia*), were the Dialecticians, who were
much like the Sophists of Greece. These men were groping toward a
system of logic by analyzing the true meaning of words and thus avoid-

ing the logical pitfalls of any language. They were both stimulated and perhaps in the long run frustrated in this effort by the ambiguity of Chinese, which, being uninflected, usually fails to express the distinctions of tense and number that are so explicit in Greek, Sanskrit, and the other Indo-European languages.

Among the Dialecticians, Hui Shih, of the fourth century B.C., is famed for his Ten Paradoxes, and Kung-sun Lung, of the early third century, for the passage in his works that starts out with the statement: "A white horse is not a horse" (by this he apparently meant that "white horse" does not correspond to the universal concept "horse," but is descriptive of only one kind of horse). The arguments of the Dialecticians were condemned by later Chinese as being frivolous and unprofitable, and their particular type of thought, though revived again in the third and fourth centuries A.D., eventually died out.

Mo-tzu. An older philosophy than that of either the Naturalists or the Dialecticians is the school of Mo-tzu, who was born around or soon after the death of Confucius. His teachings have come down to us in a work known as the *Mo-tzu*, which includes, besides the later additions, certain prolix and clumsy sections which he himself may have written. Made up of essays as well as dialogues, it shows a definite advance in logical presentation over the Confucian *Analects*.

Mo-tzu's concentrated attacks on Confucianism suggest that he represented a heretical offshoot of this school and also that Confucianism was the only recognized philosophy in his day. Since he was consciously combating another school of thought, he was interested in questions of dialectics. In fact, the later Dialecticians may have got their start from him, as did a group of later logicians within his own school, one of whom set out to prove that "A white horse is a horse."

In most matters Mo-tzu took a more extreme stand than Confucius. Where the latter had looked back to the golden age of the early Chou, from which some traditions had survived, Mo-tzu advocated a return to the much earlier Hsia dynasty, for which "traditions" could be made virtually from whole cloth; and where Confucius advocated that men of learning should guide the rulers, Mo-tzu saw no reason why hereditary princes should not relinquish their thrones to their obvious superiors. By this time the myth of the sage rulers Yao and Shun, who passed on their thrones to their most worthy ministers, had taken shape.

Confucius, for all his innovations, had been a traditionalist at heart; Mo-tzu was strictly a utilitarian. He advocated measures to enrich the country, increase the population, and bring order to the state. Anything that did not contribute to these ends he attacked with vehemence. Food, clothing, and housing should be limited to bare necessities. Music and all the ceremonial *li* of the Confucianists were useless and wasteful.

In particular, Mo-tzu inveighed against elaborate funerals and the three-year period of mourning for one's parents, which was part of the Confucian system. He had no use for any aesthetic expression and advocated the suppression of all the emotions.

The greatest waste of all is, of course, aggressive warfare, which Mo-tzu condemned on utilitarian as well as moral grounds. His solution to the problem was to develop the defense until offense became impractical. Several chapters in his book are devoted to defensive warfare, and he schooled his disciples in this art. The history of the next two centuries presents overwhelming evidence of the failure of Mo-tzu's pacifistic views, and later ages esteemed his writings far less than they did the *Sun-tzu*, the late Chou classic on the military arts.

Mo-tzu's panacea for achieving his utilitarian utopia was the doctrine of universal love. The Confucians, accepting the family system and the complexities of society, were developing at this time a theory of graded love, dependent on the specific relationships among individuals. Mo-tzu felt that the interests of all would be better served if "everyone would love every other person as much as he loves himself."

Mo-tzu felt that the increasingly agnostic Confucians were too fatalistic and erred in ignoring the spirits. But, again, his motives in stressing the supra-human may have been essentially utilitarian. Sacrifices to the spirits, he believed, would bring worldly blessings, and the moral Heaven he envisaged would provide the final sanction for his teachings because it would mete out appropriate rewards and punishments.

There was a definitely authoritarian strain in Mo-tzu's teachings. He was a dogmatic proselytizer. From his large following he demanded strict obedience and he bequeathed his authority to a line of Grand Masters of the school. Not unnaturally, he thought in terms of a rigidly disciplined state, in which the subordinate at each level would follow the lead of his superior in all matters and feel a strong sense of identity with him.

It is an interesting question why Mo-tzu's school did not survive the third century B.C. and his philosophy disappeared almost without a trace. He had a better organized following than Confucius, and for a while his ideas may have had greater currency. The Westerner recognizes in his "universal love," utilitarianism, pacifism, awareness of the otherworldly, and interest in problems of logic concepts that could have greatly enriched Chinese thought. Then why did they fail? Insofar as the answer lies in the content of his ideas, it appears to be the reverse of that given for the success of Confucianism. Mo-tzu's ideas were too extreme. The Chinese did not care for his austere utilitarianism and complete lack of psychological subtlety; they preferred the moderate but practical graded love of the Confucians to his lofty but seemingly impractical "universal love."

MENCIUS, HSÜN-TZU, AND THE LEGALISTS

Mencius. A philosopher who succeeded where Mo-tzu failed in passing on his doctrines to later ages was Meng-tzu, known to the West in the Latinized form, Mencius. His book, the *Mencius*, was in the twelfth century elevated to the status of a classic, second only to the *Analects*. A long work of great literary merit and deep psychological perception, the *Mencius* has left a profound mark on East Asian civilization.

Mencius, a native of a small principality bordering on Lu, lived from about 372 to 289 B.C. He was an ardent champion of Confucianism, arguing, often with more vehemence than logic, against its opponents, particularly Mo-tzu and the Taoistic hedonist Yang Chu, whose doctrines, he complained, "filled the world." Like Confucius, he wandered from state to state, seeking high government office without success; but by his time the itinerant philosopher-statesman was a much more honored figure than in the days of Confucius. Though Mencius seems never to have been more than a guest consultant to the kings and princes he visited, he and his retinue of disciples, which is said to have numbered in the hundreds, were well received and handsomely supported in state after state, especially in the great principality of Ch'i. He took this generous treatment for granted and apparently treated his princely benefactors with surprising disdain.

Mencius evidently thought that he was simply transmitting Confucius' Way of the ancients, but in fact he added important new facets to his master's doctrines. One of his major concepts was that man is by nature good — by which he meant that all men share an innate moral sense, which can be developed into the full-fledged Confucian virtues. Anyone, he pointed out, will spontaneously feel alarm and pity if he suddenly sees a child about to fall into a well. However, this natural bent toward morality can be perverted by an adverse environment, just as Bull Mountain was deforested by the woodman's axe. (Such reasoning by example and analogy is typical of Mencius and most of the philosophers of his day.)

Man's inborn goodness, Mencius felt, could be developed by an effort at inner self-cultivation, not unlike the mystical experience of the Taoists, and also by education. Starting with those who are near and dear and therefore spontaneously evoke a feeling of love (*jen*), men should consciously strive to extend their love to those who are more distant. They should also conduct themselves in daily life in such a way as to foster the growth of the virtues.

In the political field, Mencius was even more insistent than Confucius that government was primarily an exercise in ethics. He identified Mo-tzu's utilitarianism with gross opportunism and maintained that the guiding principle of government should be not profit but what is right.

He confidently believed that if any ruler showed himself to be a fully moral man the whole land would inevitably gravitate into his hands. This was the "Kingly Way" (*Wang Tao*), not the attempt to conquer or dominate the land through force, as the hegemons had done without success.

The "Mandate of Heaven." The rule of the truly moral king, Mencius argued, is characterized by his benevolence toward his people. He provides schooling for them and sees to their economic well-being. In this connection, he condemned the current system of taxation through grain tributes and extolled the benefits which would derive from the communal ownership of property under the "well field" system, as he interpreted this supposedly ancient institution. There is no way to become a true king, he felt, except by winning the support of the populace. In fact, the "Mandate of Heaven," the basic justification for the ruler's power, manifests itself only through the acceptance of a ruler by his people; if the people kill or depose him it is clear that he has lost Heaven's support. In this way, Mencius took the argument that the Chou had used to justify their overthrow of the Shang and turned it into a general justification of revolution. But of course this "right of rebellion," as some have called it, would be an effective right only if the rebels proved successful.

The contributions of Mencius to the main stream of Chinese thought seem to have been, as later thinkers judged them, second only to those of Confucius. His concept of human nature, which meant, in essence, that all men are created morally equal, contributed much to the dominant egalitarianism of subsequent Chinese society; his insistence that government must be on behalf of the people and requires the tacit consent of the people helps to account for the high political ideals the Chinese were able to maintain throughout much of their history.

Hsün-tzu. Another later Confucianist left perhaps as great a mark on Chinese civilization, even though the eleventh- and twelfth-century scholastics were to condemn him as heterodox because of his disagreement with Mencius. This was Hsün-tzu, who, living from about 300 to 237 B.C., seems in his own day to have been a greater success than Mencius both as a practical politician and as a teacher. Large sections of his book, the *Hsün-tzu*, were even incorporated into the *Record of Rituals*. The *Hsün-tzu*, as a series of well-organized essays, marks a considerable logical advance over the dialogue style of the *Mencius*.

Though Hsün-tzu was interested in dialectical problems and developed a whole theory of language, he is known chiefly for his flat contradiction of Mencius' basic tenet that man is by nature good. Human nature, he argued, is derived from an impersonal, amoral Heaven; man's emotions and natural desires lead to conflict and therefore are bad. The cure for this situation is education. All men are equal in their innately evil natures, but they are susceptible to improvement through education. The teacher is all-important and therefore to be revered. The process of learning "begins with reciting the classics and ends in learning the *li*."

Here for the first time we find taking shape the concept of "the classics" as the repository of all human wisdom. In Hsün-tzu we find also a strong emphasis on formal education, on the key role of the teacher, and on the central educational and ethical value of rituals and ceremonies. All these concepts are characteristic of most subsequent Chinese thought. His flat disbelief in spirits also, no doubt, contributed to the growing agnostic element in Confucianism.

The careful organization of Hsün-tzu's thinking and its dogmatic tone may also have played a part in the hardening orthodoxy of the Confucian tradition. In any case, his emphasis on education and on *li*, or proper conduct according to status, undoubtedly contributed to the growing authoritarianism of Chinese government. He believed in a strict hierarchic order, in which the distinctions expressed in *li* should be properly observed, and he admired strong discipline in government, advocating that the rulers control their people by admonishments, proclamations and punishments.

The Legalists. These authoritarian tendencies and Hsün-tzu's pessimistic evaluation of human nature were developed further by a group of philosophers and practical politicians known as the Legalists (*Fa-chia*). The leading thinker in this group, Han-fei-tzu (died 233 B.C.), and a prominent Ch'in statesman identified with this philosophy, Li Ssu (died 208 B.C.), were both disciples of Hsün-tzu.

The *Han-fei-tzu*, a work which contains some essays by the philosopher of this name, is the fullest exposition of Legalist thought. Another third-century Legalist work is the *Shang chün shu* (*Book of Lord Shang*), falsely attributed to Shang Yang, a great Ch'in statesman who died in 338 B.C. The *Kuan-tzu*, a book of doubtful date erroneously attributed to the seventh-century Ch'i statesman of that name, also contains much Legalist material.

Hsün-tzu's thought was not the only philosophical influence on the Legalists. They may also have been influenced by Mo-tzu's insistence on discipline and on the complete subordination of the inferior to the superior, as well as by his crude utilitarianism and his scorn for *li*. They owed even more to the Taoists, deriving from them a concept of an amoral natural order and a complete contempt for conventional ethics and all book learning. Their ideal state, in which an uneducated citizenry would be blindly obedient to an all-powerful king, is related at least in theory to the Taoists' ideal of a primitive society ruled without effort by a sage.

The Legalists felt that human nature is incorrigibly selfish and inevitably produces conflict. Moralists and do-gooders who pander to human desires are in fact merely perpetuating chaos. Severe laws and harsh punishments, though hateful to the people, are the only means of bringing them the order and security for which they yearn. The people, in fact, are like the baby who howls when its boil is lanced. The wise ruler must expect to find himself in conflict with the world.

The appeal of other philosophers to the Way of the ancients was simply dismissed by the Legalists: different times require different methods. Since his people are stupidly selfish and his ministers untrustworthy self-seekers, the ruler cannot rely on their moral virtues but must control all alike by clearly defined rewards and punishments — in other words, by a detailed code of penal laws. Men should be judged not by their motives but by their accomplishments. Anyone who fails to achieve what he is assigned to do must be punished; even the man who accomplishes more than his assigned task must be punished, however good the results, for "the discrepancy is not atoned for by the additional work done." People are to be made "mutually responsible" for one another's actions, and those who fail to denounce a transgressor are to be considered guilty of the same crime. If the penalties are made harsh, the people will be forced into such complete obedience that there will, in fact, be no penalties.

The Legalist State. Right, to the Legalists, consisted simply in what the ruler desired. Though denying all hereditary rights except those of the ruler, they assumed hereditary kingship, and their whole philosophy was designed to aid the ruler in consolidating his position and power. They took for granted that the ruler's objective would be the creation of a prosperous and militarily strong state. All the people must be forced into productive work, and every effort should be devoted to building up a martial spirit and the arts of war. Merchants, intellectuals, and other unproductive and un-martial groups should not be tolerated. The only nobility should be that based on military merit — this was an extremely revolutionary stand against the existing aristocratic society. All aspects of life should be so regulated as to produce the maximum wealth and military might for the state.

In recent years, the Legalists have often been called totalitarians. The name might be fully justified if they had had the technical means of popular control and propaganda of their twentieth-century counterparts. In terms of their own day, they were, like the modern totalitarians, conservatives and innovators at the same time. Their simple acceptance of royal absolutism and of a society of strict hierarchy and their glorifying of a purely agricultural economy all smack of an earlier age. In this connection it is worth noting that the state of Ch'in, which is closely associated with the rise of Legalism, was thought of as a culturally laggard if not semi-"barbarian" area.

On the other hand, the Legalists were undoubtedly part of the wave of the future in their stress on a universal system of law. In some degree, this emphasis was a response to the need of the larger, more complex political unit of the day for an impersonal, mechanistic system of government. The state could no longer be just an extended family. In place of the archaic system of communal land ownership and a society tied together by family relationships and hereditary loyalties, the Legalists championed the more modern political and economic ideal of an all-powerful centralized state ruling impersonally over a vast mass of individual, small-peasant proprietors.

The concept of law is one of the glories of Western civilization, but in China Legalism, although it profoundly influenced the Chinese attitude toward all law, has been a despised term for more than two thousand years. This is because the Legalist concept of law fell far short of the Roman. Whereas Western law has been conceived of as a human embodiment of some higher order of God or nature, the law of the Legalists represented only the ruler's fiat. China developed little or no civil law to protect the citizen; law remained largely administrative and penal, something the people attempted to avoid as much as possible. Whereas Westerners have felt it safer to be ruled by impersonal laws rather than by personally fallible judges, the Chinese, presumably following Mencius in his estimate of human nature, have felt it safer to be ruled by ethically-minded administrators rather than by impersonal and, in their estimate, purely arbitrary laws.

Despite the condemnation of later ages, however, Legalism left a lasting mark on Chinese civilization. Through the triumph of Ch'in and the imperial system that Ch'in created, it became an important part of actual Chinese society, partially accounting for the highly centralized state of later times and the harsh and often arbitrary rule of a controlling elite over the peasant masses. One could say that the Legalist spirit is more obviously alive in Communist China today than either Confucian morality or Taoistic nature mysticism. In any case, Legalism naturally leads us back to the great political transition in Chinese history of the late third century B.C., when Ch'in unified the whole country and founded the Chinese Empire.

The First Chinese Empire:

The Ch'in and Han Dynasties

CH'IN CREATES THE EMPIRE

It is significant that the state of Ch'in had as its capital region the Wei Valley, where previously the Chou had risen to power. The area had certain strategic advantages. The only easy access to this mountain-girt valley from the rest of China was through the narrow strip of land between river and hills at the great bend of the Yellow River. Defense, therefore, was simple, and the Ch'in, by controlling this strategic point, could sally forth at will from "the land within the passes" to wage war on their eastern rivals.

The Wei Valley also had the advantage of being a peripheral area. There was room for growth at the expense of the neighboring nomadic "barbarians" to the northwest and of the less advanced agricultural peoples of the Szechwan Basin to the southwest. The Ch'in are said to have annexed the semi-"barbarian" states of Shu and Pa in Szechwan in 318 B.C. Contact with the "barbarians" maintained the martial arts, while remoteness from the cultural centers of the east kept the people of Ch'in unsophisticated; in fact, they were semi-"barbarians" them-selves in the eyes of other Chinese. Finally, the position of Ch'in in the extreme northwest meant that technological advances from the rest of the civilized world were likely to come to it as soon as to any of the Chinese states. Ch'in, for example, was second only to the state of Chao in north Shansi in developing cavalry in the fourth century B.C.

Ch'in may also have been aided by the relative simplicity of the water-control problem it faced compared with that of the states which sought to control the waters of the Yellow River. In any case, we know that in the middle of the third century B.C. Ch'in was eminently successful in building an irrigation and transport canal in the Wei Valley, which greatly increased the productivity and population of the area. A Ch'in official is also usually given credit for having created an irrigation system on the Chengtu Plain in Szechwan that is still one of the engineering wonders of China.

Shang Yang's Reforms. Another reason for Ch'in's triumph was its wholehearted application of the new techniques of political and military organization which, if not devised by Legalist theoreticians, at least received philosophical justification at their hands. The first great surge forward to power took place under the leadership of Shang Yang, whose name we have seen linked with the Legalists. A native of East China, Shang Yang was the leading official of Ch'in from 361 until his disgrace and death in 338 B.C. He is said to have instituted a strict system of rewards and punishments in Ch'in, forced all persons into "productive" occupations, set up a system of mutual responsibility and spying among the people, and attempted to replace the old hereditary families by a new, purely honorary aristocracy based on military exploits.

The most important of Shang Yang's reforms was the effort to bring all the territory of the state under the direct control of the central government. For some time in Ch'in and some of the other large peripheral states, newly acquired territories had been made into prefectures (*hsien*). Each of these probably represented an old administrative unit of a walled town and its supporting countryside. Also, along the borders large military units had been set up under the name of commanderies (*chün*). Shang Yang in 350 divided the whole of Ch'in into thirty-one prefectures, each under an officer of the central government known as a prefect (*ling*), thus applying this centralizing technique to the whole of a realm for the first time and leaving no room for large hereditary holdings.

In Shang Yang's day, Ch'in was not yet considered one of the major powers — the so-called "Six States." These were Chao, Wei, and Han (the three succession states of Chin), together with Ch'i, Yen, and Ch'u. By 318 B.C., however, Ch'in was able to crush the united forces of the five northern of these states and six years later administered a sharp defeat to Ch'u in the south. As we have seen, Ch'in felt itself powerful enough by 256 to exterminate Chou.

Unification and Standardization Under the First Emperor. The unification of China was eventually accomplished by a Ch'in king who came to the throne as a youth in 246 B.C. In the early years of his reign the land was administered by Lü Pu-wei, a remarkable man who had originally made his fortune as a merchant in the east and who was reported to be the natural father of the king, though this may simply be a later malicious invention.

After Lü Pu-wei's downfall in 237 and death two years later, one of his former henchmen rose to prominence. This was Hsün-tzu's former disciple, Li Ssu, who, though a native of Ch'u, had entered the service of Ch'in in 247. Li Ssu probably played an even more important role than the Ch'in ruler himself in the triumph and consolidation of Ch'in rule. Curiously enough he seems also to have been responsible for the imprisonment and death in 233 of the great Legalist philosopher, Han-fei-tzu, who like him had studied under Hsün-tzu. This incident occurred when Han-fei-tzu, who was a member of the royal clan of Han, came on a diplomatic mission to Ch'in.

The final unification of China by the invincible armies of Ch'in came with amazing speed. Between 230 and 221, Han, Chao, Wei, Ch'u, Yen, and Ch'i fell in rapid succession. By 221 the King of Ch'in had created what he believed was a universal and everlasting empire. Grandiloquently he adopted the title *Shih Huang-ti*, "First Emperor," using for the new term "emperor" two words that previously had been used for deities (Shang Ti) and the mythological sage-emperors of antiquity (the Three Huang and Five Ti). (See Plate 14.)

It might have seemed natural for the First Emperor to parcel out his vast conquests among his relatives and generals as satrapies. The newly risen empires of the West, those of the Persians, Alexander the Great, and the Maurya in North India, had relied on such a system. On Li Ssu's advice, however, the First Emperor applied the centralized system of Ch'in to the whole land. China was divided into thirty-six (later forty-two) commanderies and these subdivided into prefectures. Over each commandery was placed a Civil Governor (*shou*), a Military Governor (*chün-wei*), and a third officer, known as an Overseer (*chien-yü-shih*), who represented the central government and helped keep the balance between the other two.

At the same time the Ch'in system of private landholding and equal, impersonal laws and taxation was applied to the whole land. The First Emperor also deprived all but his own soldiers of their weapons and collected the whole of the hereditary aristocracy of China, supposedly 120,000 families, at his capital, Hsien-yang, near the site of the ancient Chou capital of Hao. Here he built himself a vast palace and erected a huge mausoleum in the neighborhood. The great tumulus in the Wei Valley that is said to be his tomb is a veritable man-made mountain.

The First Emperor did not attempt to consolidate his vast conquests merely by administrative centralization. He unified weights and measures, standardized the coinage, and even unified the axle lengths of wagons. This last measure was important for communications in northwest

China, where wagon wheels cut miniature canyons through the loess soil. Li Ssu is also said to have standardized the writing system, for previously many different types of calligraphy and composition had flourished in the politically divided land. As a result of his efforts and of the unifying influence of a centralized state, both the Chinese characters and the formal style of Chinese composition had become standardized by the second century B.C. in what are essentially their modern forms.

Because of their Legalist background, the Ch'in rulers had no compunction against attempting to control thought. To them such ancient books as the *Classic of Documents,* the *Classic of Songs,* the works of the various philosophers, with their praise of outmoded institutions, and the histories of other princely houses were all obviously subversive to the security of the state. Li Ssu in 213 B.C. accordingly set about destroying undesirable books in a literary inquisition that has come to be known as the "Burning of the Books." The only books spared were utilitarian ones, such as works on medicine, divination and agriculture, and the historical records of Ch'in itself, as well as the collections in the imperial library and in the hands of the seventy official court scholars. All others were to be destroyed, and recalcitrant scholars were to be punished by banishment or death, hundreds reportedly being buried alive.

For this desecration of the written word, Li Ssu has earned the undying hatred of Chinese historians. Unquestionably his effort to blot out dangerous doctrines did help to put an end to the golden age of Chinese thought. Other factors were the burning of the Ch'in imperial library when the dynasty fell and the violent wars that bracketed the short span of Ch'in rule. A more basic reason for this sad loss, however, was the empire itself, which, as a highly organized and centralized state, had less place for the freedom and diversity that had formerly characterized Chinese thought. There is a great and sudden break between pre-Ch'in and post-Ch'in philosophy. In fact, the vigor and richness of late Chou thought was seldom if ever again matched in China.

Foreign Conquests and the Great Wall. Despite this intellectual loss, the unification resulted in a great outburst of physical energy. Drawing on almost unlimited levies of peasants, Ch'in commanded far greater power than had ever before been known in East Asia. The First Emperor laid out a radiating system of great roads, along which he raised stone tablets commemorating his deeds. His armies incorporated many of the "barbarian" peoples of the South into the empire. They penetrated to the northern part of present-day Vietnam and established Ch'in rule along the southern coast of China in the neighborhood of modern Canton. Thus, for the first time, the map of China began to approximate its present borders.

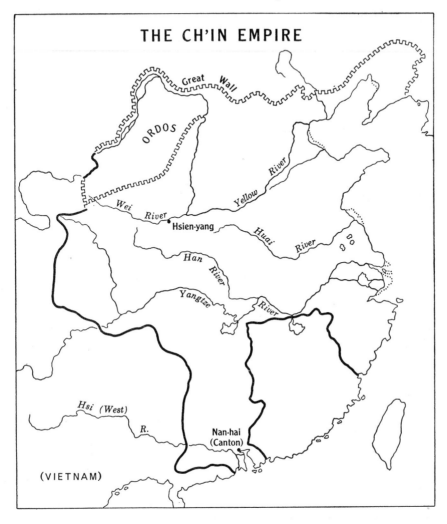

THE CH'IN EMPIRE

Along the northwestern frontier the Ch'in armies drove back their old nomadic rivals, who in this period were themselves forming for the first time a large political union. To secure the border against the nomads, the First Emperor had his greatest general, Meng T'ien, mobilize huge levies of forced laborers to construct a system of defensive walls across the northern frontier. Incorporating sections previously erected by such northern states as Yen, Chao, and Ch'in itself, the Great Wall ran for some 1400 miles, from southwestern Kansu, along the southern edge of Inner Mongolia, to southern Manchuria. It was designed to be a permanent barrier separating the agricultural Chinese on the south from the nomadic "barbarians" on the north. As a military defense it was reasonably effective if properly manned, because it could hold up a raiding party of nomad horsemen until adequate defense units could be concentrated against it. Under later dynasties new walls were erected north or south of the old ones, depending on military and climatic conditions, and there was a great deal of reconstruction and new construction up until the sixteenth century, but the Great Wall always remained essentially the same unified defensive system that the Ch'in had first created.

Although the First Emperor thought that he had founded an empire that would endure for "ten thousand generations," it outlasted him by less than four years, and succeeding generations have always excoriated its memory. He was successful, however, in one sense. The imperial system he inaugurated proved as durable as his own dynasty was transient. The Chinese Empire persisted, with only occasional interruptions, for more than two thousand years; in fact, it continues in modernized form even today. It proved to be the most long-lasting of all human political institutions, and it is therefore quite fitting that our Occidental name for China still reflects the name of Ch'in.

HAN RECEIVES THE MANDATE

The Failure of Ch'in. The very success of the First Emperor in centralizing power contributed to the early demise of his dynasty. The government was so thoroughly controlled from the top that a failure of the leadership immediately affected the whole country.

The First Emperor himself was prodigiously active, reportedly handling 120 pounds of bamboo or wooden documents a day and traveling indefatigably throughout his empire. At the same time he seems to have suffered from megalomania, and he hid his whereabouts and movements under a cloak of elaborate mystery. He also was obsessed with the idea of achieving physical immortality through magical practices, which was a rising Taoistic concept at this time. Some of his travels were to visit magicians along the coast of Shantung, whence he had expeditions dispatched to search for the "islands of the immortals" in the Eastern Sea. The legend about these islands possibly reflected some knowledge of the existence of Japan.

When the First Emperor died in 210 B.C. during one of his trips to the Shantung coast, Li Ssu and the chief eunuch, Chao Kao, were able to conceal his death until they had returned the corpse to Hsien-yang and had engineered the suicides of the heir apparent and the great general Meng T'ien. They then put on the throne a young and inexperienced son of the former ruler, under the title of Second Emperor (*Erh-shih Huang-ti*). Within two years Li Ssu had in turn fallen prey to Chao Kao's machinations, and the empire, now bereft of all its chief original leaders, rapidly disintegrated. Chao Kao soon did away with the Second Emperor and was in turn destroyed by the latter's successor. By 206 Ch'in had disappeared entirely.

The sudden collapse of Ch'in should not be attributed solely to a failure in leadership. A more basic reason was that the new empire lacked the support of the vast majority of the people over which it ruled with such rigid severity. Most of them seem to have retained some loyalty to the ancient principalities and royal lines that Ch'in had recently destroyed. This was particularly true of the upper classes, which had been the ruling element in the old states. Moreover, many of the best educated men of the land, the potential bureaucracy of the new regime, had little sympathy for the Legalist system of rule and secretly maintained their attachment to other philosophical schools. Ch'in thus found itself pitted against the vast inertia of tradition.

The very magnitude and speed of the Ch'in triumph also militated against its enduring success. The Ch'in rulers, by using their new un-limited power without restraint, had rapidly extended China's frontiers and moblized China's human resources for unprecedented building pro-grams: palaces, roads, canals, and the Great Wall. But in the process they had overstrained the peasant masses. The constant drafting of men for campaigns abroad and construction work at home made the new imperial order seem less desirable than the old inter-state anarchy. In proving the efficacy of Legalist concepts of rule, the Ch'in also demonstrated the validity of one of Mencius' ideas: that government ultimately depends upon the tacit consent of the governed. The Chinese people simply deserted Ch'in, and the invincible empire collapsed.

The Struggle Between Hsiang Yü and Liu Pang. In 209 B.C., only a year after the First Emperor's death, a soldiers' revolt broke out in the old Ch'u area, and rebellions followed in quick succession throughout the empire. In 206 the most powerful of the rebels, Hsiang Yü, who was the aristocratic descendant of generals of the state of Ch'u, wiped out the last of the loyalist armies and the ruling house of Ch'in as well. The previous year, the capital city, Hsien-yang, had meekly surrendered to one of his generals, Liu Pang (or Liu Chi), and the city was sub-sequently sacked and burned by Hsiang Yü.

Most of the rebel bands were led by turncoat soldiers or bandits, but they commonly espoused the cause of one or another of the old royal lines. Thus, Hsiang Yü gave the title of emperor to a member of the old Ch'u royal family and allowed the land to be divided among the other royal houses and the various rebel generals, reserving for him-self only the title of Hegemon King.

This compromise with the former system and the attempt to recreate the old states, however, proved entirely unrealistic. Ch'in had succeeded in destroying the old order, and it could not be revived. Hsiang Yü himself set aside his Ch'u emperor and soon found himself engaged in a life-and-death struggle with his former associate Liu Pang for the complete mastery of all China.

Liu Pang already controlled the Wei Valley, and once again West China proved stronger than the eastland. Finally, in 202 B.C., he annihilated his militarily more brilliant but politically less astute rival. He then set himself up as emperor, establishing as his capital the city of Ch'ang-an in the close vicinity of Hsien-yang, the old capital of the Ch'in. His dynasty he called Han, deriving the name from the upper valley of the Han River, where he had been given the title of King of Han by Hsiang Yü in 206, the date traditionally used for the founding of the Han dynasty.

The rebellions against Ch'in had been motivated in part by the desire to restore the old order, but in fact they completed the break with the past. The First Emperor had dethroned the other kings but was himself a member of the old hereditary aristocracy, and his empire had evolved gradually out of one of the princely Chou states. Liu Pang, by contrast, was of peasant origin — a former village official from East China who had turned bandit before joining Hsiang Yü. He and his henchmen were rough plebeians unconnected with the aristocratic rule of the past. Moreover, the wars through which they had triumphed had probably been more destructive to the old traditions, the old books, and the old philosophies than had any of Ch'in's harsh measures. Han's role in Chinese history, in actuality, was to consolidate the new imperial system that Ch'in had started.

The Two Han Dynasties. Han's success, where Ch'in had failed, in founding a lasting empire is probably to be attributed to the passage of time and to the greater shrewdness of Liu Pang and his followers. As self-made men, rather than proud aristocrats, they showed themselves more pragmatic and flexible than their predecessors. They moved more slowly in consolidating their power, subjected the peasants to fewer demands for taxes and labor, and allowed more room for a diversity of interests and opinions than had the doctrinaire Ch'in Legalists. Moreover, the pre-Ch'in system had sunk another decade back into the past and had been made to appear even more remote by destructive wars and the failure of the efforts to revive the princely states. The new imperial order seemed better than it had under the Ch'in, and memories of the old system had become much vaguer and less appealing. Han, in other words, had received the tacit acceptance of the people, that is, the Mandate of Heaven as Mencius understood the term.

The empire that Liu Pang founded lasted a little over two centuries without significant break; then, after a temporary collapse, it revived and continued for another two centuries before it finally began to disintegrate. As it was stumbling toward its first failure, Wang Mang, the leading statesman of his day, usurped the throne in 8 A.D. and adopted the name of Hsin (or New) dynasty. Despite heroic efforts to revive centralized power, his reign ended in chaos and revolution in 23 A.D., but two years later a descendant of the ruling Han family of Liu managed to reunite the land. The empire that he founded lasted until 220 A.D. and is usually known as the Later Han, in distinction to the Earlier Han of Liu Pang. Thus the two Han empires together cover the four centuries from 206 B.C. to 220 A.D. Corresponding roughly in time to the heyday of Rome, the Han empires also paralleled Rome in power, prestige, and historical significance. Even today the Chinese refer to themselves as "men of Han," and the Japanese call the Chinese writing system "the Han characters."

The Consolidation of Han Rule

Liu Pang, like most later Chinese emperors, is best known by his posthumous title, which is Kao Tsu ("High Progenitor"). He was apparently a gifted leader of men, but he faced many serious problems in consolidating his power. The new empire was threatened by internal dissension and by foreign conquest, and it was actually several decades before Han rule was securely established.

For the most part the early Han rulers merely continued the Ch'in system of government. In one respect, however, Han made a notable retreat from the centralization of Ch'in rule. Kao Tsu and his successors allowed the reconstitution of vassal kingdoms and marquisates. Large parts of the empire were so far from the capital region that, with the primitive means of transportation then available, they could not contribute effectively to the support of the central government. It seemed reasonable, therefore, to assign the responsibilities of government in the more distant areas, as well as their income, to vassals of the emperor. Such a policy also recommended itself as a means of retaining the loyalty of powerful military figures and maintaining collateral branches of the imperial family.

This partial reversion to the divisions of earlier times was perhaps a necessary tactical retreat. Nevertheless, the Han emperors had to spend the first half century of their rule liquidating the resultant menace to centralized power. Kao Tsu, in fact, devoted his few years on the throne largely to the elimination of the seven kings he had created who were not members of his own family, and before his death in 195 B.C. he established the rule that only members of the imperial clan henceforth should hold this rank. His successors whittled away the power of the remaining kings by reducing their territories, by dividing realms among the sons of the kings, and eventually by appointing officials of the central government to control each kingdom. Even before this last measure was adopted, the menace of the kings had been eliminated when seven of the strongest kingdoms were forced into rebellion in 154 and then either destroyed or greatly reduced in size. Kingdoms and marquisates were allowed to continue throughout the dynasty, and at the end there were 20 kingdoms as compared with 83 commanderies, and 241 marquisates as compared with 1314 prefectures. These private realms, however, were never again after 154 B.C. a threat to the central government.

A second early menace to Han rule, and one which was to arise repeatedly throughout Chinese history, was posed by the family of Kao Tsu's empress. The Chinese emperors had many consorts, but when a child of one of them was made heir apparent that consort usually was recognized as empress, and on the accession of her son she, as the Empress Dowager, often became a dominant figure at court. This happened for the first time when the Empress Lü became the real ruler of China on Kao Tsu's death. A mere child was on the throne, and most of the more important members of the imperial clan were in their distant kingdoms and marquisates. This situation permitted the Empress Lü to rule through the members of her own family. For a while it appeared that she might usurp the throne for her family, but on her death in 180 B.C. Kao Tsu's old loyal henchmen massacred the whole Lü clan and placed one of Kao Tsu's sons, Wen Ti (the "Cultured Emperor") on the throne.

The Hsiung-nu Menace. The third threat to the early Han state was that of conquest by the nomads on its northern frontiers. The tribal societies of the northern steppes, as we have seen, evolved from the same basic Mongoloid stock as the Chinese but were linguistically distinct. While the agricultural society of the Middle Kingdom was developing in the Yellow River basin, the peoples of the grasslands were developing their own way of life, which differentiated rapidly after they began to use the horse. These nomads were called by the Chinese the Hsiung-nu, which very probably was an early form of the name known in the West as Hun, for elements of these Turkish-speaking peoples were later driven out of East Asia by Chinese military power and subsequently appeared in the West under that name.

The nomads, impelled by occasional failures of their food supplies, as well as by the aggressive military nature of their tribal society, were a constant menace during much of Chinese history. Particularly during periods of civil war and military weakness, China seemed an irresistible attraction to these predatory neighbors. Even in the fifth century B.C., when the Hsiung-nu first appeared on the northwest frontier, their mobility on horseback enabled them to outmaneuver the fighting chariots of the Chinese. (See page 56.)

In the same period that China was first becoming a unified empire, a comparable process of unification was occurring in Mongolia. By the third century B.C. the Hsiung-nu tribal federation spread roughly from western Manchuria across Mongolia and southern Siberia into Chinese Turkestan as far as the Pamirs. From the Chinese records we know that the Hsiung-nu emperor had a title, *Shan-yü*, which was roughly equivalent to "Son of Heaven." His horse-archers, said to total as many as 300,000, often raided and looted North China in the winter when the cultivated ground was hard. Chinese rebels from the Han also fled to the Hsiung-nu, teaching them useful military secrets.

Kao Tsu, while at war with the kings he was attempting to destroy, found himself hard pressed by the Hsiung-nu and bought them off by offering a Chinese princess in marriage to their emperor, a strategem which became routine in later Sino-"barbarian" relations. The Hsiung-nu, however, continued to invade China periodically during the next several decades and in 166 B.C. even got within sight of the capital.

Government and Society. Despite all these difficulties, the Han rulers gradually established a firm and highly centralized government, and the whole country prospered greatly after centuries of almost uninterrupted warfare. In 2 A.D. the "census" figures showed a population of 59,594,978. Traditional Chinese population figures are notably unreliable. They were essentially tax registers, which might be falsified downward in an effort to escape tax responsibilities or upward to indicate administrative efficiency, and numerous groups did not appear on them for one reason or another. The Han figures, however, seem to be more reliable than many of the later returns and do give a rough indication of the population. It seems safe to conclude that the Han ruled over a greater mass of people than ever recognized Rome's authority. Even though many of these people were in economically independent kingdoms and marquisates or lived in remote regions that contributed little or nothing to the finances of the central government, enough remained under the close control of the capital to give the Han regime vast surpluses during its early decades of rule.

The tremendous success of this first sustained attempt at centralized government in China permitted the Han to relax some of the harsher features of the Ch'in system that had created this unity. Punishments were reduced in severity, basic agricultural taxes were progressively lowered, and some reductions were even made in forced labor, or *corvée*. This *corvée* labor was an even more important support of central government than were taxes. It usually required each farmer to spend a month every year in local work on roads, canals, palaces, and imperial tombs, and various less frequent periods for military service, frontier-guarding, and service at the capital.

The government of so vast an empire naturally required elaborate administrative institutions and a huge salaried bureaucracy, which was concentrated largely in Ch'ang-an, the capital. Specialized organs of government were developed for the military, the central civil government, the imperial household, and the provincial administration. By the first century B.C. the bureaucracy is said to have consisted of 130,285 officials. These constituted a favored elite. They and other persons of distinction held ranks in eighteen grades, which entitled them to reduced sentences for crimes and, in the higher brackets, to exemptions from taxation.

Although the Han bureaucracy can be rightly described as huge, it was actually very small when compared with the population over which it ruled: perhaps one person in 400 or 500. This situation was to remain typical of all later Chinese empires. The central administration simply was not constituted to provide what we today would consider the full services of government to the citizenry. It devoted its attention primarily to the lavish support of the emperor and his relatives and the defense of the dynasty. The people were a major concern of the government only as taxpayers or *corvée* labor and as potential rebels. Since the government was extremely suspicious of any large grouping of citizens, such bodies could exist only as secret societies, and these, consequently, have had a large role in Chinese history. So long as tax and *corvée* labor schedules were met and all subversive activities were avoided, the people were usually free to administer their own village affairs and carry out their own customary justice as they saw fit. The government thus was a relatively small, highly centralized body that floated on a sea of isolated peasant communities. The point of contact between the two was the prefectural town, where a governor and perhaps two or three other central government appointees dealt with the village heads, landed magnates, and other local leaders.

The ruling elite was in no sense a hereditary aristocracy like that of the Chou period. Even the families of the kings and marquises rose and fell with astonishing rapidity, rarely retaining these ranks for more than three or four generations. The bureaucracy and the whole upper class consisted simply of those persons with sufficient talent, education, or wealth to play a part in the central government. Wealth and education were naturally associated, for the first was usually necessary for the second. The merchant class, however, was specifically excluded from leadership. The Han, like the Ch'in before it, and like most other despotisms based on agricultural taxes, had a strong prejudice against merchants, who were considered to be economic parasites. They were forbidden to buy land, the safest method of capital investment, and were otherwise discriminated against. The class of wealth and education from which the bureaucracy was largely recruited, therefore, was primarily the richer landowners.

Thus in the Earlier Han we already see the old distinction between hereditary aristocrat and commoner transformed into a cleavage between officialdom and the common taxpayer — a division that was to characterize all subsequent Chinese society. One major stratum was the rich landowning class, which provided the bulk of the bureaucracy. These landowners were to some extent tax-exempt, and, as local leaders with interests in the national scene, served as the link between the central government and the countryside. The other major stratum was the peasantry, which supported the landowners through rents and the central government through taxes and *corvée* labor.

Above and below these two strata were two other minor groups. There was a small hereditary aristocracy consisting of the imperial clan, great generals, and the relatives of empresses and imperial consorts. Members of this class often wielded great power, but even the imperial clan did not outlive the dynasty as a privileged group, and the rest of the aristocracy was even more ephemeral. At the bottom of the scale, some of the peasants were virtual serfs, and there was an insignificant group of domestic slaves, constituting perhaps less than one per cent of the population. These social groups were not castes in the Indian sense; nor were they even comparable to the strictly divided classes of European feudal society. A spin of the wheel of fortune could plunge an aristocrat into slavery or elevate a commoner like Liu Pang to the imperial throne.

THE APOGEE OF HAN POWER

The Reign of Wu Ti. The first sixty years of Han rule were a period of national recuperation and dynastic consolidation. Then followed a sudden expansive burst of Chinese power such as had taken place under the First Emperor and was to be repeated under all of the stronger dynasties of later times. This occurred during the long reign of Wu Ti (the "Martial Emperor"), which lasted from 141 to 87 B.C.

A man of unlimited energy, Wu Ti personally supervised the mechanism of government in a way no ruler had attempted since Kao Tsu. The intervening emperors had been content to lend their approval to decisions made by their great ministers, but Wu Ti ruled directly through a palace secretariat. Thenceforth, Chinese government tended to alternate between periods of personal administration by dynamic emperors and periods in which the high bureaucrats actually ruled. Under the former, policies could be more vigorously and consistently pursued, but, since the emperor was beyond criticism, there could be no check on his follies. Wu Ti was no exception to this rule. He dealt harshly and unjustly with his generals and officials and himself was frequently the dupe of magicians. Under bureaucratic rule there tended to be less decisiveness, but more flexibility and stability.

In order to marshal the resources and manpower of his empire for his policy of expansion, Wu Ti made the laws more severe and administered them more rigorously than had his predecessors. The "slave labor" of criminals became an important source of military manpower as well as of construction labor. With this labor and the *corvée* services of the peasants as part of their tax duties, he reinstituted a major program of canal construction, connecting the capital directly with the Yellow River and thereby greatly facilitating the transportation of tax grain from East China to Ch'ang-an. He also embarked upon a long series of foreign conquests.

Wu Ti's foreign wars, particularly those against the Hsiung-nu, were partially justified on grounds of self-defense, as so many foreign conquests have been throughout world history. Despite the anti-merchant bias of the Han, there may also have been an interest in some quarters in capturing control of the lucrative trade between East and West that passed through Central Asia. There was also, no doubt, an element of the "Alexander complex," the desire for "more worlds to conquer," to which strong Chinese rulers have been as susceptible as their counterparts elsewhere in the world. In fact, the Chinese Empire, like most other empires, tended always to expand to the practical limits of military control, and often enough beyond those limits.

The conquest of the weakly organized and culturally assimilable peoples of South China was a relatively easy matter. Native states in southern Chekiang and Fukien were destroyed and their coastal populations were moved inland. Then in 111 B.C. came the conquest of the semi-Sinicized state of Nan-yüeh (South Yüeh), which controlled modern Kwangtung, Kwangsi, and North Vietnam, an area which had first been conquered by the Ch'in. Some native states in the Kweichou and Yunnan area in the extreme southwest were also brought under Chinese suzerainty, partly because the Chinese had learned enough about geography to realize that Burma and India might possibly be reached by penetrating far enough in this southwesterly direction.

More than a millennium was to elapse before the Kweichou and Yunnan area was fully incorporated into China. It also took several centuries of steady immigration of Chinese from the North and assimilation of the local population before the southern coastal areas became predominantly Chinese-speaking. This area, however, always remained politically a part of China after Wu Ti's conquests. His reign thus witnessed a greater filling out of the borders of China proper than any other comparable period in Chinese history.

The Hsiung-nu Wars. Despite the historical significance of the southern campaigns, the greatest wars of Wu Ti were against the Hsiung-nu along the northern frontier. As a result of these wars China for the first time came to control the huge waste lands of Central Asia that today, as during much of the intervening period, form part of the Chinese domain.

Wu Ti hurled one army after another against the Hsiung-nu. A single one of his expeditions might number 50,000 to 100,000 cavalry supported by infantry and supply trains. Some of these armies were all but annihilated in the vast steppes and deserts of the north; others returned thoroughly decimated. The loss of life was prodigious. But nomad power was gradually whittled away. By 127 B.C. Wu Ti had driven the Hsiung-nu out of the Ordos region north of Shensi, and in 119 his armies pursued them as far as the Gobi (a name which means "desert"). The wars continued, however, throughout the remainder of his reign, and for decades thereafter.

Eventually, in 52 B.C., the ruler of the southern half of the Hsiung-nu horde submitted to Han and came to Ch'ang-an to pay homage. About this time others of these troublesome neighbors started on the westward migrations that were to eventuate indirectly in the sack of Rome.

Wu Ti's Hsiung-nu policy was not merely military. He also sought to find allies against them. As early as 139 B.C. he dispatched an officer, Chang Ch'ien, to make an alliance with a Central Asian people known to the Chinese as the Yüeh-chih. The Yüeh-chih, who may have been the easternmost extension of the Indo-European-speaking peoples, had been driven out of western Kansu by the Hsiung-nu some decades earlier. They had then moved westward and had by Chang Ch'ien's time displaced the Greek kingdoms in Bactria, or northern Afghanistan, and were on the point of invading North India, where they subsequently set up the Kushan dynasty.

Chang Ch'ien, after years of imprisonment at the hands of the Hsiung-nu, finally found the Yüeh-chih, but the latter, now safely across the great Pamir mountain barrier from Hsiung-nu power, had no desire to become embroiled again in the wars of East Asia. Chang Ch'ien eventually returned to China, in 126 B.C., without the alliance he sought but with much detailed knowledge about Central Asia and some glimmerings of the rich civilizations that lay beyond. In 115 Chang Ch'ien's second diplomatic embassy, this time to the Wu-sun, another Indo-European tribe living in the Ili Valley north of the Tarim Basin, proved no more successful than his first mission but helped to broaden Chinese contact with these distant areas.

The Occupation of Korea and Central Asia. Another aim of Wu Ti's policy was to outflank the Hsiung-nu. In the east this led to the con-

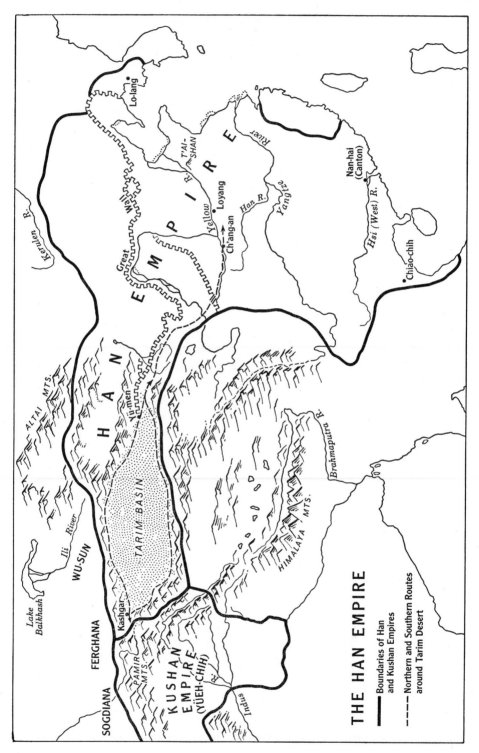

THE HAN EMPIRE

—— Boundaries of Han
and Kushan Empires

- - - Northern and Southern Routes
around Tarim Desert

quest in 108 B.C. of Chosŏn, a semi-Sinicized Korean state occupying North Korea and southern Manchuria. At its capital, the modern North Korean capital of P'yŏngyang, the Han commandery of Lo-lang (Nangnang in Korean) was created. Three other commanderies were subsequently set up in the peninsula. Lo-lang, which lasted as a Chinese outpost until 313 A.D., was said to have had a population of around 400,000, and some of the finest artistic remains of Han times have been found in tombs in the vicinity.

The flanking policy in the west resulted in the extension of the Great Wall westward into the deserts as far as Yü-men, "the Jade Gate," enclosing the area that was to become the great Kansu panhandle and the channel of contact between China and Central Asia. Some 700,000 Chinese colonists were moved into this barren corridor, which has remained ever since part of China proper. Han rule was then extended over the Indo-European populations of the small agricultural oases of the Tarim Basin in the heart of Central Asia, and the region was placed under a Protector General. These oases were usually situated on the narrow margin between the mountains and the desert, where streams from the mountains could be used for irrigation before they sank into the desert sands and the foothills offered game for the hunter. Travelers crossed the desert by stages from one oasis to the next. Over this route passed precious cargoes of silk for the ladies of the Roman Empire.

In 104 and 102 B.C. one doughty Chinese general, Li Kuang-li, even led two Chinese armies from the Tarim Basin across the mighty Pamir range to subdue the region of Ferghana in what is now Russian Turkestan. In 42 B.C. another Chinese led 40,000 men across the Pamirs and west of Ferghana to the former Greek kingdom of Sogdiana, where the Chinese with their superior crossbows, crushed a refugee group of the Hsiung-nu and an armored force of what were possibly captive Roman soldiers. Thus Chinese armies, marching across all but impenetrable deserts and mountains, extended Han military might farther from their capital (over 2000 miles) than the Roman legions ever reached from Rome, despite the much easier communications of the Mediterranean area.

THE TRIUMPH OF CONFUCIANISM

Wu Ti was, in practice, a complete despot and almost as thoroughly a Legalist monarch as the First Emperor had been. It is commonly said, however, that during his reign Confucianism became the predominant philosophy of the Chinese court. Actually the triumph of Confucianism was a slow process, continuing over the whole Han period, and the Confucianism that won out was a curious synthesis of ancient philosophies and current superstitions, and not at all the pure, ethical teachings of Confucius and Mencius.

Early Han Thought. None of the pre-Ch'in schools of thought survived into Han times as distinct and mutually exclusive philosophical systems. The ideas that survived best were those which had the greatest appeal to the uneducated, superstitious masses. This is the clearest evidence of how completely the successive triumphs of Ch'in and Han had broken with the aristocratic past.

Among the ideas that were most vigorously continued into Han times were the concepts of the late Chou Naturalists. Their ideas of *yin* and *yang* dualism and the "five elements" came to permeate all thought and proliferated into the elaborate pseudo-science described in the previous chapter. Closely allied with these concepts was the notion that unusual natural phenomena were signs and portents which reflected the character of the ruler or foretold the future. Such ideas had lurked in the background of Chou thought, but now they became a major interest of court scholars, who sometimes may have fabricated alleged natural portents for selfish political purposes or to curb the ruler.

The Taoistic tradition survived the political upheaval of the late third century better than most schools of thought, but in the process the philosophy of the *Tao te ching* and the *Chuang-tzu* was almost lost among the more primitive beliefs that had probably always underlain it. The search for long life, and eventually for gross physical immortality, became the primary concern of the Taoistically inclined. The magicians of the Shantung coast fostered a growing interest in visits to the "fairy immortals" (*hsien*) of the mysterious islands in the Eastern Sea and developed the idea that humans could achieve this type of immortality. One method was by finding an elixir of life. Cinnabar (red mercuric sulphide), actually a poison, was early thought to provide one of these, and we find in 133 B.C. a magician persuading Wu Ti to seek immortality by transmuting cinnabar into gold. This incident is very significant, for it is the first clear sign anywhere in the world of the proto-science of alchemy. Other methods of achieving immortality were by dietary regimens, especially avoidance of cereals, and by yoga-like breathing exercises. All these ideas were widespread in the Han and continued to be extremely popular for many centuries thereafter. As we have seen, the First Emperor was much given to such Taoistic interests, and Wu Ti was under the influence of one Taoist magician after another, heaping each in turn with honors and riches before becoming disillusioned and destroying him.

Various popular cults, such as the worship of ancestors and sacrifices to nature deities, also survived among the masses. The nature cults became more and more identified with Taoism and gradually developed a rich mythology which greatly influenced the art of the times. (See Plate 10.) The old aristocratic cults had, of course, been obliterated, but their memory continued. In 110 B.C. Wu Ti was persuaded to revive the sacrifices to Heaven and Earth in mysterious form and on a grandiose scale. He performed the *feng* sacrifice to Heaven on the summit of T'ai-shan, the sacred mountain in Shantung, and the *shan* sacrifice to Earth on a low hill at its foot. Twice again, in 106 and 98, he carried out these great symbolic ceremonies.

The Recovery of the Classics. At a higher intellectual level, men of scholarly bent busied themselves during the first century of Han rule in recovering as many of the writings of earlier times as possible. After the Ch'in ban on philosophical and historical works was formally lifted by the Han in 191 B.C., certain older scholars were apparently able to reconstitute texts that they had memorized in their youth. The recension of the *Classic of Songs* made by Mao Ch'ang early in the dynasty became so famous that this classic is sometimes called the *Mao Shih* (*Mao Songs*).

There were also many stories of ancient works being recovered from hidden recesses in old walls. The most famous of these concerns the "old text" version of the *Classic of Documents*, said to have been discovered by K'ung An-kuo, a descendant of Confucius, in the wall of the Master's house. Although the existing "old text" is in large part a later forgery, the two variant forms of this classic gave rise to endless later controversy. The very name "old text," used for a document in pre-Ch'in calligraphy, indicates how much the writing system had changed since Chou times.

The Han scholars showed little philosophical perception, lumping all the old writings together as equally valid expressions of the thought of antiquity. For the most part they also showed little historical discrimination. They tended to accept the myths and fantasies of pre-Ch'in writings as sober historical fact, and they simply assumed that the political unity of their own day must also have existed in earlier times. Their concept of a universal unified Chinese Empire stretching back to the beginning of time became the standard view of history in China until recent years.

On the other hand, the Han scholars, with their great veneration for the written word, were scrupulous transmitters of the ancient texts they discovered or reconstituted. Many of these works were no longer readily understandable, so great had been the political, cultural, and even linguistic changes in the intervening years. The scholars therefore had to explain these works through detailed commentaries, but they took care to keep their exegesis distinct from the original text. In time the practice developed, first in manuscripts and then in printed texts, of inserting the commentary in distinctive double columns after the single-column passage of the text which it sought to elucidate.

The Han scholars, as a by-product of this work of recovering old

FROM *Commentaries to the Classic of Songs*

Two pages from the Shih chuan ta ch'üan (Complete Commentaries to the Classic of Songs), *compiled on the order of the Yung-lo Emperor of the Ming dynasty and printed in a Palace Edition in 1417. The columns in large type (preceded by circles) are the famous commentary of Mao Ch'ang of the Earlier Han dynasty. The second size of type represents a commentary of the Later Han dynasty, and still later commentaries are given in the smaller type in double columns. In many editions of the Classics the original text in large type is interspersed with commentary printed in double-column fashion.*

texts, established the category of the Five Classics, which we have already described. Their commentaries also marked the start of what has ever since been one of the major intellectual activities of Chinese scholarship. Until relatively recent times the Chinese have seen their classical literature only through the interpretations and misinterpretations of the Han scholars or through the endless reinterpretations of the work of the Han pioneers by successive generations of later scholars.

Lexicography was another aspect of Han scholarship that was closely allied to the commentaries. The *Erh ya* of the third century B.C. has been mentioned as the earliest Chinese dictionary. Around 100 A.D. a much more complete and modern type of dictionary was compiled. This was the *Shuo wen (Explanation of Writing)*, in which, under 540 radicals, more than 9000 Chinese characters are listed. This system of classification is still used, though the number of radicals has since been reduced to 214.

Philosophical Syncretism. At first there was little that was specifically Confucian about the activities or ideas of the Han scholars, but increasingly they came to identify themselves with the Confucian tradition. This may have been because the Confucian school of thought was remembered in Han times more clearly and with greater respect than any of its Chou rivals. The very name of the Confucianists, "the school of the literati," suggests what happened. It was not so much that Confucian philosophy completely won over the thinkers of Han times as that Han scholars gradually adopted Confucius as their ideal prototype.

The thought of Han times was certainly syncretic rather than specifically Confucian. This eclectic tendency is perhaps first clearly seen in the *Lü-shih ch'un ch'iu* (*The Spring and Autumn Annals of Mr. Lü*), a compendium of Taoistic and pseudo-scientific writings probably compiled by men in the entourage of Lü Pu-wei, the great Ch'in statesman. It is even clearer in the *Huai-nan-tzu*, which was compiled under the patronage of the King of Huai-nan, a grandson of Kao Tsu. This work, while predominantly Taoistic, is full of omen lore, cosmological speculations, and concepts from diverse other philosophical sources.

The so-called Confucianist writings of the Han also show this same syncretism. The *Record of Rituals*, which was compiled at this time from earlier elements, includes Legalist ideas, numerology, and methods of predicting the future, as well as more specifically Confucian concepts. The appendices to the *Classic of Changes*, which also may date from this period, show how this entirely non-Confucian work was swallowed whole by "Confucianism."

Even Wang Ch'ung (died about 100 A.D.), perhaps the most original thinker of Han times, shows this same syncretic tendency in his *Lun heng* (*Disquisitions*). Although avowedly a Confucianist, he was at heart an extreme iconoclast and felt free to attack the inconsistencies he found in Confucius and Mencius. Fundamentally he was a believer in the impersonal natural order of philosophical Taoism. This led him to a rationalistic condemnation of many of the superstitions of his time, including a frontal attack on the concept of omens and portents, which was a central theme of Han Confucianism.

Confucian Scholars at Court: the University. The triumph of Confucianism in the Han consisted not merely of the adoption of the label by men of scholarly bent. More important was the incorporation of such scholarly men, labels and all, into what had started as a purely Legalist type of government.

Kao Tsu was scornful of scholarly affectations (he once made clear his attitude by urinating into a scholar's formal hat), but he saw clearly the need for educated men in government. As early as 201 B.C. he had a scholar devise fitting ceremonial procedures for his court, and in 196 he sent out a call for the services of men of talent. His successors continued to do the same and held various sorts of written examinations for the candidates who presented themselves in response to these calls.

Two "Confucian" scholars who rose to prominence at Wu Ti's court as a result of this procedure were Kung-sun Hung (died 121 B.C.) and his junior contemporary, Tung Chung-shu. Significantly enough, both men were noted for their ability to interpret omens and portents and for their analysis of the *Spring and Autumn Annals* as a book which supposedly indicated the judgment of Confucius through its choice of words. Tung Chung-shu's work, the *Ch'un ch'iu fan lu* (*Luxuriant Dew of the Spring and Autumn Annals*), is full of pseudo-scientific reasoning about the relationship between the "five elements" and historic occurrences — a far cry from the thought of Confucius and Mencius. Thus the "Confucianism" that seems to have appealed to Wu Ti was a complicated sort of cosmology and utilitarian omen lore rather than ethical teachings.

It can be said, nevertheless, that by Wu Ti's time there was a definite bias at court in favor of the Confucian tradition, however much the Sage's teachings may have been misunderstood. One of Wu Ti's first acts, perhaps under the influence of Confucianist tutors, was to ban all students of Legalist philosophy from court. Nothing could better illustrate the eclipse of Legalist theory and the self-assurance of the still essentially Legalist government. Wu Ti followed this measure in about 135 B.C. by setting up Erudites (*Po-shih*) of the Five Classics, the latter being now thought of as works of the Confucian tradition. The Ch'in had had official court scholars, and Wu Ti's predecessor, Wen Ti, had created Erudites to represent various schools of thought; but it was under Wu Ti that the court scholars for the first time became definitely identified with Confucianism.

A more important innovation was the creation in 124 B.C., at the suggestion of both Tung Chung-shu and Kung-sun Hung, of a sort of imperial university, at which fifty official appointees, destined for government service, were to study under the Erudites. The setting up of a government school for training officials had been pioneered some twenty years earlier by a governor in Szechwan, but now this technique was used for the first time by the central administration. Details are lacking about the university, but it is said to have grown to 3000 students in the second half of the first century B.C. and to 30,000 students under the Later Han dynasty. By 1 A.D. a hundred men a year were said to be entering government service through the examinations administered by the official scholars. Thus, from Wu Ti's time on, a large proportion of the lower bureaucracy was produced through a definitely Confucianist education at government expense.

At the same time Confucianism was beginning to be recognized as the official philosophy of the state. Great conferences of scholars were held under imperial auspices in 51 B.C. and again in 79 A.D. to determine the true interpretation of the Confucian Classics, and the discussions were duly recorded. In 175 A.D. the government had the approved version of the Classics carved on large stone tablets, which were erected at the capital. Meanwhile, in 8 B.C. the descendants of Confucius had been assigned state revenues for their ancestral cult, and in 37 A.D. they had been given patents of nobility. In 58 A.D. all government schools were ordered to commence making sacrifices to Confucius.

The Balance Between Confucianism and Legalism. The incorporation of Confucianism into the Legalist state was in many ways a strange phenomenon, but it was characteristically Chinese and helps explain the superior lasting power of the Chinese imperial system over all other empires. The land, though won by the sword, could be governed only by the writing brush; that is, with the aid of men of education. The Legalist conqueror needed the efficient civil administrator, and a place of responsibility and honor was, accordingly, created for him in the government. As a result, men of education and ideas became supporters rather than opponents of the state, which now gave them this favored status.

More important, a start was made toward the development of an efficient bureaucracy through a system of education and selection of prospective officials. China in short was already beginning to develop a modern type of civil service system based on merit. It was almost two thousand years before the West adopted a system similar to, and perhaps inspired by, that of the Chinese. This great time differential in the use of one of man's most important inventions in part explains why China had greater political stability and more efficient government than Europe during most of the intervening years.

Fortunately for the Chinese, the Confucian tradition was the chief intellectual force among the educated classes. Although Han Confucianism was a strange mixture of ideas, the ethical concepts of the Chou founders of the school gradually reasserted themselves over the syncretic beliefs of the early Han scholars. The ruthless despotism that the Ch'in had created on Legalist principles, therefore, came increasingly into the hands of men who stressed moral virtues, such as loyalty to the ruler and paternal benevolence toward the common people. In these more gentle hands, the government developed the strong lasting qualities that Ch'in and most other empires of conquest have lacked.

The beautiful balance eventually achieved between the Legalist empire and its Confucian administrators once again illustrates the usefulness of the *yin-yang* concept of complementary, as opposed to conflicting, dualism. The Legalist victory, while seeming to destroy Confucianism, in reality created the stable society in which it could triumph. The Confucian victory, far from destroying Legalism, made the Legalist empire all but indestructible.

CULTURAL GROWTH DURING THE HAN

The expansion of Chinese power during the Han period and the great increase in population and wealth were naturally reflected in the life and culture of the times. The imperial family, enfeoffed nobles, great officials, rich landowners, and, despite the anti-commercial bias of the government, even prosperous merchants — all lived on a lavish scale and made a conspicuous display of their wealth.

Contacts With West Asia. Foreign trade probably contributed to the general prosperity of the land and certainly to the richness of the culture. Han control of Central Asia permitted a much greater flow of overland trade with West Asia across the great barriers of steppes, deserts, and mountains. The two chief trade routes led from oasis to oasis along the northern and southern edges of the Tarim River Basin, skirting the fearsome Taklamakan Desert in its center before crossing the mighty Pamirs into West Asia. Naturally, control over Central Asia also gave the Chinese much greater knowledge than before of this area and of the regions beyond. Just as the Romans were vaguely aware of China, so the Han Chinese knew something of Rome, or rather its eastern provinces, which they honored with the name Ta Ch'in, or "Great Ch'in."

During these centuries trade with the West was not exclusively by way of Central Asia. Contact through the Indian Ocean became frequent between the Roman Orient and India, and a thin trickle of sea-borne trade began to flow on eastward around the Malay Peninsula to South China. At that time the main Chinese port for this trade was in the present Hanoi area of North Vietnam. Subsequently Canton developed as the center of oceanic commerce with South and West Asia. In 120 A.D. a band of jugglers claiming to come from the Ta Ch'in area arrived at the Han court by way of this southern route, and in 166 a group of merchants who had reached the southern borders of Han made the no doubt specious claim of being ambassadors from An-tun, the emperor of Ta Ch'in, in other words, Marcus Aurelius Antoninus.

Through foreign trade the Chinese obtained precious stones, tropical luxury goods such as ivory, magnificent horses from Central Asia, and even glass and fine wool and linen fabrics from West Asia. But none of these imports was so important to the Middle Kingdom as the major

Chinese export was to the outside world. This was silk, which is said to have been imported into the Roman Empire on so large a scale that the economy was hurt by the resulting eastward drain of gold and silver. Pieces of Han silk, some of them polychrome figured fabrics, have been found in Central Asia, Siberia, and the Middle East. Thus, as early as Han times, we encounter a feature of China's foreign trade that was to remain characteristic until the nineteenth century: Chinese products, and especially handicraft goods, were more in demand abroad than foreign goods were in China. This situation was not a sign of Chinese prejudice but rather of the greater wealth and technological advancement of China over the regions to the west during most of this period.

Accompanying this trade, many new ideas, inventions, and products were introduced into China. Thus Chang Ch'ien is given credit for bringing back alfalfa and the grape from Central Asia to his homeland, and the high level of Han astronomical and mathematical learning may reflect stimulation from India or West Asia.

In the arts foreign influences are even clearer. The *p'i-pa*, a type of lute which was introduced from Central Asia at this time, became one of the most important of all East Asian musical instruments. Animal designs in silhouette of the so-called Scythian type from the steppe lands of Eurasia also became popular for such things as metal horse trappings. Various Mediterranean design motives also came into common use. In fact, the whole Western approach to artistic representation through realistic silhouettes, which had appeared in the late Chou, now entirely displaced the older East Asian approach, and the Chinese, who once had limited themselves mainly to rather abstract animal forms, now showed

"Scythian" Bronze

A horned herbivore attacked by a feline beast. Bronzes in this so-called "Scythian," "Sino-Siberian" or "animal" style have been found throughout the northern areas of Asia which were accessible to the steppe peoples.

almost as much interest in the portrayal of human figures as did the peoples of the Mediterranean region.

Chinese Inventions. The current of influence, however, was by no means one-way. In pre-Ch'in times the flow seems to have been largely toward China. During the Han period China drew technologically abreast of the other early centers of civilization and then apparently began to surpass them. The Han Chinese already knew of sunspots, and had developed a primitive seismograph for recording otherwise imperceptible earthquakes; the crossbow dates back to the Chou; Han textile techniques were centuries ahead of those of West Asia and Europe; in the Later Han the water-powered mill was invented; during the Han period the Chinese developed the shoulder collar that so greatly increased the efficiency of horses as draft animals; and at about the same time the technique of iron casting began to spread from China to the western areas. It is not generally realized that between the Han and early modern times, that is, during a period of more than a thousand years, a much larger number of important mechanical inventions as well as agricultural products were borrowed by Europe from China than spread in the opposite direction.

Two of the greatest of all Chinese inventions, paper and porcelain, had their beginnings during the Han period. Pure rag paper dating from about 100 A.D. has been found in the remains of Han outposts in Central Asia, which confirms the traditional account of the invention of paper at about that time. Naturally, paper soon replaced cumbersome wooden and bamboo slips for writing and also reduced the use of expensive silk cloth for this purpose. It is very significant that this particular advance should have been made in China, where the written word and scholarship were so highly regarded. It took more than a thousand years for the knowledge of paper-making to spread from China to Europe. Our whole modern civilization, however, would be quite inconceivable without this great Chinese invention.

Pottery glazes were already common during the Han, and toward the end of this period a sort of proto-porcelain appeared. The Chinese, in other words, were beginning to discover china. During the next several centuries they gradually developed the fine ware that the rest of the world eagerly imported and eventually in modern times learned to copy. Porcelaneous wares were not only a great artistic creation; they also represent a major advance in hygiene, for their smooth surfaces provided much more sanitary eating utensils than the rough pottery or wooden plates of earlier times.

Ch'ang-an was no doubt a city that rivaled Rome, but little or nothing has been preserved from this great Han capital. The failure of China's ancient architectural monuments to survive can probably be attributed in large part to their wooden frame construction, so much less enduring than stone. As a result, the only remains of the Han are crumbling walls or the rubble of military outposts in Central Asia and scattered tombs of nobles and officials. From these tombs have emerged countless funerary objects, such as terra cotta houses, stoves, farm animals, and dancing figures, which reveal something of the life of the times. Certain tombs were profusely decorated with stone bas-reliefs portraying mythological figures, famous historical incidents, and scenes of daily life, such as a great banquet, including the kitchen preparations as well as the guests and the jugglers hired to amuse them. (See Plates 10, 12, 13 and 14.) The tomb of Ho Ch'ü-ping, a famous general who fought the Hsiung-nu, has some fine figures of animals in the round. The even more remarkable tombs of Lo-lang in Korea contained intricate filigree work and many fine pieces of lacquer, some decorated with gentlemen in long-sleeved robes that look more like Japanese kimonos than like Chinese costumes of recent centuries. (See Plate 11.) Several of these lacquer pieces bear inscriptions indicating their manufacture in distant Szechwan. The most characteristic of all Han remains are beautifully executed bronze mirrors which have on their backs elaborate designs of presumably cosmological significance.

Poetry: the Fu. Most Han writing was scholarly or didactic, but one important genre developed in this period. This was the poetic form known as *fu*, which derived from and was still closely akin to the *Li sao* of Ch'ü Yüan. The *fu* enjoyed great favor at Wu Ti's court, where Ssu-ma Hsiang-ju was the outstanding master of the art, and it retained its popularity for several centuries. Since there is a certain irregularity of meter and rhyme in its long lines, Western students have frequently called it "prose poetry" or "rhymeprose," but it is in fact a rich poetic form characterized by great linguistic exuberance. The poets often used the same themes: the capitals of China, beautiful landscapes, or great imperial hunts. The *fu* are usually long descriptive pieces, full of hyperbole and tending toward balanced, paired phrases. ("A thousand chariots advance like thunder; ten thousand riders race like dragons.") These were no ballads, but a highly artificial poetry for men of scholarship at the court.

Ssu-ma Ch'ien and Historical Scholarship

The greatest literary achievement of the Han period was in the field of historical writing. This is not surprising in a civilization in which history was so strongly emphasized. No people have been more interested in their past than the Chinese, for to them it was the model for the present and the primary source of information on human society, the subject that concerned them most. No people have shown a greater realization of being actors on the stage of history or greater interest in the future judgment of history on themselves. The Chinese quite naturally made history one of the four main categories of literature, the others being the classics and their commentaries, philosophical writings, and belles-lettres.

The Historical Records.   Much of earlier Chinese literature, as we have seen, was actually historical writing of one type or another. In the time of Wu Ti, however, there appeared a history much greater in scope and far more advanced in scholarship than anything that had preceded it. This was the *Shih chi,* or *Historical Records,* of Ssu-ma Ch'ien.

Ssu-ma Ch'ien (died about 85 B.C.) inherited a post as court astrologer and had access to the resources of the imperial library. He also had traveled throughout most of the empire in his youth. He claimed to be simply completing the historical work which his father, Ssu-ma T'an, had commenced, but this may have been partly a pious excuse for what was in reality a most presumptuous undertaking — the continuation and amplification of what was supposed to be Confucius' greatest accomplishment, that is, the arrangement of the record of the past in proper form. Ssu-ma Ch'ien was obviously a man of great daring as well as prodigious learning. In 99 B.C. he came to the defense of a prominent Chinese general who had been forced to surrender to the Hsiung-nu, and Wu Ti repaid him for his audacity by having him castrated.

Ssu-ma Ch'ien not only set the pattern for most later Chinese historical works but also determined their style and scholarly approach. He limited himself to a concise and straightforward statement of the facts as he knew them, avoiding the dramatic but largely imaginary embellishments of historical incident that characterized some of the earlier Chinese histories as well as those of the ancient Occident. His technique was to quote with a minimum of alterations those sources which he felt to be the most reliable. On dubious points that he did not feel he could himself resolve, such as the variant traditions regarding high antiquity, he simply copied the different accounts side by side. His book, therefore, like those of later Chinese historians, is for the most part a complicated patchwork of passages and paraphrases from earlier books and documents. Ssu-ma Ch'ien thus set a standard for historical scholarship in China that was probably not equaled in the West until relatively modern times. His succinct prose style also set a literary standard that strongly influenced later generations of historians.

Ssu-ma Ch'ien was attempting to write universal history and came as close to succeeding as any man has. He conceived of his work on a grand scale. The *Historical Records* consist of 130 solid chapters, and in its present form, after undergoing some losses and later additions, it is a text of over 700,000 characters. Because of the conciseness of classical Chinese, this represents a work of about five times the content of the 300,000 word volume the reader has in hand.

The first twelve chapters of the *Historical Records* are known as the "Basic Annals" and contain the records of events in the reigns of the main line of Chinese rulers, beginning with the mythological emperors and including the kings of the Hsia, Shang, and Chou dynasties, a few other kings of late Chou times, the Ch'in emperors, Hsiang Yü, and, finally, the Han emperors up to Wu Ti. There follow ten chapters of chronological tables of the various ruling houses of Chou and earlier times and of the imperial clan and high officials of the early Han period.

The third section of the book is devoted to eight essays on subjects that are not susceptible of chronological treatment but are of interest in government. There are essays on rituals, music, musical scales, the calendar, astrology and astronomy, Wu Ti's *feng* and *shan* sacrifices, rivers and canals, and weights and measures (the last being actually a general essay on economic matters). The next thirty chapters are devoted to accounts of the hereditary princely houses of Chou times, together with a few biographies of Han notables. The fact that Confucius is included in this section indicates how great was the veneration for him by this time, even though Ssu-ma Ch'ien and his father both show strong Taoist leanings.

The last seventy chapters, that is, over half of the book, are devoted to what are usually called the "Biographies." A few important men have a whole chapter to themselves. Other chapters treat two or more men who are associated in some way, while whole categories of minor characters, such as famous assassins, imperial favorites, and poets, are treated briefly together. The "Biographies" also include geographical essays on other peoples and lands of the world.

Counting Time by Year Periods. Oddly enough, just at the time that Ssu-ma Ch'ien was making his great step forward in historiography, a backward step was taken in keeping the time record for history. Under Wu Ti it became customary to count years by arbitrary year periods (*nien-hao*) chosen largely for their magical potency. The development was closely associated with the Han interest in signs and portents. A year period might last a long time if conditions were stable or might be abandoned within a few months if some disaster struck or a particularly propitious omen occurred. The result has been a chaotic method of counting years, which has made the Chinese all the more dependent on dynasties for reckoning time. Despite the drawbacks of this system, it still remains in use in East Asia. The only later advance has been to make year periods coincide with reigns, an innovation adopted by the Chinese in 1368 and by the Japanese in 1868. Thus the year 1900 is known in China as the twenty-sixth year of Kuang-hsü ("Brilliant Succession") and in Japan as the thirty-third year of Meiji ("Enlightened Rule").

Pan Ku and the Dynastic Histories. Time eventually makes inadequate the work of even the most thorough universal historian, and Ssu-ma Ch'ien's great undertaking soon was supplemented by other hands. The second great work of the new historical scholarship was compiled by a whole family of scholars. Started by Pan Piao, it was in large part written by his son, Pan Ku (died 92 A.D.), and was completed by the latter's sister, Pan Chao, China's first and still most famous woman scholar. The Pans, writing in the early years of the Later Han dynasty, limited their work to the preceding dynasty, thus overlapping with the *Historical Records* for only the first century of Han rule.

The *Han shu* or *History of the [Earlier] Han* is a large work of 100 chapters which closely follows Ssu-ma Ch'ien's pattern. Pan Ku, however, dropped the whole third section on the hereditary princely houses, since he was not concerned with Chou times. He also innovated by adding essays on law, the pseudo-science of the "five elements," geography, and literature. The latter was actually a bibliographical essay on the imperial collection, based on an earlier work by a scholarly father and son, Liu Hsiang and Liu Hsin. Pan Ku also gave the essay on economics a new and more graphic name: "Food and Currency."

Pan Ku's *History of the [Earlier] Han* became the prototype for all the later dynastic histories of China, which treat either one major dynasty or a group of smaller related dynasties. The idea soon developed that each new dynasty had the duty of continuing the record of the past by compiling an official account of the preceding dynasty. If satisfactory, the work was then accepted by imperial order as one of the "standard histories." Sometimes an officially accepted "standard history" would subsequently come to be regarded as inadequate, and a second or "new" history would be compiled for that dynasty. During the eighteenth and nineteenth centuries there were twenty-four "standard histories," but in 1921 the President of the Republic of China accepted a "new" history of the Mongol Yüan dynasty, bringing the number to twenty-five. The *Ch'ing shih kao*, or *Draft History of the Ch'ing*, which was compiled under the Republic for the last of the imperial dynasties, however, has not as yet been officially accepted as one of the "standard histories."

THE DYNASTY CYCLE: PERSONAL FACTORS

The Chinese practice of compiling the records of the past in dynastic chunks is partially responsible for the traditional interpretation of Chinese history as a series of repetitive dynastic cycles. The lack of

PLATE 10. The archer Yi shooting nine of the ten sun crows which threaten to burn up the earth — a drought myth. Stone engraving on the wall of the Wu family funerary shrines in Shantung (second century A.D.).

PLATE 12. Rubbing of a Han stamped tile showing a banquet scene. Note the long-sleeved flowing robes and kneeling position, no longer characteristic of China but still seen in Japan.

PLATE 11. Detail from lacquer-painted basket found in a grave at the Han colony at Lo-lang (P'yŏngyang) in Korea (second or early third century A.D.).

PLATE 14. The First Emperor of the Ch'in dynasty attempts to recover the Chou ritual bronzes. Detail of a Han stone engraving from the Wu family shrines. The emperor stands on the bank of a river directing his men who are hauling on ropes to bring the bronze vessel up from the river bottom. The scene illustrates the dramatic moment when a dragon's head emerges from the vessel and snaps the ropes. Boats, fisherman and water birds delineate the river area.

PLATE 13. Detail of a Han stone engraving from the Wu family shrines. The upper register shows, left to right, guests arriving by chariot, kneeling guests being served a banquet (a gaming board is above the food tray), and acrobats performing. On the lower register servants, in their distinctive costumes, are preparing meats for the banquet.

DEVELOPMENT OF THE PAGODA

PLATE 15. The Great Stupa at Sanchi in central India dating from the third century B.C. to the first century A.D. Such early Buddhist structures were the origin of East Asian pagodas.

PLATE 16. Nine-story brick pagoda of the K'ai-yüan-ssu at Cheng-ting in Hopei, erected in 659 A.D. and rebuilt in 1668. Monasteries called K'ai-yüan-ssu were ordered established in every prefecture by the emperor in the twenty-sixth year of K'ai-yüan (738 A.D.).

PLATE 17. Wooden pagoda of the Yakushiji ("Temple of the Buddha of Medicine") near Nara in Japan, dating from the late seventh century. Only the finial bears any resemblance to the early stupas.

a belief in progress and the idea that there was a golden age in antiquity have strengthened this tendency, for the most that could be expected of history as it unfolded was the repetition of past glories. As a result, the fascinating story of the growth of Chinese civilization has been made to seem like one vast human treadmill. After reading the story of one dynasty, the student may feel that the next is just more of the same.

The Han historians, with their assumption that ancient China had enjoyed the same imperial unity they knew, managed to hide many of the fundamental changes between Shang times and the early Han under a surface pattern of repetitive motifs. Later historians made the succeeding 2000 years seem an even more monotonous series of more or less successful attempts to repeat the story of the Earlier Han dynasty. The concept of the dynastic cycle, in other words, has been a major block to the understanding of the fundamental dynamics of Chinese history. Even today historians are only beginning to grope their way toward the establishment of such useful generalizations as are afforded in Western history by its division into ancient, medieval, and modern periods.

It must be admitted, on the other hand, that there is considerable validity to the Chinese concept of the dynastic cycle, if one interprets it as a somewhat superficial political pattern that overlay the more fundamental technological, economic, social, and cultural developments. The two Han dynasties each lasted about two centuries; the great dynasties of later times, existing under somewhat different sociological and technological conditions, each tended to last about three centuries. And within each dynasty such matters as fiscal conditions, administrative efficiency, and power relations with the "barbarians" followed remarkably similar patterns. In fact, the Chinese concept of the dynastic cycle, if applied to the more stable periods of history in other parts of the world, might be found to have a greater degree of general validity than the more sweeping theories of cultural cycles put forth by such Western historians as Spengler and Toynbee.

Chinese historians, influenced by the Confucian insistence on the ethical basis of government, have always emphasized personal factors in explaining the dynastic cycle. Founders of dynasties, who, like Kao Tsu, successfully claimed the Mandate of Heaven, were not portrayed just as strong men but as veritable supermen, if not demigods. The last rulers, who lost the Mandate, were not considered just unfortunate or weak but were often described as evil and debauched, like the last kings of the Hsia and Shang.

Actually, the imperial lines invariably degenerated. The dynastic founder naturally had to be a man of great ability and force, and his original drive was likely to carry on for a few generations. Later rulers, raised in a luxurious and intrigue-ridden court, were more likely to be weaklings. Usually the dynasty produced at least one later strong man who either brought the regime to new power, as did Wu Ti, or gave it a sort of second start; but in general all the imperial lines showed a downward trend in ability, particularly in their last century of rule.

The quality of the men around the throne was on the whole more important than that of the emperors themselves. Here the picture is less clear. Struggles over the succession and court intrigues between rival factions characterized the history of all the dynasties almost from beginning to end. In the latter years of a dynasty, when the central government was weakening for other reasons, such factional quarrels, *coups d'état*, and palace revolutions, however, were naturally more deleterious than in the dynasty's heyday.

Factional quarrels in Han times were for the most part simply struggles over power and rewards. A typical example is afforded by Ho Kuang, a half brother of the general Ho Ch'ü-ping. A faithful administrator, Ho Kuang dominated the court during the reign of Wu Ti's successor, but his power began to fade with the accession of Hsüan Ti (the "Comprehensive Emperor") in 74 B.C., and, shortly after Kuang's death six years later, the whole Ho family was destroyed by its rivals.

In later dynasties, as we shall see, factional quarrels occasionally became more clearly ideological. Large factions, splitting the whole upper bureaucracy, sometimes feuded for generations over basic policy matters, thus impairing the efficiency of the central government far more than the briefer and more limited power struggles of earlier times.

One type of factional struggle that was endemic in all the dynasties was that between civil bureaucrats and eunuchs. The eunuchs naturally were at court to guard and administer the imperial harem, but their functions spread to other fields. As men of low social origin without descendants who could rival the imperial line, they were the natural allies of those emperors who sought to curb their more ambitious or greedy officials. The empresses, in particular, tended to rely on eunuchs, for these were the only men with whom they came in close contact in the harem. As a result eunuchs commonly came to hold high posts in the imperial household, and frequently they were made the commandants of the palace guards and in later dynasties even supervisors of the frontier armies.

The bureaucrats naturally looked with keen disfavor on these influential eunuchs, who lacked their own education, came from a different social background, and were their rivals for power and rewards at court. Since the writing of history was the prerogative of the more scholarly bureaucrats, we find the eunuchs uniformly condemned in the Chinese histories for their misrule. Whatever the truth of the matter, there can be no doubt about the bitter rivalry between eunuchs and bureaucrats. We have already noted under the Ch'in how the eunuch Chao Kao did away with Li Ssu. In 47 B.C. we find another great eunuch getting rid of his rivals at court. The high point of eunuch power came in the second half of the Later Han dynasty, when they often completely dominated the court.

The most persistent factional problem was that posed by the families of the empresses. We have already seen how Kao Tsu's empress almost took the throne for the Lü family. Wu Ti had a characteristically drastic solution for the problem: he destroyed the relatives of the woman whose son he named as heir apparent. His successors were less ruthless, and within a century Wang Mang, the nephew of an empress, was able to take the throne for himself. The son of an empress of the Wang family ascended the throne in 33 B.C., and soon her relatives came to dominate the court. By 8 B.C. Wang Mang, who was already a marquis, had intrigued his way to the highest position in the bureaucracy. After a temporary eclipse during the reign of the next emperor, he emerged again as all-powerful in 1 B.C., dominated the government during the reigns of two children, and in 8 A.D.[1] finally usurped the throne and established the Hsin (or New) dynasty.

THE DYNASTIC CYCLE: ECONOMIC AND ADMINISTRATIVE FACTORS

Despite the Chinese emphasis on the personal factor, it was by no means the chief element in the dynastic cycle. In fact, Wang Mang's usurpation is not the end of the first dynastic cycle, but rather the beginning of its last chapter — namely, the collapse of the Han central government that took place in his reign. A much more fundamental part of the story is the closely related rise and fall of the fiscal stability of the dynasty, its administrative efficiency, and its military power. The dynastic cycle, in other words, seems to be mainly an economic-administrative cycle, not a matter of personal character or genes.

All the great dynasties have an initial period of prosperity. The group that has seized the throne is relatively small and closely knit. The wars that have brought it to power have eliminated most of its rivals, and therefore the wealth of the nation pours largely into its coffers. The country prospers in its newly established peace, the population seems to increase rapidly, and the treasuries and granaries of the central government overflow.

But an excess of *yang* leads to the rise of *yin*. The affluent central government builds great palaces, roads, canals and walls. The imperial

---

[1] The actual date, according to the Western calendar, was January 10, 9 A.D., but the new year according to the Chinese lunar calendar usually begins two to six weeks later than in the West.

clan, the nobility, and the high bureaucracy grow in numbers and become accustomed to an ever more luxurious mode of life. The very military successes of the empire have established far-flung defense lines that are costly to maintain. More and more lands and their peasant-cultivators are used for the personal support of the ruling classes and fewer and fewer tax-paying contributors remain to the central administration. Because of constantly increasing expenditures and often a slight decline in income, each dynasty begins to experience serious financial difficulties within a century of its founding.

Economic and administrative reforms are then carried out and may halt the financial decline for a while. The downward trend, however, eventually reasserts itself. Economic and administrative difficulties accumulate. Official self-seeking and corruption become worse, leading to a decline in administrative efficiency and an intensification of factional quarrels at court. The potential rivals of the imperial family become politically and economically more independent of the central government and challenge it with greater impunity. To meet government deficits, the burden on the tax-paying peasant is increased to the breaking point. Because of the government's financial difficulties, canals and dikes are allowed to fall into disrepair, making floods and droughts more probable. Crop failures that once could have been offset by stores from the government granaries now result in famines, and these lead to banditry and eventually to peasant uprisings. Inadequately maintained frontier defenses begin to crumble. Provincial officials and their armies begin to defect, and the central government starts to go to pieces. Then follow the wars that liquidate the old regime and clear the slate for a new dynastic beginning.

Wu Ti's Financial Reforms. This essentially is the story of the Earlier Han dynasty. Wu Ti's canal-building program and foreign wars brought the dynasty to the height of its power but also produced a fiscal crisis. New revenues were desperately needed for the greatly expanded costs of government. Wu Ti's whole reign was characterized by a long series of efforts, some wise and others very unsound, to redeem the finances of the dynasty.

The most important of Wu Ti's economic measures was the reinstitution of state monopolies or licensing systems for the production and sale of certain commodities from which large profits could be made with minimal effort. This had been a standard practice of the Legalist state, fully employed by the Ch'in but allowed to lapse during the early prosperous days of the Han. The restoration of the government monopoly on the minting of copper coins brought in new revenue and was obviously a desirable measure, because it standardized the currency.

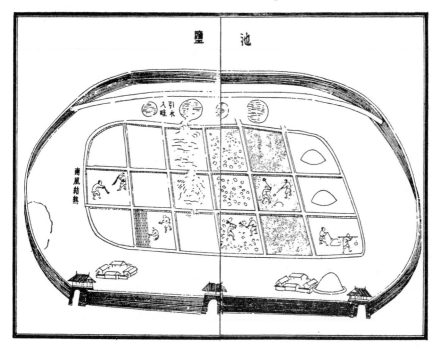

THE SALT MONOPOLY

Since salt was essential to the Chinese cereal diet, its manufacture and sale were ordinarily controlled by government licensing of both the producers and the distributors. This picture from the T'ien-kung k'ai-wu, *an encyclopedia of 1637, shows a flat salt "pan" on the seacoast, enclosed by walls and gates for control purposes. Left: The surface of the evaporation area is swept clean, and salt water is let in to cover it. Right: The salt left by solar evaporation is pulverized and collected in mounds for transport. Other methods of production were used in the interior provinces.*

In 119 Wu Ti reintroduced the government monopolies on salt and iron, which dated well back into Chou times in some areas of China, and later he added a monopoly or licensing system in liquor.

Another important economic innovation was the so-called "leveling" system, started in 110 B.C., by which the government purchased surplus produce in times and areas of glut to sell in periods and places of deficiency. Such a system naturally had some of the beneficial effects of a policy of price stabilization, but the chief motive was not price support and famine prevention but rather large and easy profit for the treasury. Both this system and the monopolies, though common practices throughout Chinese history, always remained highly controversial. As early as 81 B.C. a great court conference was held to discuss their propriety, and

the largely condemnatory conclusions were put into book form a generation later under the title of *The Discourses on Salt and Iron* (*Yen t'ieh
lun*).

The rest of Wu Ti's economic measures were less important, and many
of them were administratively or even economically harmful. He did
manage to tax commerce to some extent by special imposts on wagons
and ships and a sort of capital levy on artisans and merchants, but his
commutation of punishments to money fines for the wealthy may have
undermined his laws as much as it helped his treasury. The sale of ranks,
some for as much as 170,000 cash, though obviously contrary to the
theory of the bureaucratic state, became a practice often followed by
later dynasties. Similarly, his virtual extortion of large gifts from the
wealthy was often imitated later.

There was even some debasement of the currency, which the government now monopolized. Although nothing more than a palliative that
would eventually increase the ill, currency debasement was to prove a
favorite measure of most later Chinese rulers when they found themselves in financial difficulty. Wu Ti debased some of the coinage and even
invented an intrinsically worthless substitute for money. He had certain deerskin certificates issued which he forced the nobles to purchase
for 400,000 coins apiece.

During the latter years of Wu Ti's reign there were popular disturbances and much banditry, but his fiscal efforts were on the whole
successful, and the financial underpinnings of the dynasty were at least
temporarily restored. The government remained solvent through the
comparatively peaceful reign of Hsüan Ti (74–49 B.C.), and some of
Wu Ti's economic reforms were even relaxed.

Meanwhile, an even more serious problem, however, had developed.
The population had grown to such a point that the average peasant had
less land to cultivate than had his ancestors. Moreover, a much larger
proportion of the peasants were now on the virtually untaxed estates
of the great landowners, and therefore the tax-paying peasants elsewhere
were forced to carry a heavier load than before, on a smaller agricultural base. State revenues were declining and with them all the institutions of the central government. By 18 B.C. the fiscal situation was so
desperate that the sale price of court ranks was reduced. Beginning in
22 B.C. there was a series of large revolts, particularly among the slave
laborers of the government iron works. The general decline became
so obvious that even at court there was a spate of rumors about omens
portending the end of the dynasty.

Wang Mang's Usurpation and Reforms. It was at this critical juncture
that Wang Mang rose to power and sought desperately to stem the tide.
Two factors have served to confuse the story of his efforts. One was

his usurpation of the throne, which earned for him the condemnation of later Chinese historians. The other was the mantle of Confucian piety with which he cloaked all his actions — possibly a strategem to win the support of the now strongly Confucian bureaucracy, though it is more probable that Wang Mang sincerely believed that he was reviving the perfect Confucian state. For a while before his usurpation he allowed himself to be pictured as a new Duke of Chou, the regent who had been Confucius' ideal. He used ancient Chou titles and re-created supposedly Chou institutions. With the aid of the bibliographer and Confucian scholar Liu Hsin, he sponsored a revival of interest in ancient texts. Certain early works, such as the *Tso chuan*, the *Rituals of Chou* (*Chou li*), the Mao text of the *Classic of Songs*, and the "old text" of the *Classic of Documents*, were brought to general attention for the first time during his reign. In fact, Wang Mang's connection with these texts increased the passion with which later generations have argued their authenticity or spuriousness. At the same time, his championing of Confucianism at court contributed greatly to its ultimate triumph.

Wang Mang's return to the ideal Confucian state of Chou times, however, was merely a matter of names and theory. His actual reforms were for the most part more in the Legalist tradition. Many were no more than a revival or amplification of Wu Ti's policies. On the one hand he attempted to strengthen the bureaucracy, and on the other he strove desperately to solve the financial crisis. He built up the monopolies, returned vigorously to the "leveling" systems, and instituted a policy of agricultural loans, which might have been of some help to the hard-pressed peasants and unquestionably would have brought in substantial new revenue if they had continued long enough. He also returned to the game of currency debasement, making this easier by introducing coins of differing denominations. In fact his monetary policies were so successful that he amassed a huge store of gold, about five million ounces, in return for his debased copper coinage.

The most important of Wang Mang's reforms was his frontal assault on the major economic problem of his day. So many peasants were on the tax-free estates that not enough of them remained on the tax registers to support the central government. He therefore decreed the end of the great private estates by ordering in 9 A.D. that the land be "nationalized" and parceled out among tax-paying peasants and that private slavery be ended. Such a drastic policy would have been extremely hard to carry out even in Wu Ti's time. Now, a century later, it was entirely beyond the power of the central government to enforce. Within three years Wang Mang had to rescind it, and all that then remained of his bold bid to recapture the potential taxes of the country for the government treasury was a prohibitory tax on private slaves.

Wang Mang's effort to "nationalize" the land has won him both praise and condemnation as China's first Socialist. The term as applied to him is, of course, anachronistic. He had no concept of Socialist theory and thought of himself as a perfect Confucianist, even though his policies were more in the Legalist tradition. What distinguished him most from other strong Chinese rulers was the daring with which he attempted to turn back the dynastic cycle and re-create the conditions that had existed at the beginning of the dynasty.

The Final Collapse of the Empire. Wang Mang's vigorous efforts at reform may have hastened the collapse of the central government. Already undermined by slow fiscal and administrative erosion, it now lost the support of the powerful and rich families whose lands Wang Mang had sought to expropriate. A series of bad harvests contributed to the debacle, but these were not simply the result of unfavorable weather. Breaks in the dikes of the Yellow River, which sent part of its waters into a new course south of the Shantung Peninsula, and the breakdown of the water-control system in the Wei Valley, which resulted in famines in the capital district, were clear signs that the whole structure of government was disintegrating.

There were frequent rebellions. For example, a great peasant uprising broke out in Shantung in 18 A.D. and soon spread to the whole empire. These rebels called themselves the Red Eyebrows, from a distinguishing mark they adopted. The Red Eyebrows had originated from a secret society with strong Taoistic tendencies. Such religious affiliations were to prove typical of the great popular rebellions that usually marked the declining years of later dynasties. Though motivated by economic necessity, popular risings were commonly set off by some spark originating in the popular religions of the day.

The Red Eyebrows also had another point of similarity with the leaders of popular revolts in later times. They laid waste the land but lacked the administrative experience and understanding to substitute a central government of their own for the one they were destroying. The task of re-creating the central power fell to the hands of better educated men. Various descendants of the Han emperors, or at least men who shared their surname of Liu, had joined in the revolt, claiming to be the rightful heirs of the Han. These men were usually great landowners and in better times would have been the supporters of the central government rather than its destroyers. It was a man of this type, rather than any of the Red Eyebrows, who eventually managed to take Wang Mang's place on the throne.

Meanwhile, the frontier defenses had crumbled, and the border states had reasserted their independence. Wang Mang had planned great expeditions against the Hsiung-nu but had been unable to finance them. The nomads invaded the border regions, the capital was sacked by rebels, and Wang Mang died at their hands in 23 A.D. The great central-ized government that Kao Tsu had founded had finally disintegrated in complete chaos.

THE LATER HAN DYNASTY

The man who finally emerged victorious in 25 A.D. from the free-for-all that followed Wang Mang's downfall was Liu Hsiu, who as a descend-ant of the Han rulers revived the Han name. Liu Hsiu had been a prosperous landowner in what is now eastern Honan, and he chose for his capital the nearby city of Loyang, which had been the Eastern Chou capital. The move from Ch'ang-an was not unwarranted, because the old capital had been destroyed by the rebels and the agriculture of the Wei Valley had declined drastically since the ruin of its water-control system. Because of the location of Loyang, the Later Han dynasty is also known as the Eastern Han, and the Earlier Han dynasty by contrast is called the Western Han.

Liu Hsiu, who was given the posthumous title of Kuang Wu Ti ("Shining Martial Emperor"), spent his three decades on the throne (25–57 A.D.) consolidating the power of his regime and achieving a "restoration" that became for Chinese historians the prototype for later dynastic revivals — that is, a restoration of strong, centralized govern-ment following a great rebellion. A strong ruler, Kuang Wu Ti suppressed the Red Eyebrows and other rebels, destroyed what little power he him-self had given to the imperial princelings, re-created a powerful central administration on the pattern of his predecessors, and freed those people who had fallen into slavery during the preceding time of trouble. He no longer faced the insoluble financial problem that had proved too much for Wang Mang. The wars had wiped out the Earlier Han aristocracy and some of the other great landholders. The new dynasty, moreover, was not as yet burdened with a large imperial clan and ruling class. Tax returns, consequently, were more than adequate to meet government needs.

The Reconquest of Central Asia. As during the Earlier Han, it took several decades before the new dynasty reached its apogee of power and returned to a vigorous policy of imperial expansion. Under Kuang Wu Ti, a general named Ma Yüan had already reconquered South China and northern Vietnam, and this area had been made a more in-tegral part of the empire than ever before. But it was not until the reign of the second ruler, Ming Ti (the "Enlightened Emperor," 57–75 A.D.), that a determined effort was made to reconquer Central Asia and the northern nomads. The story of this reconquest is largely that of one man, Pan Ch'ao, the brother of the famous historian Pan Ku.

Fortunately for the Chinese, the Hsiung-nu were no longer a united empire, as they had been two centuries earlier, and were therefore less of a menace. In fact, the Southern Hsiung-nu had meekly surrendered to Kuang Wu Ti and been settled along the northern marches as defenders of the frontiers of the empire. The petty states of Central Asia also seem to have preferred Chinese rule to that of the Northern Hsiung-nu, who were culturally as well as linguistically so different from the agricultural Indo-Europeans of this area. Consequently, intrigue and the use of local levies were probably as helpful to Pan Ch'ao as the Chinese armies that were occasionally sent to him by the reluctant court.

Pan Ch'ao's first effort to win back Central Asia, in 73 A.D., was frustrated by his recall three years later, but he was allowed to return to the attack and soon had the whole Tarim Basin firmly under his control. In 91 he was made Protector General (*Tu hu*) of the Western Regions, with his headquarters at Kucha on the northern edge of the Tarim Basin. Subsequently he led a great army across the Pamirs, conquering the whole area as far as the shores of the Caspian Sea. His forces also defeated those of the Kushan Empire of the Yüeh-chih. Only Parthia then intervened between Han and the Roman Empire, and Pan Ch'ao actually sent one of his lieutenants to look for Ta-Ch'in, but the man turned back after reaching Mesopotamia and the head of the Persian Gulf.

The Chinese hold on Central Asia did not long outlast Pan Ch'ao's retirement and death in 102. Two of his sons maintained some Chinese control in the area for a while, and Han garrisons occupied the Kansu corridor until about the middle of the second century, but the Later Han by that time was rapidly declining in power.

Financial and Administrative Weakness. The Later Han, in fact, had never been able to achieve as strong a financial position as had the Earlier Han at its height. The founder of the dynasty and most of his chief supporters, like the great general, Ma Yüan, had been rich hereditary landowners, and the power of this class was never seriously challenged. Too many of the large private estates of the first century B.C. had survived into Later Han times to allow the new dynasty the same clean slate, economically and administratively, that Kao Tsu and his successors had enjoyed.

The position of the great landowners was quite secure. Land taxes in Han times were usually only about one-thirtieth of the yield, while rents ran about one-half. Paying thus only an inconsequential land tax, if any, they lived luxuriously off the exorbitant rents wrung from their peasants, gained further income by controlling trade, and protected their wealth by monopolizing the higher court posts. Although the central government repeatedly made efforts to build up an efficient bureaucracy based on merit, the great majority of the officials achieved their positions through inheritance, patronage, or the open manipulation of the official examinations by those in charge. Officials thus became the admitted adherents of one great landowner or another.

The financial and administrative weakness of the Later Han is reflected by the registration figures. As late as 57 A.D. there were only 21,007,820 people on the tax registers. Presumably this did not reflect a drastic reduction in population, from the high point of 59,594,978 in the Earlier Han, so much as the smaller proportion of the people subject to effective government control. Subsequently the census figures reached 53,256,229 in 105 A.D., but a slow, steady decline then set in, as administrative degeneration evidently outpaced population growth.

The distribution of the tax-paying, *corvée*-serving population was even less favorable than its declining size. In all North China, the area best situated to support the central government, there was a drastic reduction of the census figures after the Earlier Han. Many of the northern border regions, on which the chief burden of military defense fell, had only a small fraction of the official population that had been registered under the previous dynasty. Only in the newer lands of Szechwan, the areas south of the Yangtze Valley, and the remote south coast was there any marked increase of officially recorded population over the Earlier Han, but these areas were too distant to make much of a contribution to the support of the capital or the defense of the northern frontier.

To maintain itself, the central government was forced to levy increasingly heavy taxes on the dwindling number of tax-paying peasants in North China. The burden eventually became unbearable. Many peasants were forced to flee to the less rigorously taxed South or into the estates of the great landowners, where the rents were less crushing than the taxes on free peasants. The result of such absconding was an inevitable increase in taxation on those who remained. The hard-pressed peasants thus were forced into banditry or open revolt, which further weakened the dynasty's finances. This downward spiral, once started, was not easily stopped.

The decline of the Later Han dynasty can, of course, also be explained in personal terms. No later strong ruler arose, like Wu Ti of the Earlier Han, to restore the government's finances, and factionalism at court was even more intense than during the preceding dynasty. These, however, were merely symptoms of a fundamental malady — the financial and administrative weakness of the central administration and the strength of the great families.

Empresses, Eunuchs, and Popular Rebellions. As in the Earlier Han, the first major challenge to the imperial clan came from the relatives of empresses who found their wealth and power greatly enhanced by their fortunate connections at court. For example, Tou Hsien, who came of a great landowning family that dated back to the second century B.C., became all-powerful at court around 100 A.D. A half century later it was the Liang family which, through the influence of an empress, came to dominate the government.

In both cases the emperors finally got rid of these powerful relatives of their empresses through the aid of the high court eunuchs. Tou Hsien was killed, while the Liang were wiped out in 159. The five leading eunuchs in this second great *coup d'état* were ennobled and given huge fiefs, and at this time the eunuchs as a group achieved greater control over the Chinese empire than ever before. They were even able to make their power and wealth hereditary, for during the second century they were allowed to found families through adoption.

The other great families, naturally, were not willing to see all power monopolized by eunuchs. With the support of the petty bureaucracy and the thousands of would-be officials in the Confucian government university, certain high bureaucrats who considered themselves the "pure" party attempted to curb the eunuchs, but their efforts backfired. The eunuchs imprisoned hundreds of their court opponents in 166, and in a larger outbreak of open conflict between 168 and 170 they killed thousands of the adherents of their bureaucratic foes.

The great purges carried out by the eunuchs were both symptomatic of administrative decline and contributory to a further disintegration of the government. By 184 two great rebellions had broken out, in East China and Szechwan. Both were led by Taoist religious leaders of faith-healing sects. The uprising in East China was headed by Chang Chüeh, who had built up a huge popular following for his "Way of the Great Peace" (T'ai P'ing Tao). Since his followers wore yellow kerchiefs when they rose in revolt, they were known as the Yellow Turbans. The yellow stood for "earth," the element these religious zealots felt was now to triumph over the red "fire" that had symbolized Han rule. Chang Chüeh was killed in 184, but the Yellow Turbans remained a serious military threat for more than two decades.

In Szechwan the rebels were known as the Five Pecks of Rice band, because of the dues paid their cult masters. They were led by two successive but unrelated religious leaders called Chang Hsiu and Chang Lu. The latter was finally bought over in 215 by Ts'ao Ts'ao, the greatest of the Han generals. The Taoist rebellions had lasted for more than thirty years, and the Later Han dynasty never recovered from the disruption they caused to centralized government.

The Division of the Empire by the Great Generals. The *coup de grâce*, however, was given the Han by its own generals, as was often the case in later dynasties. The collapse of the tax-paying peasantry entailed the ruin of the *corvée* labor system and the peasant draft army associated with it. The professional armies that took its place tended to become the private forces of the generals who commanded them. These generals were usually rich landowners and thus represented just one more aspect of the continuing threat of the great families to the central government.

After the outbreak of the popular revolts the generals became virtually independent war lords within their respective commands and soon completely overshadowed the central government. In 189 one general slaughtered the court eunuchs, and the next year another general, Tung Cho, sacked the capital. Gradually a three-way division of power developed among the leading generals, with Ts'ao Ts'ao, the son of an adopted son of a eunuch, in the North, Liu Pei in Szechwan, and Sun Ch'üan in the region of the lower Yangtze and the South. This divi-

THE THREE KINGDOMS

WEI

•Loyang

Chien-yeh (Nanking)

•Chengtu

SHU HAN

WU

sion was geographically a natural one and was to reappear at various times in later Chinese history.

When Ts'ao Ts'ao died in 220 A.D., his son Ts'ao P'ei, usurped the throne, naming his dynasty the Wei after the late Chou state of that name. He tried to make his usurpation appear similar to the transfer of the throne from the legendary emperor Yao to his loyal lieutenant, Shun, a Confucian pattern that later usurpers were careful to follow. This act brought an official end to the Later Han dynasty, though it had been scarcely more than a political fiction for the past three decades.

The following year Liu Pei in Szechwan also assumed the imperial title, taking the dynastic name of Han, as befitted a man who traced his ancestry back to the old imperial line, and his dynasty has been called the Shu Han after the former Szechwanese state of Shu. In 222 Sun Ch'üan in the South followed suit, adopting the dynastic name of Wu after the Chou state that had once existed in the part of China he now ruled. The half century during which China was divided between these three states is known as the Three Kingdoms (*San-kuo*) period.

THE END OF THE FIRST CHINESE EMPIRE

According to the theory of the dynastic cycle one of the three succession states or some new rebel group should presently have reunited the country and started another two-century cycle of united rule, but nothing of the sort happened. Something much more profound than a mere administrative breakdown was occurring in China — something closer to the type of cultural breakdown that Toynbee postulates in his theory of civilizations. The whole collapse of the Han system bears a general resemblance to the decline and fall of the Roman Empire. In fact, the great sweep of this history, from the political divisiveness but intellectual vigor of the Chou, through the unification of the Ch'in and Han empires, to the disintegration of the imperial system, fits in remarkably well with Toynbee's pattern, which is so clearly based on the similar course of history in the classic West.

The close parallel between the Mediterranean area and China during this millennium of history is at first startling, but on second thought not really surprising. Since their technological levels were quite comparable, it is not unnatural that these two areas should have been capable of similar accomplishments and subject to similar weaknesses. There was a sufficient surplus of wealth and leisure time to permit a cultural and philosophical flowering in both ancient Greece and the later Chou. Parallel technological advances — such as the widespread use of iron and the speeding up of communications and the extension of military power through horseback riding — also made possible the steady consolidation of political power and the eventual appearance of "universal" empires in both areas at much the same time. But a number of the conditions essential for efficient imperial administration — such as a large tax income for the central organs of government, efficient administration throughout the empire, and cohesiveness within the ruling group — could not be maintained. The regimes in both East and West proved inadequate to surmount the problems resulting from the increase in population and the rapid economic and institutional growth that these empires themselves had made possible, and the eventual breakdowns in both areas were therefore not dissimilar.

However, the parallels, both in general outline and in certain details, between the Mediterranean world and China at this time do not necessarily mean that this particular pattern of history is a universal one. It may apply to other civilizations existing at the same cultural level; but Toynbee's effort to make it fit later Chinese and Japanese history is entirely unconvincing. In fact, the story of China's second great imperial era, lasting from the sixth century to our own day without significant break, suggests that Toynbee's classic pattern might best be limited to the period of history from which it is basically derived.

Economic and Administrative Disintegration. The decline of the first Chinese empire can be traced back to the financial difficulties at the time of Wu Ti. It became marked during the first century B.C., when the great families consolidated their hold on their large estates. Kuang Wu Ti, in recreating the centralized state of the Later Han, had to make a greater compromise with the principle of large private holdings than had the emperors of the Earlier Han. From then on the decline was rapid, and the Later Han took no effective measures to check it. In fact, throughout this period the centralized administration was its own worst enemy. Emperors were the first to award huge grants of land and peasants in perpetuity to their relatives, favorites, and outstanding generals and administrators. The great officials were unendingly avaricious in rewarding themselves and their relatives in similar fashion. Though frequent shifts of power, *coups d'état,* and palace revolutions resulted in the confiscation and return of many of these lands and peasants to the government tax registers, the outflow of these essential assets was in general greater than the inflow.

By the late second century the great local families were simply too rich and powerful to be curbed by the central government; in fact, they controlled it, and the division of the country into three separate empires after 220 A.D. was merely formal recognition of the bald fact that a truly united government was no longer possible. Nor was any of the three succession states an effectively united empire. All were more or less at the mercy of their own great families and generals. They and the dynasties that followed all sought to revive the Han imperial system, but none could achieve more than a pale imitation of it. Wei, for example, pretentiously set up stone classics at its Loyang capital to accompany those of the Later Han, but was unable to reunite the land or recreate the bureaucratic state. It and most of the other succession "empires" of the Han were merely one-man dynasties, created by a strong general and lost within a generation or two by his heirs.

The Three Kingdoms and the Chin Dynasty. The Three Kingdoms period, however, is thought of by the Chinese as an exciting and romantic time. Kuan Yü, one of the associates of Liu Pei, the founder of the Shu Han dynasty, eventually became canonized in popular Chinese religion as Kuan Ti, the God of War. Chu-ko Liang, the astute strategist of the same state, ranks as one of the greatest popular heroes of Chinese history. A whole cycle of semi-historical legends grew up about such worthies. Over a thousand years later these stories found literary expression in the sprawling historical novel entitled *San-kuo-chih yen-i*, or *The Romance of the Three Kingdoms.*

The period saw incessant warfare. Wei suppressed an upstart king of Yen in southern Manchuria and extended its sway over Korea; Shu Han conquered barbarian tribes in the southwest; and Wu extended its military control as far south as Vietnam. The three succession states were also continuously at war with one another, and finally, in 263, Wei managed to destroy and annex Shu Han.

The real power in Wei, however, had long since passed from Ts'ao Ts'ao's heirs to the hands of their great generals, and in 265 the strongest of these, Ssu-ma Yen, usurped the throne. His dynasty he named Chin, after the great state that had existed in Shansi in Chou times, and he himself is known to history as Chin Wu Ti, the "Martial Emperor" of the Chin.

This new Wu Ti conquered the southern state of Wu in 280, uniting China briefly once more, and he strove valiantly to restore the old imperial system. He tried to disband his armies, in order to reduce the costs of government and convert his soldiers into tax-paying peasants, and he attempted to carry out reforms, so that the fruits of their labor would pour into the government treasury as taxes and not into the storehouses of the landowners as rent. The official census, however, was down to 16,163,863, a sure sign that a large part of the population was beyond effective control or taxation by the government, and Wu Ti made no real attempt to break up the estates and get the peasants back on the tax registers.

In any case, the tides of history could scarcely have been stemmed by a single energetic ruler. The so-called nine-grade ranking system, which the Chin had inherited from the Wei, was indicative of the great changes taking place. While purporting to take the place of the Han examination system as a means of recruiting new talent into government, it actually institutionalized the supremacy of the great families. The most prominent individuals in each administrative area were given the duty of ranking the local families and individuals by merit for possible government service, but since the ranking was actually done by status and influence it merely helped secure the monopoly of high government posts by the great families.

The Chin was a typical one-man dynasty. Shortly after Wu Ti's death in 290 it fell apart in a civil war known as the Revolt of the Eight Kings.

"Barbarian" Invasions. A new aspect of the disintegration of the imperial system now became apparent. China was all but defenseless against the northern nomads. Fortunately for the Chinese, their troublesome neighbors were not united into a great empire, as they had been some centuries earlier, and were again to be in later periods, but now even small tribal bands of Altaic and Tibetan peoples found the border marches of China easy prey. The pendulum of conquest, after swinging outward into the steppe land for centuries, was now beginning to swing back into China.

This drastic shift in power relationship between the Chinese and the nomads can be explained in part by our useful concept of *yin-yang* dualism. The very subjugation of the nomads by the Han had sown the seeds for the barbarian conquest of China. Hsiung-nu bands that had surrendered were settled as semi-agricultural tribal groups on the northern borders of China. We have noted, for example, that Kuang Wu Ti settled the Southern Hsiung-nu along the frontiers, and toward the end of the second century the great general Ts'ao Ts'ao permitted nineteen Hsiung-nu tribes to settle in northern Shansi. This situation may explain in part why the census figures for the tax-paying Chinese in these northern areas showed such a drastic decline during the Later Han dynasty.

The "barbarians," because of their horsemanship and martial traditions, also became important elements in the Chinese armies. The fourth century marked the beginning of a millennium during which the mounted archer dominated warfare in most of Asia. Thus, the borderland and the whole Chinese defense system became permeated with semi-Sinicized "barbarians" — men who at best were only halfhearted defenders of the Chinese way of life. The situation was not unlike that of Late Roman times in Europe, where the borderlands and defense forces passed in large part into the hands of the Germanic "barbarians."

As the Chinese Empire disintegrated, the semi-agricultural "barbarians" from the north and the still purely nomadic tribes beyond them found no difficulty in penetrating deep into China in their search for better pasture or rich booty. A veritable flood of petty invasions started in 304, and for more than a century the whole North was inundated by tribal war bands of nomadic origin. Only the mountain ramparts of Szechwan and the large river systems of the Yangtze Valley and the South preserved these regions from the ravages of the northern horsemen.

Huge numbers of Chinese, naturally, attempted to escape the depredations of the "barbarians" and the generally chaotic conditions in North China. Some sought safety in the Kansu corridor, where a Chinese general founded a dynasty, the Earlier Liang, that maintained itself from 313 to 376. Many more fled southward to the safety of Szechwan and the area south of the Yangtze. As a result, the Chinese population in the South multiplied several times over between the third and fifth centuries, and the Sinicization of the non-Chinese peoples of the area was accelerated. Many of the North Chinese moved into South China as powerful family groups, demanding special privileges for themselves and establishing political control over their new homes.

The Succession States of the South. Hsiung-nu bands, which had responded in 304 to a call for aid from one of the contenders for power in the Chin state, destroyed that dynasty in 316. The next year a Chin prince in South China declared himself emperor at Nanking. His dynasty is known as the Eastern Chin, in contrast to the first Chin dynasty at Loyang, which is called the Western Chin.

The capital at Nanking (appropriately meaning "Southern Capital," though this is actually a much later name for the city, which at this time was called Chien-k'ang) grew into a great metropolis where the luxurious ways of the Han were continued. The government, however, was weak and continually at the mercy of its generals, who repeatedly seemed on the point of snuffing out the dynasty. These generals, of course, were great landowners, and, significantly, most of them were of recent northern origin. Quite naturally they were obsessed with the idea of reconquering their northern homeland. In 347 the Eastern Chin did manage to subjugate Szechwan, but its various wars against the "barbarians" in the North brought no permanent gains. At home it was constantly plagued by revolts and *coups d'état,* and a great peasant uprising, led by spiritual descendants of the Yellow Turbans, broke out in 400.

Finally in 420 Liu Yü, a general who had had considerable success against the barbarians in the North, usurped the throne and founded the Sung dynasty, usually called the Liu Sung, in distinction to the great Sung dynasty of later history. Liu Yü and his successor on the throne brought the empire centered at Nanking to its highest point of power, but after the latter's death the Liu Sung dynasty fell apart.

The next century and a half, until the final destruction of the southern capital in 589, witnessed dismal repetitions of the same story. There were constant and usually unsuccessful wars with the "barbarian" states of the North, and one general after another seized the throne from the weak heirs of the preceding usurper.

In 479 Hsiao Tao-ch'eng founded the Southern Ch'i dynasty, but in 502 one of his relatives, Hsiao Yen, who is known to history as Wu Ti (the "Martial Emperor"), usurped the throne and founded the Liang dynasty. This Wu Ti of the Liang was a great patron of Buddhism, and his reign was the longest and most stable in the history of all the southern states. Eventually, however, his capital was captured by a "barbarian" general in 549. A Liang prince then attempted to revive the dynasty at what is now Hankow, but he soon lost the whole upper Yangtze Valley to the "barbarians."

Ch'en Pa-hsien, a leading general in the lower Yangtze, then revived the southern state at Nanking in 557, but his Ch'en dynasty was wiped out thirty-two years later by the Sui Empire, which was a product of the "barbarian" North.

This brought to an end the efforts on the part of the Han succession states to restore its great imperial tradition. For a century in North China and three and a half in South China the dream had been to found another Han. The net result, however, was complete failure. No dynasty had been more than a mere shadow of the old empire, perpetuating at most the conditions of ineffectual central government and complete dominance by the great families that had characterized the dying days of Han rule.

A broken-down Han could be maintained for a while, much as Byzantium continued a degenerated Roman tradition for a much longer period in the West, but Han could not be revived — at least not by the Chinese themselves. The later history of China was to grow out of the amalgam of "barbarian" and Chinese in North China, as the later history of Europe grew out of the union of Latins and Germans. The most significant aspect of the history of this period, therefore, was not the perpetuation of the Han system in the South, but the "barbarian" challenge, and the eventual response of Chinese civilization to this challenge, which took place largely in North China.

The "Barbarian" Challenge

and the Regeneration

of the Empire

THE NATURE OF THE CHALLENGE

The Six Dynasties Period. The epoch following the fall of the Later Han dynasty is called the Six Dynasties period (*Liu ch'ao*) after the six successive dynasties that had their capitals at Nanking between 222 and 589. This span of three and a half centuries is commonly treated as a single slice of history — a sort of dynastic cycle in reverse, in that it runs from unity through prolonged disunity back to unity again.[1]

The Six Dynasties period was indeed an interregnum — a great trough between strong, unified dynasties. This certainly is the surface pattern, but it should not be allowed to obscure the deeper flow of Chinese history beneath it. One of the major stories of the period, which we have already told, centers around the futile efforts of the Chinese to restore Han unity. A more important story is that of the fundamental challenge to classic Chinese civilization that occurred at this time and the way in which Chinese civilization eventually met the crisis by incorporating the challengers into the Chinese system. Out of this synthe-

[1] The latter part of this era, variously dating from the founding of the Eastern Chin (317–589), the establishment of the "barbarian" dynasty of the Northern Wei (386–589), or the usurpation of the Liu Sung (420–589), is also known as the period of the Southern and Northern Dynasties (*Nan pei ch'ao*).

sis grew a new and richer Chinese civilization and a revivified empire that outshone the most glorious days of the Han. This story has its beginning in the Six Dynasties period but reaches its climax under the unified rule of the Sui and T'ang dynasties in the late sixth and seventh centuries. A sharp historical division around 220 A.D. leaves the last sad chapter of the decline of the first empire untold; an abrupt break at 589 divides in half the story of the re-creation of the Chinese Empire, making the Six Dynasties period appear more of a departure from the pattern of empire than it actually was and lending credence to the misapprehension that the second great empire rose miraculously like a phoenix from the ashes of three centuries of anarchy.

Internal Breakdown. The challenge to classic Chinese civilization was posed most dramatically as an external or "barbarian" threat. Nomad hordes overran North China, and an alien religion, Indian Buddhism, menaced the ideological basis of Chinese society. The challenge, however, was probably more of internal than of external origin. Only because the Han political system had collapsed of its own inner contradictions were the barbarians able to pour into China. Only because the Han synthesis of Confucian ideology, pseudo-scientific superstitions, and Legalist practices had proved spiritually unsatisfying and politically inadequate were the Chinese receptive to Buddhism. In fact, thinking men first deserted Confucianism for Taoism before turning to Buddhism. Moreover, "barbarian" invasions did not themselves necessarily pose a major threat to Chinese civilization. More extensive invasions by much more powerful "barbarian" hordes were to occur later in Chinese history without seriously menacing the continuity of Chinese civilization, because Chinese culture by that time, partially as a result of its enrichment and invigoration during the Six Dynasties period, no longer suffered from its earlier inadequacies.

The Later Han saw the breakdown of a whole social order as well as of a political system. The change was comparable to that of the late Chou, when a clan-centered society, in which authority, status, wealth, and political loyalty were all based on hereditary and semi-religious relationships, gave way to a new social order in which smaller family units, with their own private holdings, were ruled over impersonally by a centralized bureaucratic government. Now this new political order of Han was giving way in turn, because the richer of these family units had come to own so much private property that they dominated society and made centralized government all but impossible.

As during the Chou, this fundamental social change was centuries in the making. It started with the great grants of land at the beginning of the Earlier Han. It accelerated rapidly in the dying years of the Later Han and in the decades that followed. The weakened central government was less able to check the growth of private holdings than before, and the great landowners found it easier to evade all taxes and to incorporate new lands into their estates by falsifying land registers, foreclosing mortgages, or opening up hitherto uncultivated areas.

At the same time, family units among the rich and powerful drew together for self-protection into extended family groups. They also consolidated their control over their subordinates. Tenant farmers gradually declined in status into virtual serfdom. Impoverished peasants, fleeing the government tax collectors or the "barbarians," gave themselves and their services to powerful landowners in return for economic security and protection and gradually became hereditary dependents or "guests" (*k'o*) of their patrons.

Those among the dependents and serfs who had martial inclinations became the personal soldiers (*pu-ch'ü*) of the great landlords, and a system of private armies gradually replaced the former peasant levies. Each great family came to possess its own fortified manors and fortresses. It was families with this sort of private economic and military base that could usurp the throne from weak rulers or could move to the South with their thousands of dependents and quickly establish their mastery over the local populace.

As the central government declined, the large self-sufficient manor became the chief economic unit, and trade consequently languished. Administrative centers declined in size, and trading cities were drastically reduced. Copper coinage virtually went out of use in certain areas, and barter, which had always persisted in rural areas, became again the rule throughout the country.

Conditions were not unlike those in the Roman Empire at a slightly later date. In fact, they might be described as already proto-feudal. The "barbarian" invasions naturally contributed to the breakup of the old order. Under their impact a pastoral economy might conceivably have replaced the agricultural economy of North China, and Altaic languages might have taken the place of Chinese. More probably, the tribal, military traditions of the northern nomads might have contributed to the feudalization of China, as the comparable traditions of the Germans contributed to the feudalization of Europe. If the failure of centralized government had continued a few centuries longer and the dream of Han unity had further dimmed, China might very well have developed a system quite comparable to the feudalism that Europe and Japan were to experience a few centuries later.

The Failure of Confucianism. The challenge to the old Chinese ways of thought, like the challenge to government and to the social order, was also largely self-generated. Confucianism itself proved in some ways subversive to centralized government during the declining days of the first empire. It had, of course, strengthened bureaucratic rule and during later periods was to provide the perfect ideological balance to the essentially Legalist power structure within the imperial system. At this time, however, when the chief threat to centralized rule was the wealth and power of the great families, the Confucian emphasis on filial piety and family loyalties was decidedly injurious to the state. Similarly, its emphasis on civil rituals and cultural accomplishments was of little help at a time when the central government had lost military control over the land; nor did its textual scholasticism, its preoccupation with antiquity, and its growing dogmatism help meet the economic and administrative difficulties that were destroying the empire.

During the Later Han the Confucian tradition had dominated society more completely than ever before. Classical studies spread rapidly, and Confucian scholars were highly respected and much sought after. The centralized bureaucratic state, however, was sinking fast, and Confucianism was contributing at least as much to its destruction as to its maintenance.

As the political situation worsened, there was an increasing apathy toward Confucianism and all other forms of political philosophy, which had once been an all-consuming interest. Chinese thought, in other words, began to turn inward and away from the social order. Since society and government now seemed hopelessly degenerate, men again became interested in the old Taoist problem of the individual's relationship to nature and his personal perfection or salvation, irrespective of surrounding social conditions. This Taoist current of thought had no doubt always existed, particularly among the common people, but with the disintegration of the political superstructure it rose prominently to the surface of Chinese society. There was a sudden upsurge of Taoism in all its diverse manifestations.

Before long Buddhism too began to make spiritual and intellectual inroads. Appearing first in the guise of a Taoist sect, the Indian religion soon established its independence, and in time outstripped Taoism in popularity and influence. Denying not only the importance of the political and social order but even the desirability of life in this world, Buddhism was the antithesis of the main stream of Chinese thought as it had existed hitherto. The triumph of such an alien religion during these centuries thus constituted a far more serious challenge to Chinese civilization than the mere conquest of the land by "barbarian" invaders.

THE UPSURGE OF TAOISM

Even in the first century A.D. Wang Ch'ung's iconoclasm and somewhat corrosive skepticism had presaged the turning of the educated classes from Confucianism. By the third century this tendency was quite obvious. The precocious Wang Pi (226–249), the most brilliant scholar of his day, produced great commentaries on the *Tao te ching* and the *Classic of Changes*, and the outstanding scholarly achievement of the Western Chin period was an equally learned commentary on the *Chuang-tzu*.

The Ch'ing-t'an Philosophers. The Taoistically inclined intellectuals of the third century were addicted to *ch'ing-t'an*, variously translated as "pure discussions" or "purity debates." These men maintained their vaunted "purity" by holding themselves disdainfully aloof from unsavory politics and all other mundane matters. One is reminded of the Confucian bureaucrats who in the preceding century had called themselves the "pure" party in distinction to the corrupt eunuchs. The answer of the *ch'ing-t'an* group to the social and political disillusionment of the time was to develop their own aesthetic sensibilities and give individualistic expression to their every impulse. Their hedonistic escapism of course grew out of a profound pessimism. In turning their backs on government, they robbed society of some of its natural leaders, thus contributing to the general breakdown.

The most famous of the *ch'ing-t'an* group were the Seven Sages of the Bamboo Grove. These wealthy recluses, who lived at the Western Chin capital in the early years of the dynasty, loved to engage in philosophical debates, compose poetry, play on the lute, enjoy nature, and drink. They were, in fact, renowned topers. One of the group expressed his basic philosophy by always having in attendance a servant who carried a wine bottle in one hand to quench his master's thirst and a spade in the other to bury him if he fell dead. The "barbarian" invasions drove such wealthy dilettantes out of the North, but the *ch'ing-t'an* movement continued at Nanking in the South, where the Eight Understanding Ones of the fourth century were even more wildly eccentric than their northern predecessors.

Alchemy and Immortality Through Inner Hygiene. Another aspect of the Taoist resurgence was the growing interest in alchemy as a method of obtaining an elixir of life. We have encountered the concept already in the Earlier Han at Wu Ti's court. The world's earliest book on alchemy appeared in China around 140 A.D., and in the early fourth century Ko Hung completed his monumental *Pao-p'u-tzu*, which is a sort of encyclopedia on the art of achieving immortality. He had a prescription for making gold out of mercury, lead, cinnabar, and other ingredients and claimed for his various elixers not only the power to confer immortality but also a long list of other beneficial properties to suit the specific needs of magicians, generals, or government officials.

The Taoist search for elixirs probably led to the experimental eating of all sorts of organic and inorganic substances. Such experimentation may have contributed to the extraordinarily catholic tastes of the Chinese and the richness of their culinary art, which is one of the glories of Chinese civilization. Another outcome was the discovery of anesthetics and a tremendous pharmacopoeia. In fact, the whole development of Chinese medicine was closely associated with Taoism, and, like all later books of its type, the earliest Chinese medical work, dating from the second or third century A.D., is full of Taoist anatomical concepts. Most Chinese scientific inquiry, for that matter, seems to have grown out of the activities of the curious, experimenting Taoist alchemists and magicians; and perhaps one reason why later Chinese thinkers turned their backs so emphatically on scientific experimentation was its association in their minds with Taoism.

Another Taoistic movement which flourished between the Later Han period and the sixth century was an immortality cult based on concepts of inner hygiene. There were thought to be in each man's body three vital centers or "cinnabar fields," 36,000 gods (forming a microcosm of the universe), and three worms (which were the causes of disease, old age, and death). The objective was to suppress the worms, nurture the gods, and purify the "cinnabar fields," thereby creating within the physical body a pure body that would become immortal. The Taoists by this time had developed the convenient idea that the *hsien*, or immortal, went through the outward form of dying but was only discarding his useless physical body in the process.

Members of the cult eschewed wine and meat, because these were offensive to the inner gods. They also avoided the five grains, since these nourished the three worms. They opened up their inner channels by gymnastic practices and purified their bodies by breathing exercises, holding their breath for incredibly long periods and supposedly guiding it throughout their whole bodies. Breath and their own saliva were thought to be the purest forms of nourishment, and an inner union of breath and semen was supposed to build up their inner immortal bodies.

The popularity of the inner-hygiene concepts may have helped to rob Taoist alchemy of its scientific potentialities. After the sixth century, interest slowly shifted to the search for an "inner elixir," that is, a sort of internal chemical transformation through meditation. At about the same time the inner-hygiene cult itself began to change. The concept of the gods within the body was abandoned, and interest became concentrated on breathing exercises. Gradually these Taoistic practices evolved into the general hygiene system that is still popular in China. Many Chinese still believe that through carefully regulated breathing and quiet concentration they can prevent disease and retard the ravages of age.

Popular Religious Movements. The most spectacular aspect of the upsurge of Taoism during the imperial interregnum was its rise as an organized popular religion — the first thing of this sort that the Chinese had ever known. In this development we probably can see a clear "barbarian" influence. As has already been noted, Buddhism entered China in the guise of a Taoist sect. The more highly developed and organized Indian religion soon began to have a profound effect on Taoism. The very concept of collective worship and religious organization may have been borrowed from the Buddhists, as were numerous other ideas and institutions of Taoism. In fact, many of the books of the huge Taoist canon that was later developed were nothing more than close imitations of Buddhist texts.

The revolts of the Yellow Turbans and the Five Pecks of Rice band in 184 A.D. were the first clear signs that Taoism had given birth to organized popular religions. Faith-healing was at the heart of both these religious movements. The believers participated in public ceremonies intended to expiate their sins and cure their ailments through ecstatic acts of repentance. Sometimes the religious ceremonies were collective sexual orgies, justified by *yin-yang* theories and the concepts of the inner-hygiene cult.

Popular Taoism developed an enormous pantheon, headed by a triad of deities and at the lower levels composed of immortals and historical human beings. The earlier gods tended to be personifications of natural or metaphysical concepts, such as T'ai I, or "Great Unity," who once was considered the highest god. Perhaps under the influence of the story of the historical Buddha, the Taoists then developed the idea of immortals as instructors of living persons, and Lord Huang-Lao, an amalgam of the mythical Emperor Huang Ti and Lao-tzu, became the supreme deity. Subsequently, under the influence of later Buddhist concepts of the divine, the Taoists turned to supra-human gods, and Yüan Shih T'ien Tsun, the "Heavenly God of the Original Beginning," became supreme, but he was eventually displaced by his deputy, Yü Huang, the "Jade Emperor."

Meanwhile, even the basic beliefs of the Taoists were being transformed by Buddhist influence. The concept of the indestructible soul of later Buddhism led to a concern for an afterlife in heaven rather than corporeal immortality. Taoists also became interested in good works as a means of reaching heaven and escaping hell. The gods developed into a celestial bureaucracy, and hell became staffed with its own officialdom. Gradually the distinctions between popular Taoism and popular Buddhism began to disappear, and the two tended to merge in a confused mass of mythology, superstitions, and magical practices.

The History of the Taoist Church. The Han authorities had managed to break up both the Yellow Turbans and the Five Pecks of Rice band as centrally controlled religious organizations, and the Taoist religious movement was never again reconstituted as an effectively centralized church. The individual parishes, however, remained, and the religion flourished under their atomized leadership. The local priest, or *tao shih*, was supported by gifts received at religious ceremonies called "banquets" and by the traditional tithes of five pecks of rice from his parishioners.

During the Six Dynasties period, Taoist monasteries and convents also developed in obvious imitation of Buddhist monasticism. In these institutions interior-hygiene practices and the traditional search for immortality could be pursued more easily than in lay life, but Taoist monks were commonly allowed to marry, and the intellectual and moral standards of their communities tended to be very low.

Various efforts naturally were made to unify the church and to eliminate undesirable practices. One priest, for example, persuaded an emperor of the "barbarian" Northern Wei dynasty in 444 to proclaim Taoism the official religion of the empire, and he himself assumed the title of *T'ien Shih*, or "Heavenly Master," first used by Chang Ling, who had founded the Five Pecks of Rice cult around the middle of the second century. From time to time until the sixteenth century, other Taoist leaders won official recognition for their religion and high honors for themselves from later Chinese emperors. None of them, however, was able to organize Taoism into a unified church.

A more significant development was the appearance of sects, again under the influence of sectarian Chinese Buddhism. There came to be as many as eighty-six Taoist sects, including a "Northern" sect, founded in the twelfth century and subsequently centered at Peking, and two "Southern" sects. The second of the "Southern" sects was controlled by a hereditary line of Taoist priests who claimed descent from Chang Ling. In 1019 a Chinese emperor gave a priest of this line a great tract of land in Kiangsi in South China and invested him with the traditional title of *T'ien Shih*. In the late thirteenth century the Chang family was accorded official recognition as the leader of the Taoist church and during the next century was given a certain degree of official control over the Taoist priests of the whole land. The so-called Chang "popes" maintained their rich holdings and at least the theory of their leadership until 1927, when the last *T'ien Shih*, who claimed to be the sixty-third in lineal descent from Chang Ling, was ousted, apparently by Communists, from both his property and his title.

INDIAN BUDDHISM

The resurgence of Taoism at a time of political disruption is quite understandable. But the even greater popularity of Buddhism is more surprising. The Indian religion flatly contradicted the dearest concepts and ideals of the Chinese. It constituted an even more direct challenge to Chinese civilization than did Western culture in the nineteenth century, and its adoption represented the greatest borrowing from abroad that the Chinese were to know before modern times. The triumph of Buddhism can be explained only by the profound disillusionment of the Chinese at this time and the inability of the negativistic *ch'ing-t'an* philosophy and the gross popular sects of Taoism to satisfy their spiritual needs.

Buddhism is the chief cultural link between the peoples of East and South Asia. Its contrasting histories in India and China, however, highlight the differences rather than the similarities between these two spiritual and psychological ends of the earth.

Indian Buddhism was based on a series of premises that the ancient Chinese would never have understood. Although in a sense a revolt against the rising caste differences of Hinduism, it had accepted some of the other basic assumptions of Indian thought without question. The Buddhist agreed that life is essentially painful; he also assumed that it was unending, since one existence was tied to another by *karma*, a term which literally means "act" but implies causality. Each act produced the next, birth leading to old age, death, and further births, in an endless chain of causality. This was thought to be the origin of the differences in status and the injustices one sees in the world. The Indian Buddhist, however, unlike the Chinese Confucian, was not interested in correcting these injustices and perfecting the social order but in escaping the painful cycle of existence.

The Historic Buddha and His Teachings. The historic Buddha, known as Sakyamuni, "the teacher of the Sakya clan," lived around 500 B.C. He was a prince in the state of Magadha in what is now the southern edge of Nepal north of India. Distressed by the suffering he saw around him, he abandoned his wife and young son, but he found that a purely ascetic life led nowhere. It was like tying knots in the air. Subsequently, sitting in meditation, he achieved enlightenment, discovering the "Middle Way" between the extremes of self-indulgence and self-mortification. He thus became the Buddha, "the Enlightened One," and began to preach his wonderful discovery to a devoted band of disciples.

Since the Buddha's teachings were not committed to writing for several centuries, and then in confusingly abundant and contradictory forms, it is not easy to determine what were his original teachings. The essence of his ideas, however, appears to be contained in his Four Noble Truths: that life is painful; that the origin of pain is desire; that the cessation of pain is to be sought by ending desire; and that the way to this end is through his Noble Eightfold Path — that is, his rules for right living. His disciples took vows against killing, stealing, falsehood, unchastity, and strong drink; they practiced confessionals;

and they lived, at least by Chinese standards, an extremely ascetic, world-denying life, though apparently with a considerable feeling of joy.

The end objective of all this effort was Nirvana. Nirvana is not the achievement of godhood or the salvation of the soul in the Western sense. In fact, primitive Buddhism had no gods and denied the animistic soul. The human personality was considered to be a combination of "five aggregates," that is, the bodily organism and the four psychic states of sensation, cognition, mental activity, and consciousness. In seeking Nirvana the Buddhist was merely attempting to break the chain of existence through the ending of all desires. Although literally meaning "emptiness," Nirvana was felt to be not simply extinction but something more like the peaceful merging of a drop of water in the sea.

Buddhism early developed into a monastic church. The Buddha's disciples, like most Indian holy men throughout history, were primarily ascetic mendicants. The Indian rainy season forced these wanderers to take up fixed residence for a part of each year, and their abodes grew into permanent monastic communities that thenceforth dominated the religion. In time these monastic communities became ranked with the Buddha and the "Law," or body of teachings, as one of the "three treasures" of Buddhism.

After a long oral tradition, Buddhism around the first century B.C. also began to develop a tremendous sacred literature. It was originally written in two closely related Indo-European languages. The Pali scriptures have been preserved in Ceylon, and the Sanskrit scriptures have been preserved largely through translations into Chinese and Tibetan.

The Buddhist canon, known as the Tripitaka, or "three baskets," is traditionally divided into the *Vinayas*[2] or "disciplines" for monastic life, the *Sutras*[3] or "discourses," which constitute the major teachings, and the *Abhidharmas*[4] or scholastic elaborations of the teachings. It is a huge collection of writings. The Chinese Tripitaka, for example, consists of more than 1600 works in over 5000 sections.

The Spread of Buddhism. Buddhism is a universal religion, in which all men are equal in the Buddhist "law." Like Christianity and Islam, the two great universal religions of the Mediterranean area, it spread widely, over all South, Central and East Asia. By the third century B.C. it had already spread throughout India under the patronage of the great conqueror Asoka and had also entered Ceylon. Subsequently Indian traders and travelers carried it by sea throughout Southeast Asia and to South China.

Buddhism also spread northwestward among the Greek kingdoms left

[2] *Lü* in Chinese; *ritsu* in Japanese.
[3] *Ching* in Chinese, the same word as "classic"; *kyō* in Japanese.
[4] *Lun* in Chinese; *ron* in Japanese.

over by Alexander's conquests in Gandhara and what is now Afghanistan. The greatest monarch of the Kushan Empire of the Yüeh-chih, Kanishka, who ruled around 100 A.D. from North India to the Tarim Basin, was an ardent patron of Buddhism. He championed the faith in Central Asia, and from there it spread into North China.

A third wave of Buddhist propagation rolled northward a few centuries later, through Tibet and on into Mongolia. This was a late and degenerate form of Buddhism, which contained a large element of Hinduism and soon absorbed the popular demon worship of Tibet. The resultant Lamaism and the theocratic society it produced in Tibet and Mongolia bear small resemblance to the original teachings of the Buddha.

Mahayana and Hinayana.   Even the purer forms of Buddhism divided at an early date into two major trends. These are usually known as Mahayana or the Greater Vehicle and Hinayana or the Lesser Vehicle, although recently the less invidious name of Theravada, "the doctrine of the Elders," has come to be preferred for the latter. Hinayana has remained closer to original Buddhism and is still the religion of Ceylon, Burma, Siam, and Cambodia, while the Buddhism of China, Korea, Japan, and Vietnam stems largely from Mahayana.

The Greater Vehicle was "greater" in the sense of its all-inclusiveness. It contained more of the concepts of pre-Buddhist Indian thought and readily accepted the cults and religious ideas of the peoples it converted. Arising largely in North India and its northwestern borderlands, it absorbed the religious attitudes of the non-Indian peoples of this area. Since Mahayana distinguished between absolute and relative truth, it could tolerate even contradictory ideas as representing various degrees of relative truth accommodated to the different levels of understanding of its believers.

Mahayana developed a vast body of metaphysical speculation and a huge pantheon. In place of the godless religion of the historical Buddha, the Mahayanists have myriads of godlike Buddhas in aeons of time. They also developed a new type of deity, the Bodhisattva or "Enlightened Existence," who, though he has achieved the enlightenment of a Buddha, stays back in this world to help others to salvation before passing on into Nirvana himself.

Because of the concept of Bodhisattvas dedicated to saving other weaker creatures, the emphasis in Mahayana Buddhism shifted from enlightenment through "one's own strength" to salvation through "the strength of another." Faith was all that was necessary, even an unthinking act of faith, such as the mouthing of the name of a Buddha or Bodhisattva. The *Lotus Sutra,* a popular Mahayanist scripture, predicts the eventual salvation of all animal life. (Buddhism recognizes no division between humans and animals.)

Naturally Bodhisattvas became the great popular gods of Mahayana

Buddhism. The Buddha Amitabha (Chinese: O-mi-t'o Fo; Japanese: Amida Butsu), who was a Bodhisattva in origin, became the great savior as the "Deity of the Western Paradise." Avalokitesvara (Chinese: Kuan-yin; Japanese: Kannon), gradually changing in sex, emerged as the benign "Goddess of Mercy." Mahayana thus provided compassionate, comforting gods for every human need.

Nirvana also gradually changed its meaning, at least for the less sophisticated Mahayanist believers. Increasingly, it came to mean salvation in a very definite afterlife in paradise. Descriptions and portrayals of this paradise became quite specific and those of hell even more graphic and gruesomely convincing.

The Bodhisattva ideal of aid to others led to a strong emphasis in Mahayana on charity — on good works to help others and to contribute to one's own salvation. Buddhism thus was turned somewhat from its original anti-social contemplative bent. The concept of charity made social work important; the possibility of salvation through faith made monasticism, celibacy, and asceticism less necessary.

THE COMING OF BUDDHISM TO CHINA

Mahayana Buddhism's tolerance of other religious ideas and cults naturally facilitated its spread. The ideas it absorbed also made it far more palatable to non-Indian peoples than the original religion had been. It is hard to imagine the Chinese, even in the sad days following the fall of the Han, taking to the austere, anti-social religion Buddhism had been before it was transformed by the Mahayana doctrines. One should not imagine, however, that these tendencies were already full-blown when Buddhism first reached China. Much of this development actually took place on Chinese soil.

In its Mahayana form, Buddhism thus had a powerful appeal to a barbarianized North China and a demoralized South. To the superstitious it was a potent new magic, to the educated an amazing but stimulating new set of ideas. It was a great universal faith and, except for the Taoist sects, the first organized religion the Chinese had ever known. It had behind it the fruits of other great cultures — the metaphysics and early science of India and even elements of Mediterranean civilization. It was pitched on a high moral and intellectual plane. It had a noble literature, a beautiful religious art, aesthetically satisfying ceremonials, the appeal of the peaceful monastic life in a troubled age, and the promise of personal salvation at a time when there seemed to be no solution to man's worldly problems. It is not really surprising that most Chinese succumbed to this multiple appeal.

Early Buddhist Missionaries. According to Buddhist tradition, the religion was first introduced to China as the result of a dream of the Emperor

Ming Ti in 64 A.D. The story is apocryphal, but already at this time there was a Buddhist group at the court of the emperor's brother, the King of Ch'u, in the lower Yangtze Valley. By the next century Buddhism had become entrenched in the North Vietnam area on the southern edge of the empire, and stupas, the Buddhist reliquary towers, were being erected by converts in various parts of China. Modified by Chinese architectural concepts, these stupas in time developed into the stone, brick, and wooden pagodas that have become so typical a part of the scenery of East Asia. (See Plates 15, 16 and 17.)

The first transmitters of Buddhism may have been traders who came to China by the southern sea route and the northern land route through Central Asia, but the religion was soon being propagated more actively by missionaries. A Parthian prince, known to history by his Chinese name, An Shih-kao, was active as a missionary and translator of scriptures at Loyang during the latter part of the second century. An even greater transmitter of the faith was Kumarajiva, who was born in Central Asia to an Indian father, captured by a Chinese expedition around 382, and brought to China, where he headed a great translation project. No fewer than fifty-two of the ninety-eight scriptures he translated are still extant.

Chinese Student-Pilgrims. Chinese converts eventually became more important than the missionaries in transmitting the Indian religion to China. We have the names of close to 200 East Asian monks, nine of them Koreans rather than Chinese, who between the third and eighth centuries essayed the long and perilous trip to India to imbibe the Buddhist teachings at their source. This was the first great student migration of East Asian history.

Fa-hsien, who left for India by way of Central Asia in 399 and returned by sea in 414, settled at Nanking to translate the scriptures he had brought home with him. He is particularly famous for the record of his trip that he left. Since the Indians, lacking much interest in history, rarely bothered to record dates, the carefully dated accounts of Fa-hsien and the other Chinese Buddhist pilgrims have proved invaluable in establishing Indian and Central Asian chronology.

The most famous of the Buddhist pilgrims was Hsüan-tsang, who made the round trip to India between 629 and 645 by way of Central Asia. After his return to Ch'ang-an, by this time once again the capital of a united China, he became the greatest churchman of his day, devoting the rest of his life to translating seventy-four Buddhist works (in 1338 chapters). The account of his travels, the *Hsi-yü chi* or *Record of the Western Regions*, is the most important work of its sort. A third Chinese pilgrim, I-ching, who between 671 and 695 made the round trip to India by the southern route, with long stopovers each way in

Sumatra, is noteworthy for the records of more than fifty other pilgrims that he compiled.

The Spread of Buddhism in China. Buddhism, unlike Christianity in the Roman Empire, apparently was taken up by the rich and aristocratic circles before it spread downward to the peasantry. In fact, it probably did not thoroughly permeate the lower classes until the eighth or ninth century, by which time it was beginning to lose its influence among the upper classes.

At first Buddhism seems to have made more rapid progress in the "barbarian" North than in the South, perhaps because the non-Chinese rulers of this area felt no prejudice against it as a foreign religion. Already by 381, we are told, nine-tenths of the inhabitants of northwestern China had been converted. The greatest imperial patrons of the new religion were the emperors of the "barbarian" Northern Wei dynasty (386–534). The two sets of Buddhist cave temples, at Yün-kang, near their first capital in northern Shansi, and at Lung-men, near their second capital of Loyang, contain some of the finest artistic remains of early Chinese Buddhism. (See Plates 19, 21, 22 and 24.)

The South, too, was not lacking in imperial patrons. Buddhism flourished at Nanking, and Wu Ti of the Liang dynasty was so enthusiastic a believer that in 527 and again in 529 and 547 he renounced his throne for holy orders, and each time had to be bailed out, as it were, by his government. By this time, in fact, South China was perhaps as thoroughly Buddhist as North China, and the religion actually was to retain greater popularity and vigor into modern times in the South than in the North.

The Buddhist Age. Part of the success of Buddhism in China during the Six Dynasties period was due to its readiness to compromise with Taoism and Confucianism, tolerating the former as an inferior level of truth and the latter as a political and social philosophy that was not incompatible with its own basic teachings. Ever since there has been a strong tendency among the Chinese to synthesize "the three religions" or to maintain them side by side. At this time, however, Buddhism was definitely the dominant member of the trio, and a great proportion of the higher intellectual capacities and the artistic genius of the Chinese was devoted to the translation and interpretation of its scriptures and the building and beautifying of its temples and monasteries.

The whole epoch from the mid-fourth century to the end of the eighth might well be called the Buddhist age of Chinese history. In fact, it can be called the Buddhist age of Asian history or perhaps of world history, since probably more than half of the world's population were believers in the Indian religion at this time. It blanketed the whole of the Asian continent, except for Siberia and the Near East, giving to this vast area a degree of cultural unity that has never been matched since then.

This, however, was but a brief moment of religious unity. Buddhism had begun to decline in India even in the sixth century and by the fifteenth had disappeared. It was wiped out in Central Asia in the ninth century by the inroads of Islam. Meanwhile, the Hinayana of Southeast Asia and the Mahayana of East Asia had begun to drift apart, and a serious decline commenced in the latter. By the ninth century the Buddhist age was ending in most of Asia. In China its fading was in part a reflection of the fact that a fully revived Chinese Empire had long since met and overcome the whole "barbarian" challenge.

THE "BARBARIANS" AND THE CHINESE IMPERIAL IDEAL

To an observer of world history in the fourth century it might have appeared that Rome would always endure but that the days of the Chinese Empire were definitely over. North China, the heartland of the empire, was completely overrun by "barbarians"; South China was obviously incapable of restoring imperial unity; and the whole land was being swept by a foreign religion which had an otherworldly emphasis and a celibate, monastic ideal that cut at the roots of Chinese philosophy and the family-centered social system.

It was not strange that the "barbarian" conquerors of the empire quickly seized on the idea of making themselves its new emperors. Their desire to appropriate by conquest the great traditions of the empire was only to be expected. The "barbarian" conquerors of the Roman Empire had the same hope but in the long run only contributed to its demise. By the middle of the fifth century, however, the "barbarian" invaders of North China had recreated a fair facsimile of the old empire, and by the seventh century the Chinese Empire had not only been completely restored but had been made stronger and richer than ever before. The contrast with the steadily sinking fortunes of Rome is striking and constitutes perhaps the greatest single difference between the histories of the peoples at the two ends of the Eurasian continent.

Reasons for the Revival of the Chinese Empire. The collapse of Han had been more rapid and perhaps more complete than that of Rome. How then was it possible for the Chinese Empire to be reconstituted but not the Roman? There is, of course, no single answer to this question, but several possible reasons can be suggested. Perhaps the dynasties of South China maintained a greater continuity of the imperial tradition than did the Eastern Roman Empire and Byzantium in the West. More important, China was geographically more compact than the Roman Empire. Nanking was closer to North China than Constantinople was to Italy and France, and the Yangtze was not a barrier like the Alps. Hence, the influence which the South had on the rest of China may have been stronger and its reincorporation into a revived empire easier than in the case of Byzantium in the West.

Another important reason may have been the intrinsic superiority of the Han imperial concept over the Roman. Rome lacked the ideal of just and ethical rule by an emperor whose possession of the Mandate of Heaven was manifested in the ready acceptance of him by his people and who exercised his power through a bureaucracy of educated men, chosen not by chance or by birth but because of their merit. Although it had long been hardly more than a theory, this concept was more rational and less theocratic than the Mediterranean imperial tradition and perhaps was more understandable to the people than was the Roman ideal of rule by impersonal law. The old imperial system, therefore, may have seemed even more desirable to the Chinese than did the Roman system to the Europeans.

Still more decisive may have been the nature of the Chinese writing system. It could not be utilized by the "barbarians" for the writing of their own languages; nor did it reflect regional or dialectical differences in the pronunciation of Chinese. While European "barbarians" and the Romance inheritors of Latin soon found themselves split into several linguistic groups, the Chinese and their "barbarian" invaders remained closely tied to classical Chinese for all purposes of writing, and China therefore continued to be a well-knit cultural unit.

Finally, the "barbarian" invaders of China probably encountered a much heavier "specific gravity" in the local agricultural population than did the Western invaders of Rome. Chinese agriculture already was much more intensive than that of Europe and therefore supported heavier populations. This was particularly true of the irrigated areas in the heart of the empire in North China and the rice-growing areas of the South. The "barbarians" thus may have been absorbed more rapidly and completely into the local population in China than they were in the West.

The "Five Barbarians" and the Sixteen Kingdoms. The semi-nomadic invaders who overran North China early in the fourth century are called by the Chinese the "Five Barbarians." These were the Turkic Hsiung-nu; a closely related tribe known as the Chieh; the Hsien-pei (also called Hsien-pi, probably a proto-Mongolian people), who invaded from the northeast; and the Ti and the Ch'iang, who were two groups of Tibetans from the mountainous grasslands to the west. The Hsien-pei overran the edges of the North China Plain as early as 281, and the Tibetans started their depredations in 296. The "barbarian" inundation, however, really commenced in 304, when a Chin prince asked for the aid of the semi-Sinicized Hsiung-nu tribes of northern Shansi.

The Chinese have characterized the history of North China between 304 and 439 as the period of the Sixteen Kingdoms. The name gives a good idea of the military and political confusion of the epoch. There was a welter of "barbarian" pretenders to the Han throne. North China was only sporadically and fleetingly reunited by one or another of them, and at one time there were as many as nine contending dynasties.

The Hsiung-nu Earlier and Later Chao. The Hsiung-nu ruler in northern Shansi, Liu Yüan, who had adopted the surname of the Han emperors, declared himself King of Han in 304. After the destruction of the Western Chin in 316, his successors renamed their dynasty the Chao (known as the Earlier Chao), after the state that had existed in northern Shansi in late Chou times. The Earlier Chao, however, did not rule over all of North China. In the Kansu corridor a Chinese general had in 313 set up the Earlier Liang dynasty; and in the northeast one of the Hsiung-nu generals, Shih Lo, soon established his own Later Chao dynasty, and destroyed the Earlier Chao in 329.

Within Hsiung-nu society Shih Lo was a real revolutionary, because, unlike his predecessors, he was not descended from the Hsiung-nu emperors (*Shan-yü*) but was a commoner of Chieh ancestry. In another sense, however, he was less revolutionary than the highly Sinicized Earlier Chao rulers, for he returned to a more traditional, tribal type of rule. The Later Chao in turn was snuffed out in 352 by the Mu-jung

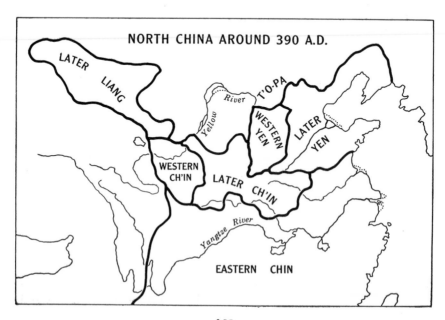

tribe of the Hsien-pei, which, rising in the northeast, called itself the Earlier Yen, after the Chou state that had once flourished in that part of China.

The Tibetan Earlier Ch'in and Its Succession States. At about this time a powerful Tibetan state began to rise in the northwest. This was the Earlier Ch'in, which revived one of China's greatest historical names. Fu Chien, the emperor of this Tibetan state, was not encumbered in his rule by the tribal divisions of the Turkish and Mongol peoples. He built up a highly Sinicized administration and a strong Chinese infantry to accompany his nomadic cavalry. More powerful than any of the "barbarian" rulers that had preceded him, he wiped out the Earlier Yen in the northeast in 370 and the Earlier Liang of Kansu six years later, thus reunifying the North. He then embarked on the conquest of South China in 383, but the campaign ended in disaster, and his empire fell apart.

A Tibetan general in 384 usurped the throne at the capital, Ch'ang-an, founding the Later Ch'in dynasty. In the same year groups of the Mu-jung tribe established the Later Yen and Western Yen dynasties in the northeast and in Shansi, respectively. The following year another Hsien-pei group proclaimed its independence in southern Kansu as the Western Ch'in, and in 386 a Tibetan general founded the Later Liang in the Kansu corridor.

These succession states of the Earlier Ch'in were of ephemeral duration, averaging only twenty-six years. They were followed by equally short-lived tribal states: the Hsien-pei Southern Yen (398–410) and Northern Yen (409–436) in the northeast; the Hsien-pei Southern Liang (397–414), the Hsiung-nu Northern Liang (397-439), and the possibly Chinese Western Liang (401–421), all in Kansu; and the Hsiung-nu Hsia dynasty (407–431) in the Ordos area of Inner Mongolia and in Shensi.

The T'o-pa Northern Wei. One tribal state that emerged from the debris of the Earlier Ch'in Empire proved to have more lasting power. It was founded by a largely Hsien-pei group, known as the T'o-pa, which had moved into northern Shansi as the Hsiung-nu had pushed on south-ward. Here they had maintained the semi-Sinicized state of Tai between 338 and 376. After submitting for a while to the Earlier Ch'in, they reasserted their independence in 386 under the dynastic name of Northern Wei.

The Northern Wei state slowly grew in power and territory, and by 439 it had eliminated the last of its rivals in North China. At the same time it had been driving back the newly risen nomad empire of the Juan-juan in the northern steppes and had been reconstructing the Great Wall. In 445 and 448 the Northern Wei armies even penetrated into the Tarim Basin in Central Asia. This was the closest approach to the military exploits of the Han that had been seen in three centuries. The Northern Wei efforts to conquer the South, however, were completely unavailing.

After the Northern Wei had incorporated into their empire the densely populated agricultural lands of the North China Plain, a subtle change began to take place in this originally "barbarian" empire. Like the Earlier Chao and Earlier Ch'in, the strongest of the previous "barbarian" dynasties, the Northern Wei from the start had been a semi-Sinicized state, but now the process of cultural absorption was accelerated. The agricultural lands were not divided among the T'o-pa tribes but were administered in the traditional Chinese manner, and the northern tribesmen were relegated to the status of a soldiery.

By the reign of Hsiao Wen Ti (the "Filial Literary Emperor," 471–499), the process of acculturation had gone so far that the Northern Wei

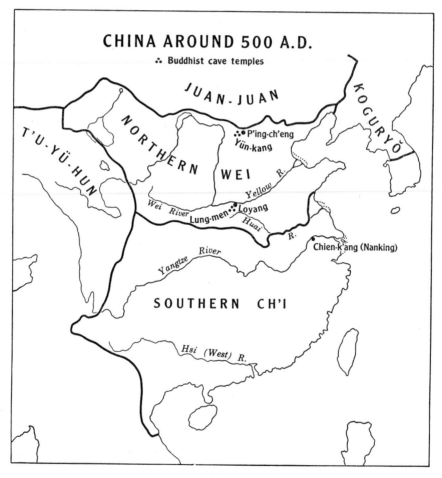

CHINA AROUND 500 A.D.

∴ Buddhist cave temples

JUAN-JUAN

KOGURYŎ

T'U-YÜ-HUN

NORTHERN WEI

P'ing-ch'eng
Yün-kang

Yellow R.

Wei River
Lung-men Loyang
Huai R.

Chien-k'ang (Nanking)

Yangtze River

SOUTHERN CH'I

Hsi (West) R.

court embarked on a conscious policy of Sinification. In 493–494 the capital was moved from P'ing-ch'eng (the present Ta-t'ung) in northern Shansi to Loyang, which had been the capital of both the Eastern Chou and the Later Han. At about the same time, Chinese was made the only official court language, and the T'o-pa aristocrats were ordered to adopt Chinese dress, customs, and surnames and were encouraged to intermarry with the local population. They were even deprived of their old status as tribal chiefs and became classed in the same hierarchy as the important families of Chinese origin.

The Succession States of the Northern Wei. The complete Sinification of the court had by 524 led to serious revolts by the still partly tribal military forces. The central government also found itself the prey of its own great families. It rapidly disintegrated after the outbreak of the revolts, and its generals seized power. In 534 the Kao family set up a puppet emperor of the Eastern Wei in the northeast and in 550 usurped the throne as the Northern Ch'i dynasty. In the northwest, the Yü-wen family in 535 created its own puppet of the Western Wei and then in 557 took the throne for itself as the Northern Chou dynasty. Both usurping families seem to have been of Hsien-pei origin and represented something of a reversion to "barbarian" military rule.

The Northern Chou, based in the Wei Valley with its capital at Ch'ang-an, once again proved the military superiority of this area over the North China Plain and in 577 destroyed the Northern Ch'i, reunifying the North.

Four years later, however, the throne was usurped by a general, Yang Chien, who is known to history as Wen Ti (the "Cultured Emperor"), the founder of the Sui dynasty. Yang Chien claimed to be of Chinese descent, though he may actually have been of Hsien-pei origin. By this time, however, the distinction between the various "barbarian" groups and the Chinese in North China had become highly theoretical, and in any case the Yang family was closely related by intermarriage with the ruling family of the Northern Chou and other members of the "barbarian" aristocracy.

SUI AND T'ANG
RECONSTITUTE THE EMPIRE

The role of the Sui dynasty in Chinese history was much like that of the Ch'in eight centuries earlier. The founder of the dynasty had by 589 easily conquered the Ch'en, the last of the Southern dynasties, thus reuniting China after almost four centuries of political division, but his successor failed to hold on to the empire. Like their Ch'in predecessors, the Sui rulers may have been overly ambitious. They attempted to achieve too much in too short a time, overstraining the endurance and loyalty of their new subjects. This was particularly true of the second ruler, Yang Ti, the "Emblazoned Emperor," who succeeded his father, probably through murder, in 604. As a man who lost the Mandate of Heaven, Yang Ti has been castigated as one of the villains of Chinese history.

Under the two Sui emperors, however, China was started on its second great imperial period. A strong centralized government was re-established for all China; the Great Wall was reconstructed, though at prodigious human cost; long canals were dug, making possible the great prosperity of the following centuries; huge palaces were erected; and the prestige of the Chinese Empire was fully restored.

The Sui Conquests. Once again, the pendulum of conquest began to swing outward from China into the lands of the "barbarians." The *yin* of "barbarian" rule in China had run its course and, by infusing new blood and new martial ardor into China, had produced once again the *yang* of Chinese imperial conquest.

In the south, Sui Wen Ti reasserted Chinese control over North Vietnam and in 605 Yang Ti even sent an expedition against the Cham state in South Vietnam. An expedition was also sent to Formosa, and Palembang in Sumatra was induced to send tribute.

Meanwhile, in the north, the Sui had been re-establishing some control over Central Asia and the steppe, though they achieved this more by intrigue than by conquest. In 552 the T'u-chüeh, a vassal people of the Juan-juan, had crushed their overlords. It is possible that some of the fleeing Juan-juan were the Avars who a few years later descended on the Near East and Europe. In the T'u-chüeh, we encounter for the first time a form of the name Turk, which was subsequently to become the generic term for the whole linguistic group. The T'u-chüeh built up a huge empire throughout Central Asia but split into eastern and western halves in 581, and some of these now divided Turks acknowledged the suzerainty of the Sui. In 609 the Chinese also conquered the T'u-yü-hun, a mixed Tibetan and Mongol people in northern Tibet, who were constantly menacing the Kansu trade route.

Yang Ti, however, had alienated his people because of his endless wars and the tremendous labor needed for the construction of canals, walls, and palaces. The prestige of his dynasty was also seriously tarnished by a disastrous campaign in 612 against the Korean kingdom of Koguryŏ in North Korea and South Manchuria. Serious revolts broke out in 613, forcing him to terminate inconclusively his campaigns of 613 and 614 against Koguryŏ. In 615 he was badly defeated by the Eastern Turks, who had hitherto been his loyal vassals. The empire then started to disintegrate, and he fled to South China, where he was assassinated in 618.

The Founding of the T'ang. The man who emerged victorious in the free-for-all that followed the collapse of the Sui was a prominent Sui official named Li Yüan. Li Yüan, who had been suppressing peasant revolts and repulsing Turkish inroads in Shansi, was urged into revolt in 617 by his ambitious and energetic second son, Li Shih-min. Although claiming to be of Chinese descent, the Li family had been ennobled under the Northern Chou and was thoroughly intermarried with the great "barbarian" families of North China.

With the aid of Turkish allies, Li Yüan and Li Shih-min captured Ch'ang-an in 617, and the father was enthroned there in 618 as the first emperor of the T'ang dynasty, known to history as Kao Tsu, "High Progenitor." By 628 order had been restored to China. The dynasty thus founded was to continue for a full cycle of three centuries, until 907. Under it China reached perhaps its most glorious height in world history, and the names of Han and T'ang came to be paired as the two golden ages of the Chinese Empire.

In 626 Kao Tsu abdicated the throne to his domineering and scheming son, who meanwhile had eliminated his rival brothers. Li Shih-min, who was posthumously known as T'ai Tsung, "Grand Ancestor," ruled until 649, and the Chen-kuan year period (627–650) of his reign is considered the first great high point of the T'ang era. Under his able rule the centralized administration was fully reconstituted, further canals were dug, palaces were rebuilt, and the Chinese returned in earnest to the subjugation of the surrounding "barbarians."

The T'ang Conquests. The Turks had broken with the emperor they had helped place on the Chinese throne and in 624 had invaded as far as Ch'ang-an, but in 630 T'ai Tsung subjugated the Eastern Turks and himself took the title of "Heavenly Khan" of the Turks, *Khan* having now replaced the Hsiung-nu term *Shan-yü* for the chief ruler of the Turkish peoples. In great campaigns in 639–640 and 647–648, T'ai Tsung then wrested the Tarim Basin from the control of the Western Turks and incorporated this region into his empire. He was aided in his victory by the Uighur tribes, who at this time broke away from the Western Turkish Empire to become the loyal allies of the T'ang and their chief source of military power in Central Asia.

Chinese suzerainty was gradually extended beyond the Pamirs over the states of the Oxus Valley and even over the upper waters of the Indus in modern Afghanistan. The administrative protectorate of An-hsi, "Pacify the West," was set up in the Tarim Basin, paralleling the administrative protectorate of An-nan, "Pacify the South," which had been set up earlier in North Vietnam and which eventually gave its name to the whole region of Annam. (There were also an An-pei, "Pacify the North," in Mongolia; and An-tung, "Pacify the East," in South Man-

churia; and two other administrative protectorates in the northern borderlands.)

Tibet, which had been unified for the first time in 607, also came
under Chinese suzerainty, and from there Chinese influence was even
extended southward toward India. A T'ang envoy, Wang Hsüan-ts'e,
who went from Tibet to North India, was despoiled by a petty Indian
king. Returning to India at the head of some borrowed Tibetan and
Nepalese soldiers, he captured the offending monarch and in 648 brought
him back as a prisoner to Ch'ang-an. This incident was the only important encounter between Chinese and Indian military power in early times,
illustrating by its uniqueness the effectiveness of the tremendous terrain
barrier that lies between these two great centers of world population.

T'ai Tsung's armies had been twice repulsed by Koguryŏ in North Korea, but under his successor, Kao Tsung ("High Ancestor," 649–683), the

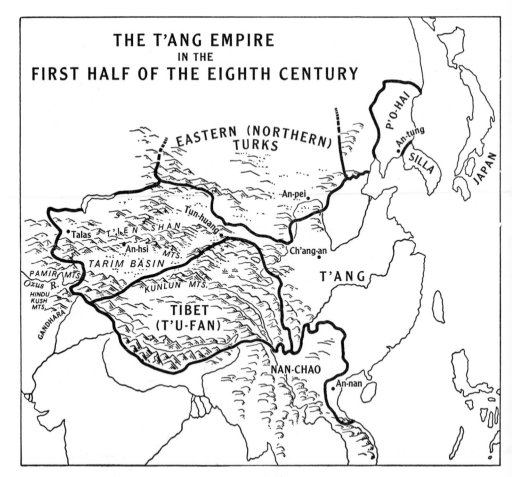

whole of the peninsula was brought under the nominal suzerainty of China. In a long series of campaigns, T'ang and the southeastern Korean kingdom of Silla defeated a coalition of Koguryŏ, the southwestern Korean kingdom of Paekche, and Japan. As a result, Korea was unified in 668 under the rule of Silla, which thereafter remained a loyal vassal of T'ang.

In 657 the Western Turkish Empire was finally broken up with the aid of the Uighurs, and Turkish groups were pushed southward into India and westward into West Asia and Europe. Toward the end of Kao Tsung's reign, however, control over the Tarim Basin was lost to the Tibetans and was not regained until the time of his successor, the Empress Wu.

The Empress Wu was a most remarkable woman. Originally a concubine of T'ai Tsung, she had been made empress by Kao Tsung and came to dominate his later years. After his death she ruled for a while through two successive puppets, and then in 690 assumed the title of emperor for herself — the only time a woman ever did this in China — and changed the dynastic name to Chou. As a usurper, and a woman at that, she has been severely condemned by Chinese historians, but actually she was a strong and able ruler.

The Reign of Hsüan Tsung. In 705, when in her eighties, the Empress Wu was set aside by a palace *coup d'état*, and the first of her puppet emperors was put back on the throne. He was subsequently murdered by his empress, who attempted to seize the throne, but she and her relatives were destroyed in 710 by the son of the second puppet emperor, who, after letting his father reign for two years, took the throne for himself in 712, thus emulating Li Shih-min's career as king-maker and king. This brilliant ruler is known to history as Hsüan Tsung ("Mysterious Ancestor") and also as Ming Huang ("Enlightened Emperor"). The K'ai-yüan (713-742) and T'ien-pao (742-756) year periods during his long reign (712-756) are considered to be a time of second blossoming of the dynasty.

The Uighurs had turned on the Empress Wu in her later years, but they now returned to their usual position of loyal support for the T'ang, and, with their aid, Chinese suzerainty was restored over Central Asia and the steppe land. The trans-Pamir regions were protected from the new surging power of the Arabs and their Islamic converts. In 747 Kao Hsien-chih, a Korean general in the service of T'ang, led an army across the Pamirs and the Hindu Kush to break up an attempted juncture between the Arabs and the Tibetans.

This, however, was the last highwater mark of T'ang power. In 751 Kao Hsien-chih was disastrously defeated by the Arabs at Talas, north of Ferghana, and Hsüan Tsung's reign ended a few years later in rebel-

lion and an apparent breakup of the empire. But with the aid of its
"barbarian" allies the dynasty was restored and continued for another
century and a half, though never again with its earlier power and verve.

The Revival of
Centralized Government: Finances

The recreation of the Chinese Empire was not merely the story of the
absorption of the "barbarians" in North China and the growing military
power that resulted from the successful union of "barbarian" tribal
military traditions with China's agricultural wealth. The reunification
of China by force of arms and the reconquest of the far-flung empire
were merely the surface manifestations of a much more profound
process — the restoration of a stable centralized government.

During the Six Dynasties period, the South devised no means of controlling the rich independent families that had destroyed Han unity
and kept the succession states feeble and unstable. In the North, the
tribal divisions of the "barbarians" only accentuated this instability and
contributed no principle by which the great families could be curbed.
In both halves of China, society remained highly aristocratic, dominated
by powerful families of noble lineage, great wealth, and unchallenged
local prestige. Buddhism, moreover, had introduced a new element of
economic disruption. Rich monasteries became great landowners and
thus joined the great families as contenders with the central government for the fruit of the peasants' toil. Strong centralized rule appeared
unattainable, and certainly throughout the fourth century there was no
sign that it would ever again be achieved.

*The "Equal Field" and "Three Chiefs" Systems of the Northern
Wei.* In the fifth century the rulers of the Northern Wei began to
solve the basic problem that had destroyed the Han. As a result they
maintained a fairly stable and powerful government for the better part
of a century, and thereafter the build-up to the Sui and T'ang dynasties
was rapid.

The solution was, in a sense, a return to Wang Mang's effort to
nationalize the land. Since land taxes were light and the main tax burden,
especially *corvée* labor, was borne by the free peasantry on a per
capita basis, a government, in order to prosper, had to keep as many
peasants as possible in a tax-paying status as free farmers. In other
words, it had to keep the peasants out of serfdom or slavery on the
great estates. During the third century both the Wei dynasty and the
Western Chin attempted, though with little success, to carry out reforms
designed to keep under the control of the central government those
lands and peasants that had not yet been incorporated into the private

estates. In the fifth century the Northern Wei, supported by its "barbarian" military power, was able to carry out such a policy more successfully.

In 485 Hsiao Wen Ti instituted an "equal field" (*chün-t'ien*) system, according to which all able-bodied adult peasants were supposed to be assigned agricultural lands of specified dimensions. The joint holdings of a man and wife were supposed to total about 140 *mou*, or about nineteen acres. Only a small part of this could be held permanently as crop lands in mulberry trees for feeding silk worms or in other tree crops. The rest was to be returned to the government at a person's death or his passing of the age limit. Although the "equal field" system was not designed to deprive the great families of their holdings and was applied only to free peasants and in a highly irregular fashion, it did help to stop the flow of lands and peasants into private hands and to stabilize the financial foundations of the central government.

In order to enforce this complicated landholding system and to insure that it would bring in the desired taxes, Hsiao Wen Ti also inaugurated the "three chiefs" (*san-chang*) system, by which the people were divided into groups that were mutually responsible for one another's conduct and tax payments. Five families constituted a "neighborhood" (*lin*), five "neighborhoods" a "village" (*li*), and five "villages" an "association" (*tang*). Each type of grouping was under a "chief," hence the name of the system. Such collective-guarantee systems, which had existed in one form or another in ancient times, have been continued until recent days in China as the *pao-chia* or "street committee" systems and in Japan as "neighborhood associations."

The New Military System. The "three chiefs" and "equal field" systems were effective enough to be continued, with variations, by the dynasties that followed the Northern Wei in North China. A third element was added by the Western Wei (535–557) and the Northern Chou (557–581). This was the "militia" (*fu-ping*) system, in which able-bodied peasants were given military training and organized into regular forces like the tribal soldiery. Under the T'ang this militia service was later integrated with the "equal field" system by being made part of the tax burden that peasants bore as landholders.

In addition to the regular militia armies, special self-supporting military colonies (*t'un-t'ien*) of soldier-farmers were placed along the northern frontier and at other strategic places. Military colonies of this type were first developed in Han times but became an important part of the military system during the Six Dynasties and remained a feature of the military scene in China until modern times.

The "Equal Field" System of the Sui and T'ang. During the Sui and T'ang dynasties the "equal field" system was greatly elaborated and became the fiscal foundation for one of the greatest periods of Chinese history. The Sui, following their conquests, applied it to the whole country and forced the great families to fit into the system by designating their holdings as assigned "rank lands," scaling downward from a maximum for the highest rank of 100 *ch'ing,* or about 1370 acres. (One *ch'ing* equals 100 *mou.*) According to the "equal field" system of the early days of the T'ang, each able-bodied adult male between the ages of twenty-one and fifty-nine was supposed to have 100 *mou* of land (about 13.7 acres), of which only one-fifth could be permanently owned "mulberry" land. (Widows received thirty *mou,* and other categories similarly reduced portions.) On this economic basis, the able-bodied male was to pay the government in taxes a fixed amount of unhulled grain; a certain length of silk or hemp cloth or weight of silk floss or hemp fiber, depending on the type of textile produced in his region; and twenty days per year of *corvée* labor for the central government and other periods of labor for the local organs of government. This *corvée* labor was sometimes commuted into textile or money taxes.

In addition, certain able-bodied peasants who were exempted from other taxes and levies had to render periodic military service, usually without pay and at their own expense. Each served one long tour of duty on the frontiers, was occasionally called to serve in one of the sixteen capital guard armies, and at other times drilled in one of the 600 local militia units.

As during the Sui, the great families and officials were integrated into the system by assignment to them of permanent "rank lands" of 100 *ch'ing* or less and sometimes lesser amounts of "office lands" to correspond to the governmental position each man held at the time. In addition, the emperor occasionally made special grants consisting of peasant households and, of course, the lands they farmed. As many as 1500 households might be given to a single individual. The organs of local government were similarly supported by "office fields" assigned them.

To operate this complicated landholding system, a careful census and land register was necessary for the whole country. Remaining examples of such surveys show that every piece of land was indeed allotted by specific category (as, for example, "permanent land," "assigned land," or "house plot") to the individual taxpayers. It was perhaps as complicated a system of landownership and taxation as was to be found anywhere in the world before the late nineteenth century, but it worked reasonably well for about a century, supporting the Chinese Empire during an outstanding epoch.

The "equal field" system during the Sui and T'ang, however, did not break the power of the great families. It was not used as an excuse for confiscating their holdings but was applied primarily to newly opened agricultural lands and fields that had gone out of use during the wars.

In fact, the collapse of the Sui may be attributed in part to the resentment of the great families against a regime that was attempting to curb their economic growth.

The T'ang had an easier time of it than the Sui. As at the end of the Ch'in, the fighting that swept China during the collapse of the Sui wiped out or greatly reduced the holdings of a large proportion of the old families, giving the new dynasty a relatively clean slate. The newer aristocracy that emerged with the T'ang from the northwestern corner of the country was as yet less entrenched as landowners than the old aristocracy had been. And with the aid of the "equal field" system, the drift of lands and peasants into private hands was sufficiently slowed to give the dynasty a century of financial stability.

T'ang Prosperity. During the early T'ang, the central government actually had an ample tax income, which was equaled by expenditures only after the imperial family and the organs of government had undergone a long period of growth. With their characteristic genius for organization, the Chinese at this time developed units of measure of approximately equal value for the principal commodities in the economy. Thus, a string of 1000 cash, an "ounce" of silver, a "bushel" of grain, a "bolt" of silk, and a "weight" of silk floss were all roughly equivalent in value. Counting by this standard "unit" of value, the tax income of the central government, according to one of several such listings, amounted to over 52,000,000 "units," almost four-fifths of which were derived from per capita taxes on the peasantry and the remainder from land taxes by area and "household" taxes by wealth. In addition, of course, the central government enjoyed as a part of the tax system the free labor and military service of its millions of peasants.

The government unquestionably was far more affluent than it had ever been under the Han. Advances in agriculture and administration were probably responsible for part of this gain, but the chief reason was the great growth in population of the Yangtze Valley during the intervening centuries. Although the government remained in the northwest and in the hands of a military aristocracy from that region, the chief breadbasket was no longer the dry wheat and millet land of the Wei Valley and the North China Plain but the rich rice-growing paddy fields of the Lower Yangtze region.

The First Grand Canal. This situation explains the great canal-building activity of the Sui. An efficient transport system was necessary between the South and the capital and frontier areas in the North to enable the empire to take full advantage of its rich southern provinces. By 584 the old canal system between Ch'ang-an and the Yellow River had been reopened; by 605 a canal had been dug between the Yellow River and the Huai and on south to the Yangtze at Yang-chou (or

CHINA PROPER AROUND 700 A.D.

•••••• Borders of Provinces

⊔⊔⊔⊔⊔⊔ First Grand Canal   ═══ Modern Grand Canal

KUAN-NEI = "Within the Passes"   HUAI-NAN = "South of the Huai"

HO-TUNG = "East of the (Yellow) River"   SHAN-NAN = "South of the (Tsinling) Mountains"

HO-PEI = "North of the (Yellow) River"   CHIANG-NAN = "South of the (Yangtze) River"

HO-NAN = "South of the (Yellow) River"   LING-NAN = "South of the Range"

LUNG-YU

River

(Peking)

Yellow

HO-TUNG

HO-PEI

KUAN-NEI

Ch'ang-an

HO-NAN

Loyang

Yang-chou

CHIEN-NAN

SHAN-NAN

HUAI-NAN

Yangtze   R.

Hangchow

MT.
T'IEN-T'AI

CHIANG-NAN

LING-NAN

Chiang-tu, "the River Capital"); by 608 Yang Ti had constructed a canal from the Yellow River to the Peking area in order to supply his armies in their campaigns against Korea; and by 610 he had extended his canal system southward from Yang-chou through the rich rice lands of the Yangtze delta to the Hangchow area. This great system of canals was not all entirely new, for parts of it dated as far back as Chou times, but there never had been a united system of water transport of comparable dimensions.

The part of this great canal system between Hangchow and Ch'ang-an can be called the first Grand Canal, in contrast to the second or modern Grand Canal between Hangchow and the later capital, Peking. The two were identical as far north as the Huai River, but the northern part of the modern Grand Canal was not dug until the Mongol dynasty in the second half of the thirteenth century. The first and second Grand Canals had the same primary purpose — to supply with food from the South the capital city and the border armies that defended it.

The Breakdown of the "Equal Field" System. In theory the "equal field" system rested on the periodic redistribution of the bulk of the farm land among the tax-paying peasants, but it is doubtful that there was ever much actual redistribution. The population grew quickly because of domestic peace, and the peasantry increased faster than the land resources. The result was that most peasants inherited from their fathers less than their full quota of 100 *mou* of land. Moreover, most of their holdings came to be registered as permanent possessions. At the same time, cumulative imperial grants and the falsification of records by corrupt officials reduced the total quantity of land available to the tax-paying peasants.

By the first half of the eighth century the whole system was obviously breaking down. Hsüan Tsung made valiant efforts to restore it, but without avail. The disintegration of the T'ang government toward the close of his reign may be attributed in part to this failure of the complicated landholding and tax system. In any case, the system was abandoned at this time and was never again attempted on the same scale. The revival of the T'ang following Hsüan Tsung's reign was achieved by shifting the emphasis from per capita taxes to outright land taxes, but this is part of the story of the next major phase of Chinese history.

THE REVIVAL OF CENTRALIZED GOVERNMENT: THE BUREAUCRACY

In the task of restoring centralized government after the collapse of the Han and the "barbarian" invasions, the re-creation of the financial foundations of government was only half the problem. The other side of the coin was the development of a dependable bureaucracy to run the centralized administration. This was an even harder undertaking in this highly aristocratic age.

During the third century, as we have seen, the Wei and Western Chin dynasties had tried to emulate the Han by having local authorities classify and recommend men of merit for government service in the "nine-grade ranking system," but the powerful local families had given this mere lip service and had placed their own members and henchmen at the top of the lists. Similarly, the Northern Wei in the fifth century had to rely on the aristocracy for its officialdom, although, because they were backed by their own tribal military power, they and the other "barbarian" rulers of the North were never obliged to be so pusillanimous as the rulers of the successive dynasties in the South.

The Revival of the Examination and School Systems. The Sui rulers, inheriting the "barbarian" tradition of centralized military power, made a determined effort to recreate an effectively centralized civil administration. For this purpose Wen Ti re-emphasized the Confucian tradition that had become a part of the Han imperial system. It seemed obvious that this tradition would contribute most to social and political stability. Only it seemed to offer the sort of political theory, the rules of organization and the ritual precedents that would be appropriate for a great centralized empire. Certainly Taoism, Buddhism and the traditions of the northern nomads had little to offer along these lines. Thus the reunification of the empire brought with it a resurgence of Confucian political concepts.

Wen Ti not only reinstituted the Han system of examinations based on a Confucian curriculum for candidates for the bureaucracy, but he carried out this policy in a much more systematic fashion than the Han had ever attempted. He also introduced the principle that the officials of the prefectures and subprefectures should not be local aristocrats but appointees from the central government, and he took the peasant militia out of the hands of the local officials and put it under a centralized system of control.

The T'ang continued and expanded the government schools and examination system of the Sui. Under the supervision of the Directorate of the Imperial Academy (*Kuo-tzu chien*), a series of national schools was organized at the capital. The higher of these might be called liberal arts colleges. The student body of the most exclusive one was made up largely of members of the imperial family and the sons of high officials. There were also technical schools for law, writing, and mathematics, but these did not lead to high office. The prefectures and subprefectures also maintained government schools where local scholars could pursue their studies, although these lacked the systematic instruction of modern school systems.

The government examinations were held for the students of the capital schools, for nominees from the local governments (often on a quota basis according to the size of the local population), and occasionally for special imperial nominees. The Ministry of Rites administered the examinations amidst an elaborate series of rituals. There were several different categories of examinations, such as "flowering talent" (*hsiu-ts'ai*) for current political problems, "presented scholar" (*chin-shih*, implying presentation to the emperor) for letters, and also examinations in classics, law, calligraphy, and mathematics. The last three, however, were considered merely technical skills leading to low positions, and the *hsiu-ts'ai* degree dropped temporarily out of use, leaving only the *chin-shih* and classics degrees leading to the higher bureaucracy. The former of these came in time to be the preferred one, since it was less limited, including as it did the whole field of literature, and it became the one important degree in later Chinese history.

The successful candidate who passed this purely literary examination, thereby demonstrating his qualification for high office, had to pass a second series of examinations administered by the Ministry of Personnel before he could be appointed to office. This consisted of a written examination, in which the man's judgment and writing ability could be assessed, and an oral examination, in which he was judged on his personal appearance and speaking ability. To supplement this system there were also so-called merit examinations, amounting to a civil service rating system, which were useful in promotions and dismissals.

The Survival of Aristocratic Privileges. It should not be supposed that this highly elaborated system was fully developed in the early years of T'ang rule. It grew slowly and did not reach its height until the eighth century. The early T'ang system was still extremely aristocratic, and there was no flood of brilliant but obscure young men coming into high office. After all, the capital schools were primarily for the aristocracy; the nominees of the local government were selected by members of the privileged central government bureaucracy; and the oral examinations and subsequent promotions in office were no doubt heavily influenced by considerations of class and family connection. And it should not be forgotten that, even under the most favorable circumstances, no one was likely to distinguish himself in these examinations without long years of careful classical education, which required a considerable financial investment. Moreover, high officials always had the privilege of recommending their sons and protégés for official rank and position without their passing through the examination system.

In terms of social and political structure, the early T'ang thus should be considered part of the aristocratic period of Chinese history that had started in the latter years of the Han. This point is illustrated by the compilation in 634 on T'ai Tsung's order of a great genealogy of the aristocratic families, known as the *Shih tsu chih* (*Compendium of Families and Clans*).

The Efficacy of the Examination System. Nevertheless, even in the early days of the T'ang the examination system helped create a bureaucracy of talent which was at least the equivalent of the best that the Han had produced. By the middle T'ang the concept of a bureaucracy of merit had progressed far beyond anything the Han had known. This was the true start of the civil service merit system that was to prove one of the greatest achievements of Chinese civilization and that was to produce most of the great political leaders of the next thirteen centuries. With the exception of the first group of T'ang leaders, who achieved power through the sword, and the leaders during the last years of dynastic collapse, the great majority of the men who reached the top posts in the bureaucracy (and apparently the majority of those in the middle grades also) first distinguished themselves intellectually by winning the *chin-shih* degree. In later dynasties the preponderance of degree holders in high posts became even greater.

The examination system not only gave to China the world's first educated bureaucracy chosen fundamentally on the basis of merit; it also helped to unify the country intellectually. All who wished to participate in national leadership were led to seek, usually at their own expense, the same classical type of education, since the examination system was the most obvious route to political and financial success. The ruling class thus came to have a uniform education, actually not unlike the classical education that produced a successful ruling class for the British Empire in modern times. Since Confucian ideology lay at the basis of this education, the ruling class was thoroughly imbued with ethical principles, concepts of loyalty to existing authority, and a strong sense of the value of proper rituals and decorum.

Men of intellectual ability, singularly favored as they were by the system, became the strongest supporters of the government, instead of its critics, as has happened in so many other societies. The system even won the support of the lower classes for the established order, because there was always the possibility that a man of humble birth might pass the *chin-shih* examination and eventually become prime minister. In fact, this dream was almost as potent a political force for the following millennium in China as the "log cabin" myth in nineteenth-century American politics.

The examination system, however, had its weaknesses too. The resulting prestige of scholarship, combined with the traditional prestige of political office, helped perpetuate a division of Chinese society by education into two major strata, long after the power of the medieval aristocracy had faded. The insistence on orthodoxy in the examinations also helped stifle creative thought, while the narrowness of the subject matter sometimes produced a ruling class that was uninformed on other things. All this undoubtedly brought into government many men who were too scholastic or too antiquarian in their interests to be effective political leaders. In times of rapid change, as during the nineteenth century, this produced a ruling class that because of its strong historical orientation was dangerously divorced from realities.

The very perfection of the system thus contributed to a slowing down of both change and progress in China. Taken all in all, however, the examination system was one of the world's greatest political inventions and a major reason for the extraordinary strength and stability of the Chinese Empire ever since T'ang times.

T'ANG GOVERNMENT

The development during the T'ang of an educated bureaucracy of merit took several generations, but the dynasty needed elaborate organs of government for its vast empire right from the start. These it developed from the political institutions it inherited from the Northern Wei, the Northern Chou, and the Sui, which had in turn been patterned partly after the old Han institutions.

Under the T'ang the legal system became carefully codified under the four categories of penal law (*lü*), administrative law (*ling*), elaborations of these two categories (*ko*), and operational bylaws (*shih*). As in earlier and later dynasties, the laws thus were primarily administrative and penal and were little concerned with civil matters, which the people were supposed to settle privately. The T'ang codes seem to have been not only more elaborate but also more humane than those of the Han (of which few remain). The theory, as in other ages, was that wise judge-administrators would in practice subordinate the law to their own independent ethical judgment.

Local Government. Wen Ti of the Sui had abolished the old commanderies (*chün*) and divided the country into a more uniform system of prefectures (*chou*) and subprefectures (*hsien*).[5] The T'ang carried on the Sui system and elaborated it. As another organ of centralized supervision, the T'ang created for the first time large provinces over the prefectures. There were originally ten of these, known as *tao* ("circuits," the same word for "way" as in Taoism), but in Hsüan Tsung's time the larger ones were divided to form a total of fifteen.

To bind the empire together, the T'ang created an elaborate post-station system on the roads and waterways that radiated out from the capital. Commonly located at ten-mile intervals on the major lines of communication, these post stations maintained hostels and restaurants for official travelers provided with government tallies and furnished them with horses or boats as called for in their travel orders. The post-station system remained thereafter a standard part of Chinese government.

The early T'ang rulers showed the same scorn for merchants as had the Han, yet they similarly turned to trade monopolies and profitable price control systems when they needed additional income. They obviously felt that all economic activity should not only be taxed but should be carefully controlled. For these purposes barriers were created

---

[5] It should be noted that with the appearance of the *chou*, which grouped several *hsien* together, the *hsien*, translated as "prefectures" in Ch'in and Han times, slipped to the status of subprefectures. In more recent times they have commonly been called counties or districts.

on the principal trade routes within China, and city market places were strictly supervised by the government authorities.

The Central Organs of Government. The three top organs of the central government were the Imperial Secretariat (*Chung-shu-sheng*), the Imperial Chancellery (*Men-hsia-sheng*), and the Secretariat of State Affairs (*Shang-shu-sheng*). The first, operating directly under the emperor, was the chief originator of government policies and imperial orders. The Imperial Chancellery, which was a stronghold of bureaucratic power, had the right to review these orders and return them to the Imperial Secretariat for reconsideration if it disapproved. In other words, it served as a check on the authority of the emperor.

The Secretariat of State Affairs had the duty of executing the orders that had been agreed upon by the other two bodies. Under it there were the Six Ministries or Boards (*Liu-pu*): Personnel, Revenue, Rites, War, Justice, and Public Works. There were also nine courts (*ssu*), such as those for Imperial Sacrifices, Imperial Ceremonials, State Ceremonials (including the entertainment of foreign embassies), Imperial Household Affairs, Judicial Review, and Agriculture (including the supervision of official salaries paid in grain, the transport of tax grain, and granaries). Another category of bureaus was that of the five directorates (*chien*), for such disparate areas as the Imperial Academy and Weapons.

An office that deserves special mention was the Board of Censors (*Yü-shih-t'ai*). This institution, which was another unique creation of Chinese political genius, was designed as an internal control organ. The members of the board were officials of high prestige who had the primary duty of ferreting out cases of treason, misgovernment, or maladministration and reporting them directly to the emperor. To a lesser degree, they also performed the ancient scholars' function of remonstrance, pointing out to the emperor (at no little risk to themselves) any imperfections in his conduct. The Board of Censors remained an important organ in the Chinese imperial government in later dynasties.

The Capital. Ch'ang-an was both the center and the symbol of the highly centralized, carefully regulated T'ang Empire. The eastern terminus of the great overland trade routes across Central Asia, as well as the capital of the largest empire the world had yet seen, Ch'ang-an was thronged with people from all over Asia. The population of the capital district, including the city, its suburbs, and a little surrounding countryside, rose to 1,960,186. There probably were more than a million people within the city walls, which stood in a great rectangle of slightly more than five by six miles. The modern provincial capital of Sian occupies only a small part of the area once enclosed within the walls of Ch'ang-an.

The city was laid out in modern checkerboard fashion, with nine

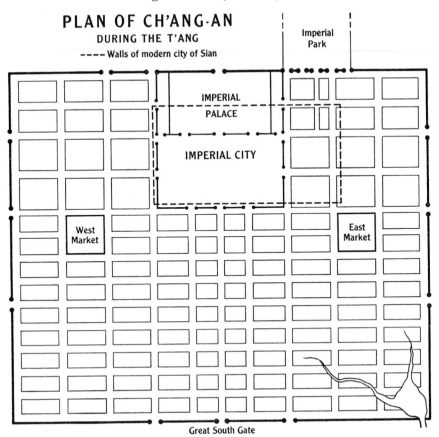

PLAN OF CH'ANG·AN
DURING THE T'ANG
---- Walls of modern city of Sian

Imperial Park

IMPERIAL

PALACE

IMPERIAL CITY

West Market

East Market

Great South Gate

great north-south thoroughfares crossing at right angles twelve great east-west roads. At the north center of the city stood the imperial palace, within its own walls. The Imperial City, that is, the government headquarters, lay immediately south of it. The main south gate of the palace led directly to the main south gate of the Imperial City and straight on down the central north-south thoroughfare, 500 feet wide, to the main south gate of the city, creating a great central axis on which the city was divided into administrative halves, the left (east) and the right (west). In each half was a large government market place. The remainder of the city was divided into 112 blocks (*fang*), most of them 650-by 350-pace rectangles. Each was an administrative "village" within the city, divided by its own internal alleyways and closed up at night within its own walls.

The whole plan and organization of Ch'ang-an illustrates the strict and careful control that the early T'ang maintained over society. The size and grandeur of the city suggest the dynasty's power and wealth.

China during the seventh century towered high above all other political units of the time. During the Han dynasty China had drawn abreast of the Mediterranean world. Now it was starting on what was to prove to be a millennium of pre-eminence as the strongest, richest, and in many ways most culturally advanced country in the world.

THE ABSORPTION OF BUDDHISM

The incorporation of the "barbarian" invaders into a new and greater empire was a spectacular phase of Chinese history, but an even more surprising story was that of the gradual absorption of Buddhism into the main stream of Chinese culture and the eventual neutralization of those of its features that were incompatible with basic Chinese ideas or the prevailing social system. Buddhism, as we have seen, was a frontal challenge to Chinese civilization, but in the long run China changed Buddhism much more than Buddhism changed China.

Buddhism reached its greatest heights under the patronage of the Northern Wei monarchs and during the brilliant first half of the T'ang. T'ai Tsung showered extraordinary honors on Hsüan-tsang when the great pilgrim returned from India, and the peace and prosperity of the early T'ang period allowed the Buddhist church to thrive economically and intellectually as never before. In fact, it probably achieved its peak around 700 under the zealous patronage of the Empress Wu. The Buddhism that flourished during this heyday from the fifth to the eighth centuries, however, was being steadily reshaped into a set of ideas and institutions that bore little resemblance to primitive Buddhism but fitted easily into the Chinese system.

The Development of Sects. This transformation of Buddhism was to be seen even in its basic doctrines. The Indian love of philosophical speculation had given rise to numerous schools of thought within Indian Buddhism; the Chinese love of classification now resulted in the organization of some of these different philosophical tendencies into sects. It should be noted, however, that these sects in China never developed into mutually exclusive churches, like the sects of Christianity, although this did happen to them after they were introduced into Japan.

Some of the Chinese sects were no more than philosophical transplants of Indian schools of thought. The most important of these was the Fa-hsiang sect (Japanese, Hossō), introduced by Hsüan-tsang, which stressed the idealistic concept of the discovery of ultimate truth through an understanding of its manifestations in transient existence. Such Indian philosophical sects, however, flourished in China only as long as direct contact was maintained with Indian Buddhism, and all had withered away before the end of the eighth century.

T'ien-t'ai (Tendai) and Chen-yen (Shingon). The sects that prospered in China were those which stressed elements that were more native to Chinese thinking. One of these was the T'ien-t'ai sect (Japanese, Tendai), which, significantly, was founded by a Chinese monk, Chih-i (538–597), and was named for Mount T'ien-t'ai, a great Buddhist center in Chekiang. Its popularity was based on its typically Chinese eclecticism, love of compromise, and skill at classification. It developed the Mahayana concept of relative truths, organizing the vast body of conflicting Buddhist doctrines into different levels of truth, each valid in its own way. T'ien-t'ai became the leading sect in the eighth and ninth centuries, and helped establish the *Lotus Sutra* as the most popular scripture of East Asian Buddhism.

Another sect that came to the fore at much the same time was Chen-yen, the "True Word" (Japanese, Shingon), a late and degenerate form of Indian Buddhism. This was an esoteric or secret doctrine, strongly influenced by the Tantric cults of Hinduism. The Chen-yen sect taught that the Eternal Buddha, Vairocana, was the ultimate source of all things and that man, like all other phenomenal existence, was merely an emanation of this deity. It also taught that ultimate reality could not be expressed by words but was best suggested by magic signs and symbols.

The incantations, magic formulas, and ceremonials Chen-yen emphasized were readily appreciated by the Chinese, who were familiar with such things from Taoism and from the Confucian emphasis on ritual. Chen-yen masses for the dead, in particular, became extremely popular, because they fitted in so well with traditional ancestor worship. The artistic representation of Chen-yen philosophy, especially in the form of huge schematic cosmological drawings known as *mandala* (Japanese, *mandara*), also appealed greatly to the Chinese, and as a consequence Chen-yen influences had a large role in later Chinese Buddhist art. (See Plate 56.)

The "Pure Land" Sect. The characteristic Mahayana concept of salvation through faith also became the basis of a strong sectarian movement known as Ching-t'u (Japanese, Jōdo), named for the "Pure Land," that is, the Western Paradise of Amida. Tracing its origin all the way back to the South Chinese monk Hui-yüan (334–416), this sect stressed the simple act of faith of calling on the Buddha's name (*nien-fo;* Japanese, *nembutsu*). By the fifth century these ideas were entrenched in China, and the popular rebellions from Sui times on drew spiritual inspiration from such popular forms of Buddhism, rather than from Taoism. T'ien-t'ai classification helped the spread of the "Pure Land" concepts, because it could be argued that these simplest of Buddhist doctrines were those that applied in the "degenerate" age in which people usually felt themselves to be living. The "Pure Land" sect naturally had the strongest appeal to the common man and numerically became the greatest force in East Asian Buddhism.

Ch'an (Zen). The last of the sectarian movements proved ultimately the most significant. This was the Meditation sect or Ch'an, better known by its Japanese name, Zen. According to tradition, Zen was introduced by Bodhidharma, a semi-legendary figure of the early sixth century who is reputed to have sat facing a wall in meditation for nine years until his legs atrophied. (The legless tumbling dolls of Japan, known as *daruma*, derive from this legend.) Actually, Zen appeared in China only in early T'ang times and did not become prominent before the ninth century.

Zen was close to primitive Buddhism in its stress on meditation and intuitive insight or "enlightenment," but it derived perhaps even more from native philosophical Taoism, which had also stressed meditation and intuition. It taught that the only true reality was the Buddha nature within each person's heart. Though it derived a sense of the other-worldly and the infinite from India, this mysticism was applied in typically Chinese fashion to the mundane life of the individual. The meditative life in China became a life of hard work and rugged self-reliance. Zen's anti-scholastic, anti-textual bias was pure Taoism. Instead of texts, it stressed oral instruction, particularly through outwardly non-sensical problems meant to shock the student out of his dependence on ordinary logic. In its love of nature and rustic simplicity, Zen was merely the old Taoistic tradition in a new guise, and therefore not un-naturally came to share with Taoism the role of a major inspiration for artistic and poetic creativeness.

Drawing as it did so directly from one of the chief springs of Chinese civilization, Zen became the strongest of the sects of later Chinese Buddhism. Although never a well-organized church in China, its discipline of meditation and emphasis on self-reliance gave it much greater strength than the other sects could derive from their monastic rules or intricate philosophies. Zen was the only type of Buddhism that continued a vigorous intellectual life after the T'ang. Gradually, the rest of Chinese Buddhism was absorbed either by Zen or by the popular "Pure Land" sect, and eventually these two lost their distinctiveness, merging in the vague mixture of superstitions into which Chinese Buddhism in time degenerated.

Buddhism's Role in Chinese Society. While Buddhism was being intellectually neutralized by the subordination of many of its original tenets to ideas more congenial to Chinese minds, it was also being absorbed institutionally into Chinese society. In other words, monastic, anti-social

Buddhism was being remolded into a religion that would serve society and buttress the state.

During the period of political disunion, Buddhist monasteries, like the Christian monasteries of medieval Europe, had an important role as centers of learning and culture in a troubled age. They also expanded their functions as havens of refuge for the persecuted, inns for travelers, hospitals, public baths, and even as primitive banking institutions where articles of value could be stored and loans of money obtained. The Buddhist church also took over the burial of the dead, retaining this function until contemporary times. Even celibacy, regarded by the Chinese as the most anti-social aspect of Buddhism, was in time mitigated by a gradual relaxation of the rules regulating the lives of priests and monks.

The most startling aspect of the Sinification of Buddhism was its incorporation into the economic and administrative pattern of the empire. The rich holdings of the great Buddhist monasteries came to present the Chinese state with the only true church problem it ever faced. Monasteries were built and endowed by rulers or prosperous individuals and tended to accumulate greater riches through further gifts of land or treasure from pious believers. They also expanded their holdings through usury and the various other legal or illegal methods by which the great families had amassed their landholdings. Moreover, wealthy monasteries tended to breed religious and moral laxity and encourage the activities of religious fakers and racketeers.

Strong rulers quite naturally felt that such evils should be controlled and that the number and holdings of monasteries should be limited, because they, like other large landowners, were potentially a fiscal menace to the state. In fact, they were felt to be a double menace to society, because they removed men from production both as immediate taxpayers and as fathers of future taxpayers.

Another typically Chinese concept was that, in so far as it was a true religion, Buddhism should serve the interests of the state as its spiritual guardian and as the performer of religious ceremonies for the imperial line. It was felt, moreover, that the government should not leave to chance the establishment of Buddhist monasteries and temples capable of performing these services, but should itself create these organs. Thus the idea arose that Buddhism should not only be controlled by the government but should be supported by it as a sort of spiritual branch of the administration. Nothing could have been further from the original role of Indian Buddhism.

The South Chinese dynasties proved no more capable of limiting the Buddhist monasteries than they were able to control the other great landowners, but in North China a regularized Buddhist church slowly emerged. As early as the fourth century, rulers were appointing "bishops" who were supposed to control the church, and the Northern Wei developed the idea that the government should limit the number of monks and monasteries and see to it that monasteries, like any other branch of the administration, had adequate lands and peasants for their support.

The T'ang had the theory that there should be one official monastery, with thirty monks, per prefecture. The government recurrently defrocked monks in an effort to keep their numbers within bounds, and by 729 had inaugurated a clerical census every three years to aid in the process. By 747 the government itself was issuing ordination permits to limit the number of new monks, and all clerics were forced to carry these official papers.

Attempts to control the number of monasteries and monks always failed in the long run. Devout rulers and government officials were constantly breaking their own regulations, and secret ordinations were common. In later dynasties the whole effort was abandoned, and frequently the government even used the sale of ordination permits as a means of replenishing its treasury. By this time, however, the shift of emphasis in taxation from the individual to the land unit had altered the problem and reduced the fiscal menace of Buddhist monasticism.

Buddhist Persecutions. During the Six Dynasties and T'ang periods, when the economic threat of monasticism was strongly felt, Buddhism was sometimes subjected to violent persecutions. These outbursts were in part motivated by resentment of Buddhism as a foreign religion. There was also general abhorrence of certain Buddhist practices, such as self-mutilation or cremation, both of which the Chinese felt were unnatural or even immoral practices, since they regarded the body as an inviolable gift from one's ancestors. Taoist priests, who increasingly found themselves in competition with the Buddhists for imperial patronage or popular support, sometimes helped whip up an anti-Buddhist furor.

The most fundamental reason for the persecutions, however, was financial. Recurrently the idea arose in government circles that the excess lands (and the monks) of the monasteries should be returned to the tax registers and their vast treasures confiscated. The gilt coverings and bronze bodies of the great images were particularly coveted, the gold for imperial treasures and the copper for currency. Unlike the religious persecutions of the Near East and Europe, the Buddhist persecutions of China were aimed solely at the clergy and the property of the organized church; individual believers were seldom seriously bothered.

There was a brief persecution of Buddhism under the Northern Wei in 446 and another in 574 under the Northern Chou. In the first case, Taoists helped stir up the trouble; in the second, they were persecuted together with the Buddhists.

By far the greatest and most significant persecution of Buddhism took place in 841–845, under a half-insane T'ang ruler who had become a fanatic searcher after Taoist immortality. According to the official accounts, 4600 monasteries and 40,000 shrines were destroyed during these years; 260,000 monks and nuns were defrocked and, together with their 150,000 slaves, were returned to the tax registers. The Japanese Buddhist pilgrim Ennin, who was an indefatigable diarist, has left a graphic eye-witness account of this particular onslaught on the Buddhist church in China.

This third great persecution proved to be a crippling blow to Buddhism because the Indian religion was already losing its inner vitality. As we shall see in the next chapter, a fundamental change was starting to take place in Chinese attitudes. The examination system had revived interest in the classical literature associated with Confucianism and, therefore, in Confucian philosophy. The upper classes were losing interest in Buddhism, and the best thinkers and greatest artists were abandoning Buddhism for other modes of expression. Coming at such a time of inner decay, the great persecution of 841–845 dealt Buddhism a blow from which it never recovered. Zen, which was so very Chinese and so little Buddhist, continued its growth and influence for a few more centuries, but the other forms of Buddhism rapidly fell into decay.

Fortunately, before all the intellectual and artistic glories of Chinese Buddhism were irretrievably lost, it left a permanent shrine at Tun-huang near the western extremity of the Kansu corridor. Here, among the elaborately decorated, rock-hewn temples known as the "Caves of the Thousand Buddhas" (see Plate 23), a great Buddhist library was sealed shut around 1035 to save it from raiding Tibetans. Not reopened until 1900, this library, with its thousands of manuscripts, many in various Central Asian languages, proved to be a unique repository of the Buddhist age in China.

The Lasting Influence of Buddhism. Although Buddhism was a major component of Chinese culture during one of its most brilliant epochs, it left relatively little permanent impress on Chinese civilization. Most of its fundamental religious concepts, as well as its basic way of life, were ultimately rejected by the Chinese. They refused to accept such practices as asceticism, self-mutilation, and cremation, and its celibacy and mendicancy were sharply reduced in importance.

Buddhism's lasting contributions to Chinese civilization tended to be additions to the inherited culture, rather than alterations of the central structure of ideas and institutions. It did contribute scores of new concepts and hundreds of new words to the Chinese vocabulary. Its ideas of salvation, *karma,* the transmigration of the soul, heaven and hell, its god concepts, and much of its mythology and ceremonials worked their way into the eclectic popular religion and decidedly influenced the way people thought about the problems of life. The Buddhist emphasis on charity contributed to a vague concept of public philanthropy, and its respect for all forms of life may have had a humanizing influence on law and custom. Buddhism unquestionably added new dimensions to Chinese philosophy, and after the T'ang period elements of its metaphysics became incorporated into the main stream of Confucian thought. Most important, it added greatly to the richness of Chinese literature and art. While Buddhism thus did not remold a whole civilization, as did Christianity in Europe, it greatly enriched Chinese culture by accretions.

THE GROWTH OF CHINESE CULTURE

Contacts With the Outside World. Despite the political disunity and chaos of the Six Dynasties period, this epoch, as well as the early T'ang, was a period of significant cultural growth. China was pervaded by a spirit of cultural tolerance. The "barbarian" invasions left the North wide open to foreign influences; Buddhism was both a vehicle for and a stimulus to close cultural contacts with distant areas; inter-regional trade by sea and by land was growing far beyond anything known in Han times; and the early T'ang empire brought the Chinese into direct contact with the borderlands of Indian and Near Eastern civilization. Never again until the twentieth century was China to prove so responsive to foreign influences.

One sign of the close contact with the outside world was the large number of foreign residents in China. During the Six Dynasties there were many Buddhist missionaries as well as traders who reached China from Central Asia or the region of the southern seas. In the early T'ang, Ch'ang-an was literally crowded with foreigners — thousands of members of the official embassies which came periodically from all over Asia, and still larger numbers of merchants, soldiers, monks, and jugglers and other entertainers attracted to this, the greatest metropolis of the world.

Near Eastern Religions. A measure of the foreign population of Ch'ang-an was the prevalence of Near Eastern religions at the capital. Zoroastrianism (or Mazdaism), the fire-worshiping religion of Persia, had reached China by the sixth century. In early T'ang times came the Nestorian branch of Christianity and Manichaeanism, which had been founded in Babylon in the third century and included Christian and Zoroastrian elements.

Although these religions were limited largely to foreigners, they had temples in many provincial cities as well as Ch'ang-an. Manichaeanism, being the official religion of the Uighur allies of the T'ang, was especially favored. A stone stele erected at the capital in 781, and rediscovered only in the early seventeenth century, indicates that Nestorianism too was flourishing at that time. All three religions were virtually wiped out in the religious persecution of 841–845 and were never strong again in China.

Two other Near Eastern religions first introduced during these centuries, however, proved to have more lasting powers. These were Judaism and Islam. Judaism survived in isolated communities until the late nineteenth century, and Islam grew steadily, until by modern times it embraced many millions, largely in the southwest and northwest.

The Imitation of the T'ang Model Abroad. Another aspect of the internationalism of the period was the way in which neighboring peoples sought to imitate the early T'ang. Never before and never again did such a large proportion of mankind look to China as the paramount military power of the world and as the obvious model for government and culture. The various peoples who surrounded China imitated the T'ang much more consciously than they had ever copied the Han. In part, this was because of increased contacts, but another reason may have been that the peoples of these peripheral lands had in the meantime reached a cultural level at which the direct imitation of Chinese culture was now more feasible for them than it had been during the Han period. Other reasons may have been the greater perfection and prestige of the T'ang system and the very cosmopolitanism of T'ang culture, which made it more attractive to foreign peoples.

The first unified Tibetan government, established in the seventh century, and the state of Nan-chao, founded in Yunnan around 740, were both directly inspired by the T'ang system of rule. The people of Nan-chao were the Thai, who later moved south to found modern Siam. The T'ang political and cultural pattern was even more fully adopted by the peoples to the east. As we shall see, the various kingdoms of Korea had for centuries shown strong Chinese influence, and Silla, after uniting the peninsula in 668, became a veritable replica in miniature of the T'ang. The first Tungusic kingdom of P'o-hai, which flourished in the woodlands of southern and eastern Manchuria and northeastern Korea from 713 to 926, also closely copied certain T'ang institutions. The efforts of the Japanese in the seventh and eighth centuries to create another small T'ang in their remote islands was an even more remarkable example.

Technological Advances. Despite the political and economic disruption of the Six Dynasties period, China made steady technological advances at this time as well as during the early T'ang. Under Indian inspiration astronomy and mathematics made great steps forward, and Indian medical knowledge, transmitted by Buddhist monks, combined with the experimental work of the Taoist alchemists to further medicine. The earlier inventions of paper, porcelaneous wares, and the water mill were greatly developed.

Gunpowder was invented, though it was not used at this time for warfare but only for fireworks, of which the Chinese are still extremely fond. By the third century detailed sketch maps with a rectilinear grid pattern were being made. The kite, too, was invented in China at this time, as was also the wheelbarrow. This useful conveyance, which greatly facilitated transportation on narrow footpaths, did not reach Europe until many centuries later.

The chair was introduced to China during the Six Dynasties period and over the centuries gradually replaced sitting pads and mats (though the Koreans and Japanese still usually sit on the floor when at home, in the ancient Chinese manner). Tea was introduced from Southeast Asia. It was valued at first for its medicinal use and as a stimulant for meditative séances, but by the late T'ang it had come into more general use in China and then spread from there to become in time the world's most popular drink. Coal was used in the coal-producing areas of North China from the fourth century on, though it was still to seem a marvel to Marco Polo in the thirteenth century.

The Arts. Buddhist psalmody had a profound influence on Chinese music, and during this period the music and instruments of Central Asia virtually displaced the older musical traditions of China. In art, and particularly in sculpture, foreign Buddhist influence was also strong. In fact, the Buddhist demand for religious images made this the one great age of Chinese sculpture. What had been a minor art form in earlier periods rose to great heights for a few centuries, and then fell again with the decline of Buddhism after the T'ang.

Chinese Buddhist sculptures, as preserved in such successive shrines as the rock temples of Yün-kang, Lung-men, and Tun-huang, show diverse artistic strains. (See Plates 19–22 and 24.) Some influences came directly from India, but the most important artistic traditions in North China during the Six Dynasties period were those of Central Asian Buddhism, which had been derived in turn from the strongly Hellenistic Buddhist art of Gandhara and surrounding areas in what is now northwest Pakistan and Afghanistan. (See Plate 18.) The early Buddhist sculpture of China, however, was quite different from the Greek in spirit, as was to be expected in a deeply religious art. The

BUDDHIST SCULPTURE

PLATE 18. Head of a Buddha in Graeco-Indian style from the Gandhara area (Northwest Pakistan and Afghanistan) dating from the second century A.D.

PLATE 19. The Bodhisattva Kuan-yin (Kannon) carved in stone, from the Northern Chou dynasty (557–581 A.D.).

PLATE 20. A Buddhist deity in a wall niche in the Yün-kang rock temples (northern Shansi), carved in the second half of the fifth century during the Northern Wei dynasty.

PLATE 21. Stone bas-relief of the empress as a donor with attendants, from the Lung-men rock temples (near Loyang) of the Northern Wei dynasty (about 522 A.D.).

PLATE 22. Giant guardian deities carved at Lung-men in the early T'ang dynasty (672–676 A.D.). Note for scale the two persons seated below the right-hand figure and the square holes and niches made to support the wooden structure that once enclosed these figures.

PLATE 23. Buddhist deities, saints and flying angels, painted during the T'ang period on the walls and ceiling of a grotto in the "Caves of the Thousand Buddhas" at Tun-huang.

PLATE 24. Entrances to some of the Buddhist rock temples at Yün-kang. The colossal Buddha at left, carved from the cliff wall in the late fifth century, is about forty-five feet high. The building and wall on the higher ground are later structures.

PLATE 25. Life on the steppe. A Mongol camp near the Altai Mountains with yurts, sheep, horses, pasture and a brackish lake of surface water (on right).

PLATE 26. Pottery figure of a lady polo player from the T'ang dynasty (seventh century), about ten inches high.

PLATE 27. Stone relief from the tomb of the T'ang Emperor T'ai Tsung (626–649), depicting one of his battle chargers attended by a bearded "barbarian" groom.

human figures, far from being naturalistic, were stiff, austere abstractions of deity, and Greek realism was limited to such superficial elements as the folds of their clothing. (See Plates 19–21.)

By the T'ang, however, Chinese humanistic interests had made the Buddhist concept of deity more intimate and human, and this change was reflected in sculpture. Images became much plumper and more lifelike, closely approximating T'ang concepts of human beauty. In post-T'ang times the steady decline of Buddhism was mirrored first by the sometimes insipid prettiness of Buddhist sculpture and eventually by its inept crudeness.

Secular sculpture also flourished during the Six Dynasties and T'ang periods. Great monumental figures, usually representing fabulous beasts, were erected around the tombs of emperors and other great men. The most famous of these are the bas-reliefs of the favorite horses of T'ai Tsung. (See Plate 27.) The making of pottery figurines for burial in tombs also had become a fine art by this time. Unknown craftsmen turned out huge numbers of small statues of dancing girls, camels, horses, Central Asian grooms, and the like. (See Plate 26.) Some of these figures were beautifully glazed, and all are now treasured as superb examples of the sculptor's craft. The mirrors of T'ang times, with their flowing floral or animal ornamentation in place of the more geometric designs of Han mirrors, also show the Chinese mastery of the plastic arts during this period.

Little remains of the Buddhist painting of the Six Dynasties and T'ang periods, except for the murals of the Tun-huang caves (see Plate 23), but the Buddhist influence on Chinese painting was unmistakably great. Though most of the artistic genius of China during this time was probably devoted to religious art, secular painting also flourished, and South China saw the beginnings of artistic trends which were to grow into the great painting traditions of the late T'ang and following periods. Though, again, little remains today of this secular art, Ku K'ai-chih, who flourished around 400 A.D., is honored as the first great figure in Chinese painting, while Wang Hsi-chih (321–379) is considered the greatest name in calligraphy, an art that ever since his time has been highly esteemed and has had a profound influence on painting techniques.

Except for brick and stone pagodas (see Plate 16), little remains of either the secular or religious architecture of the T'ang or earlier periods. Having been mainly of wood, both secular and religious buildings succumbed to the wars and revolutions that swept the country and to the vicissitudes of time. Buddhist temples built in the Chinese style in Japan during the seventh and eighth centuries, however, have survived, giving us some idea of the classic simplicity and balance of Chinese architectural forms at this time (see Plates 17 and 50), and from the middle of the ninth century there remains a small religious structure

0 5 10 15 20 25 FEET

CHINA'S OLDEST WOODEN BUILDING

Front elevation and cross section of the main hall of the Fo-kuang-ssu ("Monastery of the Buddha's Halo") on Mount Wu-t'ai.

at a monastery at the great Buddhist center on Mount Wu-t'ai in northern Shansi.

Literature. During the Buddhist age a large proportion of the best literary and scholarly talent naturally was devoted to Buddhist works, which later generations of Chinese have generally ignored. There was also a large amount of literary and scholarly endeavor along more traditional lines. There is, in fact, no clear break in the development of literature and scholarship between the Han and the Six Dynasties or between the latter and the T'ang and later ages.

Buddhist mythology and wonder stories as well as other popular foreign tales greatly enriched the subject matter of Chinese literature at this time, but for the most part writing continued to be an essentially aristocratic art, as was to be expected in this highly aristocratic age. The *fu* poetic form, which was so very artificial in language, remained in fashion during the Six Dynasties period and was matched in the field of prose by an elaborate balanced style that featured carefully paired verbal patterns, commonly in four- and six-syllable phrases (*p'ien-t'i-wen*).

The most important verse form of the Six Dynasties period was the *shih*, a lyric in five syllable meter, which first appeared in the late Han. Reflecting the disruption of the times, this lyric poetry was typically Taoistic, lamenting the corruption of the world and asserting with vehemence the point of view of the individual in conflict with society.

For all its Taoistic individualism, however, even this lyric poetry showed much preoccupation with form and a considerable degree of rigidity. This was less true of the verses of the greatest master of the art, T'ao Ch'ien (also known as T'ao Yüan-ming, 376–427). A native of the South, he abandoned his official post in true Taoist fashion to live the hard life of a farmer. Also in Taoist fashion, he seems to have found his own personal elixir of life in wine. The following is one of his many poems entitled "On Drinking Wine":

> The lovely colors of Fall chrysanthemums —
> I pick the blossoms wet with dew
> And dip them in this Thing Which Makes One Forget
> To put from me any desire for the world I have left.
> I am alone drinking my wine
> And when the cup is empty I pour myself another.
> The sun sets and all nature rests;
> Homing birds twitter as they approach the woods.
> I sing complacently at the east window
> Having recaptured something of this life's joy.[6]

Continuing into the T'ang, the tradition of lyric poetry, as we shall see, produced a glorious poetic outburst in the eighth and ninth centuries.

Literary Criticism and Scholarship. Another important innovation of the Six Dynasties was the development of literary criticism. The earliest critiques of literature appeared in the third century, and around 480 Liu Hsieh produced his great *Wen-hsin tiao-lung* or *Treatise on the Fundamentals of the Literary Art.* A short time later, Hsiao T'ung (501–531), the heir apparent to the Liang throne in South China, compiled the *Wen hsüan* or *Literary Selections*, China's most famous anthology.

The quantity of Buddhist and even Taoist scholarly endeavor during this period was prodigious, but there was no falling off in the output of standard histories, commentaries on the classics, and other traditional types of scholarship. Around 500 appeared a curious work much used in later Chinese elementary instruction. This was the *Ch'ien-tzu wen* or *Thousand-Character Classic*, which summarizes Chinese history and Confucian philosophical views in a thousand characters, none of which is repeated.

Another important book, which straddled the traditional field of history and the new field of Buddhism, was the *Kao seng chuan* or *Biographies of Eminent Monks.* Compiled by the monk Hui-chiao in 519, it became the model for later works of the same nature. By the late fifth century the study of Sanskrit by the Buddhists had also stirred Chinese interest in phonetics, giving rise to work on the Chinese system of tones and a sort of spelling system whereby the pronunciation of a character could be represented by two other characters, one indicating

---

[6] From a forthcoming book by James R. Hightower.

its initial consonant and the other its vowel and its final consonant, if it had any.

One new aspect of Chinese scholarship, which in later periods grew to colossal proportions, was the making of works of an encyclopedic nature. The earliest seems to have been a general encyclopedia, compiled in the third century for the first ruler of the Wei dynasty, which has since been lost. A compendium on the flora of South China appeared later in that same century. The first surviving local encyclopedia of the history, natural features, and political and social institutions of one small administrative unit appeared in the fourth century. Usually called gazetteers, such works in time came to number in the thousands. The *Shui ching chu* or *Commentary to the Waters Classic*, compiled around 510, might be classed with these geographical compendiums. By the fifth century there were books on Chinese painters and their works and on the canons of painting. All these new scholarly trends that grew so naturally out of earlier Chinese cultural traditions were continued and expanded under the T'ang.

In higher culture the Six Dynasties period thus represented no great break with the past and led on smoothly into the T'ang and later periods. This was perhaps because of the broad overlapping in time of the old and the new. The continuing cultural traditions of the Han in South China and the rising new semi-"barbarian," semi-Buddhist culture of the North remained for a long time contemporaneous. Despite the challenge to Chinese society of "barbarian" invaders and a foreign religion, there was much greater cultural continuity between the Han and the T'ang than between Rome and Medieval or Renaissance Europe. By escaping the proliferation of local national cultures which occurred in Europe, Chinese civilization was able to preserve itself and flourish vigorously during an era of Western decline.

6

The Late T'ang and Sung:
The Golden Age of Chinese Culture

THE NATURE OF THE PERIOD

To divide a dynasty between two major periods goes against the whole cyclic interpretation of Chinese history. The traditionalist may be especially outraged when the dynasty so divided is the T'ang, perhaps the most resplendent in all Chinese history. But this is necessary if we are to see the more fundamental patterns that underlie the dynastic cycle.

The Transition from Classic to "Early Modern" China. In political and economic organization, in relations with the outside world, in religious and philosophical attitudes, in social structure, and in higher culture, the early and late T'ang periods probably had fewer affinities with each other than with either the preceding Six Dynasties period or the following Sung dynasty (960–1279). More important, the early T'ang together with the Six Dynasties can be regarded in many ways as the last phase of ancient Chinese history, while the late T'ang together with the Sung forms the first phase of later Chinese history. One might, in fact, call it the "early modern" phase, for the culture which evolved at this time was to remain characteristic of China until the opening decades of the twentieth century. All that has proved most typical of the Middle Kingdom during the past millennium appeared at least in embryo by late T'ang times and came into early bloom under the Sung.

The period of transition between late classic China and the "early modern" period centered around the eighth century, right in the middle of the T'ang dynasty. Traditional Chinese historians, concentrating on the dynastic cycle, have failed to see the significance of the changes that occurred at that time; they may also have overlooked them because the institutional and cultural patterns that developed after the eighth century became so strong that all earlier stages of Chinese history were thenceforth interpreted in terms of these patterns. Those earlier elements which were like post-T'ang China were emphasized, and those which were alien were minimized, with the result that the magnitude of the change that took place during the T'ang has been obscured.

We are accustomed to thinking of great cultural and social changes as occurring during times of military conquest or political breakdown. Such a concept fits in with the theory of the dynastic cycle. Even greater cultural changes, however, can take place during times of peace and prosperity. Nothing produces change more inevitably than growth, and growth in population, production, trade, culture, and institutions takes place more easily in peaceful times than during periods of disruption. This is what happened during the T'ang.

The rulers of the Northern Wei, Sui, and early T'ang had solved the administrative problems that had destroyed the Han and had met the challenge of the "barbarians" and of Buddhism. They had re-created the classic empire, though in a much more perfected form and at a higher technological level. The reunified empire, therefore, quickly rose to new peaks of wealth and power. A century of relative peace and prosperity brought growth of a sort that lifted China to a significantly higher level, quite different from that of the Han. A greater degree of integration and equilibrium was achieved among political, economic, and social institutions, with a resulting increase in stability. There was, in other words, a sort of cultural and institutional breakthrough.

Unfortunately for China, the new level was not greatly altered during the next several hundred years. It proved to be a sort of plateau in time, at first high above Western attainments but in later times technologically far below. This was the "unchanging" China of both the Chinese and the traditional Western view. Certainly, as we shall see, post-Sung China did change much more slowly than the West during these centuries. But this contrast was only in part the result of increased stability and a slowing of the rate of change in China; it was heightened by the dynamic upsurge in Europe during and after the age of discovery. The acceleration of the rate of change in the West makes China seem more immobile than it actually was. In any case, the slowing down of change in China should not be read back into earlier times. Until the thirteenth century Chinese civilization seems to have grown and developed at least as rapidly as the civilization of any other major area.

The late T'ang and the Sung may be called a period of renaissance, though only in a special sense of that much-used term. There was a new awareness of the significance of some of the classic literature of the Chou and a rising interest in Shang bronzes and other features of the old culture. But the historically-minded Chinese had always been acutely conscious of antiquity, and there was, therefore, no spectacular rediscovery of the past comparable to the rediscovery of Greece and Rome in the European Renaissance. On the other hand, there was a decided shift in the basic values of the culture at this time, and new patterns were established which were to remain characteristic of early modern China. In this limited sense, the period from the eighth to the thirteenth century might be justifiably compared with the Renaissance period of Europe.

Swings of the Pendulum. We have already noted some of the ways in which the late T'ang differed from the first century of this dynasty's rule. One was in its relationship with neighboring peoples. The early T'ang saw the high point in the swing of the pendulum toward Chinese conquest which had started under the Northern Wei. The second half of the dynasty saw the start of a long swing back in the opposite direction, which was to culminate in the Mongol triumph in 1279, when for the first time in history all of China came under alien rule.

Such swings of the pendulum had occurred before and were to be repeated again in Chinese history, but at this time the swing from conqueror to conquered was accompanied by two subtle changes in Chinese society that profoundly altered the whole relationship between the Chinese and the "barbarians." One change was that the open, cosmopolitan spirit of the early T'ang gradually faded into a narrower, more exclusively China-centered and introspective attitude. The other was the decline of the martial spirit and the development of pronounced pacifistic traits. Up through the early T'ang, the Chinese dynasties had all been militaristic, in the old Legalist tradition, but by Sung times the civilian point of view had become overwhelmingly predominant, and there was a growing contempt for the military profession.

We have also noted the end of the Buddhist age in the late T'ang. Before the end of the dynasty, Buddhism, except for the Zen sect, which itself had many "early modern" characteristics, had lost much of its vigor. On the whole, the best brains and artistic talents of China were turning from Buddhism and Taoism back to the Confucian tradition, though the Confucianism that was revived in the late T'ang and brought to full maturity under the Sung was so different from that of Chou or Han times that it has been called Neo-Confucianism. It was this Neo-Confucianism of the Sung that remained the dominant philosophy of China until the twentieth century.

Economic and Social Changes. Mention has also been made of the fundamental change in taxation — from a per capita basis to land areas — that took place during the eighth century. This may seem a minor point, but it profoundly affected government finance and was accompanied and to some degree produced by important economic and social developments. One such change was the rapid growth of commerce and of a more highly developed money economy. This can best be seen in the spectacular rise of overseas trade from the eighth century on. During this time the world's first large-scale maritime commerce grew up between China and South and West Asia. This expansion of the Chinese economy, coupled with the shift in taxation from the individual peasant to the piece of land and to commercial taxes, made the financial and administrative problems of the Sung and later periods quite different from those of the Han or the early T'ang.

Economic growth helped produce an equally significant social change. Chou society had been controlled by a hereditary military aristocracy of hoary antiquity. This aristocracy had been wiped out by the Ch'in and Han empires, but a new aristocracy of landed wealth, official position, and, frequently, of personal military power had grown up and had tended to dominate both government and society between the Han and the early T'ang. During the next few centuries, however, the great families of this second aristocracy gradually faded in importance, merging in a much broader class, commonly called the "gentry." The "gentry," like the old aristocracy, was in large part a landowning class, but, as we shall see, it was very different in other ways.

With the decline of the old aristocracy came the real triumph of the bureaucratic system. Or, to put it the other way, with the appearance of the fully developed examination system in the T'ang, the decline of aristocratic society commenced. Until the seventh century the organized bureaucracy, itself drawn largely from a hereditary aristocracy, had been used to buttress the rule of a military empire of aristocratic traditions. In post-T'ang times, Chinese or "barbarian" warriors continued to found dynasties by force of arms, but for the most part both government and culture were dominated by bureaucrats who owed their position more to their own talents than to birth. This meant the acceptance of a basically egalitarian ideal. The concept that leadership should be in the hands of the man of moral and intellectual superiority, whatever his origin, had always been implicit in Confucianism, but it did not really triumph in Chinese society until the late T'ang and the Sung.

Another profound change that took place during this era was the shift in the geographical center of Chinese civilization from the dry lands of North China to the better watered and richer Yangtze Valley and the regions to the south of it. In classic times the North had been the only part of China that had counted, and up until the early T'ang period the government remained largely in the hands of men from the North. Since the Sung, however, the South Chinese, and particularly men from the lower Yangtze Valley, have played an often dominant role. This change reflected the earlier shift of the economic heart of China from the North to the South. The T'ang was the last dynasty to have its capital in the Wei Valley in the northwest, later Chinese capitals being all to the east, either out on the North China Plain or south of the lower stretches of the Yangtze.

Still another significant change was the shift in the cultural center of gravity from rural China to the cities. The new gentry class did not necessarily live on its agricultural holdings and lead a rural type of life, but usually joined the officials and merchants in the cities and towns. Chinese society did not become urbanized in the sense that we apply this term to the nineteenth century, but it was very much more citified than in previous periods and began to display certain cultural traits that we associate with the urbanization of Western society during recent centuries.

The various developments outlined above naturally had an influence on the higher culture. There was a marked falling off in work of Buddhist inspiration — a pronounced secularization of both artistic endeavor and scholarship. The growing introspection of Chinese culture was revealed in a strong reaffirmation of artistic, literary, and scholarly traditions from earlier times. In fact, the great achievements of this period were for the most part a flowering of tendencies already inherent in the culture, and they set a pattern from which Chinese of later ages usually departed only in detail. Urbanization was accompanied by a growing sophistication of art, literature, and scholarship and by a great expansion in scope and sheer quantity of production. There was, indeed, such an outburst of activity in these fields between the eighth and thirteenth centuries that this period above all others deserves to be called the golden age of Chinese culture.

Naturally, the great changes briefly outlined above took place slowly, and some of them had only just begun by the late T'ang. There was a strong continuity of cultural development, however, between the latter part of the T'ang and the Sung, and it would be difficult to draw as valid a line of cultural demarcation anywhere between the eighth and thirteenth centuries as can be drawn between the seventh and eighth centuries. But before examining in more detail the chief cultural and institutional features of this period, we shall first look at its major political developments.

COLLAPSE AND REFORM IN THE
MIDDLE T'ANG

Hsüan Tsung's long reign (712–756) was perhaps the key period in the transition from ancient to early modern China. It was also, and more obviously, the crucial turning point in the dynastic cycle, which revolved as inexorably during the T'ang as in the Han. In fact, if one looks only at the T'ang period itself, it is this pattern that stands out clearly in Hsüan Tsung's reign, while the great cultural transition taking place beneath the surface phenomena of the dynastic cycle can be discerned only by looking at a broader segment of history.

Under Hsüan Tsung the dynasty reached its second great peak. In wealth, grandeur, and cultural brilliance his reign far outshone that of T'ai Tsung a century earlier. The population had increased considerably, as had also the wealth of the empire. But the costs of maintaining the imperial family and the government had multiplied many times over, and income had by no means kept pace. The whole system of government was operating less smoothly and was beginning to break down in such vital sectors as taxation and military defense.

The tendency to increase government expenditures, which was perhaps the most inevitable aspect of the dynastic cycle, has been described in an earlier chapter. The breakdown of the tax system, too, was not unlike that of Han times. The use of the "equal field" system slowed the process but could not stop it.

The Breakdown of the Tax and Military Systems. The rapid growth of population under the T'ang made it quite impossible to redistribute the land periodically and assign 100 *mou* to each peasant family. Before the end of the seventh century most agricultural lands had become classified as permanent holdings, and a large proportion of the best lands had passed, through legal or illegal means, into estates owned by the wealthier classes. Thus the main tax burden fell on peasants whose individual holdings were smaller than before and who collectively farmed a smaller proportion of China's agricultural land than had their ancestors. But per capita taxes in produce and labor, the major part of the tax burden, remained as high as when the peasants had had a larger agricultural base on which to carry them. The burden often became unbearable, forcing peasants to flee their farms or transfer their holdings through shady deals to the estate of some wealthy man, where the 50 per cent of produce paid in rent (60 per cent if tools as well as land were rented from the owner) would actually be less oppressive than the government taxes. But for peasant families to drop in this way from the tax registers, though a personal solution of the problem, only aggravated the situation for the remaining free peasants and the government treasury.

As the "equal field" system collapsed, the yield from the per capita tax system associated with it declined drastically, and the government had to find substitute forms of income. Efforts during Hsüan Tsung's reign to force peasants back onto the tax registers, while partially successful, did not basically alter the situation. Some of the estates being formed at this time were government-owned and therefore helped to support the dynasty. Innovations in the tax system were a more important source of new income. The very light land tax, which applied to the estates as well as to peasant holdings, had originally been designed merely to provide emergency supplies in case of famine. It was now gradually increased and made a regular part of the government income. Various new and extraordinary land taxes and commercial taxes were also devised, and a tax on all households, which were divided into nine categories according to wealth, was developed into an important fiscal support of the state.

The collapse of the original tax structure naturally involved the decline of *corvée* labor and the militia system, which had both been part of it. The militia had provided a cheap, loyal army that was eager to defend its native soil, but the military burden had fallen with disproportionate weight on the peasants of North China, because both the capital and the frontiers that needed defense were in this region. Richer taxpayers commonly escaped service by hiring substitutes. The poorer peasants, on whom the main burden fell, were least able to support themselves during their terms of military service and were the most prone to desert, since they had least to defend.

During the first half of the eighth century the whole *corvée* and militia systems degenerated rapidly. Bit by bit, *corvée* labor was eliminated in the key function of transportation of tax grain up the Grand Canal to the capital. Professional military men also gradually replaced the militia in certain important units. By 723, some 120,000 mercenaries had taken the place of the militia in the capital guards, and professionals had also begun to replace the militia in the frontier armies. Although both the *corvée* and militia systems were to continue in use in various forms until contemporary times, never again did the government rest so heavily on them as before the eighth century.

While these changes in part represented an institutional advance connected with a developing money economy, they entailed some grave new difficulties. Professional soldiers, who were commonly recruited from the dregs of society or from "barbarian" tribes, were less ardent defenders of the Middle Kingdom than the militia, who had farms to protect. Moreover, because of their long terms of service they frequently developed a primary loyalty to their generals rather than to the dynasty. The partial substitution of paid workers and mercenaries for *corvée* laborers and militia also increased the government's need for tax income and hence for new forms of revenue.

Factional Struggles and Regional Commanders. Another problem in Hsüan Tsung's reign was a growing factional struggle for power at court between the bureaucracy and the old T'ang aristocracy from northwest China. A century of successful use of the examination system had created a true merit bureaucracy drawn from the whole country, and for the first time in history this group was seriously challenging the aristocracy for leadership in government. The bureaucracy had become particularly powerful under the patronage of the Empress Wu, who, as an outsider herself, had relied more heavily on these new men than on the aristocrats.

A complicating factor was the growing rivalry between provincial military leaders and the central government. During the seventh century various types of imperial intendants had been dispatched periodically from the capital to the provinces, and by the early years of Hsüan Tsung's reign one category of these intendants, the Regional Commanders (*Chieh-tu-shih*), had become permanent officials controlling the military and civil affairs of large border regions. There were eight Regional Commanderies stretching across the northern frontiers from the sea near Peking to Central Asia and two others in Szechwan and the Canton area.

The Regional Commanders themselves, as professional military men, were frequently of foreign origin, as were a large part of the mercenaries they commanded, while the more distant defenses of the empire were entirely in the hands of "barbarian" allies. Once again the defeated "barbarian" was falling military heir to the empire that had conquered him.

These were the causal elements in the sudden collapse of the T'ang that brought Hsüan Tsung's brilliant reign to a tragic end. Government finances depended largely upon improvisations; dangerous administrative cracks were appearing between the central government and the border areas and within the central government itself; and the defenses of the empire depended to a large extent on non-Chinese generals and soldiers.

Defeat Abroad and Revolt at Home. One obvious turning point in the fortunes of the T'ang came in 751. In that year the Chinese armies were defeated by the Thai state of Nan-chao in Yunnan and thereafter remained on the defensive even in the southwest. In 751 also the

Arabs defeated Kao Hsien-chih, the Korean general of the T'ang, at Talas, west of the great mountain system of Central Asia. This encounter, although fought in an area remote from the centers of Chinese and Arab power, was one of the most fateful battles of history. It presaged the collapse of Chinese control over Central Asia, which took place four years later during the great revolt that swept China. Thus it marked the beginning of five centuries of steady military decline for the Chinese Empire and also the beginning of the Arab conquest of Central Asia. Soon the area was permanently converted to Islam, and at much the same time the Turkish language began to replace the Indo-European tongues of the oasis states of the Tarim Basin. In other words the Buddhist and Indo-European culture of Central Asia, which had played so important a role in the introduction of the Indian religion to China, began to disappear from history.

The internal collapse of the T'ang was not long delayed. The final disaster was connected with a dramatic personal story which traditional Chinese historians have interpreted as the basic cause of the debacle. In 745 the sexagenarian Hsüan Tsung took as his favorite the beautiful young consort of one of his sons. This was the infamous Yang Kuei-fei ("Consort" Yang), under whose influence Hsüan Tsung is said to have given himself over to unseemly frivolities.

Both the emperor and Yang Kuei-fei were much taken by a boisterous, fat young general of "barbarian" origin, named An Lu-shan. Yang Kuei-fei even adopted him as her legal son and was rumored to have made him her lover. Under such powerful patronage, An Lu-shan came to control almost 200,000 troops as the head of the three Regional Commanderies along the northeastern frontiers. His ambitions eventually led him into conflict with Yang Kuei-fei's brother over control of the central government, and in 755 he revolted. He easily captured Loyang, which was considered the Eastern Capital, and then Ch'ang-an itself. Hsüan Tsung fled to Szechwan, but on the way his discontented soldiers forced him to let Yang Kuei-fei and her brother be executed, and the heartbroken emperor abdicated in favor of one of his sons. This pathetic story of imperial romance, with its contrast of youth and age and conflict of love and duty, became one of the most celebrated incidents in Chinese history and a favorite subject for poets and writers.

An Lu-shan was killed by his own son in 757. His successor as the leader of the rebellion, another "barbarian" general named Shih Ssu-ming, suffered the same fate. The new T'ang emperor was put back on the throne with the aid of the Uighurs and other "barbarian" troops, including even a body of Arabs, and peace was finally restored in 763.

The Weakness of the T'ang After An Lu-shan. The earlier grandeur of the T'ang was never again recaptured. The rebellion had been a serious blow to centralized government, as was reflected in the drop of the official census figures from 52,880,488 in 754 to a mere 16,900,000 in 764. Moreover, the dynasty thereafter remained entirely dependent on foreign troops and never again exercised any real power outside of China proper. The Uighurs continued to dominate much of Central Asia, until they were supplanted around 840 by the Kirghiz. The Tibetans, until their internal dissensions in the middle of the ninth century, kept raiding China from the west, even entering Ch'ang-an itself briefly in 763.

After An Lu-shan's revolt the central government was never again able to control even the provinces of China proper so closely as in earlier days. The system of Regional Commanderies was extended to the whole country. Gradually the Regional Commanders turned their areas into personal satrapies, and in some cases even succeeded in making their positions hereditary. Occasionally, spurred by their own ambitions or incensed at the efforts of the central government to reassert its authority, they revolted against it. The most serious such outbreak occurred in northeast China between 781 and 786.

At court, too, there was increasing friction between factions within the bureaucracy and between the bureaucrats and the eunuchs. As generals of the capital guard armies, powerful eunuchs commonly made emperors into their virtual puppets and contended openly with the bureaucrats for control of the central organs of government.

Because of such conditions, the second half of the T'ang is often portrayed as a time of little centralized authority and of general political and economic confusion. But such matters are always relative. During his stay in China between 838 and 847 the Japanese diarist Ennin described a prosperous and well-ordered society with a degree of bureaucratic meticulousness and centralized control that probably was not matched in other parts of the world until much later times. Despite Tibetan inroads and occasional revolts, China enjoyed another full century of comparative peace, particularly in the prosperous South, where no major disturbances occurred during this period.

Administrative Reforms: the Double Tax. One fundamental reason for this relative peace and stability was the new financial basis of government developed during the restoration that followed An Lu-shan's revolt. The minister Liu Yen (715–780) is credited with restoring and improving the indispensable operation of transporting grain from the Yangtze Valley to the capital, completely replacing *corvée* labor by the services of professional transport workers and improving the water route and the boats used on it. Another statesman, Yang Yen (727–781), carried out an even more important reform. In 780 he consolidated the various land, personal, and household taxes into the so-called Double

Tax, which was levied in the sixth and eleventh months of each year on land areas, regardless of ownership, rather than on the peasants as individuals.

This reform capped an epoch-making transition which had been a century under way. Thenceforth in Chinese history land areas rather than individuals remained the basic units of agricultural taxation, and the collecting of taxes became a much simpler problem. Thenceforth also the central government could be less concerned about the development of private holdings, for such holdings no longer represented a menace to the financial underpinnings of the state. In fact, the whole landholding system of China changed. Big landowners no longer were powerful aristocrats who controlled virtually tax-free estates but simply landlords whose tenant-operated farms paid their share of taxes. This was, in other words, the beginning of the widespread landlordism that was to characterize China's rural economy from then until the twentieth century.

The revenues from the Double Tax, as well as those from the increased taxes levied on wealth and on commercial transactions, were all divided among the central government, the local governments, and the Regional Commanders, giving each a reasonably adequate income. The old Han policy of monopolies and licensing systems was also revived and, particularly in the case of salt, tea, and liquor, these monopolies became an important source of revenue.

The T'ang dynasty thus gradually acquired a much wider and more diversified fiscal basis than earlier Chinese governments had enjoyed. This and its superior administration, based on the examination system, might be coupled as the two major reasons why the T'ang and the great dynasties that followed it averaged three centuries in duration, as compared with the two centuries of the Earlier and the Later Han.

THE POLITICAL TRANSITION FROM THE
T'ANG TO THE SUNG

Although given a new start, after An Lu-shan's revolt, in a dynastic "restoration" which has been traditionally ranked with that of Kuang Wu Ti of the Later Han, the T'ang government slowly deteriorated again. Population growth and declining administrative efficiency led to increasing numbers of impoverished people, so that, consequently, unfavorable weather conditions easily produced famine and widespread unrest. The growing independence of the Regional Commanders also spelled the inevitable ruin of centralized rule.

The breakup started with great uprisings in the North China Plain in 874. One of the rebel leaders, Huang Ch'ao, who was a product of the new age in that he was a frustrated would-be bureaucrat, that is, an unsuccessful candidate in the government examinations, achieved prominence first by defying the government salt monopoly. He pushed south, sacking the rich commercial city of Canton in 879. Then he turned north and in 880 captured Ch'ang-an, forcing the emperor to flee, as had Hsüan Tsung, to Szechwan. Not until 884 was the revolt finally suppressed by Li K'o-yung, a general of Turkish origin.

As usual, the popular uprisings fell short of destroying the dynasty, but the latter's defenders completed the task. All semblance of control over the Regional Commanders had been lost during the ten-year revolt, and the stronger of them now became in effect independent kings in their own domains. Meanwhile, a contest over the control of North China had broken out between Li K'o-yung and Chu Wen (also called Chu Ch'üan-chung), a lieutenant of Huang Ch'ao who had come to terms with the government. Eventually Chu Wen emerged victorious, set up a puppet emperor in 904, and then usurped the throne in 907, replacing the T'ang with his own Later Liang dynasty.

The Five Dynasties and the Ten Kingdoms. The following fifty-three years are called the period of the Five Dynasties (*Wu-tai*) and the Ten Kingdoms. These names are derived from the five would-be dynasties that followed one another in quick succession in the capital region of North China and the ten other regimes, largely in the South, which maintained themselves through all or part of this period.

The political breakup was more complete and the military situation more confused than at the end of the Han, but there was no comparable challenge to the continuity of Chinese civilization. In fact, there was no cultural break at all. Some of the kingdoms in the South were relatively stable and saw rapid economic and cultural growth. Even North China, though economically disrupted by constant wars, suffered only minor "barbarian" incursions.

The most significant fact about the Five Dynasties period is that it lasted only a little over a half century, in contrast to the three and a half centuries of political division during the Six Dynasties period. Perhaps the traditions and techniques of centralized rule had become so much stronger by the tenth century that a long multiple division of the country was no longer possible. In any case, it should be noted that China was never again divided into a number of competing political units for even so long as half a century. Foreign conquest was to divide it between a purely Chinese South and a "barbarian"-ruled North, but not until the collapse of the old system in the early twentieth century was the empire again broken up into a number of independent or autonomous units, and this recent period of division was even shorter than that of the tenth century. In other words, China since the T'ang has proved to be an almost indestructible political unit.

The Ten Kingdoms, some of which called their rulers kings and others emperors, were actually more important than the Five Dynasties, because they were more permanent. For their dynastic titles they revived local or historical names. In the lower Yangtze there was at first a Wu dynasty (902–937), with its capital at Yang-chou, and then a Southern T'ang (937–975), centered at Nanking. In the middle

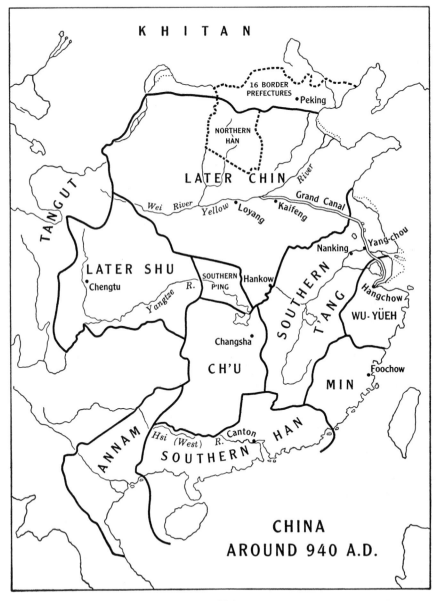

Yangtze was a small state called Ching-nan or Southern P'ing (907–963), and south of it in Hunan a Ch'u dynasty (927–951), with its capital at Changsha. In Szechwan there was an Earlier Shu (907–925) and a Later Shu (934–965), both with their capitals at Chengtu. Along the south coast was Wu-yüeh (907–978) at Hangchow in Chekiang, Min (909–944) at Foochow in Fukien, and a Southern Han (907–971) in Kwangtung and Kwangsi, with its capital at Canton. Finally there was a Northern Han (951–979) in northern Shansi.

"Barbarian" Encroachments. The five successive northern "dynasties," which had their principal capitals at Loyang and at Kaifeng to the east, were all ephemeral. Chu Wen's Later Liang was the longest-lived, but it lasted only sixteen years. Moreover, it never succeeded in subduing the Turkish general Li K'o-yung, who maintained his independence in Shansi. Chu Wen was murdered by his own son, and the dynasty was extinguished in 923 by Li K'o-yung's son, who then set up his Later T'ang dynasty. After thirteen years of fairly successful rule, this regime in turn was replaced by the Later Chin, founded by Shih Ching-t'ang, another general of Turkish origin, who was the emperor's son-in-law.

Shih Ching-t'ang won the throne in 936 with the aid of a semi-agricultural, semi-nomadic Mongol people known as the Khitan (Ch'i-tan in Chinese). Recently risen to power in the Liao River Valley in South Manchuria, they had extended their sway over Inner and much of Outer Mongolia and in 926 had destroyed the Sinicized Tungusic state of P'o-hai to the east. Now, as a reward for their aid, the new ruler of North China gave them, in addition to tribute, sixteen border prefectures around Peking in northern Hopei and around Ta-t'ung in northern Shansi. The Khitan made Peking their southern capital, thus starting its history as a capital city. (Incidentally, Khitan, in another form, Khitai, is the origin of Cathay, the name for North China in medieval Europe, and of Kitai, the Russian name for China.)

When Shih Ching-t'ang's successor stopped his tribute to the Khitan, they destroyed the Later Chin dynasty in 946 and, under the dynastic name of Liao, claimed the Chinese throne for themselves. Though the Khitan were able to retain only a small part of North China as the southern component of their dual Sino-"barbarian" kingdom, this holding was enough to give their Liao dynasty a place in the Chinese dynastic annals, and we shall discuss it more fully in the next chapter.

After the Khitan had been forced back to their northern border region, another North Chinese general of Turkish origin took the throne in 947. His Later Han dynasty lasted only four years before still another general usurped the throne, founding the Later Chou. The second ruler of this line was an able soldier and efficient administrator. To strengthen his financial position he carried out a great persecution of

Buddhism, reportedly destroying more than 30,000 monasteries and shrines and confiscating their property. He also started to reunify China, expanding his territories considerably, but he died prematurely, leaving a small child on the throne.

The Founding of the Sung. Another usurpation inevitably took place. Chao K'uang-yin, a leading general of Chinese origin, was dispatched in 960 to stop a new Khitan incursion but he seized the throne instead. Unlike his predecessors, he succeeded in establishing his dynasty on a more permanent basis. Chao K'uang-yin is famed in history as T'ai Tsu ("Grand Progenitor") of the Sung dynasty, which lasted for more than three centuries, from 960 to 1279.

After five unsuccessful attempts, a stable government had at last been recreated in the North, and China was soon reunited. The reconquest of the South was relatively easy. Before T'ai Tsu died in 976 he had either subjugated by force of arms or overawed into submission all the other states except the Liao dynasty on the northern border, Wu-yüeh in Chekiang, and the Northern Han in Shansi. The last two were annexed in 978 and 979 by his brother and successor, T'ai Tsung ("Grand Ancestor," 976–997).

SUNG GOVERNMENT

T'ai Tsu's success in establishing a lasting dynasty can be attributed in part to his relatively long reign of sixteen years, twice the length of any reign during the Five Dynasties. He also passed on his throne, possibly against his own will, to an adult brother rather than to an infant son. A still more important reason for his success was the determination with which he tackled the gravest political problem of the day — the almost unrestricted power of local military commanders.

T'ai Tsu managed to transfer his own leading generals to minor posts or to retire them with suitable rewards, and in the provinces he limited the Regional Commanders to a single prefecture and, as they died or retired, replaced them with civil officials from the central bureaucracy. He also followed a policy of transferring the best military units to the capital armies, replacing them in the provinces with inferior soldiers, and he placed all military forces directly under the central government. In these various ways he assured the central government of preponderant military power and eliminated the warlordism that had destroyed the T'ang and kept China unstable and divided during the Five Dynasties period.

T'ai Tsu's success in carrying out these crucial military reforms without provoking serious revolts was due to his extraordinary administrative ability and his policy of leniency and benevolence toward his former rivals and recalcitrant subordinates. He set a standard of generosity toward his officers, deference to his ministers, and modesty in his own scale of living that approximated the Confucian political ideal and influenced his less able but often equally conscientious successors on the throne.

Military Weakness: the Liao and the Hsi Hsia. The relative weakness of the Sung dynasty in arms was perhaps partially the result of T'ai Tsu's deliberate policy of undermining the provincial military and subordinating the army to the civil government. A more fundamental reason for this condition may have lain in the social and ideological changes of this period.

The Sung, in any case, never achieved the military prowess of the Han and the T'ang. Annam (North Vietnam) was not reincorporated into the empire, and the Sung never controlled any part of Central Asia or the northern steppe. In fact, they even failed to recover the sixteen northern prefectures lost during the Five Dynasties period to the Khitan Liao dynasty. The early hopes of reconquering this area were dampened by a disastrous defeat in 986. After two more decades of indecisive fighting, the Sung in 1004 acknowledged in the Treaty of Shan-yüan the permanent loss of this region and agreed to pay an annual tribute to the Liao.

This settlement brought more than three decades of peace which was broken only by the rise of new "barbarians." Tangut tribes of Tibetans had created a strong state in the Ordos, the Kansu corridor, and adjoining parts of Inner Mongolia. After adopting in 1038 the Chinese dynastic name of Hsia (the Chinese call them the Hsi Hsia or Western Hsia), they started out to conquer China. Eventually they were beaten off and in 1044 they made a peace agreement with the Sung, which included an annual tribute payment for them too. Meanwhile, the Liao, who had taken advantage of the Hsi Hsia invasion to move against the Sung, had been bought off in 1042 by a substantial increase in the tribute they received. This three-way balance of power in North China preserved the peace along the frontier for another eighty years, until it was eventually shattered by the rise of still another "barbarian" people.

The Concentration of Power in the Emperor's Hands. Bridling the powers of the local military leaders was only half of T'ai Tsu's problem. The other side of the coin was the creation of a strong civil government on the ruins of the T'ang administrative system. He and his successors allowed most earlier posts to become purely honorary and built up in their place a new set of administrative offices which were more directly under the personal control of the emperor than the T'ang organs of government had been. For example, two minor offices, close to the throne, which had appeared in the second half of the T'ang,

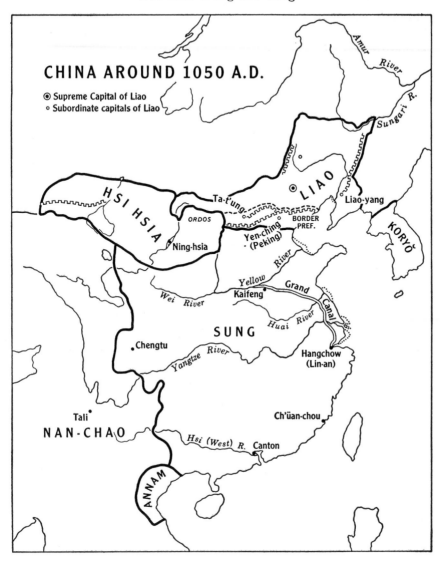

CHINA AROUND 1050 A.D.

◉ Supreme Capital of Liao
○ Subordinate capitals of Liao

were now made into major government agencies and grew to have an important role in later Chinese history. The first was the Board of Academicians (*Hsüeh-shih-yüan*), originally a sort of document-drafting body, which now became a major advisory group to the emperor. The other was the Privy Council (*Shu-mi-yüan*), which during the Sung was one of the three main administrative branches of the government and actually operated as a Bureau of Military Affairs.

This conscious effort to gather all the reins of government into the emperor's own hands made the Chinese government thenceforth more obviously autocratic than it had been before. Some historians, therefore, call the millennium of Chinese history beginning with the Sung the period of "autocracy," as opposed to the preceding "aristocratic" age. The term, however, is misleading. The Chinese empire had always been entirely autocratic in theory and highly autocratic in practice, too, whenever a strong ruler was on the throne. By the tenth century, the rulers had apparently become more conscious of the problem of keeping their absolute power out of the hands of their ministers and more sophisticated in the measures they adopted to accomplish their aim. But the important change was in the nature of the officialdom through which they worked. During the first half of the history of the Chinese Empire, high officials had usually had behind them great independent wealth and aristocratic status and, consequently, they had been more prone to challenge the ruler's claim to despotic power. From Sung times on, the bureaucracy, as we shall see, was largely the product of the examination system and thus lacked the independent wealth and status with which to challenge the emperor's absolutist tendencies. The governments of both epochs were basically "autocratic," and if the first is also to be called "aristocratic" the second might, in contrast, be called "bureaucratic."

The Organs of Government. The principal policy-making body under the emperor in the Sung period was a sort of informal cabinet made up of a group of five to nine councilors. The Chief Councilors, from one to three in number, were known as *Tsai-hsiang,* but had none of the independent powers of the *Tsai-hsiang* of the T'ang, who had been virtual prime ministers.

The chief administrative organs of the government during the early Sung period were the Secretariat-Chancellery (*Chung-shu Men-hsia*), the Privy Council (or Bureau of Military Affairs, *Shu-mi-yüan*), and the Finance Commission (*San-ssu*). The Chief Councilors were also the heads of the Secretariat-Chancellery, and the other councilors were high officials in it and in the Privy Council. Under the Secretariat-Chancellery was a proliferation of ministries, courts, and directorates, similar to those under the Secretariat of State Affairs of the T'ang.

The Finance Commission supervised the treasury, the accounts, taxes, the registration of land and population, and the monopolies. Through it, the central government, in sharp contrast to T'ang practice, kept close and direct control over the entire tax yield of the empire. Because of these improvements in financial control, and also because of general economic growth, the government's income in the early eleventh century was three times that of the T'ang at its height, and a huge surplus was soon built up.

A Board of Censors criticized policy, transmitted complaints, and in time developed an elaborate system for checking on all the operations of government. It shared some of these regulatory functions with the Bureau of Policy Criticism (*Chien-yüan*) and other similar bodies.

The administration of the whole empire during the Sung was more thoroughly centralized at the capital than ever before in Chinese history. The capital itself was Kaifeng, as during the latter part of the Five Dynasties. Although poorly situated for defense, because it was out on the North China Plain, Kaifeng had a strategic economic location at the head of the Grand Canal system just before the Canal joined the Yellow River. Thus, while still in the North, which was probably necessary for the defense of the empire, Kaifeng was almost 300 miles closer than Ch'ang-an to the rich rice-producing areas of the lower Yangtze. More important, its location eliminated the difficult Yellow River stretches of the earlier transport system between the South and the capital.

The Sung continued unchanged the T'ang system of prefectures and subprefectures but increased the number of provinces or "circuits" (called at first *tao* and later *lu*, literally meaning "road" or "route"). These "circuits" had no chief officer but four categories of intendants: fiscal, judicial, military, and one which was concerned with commodity storage and transport. This group of intendants oversaw, but did not control, the work of the local officials in their respective fields.

The Civil Service. The chief strength of the Sung government was its civil service. This in turn depended in large part on the examination system, which had been so greatly developed during the T'ang and now reached its ultimate stage of perfection. The high standards of government service at this time are indicated by the practice of prohibiting close business contact among officials related by blood or marriage and by the rule barring relatives of empresses and other imperial consorts from holding any of the higher positions.

The civil service was the apex of a great officialdom which also included military officers, a clerical service, and various types of irregular officials. The civil service was built up partly by the transfer of able men from the other services, by permitting high officials to nominate sons or relatives for appointment, and even through the sale of offices, whereby some members of the merchant class were permitted to enter the government. By far the most important source of civil servants, however, was the examination system. Between 997 and 1124 an average of well over 200 men a year entered the civil service through the ordinary examinations, constituting probably a slight majority of the 12,000 or more civil officials of this category. Since men who had passed these examinations were probably more capable and certainly enjoyed far more prestige than the other civil servants, they virtually monopolized all the higher posts in the bureaucracy. In fact, throughout the Sung dynasty a very high proportion of the leading officials were also famous scholars and men of letters who had first distinguished themselves in the official examinations.

The Examination System. As during the T'ang, there were various categories of examinations in such fields as law, history, rituals, and classics, as well as the *chin-shih* degree in letters. Since only the last of these put much emphasis on originality and skill in reasoning and composition rather than on mere memory, it was much more esteemed than the other degrees and all but eclipsed them by the late eleventh century.

The examinations were at first administered sporadically, but after 1065 they were held regularly every three years. There were three successive levels of examinations. First came the examinations held by the individual prefectures or government schools. Scholars who passed these, reportedly varying between one and ten per cent of the candidates, went on to an examination given by the central government at the capital. About ten per cent of these were passed and were then subjected to a "palace examination," which rejected a few more and ranked the remaining successful candidates. Initial appointment and future promotion depended to a large extent upon the rank achieved in this final examination, and men who were listed at the top frequently reached the highest levels of government within a few years.

Unsuccessful candidates usually took the examinations time after time. As a result, those who passed could range in age from their late teens to the seventies, though they probably averaged around thirty-

EXAMINATION CELLS

Drawing of the examination cells (no longer in existence) at Nanking, based on nineteenth-century photographs. The inset shows individual cells in which the examinees were isolated.

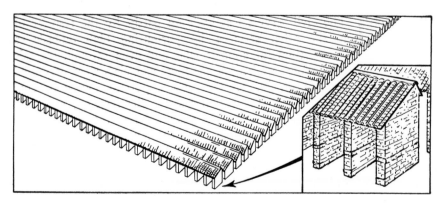

five. To reward the perseverance of those who had failed repeatedly, and possibly to prevent disappointed candidates from becoming subversives like the T'ang rebel Huang Ch'ao, older men (those past fifty or sixty) who had failed repeatedly (on an average, six times, though in some cases fifteen times) were taken into the civil service through special facilitated examinations.

Promotion of officials depended on several factors — the length of their tenure of office, a system of merit ratings, special examinations for certain specific assignments, a candidate's rank in the original examinations, and the sponsorship of higher officials. According to the sponsorship system, the higher officials in the prefectures and "circuits" and some of the capital officials had the duty of nominating for promotion promising junior officials who might otherwise be overlooked. The sponsor was not supposed to recommend anyone related to himself in any way, and he was responsible for his protégé to the extent of being punished if the latter subsequently committed an offense.

The civil service and examination systems succeeded in bringing a large measure of real talent into government service. They also seem to have kept men of ability out of subversive activities by opening a more attractive door to them, for the Sung dynasty was relatively free of serious rebellions. The degree to which the examination system discovered new talent is suggested by the lists of successful candidates in 1148 and 1256, which reveal that more than half of the men came from families with no record of civil service status in the paternal line during the three preceding generations.

Naturally, the examination system drew into government service only men who were either from relatively prosperous families which could afford to educate their sons, or from poorer families with a scholarly tradition. No one at the time felt this to be an undesirably limiting feature of the system, but there was criticism of the preponderance of successful candidates from the capital and the lower Yangtze region, both of which enjoyed greater wealth and, therefore, better educational facilities than the rest of the country.

DECLINE AND REFORM IN THE MIDDLE SUNG

The Sung had devised so stable a political system that Chao K'uang-yin's usurpation was to prove to be the last in Chinese history. In early periods emperors had repeatedly been robbed of the throne by their great generals, empresses, or civil officials. After 960 this never happened again. Dynasties continued to be snuffed out by foreign conquest or by popular revolution, and members of the imperial family stole the throne from one another, but no subject ever again succeeded in usurping the imperial prerogative.

The early Sung was also more prosperous than any previous dynasty had ever been. The usual administrative decline and financial difficulties of the old dynastic cycle, however, had reappeared by the time the Sung had completed a century of rule. Government income had risen rapidly during the first six decades of the Sung to a high point in 1021 of 150,850,000 units, each roughly equivalent in value to a string of 1000 cash, but thereafter receipts gradually dropped off, until by 1065 government income had fallen, by nearly a quarter, to 116,138,405 units.

Population Growth and the Declining Tax Yield. One underlying cause for this decline may have been the increase in population. In the early Sung the number of registered households was lower than half of what it had been just before An Lu-shan's revolt, but in the early eleventh century it climbed back to this high-water mark of the T'ang and by the early twelfth century had more than doubled it. Although these figures cannot be accepted at full face value, they are indicative of general trends.

The dynamics of the relationship between population and government income are not entirely clear. Population growth in a rapidly expanding economy was obviously beneficial to the administration, but beyond a certain point it does not seem to have been accompanied by a corresponding growth in production. Thus, the more mouths there were to be fed, the less surplus remained for the tax collector to harvest for the treasury. In other words, population growth beyond this certain point may have contributed to a decrease rather than an increase of government revenue.

Although taxes had been levied since the middle T'ang primarily by land areas rather than on a per capita basis, the burden still fell most heavily on the small peasant, who had the least financial resources. Population increases meant smaller farms and overworked soil, with the result that a declining per capita production left less surplus above minimal living needs for the peasant to devote to tax payments. As a consequence, more and more small peasants were reduced to pauperism or were driven into tenancy on the holdings of the landlord class. As the number and wealth of the landlord families increased, they naturally consumed a greater proportion of national production. While their holdings theoretically were as subject to taxation as peasant farms, the large landlords, because of their government connections and privileged position, frequently escaped some of the burden, and consequently the increase of their holdings was accompanied by some decline in government revenue.

Increasing Expenditures. Government expenditures, however, could not be tailored to fit declining receipts. The great surpluses of the early eleventh century had all been used up by the middle of the century. In the single year of 1065 the government ran a deficit of about 15,000,000 units.

The financial difficulties of the Sung have been attributed by some to the annual tribute paid the Liao and the Hsi Hsia, but this was only a small part of the problem. The original tribute agreed upon with the Liao in 1004 had been only 300,000 units. This was increased in 1042, to 500,000 units, and two years later 255,000 units were added for the Hsi Hsia. The total of 755,000 was perhaps worth more than the figures indicate, because it included a high proportion of silk and silver units, which were actually more valuable than grain or cash units, but, at the most, these tribute payments never amounted to so much as two per cent of Sung revenues.

A more important reason for the Sung deficits was the phenomenal increase in military expenditures. The relatively cheap militia system of the early T'ang had long since been abandoned as the chief military support of the empire, and T'ai Tsu, in order to insure domestic peace, had destroyed the comparatively efficient system of local armies under Regional Commanders. Instead, he had chosen to concentrate military power in great professional armies centered in the capital. These mercenaries were recruited largely from among the paupers and, consequently, were not very good fighting men. The Chinese armies were also handicapped by the weakness of their cavalry, because, holding none of the steppe lands, the Sung Empire was poor in horses. Although new techniques, such as the use of explosives, gave the Chinese some advantages, they sought to make up for their lack of military quality primarily by the size of their armies, constantly increasing the number of troops and expanding military expenditures. The number of men recorded as under arms shot up from 378,000 in 976 to 1,259,000 by 1041. Military expenses came to absorb about 80 per cent of total government expenditures.

Another reason for soaring expenses was the steady increase in general administrative costs and the expansion of the civil bureaucracy. In the early years of the dynasty there had been a dearth of experienced officials, but by the middle of the eleventh century the civil service was overstaffed. Because of the financial difficulties of the government, rates of pay were allowed to become inadequate, which hurt the morale of the bureaucracy and encouraged the misuse of office.

Bureaucratic Factionalism. These conditions may have stimulated the growth of disruptive factionalism within the bureaucracy. In a now thoroughly bureaucratized state, there were no longer the crude rivalries that had wrecked earlier dynasties, such as the fights between the emperors and the relatives of their consorts, between scholar-officials and eunuchs, or between civil officials at the capital and military commanders in the provinces. The rivalries were now largely within the bureaucracy itself, at first between groups from different parts of China and then between advocates of different policies.

The bitterness of policy disputes became accentuated as the economic and military situation worsened. There grew up on the one side the traditionalists, who supported the system of government as it had developed over the past century and, confident in the ultimate efficacy of moral example, saw no reason for drastic reforms. In opposition stood the innovators or reformers, who believed that the evident ills of the time called for positive action.

The Reforms of Wang An-shih. In 1069 the new young emperor, Shen Tsung ("Inspired Ancestor," 1067–1085), appointed as Chief Councilor the able but opinionated reformer Wang An-shih (1021–1086). Wang immediately embarked on a series of sweeping reforms to bolster the government's finances and strengthen its armies. He took over the control of financial policy from the Finance Commission and plunged the government into economic manipulations of a sort that had not been tried for several centuries. He had the government buy the specialized products of one area for sale in other regions, thereby facilitating the exchange of goods, helping to stabilize prices, and making a profit for the government. He instituted government loans to peasants at 20 per cent, a very low rate for the time, thereby helping poorer farmers to maintain themselves and pay their taxes and diverting the profits of moneylending from private usurers to the treasury. He had new land surveys made to eliminate old inequalities and established a graduated scale of land taxes according to the productive capacity of the soil. He commuted the remaining *corvée* services, which fell most heavily on the poor peasants, into taxes, which fell more heavily on the rich. He also had all personal wealth assessed, attempted to regulate prices, extended relatively cheap credit to small enterprisers through government pawnshops, and carried out needed water-control undertakings.

On the military side, Wang An-shih revived under the name of *pao-chia* the old collective-guarantee methods of the "three chiefs" system of the Six Dynasties period, and decreed that the various units under this system were to provide at their own expense certain quotas of trained and armed militia. To built up a cavalry, he had horses procured at government expense and assigned to the peasant families of North China, in return for which one member of each family was to serve with his horse in cavalry militia in time of need.

Like Wang Mang in Han times, Wang An-shih claimed the support of the classics for his reforms, selecting the *Rituals of Chou* and some of the other texts championed by Wang Mang as his specific inspiration. He also applied his ideas to education and the examination system. He greatly expanded the number of government schools to compete with the endowed private academies (*shu-yüan*) that dominated education at this time, and he insisted that the government examinations should be less strictly literary tests and should be directed more toward practical problems of policy and administration.

Wang An-shih, again like Wang Mang, has been both castigated and praised as a Socialist, but he was no more motivated by concepts of social equality than was his famous predecessor. Some of his reforms, such as the graduated land tax, cheap credit systems, and the complete abandonment of the *corvée*, obviously were steps forward economically and administratively. Other measures, such as price regulating, government commodity controls, and the collective-guarantee and militia systems, were merely revivals of earlier institutions. Still other reforms, such as his cavalry militia, were no more than improvisations. Although his reforms appear for the most part to have been economically favorable to the peasantry and poorer classes and injurious to the interests of the bigger landowners, large merchants, and moneylenders, they were not dictated by ideology but were designed merely to solve specific current problems.

The reforms naturally roused the determined opposition of the groups they hurt — large landowners, big merchants and moneylenders. The bulk of the bureaucracy, drawn as it was from the landowning classes, was also in opposition. Some scholars have seen a distinction between the support given Wang by men who, like himself, came from South China, where a new pattern of relatively small landholdings was developing, and the bitter opposition of men from the North, where the older pattern of large landholdings still prevailed. Whether or not this distinction is a valid one, there can be no doubt that most of the great scholar-statesmen of the day, such as Ssu-ma Kuang, Ou-yang Hsiu, and Su Tung-p'o, were solidly ranged against the innovations. As a consequence, the verdict of history, at least as represented by traditional Chinese historians, has gone against Wang An-shih and his reforms.

This bureaucratic opposition may not have been merely a matter of class interests. It also seems to have reflected the natural administrative inertia of a bureaucratized state — a growing inflexibility which was to characterize the Chinese government from this time on. The entrenched bureaucracy refused to tolerate any sudden change in the system to which it had become accustomed. It also reacted strongly against the way Wang An-shih was concentrating power in his own hands, since his methods threatened the delicate balance of power among bureaucratic offices and cliques that had been built up over the years. Wang An-shih's reforms, though not very revolutionary and often merely a reversion to older practices, stirred up such a whirlwind of intense partisan feeling that they have remained, ever since, a live and sometimes emotional topic of debate in Chinese intellectual circles.

The reforms did not produce the disasters prophesied by Wang An-shih's enemies, but, sabotaged by hostile bureaucrats and mismanaged by supporters who were unprepared to administer the necessary economic controls, they achieved no conspicuous successes. Wang An-shih himself was forced to resign in 1076 because of the violent personal animosities he had stirred up, and after Shen Tsung's death the traditionalists came back to power and reversed the whole program.' For the next four decades, the reformers and traditionalists alternated in power, nullifying through their bitter factional struggles whatever financial and military benefits Wang An-shih might have accomplished.

THE SOUTHERN SUNG

The Conquest of North China by the Chin. The financial and administrative decline of the Sung continued until disaster finally struck in the reign of Hui Tsung ("Excellent Ancestor," 1100–1125). A talented painter and a great patron of the arts, Hui Tsung presided over a brilliant and luxurious court that further strained the dynasty's finances. As might have been expected of an emperor with such a strong artistic bent, he was an ardent Taoist and at times a liberal patron of the Buddhists.

In Hui Tsung's later years the empire was wracked by peasant uprisings, but the chief blow came from outside. Beyond the northern territory held by the Liao, Tungusic tribes known as the Jürched (Ju-chen in Chinese) had gradually risen to power in northeastern Manchuria, in the upper basin of the Sungari near modern Harbin, north of the region where the earlier Tungusic state of P'o-hai had once flourished. In 1114 the Jürched rebelled against the Liao and the next year adopted the Chinese dynastic name of Chin (also spelled Kin), meaning "Golden." The Sung, intent on regaining the sixteen border prefectures lost to the Liao two centuries earlier, unwisely allied themselves with the Chin against the Liao. The Chinese armies, however, met with no success, while the Jürched hordes swept on to the complete destruction of the Liao by 1125. When the Sung showed themselves dissatisfied with their share of the spoils, a mere six prefectures around Peking, the Chin continued south. Hui Tsung, in consternation, abdicated, and his successor attempted to buy the Chin off, but the treasury was empty. In 1126 the Chin captured Kaifeng, the Sung capital, together with Hui Tsung and the new emperor.

The Establishment of the Southern Sung. A son of Hui Tsung, known to history as Kao Tsung ("High Ancestor," 1127–1162), continued the struggle, but Sung rule henceforth was limited to the central and southern parts of China. Consequently, the second half of the dynasty, from 1127 to 1279, is commonly called the Southern Sung, and the period before that from 960 to 1127 is known by contrast as the Northern Sung.

The Chin pursued the Chinese armies across the Yangtze, even capturing the cities of Hangchow and Ningpo in Chekiang, but the many rivers and canals of the South made it unfavorable terrain for the nomad cavalry, and their able emperor died just at this point. For these reasons, they withdrew from the South, though they continued their hold over North China, ruling it for about a decade through two successive Chinese puppets and then incorporating it directly into their empire. In 1153 the Chin moved their capital from Manchuria to Peking (then known as Yen-ching), becoming thereafter an increasingly Sinicized state.

Meanwhile, in 1135 the Southern Sung had established their capital at Hangchow, or Lin-an, as it was then called. For a while they fought desperately to recapture the North under the able general Yo Fei, who has been extolled by modern patriots as a symbol of national resistance to foreign domination. The big landlords of the South, however, favored peace, and a peace party under Ch'in Kuei eventually won out. After executing Yo Fei, this group concluded peace with the Chin in 1141. The treaty established a boundary between the two states, which the Sung agreed not to defend. It also stipulated that the Sung was the vassal of the Chin and should pay an annual tribute of 500,000 units, half in silver and half in silk.

The peace was not always preserved between the Chin and the Sung. An unsuccessful attempt by the Chin to conquer the South led to the reduction of the tribute by 100,000 units in 1165 and the dropping of the Sung's status of outright vassalage. Between 1205 and 1207 a Sung leader, Han T'o-chou, made an even less successful effort to reconquer the North, losing further territory for the Sung and paying for the failure with his own life.

The military and political ills of the later decades of the Northern Sung continued throughout the Southern Sung. The government remained relatively weak in arms and torn by political factionalism. The early struggles within the bureaucracy between the war and peace parties continued in various forms. Han T'o-chou, for example, before embarking on his ill-fated northern campaign, in 1195 carried out a sweeping purge from office of his opponents, including the great philosopher Chu Hsi.

On the surface the position of the Southern Sung in history may seem much like that of the Southern dynasties which followed the Han.

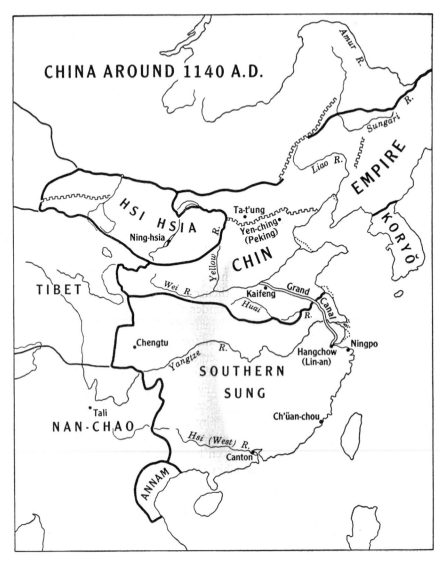

CHINA AROUND 1140 A.D.

Like them, the Southern Sung was driven out of the historic heartland of China. It, too, maintained in the South, in somewhat ineffectual and degenerated form, a political and military system that in happier years had been used to govern the whole country. The comparison, however, is more misleading than helpful. Although the North had been conquered once again by "barbarian" rulers, this time the population and culture of the area were little affected. The admixture of "barbarian" blood was not on a large scale. There was no appreciable break in cultural or economic patterns. Furthermore, the South, far from being a semi-barbarous and relatively underdeveloped area, as it had been at the time of the nomadic invasion of the fourth century, was now the economic center of China and was fast displacing the North as the center of Chinese culture. Under the Southern Sung, the South continued to grow rapidly and to establish beyond question its economic, intellectual, and cultural leadership over the rest of China. In fact, this was economically and culturally one of the greatest periods in all Chinese history.

The Southern Sung, despite its poor showing on the map, was in most ways a wealthier country than the Northern Sung had been. Because of rapid economic expansion, the government could devote much larger sums to military defense than had the Northern Sung at its height, and it supported a far larger bureaucracy. The capital at Hangchow was apparently a grander city than Kaifeng had ever been. Even after its ultimate capture by "barbarians," it struck Marco Polo as being "beyond dispute the finest and noblest" city in the world.

During its century and a half of existence the Southern Sung was, of course, no more impervious to the dynastic cycle than previous dynasties had been. The administrative decline continued throughout the period. Even so, the government showed no sign of collapsing from inner pressures. As in the case of the Northern Sung, it was destroyed only by a powerful foreign enemy, the Mongols, and only after many years of bitter fighting.

THE "COMMERCIAL REVOLUTION"

The political history of China shows a steady military decline from the high point of empire in the eighth century to the eventual conquest of all China by the Mongols in the thirteenth; but, as we have seen, this was nonetheless a period of steady institutional and cultural growth. Underlying this growth was a great expansion and development of the Chinese economy which made it possible for the Southern Sung, though it did not rule all the country, to be far richer in state income than any previous dynasty had been. The economic expansion of these centuries was so great that it might with justification be called, by analogy with the later European experience, the "commercial revolution" of Chinese history. It brought China up to an economic level that was distinctly higher than that of earlier ages and produced an institutional framework that remained in many ways unchanged into the nineteenth century.

One of the reasons for this spectacular development of the economy was probably a general growth of population. Chinese census figures, as we have seen, are generally more indicative of administrative than of demographic conditions, but those for the Sung do suggest a considerable increase of people, and there can be no doubt of the spurt in population that took place in the prosperous South. Certain areas of the North probably suffered a decline in inhabitants, but the statistics seem not far wrong in indicating more than a tripling of the population in South China between the eighth and the eleventh centuries. During the Northern Sung the total Chinese population may already have passed the 100,000,000 mark. Presumably it never fell much below this level subsequently.

Technological Advances. Technological advances, no doubt, were another reason for economic growth. There were no spectacular industrial inventions at this time, but there were many significant technical advances. The perfection of traditional industries produced more and finer silk textiles, lacquer ware, and porcelaneous wares, stimulating the demand for such Chinese manufactures abroad. Another step forward in technology was the development of gunpowder for explosive weapons. By the early eleventh century mines, a type of hand grenade, and other explosive projectiles had been developed, helping to compensate for the weakness of the Sung in cavalry. (See Plate 59.) Medical science made a forward step with the discovery by the fourteenth century of chaulmoogra oil for the treatment of leprosy. The abacus came into use in late Sung times and has remained ever since the prime calculating device for East Asian merchants. The expanding economy was already putting a heavy strain on available mineral resources and the primitive mining technology of the period. Most mines were under government control and were assigned minimum quotas of production.

There seems to have been a considerable increase in agricultural production during these centuries. For example, the introduction from Champa in South Vietnam in the early eleventh century of a quickly maturing strain of rice greatly increased rice yields in the South. Another factor was the large number of major water control projects undertaken during the Sung, which greatly increased the total area devoted to irrigated paddy fields. The rice crop may have been almost doubled between the eleventh and twelfth centuries. The cultivation of tea on hillsides also increased, and around the twelfth century cotton began to be a common crop, adding greatly to the textile resources of the country. A still more important factor was the rapid growth in the volume of trade, which permitted much greater regional specialization in crops and therefore much higher total yields in most areas.

The Development of Private Trade. Although statistics and other proofs of an over-all growth of production in China between the eighth and thirteenth centuries are at best extremely sketchy, there is ample evidence of the great expansion of trade that took place at this time. The early T'ang rulers, with the traditional Chinese scorn and suspicion of commercial activity, had attempted to control and restrict trade. The two great government-operated market places of Ch'ang-an had been symbols of this attitude. During the late T'ang and the Sung, however, trade broke out of this government strait jacket. The supercilious scorn of officials and scholars for merchants remained, but the society as a whole became commercialized as never before. Trade outgrew the restrictions of place and hour imposed by the government in earlier times. It spread beyond the old official market places, until under the Sung the main streets of the cities became lined with shops, as in modern China. The whole *fang* system of self-contained, walled blocks within the capital had largely disappeared by the twelfth century. Great commercial cities also began to appear for the first time — that is, great population centers which, unlike earlier Chinese cities, were not largely centers of political administration but were primarily great emporiums of trade. China was well on its way to becoming the nation of shopkeepers and shrewd businessmen that it has appeared to be, at least from one point of view, in modern times. (See Plate 32.)

Local trade in rural areas continued to be carried on as usual through the barter and exchange of everyday commodities. Above this level the inter-regional exchange of goods had in earlier times been conducted in large part by the government through taxation, the operation of monopolies, and other measures of economic control, with private traders serving mainly as dealers in luxury goods. During the late T'ang and the Sung, however, there was so great a development of private trade that it came to overshadow the government's operations.

There was also a tendency toward greater specialization in commercial activities. Local tax collectors developed the corollary function of wholesalers or brokers, gathering the local surplus of agricultural or manufactured goods for sale to transport merchants. The latter ranged from itinerant peddlers to large-scale, monopolistic operators. An extensive network of inns that developed to accommodate these traveling merchants became the inn system that was to continue with little change until recent times. Individual peddlers sold directly to the consumer, while the large transport merchants disposed of their goods through local brokers to a multitude of individual shops.

The growth of commerce was also accompanied by a proliferation of trade guilds. These originally grew out of the merchant associations which had been grouped by trades in the various streets (*hang*) of the market places of early T'ang times. *Hong*, the Cantonese pronunciation of *hang*, was still the generic name for licensed firms when trade with the West was a *hong* monopoly in Canton in the early nineteenth century.

Each guild was organized under one member, selected as head, who was responsible to the government for the collection of all the members' taxes or the payment of a collective quota in the case of a government monopoly farmed out for a fee to the guild in question. The more important guilds were usually those which transported and sold such basic commodities as grain, salt, tea, or silk or had the banking functions of storing and lending currency. The scale of operation of the larger guilds is indicated by the case of a guild of 100 grain transport merchants in the capital region during the eleventh century which reportedly did an annual business worth 10,000,000 units.

THE GROWTH OF FOREIGN TRADE

The growth in foreign trade that took place during the late T'ang and the Sung is one of the clearest indications of the commercial expansion of the time and presumably was a major stimulant to the whole "commercial revolution." In earlier times foreign trade, such as the silk trade with the Roman Empire, had been conducted mainly by camel caravans traversing Central Asia. This land trade naturally continued during these centuries. In fact, the wide conquests of the early T'ang made that period a high point in overland commerce.

The trade that passed across China's land borders in T'ang and Sung times, however, was by no means largely transcontinental. These centuries saw the development of a vast exchange of goods between the Chinese and their immediate nomadic neighbors. The Sung were constantly importing horses for their cavalry from the Tibetans, Turks, Mongols, and Tungus. They paid for them with the Chinese products which many of these peoples had by then become accustomed to use — tea, first of all, but also silks and other manufactures. The incorporation of millions of Chinese into the empires of the Liao, Hsi Hsia, and Chin naturally increased the demand in these states for the products of South China, and the trade between the Sung and the northern areas grew to huge proportions.

Maritime Commerce. Overseas trade seems to have served as an even greater stimulus to economic development in China in the T'ang and the Sung than did overland commerce. A significant maritime trade with India and the Near East had existed since the Han, but in the eighth century it began to grow to proportions undreamed of in earlier periods. By the Sung it had ushered in what might be called the first period of great oceanic commerce in the history of the world. The entrance of the Europeans into this lucrative trade along the southern littoral of Asia in the early sixteenth century was to mark the beginning of the oceanic phase of Western history and became a primary cause of the subsequent commercial revolution in Europe.

The great development of maritime commerce in China and all

South Asia between the eighth and thirteenth centuries of course had multiple causes. One was the gradual improvement of navigation, largely at the hands of the West and South Asians. The ships engaged in this trade between China and the rest of Asia had come to be large vessels, relying on both sails and oars and sometimes capable of carrying several hundred men. In the thirteenth century Marco Polo claimed that some ships had as many as thirteen watertight compartments. The Chinese had known of magnetic polarity at least as early as the third century A.D., and a Chinese text clearly indicates that the compass was in use in this southern trade by 1119, several decades before it was introduced to Europe by the Arabs.

Another factor in the growth of oceanic commerce may have been the outburst of energy in West Asia following the rise of Islam. In fact, the overseas trade of China was at first largely in the hands of Islamic Persians and Arabs. Their great commercial activities throughout South Asia at this time can probably be associated with the surge of power that took Islamic armies all the way to Spain and France in the west and to the Central Asian borders of China in the east.

Oceanic trade between China and the rest of Asia during these centuries was also stimulated by the unprecedented prosperity of China under the T'ang and the Sung. China's wealth inevitably drew traders to her ports and created an insistent demand for Chinese manufactures in all regions from Japan to East Africa.

The spectacular rise of oceanic commerce completely changed the orientation of China to the outside world. In earlier times the land frontiers of the northwest had been China's front door and the seacoast a rather remote and unimportant area. But now the eastern and southern coasts gradually became the chief areas of contact with the outside world, and the northwestern provinces started to sink to the status of a remote hinterland. This change naturally was an important part of the growing economic and cultural dominance of the southern coastal areas over the rest of the country.

During the Sung, overseas trade was concentrated at a few large ports along the south coast and on the lower Yangtze, where it was supervised by the Superintendencies of Merchant Shipping (*Shih-po-ssu*). The system of limiting foreign trade to certain official ports where custom duties could be collected had started in the eighth century, and during the Sung these custom duties became an important source of government income. The ships' captains paid anchorage fees, while the merchants gave certain presents to the officials and the government and paid taxes ranging roughly between 10 and 20 per cent of sales value, depending on the nature of the goods. The great bulk of the foreign trade had flowed through Canton during the late T'ang and the Northern Sung, but, under the Southern Sung, Ch'üan-chou (Marco Polo's Zayton), situated near the great tea- and porcelain-producing areas in Fukien, became the leading port.

Chinese Imports and Exports. An examination of the imports and exports in this trade indicates the leading place that China occupied in the world's economy during this period. Fine cotton textiles were the only manufactured goods imported on a large scale by the Chinese. Otherwise imports were largely horses and hides from the steppe lands and luxury raw products from the tropics, such as fine woods, gems, spices, and ivory. On the other hand, Chinese exports, though they included minerals such as gold, silver, lead, and tin, were made up for the most part of fine handicraft manufactures.

Chinese silks naturally continued to be much prized abroad but were now rivaled in value by other exports. Books, paintings, and other art objects were eagerly sought in countries such as Korea and Japan that had derived much of their higher civilization from the Middle Kingdom. Chinese copper cash were in great demand throughout East Asia and were even exported as far as East Africa. They remained, for example, the primary currency of Japan until the sixteenth century.

Porcelains were perhaps the greatest of all Chinese exports, going in huge quantities to all areas reached by the oceanic commerce of the time. Korea and Japan naturally imported them with great eagerness, but so also did the lands of Southeast Asia, India, West Asia, and the east coast of Africa. Fragments of Sung porcelains are to be found as far afield as Zanzibar, and the sites of medieval trading cities on the Persian Gulf and in Egypt are said to be virtually littered with Sung porcelain shards. The great importation of Chinese porcelains to Europe following the opening of oceanic commerce between the West and East Asia was for China only a continuation into modern times of a large-scale export trade that dated back at least to the eighth century.

Foreign Trade Communities. During the T'ang and the early Sung the overseas trade of China was dominated by foreigners. The commerce with Korea and Japan during the ninth century was largely in the hands of Korean traders who lived in large numbers along the southern coast of the Shantung Peninsula and in the cities on the lower Huai River. The Persians and Arabs, who controlled the trade with South and West Asia, were established in the ports of the south coast and the lower Yangtze.

These foreign communities all lived under their own customary laws in designated quarters of the port cities. In other words, they were accorded what were later to be known as extraterritorial privileges. This arrangement was primarily for the convenience of the Chinese authorities. Although the West Asians tended to retain their Islamic religion and built their own mosques in China, they sometimes became quite

Sinicized in other respects. They frequently took local wives, and we hear of foreign trading families that remained in China for five generations and even produced learned men who succeeded in entering Chinese officialdom through the examination system.

The foreign trade communities seem to have been very sizable. We are told, for example, that in 758 the Islamic group at Canton seized the city, that in 760 "thousands" of foreigners were killed in the great commercial city of Yang-chou on the Yangtze, and that 120,000 foreigners were killed at Canton in 879. Even though these statistics, like many figures of casualties in Chinese accounts, might best be divided by ten, there can be no doubt that the foreign communities were indeed very large and that the trade they conducted was on a tremendous scale.

During the Sung the Chinese themselves began to participate increasingly in overseas trade. In fact, by late Sung times Chinese merchants had come to dominate the trade routes across the East China Sea to Korea and Japan and also those through the South China Sea as far as Sumatra. The Chinese thus were becoming for the first time a seafaring people, and the Chinese Empire was at last beginning to be a power on the high seas.

THE DEVELOPMENT OF AN
ADVANCED MONEY ECONOMY

One of the clearest signs of the economic growth that took place in China during the late T'ang and the Sung was the great expansion of the currency system. Copper cash had appeared as early as the late Chou and had been used extensively ever since, but there was now a huge increase in the quantity of currency in use, a great development in the complexity of the currency system, and a corresponding increase in the role of money in trade and government finance. In other words, China during this period reached a new level of money economy.

One measure of these changes is to be found in the records of government income. Annual receipts in cash, as opposed to textiles or grain, had amounted to only 2,000,000 strings of 1000 cash each in 749, when the T'ang dynasty was at its height. The great tax reform of 780, however, led to a considerable increase in the proportion of taxes paid in money. By 1065 the Sung was receiving 37,000,000 strings of currency a year in payment of taxes. During the Southern Sung, when the dynasty had lost the agricultural North and was dependent on the more commercialized South, the government's income in money completely overshadowed its grain and textile receipts.

At the same time the government's dependence on revenue from commerce increased greatly. The early T'ang, like most previous Chinese regimes, had relied almost exclusively on agricultural taxes. During the late T'ang and Sung periods, revenue from the government monopolies, particularly those in salt, tea, and wine, and from various commercial taxes, including customs duties, rapidly increased. By the time of the Northern Sung, income from these sources was beginning to outbalance the land tax, and during the Southern Sung the state revenue came overwhelmingly from such commercial sources. Never before, and for that matter never again, was a Chinese imperial regime so little dependent on land taxes. This development of the monopolies and commercial taxes — to a point where they could, if desired, equal or exceed the land tax as a source of government income — created a second major financial support on which the imperial government could rest. It thus contributed to the greater fiscal stability of Chinese regimes from Sung times on.

The Expansion of Currency. The extensive growth in the use of money during the late T'ang and the Sung put a heavy strain on China's currency resources. The story is revealed in part in the greatly increased production of copper cash. Under the T'ang, production had averaged between 130,000 and 310,000 strings per year. By the late tenth century production was around 880,000, and in the eleventh century it rose to as much as 1,830,000 strings a year.

Even then the demand for cash commonly outstripped production, and the government was constantly struggling with the problem of increasing the supply of coins on hand. The official monopoly on copper mining was used to maximize production, and at various times the regime attempted, though with little success, to limit the use of copper to coinage alone. The standard unit of 1000 coins was sometimes reduced in number, but this, of course, was no solution to the problem, since a shortened string of cash fell correspondingly in value. A more important measure was to prohibit the export of cash. When this ban was not in effect, an alternative policy was to place a 50 per cent export tax on coinage. Neither effort, however, was successful. The profits from exporting cash to countries like Japan were so great that daring merchants could not be stopped from running currency as contraband. The government also experimented with the use of iron coins in such border regions as Shansi and Szechwan, in order to create an iron curtain, so to speak, between China's copper cash and the purses of its nomadic neighbors, but iron proved to be too cheap to serve as an effective currency.

One way of solving the currency shortage was to use more gold and silver as money. Oddly enough, the Chinese only rarely minted these precious metals, but both came into common use for large currency transactions — gold dust by weight and silver in the form of ingots of supposedly standardized weight and purity. The growing use of these precious metals was reflected by the increase of silver in the government's tax income from 800,000 units in 1021 to 10,000,000 by 1180.

The Development of Paper Money. The most interesting solution of the currency problem and the one that best illustrates the growth of an advanced money economy in China was the development of paper currency. Both the government and the great transport merchants faced the problem of transferring large sums of money over great distances. The dependence of the capital and the border armies of the North on the agricultural yield of the distant South made this problem more acute than in earlier periods. Copper cash were too bulky for convenient transfer, and consequently various types of paper credit and paper money were developed to meet the need.

As early as 811 the T'ang were issuing so-called "flying cash" to pay for goods acquired in distant areas. These money drafts were reimbursable at the capital. The system proliferated under the Sung, which put out many separate issues of drafts of this sort, each issue commonly limited to an over-all figure of 2,500,000 strings of cash a year. Because of their convenience, such government money drafts were exchanged between merchants who wished to transfer credits and thus were used as currency.

Meanwhile, another type of paper money was being developed by private bankers, who issued certificates of deposit which could be cashed for a three per cent service charge. Such certificates, because of their convenience, came to circulate freely at face value. There were many types of such private certificates issued by different local groups of bankers. Those issued by the bankers of Chengtu in Szechwan were among the most famous, and when they were taken over by the government in 1024 they became the world's first genuine paper money. Issued in denominations of between 200 and 1000 cash (or one string), these government notes were subject to the usual three per cent service charge, and they were limited to three years' validity because of the deterioration of the paper. The Chengtu paper money was at first limited to 1,256,000 strings in value and in the early days was soundly backed by 360,000 strings of cash, a 28.66 per cent coverage.

The Sung government also put out various other local issues of paper money. These and the paper currencies of later dynasties, as we shall see, were all eventually ruined by over-issue. In currency development, however, as well as in many other features of the economy, the late T'ang and the Sung achieved a very high level — a level, in fact, that was not to be greatly surpassed from then until the late nineteenth century.

THE EARLY MODERN SOCIETY OF CHINA

The "commercial revolution" that took place in China between the eighth and thirteenth centuries helped maintain its position as the most advanced country in the world, but it did not produce such great changes in society and government as did the later commercial revolution of Europe. At first glance this may seem strange, but the reasons for this difference between China and Europe are not hard to find. The commercial growth of early modern Europe took place in a feudal social and political setting that was quite incapable of accommodating itself to these changes, so that a real revolution or metamorphosis resulted. The commercial growth of T'ang and Sung times took place within a highly organized bureaucratic empire which easily adjusted to and drew strength from the new economic activity. However much commerce grew, the merchants never became strong enough to challenge the monolithic state but always remained at its mercy. Herein, no doubt, lies one of the basic reasons why the commercial revolution of Europe led on to a further "modernization" of Western society, while the "commercial revolution" of China appears by comparison to have been a truncated development. But it is actually the European experience, with its unusual feudal background, rather than the Chinese case, which represents the aberration from the more common pattern of history.

On the other hand, one should not minimize the political, social, and cultural changes that did take place concurrently with the growth of the economy in China. While most of these changes were merely a strengthening of tendencies that had already appeared earlier, cumulatively they produced a society which was quite different in general level and tone from that of pre-T'ang times. Since this society was to remain, with only minor changes, characteristic of China until the nineteenth century, and since it contained many features which appear to be characteristic of modern urban civilizations, it may be not inappropriate to call it the "early modern" society of China. Whereas the twelfth-century culture of Europe seems to be only a rather remote ancestor of the nineteenth-century West, the twelfth-century civilization of China appears to be only a younger and more exuberant stage of the China that the West came to know in the nineteenth century.

The Fading of the Aristocracy. It would be difficult to trace the exact steps by which the highly aristocratic society of the Six Dynasties and the early T'ang became the essentially non-aristocratic and more egalitarian society of the late Sung. Let it suffice to outline some of the major changes that took place over these centuries.

In earlier times the land had been divided between the holdings of free peasants, who paid virtually the whole of their surplus produce and energy as taxes to the government, and the estates of families so privileged and powerful that they could protect their lands from the government tax collectors. Residing on their hereditary, relatively tax-free estates, these aristocrats had tended to dominate society and government. Their subordinates had usually been loyal retainers on whom they could count in time of trouble for military support. The influence of the landowner in society had usually been directly dependent on the wealth and military power he commanded. In short, the proto-feudal conditions of the Six Dynasty period had survived in part into the early T'ang.

After the change in the tax system in the eighth century, the government no longer opposed the private accumulation of agricultural land, and consequently it no longer took exceptional power and influence to protect private holdings. As a result, large numbers of small and medium landowners appeared. On the other hand, the new simplified tax system made it more difficult for the old aristocrats to maintain their tax-free status, and their influence in the government was seriously reduced both by the growing role of the examination system in producing leadership and by the success of the Sung emperors in concentrating power in their own hands. The rapid rise of commerce and a more widespread money economy also outdated the old type of economically self-sufficient estate. Scattered parcels of land became a more common landholding pattern. For these various reasons the old aristocracy was gradually absorbed into a much broader new class, commonly called the "gentry."

Although the old landed aristocracy disappeared during these centuries, the economic gulf between landowner and peasant remained almost as great as ever. There was, however, a significant change in the relationship between these two groups. The landlord's subordinates, even in the Sung, sometimes found themselves still bound to the soil by customary law as semi-serfs, but they were not hereditary retainers, as their predecessors had been in the great estates. They were, in fact, little more than tenant farmers, paying roughly half their yield to the landlord as rent. The extent of landlordism at this time is indicated by the fact that during the Northern Sung about half of the population was made up of such tenant farmers.

The New "Gentry" Class. The power of the old aristocracy had been based almost entirely on landownership. The new "gentry" class that took its place, though still in many ways a landlord class, depended for its influence much less exclusively on agricultural wealth. In fact, from Sung times landownership seems to have become economically a losing proposition. Great landowners tended to lose money rather than to accumulate it. Moreover, since primogeniture was not customary, large landholdings often broke up, as a once prosperous family increased too greatly in numbers over the generations. Certainly wealth was made much more rapidly and easily through government service and trade than in agriculture, and it could be protected best by high government office. Because of the old prestige of landownership and its relative safety, surplus capital was most frequently invested in land, but the wealth of the "gentry" landowners was probably often of merchant origin, even though this fact might be looked upon as a skeleton in the family closet. Moreover, merchant families who had not yet made themselves fully respectable by transferring their wealth from commerce to agriculture also participated directly in the leadership group by their role under the government as operators of official monopolies and controllers of commercial taxation.

There was also another way in which the new "gentry" was not simply a landowning class. Only rarely did great landlords command personal military power or even much influence in the central government simply because of their landholdings. Their wealth could be effectively translated into power in the central government only through education and the achievement of high political posts by way of the examination system. In other words, the "gentry" as a class of national political influence was actually a class based on education, depending much more directly upon intellectual accomplishments as displayed in the examination system than upon wealth. This fact makes the term "gentry" ambiguous as writers have used it in books about China. Some have meant by it the "landlord gentry," others the "scholar gentry." The latter concept is the more precise, as we shall see in considering the "gentry" of later periods.

While wealth remained important and educational attainments had become of paramount significance, hereditary status by Sung times had sunk to a minor role. Social mobility had greatly increased in an economically diversified society and had become justified by the acceptance of egalitarian principles. Thus the new "gentry" was by no means an aristocracy in the older sense. The almost proto-feudal society of the sixth century had given way by the twelfth to a much more complicated society characterized by a broad landlordism and the political leadership of a bureaucracy chosen by intellectual standards.

The Urbanization of Society. Another feature of the new society of late T'ang and Sung China was its growing urbanization. It was not urbanized in the modern sense that a majority of the people now lived in cities, though there was a considerable increase in city populations. In the late eleventh century there were forty-six local districts with more than 100,000 households, compared to thirteen for the middle of the eighth century. Kaifeng is said to have had 260,000 households in 1105 and Hangchow 391,000 in 1270. These were great concentrations of population, but the real urbanization of Chinese culture was not so much a matter of numbers as it was the domination of society from this time on by city and town dwellers.

The new "gentry," unlike the old aristocracy, usually lived more of the time in cities and towns than on their rural holdings. Thus they were frequently absentee landlords rather than country squires. With many landlords and nearly all officials and rich merchants residing in the cities and towns, a large proportion of the leadership group became concentrated in the urban areas. The higher culture, therefore, naturally became heavily urbanized, developing interests and attitudes that seem more characteristic of city people than of rural populations.

In the city environment, the higher culture became much more sophisticated and diversified than before. Moreover, a much larger segment of society began to participate in it. Such a development is hardly surprising in this more egalitarian age, when the examination system appreciably widened the leadership segment of society and gave strong incentives to scholarship and the practice of the arts.

The triumph of the civilian as opposed to the military point of view was one of the chief characteristics of the new urban culture. Despite the common opinion that Chinese civilization has always been pacifistic, the Chinese until the early T'ang had exulted in military power as much as other strong peoples. The governments had been civil only insofar as any great and lasting empire has to have an efficient civil administration. But by the Sung there had appeared the overwhelming emphasis on civil accomplishments and the undercurrent of pacifism that have since been characteristically associated with Chinese civilization. There was a growing disregard and even contempt for martial life and prowess that was not unlike the attitudes that appear to be in the ascendant in modern urban societies of the Occident. Military service, it was felt, was only fit for the dregs of society; or, as the Chinese put it, the best men were no more to be used for soldiers than the best iron for nails.

Quite understandably, the Chinese after the Sung never again achieved the military dominance in East Asia that they had enjoyed in the Han and the early T'ang. Of course, the later Chinese dynasties, like the earlier ones, were all founded and supported by men of the sword; but it is significant that of the last four great Chinese dynasties only the two of "barbarian" origin conquered far afield, while the Sung and the Ming were relatively weak in their foreign relations.

Allied with the emphasis on civil as opposed to military arts was the growing dominance of urban ways of life and citified amusements among the upper classes. While rural pleasures such as hunting and horseback riding have been enjoyed by certain aristocratic groups in the West until the present, most cultivated Chinese turned their backs on such rustic pastimes almost a millennium ago. The hunt had been the sport of aristocrats in Chou and Han times, but the upper classes of the Sung eschewed it for literature, art, and scholarship. To most of them the countryside did not offer a Chinese equivalent of riding to hounds but was a place to commune poetically with nature. Although it may seem paradoxical, this romanticized love of nature, which came so early in China but did not become pronounced in the West until recent centuries, appears to be one of the prominent features of modern urban culture in general.

City life in the Sung was free and luxurious. Cities were no longer conglomerations of walled villages dominated by the imperial palace or some other center of political authority. Amusement quarters, instead, were now the centers of social life. Here were to be found countless wine shops, tea shops, and restaurants specializing in various types of cuisine — the ancestors of the Chinese restaurants which have become a ubiquitous element of our modern world civilization. There were houses featuring professional female entertainers comparable to the geishas of a later period in Japan. Both these houses and the restaurants frequently shaded off into brothels. There were also theaters, puppet shows, jugglers, storytellers, and other entertainments of all types to add to the color and interest of life in the amusement quarters.

The evils of urban society also first made themselves felt in this age. Absentee landlords and tenancy created problems in Chinese agriculture that have continued until contemporary times. Widespread pauperism also appeared among the city proletariat, which had become in large part divorced from its rural origins. Relief measures became necessary. The Sung army was the chief means of taking care of the unemployed, but the government also set up special storehouses, supported by separate taxes, for the care of the indigent. Private charity agencies also made their appearance in the late T'ang, performing such services as caring for orphans and indigent old people or burying dead paupers. Philanthropy sometimes took the form of setting up "charitable estates" to provide schooling or poor relief for members of an extended family.

The Decline in the Status of Women. A change in the position of women might also be associated with the urbanization of culture. Women had always been subservient to men, but the concentration of the upper classes in cities, where the work of women was less essential than on the farm, apparently contributed to a further decline in the status of women in the upper levels of society. In any case, women became even more than before the servants and playthings of men. This change is suggested by the growth at this time of the institution of concubinage, that is, the taking of secondary wives, and, in polite society, the strengthening of the social rules against the remarriage of widows.

The declining status of women is even more clearly indicated by the introduction during the Sung of foot-binding among the upper

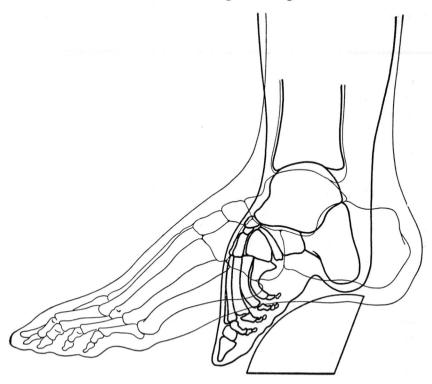

A BOUND FOOT

This diagram shows the twisted and cramped bone structure of a bound ("lily") foot, as compared with that of a normal foot. Bound tightly with cloth from the age of five, a little girl's foot grew painfully into this deformed but erotically admired shape.

classes. When still quite young, girls would have their feet tightly wrapped and gradually bent until the arch was broken and the toes were turned under. This produced a foot only about half the normal size, virtually crippling girls for life and thus accentuating their economic uselessness and the wealth of the men who could afford such obviously handicapped womenfolk. While this whole practice and the resultant stiff walk of Chinese women have appeared repugnant to foreign observers, bound feet developed strong erotic associations for the Chinese, and the custom gradually spread throughout the society, remaining a major curse until the twentieth century.

THE DEVELOPMENT OF THE ARTS

The wide-reaching empire of the early T'ang and the growing foreign trade of the late T'ang and the Sung made this a period of manifold foreign contacts. The higher culture of the epoch, however, though sometimes enriched by these contacts, was not basically modified by them. It was mainly a brilliant development of cultural traits already well established in China.

This tendency is to be seen as clearly in the fine arts as in any field. Architecture, turning its back on whatever influences had come with Buddhism from India and on the new influences from the Islamic world, remained true to its original Chinese tenets of wooden post-and-lintel construction. A towering multi-storied development of the classic one-storied architectural theme was evolved in the late T'ang and the Sung. Pagodas with as many as a dozen stories, each story having a roof of colored glazed tiles, were also built. The lines of the eaves of the massive tiled roofs of public buildings, which in earlier times had been straight, began to be curved upwards at their ends, a feature of Chinese architecture which has remained more pronounced in the South than in the North.

Under the Sung, religious sculpture reached a high point of realism, but with the waning of the Buddhist spirit it lost much of its inspiration and became ornate and stereotyped. The making of funerary sculptures also became rarer.

After many centuries of steady development, porcelains reached the height of perfection under the Sung. Such favorite Sung wares as the lustrous green celadons, the delicately figured white porcelains, and the roughly shaped rich brown *t'ien-mu* ware (highly prized in Japan under the name of *temmoku*) are often regarded as the finest works of the potter's art ever produced anywhere in the world. The great porcelain tradition of China was further developed in later ages, though not necessarily with greater aesthetic success, in the rich "blue and white" wares of the Ming dynasty and the technically superb polychrome porcelains of the succeeding Ch'ing dynasty.

Painting. Ever since the Sung most Chinese have, with good reason, felt that the greatest of their fine arts is painting. Drawing from a rich, continuous tradition stretching well back into the Han period, Chinese canons of painting became fully established during the Sung, and painting itself reached a level of perfection that was probably not surpassed in succeeding dynasties. Looked at closely, later Chinese painting reveals great variety and vitality but, scanned more broadly, it gives the impression of being not much more than variations on themes already well developed by Sung times.

Buddhist painting, with its strong iconographic elements, remained prominent through the Sung, though it was fast losing place to purely secular art. In the latter, the emphasis shifted from figures and depictions of human events to landscapes, in which the human element was

PLATES 28 and 29. Life in Mongolia and in China. Details from two Sung dynasty (eleventh or early twelfth century) paintings of the story of Lady Wen-chi, captured by the nomads in 195 A.D. and later ransomed and returned to China. Above: Leaving her husband and children in Mongolia (note the round yurts, rugs, low tables and camel carts). Below: Her arrival back in China (this style of entrance gate and inner courtyard has remained typical of China's domestic architecture until today).

SUNG PAINTING

PLATE 30. Clearing autumn skies over mountains and valleys. Detail from eleventh-century ink and tint on silk, attributed to Kuo Hsi.

PLATE 31. Ladies ironing silk, detail from a painting by the Northern Sung Emperor Hui Tsung (1100–1125), after a T'ang original.

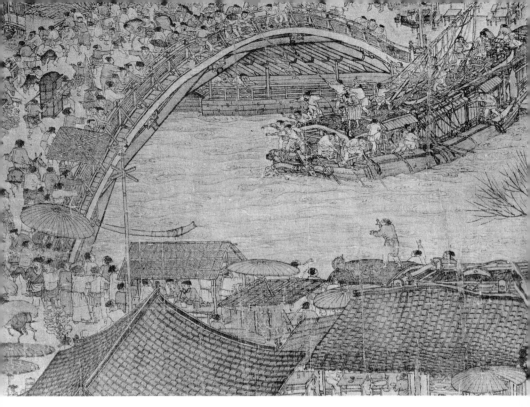

PLATE 32. City life. Scene from a long scroll, "Spring Festival on the River," by Chang Tse-tuan (twelfth century). Note the street stalls and sedan chair on the bridge, the boat crew lowering their mast to pass under it, and the tea shops on both sides of the canal.

PLATE 33. Landscape painted on a round fan by the Southern Sung artist Ma Yüan in the late twelfth or early thirteenth century.

MING PAINTING

PLATE 34. Two afghan hounds, painted by the Hsüan-te
Emperor of the Ming dynasty in 1427. The seals are those
of the painter and of successive owners of the painting.

PLATE 35. Poet on a mountain, by Shen Chou (1427–
1509), a leading painter of the Ming dynasty. The poem
is descriptive of the scene.

at most a small detail, or to vignettes of nature, such as a spray of bamboo. It is perhaps significant that Yen Li-pen (died 673), the greatest artist of the early T'ang, was still primarily a figure painter in the tradition of Ku K'ai-chih of the Six Dynasties period, while by the eighth century the great artists were generally famous for their landscapes.

As the new landscape and nature painting developed, it became highly impressionistic rather than realistically complete. The artist was selective in details and concentrated on what he felt best conveyed the true essence of his subject. Color was felt to be relatively unimportant, and consequently monochrome painting predominated. In fact, monochrome landscapes done with a minimum of detail in amazingly bold brush strokes might be regarded as the epitome of the artistic trends of the time. (See Plates 30, 33, and 35.)

Landscapes, to the artist, represented nature as a whole; a spray of bamboo or some other small sampling of nature was a microcosm of the universe. The philosophical implications of the art were important and its Taoistic inspiration was quite obvious. Some of this inspiration expressed itself specifically in Zen Buddhist forms, but nonetheless it drew from the old Taoist wonder at nature and the fundamentally aesthetic approach of the Taoist to life.

While the Chinese painting that achieved its full maturity during the Sung is extremely different from the art that the West developed between antiquity and the nineteenth century, it needs no defense or explanation to the modern Occidental, to whom Sung painting may be more immediately understandable than the art of medieval Europe or that of the Renaissance. The genius of Sung painting is revealed by the simple fact that to us it seems extremely modern.

The whole Chinese attitude toward art and the artist, as developed by the Sung period, also seems modern, especially when contrasted with the attitudes in Europe at that time. Sung art was no longer just the handmaid of religion but was practiced for its own sake. Paintings, for example, which formerly had been made largely for religious purposes or else as architectural decorations, were now produced as independent works valued purely for their own aesthetic qualities. China also had passed the age of the nameless craftsman-artist. This was a time of known painters — of men whose work was often valued as much because of their reputations as for its own merit.

The names of the great painters of the eighth to the thirteenth century are legion. Wu Tao-hsüan (also known as Wu Tao-tzu), who was active at Hsüan Tsung's court, is considered to have been the first great landscapist and the originator of the rhythmically varied, calligraphic brush stroke that has so greatly enriched Chinese painting, although he was also famous for his paintings of Buddhist figures. Li Ssu-hsün (651–720) and Wang Wei (699–759), who was equally famed as a poet, are said to have been the originators of the Southern and Northern Schools of landscape painting, two categories which are more illustrative of the Chinese love of classification than indicative of the styles or geographical origins of the painters. Mi Fu (also known as Mi Fei, 1051–1107) was an outstanding painter and calligrapher during the Northern Sung. Even the ill-fated Emperor Hui Tsung was a distinguished artist (see Plate 31), though he was even more outstanding as a patron of the arts. He helped assemble an imperial collection which, according to its catalogue, contained 6192 paintings. In the Southern Sung the two most famous landscapists were probably Ma Yüan and Hsia Kuei. (See Plate 33.)

Antiquarian Artistic Interests. There was a clearly defined antiquarian interest in art and archaeology in this period. The *Li-tai ming-hua chi,* or *A Record of the Famous Paintings of All Periods,* was compiled in the middle of the ninth century by a connoisseur who was distressed at the tragic destruction of art objects in the great Buddhist persecution of the time. During the Sung many great private and public collections of art objects were built up. Famous collectors affixed their seals to great paintings as marks of authenticity, thereby increasing rather than detracting from the value of the works. Detailed art catalogues were published; those for the ancient bronze ritual vessels contained careful descriptions as well as illustrations of each item. There were specialists on the various branches of art who wrote supposedly authoritative books on their subjects. Antiquarian interests also stimulated the faking of antiquities, which itself became a sort of minor branch of the fine arts. All in all, the interest in objects of art and the attitude toward art in general were surprisingly like what we know in the Western world today.

The Literary Arts. While the ability to paint was a prized talent among the elite of China, literary skill, and especially the ability to compose poetry, was a virtual necessity. Of all civil accomplishments in a now essentially non-military culture, writing, including its expression in the art of calligraphy, was the most prized and remained so until the contemporary period. This was only to be expected at a time when literary skills (as the civil service examinations demonstrated) had become the broadest and most respected road to fame and fortune.

In China the written word had always been accorded a higher degree of respect than in most other civilizations, but the increasing emphasis on literary skills in T'ang and Sung times gave to the two principal forms of writing, belles-lettres and works of scholarship, an even more important place in the culture than they had occupied before. There was a great increase during the tenth century in the number of private schools and academies; general literacy, as well as higher literary skills, increased proportionately; and both scholarship and belles-lettres flourished as never before, not only in terms of quantity but also in variety and quality.

Printing and Scholarship

The examination system was not the only stimulus to this great spurt in learning and literary output. The economic growth and increased wealth of the empire were other important factors, as was also the greater availability of texts made possible by printing. This great invention was originally motivated by the desire to establish and spread authentic versions of important texts. This it helped to do, but an even more important effect of printing was to increase greatly the availability of all written materials. Printing eventually contributed to a general popularization of literature and learning, though not on the same scale as in the modern West because of the difficulty of the Chinese writing system.

The Invention of Printing. As we have seen, as early as Han times the Chinese had erected stone tablets on which the officially authorized version of the classics was inscribed. These stone texts were commonly transferred to paper through a process known as "rubbing." A large sheet of soft, thin paper would be dampened and made to adhere to the carved face of the stone and then would be patted or rubbed with a bag of lampblack (or India ink) until all but the paper adhering to the indented portions of the carving had been blackened. The result would be a white-on-black reproduction of the carved text — that is, a primitive sort of block print.

The concept of printed texts may have come from such rubbings, but printing actually evolved from a different source. Since ancient times Chinese carvers had produced large seals for official use — at first made of metal but later also of wood. By the seventh century these had developed into full-page wood-block pictures or texts. A pious Japanese empress, for example, in 770 used this Chinese invention to produce a million identical Buddhist charms. A series of consecutive printed blocks would produce a whole text in traditional scroll form, and the spacing of the block prints, so that a long sheet of paper could be folded at regular intervals and one side of the folds stitched together, produced the standard Chinese printed book with its continuous double-folded pages.

A whole Buddhist sutra had been printed in China by 868. In the middle of the tenth century the printing of all of the Chinese classics and the whole of the Buddhist Tripitaka was undertaken by some of the independent regimes in Szechwan and South China. By the early

SUNG PRINTED BOOK

A page from the Fa-yüan chu-lin *(Forest of Pearls in the Garden of the Law), a Buddhist work compiled in 668 by Tao-shih, a famous Ch'ang-an monk, and printed in 1124, more than three centuries before the Gutenberg Bible. The small type on the right explains the reason for the printing of this book and gives the names of those who financed and supervised the project. The first line in large type on the right is the heading for Chapter 48 and is followed by a line in small type stating that the compiler was Tao-shih, a monk of the Hsi-ming-ssu ("Monastery of the Western Light") at the capital of Great T'ang.*

eleventh century even the Taoist canon had been printed. During the Sung, printing became extremely widespread, and printed books of all types appeared in large numbers.

Because of the huge number of different characters used in writing, the Chinese usually found it simplest to have a whole block of wood, usually representing the two sides or pages of a single folded sheet of a book, carved as a unit. When printing eventually reached the West in the fifteenth century by way of Central Asia and the Near East, the Europeans quickly discarded wood blocks for movable type, because of the small number of writing symbols they employed. But movable type in wood, porcelain, and copper had actually been developed long before in East Asia, appearing in China around 1030 and being much utilized in Korea during the first half of the fifteenth century.

Printing was a purely Chinese invention which put scholarship and learning on a new level in East Asia, just as it was to contribute to an even more thorough transformation of Western society a few centuries later. It is perhaps significant that printing and paper, the two technological underpinnings of the literate aspects of modern civilization, were both contributed by China, the literary civilization par excellence.

Historical Writings. In scholarship the T'ang and the Sung saw a tremendous expansion and enrichment of earlier forms. Standard histories were compiled with even greater enthusiasm and care than before and were also supplemented by new types of historical scholarship. Liu Chih-chi (661–721), for example, wrote the *Shih t'ung* (*On History*), the first full study of historiography, in which he discussed how history had been written and how it should be written.

The historical record had grown to such enormous proportions by the Sung that a new effort at a single comprehensive history of China's past seemed necessary. The *Tzu-chih t'ung-chien*, by Ssu-ma Kuang (1018–1086), a statesman who had been a leading opponent of Wang An-shih, was the first effort at a comprehensive history since Ssu-ma Ch'ien's time. It is a strictly chronological presentation covering the years 403 B.C. to 959 A.D. in 294 chapters. Its name, which was given by the reigning emperor, reveals the whole philosophy of the Chinese historian, for it literally means *The Comprehensive Mirror for Aid in Government*. The materials of this bulky book were abridged and reworked in the twelfth century under the direction of the famous philosopher Chu Hsi. In the resulting *T'ung-chien kang-mu*, or *The Outline and Details of the Comprehensive Mirror*, the main points of history are sorted out from the supporting factual data, and a great deal of emphasis is given to moral judgments and to the differences between legitimate and false claimants to the Mandate of Heaven. The *T'ung-chien chi-shih pen-mo*, or *Narratives from Beginning to End from the Comprehensive Mirror*, by Yüan Shu (1131–1205), was another reworking of these same materials, divided up by major incidents, more in the manner of the modern historical writing of the West. These three works became the chief introductions to history for later generations of Chinese students.

Encyclopedic Compilations. A tendency toward encyclopedic compilation was already strong in Chinese scholarship by the beginning of the T'ang, and in the following few centuries it markedly increased. Local gazetteers were produced in numbers, and many other types of encyclopedias, or, more strictly, carefully organized collections of excerpts from earlier books, made their appearance. The *T'ung tien* (*Comprehensive Compendium*), completed in 801, and the *T'ang hui yao* (*Assembled Essentials on the T'ang*), a great collection of materials on T'ang government and economics, completed in 961 on the basis of earlier compilations, became the prototypes of whole new categories of an encyclopedic literature which thenceforth supplanted the standard histories as the chief sources of information on political institutions and economic developments.

THE DEVELOPMENT OF LITERATURE

Poetry: the Shih. The literature of the T'ang and the Sung, like painting and scholarship, was for the most part a glorious flowering of earlier tendencies. There was an outburst of poetic production, and from the T'ang dynasty alone literally thousands of poets have left their names to posterity.

The chief poetic current during the T'ang was the continuation of the type of lyric poetry that had become popular during the Six Dynasties. This poetry was known as *shih*, a word we have already encountered in the name of the *Classic of Songs* (*Shih-ching*). The lyric poets of the T'ang were on the whole freer and less rigidly bound by form than most of their predecessors had been. There were also some innovations at this time. The seven-syllable line, for example, was developed to parallel the more standard five-syllable meter, and the *chüeh-chü* or quatrain, a very concise and highly evocative type of poetry, also became popular.

Chinese lyric poetry perhaps reached its apogee in the eighth century at the hands of such great masters as Li Po (also known as Li T'ai-po, 701–762) and Tu Fu (712–770). Though contemporaries and actually friends, these two men represented opposite extremes in poetic personality. Li Po, perhaps the greatest name in all Chinese poetry, was a complete Taoist, wine lover and carefree libertine wanderer. The story of his death, though entirely apocryphal, characterized his attitude and the Taoistic strain among Chinese poets. He is said to have drowned while boating when he reached out for the moon in drunken ecstasy. The following two poems are typical of his work: [1]

THE MOON OVER THE BORDER MOUNTAINS
The full moon rises over the T'ien-shan range
In the midst of a vast ocean of clouds;

[1] Both are from a forthcoming work by James R. Hightower.

The unceasing wind from a thousand miles away
Blows across the Jade Gate Pass.
Our troops have left by the Po-teng Road;
The barbarians watch from Kokonor Bay.
Since Han times when this became a battlefield
No man has been known to return.
The frontier guards stare out from the border town,
Many sad faces longing to go home,
Where, in upstairs rooms, on this very night
Sighing and sobbing never cease.

AT A FAREWELL DINNER IN THE HSIEH T'IAO PAVILION, TO MY UNCLE LI YÜN, THE COLLATOR

They have gone and left me — the yesterdays there was no holding
    back;
It confuses my heart — this day, today, with all its trouble and care.
A thousand-mile-long wind drives the autumn geese,
Excuse enough to get drunk in the high pavilion. . . .
Draw a knife and cut the water — yet the water flows;
Lift a cup to drown your grief — grief still is grief.
Man lives in the world and never gets his desire;
Tomorrow I shall let down my hair and drift away in a boat.

Tu Fu, though only a minor official, was idealistic and painfully conscientious. Buffeted by fate, he was deeply aware of the suffering of humanity and the injustices of life. Where Li Po was essentially the Taoist hedonist, Tu Fu was the grave Confucian moralist.

A third great T'ang poet of somewhat later date is usually linked with Li Po and Tu Fu. This was Po Chü-i (772–846). Unlike his illustrious predecessors and most other T'ang poets, he wrote in a simple style not far removed from the vernacular, with fewer of the heavy literary allusions that characterize most Chinese poetry. Perhaps for this reason he was vastly popular in his own day, not only in China but in Korea and Japan as well.

The traditions of the *shih* form of lyric poetry as perfected in the T'ang were continued by hosts of Sung poets, many of whom have great fame in China; but the *shih* of Sung times, though not markedly different from those of the T'ang, had through constant repetition of earlier themes lost some of their earlier vigor and become more stereotyped. Of the Sung *shih* poets perhaps the only one we need mention is Su Shih (better known as Su Tung-p'o, 1036–1101), who was the greatest member of an illustrious family of poets and philosophers and was also famed as a prose stylist and calligrapher.

Tz'u and San-ch'ü. As the *shih* type of poetry gradually became more stereotyped, a new poetic form rose to popularity. This was the *tz'u*, which originated in the lyrics for popular songs sung in the city teahouses and brothels. The *shih* too had been chanted, but the only "tune" to these chants was provided by their own strict pattern of word tones. The *tz'u* were now sung to real tunes and thus had freer tonal patterns and were naturally quite irregular in meter. They were also freer in vocabulary than the highly literary *shih* and made considerable use of the colloquial language. As a result, they were a much less restricted poetic medium. In time, however, they became divorced from actual songs and came to be patterned largely on earlier *tz'u*, evolving thus from song lyrics into a real poetic genre.

The *tz'u* at first were looked down upon by literary men and were not committed to writing, but by the ninth century respectable poets were beginning to compose them, and during the Sung every major poet wrote at least some *tz'u*. Among the greatest of the *tz'u* poets were Li Yü, the last king of the Southern T'ang dynasty, in the tenth century; Su Shih, who, of course, was even more renowned for his *shih;* and, in the twelfth century, Hsin Ch'i-chi, who in his youth was active in the wars against the Chin and later had a prominent political career under the Southern Sung.

After the Sung the *tz'u* became increasingly literary and fossilized, and a new type of song lyric rose to take its place. This form was known as *san-ch'ü*, or "popular songs." The *san-ch'ü* were written to go with new tunes that had appeared since the time of the *tz'u* tunes, and they were even freer in vocabulary and in meter than the *tz'u* had been. Although the *san-ch'ü* remained the favorite song form through the Ming dynasty, it probably reached its height in the early Mongol dynasty at the hands of Ma Chih-yüan, who happens to have been even more renowned as a playwright.

Prose Writing. The T'ang and the Sung were also golden ages for formal prose writing. Han Yü (768–824), rejecting the ornate, balanced prose style that had flourished since the Six Dynasties, returned to a simple and straightforward though slightly archaic style. The revolt against literary artificiality that Han Yü started, however, was to some extent self-defeating. In fact, the tendency of many of its proponents to fall back on ancient models helped widen the gulf between literary and colloquial Chinese. But others continued the fight to free prose writing from cramping artificialities. Ou-yang Hsiu (1007–1072), a leading historian and thinker of his day, felt that writers should be entirely free to express ideas in whatever form seemed best. Back of such a concept, no doubt, was the rising use of the vernacular for philosophic writings and for the recorded dialogues of Zen masters. Both Han Yü and Ou-yang Hsiu were also famous poets, the former being noted for the serious subject matter and heavy, prosaic style of his poetry.

While the main stream of Chinese literature, as it is recognized in China, always remained true to the traditions that antedated the T'ang and were perfected in the T'ang and the Sung, two entirely new literary currents also made their appearance during this period. These were the popular drama and the novel, which, though customarily depreciated by well-educated Chinese as plebeian and vulgar, were to achieve great literary heights in later periods. The rise of these popular literary forms at this time is clearly to be associated with such factors as the development of printing, the spread of literacy, and the general urbanization of Chinese culture.

The Statesman-Literatus Ideal. An outstanding characteristic of the literature of the late T'ang and the Sung is that most of the great poets, prose writers, and scholars were also officials, even if sometimes relatively unsuccessful ones, as in the cases of Li Po and Tu Fu. Conversely, most of the great statesmen were also distinguished men of letters. Wang An-shih was a poet of note as well as the leading political personality of his day. In earlier periods, the roles of poet, scholar, and statesman had each been relatively distinct; but the ideal Confucian type that had evolved by the Sung was that of the "universal man" who was scholar, poet, and statesman all at the same time, and possibly a philosopher and painter as well. From the Sung until contemporary times many leading figures have combined two or more of those roles, most frequently the roles of statesman and poet or scholar.

Neo-Confucianism

In intellectual attitudes and formal philosophy, the late T'ang and the Sung periods saw the clear appearance of patterns that were to remain characteristic of China until the nineteenth century. The philosophical synthesis, known in the West as Neo-Confucianism, which emerged from the intellectual ferment of these centuries was to be the almost unchanging core of Chinese thought from then until its collapse under the impact of Western ideologies in the twentieth century.

Anti-foreignism and the Return to the Native Tradition. Behind the philosophical developments of the T'ang and the Sung was an equally significant change in attitudes toward the outside world. This change took place during the long losing battle between the Chinese and their nomad foes from the eighth to the thirteenth centuries and was, no doubt, strongly conditioned by this sad phase of history. It also may have been related to the simultaneous turning of the Chinese from a martial to a pacifistic ideal.

The early T'ang Chinese had still been aggressive, expansive, inquisitive, and tolerant toward the outside world. Ch'ang-an was so much a world capital that there was no need to fear or resent foreign influences. In fact, the strange and the bizarre were often prized. When the first ambassadors from the Islamic caliphate came to China in 713 and refused on religious grounds to prostrate themselves before the emperor in the traditional kowtow, the Chinese readily waived the requirement, in significant contrast to their rigidity on this point with European embassies some centuries later.

By the late T'ang, however, a growing fear and resentment of the "barbarians" was becoming evident. Buddhism had always been criticized on the grounds that it was a foreign religion, but now attacks of this type became more common and had greater influence. A sign of the times was the famous memorial presented to the throne in 819 by the great scholar and essayist Han Yü, criticizing the emperor for paying honor to the supposed fingerbone of the Buddha. Han Yü was banished for his temerity, but only a few decades later the court itself had become so anti-Buddhist that the great persecution of 841–845 was possible.

The turning of Chinese intellectuals away from Buddhism and back to Confucianism was not merely the result of the rising anti-foreign tide in China. The collapse of Buddhism in India and its extinction in Central Asia around the ninth century must have been contributory factors. No doubt an even more basic reason was the obvious success of the old Chinese political ideal.

It would be a mistake to picture the rise of Neo-Confucianism merely in negative terms as the result of the fading of Buddhism. It was primarily the product of a vigorous resurgence of Confucian concepts, as the old Chou and Han ideal of a politically oriented society once more proved successful. The political disillusionment of the Six Dynasties period, which had contributed so much to the rise of Taoism and the triumph of Buddhism, had now receded into the dim past. The need for an educated officialdom in the revived bureaucratic state had led to the re-creation of the examination system, which had come to have a much more important role in government than it had under the Han. The Confucian curriculum on which the examinations were based had helped to spread Confucian ideas among the educated classes. Confucian concepts, of course, had never died out even at the height of the Buddhist age, but after the reunification of the empire they grew steadily in strength and popularity. As early as 630 the T'ang ordered temples to Confucius erected in every prefecture and the old sacrifices to him reinstituted. By the ninth century the educated classes were so thoroughly imbued with Confucianism that they naturally began to reject the anti-political concepts of Taoism and to condemn what they regarded as the anti-social aspects of Buddhism. Thus it would be more accurate to say that the rise of Neo-Confucianism caused the decline of Buddhism rather than the reverse.

The Diversity of Neo-Confucianism. The Neo-Confucian upsurge of the late T'ang and Sung was not simply the continuation of earlier concepts as they had existed in the Chou or Han. The revived interest in early Confucian ideas was at least to some extent an exciting rediscovery. It was obvious to the scholars who participated in this work that the society in which they were living was quite different from that described in the classics. Confucian rituals had become the concern of only a few specialists and were not part of the life of the people, as it was assumed they had once been. The Neo-Confucians hoped to recapture the original vision — to recreate the ideal Confucian society that they believed had existed in ancient times.

There was, however, considerable diversity in the ideas and aspirations of the Neo-Confucian thinkers. All of them accepted the authority of the classics, but, since these texts were quite varied in content, they could be cited to support widely different points of view. Confucianism did not as yet possess a consistent, homogeneous body of doctrine.

Nor was Neo-Confucianism limited purely to the older Confucian tradition. Buddhism had conditioned men to think in its metaphysical terms. A new Confucian metaphysics, therefore, was now needed to support traditional Confucian ethics and to win men's minds from a Buddhist view of the world. To develop this metaphysics, the Neo-Confucian philosophers turned freely to Taoist terminology and Buddhist concepts. The influence of Zen, the intellectually dominant type of Buddhism at this time, was particularly marked. Many of the leading Sung Neo-Confucian philosophers had been students of Taoism and Buddhism before they turned to Confucianism, and some had even lived in Buddhist monasteries. Thus, from a genetic point of view, Neo-Confucianism was drawn from all the major philosophies of the day. It incorporated into the main stream of Confucianism many of the ideas of Taoism and Buddhism, just as Han Confucianism had absorbed important elements from all of the Chou philosophies as these had survived into the Han period.

Much attention has been paid to Neo-Confucian metaphysics because it was something quite new in Confucianism. It was, however, a relatively peripheral element, since Neo-Confucianism naturally centered around the traditional ethics and political philosophy. The Neo-Confucians, despite the influence of Taoism and Buddhism, consciously rejected the central focuses of these two rival religions — the Taoist search for immortality and the Buddhist emphasis on the divine and on the afterlife. The this-worldly, practical bias of ancient Chinese thought and its agnostic, non-theistic tendencies were also strongly revived by the Sung philosophers and thenceforth became the over-whelmingly dominant attitudes of Chinese intellectuals.

The Great Neo-Confucians: Chu Hsi. Han Yü (768–824), the distinguished prose stylist and critic of Buddhism, might be called the first of the great Neo-Confucians. He "rediscovered," so to speak, the *Mencius* and the chapter of the *Record of Rituals* known as the *Great Learning (Ta hsüeh)*, giving them a new prominence which in time was to make them two of the most esteemed Confucian texts. In the early Sung period Fan Chung-yen (990–1053) helped draw atten-tion to the essentially non-Confucian *Classic of Changes* and the *Doc-trine of the Mean (Chung yung)*, while Ou-yang Hsiu (1007–1072) contributed to a general revival of interest in ancient texts.

The eleventh century witnessed a great intellectual ferment and the development of many variant schools of Confucian thought. Wang An-shih, for example, represented a pragmatic, activist type of Confu-cianism. Ou-yang Hsiu and the poet Su Shih were leaders of other im-portant philosophical trends. In the twelfth century, Lu Chiu-yüan (also known as Lu Hsiang-shan, 1139–1192) developed a Zen-like emphasis on personal intuition that was to reach its height, as we shall see, under the great Ming statesman Wang Yang-ming. Meanwhile, however, still another school of Sung Confucianism, of which Chu Hsi (1130–1200) was the unifier and synthesizer, had been established as Neo-Confucian orthodoxy.

The early developers of what was to become the orthodox doctrine were largely identified with the opposition to Wang An-shih, and the eventual triumph of their philosophical school and the traditional politi-cal disrepute of Wang An-shih are, no doubt, related phenomena. Chou Tun-i (1012–1073) took from the entirely non-Confucian *Classic of Changes* the term T'ai-chi, or "Supreme Ultimate," and devised an ex-tremely Taoistic cosmological chart showing how *yin* and *yang* and the "five elements" derived from this unchanging basic principle. Chang Tsai (1020–1077) and the brothers Ch'eng Hao (1031–1085) and Ch'eng I (1032–1107) contributed to the elaboration of these metaphysi-cal concepts. Ch'eng I was also largely responsible for establishing the category of the Four Books as the central scriptures of Confucianism. These four, as we have seen, were the Confucian *Analects*, the *Mencius*, and two chapters from the *Record of Rituals*: the *Great Learning* and the *Doctrine of the Mean*. From Sung times until the twentieth cen-tury these four works remained at the core of all Chinese education.

Chu Hsi, who has sometimes been compared with Thomas Aquinas in Europe, was in many ways the perfect Confucianist. He was not only a statesman, even if not a very important one; he was also a famous historian, as we have seen, and the greatest of the commentators on the classics, as well as China's leading philosopher after the classic age. He put his stamp so heavily on Neo-Confucian thought that in East Asia it has often been known as Chu Hsi-ism.

Neo-Confucian Metaphysics. In the Neo-Confucian metaphysics of Chu Hsi's school, all varieties of things were thought to have their respective *li*, or fundamental principles of form.[2] These, when brought together into a single whole, constituted the limitless, timeless Supreme Ultimate, the great principle underlying all phenomenal existence. According to Chu Hsi's commonly quoted metaphor, the Supreme Ultimate, though present within all things, "is not cut up into pieces; it is merely like the moon reflecting itself in ten thousand streams." The influence of Buddhism is evident in this theory that all things have their all-perfect normative archetypes, that is, their share of the Supreme Ultimate. It also naturally reminds us of Plato's theory of ideas.

While the *li* provides the plan of a boat or house, actual boats and houses are made of wood and brick. These are their *ch'i*, literally "ether," or what we would call matter. Elaborate theories specified the relationships between the Supreme Ultimate, *li* and *ch'i*, *yin* and *yang*, and the "five elements," and there was a concept of a cycle of change from creation to chaos that is reminiscent of Buddhist cyclic theories. All this was carefully schematized and diagramed in typically Chinese style.

Neo-Confucian metaphysics proved in the long run relatively unimportant in Chinese thought. The Sung philosophers themselves were close enough to Buddhism to put strong emphasis on this type of problem, but the Indian, Buddhistic approach to philosophy became of so little real interest to later Chinese thinkers that they were willing to accept Chu Hsi's metaphysical formulations without question while they directed their attention to other matters.

The application of these theories to human nature, and, through human nature, to society, always retained a much livelier interest for Chinese thinkers. The old conflict between Mencius' belief that man is by nature good and thus only needs self-development and Hsün-tzu's view that man is by nature evil and thus needs strict control and education came to a head during the Sung. Chu Hsi and his school settled the argument in Mencius' favor. The *li* of man's nature, they argued, is of course pure and good. It is the origin of the five basic virtues, which can be translated as love, uprightness, propriety, knowledge, and reliability. Human nature in actuality is the manifestation of its *li* through its *ch'i*, or physical aspects. The pearl of man's *li* is always found in the mire of his *ch'i*. It needs polishing to be given its full potential luster.

[2] This *li*, meaning "principle," is a different word from the *li* for "rites" or "ritual," and is written with an entirely different character.

Thus, education is desirable, though self-cultivation is even more important and leads to a type of "enlightenment" that is, as described by Chu Hsi, strongly reminiscent of Zen ideas.

Neo-Confucian Ethics. While Neo-Confucian metaphysics helped restore Confucianism to intellectual supremacy in China, the heart of Neo-Confucianism, like that of all earlier forms of Confucian thought, remained the application of its ideas through the ethical, social, and political institutions that had evolved over the centuries. Although we have touched upon this before, it may be helpful to describe again briefly this central core of Confucianism as it reached full maturity in the Sung period.

There was, first of all, the particularistic, family-centered Confucian ethic, stressing the five human relationships first spelled out in the *Mencius*. These were between the ruler and his minister or subject, father and son, husband and wife, elder brother and younger brother, and friend and friend. It should be noted that, except for the last, all of these were relations of authority and obedience.

Next there was the Confucian political ideal of benevolent paternalism. The state was regarded as the family writ large. The authority of the ruler, like that of the father, was considered to be essentially ethical. Good government, that is, the achievement of the unsullied *li* or *tao* of government, depended upon the moral character or sincerity of the ruler. It was best achieved, as Mencius had said, by the influence of the ruler's good example.

Finally, there was the bureaucratic ideal — the realization that even the ethically perfect ruler needed the aid of a large body of morally excellent officials through whom he could exercise his benevolent paternalism. This ideal was institutionalized in the civil service and the examination system, through which bureaucrats were most properly chosen. Having once been trained in the classical principles of right conduct and good government, the scholar-officials bore a responsibility to advise the Son of Heaven, even at risk to themselves. The ideals of the bureaucracy, while apparently only peripheral to Neo-Confucian philosophy, were in fact at the very heart of the whole Confucian ethic as it took final shape in the Sung period.

After Chu Hsi's death, his Neo-Confucian synthesis gradually became established as a rigid orthodoxy. By 1313 his commentaries on the classics had been made the standard ones to which all answers in the civil service examinations had to conform. Thus, through no fault of his own and only because of the comprehensiveness and persuasiveness of his views, Chu Hsi's scholarship and philosophical speculation became a check to further Chinese philosophical development. Strengthened by the traditional respect for both the past and the written word, Chu Hsi-ism, once established as orthodoxy, proved to be a sort of intellectual strait jacket, reinforcing the growing rigidity of Chinese society. Even Chu Hsi's emphasis on "the investigation of things" as the key to knowledge, an idea taken from the *Great Learning*, failed to encourage Chinese minds to advance into new fields, for the phrase was interpreted as meaning merely an examination of the classics and history as expounded by Chu Hsi and thus led to arid scholasticism rather than to new discoveries.

CULTURAL STABILITY

The establishment of Chu Hsi-ism as a rigid and rarely challenged orthodoxy was one of the most obvious manifestations of the way in which Chinese culture became fixed in a pattern which remained dominant from late Sung times until late in the nineteenth century. Being the only set of ideas recognized as valid in the examination system, and thus the only set of ideas that most ambitious students wished to acquire, Neo-Confucianism helped create the uniquely stable and traditionalistic society of early modern China — a society which changed so little in comparison with Europe that both Occidentals and Chinese have been prone to accept the myth that China has always been "unchanging."

The relative slowness of cultural and institutional change in China after the thirteenth century left the country weak and defenseless in the nineteenth century before the cultural onslaught of the West, which had grown so spectacularly during those same centuries. China's comparative inertia, therefore, is usually viewed as an historic tragedy, if not a cause for national shame. It can, however, be looked at in an entirely different perspective. For the successive generations of Chinese who lived during this long period, the high degree of political, social, and spiritual stability which they enjoyed was probably preferable to the constant turmoil of life and thought during these same centuries in Europe. We moderns, living in the notably unstable world civilization that has grown out of the rapidly changing culture of the West, may also look with envy at the peace and stability of China between the thirteenth and nineteenth centuries.

The question remains how China was able to achieve so long a period of cultural stability. There are few historic parallels except among primitive peoples. One answer to this question might be the geographical isolation of China from the rest of the civilized world, but this is not very convincing, since isolation had not slowed the rate of change in earlier periods of Chinese history and this was, in any case, a time of growing rather than decreasing foreign contact.

A more plausible reason is the very perfection that Chinese culture and social organization had achieved by the thirteenth century. The political, social, and intellectual systems were basically so viable and so well balanced that not until this balance was destroyed by massive external blows in the nineteenth century was Chinese society again set in rapid motion. In retrospect, the Chinese have every right to view with pride the stage in their civilization in which they created a society so perfect within its own guiding ideals and technological limits that it achieved a degree of stability no other high civilization has ever been able to approach.

7

China and the "Barbarians":
The Mongol Empire

"Barbarian" Participation in the Chinese State

The stability of the Chinese way of life from the thirteenth to the nineteenth century was as marked in the political as in the cultural sphere. Three great ruling houses held power during three dynastic periods: Yüan (1271–1368), Ming (1368–1644), and Ch'ing (1644–1912). Disorder occurred principally during the years of dynastic change, in the middle of the fourteenth and the seventeenth centuries.

Yet this stable political record has a puzzling aspect. The Yüan and the Ch'ing were non-Chinese dynasties of conquest. Under them, small groups of "barbarians," either Mongols or Tungusic Manchus, ruled over the immensely more populous Middle Kingdom. To be sure, they ruled with Chinese help and made little effort to change Chinese ways — so little, in fact, that they may almost be regarded, especially in the case of the Manchus, as integral parts of the Chinese political order. To take this idea further, we may view these non-Chinese rulers of China as conventional or at least regular participants in the government of the Chinese Empire.

The empire from this point of view was not merely the agricultural area within the Great Wall — China proper. It also embraced the peripheral regions of Central Asia, especially Mongolia and the region we call Manchuria. It would normally be expected that a strong Chinese dynasty, such as the Han, T'ang or Ming, would dominate these regions.

But periodically, as we have suggested, the *yang* of Chinese expansion would give way to the *yin* of "barbarian" invasion. Tribal peoples outside the Wall would seize power by force of arms and rule part if not all of the empire. Yet invariably they would make use of the traditional political institutions of the Son of Heaven and his bureaucracy. The stability of the Chinese political order lay partly in its capacity to let non-Chinese, when they were strong enough, rule over it without changing its fundamental features. This non-Chinese participation in China's political life, however, was neither passive nor purely imitative. More than once "barbarian" vigor helped to regenerate the political process by setting the dynastic cycle in motion at times when the empire under Chinese rulers had fallen into chaos or decay.

These generalizations are of course oversimplified, but they will serve to focus our attention on the fascinating problem of Sino-"barbarian" relations. Although the Mongols were the first non-Chinese to rule all China, they had their predecessors in smaller "barbarian" dynasties in the North. There are enough examples of non-Chinese ruling over Chinese to make this a major motif in East Asian history.

The Sequence of Alien Rulers. This alien influence in Chinese politics becomes increasingly prominent as time goes by. We have noted (page 49) how the Chou people who conquered the Shang are thought by some to have been partly "barbarian" in origin, and (on page 85) how the border state of Ch'in, which also expanded from the northwest to create the unified empire, was regarded by other Chinese as semi-"barbarian." Subsequently, the Han had faced the nomadic Hsiung-nu as their chief enemy (pages 94–95, 99–101, and 123–124). After the fall of the Han came the invasions by the "Five Barbarians" (pages 131–132 and 148–152) and the rise of non-Chinese rulers in the North, especially the Northern Wei dynasty (386–534) set up by the T'o-pa tribes. The Sui and early T'ang emperors who revived the united empire sprang from a mixed Sino-"barbarian" background. Subsequently, as we have noted (pages 198 and 208–210), the Sung had to cope with the full-fledged non-Chinese dynasties of Liao and Chin. The "barbarians" thus had continually played a role in the political life of the Chinese people. Moreover, this role had grown greater. The Mongol conquest was the climax of a long development.

This ever-present "barbarian" influence on China's political life was based upon a major geographical fact — the close juxtaposition of the steppe and the sown areas, of two irreducibly different ways of life and two contrasting types of social organization suited to these different geographical regions. Neither way of life could ever be fully incorporated into the other. From early times, these two worlds of East Asia had been in continuous contact, permanent factors in each other's history.

CENTRAL ASIAN PEOPLES AND KINGDOMS

(Note: The data below are not by any means permanently established, many points being still in dispute among scholars.)

People	Language Group	Period and Region
Hsiung-nu (Huns?)	Turkish	Founded first steppe empire in third century B.C.; conquered by Han in first century B.C. and first century A.D.
Yüeh-chih	Probably Indo-European	Second century B.C., sought by Han China as allies against Hsiung-nu; migrated from Kansu to Ili to Bactria, thence to Northwest India and set up Kushan Kingdom.
Hsien-pei	Mongolian	Third century A.D., in eastern Mongolia; invaded China in fourth century A.D.
Tabgach (T'o-pa)	Largely Mongolian	Founded Northern Wei dynasty, 386–534 A.D., in North China.
Turks (T'u-chüeh)	Turkish	Empire established c. 552; split into Eastern Empire (c. 600–744) on the Orkhon River, and Western Empire, in contact with Sassanians in Persia; groups penetrated India and Europe after 659.
Uighurs	Turkish	Conquered Eastern Turks and set up empire on the Orkhon River, 744–840; forced out by Kirghiz, set up empire in Tarim basin (Turfan) during 840 and after.
Khitan (Ch'i-tan)	Mongolian	Founded Liao dynasty in North China and adjacent area, 947–1125; driven west by Jürched; set up Kara-Khitai (Western Liao) Empire in East Turkestan, 1124–1211.
Jürched (Ju-chen, ancestors of the Manchus)	Tungusic	Founded Chin dynasty in North China, 1122–1234.
Tanguts	Tibetan	Founded Hsi Hsia Kingdom in Northwest China, 1038–1227.
Mongols	Mongolian	Founded Yüan dynasty over all China, 1271–1368.

The chart of Central Asian peoples and kingdoms on page 245 indicates the names and habitats of the groups of "barbarians" who have appeared and disappeared in the grasslands on China's northern horizon throughout history. It may be noted that a westward drift characterizes this record, one people after another being driven by the Chinese or by their own nomadic successors toward the West. It is noteworthy also that the earlier peoples belonged generally to the Turkish-speaking language group, while the Mongolian-speaking peoples became dominant later. From these tribes of the steppe emerged periodically a leadership and a fighting force that succeeded in ruling part or all of China.

Underlying the contrast between the Chinese and "barbarian" ways of life was, first of all, the difference in rainfall. The aridity of the Central Asian steppe, from which no rivers flow out to the sea, has made extensive agriculture impossible. Lacking adequate water resources, the high uplands of Tibet and the grasslands of Mongolia have had a very sparse population. The Central Asian regions, including Outer Mongolia, Chinese Turkestan, Tibet and the eastern Tibetan marches (which have recently become Chinese provinces) total something like 3,000,000 square miles, roughly double the area of China proper. But even in recent times, when the population within the Wall is estimated at more than six hundred million, the total population of Central Asia can hardly have gone much beyond fifteen or twenty million. Roughly the same proportions must have obtained in earlier centuries. The "barbarians" had on the order of twice the area of China, but only about one twenty-fifth or perhaps one-fortieth of the population.

The source of "barbarian" power is therefore a very interesting question. The military superiority of the "barbarians" was frequently demonstrated when their mounted archers came within the Wall. But what lay behind this capacity to produce fierce and mobile fighting men?

THE SOCIETY OF THE STEPPE

Economy. In the scattered society of the grasslands, life was sustained primarily by the raising of animals rather than crops. (See Plates 25 and 28.) The full nomad lived on a sheep-and-horse economy. Sheepskins formed his clothing. The wool made felt for his tents. He ate mutton and from the milk of his animals made cheese and butter. His women gathered dung for fuel, especially when it had been trampled into cakes in a penned enclosure. His main reliance was upon the horse for transport and the management of his flocks, and for hunting and warfare. The horse was supplemented by the camel for crossing desert regions, and by oxen for pulling his carts.

The resulting pastoral economy had little need of agriculture so long as it could maintain a minimal trade with settled areas in order to secure certain essential commodities. The most important of these was grain to supplement an animal diet. As time went on, the nomads also sought textiles, tea and other "luxuries," and metals with which to make weapons. Thus the nomad of the open steppe was self-sufficient in the short run, but could not be wholly cut off from the civilization of populated farmlands and commercial centers. He lived far beyond their frontiers but remained connected by trade.

The nomad needed mobility, but his migration was not an aimless wandering about. It occurred on a seasonal basis, usually to move his flocks and herds from summer pasture on the open plain to winter pasture in some more sheltered area such as a mountain valley, and back again. The distance might be no more than a hundred miles. His essential rights were those of movement for pasture rather than of land monopoly for agriculture. The tribal chieftain sought the right to perform a cycle of migration using certain grasslands at certain seasons. He had little interest in the settled activities of hay-cutting, well-digging, mining or industry.

Yet these herdsmen remained precariously dependent upon nature, for a severe winter could destroy their flocks. To a lesser degree the semi-nomads, who lived on the fringes of sedentary agricultural societies, shared this constant economic instability. Their lack of accumulated resources gave both types of nomads a periodic incentive not only for increased trade but for military expansion. When so motivated, they might at first fight one another but would ultimately join forces to attack the settled areas from which they could obtain greater supplies of grain and arms. The nomads were the have-nots of antiquity. Their way of life kept them always poor, in comparison with the rulers of more thickly populated farming regions.

Society. The social organization of the tribes contributed to their military strength. Their clans were organized under chieftains who rose to their positions through personal prowess. They could not linger on in power like the patriarchs of a sedentary society. When old or weak, they would be displaced by younger and stronger leaders. The personal relations of fealty and protection, reciprocally maintained between major and minor chieftains as well as among warriors, produced a type of political organization in which a leader of strong personality could rather quickly rise to the top of a hierarchy of personal relationships. Command over chieftains and their warriors would in turn bring an able leader control over the sheep-and-horse economy of whole tribes.

Unlike peasants, who could not leave their fields without loss of production, the herders and huntsmen of the steppe, when they had strong central leadership, could be quickly mobilized, especially if plunder were in prospect. The men of this society from boyhood spent their lives in the saddle. They were not just herdsmen but were also hunters and warriors, whose energies could be turned in a moment from the care of their flocks or the pursuit of game to the destruction of their enemies. Their active outdoor life produced a type of individual (not unlike the early American cowboy) who was independent, self-reliant and omnicompetent because he was unspecialized. The herdsman-warrior-hunter of the steppe had to be ready for anything and could not restrict himself to a single profession. His women served as the workers and managers of the camp and were themselves competent to handle all the problems of nomad life, except war and politics.

Since cities could not flourish on the thin population of the Central Asian grasslands, there were strict limits to the culture and technology of the nomadic herdsmen. Compared with the Chinese, they necessarily seemed uncultured, in short, "barbarians" in the Greek sense of the term. Wealth was stored in the form of silver ornaments worn by the women. The chief art form was the so-called Scythian or animal style of metal work found all across the Eurasian steppe from the lower Volga and the Caspian Sea to the Amur River. (See page 109.) Literacy and literature remained undeveloped.

The religion of the tribes was a primitive shamanism, practiced by medicine men, not unlike that of those far-distant cousins of the Tungusic peoples, the American Indians of the great plains of the United States. The one great deity of the steppe was the Eternal Heaven. Buddhism in its Tibetan form, known as Lamaism, was eventually to spread among the Mongols in the thirteenth century, but, until the establishment of the Yellow sect of Lamaism as a theocracy in Mongolia in the sixteenth century, there was no organized church or other religious influence to rival the nomad's preoccupation with hunting and fighting; there were, in other words, few religious concepts or social institutions of a sort to check the occasional unification of the tribes and their mobilization for aggression against North China.

The Nomad Menace. Post-Han China saw not only a decline of unity within the Wall but also an increase in the striking power of the "barbarians." By the third and fourth centuries A.D., if not before, the nomad cavalry had begun to use the iron stirrup, which had had a long history of early development, evident in the Assyrian footboard and the Scythian-Indian foot sling. Eventually the use of iron to make stirrups gave the nomads of Eastern Asia as well as the Arabs of the Near East an effective basis for mounted archery. The horseman could stand securely in his stirrups while shooting. This was illustrated by what is known in the West as the "Parthian shot," back over the horse's rump. The archer, firmly mounted on a well-trained horse and armed with a compound bow small enough for use from the saddle, became the dominant fighting man. (See page 56.) For the next thousand years (c. 400–1400) he maintained a tactical military superiority over the peasant foot soldier. During this millennium, up to the introduction of firearms, the balance of military technology in Asia remained in favor of the horseman.

The steppe society of the nomads was in constant contact with the settled civilization of China on a frontier which lay roughly along the line of the Great Wall. This boundary, where cultivator and herdsman met, remained unstable. Rainfall was marginal in this region and farming met periodic disaster. The continual trade with the nomad, in grain, silk, and later tea, in exchange for horses, easily became intermixed with political relations. From one generation to the next, semi-nomads on this frontier might settle down as Chinese vassals and even become Sinicized under vigorous Chinese rule. Conversely, if Chinese rule proved ineffective, the mixed Sino-"barbarian" populace of the frontier region might give its allegiance to a rising nomad leader.

The secret of the rise of a nomad leader along the borderland lay usually in his capacity to learn Chinese ways of administrative organization, so that he could set up a hybrid regime based on control of merchants, farmers, and tribal warriors. The Chinese inevitably played a part, willingly or unwillingly, in the rise of such a "barbarian" ruler on the frontier. In this uneasy partnership the alien rulers functioned in special roles — as fighters and power-holders — and so maintained their domination over the much more numerous local Chinese populace. Sometimes, as we have seen, they were able to go further and move in from the border region to set up dynasties in China.

THE KHITAN EMPIRE

The history of the Liao Empire of the Khitan (already touched upon on pages 198 and 208) illustrates the characteristic features of "barbarian" rule over a dual state. From the tenth to the early twelfth centuries, this regime extended over much of Manchuria and Mongolia and the northeast corner of China proper within the Wall. (See map, page 199.) Thus it included several economic regions: an agricultural area in North China and southern Manchuria, grasslands in western Manchuria and Mongolia, and the forested valleys of eastern and northern Manchuria. The empire centered geographically and administratively in the northern part of the modern province of Jehol, just north of Peking and the Great Wall. This region was inhospitably cold (in Jehol only about a hundred days of the year are frost-free) and had only a marginal rainfall of ten to fifteen inches.

The non-Chinese part of this kingdom included several tribal groups. In eastern Manchuria were the Tungus (ancestors of the Manchus), who lived by a combination of hunting and agriculture together with pig-raising. On the Mongolian steppe to the west were Turkish tribes, full nomads who had neither agriculture nor pigs, but many sheep, horses and camels as their mainstay of subsistence. Between these tribes, in Jehol, were the semi-nomadic Khitan people, who by their speech belonged to what were later called the Mongolian-speaking peoples (the term "Mongol" became current only later). The Chinese chroniclers had recorded them as being originally tributary to the Northern Wei and then to the T'ang. They lived by a mixed economy in which agricultural crops, camels, pigs, horses and oxen all played a part. It was these Khitan tribes in the central region of mixed economy who led the way in building the empire.

The Khitan Tribal Society. Each of the Khitan tribal units was under a chieftain, who led it in military action. Each unit had its own tribal myth and ancestor. The number of tribes fluctuated. They were grouped in confederations, with some subordinate to others, and they occasionally split up to form new units. Beginning with a nucleus of eighteen tribes which followed the founder of the empire, the number eventually grew to a total of fifty-four.

In the Khitan economy, which combined pastoralism with agriculture, the main crop was millet, the poor man's grain, but chief attention was devoted to sheep-raising, at least until the conquest of parts of North China made an adequate grain supply readily available. Wealth was measured first in terms of flocks of sheep and also horses, which represented military power. These were kept in large herds of perhaps several thousand head. After the establishment of the semi-Sinicized Liao Empire in 947, horses were used to maintain the imperial postal service, which could relay messages as fast as 700 *li*, about 230 miles, a day — a speed that remained the top limit for this service down to modern times. As the empire developed, its few industries and meager technology followed in the train of Chinese models. Smelters were maintained for iron-working, and salt was handled as a government monopoly.

Khitan society was headed by the Yeh-lü clan, divided into eight main lineages, together with the Hsiao clan, which regularly provided wives for the Yeh-lü men. Non-Khitan tribes which were conquered or which surrendered voluntarily were incorporated into the society. So also was the settled Chinese population of agricultural villages and cities. The status of the Chinese varied all the way from slavery, through various forms of bondage and partial freedom, to complete freedom. Chinese officials were regularly used in the civil administration over the Chinese populace. At the bottom of the social scale were the conquered peoples of the state of P'o-hai (713–926) in eastern Manchuria, who received the most severe treatment.

Unlike the Chinese clan system, in which an unbroken line is maintained indefinitely, most of the Khitan clans lacked clan names and tended to lose their identity after several generations. The Chinese clan system, however, was used to hold the ruling house together. Ancestral sacrifices were maintained only by the Yeh-lü clan, following the Chinese example.

In the nomad fashion, the women were camp managers and on occasion might lead troops and act in public ceremonies. A wife could divorce her husband. The wife of the founder of the Liao Empire actually ruled as regent for a time after his death. Marriage similarly followed the tribal custom, which was quite at variance with Chinese practices. That is, a man might marry his mother's or his father's sister, or his brother's widow, in complete disregard of the Chinese rules of generation. He could also practice polygamy without special recognition of the first wife, as was required in the Chinese custom of concubinage.

The Khitan religion included a simple belief in supernatural spirits and in magic to win their support or ward off evil. The shamans, or "witch doctors," were intermediaries with the spirit world, and were thought to have received power directly from the spirits, who included the tribal ancestors.

The Rise of Khitan Power. By the year 907 the Khitan had formed a tribal confederation comparable to that of the Hsiung-nu of earlier times. In that year the chieftain, whose name is known to us only in Chinese transcription as Yeh-lü A-pao-chi (872–926), declared himself emperor of the Khitan. After continuing in power for three three-year periods, according to the nomad custom by which the ablest man was chosen as leader for a limited number of years, he succeeded in shifting to the Chinese political pattern and set up a dynasty with his own son as the acknowledged heir apparent. His role as dynastic founder involved A-pao-chi in constant warfare, not least with his own brothers. Tribal disputes arose over the succession, but, as the empire expanded, it firmly adopted the Chinese system of hereditary monarchy, which provided an important focus of leadership.

Next to their capacity for maintaining central leadership, the Khitan owed their empire to their cavalry, which gave them a superior combination of mobility and striking power. A-pao-chi's mounted archers were organized in his *ordo*,[1] which formed his camp bodyguard. As early as 922 he had some two thousand braves in this elite guard drawn from all the tribes. Later, twelve *ordos* were organized in administrative districts. They included both Khitan and other nomadic tribal units and also Chinese. The men, married and living in households, constituted

[1] *Ordo* was the prototype of what Westerners later called a "horde"; it is the origin of this word as well as of the name "Ordos" for the area north of Shensi.

a mobile shock force held in reserve. Beginning as a bodyguard like those of Western emperors, this elite cavalry grew to include some fifty to seventy thousand horsemen. To back up this striking force Chinese militia were conscripted in the southern region to provide a territorial infantry. There were also border garrisons and other special armies.

In warfare the cavalryman might use three horses (leading two remounts). He wore some armor, though not the complete covering of a European knight, and sometimes put pieces of armor on his horse. In battle he used two kinds of bows and carried an axe, a sword, a rope and dried food. Training was carried out in the form of hunting exercises in units of five or ten horsemen, who were strictly disciplined to follow their leaders.

As they expanded into North China, the Khitan warriors learned how to combine their cavalry striking power with siege techniques against fortified cities. Their invasions were remarkably successful on the open plain, for they developed a clock-like precision of organization based on units of tens, hundreds and thousands, with a vanguard, wings, a center and an imperial guard. Their army was preceded by a scouting force, perhaps ten thousand strong, and they used night patrols and complicated signals consisting of beacons, drums, horns, banners, shouted code names, gongs and even birdcalls. In advancing they kept the two wings on parallel routes; armor, transported in carts, and fresh horses were always at hand. They avoided close combat with superior numbers but would cut off the enemy's supplies and use tactics of ambush and maneuver. In siege operations they enlisted the Chinese populace to fill in moats and used Chinese catapults to break down walls. In storming a city they would drive their Chinese captives ahead against their own townsmen and relatives.

THE LIAO DYNASTY

By 947, the Khitan, as we have seen, had extended their power southward over sixteen prefectures in North China and had captured towns and cities. In that year they adopted a Chinese dynastic title, calling themselves the Liao dynasty (947–1125). As the most successful of the "barbarian" peoples in taking advantage of the collapse of the T'ang Empire, they had now created a dual state composed of "barbarian" elements in the north and Chinese in the south. In this process they had essential help from Chinese advisers who joined their cause, bringing with them the culture of cities and the methods of bureaucratic government. The principal adviser who helped A-pao-chi was a political refugee named Han Yen-hui.

Government. The Liao political administration was organized under five capitals: the Supreme Capital in northwestern Jehol; the Eastern Capital on the south Manchurian plain at Liao-yang; the Central Capital in southern Jehol; the Southern Capital, called Yen-ching, on the site of modern Peking; and the Western Capital in the area of Ta-t'ung in northern Shansi. Each capital was the center of a circuit with a hierarchy of territorial units below it and with its own military commanderies, forts and fortified cities to protect it. Garrisons were posted, particularly on the north and northwest, to control the Central Asian tribes.

In this dual government each half had its own prime minister, chancellery and ministers. The heads of both governments held office at the Supreme Capital. The government of the southern region retained the inherited forms of the T'ang, such as the Six Ministries and the Board of Censors, together with the three administrative secretariats or chancelleries (*sheng*). The emperor not only held court in his palace, but, during the hunting season (which lasted much of the year), conducted his administration from his traveling camp.

One factor for success in holding this dual state together was the growth of the Liao monarchy into a Chinese type of ruling institution. A-pao-chi and his successors took over the Chinese custom of naming year periods, selected an heir apparent, made Confucius the supreme sage of the state, adopted traditional Chinese administrative titles and court ceremonies, practiced Confucian ancestor worship, used the Chinese language and script as their administrative lingua franca, and even wore Chinese clothes when in the southern region.

As against this Sinification, the Khitan retained their own tribal organization and rites and, in the main, their own style of food and clothing. Unlike earlier "barbarian" invaders, they consciously avoided taking over the Chinese spoken language as their own tongue, lest they be submerged in the sea of Chinese. They developed two forms of writing for their own type of Mongolian speech, the smaller one being alphabetical and the larger one based on Chinese characters. (See page 257.) In spite of the invention of their own writing systems, however, the literacy of the Khitan remained limited. The two Khitan scripts were used for administration, but no true literature developed in them, and there was only meager study of the Chinese classics. The Confucianism of the Khitan also was more a matter of lip service than of philosophy. Instead, they became great patrons of Chinese Buddhism.

In general, the achievements of the Liao rulers, as distinct from their Chinese subjects, were military and administrative rather than cultural. While the Liao laws have not survived, they were at least as detailed as the famous Mongol code (*jasagh* or *yasa*) of two hundred years later. The code of 1036 is said to have included 547 items. The laws differed for the Chinese and the Khitan populations. The Chinese examination system was adopted after 988 to determine eligibility of

Chinese for office. The government also used the Chinese custom of purchasing official status (which gave one the right to apply for office) and the system by which officials had the prerogative of sponsoring their sons or other protégés for official life.

Relations With the Sung. The Liao Empire at its height seems never to have had a population of more than about 4,000,000, which left it very small in comparison with the Northern Sung, who ruled almost all of China proper. Out of this small total, the actual Khitan population was only about 750,000, while the P'o-hai and other non-Chinese peoples came to perhaps another 650,000, and the Chinese populace to about 2,400,000 at a minimal estimate. Constituting only one-fifth of the population of their empire, the ruling Khitan tribesmen had to be on their mettle to maintain control. Their small numbers may be compared with the later total number of Mongols, about 2,500,000, when they ruled most of Asia three centuries later.

After its growth and final establishment as a Chinese-type dynasty in 947, the Liao state came into conflict on the south with the newly risen Sung dynasty, founded in 960. The "barbarian" incursions indeed had been a factor stimulating Chinese unification; the first Sung emperor had originally risen to prominence as a general of armies sent against Khitan invasions. In the years from 979 to 1004, a border war was carried on, though with interruptions, between the Liao and Sung. The result, as we have noted (pages 198 and 205), was that from 1005 the Sung paid a regular tribute to the Liao. At first this amounted to 100,000 taels (ounces) of silver and 200,000 bolts of silk and later to 200,000 taels of silver and 300,000 bolts of silk. The Chinese felt that these subsidies did not constitute Chinese submission to the Liao, but rather were payments to keep the frontier quiet. In self-defense, the Sung, as we have seen, sought to build up an effective cavalry. For example, in 979 they bought 170,000 horses from the Khitan for this purpose. They also defended the frontier, trying to hold the passes in the mountains and maintaining a border on the plain marked by the planting of willows and elms, the digging of canals and ditches, and the stationing of garrisons. The Chinese walled cities proved difficult for the Khitan to capture, and on the whole the much larger Sung Empire did succeed in holding off the Liao invaders.

Except for architectural monuments such as temples and tombs, the Khitan people seem to have left little cultural heritage. The Chinese populace remained of unreliable loyalty, and the other "barbarian" tribes within the empire had to be kept constantly under control. In the end, as we have noted (page 208), it was another tribal people, the Jürched, who destroyed the Liao power, took over their empire and expanded it.

The Hsi Hsia Kingdom. As has been suggested, one reason why the Sung had been able to withstand the Liao was the three-way division of power that had developed at this time in the northwest. A Tibetan people, the Tanguts, had built in the area of modern Kansu a kingdom known as Hsi Hsia, or West Hsia. Their capital at Ning-hsia, on the upper waters of the Yellow River, stood between Mongolia on the north and the Central Asian trade route to the west. They had a semi-oasis economy, combining irrigated agriculture with pastoralism and trade. After many years of sending tribute to the Sung, the Tangut ruler Li Yüan-hao in 1038 declared his independence by proclaiming himself emperor of the Hsia. During most of the eleventh century, the Hsi Hsia figured in the uneasy relations between the Liao and Sung empires.

The Tanguts modeled their government and education on that of China but, being much attracted to Buddhism, which flourished in the monasteries along the ancient route to the west, they made this their state religion. The unparalleled collection of some ten thousand religious paintings, books and manuscripts in Chinese, Tibetan, Uighur and other languages, discovered at Tun-huang in 1900, was walled up for safe-keeping there about 1035. It reflects the rich mixture of influences which underlay the Tangut culture of this era. Like A-pao-chi of the Liao, with which the Hsi Hsia had extensive contact, Li Yüan-hao had a new writing system invented for his people. It used extremely intricate Chinese-type characters to record the Tangut speech. The resulting literature remains today still largely undeciphered, despite extensive materials unearthed in Kansu.

THE CHIN DYNASTY OF THE JÜRCHED

Although similar to the Khitan in many ways, the Jürched were linguistically distinct, belonging to the Tungusic rather than Mongolian branch of the Altaic peoples. They also had a somewhat different economy. In the forested river valleys of north and east Manchuria, they depended more on hunting, fishing, and agriculture than did the Khitan herdsmen of the drier valleys of Jehol.

Since the Jürched tribes were obliged to render tribute to the Liao and were also prevented from moving down into the attractive southern region of Manchuria, they became restive as Khitan vassals. Their rise to power depended first, of course, upon the unification of the tribes, which in turn required an outstanding leader. This man is known by the Chinese transcription of his name, A-ku-ta. When in 1112 the feckless last emperor of the Liao paid his usual visit to the Sungari region in northern Manchuria for the spring hunting and fishing, he received tribute from the Jürched chiefs and at a banquet ordered them to perform their customary dances. A-ku-ta refused to dance. Soon after, he rose in revolt and in 1115 declared himself emperor. He quickly seized the Liao Eastern Capital at Liao-yang and then the Supreme Capital in northwestern Jehol. The Liao power collapsed and in 1122 A-ku-ta installed in its place the Chin ("Golden") dynasty (1122–1234), named for a river in the early homeland of his people.

The rapid supplanting of the Liao by the Chin was aided, as we have already noted (page 208), by the ill-advised effort of the Sung to "use barbarians against barbarians." In 1120 they had made an alliance with the Jürched against the Liao, promising to make their annual gifts of silk and silver to the new state as they had to the old. After the final extinction of the Liao line in 1125, however, the Chin kept on expanding. They soon overran a larger part of North China than the Liao had ever controlled, captured the Sung capital Kaifeng in 1126, and kept on pushing south of the Yellow River all the way to the Yangtze. Their boundary with the Southern Sung was finally stabilized roughly along the line of the Huai River, on the approximate northern limit of rice cultivation. They also expanded northwestward to the borders of the Hsi Hsia Kingdom. This kingdom on the west and Korea on the east acknowledged themselves vassal states. (See map, page 210.)

Kara-Khitai. In this period another nomad regime had a brief history as a remnant of the Liao dynasty. The Western Liao Empire (1124-1211), called by the Mongols Kara-Khitai or "Black Khitan," was created by a scion of the Liao imperial family, Yeh-lü Ta-shih, who fought the Jürched and then fled west to Turkestan about 1130. He gathered a mixed following of Khitan and other tribesmen and, assuming a supreme title (Gurkhan), imposed his suzerainty over the oases both east and west of the Pamirs, from the borders of the Hsi Hsia Kingdom of the Tanguts in Kansu across to the Amu-Daria (the ancient Oxus River). Yeh-lü Ta-shih's spectacular conquests were inherited by four succeeding rulers. With their cavalry forces, they dominated this sparsely populated region of herdsmen, irrigated oases and intra-Asian trade until overwhelmed by the Mongols in 1211.

Government Under the Chin. Under the Jürched, "barbarian" rule in China reached a broader geographical scope than at any time since the Northern Wei. The Chin Empire was not confined, like the Liao, to the northern border but ruled a major segment of the Middle Kingdom and its people. The Jürched migrated in large numbers into North China, but even so, the Chinese component of this new empire was proportionally much greater and the non-Chinese power-holders were much fewer than the Khitan had been.

At the time of their conquest, the Jürched were still in the early stages of learning how to maintain themselves in power within the Chinese scene. They inherited the dual administration and hybrid cul-

CHARACTER SCRIPTS

Chinese	Khitan	Jürched	Hsi Hsia		'Phags-pa	Syriac	Uighur	Mongolian	Manchu

SCRIPTS USED OR CREATED BY INNER ASIAN PEOPLES

These examples are given to show form without any reference to meaning. For each type of script two columns are shown. All of them usually read from top to bottom and from right to left, although there are sometimes exceptions. For example, Syriac and Uighur almost always read from top to bottom in the Far East and in Central Asia, but they normally read horizontally from right to left in the Near East. The scripts in non-Chinese characters are believed to have been developed mainly on the model of Chinese, but are still largely undeciphered. The alphabetic scripts (except 'Phags-pa) trace back indirectly to Aramaic, which had a common origin with our own alphabet. The 'Phags-pa script was derived from the Tibetan which ultimately was derived from the Sanskrit.

ture which the Khitan rulers had developed and were inevitably drawn further into the Chinese pattern. Moving their main capital from central Manchuria to Yen-ching, on the site of modern Peking, they soon built up a Chinese-type centralized and bureaucratic state. It had five regional capitals like the Liao, but its enlarged territory was divided into nineteen small provinces and was subdivided into prefectures and subprefectures (*hsien*) on the model of the Sung. The whole was governed by the Six Ministries and a bureaucracy in the style inherited from the T'ang. Chinese officials eventually outnumbered non-Chinese three to two.

From the beginning, the Jürched had been fully conscious of their ethnic identity. Like the Khitan and the Tanguts, they sought both to maintain their power over a large mass of Chinese subjects and to preserve their own culture in the face of the imperial Chinese tradition left by the T'ang. These post-T'ang non-Chinese peoples are in this respect reminiscent of the European tribal peoples who asserted their own nationality as Frenchmen or Germans against the tradition left by the defunct Roman Empire. Thus the Jürched used the Khitan alphabetic script and also devised two styles of Jürched script, one of them alphabetic and one in characters derived from Chinese.

In their military establishment the Chin greatly improved upon the unsystematic Sung levies, for the Jürched tribesmen, together with Khitan and other non-Chinese allies, were kept in readiness for instantaneous warfare, to which all their day-to-day activities were subordinated. Though quartered on plots of land scattered within Chinese farming areas, they were expected to respond at once to the call of their captains of "hundreds" and of "thousands." During the early decades of the dynasty, these professional warriors remained invincible. Chinese were excluded from these armies. The Jürched speech was kept alive among the soldiers, and Chinese-style names, clothing and customs were banned.

Inevitably, however, the military personnel of the original Jürched nation-at-arms, once settled in farming households on Chinese soil, became less capable as warriors. Although these transplanted tribal groups did not become fully Chinese, they could not, in spite of their rulers' protective policies, remain effective warriors, aloof from Chinese life. Through economic relations with Chinese, they often became tenants on their land and sometimes paupers. Intermarriage between the two peoples was eventually permitted. Where the unit of 100 warriors had at first been based on 300 households, and ten such units had formed a unit of 1000 warriors, the numbers in both were gradually reduced until at last twenty-five men formed a "hundred," and four such units a "thousand."

A peace with the Southern Sung in 1141 confirmed the nominal suzerainty of the Chin, to whom the Sung paid tribute. This established more or less stable relations and facilitated the continuation of extensive trade between the two areas. While the Jürched nobles intrigued and fought among themselves over the succession at court, their Chinese subjects creatively pursued the arts of peace, in printing, scholarship, painting, literature and also the drama. These accomplishments will be viewed in more detail in conjunction with China's cultural development under the Mongols (see pages 285–289). It should be noted, however, that the Chin rulers themselves were attracted by the higher culture of their Chinese subjects. They too came to follow Confucian norms, studying the classics and writing Chinese poetry.

After one relatively peaceful and constructive reign (1161–1189), the Chin became involved on two frontiers in exhausting wars with the Mongols and the Southern Sung. Friction also grew between Jürched and Chinese officials within the empire. The Chin inflated their paper currency, which they had inherited from the Northern Sung, with the usual unfortunate consequences. By 1215, under Mongol pressure, they were forced to move their capital south from Peking to Kaifeng, where the Mongols extinguished the Chin dynasty in 1234.

Chinese historians have always depicted the gradual cultural absorption of the Jürched and other northern peoples as an unavoidable surrender on the part of less civilized "barbarians" to the older, more sophisticated and superior culture of the Middle Kingdom. It is true that the Jürched rulers attempted, for example, to promote the use of their script by having the Chinese classics and histories translated into it, only to be frustrated by the fact that, even among the Jürched people, their own newly invented writing was not as widely read as Chinese. Such examples of the superior attractiveness of China's ancient culture, however, should not obscure one basic fact which did much to account for the cultural absorption of the non-Chinese invaders — namely, that in North China they were at all times very heavily outnumbered by the local Chinese population.

THE MONGOLS

Patterns of "Barbarian" Conquest. Thus by the time of the Mongols there had already been a series of nomadic conquerors in North China, and certain major characteristics of the dynasties of conquest were already evident. In the history of the Northern Wei, the Liao, and the Chin we can already see a number of repetitive features which become still clearer in the periods of Mongol and Manchu conquest:

(1) Invaders were able to seize power in North China usually during periods of disorder, when a previous dynasty had declined and cavalry raiders could establish territorial control as conquerors. (2) In organ-

izing their effort at conquest, the "barbarians" invariably enlisted Chinese advice and guidance, which they got most easily from Chinese of the border region. Chinese armed forces were similarly absorbed into the invading hordes. (3) The superior military striking power of the "barbarians" was shown in their cavalry, which was supplied with more and better horses from the grazing land of the steppe than could be maintained in an intensely farmed agricultural region. (4) As they acquired control over Chinese farming areas, the invaders often pursued a policy of tolerance, if not appeasement, of the local leadership. Chinese leaders were used to help enlist a larger corps of Chinese tax collectors and administrators. (5) The invaders had to recognize the near impossibility of imposing their own culture upon the settled masses of China, which of course was made the more difficult by their great inferiority in numbers. They therefore made use of Chinese institutions of government and, after the early period of destructiveness, let the traditional forms of administration and of social and cultural life continue. (6) As a corollary to the principle of ruling China in a Chinese way, the invaders usually found it desirable to maintain a homeland of their own beyond the Wall whence they had come. Thus the Liao divided the region under their rule into two areas — one within China and one outside the Wall, where the "barbarian" culture and way of life could be preserved. By this means they attempted to preserve their own conscious existence as a people and avoid absorption. (7) The preservation of Chinese ways in the government of China meant in effect a dual, Sino-"barbarian" administration within the Wall, conducted, at least at the local level, largely by Chinese but under the supervision of the alien conquerors. The use of both types of personnel, with various checks and balances, was an inevitable feature of every foreign dynasty. (8) In addition, the invaders found it useful to employ other foreigners in their administration. Thus the Chin used personnel remaining from the Liao, and we shall find the same principle followed by both the Mongols and the Manchus in their time. (9) Once the conquest had been consolidated, the continuing task of the "barbarians" was to preserve control through military force held in reserve. A territorial army organization had to be built up, into which Chinese could be recruited, but which would represent the alien dynasty. Units of the invading hordes also had to be garrisoned to protect the capital and to hold key areas. (10) Toward the tribal peoples who remained behind them in Central Asia, meanwhile, the dynasties of conquest typically developed a divide-and-rule policy, setting tribe off against tribe, so as to protect their rear and prevent the rise of competitors in that quarter. (11) In the long run, the invaders found it extremely difficult to maintain their cultural and racial identity in the midst of overwhelming numbers of Chinese subjects. Either willingly or reluctantly, they would begin to borrow elements of Chinese culture: food, clothing, names, and even the language. Intermarriages would also occur. The result was usually a decline of military strength and eventual absorption or expulsion by the Chinese or some new invading group. All these factors were illustrated once more during the period of Mongol conquest.

The Rise of Mongol Power. The emergence of world conquerors out of the arid wastes of Mongolia has always demanded explanation from historians and is even now not too well understood. The Mongols were not fanatical religious crusaders like the Arabs of the seventh century, who had spread Islam. The old theory that the progressive drying up of Central Asia "forced" the Mongols to move out has not been sustained. A better explanation is the one we have already suggested — that any pastoral society like that of the Mongols, who were fully nomadic and not semi-nomads like the Khitan or Jürched, was bound to suffer chronic economic instability. The lack of self-sufficiency in grain and weapons was a constant incentive for expansion toward settled areas of supply. In the military technology of the day, moreover, cavalry had become the dominant weapon, a ready means of conquest possessed by the Mongols. To catalyze these elements a dynamic centralization of political authority among the tribes of the steppe under a leader of genius had to coincide with a period of disorganization and weakness among the sedentary societies on the periphery. This is what occurred in Asia in the early thirteenth century.

China had already been divided for a century between the Sino-"barbarian" dynasty of the Chin and the unwarlike Southern Sung. On the northwest frontier of China in modern Kansu was the Hsi Hsia Kingdom of the Tanguts. Farther west were the Uighur Turks, who had settled down in the small oasis states of Central Asia, like that of Turfan, and were no longer the military power they had been in the T'ang period. The Arab-Turkish society of the Middle East similarly was in military decay five hundred years after the Arab conquest of those regions. It included the empire of Khorezm (also spelled Khwārazm, etc.) on the Amu-Daria south of the Aral Sea, the Abbassid Caliphate at Baghdad and many smaller states. Against these disunited, semi- or fully-agrarian and commercial states all across Asia, the Mongols brought to bear an invincible military power. They were organized for conquest, and they succeeded both in conquering and in administering vast areas.

Mongol Society. When Chinggis (also spelled Genghis, Jenghiz, etc.) Khan, the creator of the Mongol Empire, was born, about the year 1167 (some say earlier), the Mongolian-speaking tribes still lacked a common name. Some were composed of hunters and fishermen living in small groups on the fringe of the Siberian forest. The greater part

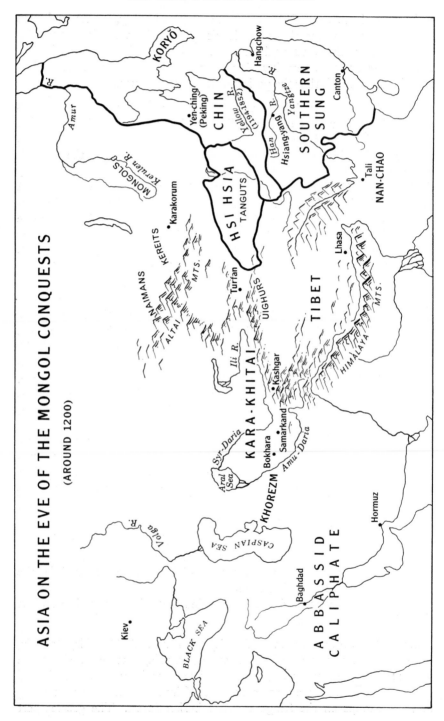

ASIA ON THE EVE OF THE MONGOL CONQUESTS

(AROUND 1200)

of the Mongol people, however, had long since taken up a life on horseback on the open steppe. Here they lived in small groups of a few families, each family in its felt tent or yurt. At the times of seasonal migration these scattered units might form larger groups of several hundred yurts.

The basic social and political units were patriarchal clans. The individual's spiritual life was focused on loyalty to his clan, which was expressed in a cult of the hearth. Since a group of clans, bound together by their blood relationships, formed a larger tribal unit, the individual felt a similar loyalty to his tribe. Within this social framework, one Mongol might choose to become a "sworn brother" of another by a personal alliance between the two of them as members of different clans; adoption was also practiced in this society which remained rather open and fluid.

The traditional institution of polygamy heightened the demand for wives, but these had to be acquired from outside the clan because marriage was considered impossible within a clan or even between members of closely related clans. Consequently, wives were often acquired by seizure, a practice which naturally fostered feuds, raids of vengeance and petty warfare between clans or even whole tribes.

As a result of tribal warfare, clan groups of families would become vassals subordinate to other clans, and whole tribes would become subordinate to other tribes, enhancing their power. On the personal level, a defeated individual might become a servitor or "slave" of a stronger man, even though they both continued to subsist in the same manner and had more or less the same standard of living. A hierarchy of feudal-type relations of fealty and protection among "lords," "knights," "commoners" and "serfs" (to borrow European terms which are not entirely appropriate) had thus developed among the Mongols, to the point where a strong personality might rise to a position of commanding leadership.

The Career of Chinggis Khan

Before the twelfth century certain Mongolian-speaking groups had played an important political role in China, but the empires of the steppe had been created chiefly by Turkish-speaking tribes such as the Hsiung-nu or the Uighurs. The empire Chinggis Khan created thus was the first great Mongol Empire of the region we call Mongolia.

Chinggis Khan enters history chiefly as an organizer and unifier of the Mongol tribes. His personal name was Temüjin. He was of aristocratic birth but lived in humble circumstances in his youth. His father had been slain when he was a boy, and he struggled through hard times to avenge him. He rose only slowly, and after reaching maturity was still merely the vassal of a minor chieftain. The establishment of personal loyalties was a gradual process, for among nomads it had to be based partly upon consent. Before he could build up a personal following, Temüjin had to master the complicated art of tribal politics, which required a creative mixture of loyalty, rivalry, cunning, and ruthless treachery, as well as physical prowess. Rebelling against his over-lord, he subjugated the Kereit tribe and then the Naiman and others. Finally at the great meeting of the Mongol tribes, the *khuriltai* of 1206 on the Kerulen River, he was confirmed in the title of Chinggis Khan, which seems to have had some connotation of "universal ruler." At that time the chieftains of all the Mongol clans and tribes committed them-selves to his leadership.

From the few accounts which have come down to us, written for the most part long afterward by Persian, Chinese and Arab chroniclers on the basis of oral legends, we can see some of Chinggis Khan's methods of organization. To secure a religious sanction, he asserted his own divine mission, delegated to him by the Eternal Heaven, the deity of the steppe. The political structure he built up was organized on the family principle, families forming clans, clans forming tribes, tribes grouped in larger units, and the latter forming an empire.

As a permanent basis of rule, superior to the Khan himself, he drew up an imperial code of laws (*jasagh*, better known in the Turkish form of *yasa*) and made it supreme over his people. The Great Yasa was first promulgated in 1206 and further developed during the remaining twenty years before Chinggis' death in 1227. While no complete text has survived, we know that it was venerated by Chinggis' descendants as the divinely inspired wisdom of the founder of the empire. It formulated, no doubt from customary sources, the basic rules of organization for the imperial family and regime, and for the Mongol nation, the army and the administration, and also laid down criminal, civil and commercial laws.

Through this imperial code and the structure of power which it embodied, Chinggis Khan's influence was to reach far and last for gen-erations. No doubt one can see behind this idea of the imperial "Con-queror of the World" the ancient Chinese concept of the omnipotence of the Son of Heaven. One source of the strength of this untutored nomad chieftain, at any rate, lay in his ability to learn from others and his refusal to follow a single, inflexible pattern. For example, in build-ing up a civil administration, he made use of the Uighur Turks, by then a commercial people, many of them Nestorian Christians, centered around the oasis of Turfan in Chinese Turkestan. Through Turkish influence, many Mongolian names and terms became known to Europe first in Turkish forms, which differ from modern transliterations made directly from Mongolian.

The Mongols adapted the alphabetic Uighur script to their needs, and this was used to codify the Mongol law. The Uighur alphabet, derived from the Sogdian, had come indirectly from Syriac and thus ultimately from the ancient Phoenician alphabet. By using an alphabetic system akin to that of European peoples, the Mongols avoided the difficulties encountered, for example, by the Japanese in their adoption of the Chinese writing system (see pages 494 and 511–515).

The Mongol War Machine. Military organization was of course the first secret of Mongol success. Chinggis' personal bodyguard as early as 1203 posted eighty men around his tent by night. Eventually his guard grew to an elite corps of 10,000, recruited from the sons of clan leaders, generals and kinsmen, many if not most of them known personally to Chinggis. The guard members were kept under fierce discipline. They were beaten if they did not arrive promptly for duty and they stood watch for three days and nights at a time. In return they enjoyed a high status and many privileges. A private of the guard rated above an army captain of 1000.

From this elite group, which was comparable to a modern officer academy or training corps, Chinggis chose his generals and top administrators, some at the age of twenty. Under them the army was organized on a decimal system in units of tens, hundreds and thousands, usually with clan members carefully intermixed. The whole force at the time of Chinggis' death in 1227 amounted to about 129,000 men, a huge army by nomad standards but small as compared with those of China. Even at the height of his campaigns, he probably never had more than 250,000 men under his command, many drawn from the non-Chinese (especially Turkish) allies of the Mongols. The total population of the Mongols cannot have exceeded 2,500,000 and perhaps was closer to 1,000,000 at this time.

In view of what we know of the Khitan armies of three centuries before, it is plain that the Mongol war machine was the climax of a long development. Its success lay first of all in the quality of its individual warriors and in their coordination with one another. The Mongol cavalry had been trained in the saddle from boyhood as scouts and hunters. They fought under hereditary, aristocratic leaders who maintained personal control and discipline. Clad in leather and furs, leading extra horses as remounts, and capable of living in the saddle as long as ten days and nights at a time, these troops could cover distances which seemed incredible to the world of the thirteenth century. They were said to have once covered 270 miles during three days in Hungary. They could live on mare's milk or even, so it is said, on the blood of their horses. They carried leather bags for water, which when empty could be inflated to help them in swimming streams. Their herds followed them, but the troops lived mainly on their plunder. Bases of potential supply ahead of them were a constant incentive for expansion.

In battle the Mongols used flying horse columns, seeking to encircle and gradually compress the enemy forces, just as they compressed the game caught in the ring of a great hunt on the steppe. They carried both light and heavy bows, more powerful than the English longbow, with armor-piercing arrows which could kill at 600 feet or more. They were masters of deception. Their favorite tactic was to get their enemy to pursue, and then to turn back, surround and cut up the pursuing column. "In this sort of warfare," Marco Polo remarked, "the adversary imagines he has gained a victory, when in fact he has lost the battle." Another tactic was in the classic mold: heavy forces concealed on the wings would wait for the enemy to be enticed through the center and so expose his flanks.

To coordinate these rapid maneuvers, commanders used colored pennants or lanterns, smoke signals and messengers. Each unit ideally had horses of a separate color. All these devices increased mobility and coordination through which crushing force could be concentrated against an opponent's weak point. The Mongols thus brought offensive power to its highest point in the age before the development of firearms. Even against walled fortresses they soon mastered the medieval art of siege warfare.

The Mongols were also masters of espionage and psychological warfare. Spies were ready at hand among the merchants on the trade routes, so that the Mongols had little difficulty in learning what they wanted to know about their victims. By putting whole cities to the sword, they let terror run ahead of them as a weapon in itself. Many ancient centers of culture were all but wiped out, the women and children enslaved, the men forced to be the front line of assault on the next city. To capitalize on this terrorism, the Mongols also spread fair promises of toleration for religious minorities and freedom for merchants and the oppressed, providing they all surrendered without delay.

Chinggis' Conquests. Once the Mongols' formidable mechanism of destruction got under way, nothing could stand against it, for they learned quickly from experience and seized every opportunity. Chinggis Khan subjugated the Hsi Hsia between 1205 and 1209, and their kingdom was finally extinguished in 1227. His first campaign against the Chin Empire of North China in 1211–1215 not only destroyed their capital (on the site of Peking) but also gained the services of Chinese who knew how to besiege cities and others who knew how to govern them. The most famous of these experts in Chinese-style administration was a descendant of the Khitan royal house, Yeh-lü Ch'u-ts'ai (1190–1244), who taught the Mongols how to tax farmers, merchants and artisans and how to foster mining and industry. He is said to have persuaded his new masters that it would be more profitable *not* to turn North China into an empty pasture!

Meanwhile Chinggis had turned westward and taken over the Western Liao or Kara-Khitai Empire, established a century before by Khitan remnants. He then overran the adjoining Turkish empire of Khorezm (in Russian Turkestan) in 1219–1221. Here again he acquired not only rich, irrigated oasis-cities like Bokhara and Samarkand, which were centers of handicraft production, caravan trade and Islamic culture, but also the invaluable services of Moslem merchants and financiers adept in money matters. Turkish tribes were also incorporated into the Mongol hordes. Thus Chinggis Khan before his death in 1227 laid the foundations of a far-flung Eurasian empire by conquering its inner zone across Central Asia.

Many in later ages have speculated as to the true personality of this great organizer and conqueror. According to one account, for all his ability his motives were simple. "Man's highest joy," he reportedly said, "is in victory: to conquer one's enemies, to pursue them, to deprive them of their possessions, to make their beloved weep, to ride on their horses, and to embrace their wives and daughters." Other chronicles endow Chinggis Khan with a consuming vision of worldly glory. To his sons he said, "Be brotherly to one another and live in friendliness . . . making the whole great people walk on the road of the true state and of the law for the sake of attaining honor and glory." Again, "If Heaven grants a way, you will embark on campaigns beyond the sea. . . . Beyond the mountain rocks you will launch campaigns. . . . Send back news on wings."

THE MONGOL EMPIRE

In the customary tribal fashion, Chinggis divided the empire among the four sons of his principal wife (including actually the son of his eldest son, who had died). Eventually, after his numerous grandsons had helped to expand it, the empire was composed of four main khanates, whose areas and chief rulers are listed below. Chinggis' third son, Ögödei, was chosen Great Khan and built his capital at Karakorum in Mongolia.

DIVISIONS OF THE MONGOL EMPIRE
UNDER CHINGGIS KHAN'S SUCCESSORS
(The asterisk designates grandsons of Chinggis Khan.)

(a) *Great Khan* (East Asia): Ögödei (third son of Chinggis), 1229–1241; Möngke (Mangu),* 1251–1259; Khubilai,* 1260–1294 (ruled over all China after 1279); Mongols expelled from China by Ming, 1368.

(b) *Khanate of Chaghadai (Djaghatai*, in Turkestan): Chaghadai (second son of Chinggis), 1227–1242; western part incorporated after 1370 in empire of Timur or Tamerlane (1336–1405).

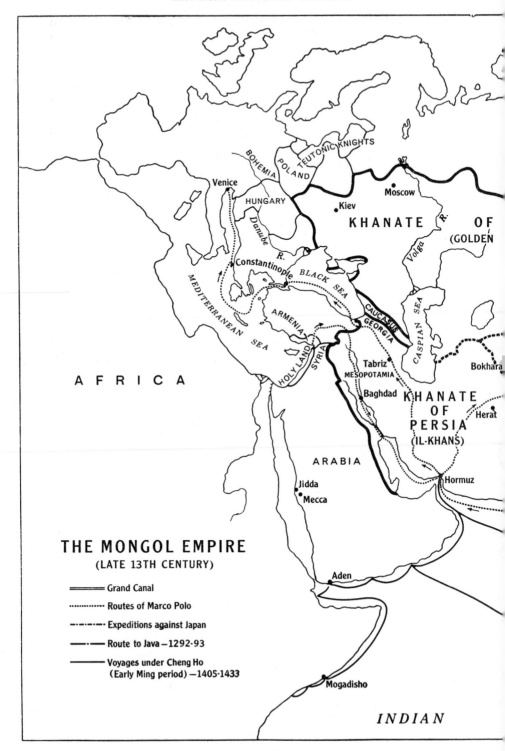

THE MONGOL EMPIRE
(LATE 13TH CENTURY)

═══ Grand Canal

············· Routes of Marco Polo

─·─·─· Expeditions against Japan

──·── Route to Java – 1292-93

─── Voyages under Cheng Ho
(Early Ming period) – 1405-1433

Venice

BOHEMIA
POLAND
TEUTONIC KNIGHTS
HUNGARY
Moscow
Kiev
KHANATE OF (GOLDEN

Danube R.
Constantinople
BLACK SEA
Volga R.

MEDITERRANEAN SEA
ARMENIA
CAUCASUS
GEORGIA
CASPIAN SEA

HOLY LAND
SYRIA
Tabriz
MESOPOTAMIA
Bokhara

Baghdad
KHANATE OF PERSIA (IL-KHANS)
Herat

AFRICA

ARABIA

Jidda
Mecca

Hormuz

Aden

Mogadisho

INDIAN

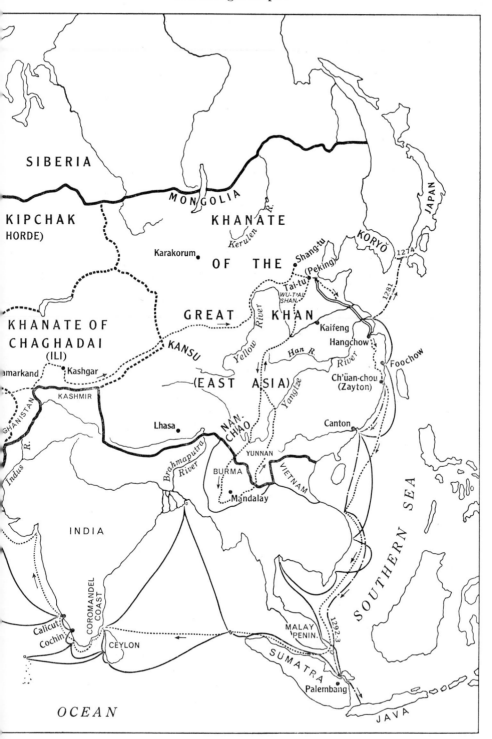

(c) *Khanate of Persia* (Il-khans): built up by Hülegü *; capture of Baghdad, 1258; dissolution after 1335.

(d) *Khanate of Kipchak* (Golden Horde) on lower Volga: built up by Batu,* 1227–1255; dominated Russia; conquered by Tamerlane and broken up in fifteenth century.

In completing their expansion over most of the known world, Mongol commanders and their mixed Mongol-Turkish armies overran Persia by 1231, plundered Mesopotamia, took over Armenia and Georgia, and subsequently extinguished the Abbassid Caliphate at Baghdad in 1258. In the same period, when other forces in East Asia were completing the conquest of the rest of North China (by 1241) and Korea (finally conquered in 1258), the West Asian armies erupted westward toward Europe. Under Batu they crossed the Volga (1237), burned Moscow, seized Kiev, and invaded Poland, Bohemia, Hungary and the Danube Valley (1241). At the western end of the great Eurasian steppe, they reached the Dalmatian coast of the Adriatic Sea. Poised for the invasion of Western Europe, Batu received news of the "Great Khan" Ögödei's death in 1241 in Mongolia and withdrew his whole army to South Russia so as to participate in the choice of a successor. Western Christendom, disunited and unprepared, was saved by Mongol domestic politics.

Batu's successors of the so-called Golden Horde ruled for two hundred years in South Russia, and thus the two giant countries of Russia and China have a certain degree of common background, both having felt the heavy hand of Mongol despotism. Meanwhile the so-called Il-khans (meaning vassal khans who were subordinate to the Great Khan) ruled for a century in Persia. Both the western khanates formed centers of power far from the Great Khan's rule in China. These three predominantly agricultural areas — South Russia, Persia, China — were in fact peripheral to the central communications zone of the grasslands of Mongolia and the oases of Turkestan. This inner core of Mongol-Turkish power, centering around the khanate of Chaghadai, was the strategic center of politics and rivalry among Chinggis' numerous descendants. Keeping it under control demanded much attention from the Great Khan.

The famous Mongol post routes combined traditional Chinese and nomad features. The post stations not only marked the routes across the grasslands and deserts of Central Asia but also, in the absence of cultivation and habitation, provided shelter and supply as well as protection against banditry. Over these routes, from one caravansary and military post to another, stage by stage, day after day, moved traders and travelers of all sorts. Thus the Mongol post system brought greater security to the long Central Asian trade routes. Like the systems of earlier Chinese and Sino-"barbarian" empires, the official post moved goods and persons on government business. Most important, it gave the rulers prior intelligence of events. Tough Mongol couriers, binding their stomachs, chests and heads tightly and using relays of horses, could cover two hundred miles a day.

Imperial unity was fostered at first by the participation of all four khanates in each conquest and its plunder. Each succeeding Great Khan was confirmed by a *khuriltai* representing all the princes and nobles of the empire. Yet, in spite of their common lineage and interests and the rapidity of their communications, the descendants of Chinggis Khan were subjected to strong centrifugal forces within their far-flung domains. In general, the Mongol rulers in West Asia accepted Islam and its culture and became absorbed in the complex relations and endemic warfare of the Near and Middle East, while the Mongol rulers of China became Buddhist believers and Confucian statesmen. The dissimilar Chinese, Russian and Persian states had their separate languages, cultures, official systems, court politics, and local needs. These differences were bound to create disunity among the relatively few Mongol-Turkish overlords. The very establishment of the Mongol-dominated regimes in the sedentary societies of Persia and China, and to some degree in South Russia, had indeed led to a revival of local bureaucratic administrations. By their nature these governments were oriented inward, toward their own domestic problems. It is really surprising that the Mongols' conglomerate superstate held together for even a century.

Conquest of the Southern Sung. The Mongols' take-over in China, in contrast to their quick sweep across Central and Western Asia, was a relatively slow process. It occupied more than a generation up to 1279 and left a correspondingly deep impress on Chinese life.

Aided by the dry open terrain of North China, the invaders by 1223 had driven the Chin for the most part south of the Yellow River. After the Chin line was extinguished in 1234, uncertain Mongol leadership delayed the attack on the rest of China for a brief decade (1241–1251), but its resumption was only a matter of time, for the Southern Sung Empire, as one of the most prosperous regions of the world, was an irresistible lure.

The Southern Sung, unmindful of the catastrophe that had overtaken Hui Tsung when he had aided the newly risen Jürched in crushing the Sinicized and effete Liao, had repeated this earlier mistake by joining the Mongols against the Chin. Thus they helped to remove the buffer that stood between themselves and their eventual conquerors. Yet the conquest of South China was no easy matter even for the invincible Mongols. It took several decades of intermittent but large-scale fighting. This alone is clear evidence of how strong the Southern Sung was, at least on its own terrain. Though rated a weak dynasty by Chinese standards, it proved a much more difficult conquest for the Mongols than the empires of West Asia, which were two to three times farther than South China from the center of Mongol power.

On the principal invasion route down the Han River from Northwest China to the Yangtze at Hankow, the Mongols had to besiege the twin cities at Hsiang-yang for five years (1268–1273). Here they used big catapults and perhaps primitive cannon. We know that Sung China had already developed catapults so big they required a hundred men to service them. Gunpowder had long been used in Chinese firecrackers and was now being employed in explosive bombs. Thus the art of warfare in Mongol hands was developing toward the new age of fire-arms which would end the nomads' era of military supremacy.

Already the invaders had outflanked the Southern Sung on the west. In 1253 they had taken over the non-Chinese kingdom of Nan-chao with its capital at Tali in Yunnan (literally, "south of the clouds," re-ferring to the mists and clouds which cover Szechwan much of the time). This conquest was to make Yunnan for the first time an integral part of China. It also brought Moslem administrators from Central Asia into Southwest China, where the religion of Islam has ever since retained a firm hold. Meanwhile the Thai people of Nan-chao began their south-ward migration which led indirectly to the founding of the modern state of Siam in 1351.

The conquest of the Southern Sung was finally completed under Chinggis Khan's ablest grandson, Khubilai (1215–1294), who became the Great Khan in 1260 and ruled for thirty-four years. Khubilai de-feated a brother who claimed the throne at Karakorum. He built up Peking as his winter capital and centered his attention on China. By 1276 his forces had moved down the Yangtze and taken the Sung capital at Hangchow. Next they took Canton, southwest of which the rem-nants of the big Sung fleet (most of which had already defected to the Mongols) were finally destroyed in 1279 together with the last claimant to the Sung throne.

Meanwhile Khubilai, in 1271, had already adopted the Chinese dynas-tic name of Yüan, meaning "The First Beginning" or "The Origin," thus choosing for the first time a major dynastic name not derived from a place or region. Chinggis was given the posthumous title of T'ai Tsu ("Grand Progenitor"), as had also been done for the founders of the Liao and Chin houses previously. Khubilai now became a Chinese-style emperor and has been listed in the Chinese annals under his posthumous title, Shih Tsu ("Regenerating Progenitor").

The Mongols in Southeast Asia. Conquest having become a way of life among Chinggis Khan's descendants, it is not surprising that Mongol envoys and expeditions went on to penetrate outlying parts of East Asia. Mongol-Chinese fleets used the naval power inherited from the Sung. As will be discussed more fully later, large but unsuccessful armadas were sent against Japan in 1274 and 1281, and Khubilai did not cease preparations for the conquest of Japan until 1286, when a defeat in Vietnam turned all his energies to the south. Altogether, at least four land expeditions invaded Vietnam and five penetrated Burma. Envoys visited Ceylon and South India by sea, and in the 1280's ten states of Southern Asia sent tribute by way of Ch'üan-chou in Fukien. These included states on both coasts of India and in Sumatra and the Malay Peninsula. In 1292 a Mongol fleet attacked Java but without permanent success. None of the ventures amid the unaccustomed heat and diseases of the tropics or across the unfamiliar sea established Mongol control in these distant areas. The fleets followed the routes of commerce to their sources, but neither Mongol diplomacy nor the lure of Chinese trade were as yet adequate to establish continuing tributary relations, as the Chinese were later to do in the fifteenth century.

This continued effort to conquer the known world by land and sea, which Khubilai maintained throughout his life, is all the more remarkable in view of his long struggle with the rebellious leader of a western branch of the imperial clan, Khaidu, a grandson of Chinggis' successor, Ögödei. Khaidu revolted in 1268 and seized the khanate of Chaghadai. Thenceforth, though defeated by Khubilai's trusted general, Bayan, at Karakorum in 1277 and later, Khaidu remained until his death in 1301 a continual threat to the power of the Great Khan in China.

MONGOL RULE IN CHINA

To conquer South China, the Mongols had to dismount, maneuver through rice fields and waterways, recruit Chinese collaborators and deal with dense, settled populations and many new problems. Time was required for them to master the rudimentary principles of administration.

Administrative Structure. Chinggis Khan's immediate successors in the annihilation of the Chin state had divided up its territory and population among the conquerors according to nomad custom. Only gradually did they face the fact that conquered Chinese villagers, merchants and city artisans could not be incorporated into the Mongol tribal society and that a bureaucratic state must be created. As Yeh-lü Ch'u-ts'ai is said to have put it, in the simple terms of advice long before offered to the founder of the Han, "The empire has been conquered on horseback, but it cannot be governed on horseback." Yeh-lü Ch'u-ts'ai was chief minister in the conquered parts of North China after 1230. He set up schools and held examinations to recruit Chinese into a bureaucracy. This trend continued. The Mongols, like the Jürched, found they could not use the rather simple dual type of divided Sino-"barbarian" administration which the Liao had developed.

The Yüan continued the administrative structure of the T'ang and

Sung, particularly the sixfold division of government activities under the Six Ministries (*Liu-pu*) at the capital. During the 1300 years from the early T'ang to 1906, this basic structure remained the same. Changes in the names and sometimes in the functions of offices and agencies occurred chiefly at the top of the imperial administration, in the various bodies (called chancellery, secretariat, grand council or the like) which stood above the Six Ministries and directly below the ruler. (See page 168 for T'ang administrative structure and pages 200–201 for Sung.) Of the three top bodies (*sheng*) of the T'ang administration, which had partly coalesced under the Sung, only the name of the *Chung-shu-sheng* was revived under the Yüan for the Central Chancellery at the head of the civil government. It was paralleled by the Bureau of Military Affairs (*Shu-mi-yüan*), inherited from the Sung, and by the Board of Censors (*Yü-shih-t'ai*), the latter being almost as long-lived as the Six Ministries in Chinese history. Thus the Yüan continued a threefold division of central government among civil administrative, military, and supervisory branches. First and second prime ministers usually headed the civil administration.

Innovation was greater in the Mongol's provincial administration. As conquerors they followed the Chin example and made the provincial governments into direct extensions of the Central Chancellery. (From this has come the modern name for a province, *sheng*.) This extension of central administration, imposed by dynasties of conquest, was an important further step in perfecting the Chinese imperial structure of government. The dozen Yüan provinces were mainly natural regions, including Yunnan for the first time, Szechwan, Shensi, and Kansu on the west, and part of Mongolia, southern Manchuria, and Korea on the north. Mongol garrisons in the provinces further insured the exercise of the strengthened central power. Troops from North China were stationed in the southern provinces.

Mongol-Chinese Relations. The Mongol conquerors, like others since their time, faced the problem of how to rule in a proper Chinese fashion and still retain power in their own hands. The Chinese populace could not be governed by force alone; rather, it had to be persuaded to acquiesce and assist in foreign rule. To accomplish this, an alien dynasty had to meet certain qualifications: to maintain local order under a vigorous central government, give Chinese talent the opportunity to rise in bureaucratic political life, lead the scholar-official class in each locality by fostering the traditional Confucian ideology and culture, and sustain the economic livelihood of the big landholders and common farmers.

For this exacting multiple task the Mongols as a whole were inadequately prepared. Much of their success in the early Yüan era must therefore be ascribed to the commanding personality of Khubilai and to his use of Confucian principles and collaborators skilled in applying them. He himself became adept in Chinese ways. His accomplishment was first of all a feat of intellect, to grasp and apply the Confucian philosophy of universal rule under the Son of Heaven. This Khubilai did with a non-Chinese emphasis upon its universality.

Preserving the invaders' identity in China was not difficult, because the Mongols had such different social institutions, laws and religious interests. Moreover, unlike the rulers of the T'o-pa Northern Wei, the Jürched Chin and the later Manchu Ch'ing dynasties, the Mongols' non-Chinese traits were constantly reinforced by their contact with a vast area outside China, in their homeland and the other khanates. They were also the only *full* nomads to achieve a dynasty of conquest. The gap between them and the Chinese was thus greater culturally to begin with and was more strongly perpetuated politically. Even their first instruction in the higher arts of civilization had come less from the Chinese than from the Uighur Turks of the Turfan area, whose alphabet was adapted, as noted above, to make the Mongolian script. Another early non-Chinese civilizing influence had reached the Mongols through Nestorian Christianity, which had found converts among the Kereit tribe.

Consequently, in China the Mongols differed from their subjects in very striking ways — not only in language and customs, but even in costume, since they preferred the leather and furs of steppe horsemen. For food they liked mare's milk and cheese, and for liquor the fermented drink made of mare's milk. Bred on the almost waterless grasslands, the Mongols were unaccustomed to washing. They lacked even surnames. Their different moral code gave greater (and in Chinese eyes, immoral) freedom to women; for example, a daughter could inherit if there were no son. Still other cultural and social traits, both superficial and fundamental, set them apart from the Chinese, as we shall see.

To make the division between conquerors and conquered even more complete, the recruiting of Southern Chinese talent for the Yüan bureaucracy was impeded by the heritage of Sung hatred for the plundering "barbarian." Reflecting this feeling, the later Chinese chroniclers, who have always had the last word on their conquerors, have generally depicted the Mongols as primitive savages capable only of destruction and orgiastic excess, heavy drinkers, superstitious and brutish. One Chinese account of Mongols in their homeland at a later date states with evident relish, "They smell so heavily that one cannot approach them. They wash themselves in urine." In the thirteenth century, cultured Chinese feelings were outraged by the Mongols' conduct in South China. The brutality of the conquest left a residue of mutual suspicion and ill-will. Marco Polo noted that in every province "there were many disloyal and seditious persons, at all times disposed to break out in rebellion." The Mongol garrisons outside the large cities, he says, were changed every second year and kept the Chinese populace in "quiet subjection."

In the face of native hostility, the Mongols in China as elsewhere employed many foreigners, particularly Moslems from Central and Western Asia, in a sort of international civil service. This was feasible because of the great number of such persons who came into China in this period. As Marco Polo recorded, "All the Cathaians detested the Great Khan's rule because he set over them governors who were Tartars, or still more frequently Saracens, and these they could not endure, for they were treated by them just like slaves. You see the Great Khan had not succeeded to the dominion of Cathay by hereditary right, but held it by conquest; and thus, having no confidence in the natives, he put all authority into the hands of Tartars, Saracens, or Christians, who were attached to his household and devoted to his service, and were foreigners in Cathay."

As a divide-and-rule tactic, the Mongols set up a hierarchy of social classes in which they themselves were the top class, and their non-Chinese collaborators second, followed by the Chinese of the North (called literally "Men of Han"), who had capitulated earlier with the Chin Empire, and, at the bottom, by those of the South (called simply "Southerners"). The last of course outnumbered all the rest.

Meanwhile the Mongol ruling class remained unassimilated and separate from Chinese life. Separate systems of law were maintained for Chinese and for Mongols and also for the Moslem collaborators. The Great Khan kept his summer residence at Shang-tu (Coleridge's "Xanadu," meaning "Superior Capital" in Chinese) north of the Wall in eastern Mongolia. He maintained his position more by force than by consent, with the result that his alien rule injected a heightened degree of centralized and ruthless despotism into the traditional Chinese Empire. The "barbarian" influence on the Chinese state system, transmitted through successive dynasties of conquest, had now reached a high point. The influence seems to have been marked by the greater importance of the military, more stress on orthodoxy and less tolerance of criticism.

LIFE UNDER THE YÜAN DYNASTY

Mongol policies of administration continued to antagonize the Chinese scholars, in spite of the emperor's gestures toward them. Khubilai on his accession had protected the Confucian temples and soon ordered the revival of the state cult of Confucius. Later he exempted Confucian scholars from taxation. He also performed the proper imperial functions of encouraging agricultural husbandry and sponsoring public works, including granaries and relief for orphans, the aged, the sick and the poor. But these traditional activities were rather superficial.

On the more fundamental issue of the recruitment of personnel for government service, Khubilai did not seek out the talent of South China. The competitive examination system had ceased to function in North China after 1237 and in South China after 1274. Its revival was delayed until 1315. Even then, Southerners were given a stiffer test than North Chinese or other persons, and were allotted only one-quarter of the available posts in spite of their greater numbers. Chinese clerks of course staffed the bureaucracy, but Confucian scholars did not often rise to the top.

Religious Developments. The scholar class was antagonized also by the Mongols' acceptance and patronage of foreign religions. In Persia many of the Mongols had embraced Islam, and in Central Asia, Nestorian Christianity. In China they followed a policy of religious toleration. Religious establishments of the Buddhist, Taoist, Nestorian and Islamic faiths, like the Confucian temples, were all exempted from taxation, and their clergy acquired local land rights and economic interests. Taoism in the late Chin, an era of disaster, had developed three new sects, with simpler doctrines, more able leaders, and new methods of proselyting. The Chin and Yüan periods saw extensive building of new Taoist monasteries in North China, while the old established sect of Taoism flourished under imperial patronage, especially in the Yangtze Valley. Ch'an (Zen) Buddhism, from which Taoism continued to borrow, also received imperial patronage. Thus older religions were revived and new ones, like Islam and Christianity, were aided. Naturally, this pattern of multiple religious growth under the Yüan was a distinct setback for the Neo-Confucian doctrines of the Chu Hsi School which had dominated the Southern Sung.

For their own part, the superstitious and untutored Mongols, with their background of shamanism, tended to accept Tibetan necromancy and take up the debased form of Buddhism that had developed in Tibet, namely Lamaism. The introduction of Buddhism into Tibet is traced traditionally to the teacher, Padmasambhava, who was invited there from northwest India in the eighth century. Once introduced, Buddhism was influenced by the native Tibetan cult known as Bon, which made much of magic and divination. The fusion which resulted is called Lamaism (the term "lama" means "superior one"). Bearing some resemblance to the traditional shamanism of the Mongols, it appealed strongly to them. In the thirteenth century it spread rapidly into Mongolia and also China, with imperial support.

A young Tibetan lama generally known as 'Phags-pa early acquired great influence over Khubilai and his court and was given the title of "National Mentor" or "Imperial Mentor" *(Kuo-shih, Ti-shih)*. Out-ranking all other Buddhist dignitaries, 'Phags-pa officiated as high priest of the court, performing elaborate ceremonies and enjoying unique honors. Following "barbarian" precedents already mentioned, Khubilai commissioned him to invent a new "international" script in which to write Mongolian and all the other languages of the empire. Fortunately, the forty-two clumsy, square, alphabetic symbols that 'Phags-pa devised, though officially promoted, never supplanted the modified Uighur alphabet for written Mongolian.

By the Buddhist clergy Khubilai was hailed as a Chakravartin ruler (i.e., an ideal Buddhist monarch who fully supports the true Buddhist teaching and so creates a universal empire). Under his patronage the number of Buddhist establishments, including the great mountain retreats at Mount Wu-t'ai in Shansi, rose to 42,000, with 213,000 monks and nuns, a great many being Lamaists. Eventually Tibetan lamas came to act like lords in the provinces and became a symbol for extortion and earthly corruption. They introduced new dances at court to please the emperor, and a mad lama even rifled the tombs of the Sung.

All this patronage and extensive financial subsidy given to a religious cult could not be offset, in the eyes of the Confucian scholar class, by the emperor's performance of Confucian ritual. Moreover, he lacked both the personnel and the policies with which to patronize Chinese accomplishments in literature, the arts and thought. Instead of performing this function of upper-class leadership in the society of China, as the Manchus were later to do with relative success, the Mongols maintained a cosmopolitan regime, under which the Chinese bureaucratic class was given little scope.

Thus in matters of administration and material construction, as in matters of warfare and destruction, the Mongols showed a degree of ability, but on the more subtle and cultural levels of Chinese life they certainly failed to perform the functions of a ruling house and did not secure an adequate flow of Chinese talent into official life in support of their regime.

Economic Conditions. In fostering the people's livelihood, on the other hand, Khubilai had some temporary success, although the extent of it is still disputed. The landholding element of the Southern Sung was not dispossessed and so generally acquiesced in the change of central power. Taxation of land and labor and the usual government monopolies were developed. The establishment of peace ushered in a period of trade and relative prosperity. This was facilitated not only by the establishment of order and public works but also by far-flung commercial contact with the rest of Asia. Foreign trade was chiefly conducted by Moslem merchants of Central Asian origin. Their corporate groups (*ortaq,* or *wo-t'o* in Chinese transcription) not only served as trading associations but also became tax-farmers of all sorts for their Mongol patrons. Performing this function with government support, these merchant "companies," whose members guaranteed one another, played a key role in collecting the agrarian surplus of the Yüan Empire and channeling some of this accumulated capital into an expanded commerce. Helping the conquerors, they also shared in the inordinate graft and corruption which accompanied Mongol rule.

Commerce was aided by widespread local issue of paper money, later replaced by a unified nation-wide system of paper currency. The Mongols used standardized notes which circulated not only in China but also in Korea, Central Asia, and parts of Southeast Asia. The Yüan government for a time even accepted paper money for tax payments. Thus they brought the Sung innovation of paper currency to its highest peak of development in traditional China. Marco Polo, coming from a much less economically advanced Europe, was amazed at this use of paper for money and repeatedly commented upon it.

Trade between North and South China was also stimulated by the growth of the new capital. Khubilai had moved the Great Khan's capital from Karakorum to Peking, where the main entrance through the Great Wall at Nan-k'ou leads down to the North China Plain. There on the plain he built a new city. Even today the long, pounded-earth mounds left from its northern walls stand out clearly on the farm land just north of the present walls of Peking. The Mongols called this their "great capital," Daidu (in Chinese, Tai-tu). It was also called Khanbaligh (Marco Polo's "Cambaluc"), meaning in Turkish, "city of the Khan." Within it was a palace enclosed by double walls and complete with parks, treasuries, a lake and a big hill dredged from it. (See page 297.)

To feed the new capital's swelling population, grain had to be transported from the fertile lower-Yangtze rice basket. The Yüan inaugurated a sea transport service around the dangerous Shantung coast and also developed the inland river and canal routes, as the Northern Sung had done to supply their capital at Kaifeng. A vast project, the digging of a canal across the Shantung peninsula, was begun but eventually given up. The problem of transporting food to the capital was met in the end by extending the Grand Canal system north to Peking from the Yellow River. This involved, among other things, the use of 2,500,000 laborers to complete in 1289 a "Connecting Canal" (*Hui-t'ung ho*) running through western Shantung north of the modern course of the Yellow River. Eventually on the stone embankments of this second Grand Canal system there ran a paved highroad from Hangchow to Peking, a total distance of eleven hundred miles, which took forty days to traverse.

Dynastic Decline. Khubilai's grandson Temür, who succeeded him in 1294, maintained a strong central administration, but after his death in 1307 the Mongols' hold on China rapidly weakened. In the next twenty-six years, seven rulers occupied the throne of the Great Khan, but none lived beyond the age of thirty-five. Internal dissensions among the Mongol princes broke out into open civil war after 1328. The last Mongol emperor of China, who reigned from 1333 to 1367, was highly cultured in Chinese ways but is said to have become absorbed in the supersitions of Lamaism and the debauches of the court.

This decline at court was accompanied by the regime's over-issue of paper money which, though it had stimulated trade earlier in the dynasty, was now issued in increasing quantities without backing — as much as 300 million strings of cash a year. Naturally paper notes were no longer accepted for tax payments. Inflation was followed by repeated conversions to new paper, which in turn steadily depreciated.

In addition, the Yellow River was causing recurrent floods, devastation, famine and government expense. It had changed its course from the north to the south of the Shantung promontory in 1194, reaching the sea through the mouth of the Huai River. (It was to remain in this course until 1852.) Its floods therefore ruined the agriculture of the relatively well-watered productive areas of northern Anhwei and Kiangsu and southern Shantung. Financial, moral and political bankruptcy thus came hand in hand.

The First Direct Contact With the West

In the retrospect of later ages, one significance of the Mongol Empire is that it made possible a century of direct, though not extensive, contact between China and medieval Europe. The Mongols' control over the whole sweep of the Central Asian trade routes permitted the travel of many Europeans to the court of China. Marco Polo was only one of many who brought back direct word of "Cathay" (a name derived from "Khitai" and referring specifically to North China).

In Europe of the thirteenth century, the Mongol conquests, which covered almost all of the known world except the states of Western Christendom, left a shock of fright which has been long remembered. Chinggis Khan, the universal conqueror from the East, his barbarous hordes and their irresistible destructiveness, became a legend to terrify children and echo in the minds of statesmen. The Western dread of the "yellow peril" no doubt harks back to this experience.

The century from about 1240 to about 1340, during which the Mongol Empire permitted safe travel between China and Western Europe for the first time, was an interlude between earlier and later eras in which Arab-Turkish control of Central Asia and the Near East kept a barrier between China and the West. During this Mongol century, European travelers reached Cathay by several routes: either through South Russia and Ili across the steppe, a hard journey; or across the Black Sea and through the Central Asian oases of the ancient Silk Route, the way taken by Italian merchants like the Polos; or by sea to Syria and the Latin states set up by the crusades, and thence through Baghdad and Central Asia; or, finally, by the sea route through the Indian Ocean and around Southeast Asia to Canton, a passage made difficult by Arab obstruction.

Over these routes, thronged by people of West Asia, many Europeans reached China during this period and a few left accounts of their travels. They recorded the presence of many Greek Orthodox Christians at the Great Khan's court, mainly captured Russian artisans or soldiers (the later Yüan emperors kept a whole division of Russian troops). We also hear of a Parisian goldsmith who had been captured in Belgrade, a Norman who was the nephew of a bishop from near Rouen, a woman from Metz in Lorraine, and numerous other Western Europeans.

Nestorianism and Papal Diplomacy. This contact between medieval Christendom and farthest Asia was facilitated by the fact that the heretical Nestorian Christian faith had earlier penetrated from Persia into East Asia. Although it had died out in China, it was revived among the Khitan and Jürched and became widespread among the Uighur Turks and several Mongol tribes, as we have noted. Khubilai's own mother was a Nestorian Christian, and it is probable that the Great Khan Guyug (reigned 1246–1248) was a convert. At this time the Nestorian church had some twenty-five metropolitan sees; in 1275 its patriarch at Baghdad created an archbishopric at Peking. There were Nestorian Christians in several regions of China and some became officials. Though deemed heretical, the Nestorian church had contact with the papacy.

European curiosity about the East was heightened by the legend of "Prester John," a supposed descendent of the three wise men. He was said to have become a proper Christian ruler in Asia, and forged letters from him were circulated. He was also rumored to be Chinggis Khan himself. In reality, the figure to whom the legend originally became attached in Asia was probably Ong Khan of the Kereit tribe of the Mongols.

Meanwhile, Western Christendom was absorbed in the fervor of the crusades. The crusaders not only attacked the infidel Saracens in the Holy Land, but also captured the citadel of the Greek Orthodox faith at Constantinople (1204), while others turned inward against heretics like the Albigensians (1209) at home. When the Mongols attacked South Russia in 1240, the Swedes and Teutonic Knights proceeded to attack the North Russians, because they were Greek Orthodox schismatics. European crusaders were evidently prepared to accept any ally against religious foes.

The stage was thus set for diplomatic relations between Western Christendom, the Mongols and Islam. Saracen envoys sought French and English help against Mongol expansion in the Near East in 1238 but were rebuffed ("Let us leave these dogs to devour one another," as the Bishop of Winchester put it). After the Mongols' conquest of Persia and Baghdad, their Il-khans sent at least seven embassies to the West between 1267 and 1291 to get help against Islam.

On its part the papacy, when the Mongol threat to Europe had receded after 1241, sent a notable series of Franciscan monks on diplomatic and evangelical missions to Persia, Mongolia and China, evidently to explore the possibility of obtaining Mongol help against the Saracens. King Louis IX of France also sent ambassadors. Among them William of Rubruck was a most astute observer. He had a somewhat tipsy audience with the Great Khan, and his report noted the tones of the Chinese language and identified Cathay with the ancient Roman Seres. It is quoted some forty times in the book of the schoolman Roger Bacon, whom he probably met in Paris.

While no diplomatic result was achieved by these envoys between East and West, the papal missionary effort finally established a Roman Catholic outpost in China under John of Montecorvino. Under the Great Khan's protection he preached, built a church with help from an Italian merchant, and taught 150 choirboys, whose Gregorian chants pleased the imperial ear. Six thousand converts were baptized in Peking in 1304, many of them probably non-Chinese. After twelve years' silence, Friar John succeeded in getting a letter back to the Pope and was made an archbishop in 1307 and sent reinforcements. Roman Catholic missions made increasing progress toward the end of the Yüan dynasty (as was to happen again in the late Ming period), only to be snuffed out afterwards.

One of the last monks to reach China was Friar Odoric. He later gained great repute as an ascetic devoted to a hair shirt, although the evidence indicates that he was given to wanderlust as much as to asceticism. He eventually became a saint to whom some seventy miracles were ascribed. At least seventy-six manuscript versions of his travel narrative were spread about medieval Europe, and Sir John Mandeville, the fanciful chronicler of strange peoples and places, borrowed extensively from him. His narrative in fact makes the first references in the West to the island of Sumatra, to bound feet in China, to long fingernails (the symbol of the non-laboring, scholarly gentleman in China), and to cormorant-fishing, an East Asian method of catching fish by using these large aquatic birds tethered on a rope and wearing rings around their necks to prevent their swallowing their catch.

The Mongol Empire

MEDIEVAL EUROPEAN TRAVELERS TO CATHAY

Friar John of Plano Carpini, Italian Franciscan; sent by Pope Innocent IV; left Lyon, April 1245, accompanied by Friar Benedict of Poland; received by Batu at the Volga camp of the Golden Horde; reached Karakorum, July 1246; witnessed the enthronement of Great Khan Guyug; returned to report to the Pope at Lyon, 1247.

Friar William of Rubruck, Flemish Franciscan; sent with companions by King Louis IX; left Constantinople, May 1253; reached Batu's headquarters in July and Karakorum in December; left in August 1254; reached Cyprus, June 1255.

Maffio and Niccolo Polo, Venetian merchants; left Constantinople in 1260; went via Bokhara and Chinese Turkestan; reached China, 1262; left in 1266 with Khubilai's request to the Pope for a hundred Christian scholars and technicians; returned via Central Asia and Syria; reached Rome, 1269.

The Polo brothers with Niccolo's son Marco set out in 1271 with Pope Gregory X's blessing but with no scholars; went via Central Asia to Khubilai's summer residence Shang-tu ("Xanadu") and Peking ("Cambaluc"); Marco spent seventeen years in Khubilai's service (1275–1292); the Polos returned by ship in 1292 via Sumatra to Hormuz on the Persian Gulf; reached Venice, 1295.

Friar John of Montecorvino, Italian Franciscan; sent in 1289 by Pope Nicholas IV with letters to Il-khan of Persia and to Khubilai; reached Tabriz, 1290; proceeded via India and sea route; arrived Peking, 1295; appointed Archbishop of Cambaluc by Clement V in 1307 (three Franciscans arrived in 1313 to be his suffragans); died about 1332; succeeded by *Friar Nicholas,* a French Franciscan, former University of Paris professor, who brought twenty-six friars with him to China, one of whom took the Great Khan's letter to Pope Benedict XII in 1336.

Friar Odoric of Pordenone, Italian Franciscan; left Venice c. 1314–18; proceeded via the Black Sea, Baghdad, Ceylon and Sumatra, and reached Canton c. 1324–25; lived in Peking for three years; returned via Central Asia; reached Padua in 1330.

Friar John of Marignolli, Franciscan; sent by Pope Benedict XII in 1340; proceeded via South Russia and Turkestan; received by the Great Khan at Peking, 1342, and presented to him a large Western horse; embarked at Ch'üan-chou, 1347; returned via India; reached Avignon in 1353.

Marco Polo and His Counterpart. Western merchants must have greatly outnumbered the friars who crossed Asia, but Marco Polo was the only one to leave a record. Going East as a young man, he evidently picked up the languages easily; yet, after seventeen years (1275–1292) under Khubilai Khan, including official service in the salt administration and trips through the provinces of Yunnan and Fukien, he still knew Persian better than Chinese — evidence of the chasm between the Mongol regime and the Chinese populace. Marco Polo's *Description of the World* was dictated to a professional romance writer in a Genoese prison. It is not a travelogue but a systematic, scientific treatise, well informed and objective. The original has not survived, but about 120 manuscripts, containing many variations, have been found in Italian, Latin, French, and other languages. As late as 1932 a new version, known as the Latin "Codex Z," with eighty unique passages, was found in Toledo.

No other traveler has ever had so great a tale to tell as Marco Polo. His was the first connected exposition of the geography, economic life and government of China to be laid before the European public. It was more than could be believed, for the China of the late thirteenth century was superior to Europe not only in size but also in culture and technology. It is not surprising that Marco Polo in late medieval times was a byword for the incredible. Yet his influence persisted. Columbus had a copy of Marco Polo's book and made marginal notations in it. Time vindicated the Venetian. His burnable "black stones" dug from mountains, for example, proved to be coal. In the nineteenth century his itineraries were verified in detail.

Marco Polo had his East Asian counterpart in Rabban Sauma, a Nestorian monk born in Peking. He crossed Central Asia to the Il-khan's court in Mesopotamia in 1278 and was one of those whom the Mongols sent to Europe to seek Christian help against Islam. In 1287 Sauma went through Constantinople to Naples, Rome, and Paris. He saw Philip IV of France, and, in Gascony, Edward I of England, and left an interesting record in which he notes, for example, that there were thirty thousand students at the University of Paris. He expounded the Nestorian creed to the College of Cardinals and celebrated the Eucharist before the Pope in order to show that, while the language might differ, the ritual was the same. His chief interest, however, seems to have been the typically medieval concern for relics, such as "a piece of board upon which Our Lord slept when he was a child."

All this knowledge of the East in medieval times, however, remained exotic. Direct contact by sea was necessary before China could bulk large on the European horizon.

China's Contact With West Asia. Meanwhile, for almost a century under the Mongols, the whole of China had lain open to foreign influences, which were more numerous and vigorous than ever before. They were part of a give-and-take between the eastern and western parts of the Mongol domain. Although European scholars have naturally been interested in the direct relations between Europe and China as mentioned above, it should not be forgotten that European contact under the Mongols was miniscule compared with the contact between China and West Asia. When the Mongols opened North China to closer contact with the Near East by land, they found the latter area already in close contact with South Asia, and even South China, by sea. Mongol conquest greatly facilitated Arab trade. This trade now went both by caravan from Baghdad to Peking and by ship from Hormuz on the Persian Gulf to Zayton (the Arab name for Ch'üan-chou in Fukien) and the other South China ports. The Arab trade routes actually encompassed Asia more completely than did the Mongol Empire itself.

An illustration of Arab trading influence in thirteenth-century China is afforded by the rise of an Arab, named in Chinese style P'u Shou-keng, who about 1250 became a Sung official in charge of the Super-intendency of Merchant Shipping *(Shih-po-ssu)* at the principal port of Ch'üan-chou. Profiting from many years' control of the customs admin-istration, he acquired great wealth and influence, and eventually went over to the Yüan, still as a high official.

Of all the medieval travelers, the Arabs, though largely unknown to Europe, were most conversant with East Asia. The fullest travel narrative of the Mongol period is by Ibn Batuta, who roamed across Southern Asia in the period 1325–1355, settling down and having families in several places as he circulated along the routes of Arab trade. He claims to have met a certain Arab in China and the Arab's brother on the Sahara Desert.

In the period of Mongol power we can imagine that thousands of Chinese, bent on warfare or trade, spread over the Mongol Empire all the way to Russia, Persia and Mesopotamia. These regions received a definite Chinese cultural impact. Coming at the end of a millennium during which Chinese technological achievements had generally sur-passed those of the rest of the world, the Mongol century saw a flow of many things from China westward — gunpowder, paper money, print-ing, porcelain, textiles, playing cards, medical discoveries and art motifs, to mention only a few. This cultural influence was strongest in Persia and the Arab world, from which it often reached Europe indirectly.

In return, China was most influenced by the Arab-Turkish culture. Islam took permanent root in the Middle Kingdom, while Christianity did not. Many mosques were built. In the northwestern and southwestern provinces, notably Kansu and Yunnan, the Moslem faith has remained strong among the population ever since. In seaports like Canton and Ch'üan-chou on the southeast coast, Arab communities, as during the late T'ang and Sung, were allowed to live under their own legal customs and responsible headmen. From Persia came influences in astronomy, ceramics, music and other lines.

CHINESE CULTURE UNDER THE MONGOLS

Despite this century of contact, however, the main cultural tradition of the Middle Kingdom proved impervious to outside influences. Things foreign remained superficial, as did the Mongol conquerors themselves. Some traditional institutions such as the examination system were only partially maintained, but they were not supplanted. On the other hand, the attraction of China's culture was so strong that a number of Central Asians — Tanguts and Uighurs, Nestorian Christians and Moslems, descendants of tribesmen from west of the Pamirs — made their mark as Confucian scholars or as typically Chinese painters and calligraphers. Meanwhile, the compiling of the official dynastic histories of the Sung, Liao and Chin went forward in the usual fashion, under a Mongol as head of the bureau of historiography. Chinese scholarship did not flourish notably, but neither did it wither away. The great Sung traditions of landscape and nature painting were brilliantly maintained, and many works of Yüan masters were added to the heritage.

Drama. The Mongol period also saw the flourishing of two new Chinese literary forms, the drama and the novel. Both were connected with the increased use, during this period, of the written vernacular (*pai-hua*) in place of the traditional literary language. Dramas and novels both had to use a less classical written form, closer to everyday speech, in order to reach the wider, less highly educated urban audiences of the day. For a similar reason the Yüan administration itself used a more vernacular style in its documents so that these would be more easily intelligible to the many officials who lacked a Chinese classical education. Meanwhile, Chinese scholars on their part, finding less opportunity in official life and less patronage of classical studies, turned their talents to these new fields, which already had a considerable tradition behind them.

Dramatic performances, apparently under strong Central Asian influence, had become popular as early as the eighth century at the court of Hsüan Tsung, who subsequently became the patron deity of actors. Playwriting began to flourish in the capitals of the twelfth century, both at Peking under the Chin and at Hangchow under the Southern Sung. Titles of nearly a thousand plays survive from this period. From the Yüan there exist the printed librettos of many plays, normally in four acts, which are considered to be finer literature than more recent productions. Their themes are typically Chinese, often involving conflicts of human passion with the social bonds of filial piety, fidelity or loyalty.

In style the Chinese drama was semi-operatic, with orchestral music to accompany a great deal of singing and dancing. Scenery and properties were dispensed with, as in Elizabethan England. In their place were developed a great variety of conventions which in time became very elaborate — stylized movements of the hands, sleeves, eyes and feet, as in stepping over an imaginary doorsill, climbing non-existent steps, or mounting an imaginary charger. Eventually, female roles generally came to be played by men, whose falsetto singing, dancing, and delicate gestures were especially appreciated. Romantic plots of adventure and legendary events, technical virtuosity in singing and dancing, humorous dialogue, brilliant costuming and violent action all combined to create an urban art of very wide popularity. During the Yüan period the drama appealed not only to the literate and illiterate alike among the Chinese, but also to the many non-Chinese who participated in city life under the Mongols. A raucous orchestral accompaniment of guitar, flute, drum and castanets lent vigor to the performance.

The Novel. While the drama grew up primarily at the capital cities, there had been a parallel development of the novel by professional story-tellers among the populace. The Chinese novel originated in the Buddhist wonder stories of T'ang times. These grew into historical or purely imaginative love and adventure tales, which at the hands of professional storytellers developed into long and loosely constructed sagas. Prompt-books for itinerant storytellers were the earliest written form of these episodic tales, and, as the books were gradually filled in with details by many different hands, they became the early novels as now preserved. Most of them are of prodigious length.

The plebeian associations of this literature are revealed by the status of the heroes, who usually are not scholar-bureaucrats but men of low class or military origin. All the novels are written in a style close to the vernacular of the day, rather than in the traditional literary language of scholarship and belles-lettres. The later novels were usually the work of single authors who were obviously men of considerable education and great literary talent, though they often concealed their identity because they considered the novel form an improper use of their literary skills. These authors often gave finished form to stories that had circulated for generations among professional storytellers and drama-tists. Cited below are the principal novels, some of which will be discussed more fully in Chapter 9. (See pages 386–388.)

The earliest of the novels that remain is the *San-kuo-chih yen-i* (*The Romance of the Three Kingdoms*), a rambling romanticized ac-count of the Three Kingdoms period in the third century, which ap-parently dates in its present form from the fourteenth century. The *Hsi-yu-chi* (*Record of a Journey to the West*, translated under the title of *Monkey*), an allegorical tale of supernatural marvels in a Buddhist setting, was written in its final form in the sixteenth century but harks back to a long tradition. The *Shui-hu-chuan* (variously translated as *The Water Margin* or *All Men Are Brothers*), which reached its present form during the Ming dynasty, is a loosely organized adventure tale of banditry and Robin-Hood exploits during the Northern Sung period. Incidents and

ILLUSTRATION FROM THE *Shui-hu-chuan*

Outlaws, led by one of their number who wields an axe, ambush an official (with black hat, on horse) and his entourage, in order to rescue a comrade who is being led to execution. From a Ming wood block of a type easily reproduced for wide distribution.

characters from it figure in many dramas, evidently expressing a popular tradition of sympathy for the brotherhood of rebels.

One of the greatest of the Chinese novels is the *Chin P'ing Mei* (translated under the title of *Golden Lotus*), which is the work of a single author perhaps in the sixteenth or early seventeenth century. Though often highly pornographic, it is a well-organized work and reaches great heights of realism and character portrayal. The most famous of the later novels, dating from the eighteenth century, is the *Hung-lou meng (Dream of the Red Chamber)*, most of which is the semi-autobiographical work of a single author, describing the complexities of relationships in a large and wealthy family. Although most of the major novels attained their mature form, or were actually first composed, in the Ming and Ch'ing periods, their roots go back to the Yüan or earlier.

The novel became the kind of literature that the majority of literate Chinese, like foreigners today, could most readily appreciate. Though customarily disesteemed by the traditional scholar trained in the classics, it became a principal literary form, with wide influence as a repository and mirror of social values. The emergence of both the novel and the drama in the Yüan period illustrates the vitality of Chinese culture as well as the frustration of the scholar class under the Mongols.

8

State and Society under the Ming

Chinese "Culturalism"

The Ming period from 1368 to 1644 is one of the great eras of orderly government and social stability in human history. A total population of around one hundred million, possibly rising toward two hundred million — in any case far greater than that of Europe and America in that era — was maintained during 276 years in comparative peace.

The subsequent change from Ming to Ch'ing rule was a relatively easy one. The decline of Ming power saw the spread of banditry and desolation over wide areas, and the Manchu capture of Peking in 1644 was followed by their conquest of all China and suppression of Ming adherents. But this warfare and devastation in the vast terrain of the Middle Kingdom seem limited in comparison with the organized looting and massacres and the incessant marching and countermarching of contemporary European armies during the Thirty Years' War of 1618–1648.

In any case, whatever the rate of bloodshed East and West, the institutions of Chinese society maintained a remarkable continuity throughout the Ming and Ch'ing periods. So stable was the political and social order of the Ming that it persisted, basically unaltered, under the alien Ch'ing dynasty for another 267 years from 1644 to 1912. During this long epoch from the middle of the fourteenth century to the beginning of the twentieth, China followed traditional ways. The village economy, the family relationships extolled in the classics, the examination system for the selection of officials, the revered rule of the Son of Heaven at Peking, all continued in established patterns which had been inherited largely from the Sung and earlier periods.

The Consequences of Stability. Unfortunately for the Chinese people of recent times, this remarkable social stability was maintained during those very centuries that saw the dynamic rise of Modern Europe — the Renaissance, the Reformation, the growth of national states, their expansion into the New World and over the earth, followed by the French Revolution and the Industrial Revolution. None of these fundamental Western transformations of the last six centuries had a real counterpart in China's own experience. Under the Ming and early Ch'ing, the Chinese people remained outside the turbulent stream of Western history which was moving to engulf the world. It was during this period that they fell behind the West in many aspects of material culture and technology as well as in certain forms of economic and political organization.

The long period of comparative stability in East Asian civilization has been one chief cause of its "backwardness" or "underdeveloped" nature during the past century of Western contact. This "backwardness" in turn, as we shall see, has been a primary cause of East Asian efforts to "modernize" in our own day, efforts that have sometimes endangered our own security and still affect the stability of international relations.

The comparison with the revolutionary and expanding society of the West should not be permitted to stigmatize the Ming and Ch'ing periods as retrogressive, or to overshadow their real achievements, for the Ming and Ch'ing saw many important developments in Chinese civilization. As we learn more about these centuries, we may expect to find many more evidences of innovation and growth. Chinese society, though stable, was far from static or unchanging, but in this period the pace was slower and the degree of change less than in the West.

One factor making for stability during this period was the Chinese view of history as "change within tradition." The leaders of society, by training and circumstance, were so strongly devoted to tradition that change could be conceived of only within the limits of the traditional order: anything that happened in the present must be fitted into the rich pattern of experience inherited from the past. Instead of an ideal of progress toward new and better ways, which the modern world has inherited from the nineteenth century, the Chinese of the Ming and Ch'ing periods saw their ideal models far in the past.

Ethnocentrism. This turning back for inspiration to the great ages of Han, T'ang, and Sung was accompanied, and no doubt partly caused, by a deeply ingrained resentment against the Mongols who had conquered and ruled the empire. Alien rule inspired in some Chinese an attitude of hostility toward alien things in general, in addition to an almost instinctive scorn for anything that could be labeled "barbarian." Gradually this view hardened into a lack of interest in anything beyond the pale of Chinese civilization. The great maritime expeditions of the early fifteenth century were to be almost the last overt sign of serious Chinese interest in the outside world. Thereafter, until the nineteenth century, most Chinese simply took for granted that the benighted "barbarian" might come to seek culture in China, if he wished, but it was below his dignity, or at least unrewarding, for the civilized Chinese to be interested in the "barbarian" or his ways.

The turning away from the outside world and the rejection of foreign influences were accompanied by a growing introspection within Chinese life. We have already seen this phenomenon in the antiquarian interest in art and in the burst of historical scholarship that took place in the Sung. From that time on a degree of mingled fear and contempt for the outside world and a narrow concentration of interest on the exclusively Chinese way of life seem to have produced a growing ethnocentrism, which eventually dominated China's foreign relations and gave her an intellectual and psychological immunity to foreign stimuli, including those offered by contact with the West.

This attitude has had much in common with the modern complex of ideas known as nationalism. But there were also differences. Nationalism seems to be typical of a group which vehemently asserts its own distinctiveness and superiority because it has reason to fear not only political but also cultural inundation by some other group. Nationalism thus seems closely tied, especially in its most virulent forms, to a general feeling of competition and insecurity or even inferiority. It is commonly asserted with greatest strength against neighbors of a similar basic culture, most typically by a cultural sub-unit, particularly a linguistic sub-group, against other and perhaps stronger sub-units within the same culture. The classic example is the rise of national states within the common culture of Western Christendom.

The Chinese attitude, by contrast, showed no sign of a feeling of cultural inferiority. Political subjugation may have been feared, but cultural conquest of the huge Chinese unit by the thin nomadic populations of the north was unimaginable. Thus Chinese xenophobia, in so far as it existed, was combined with a complete confidence in cultural superiority that is notably lacking in nationalism.

Another basic difference is that modern nationalism has depended for its strength on the identification of the individual with the national political unit. In pre-twentieth-century China, however, as in so many other pre-modern societies, the individual commonly felt no particular identification with the state. He might accept alien rule even though, in contrast with the modern nationalist, he could be counted on to remain culturally Chinese to the core. The Chinese attitude might be characterized not as the fearful reaction of a cultural sub-unit, but as the sometimes frustrated reaction of a large ethnocentric universe which remained quite sure of its cultural superiority even when from time to time it found itself relatively inferior in military power to fringe elements of its universe.

Because of these similarities to and differences from nationalism, a distinct but analogous term should be used for this earlier Chinese attitude. For this purpose we have coined the word "culturalism." By it we mean to suggest that in the Chinese view the significant unit was really the whole civilization rather than the narrower political unit of a nation within a larger cultural whole.

The Tradition of Unity. Underlying this devotion to the Chinese way of life was one primary political fact, namely that the whole Middle Kingdom remained an administrative unit under a central government. Despite the great size and geographical diversity of an empire with a population several times as large as that of Europe, disunity was regarded as an abnormal and temporary evil. If disunity occurred, reunification was expected.

This remarkable cohesiveness, compared with the constant disunity among the relatively smaller European states, cannot be attributed to geography. On the contrary, it normally took a month or so for the emperor's writ to be carried by horse to the borders of the realm in Kwangtung, Yunnan, Central Asia or the Northeast, farther than any distances in Western Europe. China's inveterate unity must be explained on institutional grounds, by the habits of thought and action which had become established in the society. We may say, in short, that the Chinese state was regarded as coterminous with Chinese culture. The spread of one carried the other with it. In Chinese thinking they were not distinguished. In Chinese "culturalism" there was such a close identification of the entire way of life with the unified empire that the one implied the other. It was somewhat as if the Roman Empire had persisted in the West and had succeeded in preventing the rise of France, England and the other nations. There could be but one sovereign, the Son of Heaven.

No doubt this political achievement of the Chinese must be attributed to the whole past development of their institutions, but one feature of this development stands out: the stress on a rational social and political order, which kept religion and commerce, learning and technology, city and countryside, all subordinate to the imperial government. Since the Chinese order found its intellectual sanction in the so-called Confucian Classics, some call this political system "Confucian." But the term "Confucian state" is unfortunately ambiguous, for the imperial administration used devices and concepts inherited from the Legalists, and Neo-Confucianism had absorbed elements of Buddhism. Chinese society and government were the products of a great variety of factors, not merely of the doctrines of the ancient Sage nor even of Neo-Confucianism, which was itself a blend of many influences.

If we want to picture a "Confucian" or "Neo-Confucian" state as an overarching entity in Chinese life, this should not lead us into simplistic assumptions that all Chinese thinking was in a "Confucian" mold or that dissent and deviance, strange ideas and original practices, did not continue to enrich China's experience. The "culturalism" of the Middle Kingdom was a unity only in comparison with the diversity of the West.

The identity of culture and polity made the Chinese leadership of the Ming and Ch'ing periods automatically uninterested in, and at times hostile to, things foreign. One of the major ways in which this "culturalistic" reaction against the outside world was expressed during the late T'ang and Sung was in the rejection of Buddhism, which had played so dominant a role in Chinese civilization during the preceding half millennium. (See pages 235–236.) The antagonism of the scholar class against Mongol rule was also in large part cultural in origin. "Culturalism" rose to a new height after the country-wide rebellions to expel the Mongols and after the founding of the Ming dynasty in the latter half of the fourteenth century.

THE FOUNDING OF THE MING

The gradual weakening of Mongol rule in the second quarter of the fourteenth century was hastened by fratricidal rivalry within the imperial clan. This disunity within the Mongol leadership set the stage for a great rebellion. Fifteen years of frequent famine in North China after 1333 were capped by severe floods of the Yellow River. Flood and famine depleted the granaries and undermined the Yüan administration.

During the 1340's, uprisings occurred sporadically in nearly every province. In 1351–53 several major rebel leaders emerged among the native Chinese, and a typical interdynastic contest began among them to determine who should survive as the fittest to inherit the Mandate of Heaven. These rebel leaders were quite comparable to the rival warlords or local leaders during other periods between dynasties — resourceful, intrepid fighters, often from humble origins. They have been regarded by Chinese historians as a "group of heroes." Their exploits and stratagems added much to the Chinese lore of rebellion.

In their rise to local power, some of these men claimed descent from the Sung emperors, some invoked a religious sanction by prophesying the advent of the Bodhisattva Maitreya, the Buddha of the Future, and others had the help of secret societies. The more enterprising used all three of these aids in the founding of dynastic power. The most famous of all secret societies has been the White Lotus society. Its origin as a sect of T'ien-t'ai Buddhism has been traced back directly to the first half of the twelfth century; indirectly, its genealogy is claimed to date from the fourth century. As with any group that opposed the ruling dynasty, this society had to be secret in order to survive, since the government claimed a monopoly of all political organization. Even with the help of secret societies, the mobilizing of dissidents was no easy task. One chieftain in Honan, claiming descent from the Sung, recruited his rebel army among the *corvée* laborers assembled to repair Yellow River dikes. Another in the lower Yangtze delta drew upon the local salt workers. Others arose in the central Yangtze region.

The Rise of Chu Yüan-chang (Hung-wu). The eventual winner among all these Chinese rebel heroes was Chu Yüan-chang (1328–1398), whose name ranks with that of Liu Pang, the founder of the Han, as a humble commoner who through native ability in a time of opportunity became the Son of Heaven. He was born in the Huai River region northwest of Nanking. Left an orphan, he entered a Buddhist monastery as a novice, which gave him a chance to become literate. For a time he even begged for a living. But in 1352, at the age of twenty-five, he joined a rebel band. (Probably he also joined the White Lotus society, but he later denied this — it was an unwise precedent to leave in the historical record.)

Gradually Chu Yüan-chang attracted his own following. He and his band crossed the Yangtze and in 1356 seized Nanking as a centrally located strategic base close to the key economic area of the Yangtze delta. During the next decade he consolidated his power, defeating rivals to the east in the Yangtze delta and upstream in Hunan and Hupei, and created a local administration that could govern as well as fight. By 1367 he controlled all the Yangtze valley and could send his generals by sea and land to take over the provinces to the south.

Meanwhile, the Mongol commanders, who had suppressed a rebellion in North China, remained split by their fatal rivalries. Instead of attacking the Chinese rebels in Central China, they fought among themselves in the northwest. In 1368 Chu Yüan-chang's forces, having launched a great northern expedition, seized Peking, but he continued to use Nanking as his capital. That same year he proclaimed himself the first emperor of the Ming ("Brilliant") dynasty. In the selection of this name he followed the Yüan example of choosing a dynastic name not derived from some place or region. The Mongol power was driven out, though not destroyed. Ming forces took over the northwest and later the southwest (Szechwan and Yunnan), unifying all of China proper by 1382.

Chu Yüan-chang was given the traditional posthumous title, for a dynastic founder, of T'ai Tsu ("Grand Progenitor"), but he is better known as Hung-wu ("Vast Military Power"). Hung-wu was the name of the "year period," but, by keeping it for his whole reign, the first Ming emperor transformed it into his reign title. This set a fashion, followed throughout the Ming and Ch'ing, of using only one "year period" name during a whole reign. As a result, Ming and Ch'ing emperors are generally known by their "reign titles." (Strictly speaking, the emperor of the Hung-wu "year period" should be called the Hung-wu emperor, but this nicety is generally disregarded.)

The Reign of Yung-lo. A second strong early ruler also contributed greatly to the organization of the Ming Empire. This was Yung-lo (1403–1424), whose personal name was Chu Ti. The fourth son of Hung-wu, he had his base of power in Peking, when he rebelled against his nephew, Hung-wu's grandson, after the latter had inherited the throne at Nanking at the age of sixteen. Chu Ti waged a devastating civil war all across North China until he finally captured Nanking. Like American administrations announcing "Back to Normalcy" or a "New Deal," the usurper at the age of forty-three took as his reign title Yung-lo ("Perpetual Happiness"). The imperial structure at home and abroad was largely completed under his aegis.

Nanking had been built up by Hung-wu as the imperial capital, with a city wall sixty feet high and over twenty miles around, the longest city wall in the world. Yung-lo in 1421 moved the Ming capital to Peking, leaving Nanking as the subsidiary capital. He rebuilt Peking on a traditional but more extensive plan than that of the Mongols. The main city walls, forty feet high and more than fourteen miles around, form a square with nine gates, each one protected by an outer gate and circumvallations. In the center of this city, with its grid of long major thoroughfares, stood the walls (now removed) of the Imperial City, forming a square some five miles in perimeter. Within it, in turn, stand the high red walls of the Forbidden City, the imperial palace itself, surrounded by a moat about two miles around. Running from south to north through the palace, on the main axis of the whole capital, are the imposing throne halls with their gold-tiled roofs, each one rising from a terrace of white marble. This great architectural creation of the Ming still stands today as an unparalleled monument of empire. (See Plate 41.)

The walls of the southern city of Peking with their seven additional gates, forming an east-to-west rectangle on the south, half as large as the main city, were added in the sixteenth century. A procession, if it entered the southernmost gate on the central axis, would pass successively through eight massive gateways before emerging onto the broad courtyard before the first throne hall within the Forbidden City. Peking gave a proper setting to the Son of Heaven's performance of ceremonies, which included the reception of officials from all over the empire and tribute-bearers from abroad.

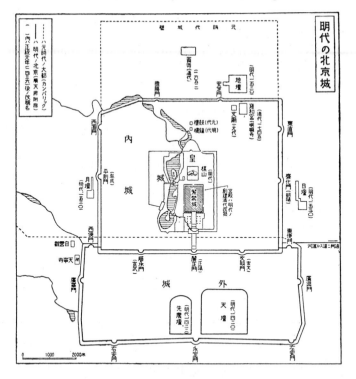

PEKING UNDER THE MING AND CH'ING

Top and center: Site of Yüan capital, Tai-tu, of which the northern walls were razed by the Ming. Center: Main city, centered on the Imperial City, with Prospect ("Coal") Hill north of the palace or Forbidden City and lakes on left. Bottom: Outer city (under the Manchus, the "Chinese City") with Altars of Heaven (right) (see Plate 9) and of Agriculture (left). Outside the main city on east, north and west, respectively, are Altars of the Sun, Earth and Moon. (From Wada Sei, Tōyō bunkashi taikei.)

THE MING ADMINISTRATION

The Ming emperors retained the inherited structure of central government: first, a civil bureaucracy under the Six Ministries and other organs; second, a centralized military hierarchy; and third, a separate hierarchy of censors, who reported on the conduct of affairs. (Khubilai Khan had referred to these three divisions, respectively, as his left and right hands and his means of keeping both hands healthy.)

The Board of Censors. In Western eyes this institution (now called *Tu-ch'a-yüan*) is perhaps the most interesting of the three. Its "chief investigating bureau" at the capital had a staff of 110 "investigating

censors." In addition, each ministry had attached to it a special censorial staff that watched its operations. Censors were drawn from
the general civil bureaucracy. Typically, they were younger officials of
rather low rank, selected for personal qualities of probity and uprightness.
When sent into the provinces, often on one-year tours of duty, they
normally investigated the conduct of justice and of ceremonies, the
condition of granaries and of schools, and received reports from officials
and complaints from the public. Their power came from their having
direct access to the throne, both to impeach other officials and to
remonstrate (at their peril) with the emperor. In addition to their surveillance duties, they had certain judicial functions and could act as
"judges at large," and they also might participate in proposing and executing regular administrative policies.

These broad powers were limited by the fact that censors usually
returned to the regular civil bureaucracy after a tenure of nine years
or less; moreover, like all officials, they depended upon the imperial
whim. Protected neither by life tenure nor by immunity from their
master's wrath, these "eyes and ears of the emperor" were in reality
bureaucrats like all their fellows, concerned for their own safety, dependent upon favorable merit ratings from their superiors, and sometimes open to bribery, intimidation or other considerations divorced
from duty.

This threefold administration, which the Ming and Ch'ing developed
on the basis of T'ang, Sung and Yüan precedents, has an interesting com-
parability with the recent regimes set up by the Kuomintang and the
Communists. Since 1928, China has been governed through the three
principal echelons of party, army and government. First Chiang Kai-
shek and then Mao Tse-tung have stood at the top of this tripod as
indispensable foci of final power, somewhat like emperors of old. No
doubt the modern governing parties in China may be viewed as the
successors of the dynastic families, the groups from whom the rulers
were chosen and to whom, if anyone, they answered. The party apparatus, however, running parallel to army and civil administration,
seems also to have inherited some of the ancient censorial functions.

Plainly this Chinese trinity is not a separation or balance of powers,
like the independent legislative, executive and judicial powers which
are kept separate under the Constitution of the United States. But
perhaps we may call it a system of balanced administration, under which
the military forces kept the regime in power, the civil bureaucracy
carried on the government, and the censors kept watch on everything.

The Growth of Autocracy. In the central administration, the first
Ming emperor, perhaps partly for temperamental reasons, became even
more of an autocrat than most of his predecessors had been. In 1380,

in suppressing a widespread plot attributed to his prime minister, Hung-wu abolished the post in perpetuity, as well as the top organ of administration headed by the prime minister, namely, the Central Chancellery (*Chung-shu-sheng*). Henceforth the emperor's rule was to be personal and direct. This institutional change, bequeathed by the dynastic founder to his successors, gave the emperors of the Ming and also the Ch'ing periods a more autocratic role than even the Sung emperors had had.

To aid him in his personal administration Hung-wu made use of Grand Secretaries, who worked with him closely, handling the flow of official memorials (as many as a hundred a day) and drafting the imperial edicts in reply. Eventually, in the second quarter of the fifteenth century, they became institutionalized informally as the Grand Secretariat (*Nei-ko*), a sort of cabinet, superior in practice to the Six Ministries and other organs. But while their influence inevitably grew, the Grand Secretaries, of whom there were half a dozen or so, remained merely secretarial aides of the ruler. They were unable to take executive action on their own initiative as prime ministers had formerly done.

Another key institution of the Ming autocracy, as in some previous dynasties such as the T'ang, was that of the eunuchs. As palace inmates, lacking family loyalties and completely dependent upon their master, these functionaries had a unique inside position, closer to the imperial person than any of the scholar-officials. Trusted agents of the emperor, eunuchs gained great influence as commanders of military forces and inspectors in the provinces.

The Ming period saw a constant tension and a struggle for power between the eunuchs and the Grand Secretaries within the palace, and also between these groups of the Inner Court, as they were called, and the top officials of the imperial bureaucracy, or Outer Court, at the capital. Bureaucratic factions and their bitter struggles eventually plagued the administration. One basis for bureaucratic friction was regional. During the first half of the Ming, three-fourths of the Grand Secretaries came from Central and South China, especially the lower Yangtze region, home of the conservative Sung tradition. Eunuchs, on the other hand, came mainly from the North.

Local Administration. The territorial civil administration of the Ming was divided into 15 provinces, which the Ch'ing later increased, by subdivision, to 18. Each province was divided into local units composed of still smaller units — prefectures (*fu*), of which there were, generally speaking, 159 in the Ming Empire, subprefectures (*chou*, also called departments), of which there were 234, and *hsien* (districts or counties), which totalled 1171. Under the Ch'ing these totals expanded to roughly

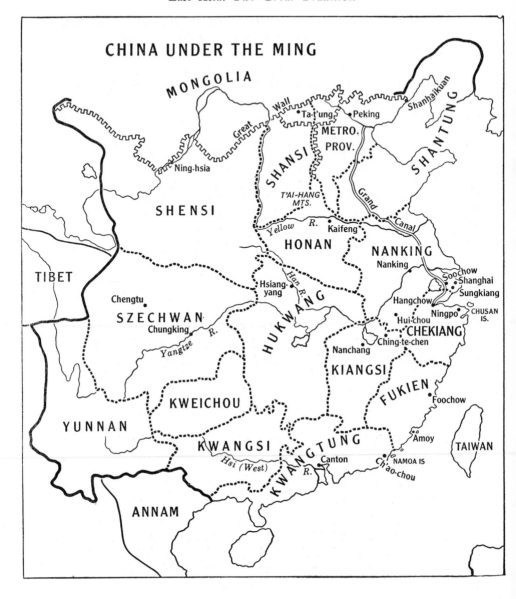

183 prefectures and 1470 districts, but precise figures, as for the various kinds of subprefectures, vary according to the definitions used and the period in question.

The local administrative hierarchy in each province was formed by the territorial magistrates, who according to the "law of avoidance" were never permitted to serve in their own native provinces lest they be seduced into collusion with kinfolk and local friends. In ascending order, these officials were the district magistrate, the subprefect and the prefect. The provincial administration was headed by an administrative commissioner. There was also a judicial commissioner or judge, with his own staff. A third top official in each province was the provincial military commander, with a hierarchy of military commands below him. Thus each province was under a sort of triumvirate, which represented the same threefold administrative, military, and supervisory functions as in the capital. A governor (*hsün-fu*) was eventually added as a coordinator at the top of each province, although this top level was not formally created by statute until the Ch'ing period. This administrative hierarchy was also watched, as already noted, by censors on tour, who formed in effect a separate hierarchy of disciplinary officials, representing the censorate at the capital.

The Ming military system developed by Hung-wu during his rise to the throne was based on guards units of 5600 men. Each unit (*wei*) was divided into five sub-units of 1120 men, who were registered professional soldiers. (The names of these guards units and their sub-units, *wei* and *so*, had been inherited from the Yüan.) By 1393 there were 493 guards units under the Ministry of War. They were now stationed at strategic spots on the Inner Asian frontier and the seacoast, along the Grand Canal and at the capital, under five main regional commands. The original guards units had thus become regional military establishments, or, in effect, garrisons, not unlike the garrisons of non-Chinese troops set up by alien dynasties of conquest. They were scattered within the territories but independent of the local civil administration. The registered soldiers' positions were hereditary, and many were given land on which to farm for their livelihood, in the hope of realizing the ancient ideal of a self-supporting army of farmer-soldiers. Inevitably, in an empire at peace, this system failed after a time to maintain an effective fighting force. Chinese garrisons, even more than Khitan, Jürched or Mongol troops, found it difficult to remain professional soldiers in a non-warlike society.

As at the capital, there was in the provinces a growth of new administrative organs which began informally and later became institutionalized. Among these were the intendants of circuit (*tao-t'ai*, often Anglicized as "taotai"), who were first appointed to handle special functions connected with the salt monopoly, police, customs, river conservancy, or the like. Eventually, the provinces were each divided for these various purposes into a number of circuits (called by the ancient name for province, *tao*), which formed a new administrative level intervening between the provincial and the prefectural levels.

Another major development was the sending of new traveling inspectors and special commissioners from the capital to deal with problems in the provinces, particularly to check corruption and misgovernment. Such officials were given certain administrative, censorial and military powers within designated areas, so as to introduce a more unified executive capacity into the territorial administration. From them developed, by the middle of the Ming era, the office of provincial governor (*hsün-fu*), already mentioned, as well as that of governor-general (*tsung-tu*), an official normally in charge of two provinces. These posts, like nearly all of the Ming system, were retained under the Manchus.

Land, People and Taxes. In governing China, the largest single unit of mankind, the Ming administration set up the innumerable categories and classifications necessary for dealing bureaucratically with vast numbers of people. Infinite variety was of course to be found in local situations over the face of this great empire. But every official was guided by the grand design of the imperial regime, which was set forth in imperial publications, first of all in the *Collected Statutes* (*Hui-tien*). These were first printed in 1511 and underwent continued growth and modification. The Ch'ing in turn completed five editions (in 1690, 1732, 1764, 1818 and 1899, respectively). Again, a comprehensive imperial geography of the realm (*I-t'ung chih*) was printed in 1461, with subsequent editions as late as 1764.

Locally, the government's control over the land and the people was signalized in the traditional way by the drawing up of detailed official registers of land and of population. In 1393 the population registers gave an estimated total of 10 million households and 60 million persons. This registration was a limited one, not based on a modern type of census. It produced a total no greater than that of the Han period fourteen centuries before. Judging by later developments, we can only wonder whether the population in 1393 may not have been double this figure.

The land registers in 1393 recorded a total of roughly 129 million acres of land in use. (This is less than half the estimated acreage of cultivated land in China in recent times.) In brief outline, this total was divided into government landholdings of many kinds, and private landholdings which could be freely bought and sold by the people. Each holding was classified according to type and productivity and was taxed according to these classifications.

Agricultural taxation followed the tradition which went back to the "Double Tax" inaugurated in the eighth century (see pages 192–193). The Ming "Summer Tax" was collected in the eighth month on the supplementary crops which had been grown during the winter and harvested in early summer, particularly winter wheat. The "Autumn Grain" was collected in the second month as a tax on the produce grown during the previous summer and harvested in the autumn, above all on the great rice crop of Central and South China. Consequently, it was by far the larger of the two collections.

In addition to payments in grain, the early Ming collected a certain number of silver ingots and rolls of silk twice a year. The usual government monopoly taxes on tea and salt were also maintained. The Ming continued to issue paper money, as the Sung and Yüan had done, but made it inconvertible into metal currency (copper cash or silver bullion), so that it became worthless and had to be abandoned by 1450. The use of metal currency to commute payments in kind at first occupied a rather subordinate position in the fiscal system.

The people were classified into military, artisan and civilian categories, the last forming the great mass under the territorial civil administration. They were registered in the tax lists under their households and land-holdings. Households were classified into three, five or nine grades (there were many complexities) and were obliged to provide labor service according to the number of registered adult males between sixteen and sixty years of age.

One kind of labor service included local responsibilities in connection with tax collections and public works. This service was organized under the *li-chia* system, in which, ideally, each 110 neighboring households formed a unit (*li* or "village"). Within this unit each year one of the ten leading families superintended one-tenth of the 100 remaining households to form a *chia* or "section," which bore the responsibility for local labor service during the year. The others served in rotation over a ten-year period. Thus the *li-chia* system had common features, but was not identical, with the *pao-chia* system of mutual guarantee developed in the Sung (pages 159 and 206).

Another kind of labor service (the *chün-yao* or "equal service") was also apportioned among the male adults. It involved prescribed tasks in the official establishments (*ya-men*, Anglicized as "yamen"), or else money payments for supplies for the yamen. There were still other forms of labor service apportioned among the populace, including service at the government post stations and in the local militia. Altogether, the official bureaucracy exacted a great and burdensome variety of tax payments and services from the people.

On assuming power the Ming had reduced the oppressive late Mongol levies and organized this rational, carefully graded, comprehensive, and minutely recorded system of taxation and labor service. But as time went on this complex system developed its own evils. In theory, for example, the burden was supposed to be heavier on the larger households which had more landed property and more male adults. But in practice, as we shall note below, the tendency was for the larger households in each locality to shift the burden onto the poorer households.

The Ming legal system showed the same pattern of reapplying traditional principles with a new vigor and thoroughness. Instead of merely copying the codes inherited from the T'ang and later dynasties, the Ming at first abolished them and then adopted those elements that proved useful, building up a comprehensive body of administrative and criminal law, which was first published as the *Ta-Ming lü* (*Laws of the Great Ming*) in 1397.

In all these ways the early Ming bureaucrats built up the imperial administration in minute detail. Yet this government remained, by modern standards, superficial. It claimed the prerogative of organizing, controlling and using all aspects of society. But in practice it did not interfere with the Chinese people in their daily lives. There were in the provinces only about two thousand principal posts and another three thousand or so accessory posts. If one adds minor incumbents and members of the central bureaucracy at the capital, the total of civil officials in the Ch'ing Empire about 1800 was only around twenty thousand. Under the Ming it was even smaller — quite insufficient for direct rule over the Chinese populace. The control of the country by such a small number of "mandarins," as Chinese officials came to be called by Westerners, was feasible only because of the functions performed by the dominant class in each locality, that is, the degree-holders or "gentry."

THE EXAMINATION SYSTEM AND SCHOLARSHIP

In the Ming revival of a purely Chinese rule over China, the animating spirit had been to return to the pre-Mongol institutions of the T'ang and Sung. Hung-wu tried to model his government on the T'ang and even decreed the revival of the T'ang style of clothing and the banning of foreign styles. In order to avoid the evils of the Yüan despotism, he stressed the careful selection of officials and the constant supervision of their local administration. For this purpose, he applied the traditional doctrines and practices of Confucianism. This soon led to restoration of the examination system as the center of official life. The system as now reconstituted remained essentially unaltered down to the twentieth century.

Under the Ming and Ch'ing there were three main levels of examination activity: On the first level were the preliminary examinations in the district town (*hsien*), which qualified the successful participants to compete in examinations held during two out of every three years at the prefectural city (*fu*). The latter gave the successful candidates the lowest principal degree, which Westerners generally translate as "licentiate" or "bachelor" (*hsiu-ts'ai*, "flowering talent"). This admitted them to the privileged class of literati, who enjoyed exemption from labor service, freedom from corporal punishments such as beating with the bamboo, and certain other prerogatives, all of which gave them enormous social prestige as members of the elite. In order to retain this status, however, the degree-holder had to take further examinations. He could advance to a higher degree by this means. But if he did not, he still had to pass periodical routine examinations, usually every three years.

For the second level there was again a preliminary test, leading to the great triennial examinations at the provincial capitals. There, with much ceremony, thousands of candidates would spend several days incarcerated with brush and paper in the long rows of individual cells at the examination field. (See page 202.) The successful candidate, one out of every one to two hundred competitors, became a "recommended man" (*chü-jen*), eligible to compete at the third level in the triennial metropolitan examinations at Peking.

If successful again at this third level at the capital, the candidate became a "presented scholar" (*chin-shih*) and was summoned to the palace for a final test by the emperor himself. After this he received his official ranking and appointment to a post. Once in office, his promotion depended upon passing further tests within the bureaucratic hierarchy. Thus the entire class of literati or degree-holders, constantly required to prove their competence in written form, lived a sort of "examination life."

One strong point of this system was its capacity to recruit the best literary minds of the country into careers open to talent. Quotas were set for the number of candidates who could succeed in each district and province, so as to insure geographical representation. Candidates could compete without securing any special recommendation or favor from those in power. Their papers were copied, without their names, before being read by the examiners, in order to insure anonymity of the authors and impartiality of the readers. For the provincial examinations, the examiners were sent out from the capital. After the metropolitan examinations the emperor himself, through the final palace examination, checked the standing of the two or three hundred successful *chin-shih*. The whole system was managed by the Ministry of Rites, instead of the Ministry of Personnel which supervised the officials' later careers. All these practices insured the impartial universality of the selection process, which somewhat counterbalanced the subsequent particularism of a government of men, not of laws.

One weak point in the examination system lay in the restriction of the subject matter to the Four Books, which had been selected as the essence of Confucianism in the Sung, and the Five Classics, again as interpreted by the Sung scholars of the school of Chu Hsi (see pages 238–241). Yung-lo had definitive editions of these works published in 1417 so as to exclude heterodox ideas and form a common core of learning for all scholars in the empire.

In accord with the Ming passion for formal organization, there was adopted finally in 1487 a set form for writing examination papers under eight main headings, with not over seven hundred characters in all and with much use of balance and antithesis. This was the famous "eight-legged essay" style (*pa-ku wen-chang*), later denounced in the Ch'ing period as imposing a tyranny of literary structure over thought. It called for systematic treatment of classical themes, such as the phrase, "Scrupulous in his own conduct and lenient only in his dealings with the people," which is a quotation from the *Analects* used as the examination subject in a provincial examination in 1738.

The Educational System. The institutions which prepared examination candidates included the government "schools," which were ordered to be set up at the district and prefectural levels. Their chief function was to hold periodical local examinations, not to provide organized instruction or residence facilities. At the capital was the Directorate of the Imperial Academy (*Kuo-tzu chien*, sometimes called by Western writers the Imperial College of Learning). In it metropolitan degree-holders (*chin-shih*) were registered and at times received instruction, principally in the form of semi-monthly lectures.

At the very top of the intellectual pyramid stood the Hanlin Academy (*Han-lin-yüan*, which is sometimes called by Westerners the National or Imperial Academy or the Board of Academicians). This was a carefully selected body of the most outstanding metropolitan graduates, who performed important literary tasks for the court, expounding the classics and drafting or compiling imperial utterances. The ethnocentric reaction of the early Ming centered in this citadel of Confucian doctrine, which abolished the elaborate sacrificial rites of the Mongol period, opposed foreign religions generally, and stressed the more austere state cult of Confucius and reverence of the ancestors.

The actual preparation of scholars was carried on first of all in the home. This fact gave the advantage to youths not only from families of wealth which could afford tutors, but specifically from scholar-official families, in which parental example and family tradition provided both incentive and intellectual guidance.

The chief primer for beginners, memorized by many millions of youths during the Ming and Ch'ing eras, was the famous *Three-Character Classic* (*San-tzu ching*) produced in the thirteenth century. Unlike the earlier *Thousand-Character Classic* (*Ch'ien-tzu wen*; see page 181), which was a tour de force that used each of its thousand characters only once, this later primer gave in jingle form a concise summary of basic knowledge and doctrine in 356 alternately rhyming lines, each of three characters. The *Three-Character Classic* begins "Jen chih ch'u, hsing pen shan. Hsing hsiang chin, hsi hsiang yüan." Substituting one English word for each character in these opening lines (a process which results in pidgin English rather than true translation), the Western beginner in Chinese may read: "Men's beginning, nature basically good. Nature mutually near, practice mutually far" — which, when properly understood, will convey to him the prime doctrine of Mencius that human nature is fundamentally good, that men are alike in this respect, but in practice they widely diverge. Needless to say, this idea, universally accepted in China, was to prove a stumbling block to several generations of Western missionaries convinced of original sin. The edifying content of this child's primer illustrated one feature of traditional Chinese education; namely, that the process of elementary learning was at the same time a process of philosophical indoctrination.

A more advanced source of training was the private academies (*shu-yüan*), some 300 of which were founded in various parts of the country, again on the model of the Sung *shu-yüan*, as centers of schol-

THE *Three-Character Classic (San-tzu ching)*

The first page of a modern edition, with the title of the book at the upper right-hand corner and the text itself starting on the third line. The passage translated above is the first line of the text. The commentary appears in smaller type.

arly study, discussion and compilation. Academies were set up usually under the patronage of high officials or rich merchants; some also received imperial encouragement and support. They brought together eminent scholars, students who received free maintenance and tuition, and small libraries for their use. Academies also published scholarly compilations and stored the wooden printing blocks.

Literary Production. The imperial sponsorship of letters was an important means of maintaining the emperor's position as head of the Confucian state and culture. This tradition produced in 1407 the great compendium, *Yung-lo ta-tien* (*Encyclopedia of the Yung-lo Period*), in 11,095 volumes and 22,000 chapters — a compilation of all the principal works on history, government, ethics, geography, etc., inherited from previous ages. Compiled by more than 2000 scholars, it was too large to print. Later, two more manuscript copies were made, but fewer than 400 volumes have survived to the present.

The next two centuries saw a continued flood of publication sponsored by the court, by officials high and low, and by academies and families all over the empire. To try here in a few pages to describe this literature, its great compilations and encyclopedias, the myriad types of monographic treatises, the many genres of belles-lettres would be no easier, and certainly no more meaningful, than to attempt it for the literature of all Europe in the same period. To cite one example, after several predecessors had led the way with smaller works, a scholar (Li Shih-chen) spent twenty-six years compiling an illustrated *materia medica* (*Pen-ts'ao kang-mu*), which described almost 2000 animal, vegetable and mineral drugs and gave over 8000 prescriptions. Completed in 1578, it described smallpox inoculation, distillation and the uses of mercury, iodine, chaulmoogra oil, ephedrine and other items of a rich pharmacopoeia upon which the modern world is still drawing. Another example, which has recently been reprinted, is a well-illustrated handbook of industrial technology (*T'ien-kung k'ai-wu*, by Sung Ying-hsing, printed in 1637; see page 335). It describes methods and instruments used in producing rice, silk, salt, pottery, metals, coal, paper, weapons and many other products of China's pre-modern technology.

By the late Ming some 1500 multi-volume local histories or gazetteers were available. In addition to official archives, several important private libraries had been built up, like that of the Fan family at Ningpo. It seems not unfair to remark, however, on the basis of present knowledge, that Ming scholarship, within the classical framework set by the examination system, was chiefly devoted to compilation, the orderly listing of things known, without much search for new ideas.

The School of Wang Yang-ming. In philosophy the chief departure from the orthodoxy of Chu Hsi was associated with Wang Shou-jen (better known as Wang Yang-ming, 1472–1529), a successful high official who carried further a line of Sung thought (see page 238). In brief, this was the Neo-Confucian school of Idealism (*Hsin-hsüeh* or "Learning of the Mind"). It had stemmed from Lu Chiu-yüan (Lu Hsiang-shan, 1139–1192), a contemporary of Chu Hsi, and had formed a minority school opposed to the dominant Chu Hsi school of Rationalism (*Li-hsüeh*). In general, this Idealist School (sometimes called the Lu-Wang School or in Japan the Wang Yang-ming School) was inclined to deny the dualism of Chu Hsi's system, the sharp distinction between Heaven and man and therefore between "Heavenly Principle" and "human desire." Instead, it viewed them both as part of a single realm, which brought it closer to Buddhism.

Building on this tradition, Wang Yang-ming's teaching represented a sort of Zen revolt within Confucianism in that it put much greater stress on meditation and intuitive knowledge than had Chu Hsi. It found strong scriptural backing in Mencius' insistence on the goodness of human nature and in his statement, "All things are complete within me." Chu Hsi's interpretation of the classical phrase (from the *Great Learning*) about the "extension of knowledge through the investigation of things" could thus be revised. Wang advocated instead "the extension of intuitive knowledge," which could be achieved through the investigation of one's own inner mind, the *li* within one. The process for doing this, as in Zen Buddhism, was essentially meditation, leading to a sort of enlightenment.

The idealistic teachings of Wang Yang-ming had an important role in East Asia, and particularly in Japan, as a stimulus to new ideas and a training for independent spirits. Wang urged that through a process of disciplined self-cultivation one might achieve the "unity of knowledge and conduct." As he put it, "Knowledge is the beginning of conduct; conduct is the completion of knowledge." This has remained a Chinese and Japanese ideal down to modern times. Today the Chinese Communists' concern for a Marxist "unity of theory and practice," though pursued in a very different way, can make use of Wang Yang-ming's terminology.

THE "GENTRY" CLASS

The processes noted above — an administration which covered the empire, examinations which produced a steady flow of degree-holders, scholarship which turned out innumerable works of compilation and description — all helped to create and give employment to an elite class of officially recognized literati trained in the Confucian ideology. The metropolitan graduates produced at the top totaled only 25,000 men in all during the whole Ming period. But the degree-holders of the lower ranks probably numbered at any one time under the Ming at least half a million persons, if we may judge by the estimate that their number in the early nineteenth century was regularly over a million. These degree-holders of all ranks have been known in Chinese as *shen-shih* (officials and scholars). In English the term "gentry" has been applied both to them and to a more inclusive group of persons prominent in the rural community.

The term "gentry" requires careful definition. It remains ambiguous, for it is applied both to individuals and to families, and may have either a political-social or an economic connotation in the mind of the user. Strictly defined, the "gentry" were individual degree-holders. This narrow definition, being more concrete and etymologically correct, is preferred. Yet in China's traditional society, where the family overshadowed the individual, the existence of "gentry families" (i.e., families that usually had members who were degree-holders) was to be expected. Similarly, individuals became "gentry" by securing degrees, not by owning land; yet, in a crowded society based on farming, land-owning was a chief economic support for scholarly study, and so might assist one to become a scholar and degree-holder. The combination "landlord-gentry" naturally was very common. Our thinking will be more precise if we distinguish between degree-holders and landlords, even though we must acknowledge that they overlapped to a considerable but imprecise extent.

One secret of the success of the examination system in forming the main avenue for social advancement lay in the fact that it permitted some to advance without examination. Degree status was not bestowed entirely according to scholarly achievement. One could also qualify by certain clearly designated non-scholarly means. The first of these was the inheritance privilege by which a son of an official of high rank could receive degree status in consideration of his father's merit. This system had been widely used under some earlier dynasties.

Under the Ming and Ch'ing, inheritance was less important than the second non-scholarly means of securing degree status, by purchase. Buying degree status by making a contribution to the imperial funds was a recognized practice under every dynasty. Indeed, sometimes it masked the officials' exactions, which took a rich man's wealth and left him an honored but less substantial title. The extent to which purchase was permitted under successive dynasties has not been fully determined. Usually it became greater toward the close of a regime, when the pressure for funds was greater. When over-indulged, the practice naturally inflated and depreciated the regular examination system. But generally the purchaser was allowed to obtain only degree status, not an actual official post. This admitted the purchaser to the "gentry" class, with its prerogatives, but not into officialdom. Thus, used shrewdly and in moderation, the practice of selling degrees could actually support the dominant examination system, for degrees acquired by purchase were clearly designated as such. They admitted certain merchants or land-lords to the scholarly elite, giving them, in return for their support of the regime, a qualified recognition within a framework that still gave the genuine scholar the highest prestige and chance for power.

In the early nineteenth century, about two-thirds of the lowest-level "gentry" members became qualified by scholarship, and one-third by purchase. In early Ming and early Ch'ing the proportion of purchasers must have been much less. But probably it was still great enough to permit big landowners to become degree-holders, thus broadening the already considerable overlap between the two groups.

"Gentry" Functions. The peculiar strength of Confucian govern-ment lay in the fact that the "gentry" performed so many public func-tions in the local community without official remuneration. They com-monly lived in the market towns or in the "big houses" in the villages, but also maintained contact or even establishments in the administrative cities. They were the bearers of the Confucian doctrine. As learned men and often also as men of wealth and political influence, they as-sumed responsibility for many activities which today are performed by officials. They raised funds for and supervised public works such as the building and maintenance of irrigation ditches and canals with their dikes and dams, and roads with their bridges and ferries. The "gentry" also took responsibility for public morals, maintaining the local Confu-cian temple or other shrines and the ceremonies which inculcated proper social behavior among the masses. They set up and supported local private schools and academies. They compiled and published the local histories or gazetteers. In time of plenty they sponsored orphanages and care for the aged, even though philanthropy in China did not become as public and impersonal an institution as in the modern West. In time of disaster the "gentry" supported relief activities. They also organized and led the local militia as defense corps for maintaining order. In most of these activities they received official encouragement or recognition but not specific appointment to office or any pay.

These public functions were of course inextricably intermixed with the private affairs of the "gentry" in their dealings with the peasantry below and officialdom above. A partial comparison might be made in this respect with other classes that have functioned in very different so-cieties, such as the equestrian order of ancient Rome, the modern Ameri-can business class, or other non-official groups that have provided local community leadership.

The "gentry" naturally tended to support the government, and it was to the interest of the latter to maintain a type of public spirit among the "gentry," as opposed to selfish opportunism. To this end the Confucian doctrines were regularly recited in the local Confucian temple and the Son of Heaven issued his moral exhortations for repetition in every community. The six imperial injunctions of Hung-wu were ordered posted in all villages in 1397. These said, in effect, "Be filial, be respectful to elders and ancestors, teach your children, and peacefully pursue your livelihood." In a similar formative period of the Ch'ing, the Emperor K'ang-hsi in 1670 issued his famous *Sacred Edict*, to be expounded semi-monthly by the officials and "gentry" in the villages. These sixteen maxims, each in seven characters, repeated, in effect, "Be filial and respect the social relationships, be frugal and diligent, esteem scholarship and eschew unorthodoxy, be law-abiding and pay taxes."

Thus the great tradition of learning, under the patronage of the head of the state, was used to indoctrinate the "gentry" class as the local

GENTRY IDEALS

From an eighteenth-century work (Pin-feng kuang-i) *illustrating the rewards of virtue. The caption (not shown) for the illustration on the left says, "In the tenth month winter cold sets in. The diligent have ample food and clothing. They feast with wine, play games, and entertain relatives. Parents live in comfort while sons pursue learning." The illustration on the right is for the eleventh month and shows a winter scene. Within their apartments women who have done their weaving sit warmly clothed around a brazier enjoying wine. On the street people who have been indolent suffer from the cold.*

elite, and they in turn provided leadership in the orderly life of the villages. Though not aristocratic in a hereditary sense, this was indeed an elitist system, for the degree-holders with their immediate families formed certainly no more than two per cent of the population but held the highest prestige and social authority outside the small official class itself. A comparison with the modern party elite of totalitarian states would be more accurate than a comparison with the hereditary elite in early modern Europe.

When the emperor's mandarin arrived at his yamen, in a province not his own (according to the "law of avoidance"), the local dialect might be quite unintelligible to him. He became at once dependent on the advisors and assistants he had brought with him and on the yamen clerks — a low-level sort of "permanent civil service" which handled his office's daily contact with the populace. His public, however, were particularly the local "gentry," who were in the best position to present local problems to him, to help him in meeting such problems, and to criticize his conduct of office. The empire of the Ming and Ch'ing, seen in modern terms, was governed by officials, to be sure, but with the indispensable assistance of the "gentry" — one might almost say, by officials and "gentry" together.

THE MING DESPOTISM

We have already decried the practice of dividing China's history into dynastic compartments, for the fluctuations of the imperial court are not a primary focus of our modern historical interest. Yet the emperor and his court bulk so large in the record that has come down to us that we can seldom avoid letting their history provide a central scaffolding around which other developments may be discussed.

The seventeen Ming emperors who began with Hung-wu presided over their dynasty's fortunes during a series of recognizable phases: (1) the inaugural era of founding and consolidation under Hung-wu (1368-1398); (2) the vigorous building and expansion under Yung-lo (1403-1424) and his successors, which, however, by the middle of the century had overstrained the imperial resources; (3) a century of gradual decline of imperial power both at home and abroad; (4) in the latter part of the sixteenth century a period of reform; and (5) by the early seventeenth century an intensification of evils and final collapse.

This profile of the Ming was studied intensively by moralistic Confucian scholars in the late Ming, who saw the Chinese state collapsing. They and their successors in the Ch'ing period made a largely political interpretation of the dynastic decline, without much reference to the economic, social and administrative factors we have discussed in Chapter 4. Thus they analyzed the personal failings of successive Sons of

Heaven, the errors of their officials, and the factionalism which rent the bureaucracy. Within this narrow political framework, however, these Chinese historians seldom questioned the fundamental premise of the whole Ming system — namely, the necessity of the emperor's final power.

Today, our first basic criticism from a political point of view might be that the emperor was subject to no higher law or constitutional checks. The state power was concentrated in him personally. He had to be either a benevolent despot or tyrant, or else let his power be exercised by others as favorites on an irregular, unstable, personal basis. The concentration of power in the Son of Heaven had greatly increased since the Sung period, as we have already noted, but the reasons for it are still uncertain. Perhaps it was mainly due to the Mongol example of arbitrary rule by alien conquerors from a tribal society, as some historians suggest. Perhaps it was largely an unavoidable result of the growth of the state apparatus and bureaucracy, requiring more vigorous executive action at the top. In any case, the Ming government had to have a great man at its head or face disaster. This problem of the effective concentration and impersonal control of power has been universal among dictatorships in all ages, and it remains a live issue also under modern constitutional regimes. Consequently the Ming experience has considerable interest.

Hung-wu's Influence. Because the founder, ruling for thirty-two years, left his imprint so strongly upon the Ming dynasty, his personality was a factor of special significance. Hung-wu was represented by most of his portraitists as a man with an ugly, porcine face. He had had a hard life in his youth, and as emperor he remained a lonely and austere figure. The abilities which had won him the throne — intelligence and foresight, cleverness in utilizing popular superstitions, respect for opponents of integrity, never-ending application — all made him an able administrator. He made a fetish of frugality, however, and in his later years apparently became subject to fears and suspicions, sometimes to delusions and violent outbursts of temper. He became very cruel and inflicted terrible tortures for slight offenses. In his final will he wrote: "For thirty-one years I have labored to discharge Heaven's will, tormented by worries and fears, without relaxing for a day." Perhaps this rather paranoid temperament of the founder helps to explain the growth of the Ming despotism.

Other factors may have lain in the circumstances of the day. Hung-wu's concentration of power in his own hands was no doubt a natural response to the problem of destroying the Mongol rulers, whose effective use of naked force as well as the weakness they suffered from their own disunity had been plain to see. Possibly Hung-wu's own experience as a self-made conqueror of pre-eminent capacity led him to institutionalize his personal role. At any rate, his abolition of both the prime-ministership and the Central Chancellery in 1380 left the Ming government without a head other than the emperor. The Six Ministries were in no position to coordinate their own activities, much less those of the military and the censorate.

As we have noted, the Grand Secretariat grew up to fill this gap, but under the Ming it remained an informal, extralegal group of individuals without statutory powers. The senior Grand Secretary might sometimes act like a prime minister, but only on sufferance as the emperor's favorite. As a member of the Inner Court, he had to rely on his personal influence and was often at loggerheads with the officials of the Six Ministries and others of the Outer Court, over whom he had no statutory seniority or control.

The Rise of the Eunuchs. Another group who moved into the vacuum left by the removal of the prime minister were the eunuchs of the Inner Court. Hung-wu had warned vigorously against this very possibility. He erected in the palace a metal tablet three feet high reading, "Eunuchs must have nothing to do with administration." He limited their numbers, ranks, titles and style of clothing, forbade their handling documents, dismissed those who commented on government affairs, and decreed that they should remain illiterate. He told his ministers, "Anyone using eunuchs as his eyes and ears will be blind and deaf.... The way to manage them is to make them fear the regulations. Don't give them rewards of merit."

Nevertheless the eunuch institution remained an integral part of the Inner Court, based originally on the emperor's need of male descendants and his consequent maintenance of a harem. In time eunuchs came to be considered a necessary type of personnel to staff the emperor's offices at the center of power. After the great days of Hung-wu and Yung-lo, who both came to power in the field, the Ming emperors grew up in the Inner Court and were often personally devoted to eunuchs who had been their childhood companions and preceptors. By the second quarter of the fifteenth century palace eunuchs were literate and active in administration. Thereafter they regularly held high rank and executed important commissions.

Their ranks and duties proliferated within the palace, their influence extended into the entire administration. In the 1420's a palace school was set up for them, headed by members of the Hanlin Academy. The number of eunuchs increased to thousands, some say tens of thousands. In a central office in Peking (the "Eastern Yard," *Tung-ch'ang*), set up in 1420, they kept secret files on official personnel, accessible only to the emperor — a forerunner of one aspect of a modern secret police system. The eunuchs became, in effect, a separate echelon of administration, not unlike a present-day security system.

The Punishment of Officials. The arbitrariness of the emperor's rule was visibly demonstrated in another custom which was practiced under the Ming, the corporal punishment of high officials at the court. Hung-wu had declared that he would follow the ancient way: officials should not be humiliated but should be moved by their sense of probity and shame. But he early followed the Mongol precedent of having officials publicly and ceremoniously beaten with the bamboo. In 1375 he had a minister beaten to death, and his successors from time to time followed this example.

This was no more frightful than the burning, racking, drawing, quartering and sundry tortures of medieval European political life or the execution of statesmen in early modern times. It also comported with the Chinese emperor's despotic rule in general. Hung-wu, for example, had a dozen officials executed at various times on suspicion of having inserted derogatory puns in their congratulatory memorials to him: thus, "you are the model" (*tse*) he suspected of suggesting "you are a thief" (*tse*); "give birth to wisdom" (*sheng chih*) seemed like a possible pun for "monk's wisdom" (*seng chih*). Whether or not such puns were intended, Hung-wu's killing of the authors hardly seems, in Confucian terms, to have made the punishment fit the crime.

Such treatment of officials had always contravened the Confucian doctrine that punishments are for the unlettered masses while the superior man is to be moved by the power of the ruler's moral example. To associate such an un-Confucian practice with "Confucian" government is anomalous and makes the term "Confucian" almost meaningless; yet the fact remains that the Ming regime, famous for exalting the letter of the classics, became notorious for contravening their spirit.

The arbitrary absolutism of the emperor and the unpredictability of his favor went along with another phenomenon of the Ming court, factionalism. As time went on, cliques of officials became violently involved in one dispute after another, hating their opponents, appointing members of their own faction to office when they could, accusing those in power when they were not. These personal, factional rivalries increasingly absorbed the officials' attention, to the point where the attainment of honors and the holding of power seem almost to have eclipsed the serious business of the formulation and application of state policies.

Our view of the Ming despotism, finally, must be kept in perspective. The unconfined power of the emperor and his favorites, as well as the factionalism of scholars and officials, was active mainly at the level of the imperial bureaucracy, which was spread very thinly and superficially over the empire. At the level of local government, on the other hand, the "gentry" class helped to maintain a stable social order in which the emperor's power was held in reserve and seldom exercised. This passivity of the central authority was in accord with the classical doctrine of government by moral example.

THE TRIBUTE SYSTEM AND JAPAN

Upon gaining the throne, Hung-wu immediately tried to re-establish the grand design of the Chinese state in his foreign relations as well as at home. Within a few months of his accession in 1368 he sent envoys to the peripheral states, Korea, Japan, Annam, Champa, Tibet and others, announcing his accession. Tribute missions from Korea, Liu-ch'iu (i.e., the Ryūkyū Islands), Annam (i.e., Vietnam) and Champa were recorded as having been received in 1369, and from Japan, Cambodia and Siam in 1371. Subsequently Borneo, Java, Sumatra, several small states on the Malay peninsula and some even on the Coromandel (southeast) coast of India were all recorded as having submitted tribute in the 1370's (as well as "Syria" from the Eastern Mediterranean). These were, in general, places to which Mongol expeditions had been sent almost a century earlier, on the established routes of China's overseas trade.

The suzerain-vassal relationship between the ruler of China and rulers of other countries was intended to create a "Confucian" world order. It expressed the traditional "culturalism" which assumed that China was not only the largest and oldest among the states of the world but indeed their parent and the source of their civilization, a concept which, as we have seen, had a good deal of historical validity as far as East Asia was concerned. Tribute relations involved much more than the mere presentation of tribute and performance of the kotow, the "three kneelings and nine prostrations," to which egalitarian Westerners objected in modern times.

"Tribute" may seem indeed a misleading term to apply to the whole institution, for it embraced all aspects of interstate relations: the exchange of envoys and conduct of diplomatic relations, the repatriation and extradition of persons, the regulation of Sino-foreign trade, and special Chinese efforts at self-defense through intimidating, cajoling, or subsidizing foreign tribes and rulers. If given this broad sense, the term "tribute system" may be properly used to indicate the basic underlying assumption of Ming foreign relations, namely, the superiority of the Son of Heaven, who in his cosmic functions represented all mankind before the unseen but moral power of Heaven. In short, the fitting of foreign potentates into a hierarchy of superior and inferior, and the expression of this in ritual observances, was merely an extension to the

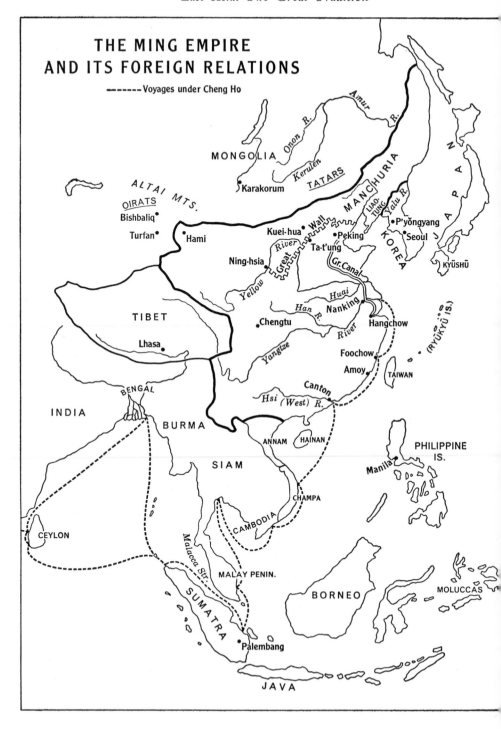

THE MING EMPIRE
AND ITS FOREIGN RELATIONS

------- Voyages under Cheng Ho

outer world of the "Confucian" social order which the ruler of China sought to maintain at home. One could not claim to be the Son of Heaven within China unless one acted like the Son of Heaven abroad, and vice versa.

Accordingly, the vassal king was given an official patent of appointment and a seal to use on his memorials, which were to be dated by the Chinese calendar, i.e., by the Chinese ruler's "year period," not by one of his own. The Son of Heaven affected a paternal interest in the orderly government of the tributary state, confirming the succession of new rulers, sometimes offering military protection against attack, usually conferring the boon of trade with China, and in any case sending down moral homilies and exhortations in the Confucian vein.

This was not an aggressive imperialism on China's part. Rather, it was a defensive expression of the "culturalism" we have already noted: foreign rulers, if they wished contact with the Middle Kingdom, must accept its terms, fit themselves into its polity, and acknowledge the universal supremacy of the Son of Heaven. Trade with China might be of great value to the vassal state. Tribute formalities were the price to be paid for it.

Like so many grand designs, this one failed of perfect execution. Yet the Chinese court and its chroniclers, by maintaining the outward forms of the tribute system in practice, or at the very least in the official record for posterity, did much to make it seem important.

Japanese Trade and "Tribute." The tribute system served many purposes. In the case of Japan, Hung-wu's main desire was to induce the "king of Japan" to curb the Japanese pirates who were raiding Chinese coastal ports. Accordingly, he sent three missions to Japan in 1369–1372, using various inducements — repatriation of captured Japanese pirates, threatening rescripts from himself, and the despatch of Chinese monks as his envoys after a great Buddhist celebration. He also seems to have used the restriction of trade as a lever, but all to no avail. Japanese piracy continued. Though tribute missions came, they were not always properly submissive, nor, for that matter, were they from the Japanese sovereign.

"You stupid eastern barbarians!" wrote Hung-wu to the Ashikaga shogun, the feudal ruler of Japan, in 1380. "Living so far across the sea . . . you are haughty and disloyal; you permit your subjects to do evil." Two years later the Japanese replied in kind: "Heaven and Earth are vast; they are not monopolized by one ruler. . . . The world is the world's world; it does not belong to a single person." Having failed to bring Japan into the tribute system, China broke off relations for a time.

When the tribute system reached its highest point of activity under Yung-lo, the third Ashikaga shogun, Yoshimitsu, inaugurated a brief period of Japanese fealty to China, expressed in very dutiful terms, which reflected his own admiration for the parent state and his interest in trade, as well as the Sinophile influence of Zen (Ch'an) monks at his court. In 1401 a Japanese mission brought a lavish tribute of native products, including a thousand ounces of gold, horses, fans and screens, armor and swords, all submitted with a proper memorial from Yoshimitsu, written "in real fear and dread and kneeling again and again."

The Son of Heaven delightedly replied, "Japan has always been called a country of poems and books, and it has always been in Our Heart. . . . Keep your mind on obedience and loyalty and thereby adhere to the basic rules."

Yung-lo in 1403 reopened the three Superintendencies of Merchant Shipping in the southern coastal provinces, which had been closed in 1374, and built hostels at each to entertain tribute envoys. Japanese missions now came annually for several years.

The tribute system's manifold uses were illustrated in the Ming commercial arrangements with Japan. In the usual fashion for tributaries, the Chinese court prepared a series of numbered paper passport tallies *(k'an-ho;* in Japanese, *kangō)*, tore them from their stub books, and sent them to the vassal ruler, retaining, of course, the stub books. When a mission came to the designated Chinese port to bring tribute and to trade, its ships, goods and persons were all specifically limited by statute. They were recorded on one of the numbered tallies, which could be verified against the stub book. A similar system operated in reverse for Chinese missions sent abroad. Thus all envoys were given bona fides, and imposters were checked. In the case of Japan, the shogun could, at least in theory, maintain his trade monopoly and the Chinese could identify pirates.

In the century and more between 1433 and 1549, eleven Japanese missions, usually of several hundred persons, came to the Chinese court under the tally system, by way of Ningpo as their port of entry. Innumerable problems arose — rivalry in Japan to get possession of the official tallies, conflicts in China with disorderly Japanese warriors, prolonged haggling at Peking over the prices to be paid for the "supplementary" tribute articles (i.e., trade goods), which included copper ore and sulphur by the hundreds of tons and Japanese swords by the thousand. Like the East India Company ship captains of a later time, members of tribute missions also carried their own goods for private trade. In addition, they received gifts from the emperor, as did the shogun, in lavish quantity — fine textiles, silver ingots and copper coins. Buddhist temples in Japan, in addition to their cultural interest in contact with China, had a lively interest in these trade privileges, not unlike the later Jesuit interest in the Portuguese trade between China and Japan.

THE MARITIME EXPEDITIONS

One of Yung-lo's major undertakings was to incorporate the states of South and Southeast Asia into the tribute system. While we know the general results of his efforts, his motives still remain a matter of speculation among historians.

The main outline of this ambitious venture is marked by seven great maritime expeditions which were dispatched to the "Southern Ocean" (*nan-yang*, the term now used for the general area of Southeast Asia). These began soon after Yung-lo's accession, in 1405, and were continued by his successors until 1433. They were led for the most part by a Moslem eunuch of the court named Cheng Ho, who came originally from Yunnan and as a Moslem was well fitted to deal with the Islamic rulers of South Asia. (See map, pages 268–269.)

The first fleet sailed in 1405–1407 with sixty-two vessels carrying 28,000 men, and reached India. The second and third, in 1407–1409 and 1409–1411, also went to India. The fourth voyage in 1413–1415 reached Aden and the head of circum-Asian navigation at Hormuz on the Persian Gulf. A fifth voyage in 1417–1419 also went as far as Aden. Another fleet was sent in 1421–1422. The seventh voyage started out with 27,500 men and reached Hormuz again in 1431–1433. Chinese vessels touched the east coast of Africa. Seven Chinese reached Mecca.

The world had never seen such large-scale feats of seamanship. These formidable Chinese armadas repeatedly sailed into and all the way across the Indian Ocean almost a century before the Portuguese in 1498 reached India by sailing around Africa, and a century and a half before the Spanish Armada of 1588 made Western history by its short and ineffectual voyage around England.

Cheng Ho's voyages were made possible first of all by the development of the requisite techniques of navigation on the Asian sea routes. Chinese seagoing junks of this period were of considerable size, sometimes over 400 feet (Chinese) in length, built with four decks and watertight compartments. They navigated by detailed sailing directions developed during many generations. They used the compass and with favorable winds could make about six knots. Distances were measured in watches, that from Amoy to Singapore Strait being figured at 9000 *li*, or 180 watches. Though the sea route around Asia from Japan to Persia generally hugged the coast from headland to headland, the Arabs had long been accustomed to sailing directly from Arabia across to India with the monsoon.

Returning after two or three years abroad, each of these remarkable expeditions brought back to court a gratifying collection of tribute envoys, lore and curiosities. They penetrated to the sources of China's foreign trade not only along the Southeast Asian coasts but also in

Ceylon, on both coasts of southern India, and in the Middle East. In addition to adjacent states which were customarily tributary, like Annam and Siam, some fifty new places were visited. The inhabitants of these states were no doubt much impressed, if not utterly terrified, by the Chinese armadas, and their rulers were enrolled by the Chinese as tributaries. Missions from Hormuz and the African coast came to China four times, from Bengal eleven times. Rulers of Palembang in Sumatra and of Ceylon were brought back by force, and the King of Malacca came to Nanking on four occasions. Back also came ostriches, zebras and giraffes. The latter were touted as the auspicious "unicorn" (*ch'i-lin*) of Chinese fable.

The Reasons for the Expeditions and for Their Ending. The complex motives lying behind these spectacular maritime expeditions are still a subject for speculation, even though several reasons seem clear. The Yung-lo reign was that of a second strong ruler, following the dynastic founder, and it saw a consolidation of political institutions at home and a great burst of expansive energy on China's frontiers, both by land into Mongolia and Manchuria and by sea to the south. Cheng Ho's voyages were an expression of the exuberance of an era of great vitality.

Personal motives played an obvious role. Yung-lo had seized the throne from his nephew but the latter, it is said, had escaped and disappeared, and it was feared he might emerge from overseas to contest the throne. For the eunuch leaders, the expeditions brought adventure, fame and presumably profit, if only from the handling of government funds. Commercial interests were also at work, connected with the well-established routes of earlier trade.

Another motive may have been broadly political, to bring all the known world within the Chinese tributary scheme of things. Far-distant places trading by land were regularly enrolled as Ming tributaries. Why not those trading by sea? This grandiose concept had been in the minds of Mongol emperors, as we have seen, and was implicit in the idea of the universal rule of the Son of Heaven. It may also have been stimulated by the fact that Chinese migration had already created large overseas communities in Southeast Asian ports. For example, Cheng Ho's fleet in a bloody affray at Palembang in Sumatra in 1407 reportedly killed 5000 local Chinese residents.

Speculation as to the causes of the Ming expeditions raises the question of why they were suddenly stopped and never resumed or imitated later. One immediately apparent reason for their cessation after 1433 was their great cost, at a time when the expansive activities of the early Ming, such as expeditions against the Mongols and the building of the capital at Peking, had begun to deplete the imperial coffers. Cheng Ho's great fleets could be criticized at court as costly adventures, largely unproductive except for pageantry and strange tales. They were also enterprises promoted particularly by the court eunuchs, whose activities were distrusted and opposed by the scholar-officials — so much so that Cheng Ho's feats were given minimal attention in the historical record.

Yet the voyages must be regarded as a spectacular demonstration of the capacity of early Ming China for maritime expansion, made all the more dramatic by the fact that Chinese ideas of government and official policies were fundamentally indifferent, if not actually opposed, to such an expansion. This contrast between capacity and performance, as viewed in retrospect from the vantage point of our modern world of trade and overseas expansion, is truly striking.

Chinese seapower, based upon the fishing fleets and trading junks of coastal centers like Canton, Amoy, Ch'üan-chou and Ningpo, had been steadily increasing. The naval strength of the Southern Sung and then of the Yüan had grown with the increase of China's overseas trade — witness the great fleets sent by Khubilai Khan against Japan and into Southeast Asia. Presumably both the volume of trade and China's naval strength reached a new high point under Yung-lo. The Middle Kingdom was on the verge of becoming a naval power that could dominate East Asia. The Ming fleets were developing the nautical and logistic capacity to bring military force and trading goods in overwhelming volume to any point in the Eastern seas.

But after 1433 the beginning made under Yung-lo and Cheng Ho was cut short and abandoned. The technological potentialities of this long development were not exploited by government policy. No Henry the Navigator came to the Chinese throne. The Ming court, unlike that of contemporary Britain, had no sustained interest in seafaring, no grasp of the possibilities of seapower. The Ming voyages were not followed up but remained isolated tours de force, mere exploits.

Ming Anti-commercialism. This contrast is significant for the light it throws on the nature of Chinese society. Cheng Ho lived and sailed a century and a half before Sir Francis Drake and the other captains of Queen Elizabeth began to lay the foundations of the British Empire. Even in the time of Elizabethan England, the Chinese Empire was greater than all of Europe in size and in the volume of her domestic, if not also her foreign, trade. Yet Ming China, having shown her capacity to do so, failed to become a maritime power. Through this default, the Eastern seas and even the China coast soon came to be dominated by a succession of non-Chinese seafaring peoples — the Japanese, the Portuguese and Spanish, the Dutch, and finally the British and Americans. Out of this commercial and naval domination of East Asian waters by non-Chinese emerged eventually those forces of imperialistic expansion on the part of many nations, which finally humbled the traditional Chinese Empire and led to its disintegration in the beginning of the twentieth century. The roots of this collapse may be traced back through at least five centuries, to the anti-commercial ideas and institutions of the Ming rulers and bureaucracy.

This traditional attitude was illustrated by the fact that Cheng Ho, as a court eunuch and high dignitary, lacked precisely those motives which later inspired the merchant-adventurers of Europe. His power and advancement, even as he cruised the Indian Ocean, still depended upon the emperor at the Ming court. Cheng Ho was evidently an organizer, a commander, a diplomat and an able courtier, but he was not a trader. No chartered companies grew out of his expeditions, empowered like the Virginia Company or the East India Company to found colonies or establish governments overseas. The migration of Chinese traders, coolies and shopkeepers into Southeast Asia was already well under way, and the Chinese in that area would always outnumber the Europeans who might come there. But the Chinese state, under both the Ming and the Ch'ing, remained uninterested in these commercial and colonial possibilities overseas.

This indifference of the Ming government toward foreign trade had already been evident in its relations with Japan. While the tribute system became a major vehicle for non-Chinese trade with China, it remained in the eyes of the Ming court primarily a political institution. The fact was that the Ming and early Ch'ing governments got their major sustenance from the land tax, not from trade taxes. In this respect they differed markedly from the Southern Sung, which had depended heavily on taxation of foreign trade, and from the late Ch'ing and Republican governments, which were to do the same centuries later. Indeed, the Ming and Ch'ing seem to have tried to turn the clock back, refusing to join in the great commercial revolution which was beginning to sweep the world, preparing the way for the subsequent Industrial Revolution of recent times.

Further examples of this Ming and Ch'ing anti-commercialism will be given below. Here we may suggest three main lines of approach to understanding it, one primarily institutional, the others ideological and strategic. The institutional explanation is of course the broader one. It goes back to the early environment in which ancient Chinese society began, on the North China Plain far from the sea, where the official class came into being as taxgatherers, fostering agriculture and gathering its products from the cultivators to maintain themselves and the state.

We have already characterized this early Chinese society as agrarian-bureaucratic, and have noted both the ideological disesteem felt for the merchant class and some of the ways in which merchants were kept subordinate to officialdom and utilized by it. In view of the growth of domestic and foreign commerce which occurred during the T'ang, Sung and Yüan periods, however, we must look to more concrete factors to explain why the Ming and Ch'ing regimes reverted to the traditional agrarian-centered attitudes of an earlier era.

One ideological development affecting these attitudes was doubtless the establishment of the Neo-Confucian orthodoxy as the matrix of Ming thought. This revived and preserved the classical values, including the ancient disesteem of commerce. As a result, the promotion of foreign trade was left to powerful eunuchs, which made it all the more distasteful to the official class.

Another part of the explanation may be essentially strategic — the Ming determination to prevent a repetition of the Mongol conquest. As we have already suggested, Cheng Ho's voyages may have ceased in 1433 because of the revival about that time of the Mongol menace from Central Asia. The result of the latter was to focus Ming attention more than ever upon the problem of controlling the "barbarians" of the grasslands, who had dominated the Chinese military and political horizon increasingly during the preceding 400 years. Insofar as Ming policy gave priority to the Central Asian frontier, it was more inclined to neglect China's sea frontier. Neither seapower nor foreign trade could curb the Mongols. The task required levies of conscripts and requisitions of food supplies and land transport.

THE MONGOL PROBLEM

Hung-wu's major preoccupation in foreign affairs had been to break the Mongol power. This remained the chief focus of early Ming foreign relations. The problem was not to subjugate and rule over the whole steppeland of Mongolia but rather to destroy the unity of the Mongol tribes, which gave them their military striking power. Accordingly, even before China had been unified within the Wall, Ming armies crossed the steppe to break up the Mongol forces, twice seizing Karakorum and even pressing on to the borders of Siberia. At the same time, Mongol chieftains who had been pacified by defeat, intimidation, purchase or other means were put in charge of Mongol settlements on the border and given titles, honors, emoluments and opportunities for trade. Mongol warriors were also recruited into the Ming armies. Using their traditional divide-and-rule policy, the Chinese generally tried to keep the closer semi-nomads of Inner Mongolia as border allies against the tribes of the full steppe in Outer Mongolia. Even so, the Mongols remained a continual threat.

In the Central Asian khanate of Chaghadai, the last great successor of Chinggis, the conqueror Timur, known to Europe as "Tamerlane"

(1336-1405), rose to power in 1369. From Samarkand as his capital, he expanded violently in all directions, overrunning Persia and Meso-potamia, defeating the Golden Horde in southern Russia, and even briefly invading northern India. Building an empire during the same decades as Hung-wu of the Ming, Tamerlane had some contact with the Chinese court and conceived the ambition to take it over. When he died in 1405, he had a vast army already on the way eastward to conquer China with fire and sword, so as to make it an Islamic state. The Ming Chinese were forewarned but hardly realized what they had escaped.

Tamerlane's death, however, marked the end of the Mongol era and particularly of the Mongol capacity to keep Central Asia united and so foster trade and contact between East and West. Under the Ming and Ch'ing, the land route across Central Asia was severed, and the tribes of Mongolia became more dependent on trade with China alone.

By the beginning of the fifteenth century the Mongol tribes of the steppe were split into two main groups. (See map, page 318.) In eastern Mongolia, along the Kerulen and other small streams in the grasslands far north of the Wall, were the Tatars *(Ta-tan* in Chinese, corrupted by Europeans as "Tartars"). In western Mongolia, in more mountainous country southwest of Lake Baikal, were the Oirats. The Oirat tribe had first appeared in history as warriors under Chinggis Khan. After the Yüan Empire collapsed at Peking, they grew to power in the remote region of the Altai Mountains north of the Hami oasis. Gradually they spread eastward until they vied in strength with the Tatars. The Chinese strategy was to play each group off against the other. Mongol bands were still capable of making devastating raids on North China, but their unity, the priceless ingredient which Chinggis Khan had supplied, was now gone.

Yung-lo's Expeditions. Ming dynastic politics reflected the impor-tant role of nomad relations in the Chinese Empire, for the Yung-lo emperor rose to power in the North at Peking by leading expeditions against the Mongols and also by finding valuable allies among them in the border region. After his usurpation of the throne in 1403, Yung-lo as emperor personally led five remarkable military expeditions far out across the steppe. This unusual activity, when the great maritime expeditions were simultaneously being launched overseas, bespoke the vigor of his reign.

Yung-lo's first campaign against the Mongols in 1410 reportedly mobilized over 100,000 men with 30,000 cartloads of supplies. Between March and September he overawed the Oirats, gave them gifts and secured their neutrality. Crossing the Kerulen River, his forces reached the Onon River and defeated the Tatars. Later, however, the Oirat chieftain seized the opportunity to expand eastward. From April to August 1414, Yung-lo led another army back to the Kerulen and this time defeated the Oirats, albeit with heavy casualties. Both Ming expeditions used cannon against the Mongols.

Within a few years the Tatar chieftain in the east, feeling stronger, raided the border. In 1422 Yung-lo led forth another host of 235,000 men. To support this army he is said to have requisitioned from North China a supply train of 117,000 carts and 340,000 donkeys. The Tatars escaped westward, however, leaving the Chinese to seize extensive booty. Further campaigns in 1423 and 1424 were likewise unable to catch the Tatar chief, and on the latter campaign Yung-lo himself suddenly died.

The Role of Peking. Already Yung-lo's removal of the capital from Nanking to Peking in 1421 had symbolized the Ming preoccupation with defense against the Mongols. Imperial strategy and politics henceforth centered on the Chinese frontier, where Peking stands athwart the principal gateway (the Nan-k'ou Pass) leading from Mongolia down onto the North China Plain. The capital of the great Chinese Empire thus was located a scant forty miles from its ancient northern boundary, the Great Wall.

This site has been used by dynasties oriented inland toward Central Asia — the Liao, Yüan, Ming and Ch'ing, as well as by the Chinese People's Republic since 1949. Southern capitals have been used by regimes originating in the South or oriented more toward overseas trade — Hangchow under the Southern Sung; Nanking in the early Ming, under the Taiping rebels (1853–1864), or under the early Republic in 1912 and under the Nationalist Government after 1927. Perhaps it is no accident that the latter have for the most part been militarily less powerful.

Some historians argue that the removal of the capital to Peking was an historical accident that had disastrous results, that it needlessly put the center of imperial administration on an unstable frontier within reach of the "barbarians," far from the centers of Chinese population and production. Certainly the strategic vulnerability of Peking to nomad inroads, and its economic dependence on grain shipments from the lower Yangtze via the Grand Canal, are startling facts — indeed, too startling to be mere accidents.

Our own view is that the capital of China had to serve as the capital also of the non-Chinese area of Central Asia. The "barbarians" were a constant military and therefore political component of the Chinese Empire, and its capital was drawn outward toward Central Asia as a result. Chinese historians have naturally wished when possible to forget this military importance of the uncultured nomad, but it was a primary fact of Chinese political life.

Overland Trade. The Ming expeditions to chastise the Mongols had been part and parcel of the effort to keep them in a harmless tributary status by carrot-and-stick methods. The Oirats, for example, had established tribute relations in 1408 and sent missions almost every year thereafter. As the Oirats grew more powerful, these missions became a thinly veiled means of keeping them pacified through subsidies, a sort of tribute in reverse.

The annual missions to Peking were headed by official envoys who presented passport tallies at the border. They might total by statute only a few score persons, but in fact the Oirat embassies of the early fifteenth century sometimes came to two or three thousand persons, including several hundred merchants from Central Asia. Entering the Great Wall at Ta-t'ung in northern Shansi, this host had to be quartered and banqueted by the local authorities; for, like cultural delegations invited to Peking today, tribute missions were the guests of the Middle Kingdom. If delayed at the border, the Oirat tribute-bearers might consume in one month 3000 cattle and sheep, 3000 jars of wine and 100 large bushels of rice, as well as fowl, fruit, fodder and other supplies, all at the local government's expense. On arrival at Peking they were quartered in the hostelry for tribute envoys, similarly provisioned, and banqueted once or twice.

As tribute, the Oirats presented their chief native product, horses, and also furs. They received in return imperial "gifts in reply," consisting mainly of silk and satin textiles, in established amounts for each grade of horse or pelt. Thus to a mission of 3000 persons the Chinese "gifts in reply" might total 26,000 bolts of gold-brocaded colored silk, 90,000 bolts of ordinary silk, and innumerable boots, hats and articles of clothing. Finer gifts might include musical instruments, folding knives, furnishings for the home, adornments for the ladies, and even articles such as weapons and copper vessels which foreigners were not allowed to buy on the market. A few days of free trade in the market followed the presentation of tribute within the sacred precincts of the Forbidden City. In this context of profitable exchange, the "barbarians" acquiesced in the "three kneelings and nine prostrations" as a regular part of the traditional court ceremony. The kotow to them seemed a convention like hat-tipping or hand-shaking in the modern West.

While gaining the nomads' submission, China had to suffer their frequent depredations on the route between the border and the capital, and their drunken roistering at Peking. Each side complained about the shoddy textiles or jaded nags offered by the other. For the Mongols, the trip to Peking spelled glamour and profit. Chinese textiles were highly valued in Central Asia, and Chinese brick tea (i.e., tea leaves packed as solid bricks) subsequently became so. Meanwhile horses and furs were highly valued in North China. Mongol princes could profit as middlemen in this exchange of goods, as well as from fees paid them by the Moslem traders to whom their tribute missions gave cover.

Ming records indicate that many bearers of "tribute" were actually merchants claiming to represent distant and sometimes non-existent potentates. Thus the Ming *Collected Statutes* listed (in the 1587 edition) thirty-eight countries of the Western Regions, all of which submitted tribute by way of Hami, the natural funnel for the caravan trade. These thirty-eight listed tributaries included Kashmir, Herat and other places in Afghanistan, Tabriz and other places in Persia, and the Alans in the Caucasus, in addition to well-known centers such as Turfan, Kashgar, Samarkand, and Bishbaliq (modern Tihwa). Also listed were Arabia (Mecca) and the Kingdom of Rum in Asia Minor (i.e., the long defunct Roman East), which were recorded as "presenting tribute" as late as 1618. A Jesuit traveler in Central Asia in 1604 (Benedict de Goes) describes the "sham embassies" of merchants who "forge public letters in the names of the kings whom they profess to represent" and "under pretense of being ambassadors go and offer tribute to the emperor." The Ming court viewed this thin trickle of Central Asian tributary trade as having political rather than fiscal value, as a means of keeping troublesome warriors quiet on the frontier.

The "Northern Robbers." In the 1430's, just as the overseas expeditions came to an end, the traditional concern for the Central Asian frontier was stimulated by a violent recrudescence of the Mongol threat. In 1439 a new chieftain, Esen, became the leader of the Oirats. As his first step toward power he subjugated Hami. He then extended his influence over the tribes to the east on the Chinese frontier all the way to Korea. In late 1449 Esen mobilized his horde along the border, threw off the forms of tribute, and approached Ta-t'ung in the north of Shansi Province.

The Ming emperor, a product of palace life, had come of age only in 1443 and was now under the ill-advised domination of his chief eunuch, Wang Chen, the first of a series of powerful eunuchs who were execrated by later chroniclers. Wang Chen was the leader of a group of eunuch henchmen who had been educated in the palace. This clique took the emperor into the field and foolishly advanced toward Ta-t'ung to meet the Oirats in battle.

Esen advanced, defeated, pursued and destroyed the Chinese force and captured the emperor. But he hesitated almost two months before investing Peking. There he found that the War Minister (Yü Ch'ien) and others had prepared a defense with cannon, enthroned a new emperor, and affected no interest in the former one. After several days before the walls, Esen, himself no Chinggis Khan, went back to Mongolia. Next year he sent back the useless emperor and soon resumed his profitable tribute relations. The Oirat power later declined.

The record of Ming-Mongol relations during the next century is a mixture of border raids and tribute missions, both of which had their attractions for the restless and impecunious nomads. The border raiding of the steppe tribes was a way of life, which the Chinese were unable to change or control. The later Ming suffered the continual harrassment of "northern robbers and southern pirates" (*pei-lu nan-k'ou*), the Mongols and the Japanese.

In 1550 a new leader, Altan Khan of the eastern Mongols, already a terror in Shansi and the northwest, united a large striking force, came through the Wall from the northeast, and pillaged around Peking again for several days before withdrawing. Ming defenses of walls and beacon towers and the establishment of military agricultural colonies on the frontier were offset by Chinese deserters who aided the raiders. Such Chinese helped Altan Khan try to establish a settled administration. He built a capital city at Kuei-hua outside the Wall, northwest of Ta-t'ung. Eventually in the 1570's he was pacified, given the hopeful title of "Obedient and Righteous Prince" (Shun-i Wang), and allowed to send tribute missions and conduct a regular market trade of horses for textiles.

Altan Khan had already become a convert to the reformed or Yellow sect of Lamaism, which as we shall note in the next chapter was spreading rapidly from Tibet into Mongolia in the late sixteenth century. This influx of a new religious teaching was to have a profound effect on Mongol life and really marked the beginning of a new era. Until the rise of the Manchu Empire, however, Mongol freebooting continued to harass the Chinese border.

TROUBLES WITH JAPAN

From the example of the Japanese and the Mongol tribute missions, we can see reasons why the Ming court may have preferred to let the tribute system rest in comparative abeyance overseas after the first half of the fifteenth century. The expense of maintaining, transporting and bestowing gifts upon a retinue of hundreds of functionaries and merchants who came to Peking was not directly compensated, at least in Chinese eyes, by the trade they conducted at the capital. The flowery protestations of humble submission from distant rulers seemed an expensive luxury. Gradually Peking enforced restrictions on the number of tribute vessels permitted to enter port, usually two or three, and on the number of persons permitted to go to the capital, usually a few score.

Missions from Southeast Asia grew fewer and fewer, the Ryūkyū Islands alone remaining a regular maritime tributary on a biennial basis and serving actually as an indirect channel for Sino-Japanese trade.

In this context of fading grandeur and frontier disorder, the first Europeans to reach China by sea, Portuguese adventurers in 1514, seemed to the Chinese little better than pirates. We can understand why the Ming court received a tribute mission from them in 1520–1521 as the price of trade but thereafter refused official contact. The Portuguese were only a small increment in a general growth of piracy and unwanted relations on the China coast.

The "Japanese Pirates." The decline of central power and rise of anarchy in Japan had given rein to maritime adventurers a full century before the Elizabethan age glorified the somewhat comparable exploits of gentleman-pirates from England. Like Drake and Hawkins, the Japanese could trade or loot by turns, as opportunity offered. Their two principal approaches to the poorly defended Ming littoral were, first, directly from West Japan to the mouth of the Yangtze and Hangchow Bay, the coasts of Kiangsu and Chekiang, and second, by way of the Ryūkyū Islands, already a principal entrepôt of trade between China and Japan, to the coast of Fukien. Their bigger ships could carry 300 men. As their ship design improved, they could make Ningpo from the Gotō Islands off Kyūshū in West Japan in three days with a favoring wind. Landing suddenly and attacking villages with their great swords, the pirates would seize provisions, hostages and loot and then make their getaway.

Although known in Chinese records as the "Japanese pirates" (*Wo-k'ou*, or in Japanese, *Wakō*, a term with pejorative connotations of "dwarf"), these raiders actually included many Chinese from coastal areas. Unlike the Mongol raids, the disloyal Chinese in these forays were not so much advisers as principal participants. By the latter decades of Ming rule, Chinese actually formed the majority among the "Japanese pirates."

The Ming response to this growing disorder on the coast was to issue a prohibition of maritime trade. This reflected the agrarian-minded and land-based unconcern for foreign trade upon which we have already remarked. It also had the effect of forcing crews and captains into smuggling or buccaneering for a livelihood, which exacerbated the problem it was intended to solve. In seeking motives for this anti-commercial policy, in addition to the classical bureaucratic disdain for merchants on ideological grounds, we can assume that regional and domestic political interests must have played some part.

Pirate raids intensified as the sixteenth century wore on, and after 1550 became actual invasions. Basing themselves on Chusan Island (later to be seized as the British base in 1840), pirates in 1552 attacked inland cities in Chekiang, while others went up the Yangtze, sacking cities on both shores. In 1555, for example, a pirate force of no more than seventy men landed and attacked Hangchow, went overland to menace Nanking, and pillaged places in between, traversing several hundred miles of countryside during two and a half months before being suppressed.

Ming pirate-suppressors bought over leading renegades with rewards and pardons and attacked the pirate lair on Chusan. But the scourge increased. In 1560 a band of 6000 plundered Ch'ao-chou in Fukien. Mustering reinforcements from the Chekiang coast and from Namoa Island on the Kwangtung border (later to be a center of the early-nineteenth-century opium trade), pirates ravaged much of the Fukien coast in 1563. Driven from Namoa, they based themselves on Taiwan, which remained a pirate lair until the arrival of the Dutch and the Ch'ing forces a century later.

The Japanese harassment of the South China coast declined only with the political reunification of Japan in the late sixteenth century (see Chapter 13). But the Japanese invasions of Korea in the 1590's concentrated Japan's military energies in a form even more menacing and exhausting to the Ming court.

The Korean Campaigns. The Ming learned of Japan's intent to invade China by way of Korea through spies in Japan as well as from Korea. In 1592, when the attack on Korea came, Peking debated whether to send a fleet from the southern provinces to attack Japan, or to put an army on the Korean frontier to watch developments, or to negotiate for peace, but decided in the end to fulfill its suzerain duty to aid Korea as the necessary way to defend Southern Manchuria (Liao-tung) and North China.

China mobilized troops and sent supplies and funds to Korea, but the Ming forces did not cross the Yalu until after the whole peninsula was in Japanese hands. When 5000 Chinese did move southward into Korea and attacked P'yŏngyang in mid-1592, they were badly defeated, and Peking started negotiations with the Japanese commander (Konishi Yukinaga) to gain time. At the beginning of 1593 a Chinese general who had pacified nomad rebels in Ning-hsia (Li Ju-sung) led an army of 43,000 across the Yalu, completely surprised the Japanese commander and drove him out of P'yŏngyang. Overconfident, the Chinese advanced to the outskirts of the capital, Seoul, and were ambushed and badly defeated. The short swords of the Chinese cavalry proved no match for the long swords, spears and guns of the Japanese infantry. Similar negotiations and exhausting conflict continued for several years more, until the Japanese finally withdrew in 1598, after they had made a second invasion in force in 1597.

The Chinese used at least 211,500 men in the first Korean war (before 1597) and spent 5,832,000 ounces of silver or "taels" (in Chinese, *liang*, "ounce," the monetary unit of account) on their grain provisions, and another 3,000,000 taels in exchange for rice and beans, to say nothing of supplies in kind. The total Ming expenditure to meet the first Japanese invasion of Korea must have come to over 10,000,000 taels, with a comparable sum required later to meet the second invasion. The Ming administration was already close to bankruptcy, after its constant subsidies to the Mongols and its building and rebuilding of the Peking palaces. Timber for the latter had now to be brought all the way from the southern and southwestern provinces because of the deforestation of North China. The Japanese invasions of Korea were a final strain on the dwindling resources of the Ming and prepared the way for the rise, after 1600, of bandits from within and "barbarian" invaders from without. Thus both the "northern robbers" and the "southern pirates" set the stage for a more direct attack by the Manchus, which proved the undoing of the Ming dynasty.

ECONOMIC GROWTH: THE SINGLE-WHIP REFORM

In seeking to penetrate the mysteries of China's economic history, we must constantly distinguish between the fiscal policies and financial state of the imperial regime, on the one hand, and the economic development of the country as a whole, on the other hand. Thus for the Ming period we have noted the court's inveterate anti-commercial attitude and the final bankruptcy of its resources. But if we now try to round out the picture by looking at the Chinese economy as a whole, we shall find much evidence of growth, particularly in commerce.

In general, from the fourteenth to the early nineteenth centuries, the Chinese economy seems to have grown in almost all its aspects — population, area of cultivated land, volume of foreign trade, production of handicraft and industrial goods, and even, perhaps, in the use of money. Unfortunately, the precise amount of growth remains unknown and so any conclusions about it must remain tentative, awaiting further research. In this situation our chief recourse is to note the institutional changes that accompanied this apparent growth in the size of the economy.

The Growth of Transport and Trade. The institution of most immediate concern to the court was that for transporting tax grain (called by nineteenth-century Western writers "tribute rice") from the rice baskets of the Huai River and Lower Yangtze to the new capital at Peking. As long as the Ming capital had remained at Nanking, this problem had not been acute. Grain for the armies on the Mongolian border and in Manchuria could still be shipped by sea around Shantung as the Yüan dynasty had done. After Yung-lo moved the capital to Peking, however, sea transport was increasingly hindered by Japanese pirates, and was in any case expensive. He therefore dug out the now unused "Connecting Canal" (*Hui-t'ung ho*) in western Shantung which Khubilai Khan had first constructed as part of the second Grand Canal system, and installed fifteen locks. Three thousand or more shallow boats were now used on the canal route, and after 1415 sea transport was given up.

The transport of tax grain to collecting depots on the canal was still part of the labor-service obligation of the peasantry. It became a heavy burden on them. Yung-lo's successors therefore placed the task of transportation entirely on certain military transport divisions of the local garrisons, which had to be increased from 120,000 to 160,000 men. From the 1430's this new system supplied usually over three million Chinese bushels, and sometimes over five million, to the capital every year. The Chinese bushel (*shih* or picul) in this period was equivalent to about three English bushels.

Trade between North and South China was of course further stimulated by the growth of Peking and the canal system. Trade on the Yangtze and in South China also increased. For example, merchants of the six districts in the southernmost part of modern Anhwei province (in an area roughly midway between Hangchow in Chekiang and Nanchang in Kiangsi) spread their operations widely into other provinces. Centered around Hui-chou and called, from an old place name, "Hsin-an merchants," they traded in all manner of commodities — porcelains from the nearby production center at Ching-te-chen in Kiangsi, teas and silks locally produced, salt, timber and comestibles. Naturally they developed the close relations with officialdom which such extensive operations required for their protection.

Specialized handicraft production for this enlarging market and even some larger-scale manufacturing grew up. One example of this was at Ching-te-chen, where the imperial kilns produced great quantities of porcelain for the palace and also for upper-class use and even export. Building on their ancient tradition, Chinese potters had developed the technique of using the particular clay now known as kaolin (named for *Kao-ling*, "High Ridge," a hill east of Ching-te-chen; chemically it is a hydrous silicate of alumina). When properly prepared with other substances and heated to about 1400 degrees Centigrade, chemical changes make it white, translucent and so hard that steel will not scratch it. This porcelain was a truly superior product in the eyes of Europeans, who lacked the technique and who properly called it "chinaware." In the use of their famous "three-color" glazes and overglaze enamels, the potters of the Ming period reached an unsurpassed height and their wares were eagerly sought by foreign traders.

Soochow, capital of Kiangsu, became a national center of trade, finance, and processing industries, particularly the weaving and dyeing of silk

MAKING SILK

Silk culture requires a maximum investment of hand labor. The silkworms are hatched from the eggs left in the previous year's cocoons and must be kept in the right condition of temperature and moisture. During their growth period they must be fed several times a day with fine-cut leaves from specially cultivated mulberry trees. This picture shows a man and woman sorting over the silk cocoons in their current crop, which is carefully kept on the trays in the background.

A later stage in silk culture requires that the strands of silk be unraveled from the cocoons in a pan of hot water. The woman here is collecting strands on a reel. This is likewise an occupation suited to the lavish application of labor in a subsidiary handicraft industry within a farm household. Home surroundings may of course be more pleasant than those of a silk filature. These pictures show only two out of a dozen stages in the complex process of silk production. (From T'ien-kung k'ai-wu, *1637.)*

335

and other textiles. The nearby Sungkiang region, inland from modern Shanghai, became a late Ming center for cotton cloth production, using raw cotton obtained from other provinces both north and south, and sending its product back for sale there. Canton meanwhile developed a special product in the form of iron pans (shallow cooking pots or frying pans for use directly over fire) which were exported widely throughout China, overseas, and to Central Asia.

One indication of this domestic commercial growth was the setting up in the sixteenth century of numerous regional guilds (*t'ung-hsiang-hui*) with guild halls (*hui-kuan*) in major centers and especially at Peking. Typically, the Kwangtung provincial guild was one of the first established there. These bodies were created by persons, chiefly officials and merchants, who came from a common region — a province, prefecture, district or city — so as to give them a convenient center of contact and mutual aid in a distant place, pre-eminently at the capital.

Meanwhile China's maritime trade seems to have developed steadily in the late Ming period, outside the framework of the tribute system. Tribute missions from Southeast and South Asia became fewer, while the Chinese merchants who went overseas became more numerous. In other words, foreign trade was no longer brought to China principally by intermediaries, like the Arab merchants who had been prominent in the Sung and Yüan periods. On the contrary, it was now carried by Chinese merchants who went abroad with Chinese products and on their return with foreign wares entered easily into the stream of China's coastwise junk traffic. The Ming and Ch'ing governments did little to encourage this trade and sometimes even banned it, but it continued to grow as an offshoot of domestic trade.

The main northern route for Chinese trading junks was from Ningpo, Hangchow Bay and the Lower Yangtze delta to Korea, South Manchuria and North China. The southern trade from Amoy and Canton down to Southeast Asia divided into an eastern route through the Philippines and east of Borneo to the Moluccas (later called by Europeans the Spice Islands), and a western route to Siam and down the Malay peninsula to the Straits of Malacca. When Europeans entered these channels of Far Eastern trade, after the Portuguese took Malacca in 1511 and first reached China in 1514, they found Chinese merchants and trading junks much in evidence at all the ports.

In time the Europeans began to make a significant contribution to China's foreign trade, principally in the form of a flow of silver from the Spanish mines in their new American colonies. This silver was imported in part by Chinese merchants who secured it in their trade with the Spaniards in Manila after 1571. Silver was also brought to China from Japan by Chinese, Portuguese and Dutch merchants, beginning in the late sixteenth century. In the centuries that followed, it was brought by traders from Europe and Southern Asia. Although the exact volume of these silver imports is still unknown, they are presumed to have contributed to an increased use of silver as currency within China beginning in the late Ming period.

The precise influence of foreign trade and silver imports on the Ming economy as a whole is hard to estimate because we still know so little of the domestic side of the economy. One approach to the latter is afforded by a major institutional development known as the Single-Whip reform. This will be briefly described before we analyze its significance.

Taxes on Land and Labor. Taxes are the aspect of the Ming economy that we know most about because, as usual in all periods, it was the one in which the officials were most interested. In the traditional levies on land and labor there was a gradual reform during the sixteenth century, which reduced them to money payments and at the same time simplified their cumbersome complexities by combining many small items of payment into one. Because of this latter reform the whole movement has become known, by a Chinese play on words, as the "Single-Whip" reform. *I-t'iao-pien,* meaning "combination in one item," sounds also like "a single whip" if one substitutes a different character for *pien*. The pun evidently caught on because the land and labor taxes were indeed a scourge upon the peasantry.

A brief look at this reform will indicate the evils which beset the Ming tax system and show how it was made more rational and efficient during the last centuries of the Chinese Empire, in a shift from payment in kind to money payments. It will also indicate the Chinese local administrators' capacity in the Ming period to adapt ancient institutions to new conditions, an adaptation which gave the imperial system another three centuries of vitality. Further, it may give us perspective on the recent Communist reforms of land tax and labor service, as variations on an ancient theme.

The evils which developed in the Ming system of land and labor taxes had begun with the falsification of the local records. As we have seen on pages 302–303, both land holdings and households were classified into grades. Each household was taxed according to the acreage and productivity of its land and the number of its male adults. It was subject to reclassification every ten years or so. One's tax burden therefore depended first of all on one's classification in the local registers of land holdings and population.

The responsibility for the local management of the system was placed on the leading households — the wealthier families, who were expected to serve in rotation as heads of the *li-chia* system in each village group of 110 households (*li*). In some provinces they were also appointed to be the tax collectors. Evidently there was little alternative to having the wealthier households assume this leadership. Yet the system automatically gave these leading families opportunity to escape their allotted burden by the simple expedient of falsifying the records. By collusion among themselves and by bribery of the clerks and petty officials, these interested parties could reduce their own tax liability, providing they could make this up by increasing that of the poorer households to meet the over-all tax quota of the area in question.

Many methods could be used: concealing the number of male adults, removing land from the record altogether, or securing a lower tax classification by registering land under the name of a servant or tenant who was helpless either to object or to assert real ownership. Other methods were to secure specific exemption by registering private land as government land or private persons as officials. Because of the special privileges enjoyed by wealthier families, smaller households often sought their protection, transferring the nominal ownership of their land in order to escape the tax burden, for a consideration paid privately to the large household.

As a result of such practices and others almost too devious to describe, the official registers within a few generations became meaningless, while taxation became chaotic and subject to the play of local interests — in short, a racket levied by the powerful upon the weak. Revenue collections naturally ran short; the government above suffered loss, and the poorer peasants beneath were milked harder than ever, while the large households and petty officials in between benefited from their mutual arrangements. It was this middle stratum of leading families in the countryside who provided many of the degree-holders through examination or purchase. Thus they became "gentry families" and, to some degree, a "landlord-gentry" class.

The confusion of this situation became compounded many times over by the complexity and variety of the tax items. The forms of land-holding were complex to begin with. Rights to the land in depth might be held by one person but rights to the use of the surface by another, who might lease the use of the surface to a tenant, who could sublet in turn. Tenantry assumed many forms. Land tax obligations were correspondingly complicated.

The labor service charges, however, became even more complex. They were subject to even greater manipulation, being apportioned on the basis of a factor less stable than land, namely, the number of male adults between sixteen and sixty years of age. Moreover, land tax rates were fixed officially, whereas labor service might vary according to local needs and was apportioned entirely by decision of the local power-holders described above. All the various forms of labor service — the *li-chia* system of households responsible for tax payments, the "equal service" (*chün-yao*) allotted among individuals, and the other miscellaneous services in all their petty variety — became more onerous as the whole institution became more corrupt. Demands for labor service bore so hard on the poorer peasantry that first households, then sections (*chia*) of villages and finally whole villages (*li*) began to abscond. Since tax quotas were seldom diminished, this increased still further the burden on those left behind, in a vicious circle.

The factor that finally made the tax system unworkable was the increasing commutation of land and labor taxes in kind to money payments. From the beginning of the dynasty some of the labor services had been levied in money form. As more and more items became commuted to money payments, the tax assessors and collectors had every opportunity to add surtaxes and extra fees, commute labor into silver inequitably, maintain assessments as tax items after the need for the original services had passed, and in general corrupt the system still further. The result was a limitless web of money taxes entangling the peasantry, levied in all seasons of the year for myriad nominal or alleged purposes, inequitably assessed and imperfectly recorded, according to no general scheme and under no superior control or direction.

The Reform Movement. The Single-Whip reform was carried out gradually by many hard-pressed provincial officials in one area after another, in a desperate effort to maintain a reliable tax structure and regular collections. It occurred chiefly in the period 1522–1619, that is, in the final century of effective Ming administration. It consisted of two principal tendencies — to combine all the various items of taxation under one or a few headings and to collect them in silver. Since this program followed no single blueprint and was worked out by many scattered individuals, it took many forms and varied widely from place to place.

For example, one basic reform was to simplify the land classification system so that, in place of as many as a hundred different land tax rates, there were only two or three rates. The classifications of male adults were similarly simplified. This inhibited manipulation. Another reform was to unify the land taxes, combining old levies like that on silk fabrics with the "Autumn Grain" levy and often abolishing the "Summer Tax" entirely. Sometimes thirty or forty different taxes would be combined into two or three items. Labor services were similarly unified. Next, the two major categories of land tax and labor service were sometimes combined to make a single item.

In this process the classification of households generally became less important, and the male adult more important. Tax quotas of a district were apportioned more simply, according to the two rather plain criteria of acreage of land and number of male adults, both being converted into money terms at established rates. Finally, dates of collection were unified, as well as the apparatus for it, which reduced the opportunities for extortion and fraud. Instead of a continuous sequence of collections for small charges, one after another, there were established a certain number of fixed dates for payment during the year, and the collecting agencies and personnel were unified accordingly.

It should not be assumed that the resulting fiscal situation was any simpler than it would be to have a separate income tax law and procedure for each county in the United States. The Single-Whip reform was no more than a combination of tendencies. It was only a partial step toward a modernized tax structure, but at least it was a step away from chaos.

Out of it came a general practice of paying taxes in silver, which was much easier to transport than taxes in kind. The government now used its tax receipts in silver to pay wages to hired laborers, who performed the labor service tasks formerly required of the common people. Communities were no longer required to transport their tax grain to a government granary. The Single-Whip reform also abolished the former indirect payment of taxes through the section and village heads. Instead, the taxpayer now put his tax silver directly into the government collector's "silver chest" in front of the local yamen and got an official receipt for it. The government then transported its tax receipts in silver to the capital.

In analyzing the significance of the Single-Whip reform we must note first how it fits into the pattern of the dynastic cycle as a reform effort which was undertaken after the Ming administration had passed its prime and become increasingly inefficient. Several dynasties had begun by relying at first on taxes and services in kind, only to have their tax system deteriorate in confusion and corruption, until a reform movement in the latter part of the dynastic period revitalized and simplified the system by a greater recourse to tax collections in money. Thus the increased use of money in government tax collections was probably in some degree related to the dynastic cycle. As a result there was a repeated growth of a money economy, as evidenced by the one phenomenon of greater government use of money, in several periods of Chinese history. Sometimes this phenomenon was part of an increased government interest in raising revenue by greater taxation of trade, an expedient to which even the most orthodox, agrarian-minded regime might be forced by dire necessity in its later days.

On this basis we may conclude that the Single-Whip reform probably demonstrated the growth of a money economy partly in this cyclical sense, as well as partly in the more absolute sense that the inflow of silver from America was beginning in the same period to increase China's total supply of silver for use as currency and to meet tax payments.

THE COLLAPSE OF THE MING GOVERNMENT

The theory of the dynastic cycle receives some confirmation from the disastrous end of the Ming dynasty. We must keep in mind the capacity of historians, both Ming and modern, to find in the voluminous record of history the evidence they may seek for almost any plausible interpretation of events. Yet even if we make allowance for this human frailty among historians, the drama of the late Ming seems to have many classic features of a dynastic decline — effete and feckless rulers, corrupt favorites misusing their power, factional jealousies among the officials, fiscal bankruptcy, the impact of natural disasters, the rise of rebellion and, finally, foreign invasion.

These cumulative evils were illustrated in the last decades of Ming rule, after the death of Chang Chü-cheng, one of the great ministers of the era, who rose to supreme power as senior Grand Secretary during the first decade (1573–1582) of the Wan-li reign. Chang was on good terms with the Outer Court and influential with the young emperor. He tried to increase the land tax revenue by getting exempted lands taxed again. He tried to restrict the ever-growing perquisites and privileges of the official class and the imperial family, including their accumulation of great landed domains. Yet Chang, for all his efforts, had to consent to raising the stipend of the court and could not check the emperor's greed.

After Chang Chü-cheng's death in 1582, the Wan-li emperor, reigning for another thirty-eight years, until 1620, became utterly irresponsible. He avoided seeing his ministers for years on end, refused to conduct business or make needed appointments, let evils flourish, and meanwhile squandered the state's resources — 90,000 taels to celebrate his marriage, 12,000,000 taels to invest various princes and more than 9,000,000 taels to rebuild palaces. Consequently, while the long Wan-li era is famous for its literary and cultural achievements, it saw great increases of taxation and corruption, and was followed by disaster.

The fifteen-year-old emperor who ascended the throne in 1620 was a dim-wit interested mainly in carpentry. He let his nurse's close friend, the eunuch Wei Chung-hsien (1568-1627), who had been butler in his mother's apartments, take over the government.

Wei Chung-hsien brought the eunuch evil to its highest point. Backed by a small eunuch army to control the palace and a network of spies and informers throughout the empire, he recruited unprincipled opportunists among the bureaucracy, organized a purge of his enemies in official life, and made extortionate new tax levies in the provinces. During four crucial years (1624–1627) he conducted what we would today call a gangster regime. While he was having numerous temples erected to himself, Wei cashiered patriotic generals who were trying to hold Southern Manchuria against the Manchus.

Factionalism: the Tung-lin Party. The Confucian resistance to these various evils was carried on mainly by a group of scholars known as the

Tung-lin party, whose long struggle and eventual failure make a poignant chapter in the annals of Chinese politics. Tung-lin, meaning literally, "Eastern Forest," was the name of an academy, originally founded in the Sung, at Wusih on the lower Yangtze. In 1604 it was rebuilt and reconstituted by a dozen scholar-ex-officials, most of whom had been in office and eventually had been dismissed during factional controversies at the court. They held monthly discussions and annual assemblies, wrote extensively, lectured at affiliated academies nearby, and soon spread their influence widely among scholars and officials elsewhere.

The Tung-lin aim was a moral crusade to reassert the traditional principles of Confucian conduct and apply them to political life. They condemned the philosophical eclecticism which had grown popular in the sixteenth century since the time of Wang Yang-ming, and which seemed to confuse Confucianism, Buddhism and Taoism. They reaffirmed the doctrine of Mencius, that man's nature is essentially good, and stressed the supreme importance of the individual's moral integrity. In these righteous terms they denounced both their opponents and various holders of power in the Inner Court, both Grand Secretaries and eunuchs.

The Tung-lin partisans of course had only an incomplete monopoly on virtue. By 1610 they were being denounced in turn as a *tang* (the modern word for "party"), that is, an organized clique of the sort that had traditionally been anathematized as subversive of imperial authority and bureaucratic harmony. The factional struggle was conducted less in terms of state policies than of the moral qualities of ministers. In the resulting game of denouncing and being denounced, the Tung-lin crusaders had their ups and downs. They became dominant in the years 1620–1623, just before the eunuch Wei Chung-hsien achieved complete power.

In 1624 a Tung-lin leader, Yang Lien, accused Wei of twenty-four high crimes, including murders and a forced abortion of the empress. Wei was able to mobilize the enemies of the reformers and in 1625–1626 retaliated with terror and a wholesale purge. Blacklists were compiled of some seven hundred Tung-lin supporters. The names of a great many were erased from the officials rolls. Leading figures were denounced, condemned, dismissed, disgraced, imprisoned, tortured and beaten to death. The most famous victims, Yang Lien and five others, were known as the "six heroes" (a title applied as recently as the late 1930's to a group of critics of Kuomintang policy). The Tung-lin group had been practically wiped out by the time Wei and his supporters fell from power in 1627.

The Tung-lin movement was not actually an organized party. Its adherents represented no one predominent region or class, although some historians see in it a commercial, middle-class interest centered in the Lower Yangtze cities. Such an interest, if discernible, was only a minor component of a movement motivated primarily by moral sentiments. The Tung-lin advocated no particular policies but rather the traditional Confucian state morality, the ideals of the scholar-"gentry." During most of its course, the movement was in political competition with other groups which also, if less self-righteously or wholeheartedly, invoked these same ideals.

At its end the Tung-lin faced the personification of immorality, a eunuch who had subverted the sacred office of the Son of Heaven and in the name of the emperor destroyed the most upright men. There were popular demonstrations in 1626 against the imperial orders arresting Tung-lin scholars. Wei Chung-hsien's manipulation of the throne for evil ends came as the climax to a long decline of leadership at the court and of financial health and solvency in the administration, as we have already suggested. In the eyes of the scholar class, which expressed the "public opinion" of the time, Wei's conduct completed the moral degradation of the Ming regime, after which nothing could save it.

The Rebellion of Li Tzu-ch'eng. It is usually forgotten that the Ming dynasty was actually destroyed by a Chinese rebel before it was superseded by the invading Manchus. Li Tzu-ch'eng (1605?–1645) rose to power as a bandit leader in Shensi in the northwest. The province was hard hit by famine in 1628, and, given the paralysis of the central government, this produced widespread banditry. Li joined his uncle, who was already a bandit, in 1631. Calling himself the "Dashing General," he made his lair on the edge of the North China Plain in the T'ai-hang Mountains of southern Shansi (in an area where the Japanese during World War II were unable to dislodge the Chinese irregular forces). Thence he pushed his raids into Honan and Szechwan, gradually acquiring more followers, organizing his armed forces and eventually setting up some of the forms of an organized government. At least two scholars joined him, after the Honan drought of 1639, and advised him how to win popular support. They spread songs and stories about his heroic qualities, helped him distribute food to the starving, appoint officials, proclaim a dynasty, confer titles on himself and others, and even issue his own coinage. By 1643 Li Tzu-ch'eng had made Hsiangyang on the Han River his capital and held much of Hupei, Honan and Shensi. Early in 1644 he took Shansi and in April descended on Peking from the northwest, taking the capital just as the last Ming emperor, deserted and in despair, hanged himself in a pavilion on Prospect Hill, overlooking the Forbidden City. Whether Li Tzu-ch'eng, even with the best scholarly advice, could have founded a strong dynasty remains uncertain. His career as a rebel had given him little opportunity to develop as an administrator.

Meanwhile his chief rival, Chang Hsien-chung, the "Yellow Tiger," who flourished during the same years, acquired a great reputation as a killer rather than an organizer of men. From about 1630 Chang had raided widely through North China, plundering with hit-and-run tactics and several times being defeated or bought off by government forces. Finally in 1644 he invaded Szechwan through the Yangtze gorges with probably 100,000 men, and took Chungking and Chengtu. He then set up a government, complete with Six Ministries and a Grand Secretariat, headed by genuine metropolitan graduates. They held examinations and minted money. But Chang Hsien-chung's main concern was military control and the stamping out of opposition. For this he used terror tactics, especially against the "gentry." The *Ming History* reports that he killed 600 million persons, meaning a great many. Even if the total were only a million, which may have been possible, he lost "gentry" support. His state collapsed, and the Manchus killed him in 1647.

The Manchu conquerors preserved and used the major institutions of government which had functioned for more than two centuries under the Ming. The downfall of Ming rule must therefore be attributed less to the structure of these institutions than to their malfunctioning under the accumulated stresses and strains which we have described already as typifying the end of a dynastic cycle.

9

Traditional China
at its Height under the Ch'ing

The Rise of the Manchu Tribes

The Ch'ing dynasty was created in the early seventeenth century, contemporary with the founding of the American colonies, and it lasted until 1911. Modern China, growing up within its shadow, has been handicapped by the fact that the Ch'ing period spanned the greater part of modern times — the whole era of American history down to our own day, for example — and yet was dominated by a regime and social order that changed relatively little. This slowness of change produced both an early strength and an ultimate weakness. As a result, the Ch'ing period saw both the zenith and the nadir of the traditional Chinese state. In the eighteenth century the population and the territory of the empire ruled from Peking were the largest they had ever been, if we except the Mongol period. The weight and sophistication of scholarly productions and the finesse and stability of administration were likewise at an unsurpassed height. Yet the nineteenth century brought unmitigated disaster in every aspect of Chinese life and thought. An entire civilization started to fall apart.

Here we are concerned only with the first act in this drama, the success of the Manchus in presiding over the Chinese state and society up to the beginning of the nineteenth century. In studying their achievement, however, we cannot help wondering to what extent their very success in maintaining the traditional order may have been a factor in its later collapse. So great was the prestige of the old order, so steady the balance which had been maintained among its various parts, that radical, thoroughgoing change of Chinese institutions and values could not easily be imagined — least of all by Manchu rulers who had taken over the whole imperial system intact from their Ming predecessors. The Manchus were successful as inheritors, not innovators, and it was not in them to remake the Chinese scheme of things.

The Manchu Homeland. The success story of the Manchus may be compared in its bold outline with that of the Mongols under Chinggis Khan. In both cases a powerful leader at a propitious time succeeded in unifying his people, giving them a common name, and setting them on the march until his descendants ruled all China. Though different in many respects, both the Manchus and the Mongols built up their military striking power in a region beyond Chinese control. Their dynasties of conquest followed a pattern which has already been suggested (see pages 259–261).

The Manchu nation-at-arms, which dominated continental East Asia for two centuries, sprang from Jürched tribes of the same Tungusic stock as the founders of the Chin dynasty (1122–1234). The Manchus rose to power on the fringe of Chinese culture and administration and therefore were in a position to learn from China on a selective basis without being completely subjugated or Sinicized. Most important of all, they were in a position to learn how to govern, at a time when the Ming administrative system was obviously running down.

Southernmost Manchuria, or Liao-tung ("East of the Liao River," including the Liaotung Peninsula), had been part of ancient China, administered within the Han Empire. This southernmost area communicated easily by sea with the Shantung Peninsula. With the wind it was only a twenty-four-hour voyage across the shallow gulf between them. Under the Ming, Liao-tung was administered as part of Shantung Province. It was also the natural corridor for land contact between North China and China's primary vassal state, Korea. Moreover, it was an area suited to the same kind of intensive agriculture as North China and so became thoroughly Chinese in culture and population and the chief source of food, revenue and wealth in Manchuria.

Liao-tung, however, being in a vulnerable strategic position, was a hostage to fortune. No natural barriers defended it from the north Manchurian region inhabited by hunting, fishing and pastoral tribes. The Ming and Ch'ing both erected walls or palisades (e.g., a ditch and embankment planted with willows) across southern Manchuria, but these served only to mark a boundary between the Chinese pale and the

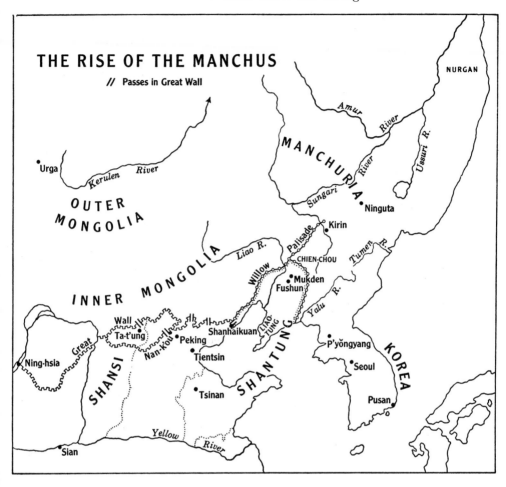

THE RISE OF THE MANCHUS

// Passes in Great Wall

tribal areas to the north. On the other hand, all Manchuria could easily be cut off from land contact with China at Shanhaikuan ("the mountain-sea pass"), where the Great Wall meets the coast. Anyone who can hold a few miles of level land between mountain and ocean there can control access to or from Manchuria like a cork in a bottle. Consequently Liaotung, though Chinese, was a place where Chinese and "barbarians" interpenetrated. If the "barbarians" grew strong, this region was a strategic liability to China, a sort of vermiform appendix prone to infection and easy to snip off. The danger in this was that any "barbarian" who snipped it off could achieve control over a genuine segment of the Chinese Empire, learn its ways, develop administrative organs over an agricultural Chinese population, and so rival the ruling dynasty.

The Ming Commanderies. The Chinese defense against this was to rely not on static walls but on human relations, to establish China's political hegemony over the tribes by "reining them in" and so subduing them (*chi-mi*). The precedent had been set by Hung-wu on the Mongol border, where he created military units (*wei*). (Because these *wei* were not regional garrison units of the Chinese army, as in China proper, but instead were tribal units under their hereditary tribal leaders, we distinguish them by translating *wei* in this case as "commandery.") Those set up in 1370–1375 were a first move in an only partly successful effort to absorb the Mongols of the frontier into a Chinese civil administration. In this process of absorption, the Mongols were first registered as "military households" and so drafted into the Ming forces with their tribal leaders as their officers. Later many were absorbed into Chinese life. As the Mongol power increased, however, this procedure became no longer effective.

Under Yung-lo this system of commanderies was applied more effectively to the tribes of Manchuria. In northwestern Manchuria the local tribes, who were mainly Mongol with a nomadic pastoral economy, had already been organized in three commanderies in 1389. Then in 1403 a first Jürched commandery, that of Chien-chou, was established among the tribes on the northeast of Liaotung. Another group of Jürched tribes was located in central Manchuria, and still another, the least civilized, was in the far north. By degrees all these tribes were given the status of commanderies and enrolled as military units under the Ming.

How far each commandery was subdivided in the Ming fashion into posts (*so*) and smaller units called banners (*ch'i*) is uncertain. They were still led by their hereditary chieftains, but the latter were now appointed or had their succession recognized by the court and were listed as loyal "barbarian" tributaries. Once this system got started, it rapidly expanded. A total of 178 commanderies and a number of smaller units of this type were set up in the Yung-lo period alone — an index of the Chinese divide-and-rule tactics. The chieftains were each given official titles and seals and expected to send yearly tribute missions.

As a Chinese writer of 1541 put it, "This is the supreme scheme for holding the reins (*chi-mi*) and controlling them: if the tribes are divided, they are weak and easy to control; if the tribal groups are separated, they become estranged from each other and submit easily. We make every one of them feel like a hero, and make them fight among themselves. This is the theory formulated: internal war among the barbarians is China's opportunity."

The Jürched tribesmen of the Chien-chou commandery, and of two adjoining commanderies set up soon afterward, were settled mainly along the southern fringe of the mountains and the upper waters of the Tumen River on the Korean border, although they moved about and in time of famine went as far north as the region of Kirin. These small groups were the direct ancestors of the Manchus.

Ming Control Over Manchuria. Yung-lo's policy was to expand Chinese influence in this area and eclipse that of the newly established Yi dynasty in Korea, since several Jürched tribes along the Tumen had become Korea's tributaries and supplied warriors for its army. Ming envoys therefore visited the Jürched with gifts in order to negotiate their acceptance of tributary status and win them away from their Korean allegiance. Typically these envoys were Jürched who had entered China's service. Once enrolled under the Ming, chieftains received Chinese support in getting their fugitive tribesmen back from Korea. The Chienchou chieftain's family was given the Chinese surname Li and his daughter entered the imperial harem. Surnames of course facilitated compilation of genealogies and so fostered the concept of legitimacy and inheritance. Meanwhile the bestowal of honors and decorations from the emperor, like those still conferred throughout the British Commonwealth, served to bind the "barbarians" into the empire. The Chinese tried also to delimit the boundaries of the tribes' territories and so attach them to the land. Another policy was to let a tribal chieftain become an absentee, moving his own residence into the pleasanter circumstances of a Chinese town in Liaotung, or even the capital, and so become Sinicized.

As part of his program, Yung-lo sent expeditions to the lower Amur River and in 1404 set up there the distant commandery of Nurgan (*Nu-erh-kan* in Chinese), maintaining contact between it and Liaotung by building boats at Kirin for use on the Sungari and Amur Rivers. The aim, as he said, was not to annex the Amur region but "to guard against a future menace," the rise of "barbarian" conquerors from the northeast.

As the Mongol threat increased in the fifteenth century, Peking's strategic aim in the northeast was to prevent the unification of the "barbarians" at all costs. The spread of Oirat power eastward roused keen fears in the 1440's. In 1448 the Ming ordered the Jürched chiefs to have no contact with the Oirats. But in the disaster of the next year, when the emperor himself was captured, the Oirats induced the Mongols of northwest Manchuria to join them, took over the Mukden area, joined forces with 15,000 Jürched, and threatened to invade Korea. Eventually, however, Peking managed to re-establish the previous situation, and the Jürched envoys again brought their tribute of horses and furs to Peking in order to receive the emperor's "gifts in reply."

As the Manchurian tribes grew in numbers and strength, the size of their missions tended to increase. Groups of 200 to 600 tribesmen at a time would now parade annually to Peking, harassing the populace en route and spying out conditions. The Chinese opened a horse market on the northern border of south Manchuria at Fushun so as to obviate this travel inside the Wall and built the usual beacon towers, each manned by five soldiers, to give warning of tribal movements.

The Ming court combined the use of the Confucian ethic with its use of rewards and punishments in maintaining peace and order among the Manchurian tribes. Its mandate of 1467, for instance, reminded certain disorderly chiefs of their titles received from the emperor's ancestors and of his many condescensions and lavish gifts. "The people of your region are all considered Our children." They were exhorted to reflect, repent and reform. The emperor also, however, threatened to chastise them with a great army. When disorder continued, this in fact was done. Ming and Korean armies now united in a common policy, since the Yi rulers of Korea continued their traditional loyalty to the emperor of China. They destroyed the Jürched chiefs but let their sons succeed to their positions. In 1478, because of continued lawlessness, another Ming and Korean military pincers chastised the Chien-chou Jürched, reporting 700 executions. But the tribes continued their unseemly raids and depredations. To protect Korean tribute missions crossing Southern Manchuria, the Ming finally built three fortresses with garrisons of 500 to 1000 cavalry and added forty-five beacon towers.

After this the Chien-chou tribes again respectfully sent their annual missions. Yet the building of fortresses was no monopoly of the Ming. As the tribes' resources increased, through the combining of their traditional hunting and pastoral economy with trade and agriculture, they too built strongholds and fortified them for use in their fighting among themselves.

It was on this frontier that the Manchu power arose as the Ming grew weak. China's defense required the Sinicizing of the "barbarian," to make him a loyal subject of the empire; yet this process in a time of imperial weakness gave the "barbarian" his chance to combine his native fighting strength with all that he had learned of Chinese ways. The result was a formidable synthesis of institutions and a new state power.

THE CREATION OF A SINICIZED MANCHU STATE

Nurhachi (1559–1626), the founder of the Manchu state, followed the tradition of Chinggis Khan in fighting his way to power on the pretext of avenging the deaths of his father and grandfather. They had been killed in 1582 in a fight which involved the Chinese commander of Liaotung and an allied Jürched chief, who therefore became Nurhachi's immediate target. While accepting the Chinese appointment to succeed his father, Nurhachi is said to have mobilized his family and tribe and exterminated this rival by 1586. He fortified his home, married the daughter of one powerful chief and the granddaughter of another, suppressed bandits and earned Chinese commendation. He accepted the fealty of smaller chieftains, and in 1590 led more than a hundred of them to present tribute at Peking. In 1595 the Ming court gave him the title "Dragon-Tiger General," the finest ever given a Jürched chief.

Nurhachi's rise to a position where he could finally defy the Ming dynasty was naturally a political, economic and administrative achievement as much as it was military. It took him thirty years of negotiation and arrangement of marriages and alliances as well as sporadic warfare to unite the four main Jürched tribes on his north. Meanwhile, he established the administrative and economic basis of his rule. He dealt in the supposedly medicinal root ginseng, which already formed a valuable luxury export from Manchuria for Chinese in need of rejuvenation, and which became an important trade monopoly for the Manchus. Nurhachi traded at the Fushun horse market.

In his own base area on the northeast border of Liaotung, Nurhachi built a fortified castle to serve as his capital. This boded ill for the Ming control of Manchuria. Nurhachi's castle, like those of other big chiefs, had three or four concentric walls. These provided an innermost fortress for himself and his clan, a middle castle of some 300 dwellings for his generals and close followers, and an outer castle for thousands of troops and their families. Blacksmiths and armorers were included, as well as a storehouse and granary. Trade and agriculture necessarily developed to supply so large a center. Chinese technicians and advisers helped this growth. One Chinese (named Kung Cheng-lu) was Nurhachi's adviser for thirty years.

The Manchu Banners. As his power grew, however, Nurhachi avoided conflict with the Ming and the Mongol tribes and concentrated on the unification of his own people. Until 1609 he sent tribute to Peking. Meanwhile, his greatest achievement was in the creation of new administrative institutions.

First in importance was the "banner" system, which came into being gradually after 1601. Companies (*niru* in Manchu) of 300 warriors were grouped at first under four banners (*ch'i* in Chinese), colored yellow, white, blue and red. Four more were later added, of the same colors but bordered with red, except for the red banner, which was bordered with white. Under the resulting eight banners and their subdivisions were enrolled all the tribesmen, in a transition from tribal to bureaucratic organization. All the people, including captives, slaves and serfs, were now registered under their respective banners and taxed, conscripted, controlled and mobilized through them as administrative units of the new state. Instead of having hereditary chieftains to lead them, the banners soon had appointed officers, as well as clerks to keep their accounts, even though the top command was reserved for Nurhachi's descendants in what was to become the imperial clan.

As the new state gained non-Manchu adherents, eight Chinese and eight Mongol banners were added, making a total of twenty-four banners. By 1644 there were 278 Manchu companies, 120 Mongol and 165 Chinese. At 300 men to a company, this would make an army of 169,000, with the Manchus forming less than half the total. This was about the size of the force that engineered the conquest of China.

Banners and their component companies did not fight as units. Rather, each company contributed a certain quota of men to make up the needed task force. For the expedition of 1634 into Inner Mongolia, for instance, each company provided twenty cavalrymen and eight guards, making a force of about 11,000. Against the revolt in China of 1673, the Manchu and Mongol companies at first each supplied ten cavalrymen and eight guards (about 9500 men), while each Chinese company supplied five soldiers (about 1000 men). The number of banner troops varied in different periods, but remained small in comparison with the traditional mass levies of untrained Chinese troops.

The banners' similarity to the Ming garrisons (*wei*) is plain, but they differed in that bannermen were allotted lands scattered in diverse places and intermixed with holdings of non-bannermen, not all located in one territorial unit. The banners thus were not attached to one place, even though they had their own lands and got sustenance from them.

Writing and Civil Administration. Another of Nurhachi's constructive steps was the development of a writing system for administrative purposes. Originally he had depended on Mongolian, written in vertical columns. (See page 257.) In 1599 he had his interpreter, who was trilingual, write Jürched words in a modified Mongolian alphabet and undertake the translation of Chinese works, such as the Ming *Collected Statutes* dealing with penal matters, into the new Manchu writing. The writing system was perfected in 1632 by adding diacritical marks (dots and circles) beside the Mongolian letters. The *Mencius* was soon available in written Manchu. Thus the new writing not only provided an easy way to deal with government business but also made possible a rapid borrowing of the Confucian ideology of the state, particularly that concerning the role of the ruler.

In 1616 Nurhachi took the title of emperor of the Later Chin dynasty, to continue the Chin dynasty of 1122–1234. Subsequently, in 1635, his successor decreed the use of the name Manchu (in Chinese, *Man-chou*) for all the Jürched tribes to supersede the names Jürched or Chien-chou, which were henceforth banned as reminiscent of Chinese suzerainty. The origin of the name Manchu is still obscure.

Nurhachi developed a civil administration with Chinese help. In 1618 he openly attacked the Ming and took part of Liaotung. At this time he captured a Chinese licentiate, Fan Wen-ch'eng, a native of Liaotung, who was a descendant of the great Confucian statesman of the Sung period, Fan Chung-yen, and grandson of a high Ming official. Fan became a trusted adviser to Nurhachi and his successors, a key figure in the new government secretariat. In 1625 Nurhachi moved his capital to Mukden (Shen-yang). After his death in 1626 he was given the posthumous title of T'ai Tsu ("Grand Progenitor"), following the custom of earlier dynasties.

Nurhachi was followed by two other capable leaders. His eighth son, Abahai (1592–1643), a hero in war and a strong ruler, soon eliminated his brothers and co-rulers and built up his personal power as monarch. He prepared the way for the conquest of North China but this was achieved only under his successor in power, Dorgon (1612–1650), fourteenth son of Nurhachi. Dorgon dutifully refused to accept the imperial title, standing aside in favor of Abahai's six-year-old son, but he actually ruled as the boy-emperor's regent for seven years after the seizure of Peking in 1644.

To reach this point of leadership, the early Manchu rulers first had to subordinate the tradition of clan government by group decision to a new principle of monarchy. Confucianism, with all its doctrines and political practices, provided a means to this end. The imperial clan leaders were brought into a state council and subordinated to it as an organ of the state. Eventually the Manchu imperial clan was kept out of administration entirely, but its members nonetheless were concentrated at the capital. Their primary state function after the conquest was to put a strong ruler on the throne and avoid the twin evils of government by women and by eunuchs, which had undone earlier dynasties. On his part, the Manchu ruler attempted to be wholly Confucian. The verbal and literary component of his monarchic rule was from the beginning couched almost entirely in traditional Chinese terms.

The success of the Manchus depended to a large extent upon the organization of state power in a Chinese fashion and the use of Chinese collaborators, two processes that went hand in hand. As bureaucracy supplanted tribalism, literate clerks and administrators were needed in increasing numbers. Many individuals were recruited into the new state administration from among the Chinese of Liaotung, who numbered about three million, some ten times the estimated number of the Manchus at this time. As Nurhachi said in 1618, "Our state has always had a generous appreciation of talented men. And if somebody is gifted and quick in administration, we elevate him, appoint him and bind him in marriage."

More and more Chinese came over to serve the new regime. They were attracted by the prospect of taking part in a strong and successful "Confucian" type of government, under which they might gain high office. The personal vigor, courage and sagacity of Nurhachi, Abahai and Dorgon, backed by their people-at-arms, provided the keystone of the new structure. The building blocks were supplied mainly by their Chinese adherents. In 1631 the Six Ministries were set up at Mukden, a simulacrum of those at Peking. Fan Wen-ch'eng was made a Grand Secretary. A censorate and other offices were also established, all on the Ming model.

The dual Sino-"barbarian" nature of the Manchu regime in its formative years at Mukden is indicated by the number of Chinese, natives of Liaotung, who rose in the Manchu service. For example, three Ming generals, all natives of that region, went over to the Manchus about 1633. Later, all three led armies to conquer South China. All three were made princes. One of these Chinese, Shang K'o-hsi, had twenty-three sons, of whom eleven became generals under the Ch'ing and three became state councilors.

THE MANCHU CONQUEST

The Manchus were able to seize Peking in 1644 partly because the Chinese commander at Shanhaikuan invited them inside the Wall as a move in the game of Chinese dynastic power politics. But this sudden and dramatic success of the Manchu invaders was by no means a mere accident of history. By building up their military and administrative capacities, the early Manchu rulers had made themselves already the leading contenders for the throne at Peking.

Nurhachi's son Abahai had steadily extended the power of the Manchu state. He attacked Korea in 1627 and 1636–1637 and made it a vassal state. He personally led expeditions through Inner Mongolia and broke through the passes in the Great Wall to descend on North China in 1629, 1632 and 1634. He sent armies there in 1636 and again in 1638, when they raided forty cities, including Tsinan and Tientsin. He defeated the Inner Mongols and made them his vassals. Meanwhile, four expeditions brought the Amur region under his control. In the midst of this furious expansion, Abahai in 1636 proclaimed the Ch'ing ("Pure") dynasty at Mukden, following the Yüan and Ming examples in taking a name of general significance rather than a place name.

The key figure in the drama of 1644 was a Chinese general of the Ming, Wu San-kuei (1612–1678), who was a native of Liaotung and had formerly been in command there. As the rebel, Li Tzu-ch'eng (see page 343), approached Peking, the Ming emperor summoned Wu San-kuei to the rescue. The capital fell before his arrival, however, and Wu withdrew to Shanhaikuan. Li Tzu-ch'eng advanced against him.

Instead of surrendering to a Chinese bandit rebel, Wu preferred to surrender to the Manchu, Dorgon, whose banners were waiting east of the pass. Together they defeated Li Tzu-ch'eng, drove him from Peking and wiped him out a year later. For three decades thereafter, Wu San-kuei helped install the Manchu dynasty while gaining great power for himself in the process.

Thus the Manchus, as rebels who had arisen on the frontier, were able with Chinese assistance to eliminate the rebels who had arisen within the country. In this case seizure of the throne proved easier from outside the Wall than from within China proper. One reason was that the Manchu state, in its strategically defensible external base, had been able to develop its administrative capacities, while rebels within China had a hard struggle to rise above the bandit level.

Against the Ch'ing invasion, the Ming princes put up only an individualistic, uncoordinated resistance. One prince at Nanking and two others on the southeast coast were eliminated within a few years. The longest-lived contender was a grandson of the Wan-li emperor, the Prince of Kuei, who moved about South China as the fortunes of war fluctuated and eventually was driven to seek refuge in Burma. Wu San-kuei, having routed the Ming remnants from Yunnan, pursued this last Ming claimant into Burma almost to Mandalay and had him strangled in 1662.

Wu then built up his own satrapy in Yunnan and Kweichou, developed his own trade monopolies, and yet milked the central Ch'ing treasury of as much as twenty million taels a year to support his armies. By this time two other satrapies had been built up, in Kwangtung by a son of Shang K'o-hsi and in Fukien by a grandson of one of the other Liaotung Chinese commanders who had joined the Manchus in their Mukden days. For many years South China thus remained under the domination of the Manchus' Chinese collaborators, whose local power rivaled that of the Ch'ing court at Peking. When Wu rebelled against the Ch'ing in 1673, the other two satraps soon followed suit, in the so-called Revolt of the Three Feudatories, which was not suppressed until 1681.

The Conquest of Taiwan. The last part of China to be taken over by the new dynasty was the island of Taiwan, as it is known in both Chinese and Japanese, or Formosa ("The Beautiful"), as it was christened by the Portuguese. Although frequented by traders and pirates of many nations in the sixteenth century and colonized to some degree by Chinese from Fukien, Taiwan had not been brought under Ming administration. From 1624 the Dutch maintained several posts on the island, principally "Castle Zelandia" at Anping on the southwest coast.

The last spark of anti-Manchu resistance was maintained in Taiwan by Cheng Ch'eng-kung (1624–1662) and his family. This man's father had risen as a pirate and adventurer, in contact with the Portuguese at Macao (who baptized him a Christian), the Spanish at Manila, and the Japanese at Hirado, where he acquired a Japanese wife who bore him Cheng Ch'eng-kung. The father having been won over to the Ming, his son became a favorite of the refugee court at Nanking and then at Foochow and received from it the imperial surname Chu and hence the popular title *Kuo-hsing-yeh* ("Lord of the Imperial Surname"), from which the Dutch derived "Koxinga." From 1646 to 1658 he controlled much of the Fukien coast, basing himself on the Amoy region (including the island of Quemoy, held by the Nationalists after 1949).

The Ch'ing tactics in dealing with Koxinga's maritime power were in the landbound tradition of the past. Echoing the Ming tactics toward Japanese pirates, they restricted foreign trade in 1655 in a vain effort to shut off the sustenance of the Ming loyalists. Koxinga retaliated in 1659 with a massive attempt to seize Nanking. Defeated in this effort, he descended on Formosa in 1661 with some 900 ships. The Dutch were expelled in 1662. Koxinga died, and in 1663–1664 a Dutch fleet helped the Ch'ing drive his son from Fukien; but he still held Formosa.

The Ch'ing now resorted to a drastic policy of forcing the population along the Chinese coast to evacuate the islands and move inland a distance of ten miles or more, behind a patrolled barrier, so as to cut Formosa off from its mainland sources of manpower, food and trading silk, and to make enemy raids unprofitable. This forcible evacuation of Chusan Island and points along the Chekiang, Fukien, and Kwangtung coasts, with all the local suffering it caused, bespoke the traditional autocracy of the Chinese state. Unlike the "scorched earth" policy of the resistance to Japan in 1937–1938, it did not commend itself on grounds of patriotism to those who suffered.

The Formosa regime, little damaged by these Ch'ing efforts, finally became involved in supporting the Revolt of the Three Feudatories. In suppressing this, the Ch'ing finally pulled together its naval forces and occupied the island in 1683. Taiwan was subsequently governed as part of Fukien.

Thus the Manchu conquest, in spite of the sudden success of 1644, actually occupied two generations, from 1618 to 1683. It was completed only by Nurhachi's fourth successor, K'ang-hsi, who was the second Ch'ing emperor to reign at Peking (1661–1722). The dynasty did not reach its height of power until the sixty-year reign of the fourth ruler within the Wall, Ch'ien-lung (1736–1795).

THE CH'ING EMPIRE IN CENTRAL ASIA

Until modern times control over China could not be easily maintained without control over Central Asia. This was partly a matter of military technology. Until the rise of modern industry and the firearms which have been one of its principal products, the mounted archer continued to decide the issue in warfare in East Asia, not least because of the superior mobility given him by that chief product of the steppe, the Mongol pony. Both the late Ming and the early Manchus used Western-style cannon supplied by the Portuguese or cast for them by Jesuit missionaries. But in the field, away from fixed fortifications, the early-seventeenth-century blunderbuss was not a decisive weapon.

The power potential of the non-Chinese tribesmen, however, was political as well as military. Being outside the Wall, they could create a new state administration to rival and supplant that of the Son of Heaven more easily than could internal rebels. The latter, being an immediate threat which the established government could not ignore, had to fight for their survival, with less opportunity to develop a settled administration than the "barbarians" might have on the frontier. Although this generalization is best illustrated by the Manchus, they are not the only example, as we have seen. In any case, the Ch'ing soon accepted the thesis that in order to control China they must control Central Asia. From the beginning, long before the conquest, they had set to work to incorporate the Mongols of Inner Mongolia into their new state. This in turn led them in the late seventeenth century to the conquest of Outer Mongolia and in the eighteenth to the conquest of Ili and Chinese Turkestan and a protectorate over Tibet. Thus the Ch'ing claims to imperial suzerainty over this vast area were eventually maintained in fact as well as in theory.

Control Over the Mongols. The Manchus had begun in 1634–1635 by defeating the Inner Mongols and then enrolling them as vassals, and yet simultaneously as allies, in the Mongol banners. Mongols thenceforth were recruited into and rose in the Ch'ing service. In the early years at Mukden, the Mongol, Manchu and Chinese languages were all three used for court business. The dynasty gave scope and opportunity for Mongol talent, both to serve in its armies and in many cases to participate in the civil government of China.

At the same time the Ch'ing preserved and strengthened the devices by which the Ming Chinese had kept the Mongols in check — assigning the tribes to fixed geographical areas, confirming new chiefs in their succession, conferring titles and honors, supervising inter-tribal councils and postal communications, permitting a regulated trade at fixed market places, and bestowing the customary gifts on regular tribute missions. In short, the Ch'ing continued to make use of China's natural advantage as the source of culture, commerce and luxuries; they maintained the Son of Heaven's role as the source of legitimacy, honors and favors. This divide-and-rule policy used Inner Mongols against Outer Mongols,

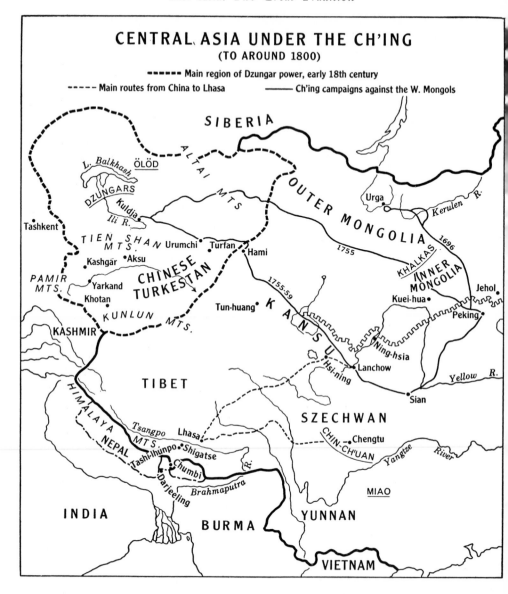

CENTRAL ASIA UNDER THE CH'ING
(TO AROUND 1800)

▪▪▪▪▪▪ Main region of Dzungar power, early 18th century

▪ ▪ ▪ ▪ ▪ Main routes from China to Lhasa   ——— Ch'ing campaigns against the W. Mongols

the principle of legitimacy against usurpers, imperial allies against rebels, and so prevented the accumulation of power by any one leader.

To operate this complex system, the Manchus in 1638 set up at Mukden the Mongolian Superintendency (or, literally, Superintendency of Dependencies, *Li-fan yüan*). This was a Manchu innovation. When transferred to Peking, it had a status roughly equivalent to that of the Six Ministries (or Boards) and eventually handled relations with Tibet,

Chinese Turkestan and Russia as well as all of Mongolia. Imperial residents or delegates were placed in Urga, Lhasa and other key spots. (In Western literature these are known as *amban*, but this is only the Manchu equivalent for "high official.")

The Conquest of Ili and Turkestan. The administration of this system, over the arid distances of Mongolia, of course required constant care and occasional fighting. In the late seventeenth century a descendant of the Oirat chieftain, Esen (who had captured the Ming emperor in 1449) rose to power in the mountains and grasslands north of Chinese Turkestan. This was the region of the Altai Mountains and the Ili River valley, which had been so often a route of access to West Asia. The new leader was Galdan, khan of the Dzungar (also spelled Sungar, Jungar) tribe. This was one of the tribes of the Western Mongols.[1]

Before taking power, Galdan had been educated as a lama at Lhasa, and he received valuable moral support from Tibet. In the 1670's he amassed a following, moved south and took over the oases and Moslem population of Chinese Turkestan as far east as Hami. Eventually he pressed eastward across Outer Mongolia and pillaged the Eastern Mongols (generally known in this period as the Khalkas) as far as the Kerulen River. Inevitably, Galdan seems to have thought of marching on Peking. The K'ang-hsi emperor of the Ch'ing mobilized accordingly, and at length in 1696, like Yung-lo of the Ming, he personally led some 80,000 troops in several columns across Mongolia to the Kerulen. Galdan's power was destroyed in a great battle south of Urga, in which the Ch'ing use of artillery symbolized the end of a millennium of nomad power. Outer Mongolia and Hami thus came more firmly under Ch'ing control.

The Western Mongols, and especially the Dzungars, though defeated in their eastward expansion, continued to be a source of disorder in the far northwest. To the usual feuds of tribe against tribe and disputes over succession had been added the devout Mongol interest and influence in Tibet, the Lamaist "holy land." The spread of the Lamaist religion had made it an important factor in Mongol life and a matter requiring Ch'ing attention, as we shall note in the next section.

The final settlement of relations between Peking and the Western Mongols, as well as Chinese Turkestan, came in the 1750's. There had been a long series of tribal rebellions, murders, usurpations, invasions and

---

[1] The Western Mongols are known in Occidental literature as Kalmuks and also as Eleuths. Eleuth is sometimes spelled Oelot, to say nothing of other ways, and the name is often confused with the earlier Oirat, in Chinese as well as English, since they each dominated the Altai region, though at different times. Actually the ancestors of the Eleuth or Oelot (properly spelled *Ölöd* in Mongolian; in Chinese, *O-lu-t'e*) of the Ch'ing era had been one of the four groups composing the Oirat (in Chinese, *Wei-la-t'e* or *Wa-la*) of the Ming era. Thus Oirat is the more comprehensive term, sometimes wrongly applied to a smaller group of a later age.

migrations in Outer Mongolia, all most distressing to the ear of any Confucian monarch. Ch'ing forces under the Manchu general Chao-hui finally occupied the Ili region three successive times in the years 1755–1757 and practically wiped out the Dzungars. Ch'ing garrisons and penal colonies were established in Ili under a military governor.

General Chao-hui in 1758–1759 also suppressed a Moslem rising in Chinese Turkestan and established Ch'ing control over Aksu, Yarkand, Kashgar and the other oases, on a basis that lasted for a full century thereafter. Following the precedent of the Han, T'ang and Yüan, this was the fourth major period in which the Son of Heaven in China ruled over the Tarim basin as far as the Pamir massif that divides East from West Asia.

THE INCORPORATION OF TIBET IN THE EMPIRE

Tibet is a country peculiarly limited by its geography. Of its three major areas, the northern plain is in large part 17,000 feet in altitude, as high as Mont Blanc in Europe, treeless, dry, cold and windy. Along the main river valley on the south (the river here called the Tsangpo flows eastward to become the Brahmaputra), the altitude is about 12,000 feet. This habitable region slopes eastward to a third region, which becomes more forested and fit for cultivation as one approaches the outer provinces of China. Cut off by the Himalayan ranges, Tibet gets little rainfall or snow although a great deal of wind. Lhasa, in the latitude of New Orleans, suffers heat by day and freezing cold at night. In short, Tibet, though about one-third the size of the United States, is an inhospitable country and so quite thinly populated. From Tibet, trade routes lead west into Kashmir, south through the Chumbi valley some 300 miles to Darjeeling and northeastern India, north to Mongolia, and east to China.

From the seventh to ninth centuries Tibet had been a small but strong military power capable of making devastating raids into India or into China as far as Ch'ang-an. The contacts between the T'ang court and the early Tibetan rulers, and the vogue of Lamaism among the Mongols in the Yüan period, have both been noted above (see pages 156, 177 and 277–278). In the early Ming period, tributary relations with Tibet were regularly recorded at Peking. Yung-lo in particular received envoys, conferred titles and confirmed appointments. Lamas came and went on the post routes and lingered long at the capital.

The Yellow Sect of Lamaism. One lama, however, who did not accept Yung-lo's invitation to come to China was Tsong-kha-pa (died 1419), a great religious reformer and the founder of a new sect of Lamaism. His reforms aimed to restore monastic discipline within

Tibetan Buddhism. This was accomplished by such measures as en-
forcing celibacy, requiring the wearing of yellow robes, and prescribing
the various routines of meetings, confession, retreat and other aspects
of the monastic life. This reform movement called itself the "virtuous
sect" (*Ge-lugs-pa*) and is generally known as the Yellow Hat sect, as distinct from the older Red Hat sect.[2]

During the late Ming, the Yellow sect spread its influence over Mongolia. The Mongols' nomadic way of life, their mobility and geographical
position gave them naturally a closer contact with Tibet than the sedentary Chinese could have, in spite of the Tibetan commercial demand
for tea and other products from China. The Mongols became involved
in the struggle within Tibet between the established Red sect of Lamaism and the new Yellow sect. Tsong-kha-pa's third successor, who
according to Lamaist belief was considered a reincarnation of his first
disciple, went to Mongolia in 1580 and died there eight years later. It
was from his host, the Mongol prince, Altan Khan (see page 330),
that this head of the Yellow sect received the title Dalai ("All-Em-
bracing") Lama. Accordingly, he has since been reckoned, retroactively,
as the third bearer of the title. After his death he was found to have
been "reincarnated" in a Mongol baby, who was in fact Altan Khan's
great-grandson, no less. In this way the Mongols were drawn directly
into the religious politics of Tibet.

The Rise of the Dalai Lamas. Under this fourth Dalai Lama the
Yellow sect teaching continued to spread. At the request of the Eastern
Mongols, the Dalai established the reincarnation of Tsong-kha-pa's third
disciple as a permanent patriarch of the church in Outer Mongolia, the
so-called "Living Buddha" (in Mongolian, *Kutugtu, Hutukhtu*) of Urga.
(The reincarnation of the founder's second disciple was the Tashi
Lama, generally known as the Panchen Lama, of the great monastery
called Tashi-lhunpo or bKra-shis-lhun-po, situated to the west of Lhasa
at Shigatse.)

Though recognized as head of the Yellow sect, the Dalai Lama
achieved his temporal power in Tibet only by degrees and by making
skillful use of Mongol and Manchu support. In 1641–1642 a Western
Mongol tribe which had moved into the region just north of Tibet intervened on behalf of the Yellow sect. It crushed the Red sect supporters,
unified the country under foreign Mongol rule, and put the fifth Dalai
Lama (1617–1682) on his spiritual throne in Lhasa. This man was an
able statesman. In response to Ch'ing invitations, he sent envoys to Mukden in 1642, and, after sending further missions to Peking, he went there

---

[2] The correct transcription of Tibetan names and terms puts initial etters, which
are still written but no longer pronounced, in lower case. Thus "g*Tsong-kha-pa*"
and "d*Ge-lugs-pa*" are the correct forms.

In person in 1652, bringing tribute and receiving high honors, exemption from the kotow, and the usual symbols of investiture — a golden tablet and seal, and a title. In Lhasa he rebuilt his great palace, the Potala, which was later imitated in the architecture of the summer palace of the Ch'ing emperors at Jehol. (See Plates 39 and 40.)

As time went on the fifth Dalai Lama succeeded in getting his natural son appointed regent, in effect, chief executive on behalf of the Mongol conquerors, who, however, soon declined in power. This regent gave his moral support to the ambitions of Galdan of the Dzungars, who challenged the Ch'ing power in the late seventeenth century, as we have noted above. This in turn drew upon Tibet the attention of the K'ang-hsi emperor, who naturally regarded the Dalai Lama as one key to the control of Mongolia, where Lamaist monasteries were already absorbing large numbers of young men into the peaceful life of the church.

Ch'ing Interventions. The upshot of this concern was another Mongol intervention, with Ch'ing moral support, in 1705. In this action the regent was killed and the death of the sixth Dalai Lama was precipitated. A new puppet Dalai was installed under a Mongol ruler.

Soon, however, religious resentment and political ambition both inspired an anti-Ch'ing counter-intervention by the distant Dzungar tribe of the Western Mongols. In 1717 their army of 6000 from Ili, feigning a friendly mission, arrived in Tibet unexpectedly over a difficult route of high passes. In the resulting struggle both sides used muskets as well as conventional weapons. The invaders stormed and sacked Lhasa and terrorized the country.

The Dzungars fled Tibet in 1720 when two Ch'ing armies reached Lhasa from the north and from Szechwan. This first direct Ch'ing intervention in force now installed in the Potala a new, legitimate seventh Dalai Lama, who had been brought along for the purpose, and a council of Tibetans to conduct his government. The Ch'ing also attached easternmost Tibet to Szechwan province, and protected the long post route between there and Lhasa.

This aggressive policy was temporarily reversed by the Yung-cheng emperor, after his accession in 1723, as part of a general retrenchment and because of the oppressive cost to the Tibetans of maintaining a Ch'ing garrison. However, a violent Tibetan civil war in 1727–1728 brought in a second Ch'ing army of 15,000. The Dalai Lama, having been involved in intrigue through his father, was exiled to eastern Tibet until 1735, and the government was put under the pro-Ch'ing victor in the civil war, Pho-lha-nas (in Chinese accounts, P'o-lo-nai). His administration was now supervised by two Ch'ing imperial residents and a garrison of 2000 men, which was later reduced to 500.

The new ruler published a new edition of the Tibetan Buddhist canon — the *Kanjur* (*Translation of Precepts*) and *Tanjur* (*Translation of Commentaries*). The Ch'ien-lung emperor made Pho-lha-nas a prince of the second class. He was called king by the Tibetans, and until his death in 1747 this exemplary Tibetan statesman maintained a peaceful equilibrium among three political forces — the regional aristocracy, the church magnates and the Ch'ing protectorate.

The third Ch'ing intervention in Tibet was precipitated by a revival of Dzungar intrigue and multiple murders in 1750, when the ruler killed his brother, the imperial residents killed the ruler, and a mob in Lhasa killed the imperial residents. For this breakdown of political control, the solution of the Ch'ien-lung emperor was to establish the Dalai Lama finally in a position of full temporal power under a continued Ch'ing protectorate. The Dalai Lama ruled thenceforth through a council (*bKa'-blon*) of four ministers (called "calons" in Western literature) under the supervision of the imperial residents and a Ch'ing garrison of 1500 men. The post routes were again taken under Ch'ing control. Thus after a good deal of trial and error, the political power in Tibet was firmly incorporated in that of the Ch'ing Empire, where it was to remain until 1912.

It is ironic that the Ch'ing had barely completed this imperial structure in Mongolia, Chinese Turkestan and Tibet, solving the age-old problem of ruling both China and Central Asia, when an utterly unprecedented problem arose — the arrival in force on the southeast coast of European "barbarians" with superior military power. This new problem proved insoluble for the rulers of China until the twentieth century.

THE PRESERVATION OF MANCHU POWER

Having become a nation of conquerors, the Manchus' basic problem was to preserve themselves as a cohesive minority capable of keeping its grip on power. Since their numbers totaled roughly two per cent of the population of their empire, this was a formidable task. First of all, the Manchus had to preserve their special status, privileges and emoluments, keep themselves separate from the Chinese, and so maintain their racial consciousness and identity.

Social Controls. The imperial clan was governed through a special office, the Imperial Clan Court, which had charge of clan records, education and discipline of clan members, and payment of their stipends. There were twelve main ranks of imperial clansmen, from princes on down. The rank inherited by a son was one grade lower than that of his father, giving the son an incentive to prove himself. Mongol men were especially sought to marry the Manchu women, so as to forge blood relationships with the Mongols. Imperial clansmen in general were kept out of administration and seldom, if ever, served in the Grand Secretariat or Grand Council.

In addition to the imperial clan, there was the Manchu aristocracy, ranked in thirty-one grades of nobility, who also received investiture and stipends from the throne. The remainder of the Manchus were all bannermen, given land to till and stipends in addition, and exempted from Chinese local jurisdiction. Mongol and Chinese bannermen, in descending order, were less amply provided for.

For all the Manchus there was a ban on engaging in trade or labor, or intermarrying with Chinese or following Chinese customs, such as foot-binding. The traditional clan system was preserved and this provided an element of social cohesion. It was supported by the totemic religion of the shamans or "medicine men"; each clan accordingly had its common ancestor. Education in the Manchu language was made compulsory. Extensive translations were made of Chinese classics and histories to help keep the Manchu language alive. Manchus were forbidden to dress in Chinese costume. On the other hand, all Chinese were required to give up the Ming coiffure, braid their hair in a queue, and shave the rest of their heads, like the Manchus. This was the origin of the queue, which the nineteenth-century Westerners regarded as the most typical feature of the Chinese costume.

Military Controls. As a second step to preserve Manchu control, the banner forces were used to insure military supremacy. The 563 companies of the year 1644 doubled in number, reaching a total of 1155 companies by 1735 — 678 Manchu, 207 Mongol and 270 Chinese companies. The totals of military forces carried on the official rolls show a doubling of personnel in the twenty-four banners, which grew from some 169,000 in 1644 to about 350,000 listed in the eighteenth century. In fact, however, this listed strength was not maintained in practice. The actual size of a company seems often to have dropped from 300 to perhaps 200 men.

The banner forces were distributed in a separate network under Manchu generals-in-chief (*chiang-chün*, whom Westerners called "Tartar generals") with Manchu brigade-generals under them. Banner garrisons were located in three sectors — first, in a military cordon of twenty-five small posts around Peking; second, in capitals and other strategic spots in the northwestern provinces, as insurance against incursions from Central Asia (three garrisons in Shansi, three in Kansu, one at Sian, etc.); and third, in major Chinese centers of population (Chengtu, Nanking, Hangchow, Foochow, Canton) and at strategic spots in the South, at the outlet of the Yangtze gorges in Hupei and where the Grand Canal crosses the Yangtze at Chinkiang. The banner garrisons, of about 4000 men, were each set apart with their families in their own fortified residential quarter of a city, instead of being outside it altogether like their Mongol predecessors of the thirteenth century. Their life of ease and increase of numbers, together with a late-eighteenth-century rise in prices, a continued lack of military duties, and an increase of corruption in the handling of their small stipends, all combined in the latter part of the dynasty to make the bannermen a demoralized, insecure and ineffective lot; but for the first century and a half of Ch'ing rule they served their purpose.

The remnants of the Ming military system and additional Chinese levies were absorbed into a Chinese constabulary, the "Army of the Green Standard." These forces in the late seventeenth century totaled 594,000 men, and by the early nineteenth century totaled according to statute about 640,000 men in 1202 battalions (*ying*), but they were decentralized in scattered small units and posts. The command over them was likewise distributed among the governors, governors-general, and Chinese provincial military commanders. The last-named were stationed in fourteen provinces with some seventy-five Chinese generals distributed under them, from two to seven in a province. Thus the Army of the Green Standard was used as a local Chinese police force to suppress banditry. Its troops were seldom concentrated and never expected to have the offensive power of the bannermen.

In general, the military command was carefully divided — between Chinese and Manchus, between the Board of War and troops at the capital and the garrisons in the provinces, and between the high civil and military officials all over the empire. The prerogative of recommending officers for appointment to the higher ranks was similarly distributed, as well as the responsibility of reporting on officer conduct. Military officers were regularly transferred from post to post, though never to their home regions, in order to forestall the growth of personal commands. These administrative arrangements, together with the limitation of the funds regularly allotted for army maintenance, prevented the growth of any military power independent of the court.

The Northeast. As a third step to preserve themselves and their military control of China, the Manchus also preserved their homeland as a base separate from Chinese life and culture. This policy was dictated by the speed with which Sinification seemed to be overtaking them in the generation after the conquest. Manchus in China were learning the Chinese language and way of life, while Chinese from Liaotung were pushing northward in Manchuria. In 1668, north and central Manchuria were therefore closed to Chinese immigration. The Willow Palisade (a ditch with willows planted along it) was extended several hundred miles in a great curve from Shanhaikuan to the north of Mukden and then south again to the mouth of the Yalu, to mark the statutory limit of Chinese settlement. Most of Manchuria, with its hunting land, forests and streams, was thus preserved for the tribal peoples. Meanwhile, Mukden remained the subsidiary capital, as Nanking had been under the Ming.

The court had also an immediate pecuniary motive in closing off the Northeast. The highly valued and supposedly medicinal root known as ginseng was gathered in the hills along the Ussuri and other streams of central Manchuria. Kirin, Ninguta and Mukden were the chief centers for collecting the annual crop. During the height of the monopoly system in the early eighteenth century, special officials annually sold licenses to some ten thousand ginseng collectors, following the general model of the salt monopoly system. These licensed persons brought in about 10,000 ounces of ginseng for sale through the official monopoly, and probably an even larger amount was gleaned for private trade. Since 10,000 ounces would bring a price of roughly four million taels, the ginseng trade had both fiscal and commercial importance, not least to the imperial household.

CH'ING RULE IN CHINA

When it came to ruling China within the Wall, the Ch'ing success was more a political than an administrative feat, for they preserved the Ming administrative structure almost as they had found it, altering it only to insert Manchu power and dynastic control into the established edifice of the state. The three essential ingredients of Ch'ing rule were, in descending order, first, ultimate military force, kept in reserve; second, ultimate political power, exercised by the Son of Heaven; and third, Manchu supervision of Chinese administration.

Though inserting themselves at the apex of the Chinese state, the Manchu rulers from the first tried to conciliate the Chinese upper strata of landlord-"gentry" families, local scholar-"gentry" leaders of community life, and Ming officials. Local landlords and administrators were generally let alone, providing they submitted to the new regime. Like earlier dynasties on their accession, the Ch'ing reduced the tax rates from the extortionate levels which had been reached in the late Ming period after 1620. But the Manchus raised no flag of social or agrarian revolution. On the contrary, they buried the Ming emperor with honors at Peking and claimed they had come to suppress the anti-Ming rebels and bring China peace and order. While this claim to Heaven's Mandate was not so easily accepted in Central and South China, it helped persuade most of the Chinese local officials in the North to accept the new dynasty.

A leading example of this class was Hung Ch'eng-ch'ou (1593–1665), a metropolitan graduate who had risen to be Ming governor-general of five provinces and had several times defeated the rebel Li Tzu-ch'eng.

Transferred in 1639 to subdue the Manchus, he was captured by them in 1642 and well treated. After Peking fell, he was made a Grand Secretary. During the next fifteen years, from 1645 to 1659, Hung played a principal administrative role in mobilizing the resources needed for the Ch'ing campaigns which overcame the Ming defense of South China.

Joint Administration. The Peking administration after 1644 became a Manchu-Chinese dyarchy. Roughly equal numbers of the two peoples (including some Mongols among the Manchus) were grouped together in major offices at the capital. Thus, of the six Grand Secretaries, three were Chinese and three Manchu. The Six Ministries each had two presidents, one Manchu and one Chinese, and four vice-presidents, two Manchu and two Chinese. Since this produced a collegial body in place of one minister at the head, the Six Ministries under the Ch'ing have been called by Western writers the "Six Boards." Actually these agencies were no more like boards of directors than they were like Western ministries, but the term "Board" has been sanctioned by long use.

Manchus (together with some Mongols) were similarly interlarded among Chinese at the top of the provincial administrations. Primarily, this device of joint or collegial responsibility met the problem of providing high positions for Chinese officials without giving them complete control. Secondarily, it also had the effect of preventing the entrenchment of any one official, whether Chinese or non-Chinese, in a position of bureaucratic power.

The Ch'ing divided three of the fifteen Ming provinces to make eighteen within the Wall. Shensi was broken up into Shensi and Kansu, Hukwang into Hunan and Hupei, and Nan-chihli (Nanking Province) into Kiangsu and Anhwei. The special commissioners (*hsün-fu* and *tsung-tu*) of the Ming were now made into additional layers on top of those which already existed in the territorial hierarchy — namely, district (*hsien*) magistrates, subprefects, prefects, intendants of circuit (or taotais), and the four heads of province-wide administrations (civil service, judiciary, examination system and salt monopoly). A single governor (*hsün-fu*) was now put over every province (except Chihli and Szechwan). A governor-general (*tsung-tu*, by Europeans often called "viceroy") was put over every two provinces, with some exceptions. Thus governors-general were in charge of the metropolitan province of Chihli (around Peking), and also of Kwangtung-Kwangsi, Fukien-Chekiang, Kiangsi-Kiangsu-Anhwei, Hunan-Hupei, Yunnan-Kweichou, Szechwan and Shensi-Kansu.

From all provinces that were under both a governor and a governor-general, important business had to come to the emperor from the two officials jointly. Two-thirds of the governors-general appointed up to 1735 were Manchu. Governors, on the other hand, were mostly Chinese.

CHINA PROPER UNDER THE EARLY CH'ING
(TO AROUND 1800)

Thus provinces were typically administered at the top level by a Chinese governor and a Manchu governor-general working together. Each had his own small force of troops, but the chief provincial military force was usually one of bannermen under a Manchu general.

Having set up a joint Manchu-Chinese headship of military forces and of major civil offices, the Ch'ing completed their system of control by appointing equal numbers of Manchus and Chinese to the Board of Censors. At Peking twenty-four censors were attached to the Six Boards and ten to various precincts of the city. In the provinces fifty-six censors were divided under fifteen circuits. Manchus and Chinese worked side by side, equal in rank and responsibility.

The Language Problem. This bracketing of Manchus and Chinese at first created a great problem of interpretation and translation. The early Ch'ing court used the Manchu language, and its regime was bilingual. Chinese interpreters, usually Chinese bannermen, were at first appointed to assist all high Manchu officials. Translation from Chinese into Manchu was particularly necessary in the Grand Secretariat, which was now more formally established to assist the emperor at the top of the administration. Translators were also attached to the Six Boards and the censorate, with high enough rank to let them participate in deliberations. A certain number of Chinese metropolitan graduates were assigned to study Manchu within the Hanlin Academy.

Until its last days, the Ch'ing continued to go through the formality of elaborately translating Chinese documents at Peking into their Manchu counterparts, but the effort at bilingual administration collapsed rather early, for the Manchus learned Chinese. By 1670 some of the interpreters' and translators' posts were abolished as unnecessary. The big examination in Manchu held in 1653 to stimulate study of that language aroused little interest. The Chinese *chin-shih* who studied Manchu became fewer and fewer, until by 1838 there were none at all. The Manchu dictionary compiled under the K'ang-hsi emperor to keep the language in use served chiefly to embalm it for posterity. Even at the court it became mainly an ornament, like the use of French in England.

The eventual Ch'ing solution was to use Manchu translations only at the court itself, where purely Manchu affairs were usually handled in Manchu and Chinese affairs in Chinese, as a means of achieving accuracy and simplicity. The dynasty, like earlier regimes of conquest, had developed a Manchu writing system (based on an adaptation of Mongolian, as we have noted) invented to facilitate its rise to power. It barely kept this writing system alive until they both collapsed. Meanwhile, local government throughout the Ch'ing period was carried on in Chinese.

THE UNITY OF STATE AND CULTURE

The insertion of a Manchu controlling or supervisory element into the inherited administration of China was only the first requirement for successful Manchu rule. The second was the recruitment of Chinese talent through the examination system. This meant that the emperor must fulfill his Confucian functions as the font of ethical instruction and the grand patron of learning and the arts.

The Ch'ing continued the Ming examination system with little change and set great store by it. But the system alone was not enough. Time-servers and sycophants could always be recruited into official life, but they would quickly corrupt it. The real test for the Manchu emperors was whether they could become such patrons of Chinese scholarship that the whole state and culture would remain unified, under the sole headship of the Son of Heaven. Only then could the best talent of Chinese society be enrolled and find expression under the patronage and control of the Ch'ing dynasty. To rule the Middle Kingdom success-fully called for cultural as well as political leadership at the court.

K'ang-hsi. Both these types of leadership were supplied by the K'ang-hsi emperor (1654–1722), a truly great ruler who reigned for sixty-one years, from 1661 to 1722. (See Plates 36, 37 and 38.) Inheriting the throne at the age of seven, he began to rule in person at thirteen. By the time he was twenty-seven, he had suppressed the Revolt of the Three Feudatories in an eight-year civil war (1673–1681) and so completed the unification of his regime. He led great armies into Mongolia, as we have noted (page 359), and fostered the warrior-huntsman tradition among the Manchus, building up his summer capital at Jehol, north of the Wall. As ruler of China he made six great tours to the South, the stronghold of the scholar-"gentry," at intervals during three decades. On these imperial progressions he devoted special atten-tion to the constant efforts that were required to check the flooding of the Huai and Yellow River systems and maintain the grain transport by canal to Peking. We have already noted (page 312) the sixteen moral maxims that he laid down in 1670, which became known as the *Sacred Edict* and were widely read and recited to inculcate proper conduct. Thus he proved himself a bold warrior, frugal administrator and proper lawgiver.

In foreign relations, K'ang-hsi had extensive dealings with Europeans, principally the Jesuits and the Russians. After the great Jesuit pioneer, Matteo Ricci (1552–1610), became established at Peking under the late Ming in 1600, Western missionaries remained attached to the imperial court there for almost two centuries, gaining some converts for Chris-tianity but principally serving to enlighten Europe about Cathay. Until the early eighteenth century, when they were finally forced by the so-called Rites Controversy to choose between the primacy of the Pope and the Son of Heaven, the Jesuits were trusted advisers of K'ang-hsi and performed many services for him in astronomy, mathematics, trans-lation and other lines, as the first "technical experts" of early modern times. Their over-all influence, however, was greater in the West than

THREE AGES OF THE K'ANG-HSI EMPEROR
(1654–1722)

PLATES 36, 37, and 38. These three portraits, from the imperial collection in Peking, show K'ang-hsi in youth (Plate 36), wearing sword and boots; in maturity (Plate 37), as a scholar in the Chinese style, surrounded by books and art objects; and finally in old age (Plate 38).

CH'ING PATRONAGE OF LAMAISM

PLATES 39 and 40. Above: The Potala, the monastery or palace of the Dalai Lama in Lhasa, rebuilt by the Fifth Dalai Lama (1617–1682). Below: The miniature Potala erected by the Ch'ing emperors at their summer residence at Jehol (Ch'eng-te) north of Peking, as an aid in their relations with the Mongols as well as Tibet.

The Palace Style

PLATE 41. The front courtyard inside the entrance of the imperial palace or Forbidden City at Peking, facing the "Gate of Supreme Harmony" (T'ai-ho men). On the main axis across the next courtyard is the great yellow-tiled "Hall of Supreme Harmony" (T'ai-ho tien), the main throne hall, on its triple terrace of white marble. In the distance on the main axis (right) is the pavilion on top of Prospect Hill ("Coal Hill") behind the Forbidden City. Note scale of figure, left foreground.

PLATE 42. Audience Hall of the Kyŏngbok Palace of the Yi dynasty at Seoul (a later reconstruction of a 1394 building), looking toward the mountains north of the city.

PLATE 43. Detail of painting, dating from the fifth century, on wall of a tomb at T'ung-kou in the vicinity of the early Koguryŏ capital of Kungnae on the Yalu River.

PLATE 44. Golden crown dating from the fifth or sixth century from the vicinity of the Silla capital at Kyŏngju.

PLATE 45. Stone pagoda at the Pulguksa ("Monastery of the Buddha Land"), founded in 751 near Kyŏngju.

in China. They did not affect the course of Chinese history as much as they did that of Europe. Similarly, the early contact by land with Russia and the Russo-Ch'ing boundary treaties of 1689 and 1727 resulted chiefly, from the Ch'ing point of view, in the stabilizing of the Central Asian frontier between the Russian and Ch'ing empires, to the advantage of the latter. In effect, Russian influence was successfully excluded from Central Asia and contained on a far frontier, just as the European trade by sea was later effectively contained (after 1760) at the single port of Canton on the southeast coast.

K'ang-hsi's chief success was vis-à-vis the Chinese scholar class. Well-versed in the classics himself, he had strong intellectual interests which fitted him to be the patron of the literati. A number of leading scholars who had grown up in the late Ming period (like Ku Yen-wu and Huang Tsung-hsi; see pages 376–378) expressed their convictions as bearers of the great cultural tradition by refusing all cooperation with the Manchus. In 1679, however, K'ang-hsi held a special examination to select the compilers of the *Ming History* (*Ming shih*) and succeeded in getting 152 top scholars to take it, out of 188 whom he invited. It is significant that, of the fifty who passed, four-fifths were from the Lower Yangtze region, the center of the Sung and Ming traditions. He also selected Chinese scholars, calligraphers and artists to serve in his personal imperial study (*nan shu-fang*) and in a studio within the palace.

In this way a score of important works were produced under K'ang-hsi's personal patronage and often with a preface by him. These included, for example, the famous *K'ang-hsi Dictionary* (*K'ang-hsi tzu-tien*), an extremely important phrase-dictionary (*P'ei-wen yün-fu*), an administrative geography of the empire in 500 chapters, the complete works of Chu Hsi, and a great compendium on painting and calligraphy. He also supported the massive encyclopedia, *Ku-chin t'u-shu chi-ch'eng* (*Synthesis of Books and Illustrations of Ancient and Modern Times*), which is a good deal larger than the *Encyclopedia Britannica*. It was finally printed in 5000 volumes, with 10,000 chapters (and about 100 million characters), in 1728. Its printing used about a quarter of a million pieces of copper type, each cut separately by hand. Thus the Manchu emperor had become as ardent and magnificent a patron of Chinese scholarship as any Ming emperor had ever been.

Yung-cheng. While K'ang-hsi perfected the union of culture and politics, it was left for his successor, Yung-cheng, who reigned from 1723 to 1736, to complete the institutional structure of the Ch'ing autocracy. K'ang-hsi from the age of thirteen had produced uncounted daughters and thirty-five sons, of whom twenty grew up. When, after 1700, the son who had been designated heir apparent grew mentally unbalanced, jealousy and intrigue arose among his brothers over the succession. The one who became the Yung-cheng emperor did so by having military support on the spot at Peking when K'ang-hsi died in 1722 and boldly announcing his own accession. It was rumored by the jealous opposition that he had disregarded his father's wishes, perhaps even killed him.

Whether because of a suspicious temperament or because of the preceding two decades of bitter fraternal rivalry, Yung-cheng took every means to safeguard his imperial power. Five of his brothers died in prison, and their supporters were victimized. He further divorced the imperial princes from control of the banner forces and set up a palace school for the indoctrination of young princes. He forbade the naming of an heir apparent, leaving the succession to the emperor's deathbed decision. Yung-cheng tampered with the imperial archives to support his own record before his accession and made widespread use of spies and secrecy in administration. He also had an interest in Ch'an (Zen) Buddhism, an unusual bent for an emperor. He was, however, a very conscientious ruler.

The main Ch'ing addition to the Ming administrative machine was made by Yung-cheng in 1729 when he set up the Grand Council to supersede the Grand Secretariat as the top center of policy decision. This illustrated an age-old tendency for the highest agency of administration to become routinized and institutionalized to the point where the monarch, as chief executive, felt it necessary to superimpose still another, less formal, body upon it. In this case the Grand Secretariat continued to handle most routine business while the new Grand Council (*Chün-chi-ch'u*, literally, "Military Plans Office," sometimes called "Privy Council") worked more immediately with the emperor on urgent and important matters, in closer contact within the palace, using less formal documents and less complex procedures than the Secretariat. The number of Grand Councilors, usually five or six, was never fixed. Usually two or three of them were concurrently Grand Secretaries, providing a useful degree of identity between the two bodies. The council ordinarily met with the emperor every day at dawn. It dispensed with clerks and minor bureaucrats. All its business was handled quickly and secretly by a specially selected group of thirty-two secretaries, half Manchu and half Chinese.

The gathering of power into the emperor's hands seems to have been a continuing tendency during the Yüan, Ming and Ch'ing periods. Where imperial orders in the T'ang had required the seal of the prime minister, under the Ch'ing all important and many unimportant decisions, executive, legislative and judicial, now had to come from the emperor himself. For example, the Six Boards at the capital did not transmit orders directly to the provinces, except on routine matters. Provincial administrations were directly under the emperor, whose edict was necessary to give effect to a policy proposed by a board.

The emperor consequently was a hard-working and hard-worked man. K'ang-hsi complained that his ministers could enter and leave the service, but he worked on and on. Yung-cheng wrote his personal comments on an inordinate mass of documents. Ch'ien-lung, during most of his long reign from 1736 to 1795, was equally conscientious. "Ten or more of my comrades," wrote one of the Grand Council secretaries, "would take turns every five or six days on early morning duty and even so would feel fatigued. How did the emperor do it day after day? When . . . military reports arrived, even at midnight he must still see them in person."

The Manchu Success. No analysis of institutions will quite explain the major conundrum — how could a limited number of Manchus conquer and rule a people some fifty or more times as numerous and far more sophisticated? Patriotic modern Chinese have felt deeply humiliated by this historic fact. There are several lines of explanation. The first begins with a point already made, that non-Chinese like the Manchus were as much a part of the great "Chinese" Empire of East Asia as were the Chinese themselves. Moreover, the small "barbarian" Central-Asian component of this empire was specialized for fighting and so for seizing and holding power. The Manchus were just about numerous enough to provide the garrisons, the imperial clan and the top administrators needed for an empire embracing both China and Central Asia. Like Europeans in their nineteenth-century colonies, the Manchus bore the burden of governing. They held and exercised power but were also exhausted by it. This is a view of history favored particularly by some Japanese and Western scholars.

Other scholars, including many in China, have generally stressed a different view — that China, even under the Ch'ing, was still ruled about 90 per cent by Chinese, that the Ch'ing regime was from the first not purely Manchu but a Manchu-Chinese synthesis, that the Manchu rulers stayed in power only by becoming as Chinese as their subjects.

These two views are not at all incompatible with each other, nor with a further consideration, namely, that the Chinese state was an autocracy in which political life was monopolized by the bureaucracy and centered in the emperor, so that the mass of the Chinese people had little to do with it in any case, no matter who was in power. This was the more possible because the imperial government was thin and superficial, confined to the upper layer of society, not present in the villages. In other words, the Chinese polity as a whole was a synthesis of state and culture. Its political or state sector was highly centralized while the culture was thoroughly diffused among the populace. The state could be dominated by an alien autocracy, while China's cultural life remained widespread and firmly rooted among the people in each locality. This broad cultural activity of the society, though led by the emperor, was nourished by the local elite, the "gentry" class, who set the model in the towns and even the villages.

It should not be assumed, however, that the state maintained its hold over the people purely by cultural means. On the contrary, we have already described the military arrangements of the Ming and Ch'ing, to which were added measures of local control by fear of punishment, as well as by moral exhortation. This can be illustrated by the reliance placed during the Ch'ing period upon the traditional device of the *pao-chia* system for maintaining local order through mutual responsibility. As we have seen above (pages 86, 159 and 206), this had been a Legalist invention used by the Ch'in and inherited by the Han, T'ang and later dynasties in turn, evidently with more variations in terminology than in practice. Thus in the Sung, Wang An-shih had grouped ten families into a *pao* and given it responsibilities for military training and for local order. The philosopher Chu Hsi, who was also a successful official, had grouped ten families into a *chia* and made it responsible for all its members' borrowings from the community granary. In these and many similar administrative devices, there were two underlying princi-ples — that the household as the kinship unit was the basic unit of political responsibility, the family being in control of the individual; and that a group of households, once defined as such, could be held accountable all together for the conduct of any individual within any household. This allotment of responsibility by groups of neighboring families was particularly suited to a static agrarian society rooted in the land.

The use of this tradition under the Ming was not limited to the *li-chia* tax system already described (page 303). The Ming also had a parallel system of mutual responsibility within village units, consisting ideally of 100 households, each unit through its chosen head trying to oversee the moral and legal conduct of its members. This parallel system was often identical with the *li-chia* organization, but its object was not economic (to insure tax payments and labor service) but political. It sought to maintain order by identifying and keeping track of all persons and by encouraging relatives and neighbors to inform on all active or even suspected evildoers.

The Ch'ing inherited and perfected this structure. Ideally, 100 house-holds formed a *chia*, and ten *chia* a *pao*. The headmen of each, selected by the villagers, became responsible for the local registry of population, for keeping the peace and for seeing that each household kept the correct information on its door placard, as to who dwelt within and their occu-pations. Although this *pao-chia* organization took responsibility for pub-lic morals and many local activities, it was less a form of self-government than an officially imposed but unofficial arm of the state, maintained under landlord-"gentry" supervision. Through it the government and local ruling class used the family system for police purposes. Mutual responsibility, as totalitarian systems have recently demonstrated, is a powerful device, especially when combined with a paternalistic morality sanctioned by a long cultural tradition.

INTELLECTUAL DEVELOPMENT: THE SCHOOL OF "EMPIRICAL RESEARCH"

Chinese scholars of the seventeenth and eighteenth centuries were primarily occupied in the study of their own tradition. The majority, no doubt, were uncritical accepters and upholders of tradition, like many scholars in other times and places. And even the creative minority, the vigorous minds who left an impress, were traditionalists, not revolutionists. They worked within the framework of the great tradition and did not seek to destroy it.

In their absorption in their own inherited literature and culture, Chinese scholars of the early Ch'ing stand in marked contrast with the leading minds of late-nineteenth- and twentieth-century China, for whom the central problem has been China's adjustment to the West. But until 1800 or even 1840, the West received little or no attention from Chinese scholarship, except in certain fields of science, which were generally on the periphery of the learned world. Possibly more detailed study will show that Western contact had a profound though subtle and un-expressed influence on Chinese thought before the nineteenth century, but thus far we lack the evidence to support such a conclusion. With few exceptions, early and mid-Ch'ing scholars seem to have been thoroughly absorbed in the digestion and reappraisal of their own inherit-ance. Their central problem was to criticize and evaluate, to winnow the written record of two millenniums and extract the essentials from it in works of compilation, annotation and criticism, without giving the out-side world a second thought. For this reason we shall take up the Western contact with Ming and Ch'ing China in the second volume of this study. Such contact did not form a major motif in the intellectual life of the Middle Kingdom until about a century ago.

Ming Loyalist Scholars. The major fact confronting Chinese scholars of the seventeenth century was the failure of Chinese rule under the Ming and the re-emergence of "barbarian" conquerors as rulers of China. The dynastic change-over, occupying most of the first three-quarters of the century, was a political process which raised many moral prob-lems, such as how to uphold Confucian ideals against eunuch corruption at the late Ming court and whether to transfer one's loyalty from the old dynasty to the new.

Inevitably, scholars of the late Ming, who still worshiped the culture of T'ang and Sung and abominated the Mongol tyranny, were deeply disturbed by the repetition of alien conquest. They rejected, as most students of China's traditional culture still reject today, any idea that the non-Chinese warrior peoples outside the Middle Kingdom could have an organic political function as potential holders of power over it. Many of the most vigorous intellectuals of the period of change remained staunchly loyal to the Ming and refused to serve under the Manchus. Instead, they sought to discover the reasons for the moral and intellectual decline which they felt had been an integral part of the Ming collapse and alone had opened the door to "barbarian" invaders. They held the traditional assumption that foreign aggression on China was made possible only by domestic disorder.

One Ming loyalist who addressed himself to this problem was Huang Tsung-hsi (or Huang Li-chou, 1610–1695) of Chekiang, who as a youth had known the leaders of the Tung-lin group (see pages 341–343) and whose father had died in prison as a member of it. Huang fought and worked for the Ming cause in South China until 1649, but then retired to a life of scholarship. The hundred or so works attributed to him range widely over the fields of history and philosophy as well as mathematics and literature. His surveys of Confucian thinkers under the Ming (*Ming-ju hsüeh-an*) and under the Sung and Yüan (*Sung Yüan hsüeh-an*) constitute landmarks in the systematic historical study of Chinese philosophy.

In political thought Huang's chief contribution was a critique of despotism (*Ming-i tai-fang lu,* which has been translated as *A Plan for the Prince*). In his work he sought to extract from the Chinese record the political wisdom necessary for a proper Confucian ruler. This attempt brings out sharply the contrast between the idealistic (and idealized) teachings of classical political philosophy and the realistic despotism of the "Confucian" monarchy as it had actually developed — a contrast which had created one of the great tensions within the "Confucian" polity.

In Huang's view, China's political development since the Ch'in unification had undergone a long deterioration, moving further and further from the ancient ideal. Within this rather utopian framework he calls for the establishment of basic laws to supplant the arbitrary edicts of emperors ("government by law should come before government by men"), for the restoration of dignity to ministers instead of their debasement by the throne, and for the revival of the prime-ministership as a token of the emperor's sharing of power with his high officials. To curb the eunuchs, Huang would reduce their numbers by reducing the number of emperor's wives. To loosen the strait jacket of the examination system, he would make education broadly available in local schools, enlarge the scope of the examinations, and provide alternative channels of advancement by recommendation. Needless to say, reforms of the land tax, currency and army also form part of Huang's plan.

It is significant that from first to last this courageous and critical-minded scholar could conceive only of ways to guide the emperor's use of power or limit his misuse of it, not of ways to supplant it. There was for him no alternative to the Son of Heaven as the source of authority and decision. Government must come from the top down. So also must reform. Huang's concern for law and the people, for universal education and military service, for moral government in its many aspects, was all within this framework.

Another Ming loyalist scholar was Wang Fu-chih (or Wang Ch'uan-shan, 1619–1692), who fought the Manchus until 1650 and then secluded himself for forty years. Among his works were historical studies arguing, like those of Huang Tsung-hsi, that government is for the people, not the ruler, though the ruler is essential to government. Wang also stated a vigorous case against alien rulers. But most of his works remained unpublished until the nineteenth century. This was true of a number of other anti-Manchu scholars also. Thus these critics had little influence during the early Ch'ing period and became influential only when discovered and quoted by Chinese patriot-reformers toward the end of the dynasty.

Ku Yen-wu (or Ku T'ing-lin, 1613–1682), on the other hand, was a Ming loyalist whose studies started new trends in the scholarship of the whole Ch'ing period. Ku fought against the Manchus, was persecuted by personal enemies, and from about 1650 lived a life of intermittent travel and study. This took him widely over North China and brought him into intimate contact with problems of farming, trade and banking, and even industry and mining. His travel notes and researches resulted in a geographical work on *The Strategic and Economic Advantages and Disadvantages of the Districts and States of the Empire* (*T'ien-hsia chün-kuo li-ping-shu*) and also a widely-read collection of thoughtful essays on many topics, entitled *Notes of Knowledge Accumulated from Day to Day* (*Jih-chih lu*).

Refusing to serve the Ch'ing, Ku Yen-wu developed a trenchant thesis as to the cause of the Ming collapse. He blamed the sterile and abstract philosophizing of the dominant Ming school of Sung Neo-Confucianism — the so-called "Sung Learning" or "Rationalism" (*Li-hsüeh*) of Chu Hsi. He also attacked particularly the metaphysical branch of Neo-Confucianism, which had been further developed by the influential Ming philosopher, Wang Yang-ming (see pages 308–309). Ku correctly discerned in Wang's idealistic stress on intuition and self-cultivation the actual influence of Ch'an (Zen) Buddhism, rather than of the classics. He attacked the routine acceptance of preconceived ideas which had resulted, and their propagation through the Four Books and the examination system as a prefabricated, orthodox interpretation of the classics. This, he felt, had so confined Chinese thinking within set patterns that it had become incapable of facing political realities or of saving China from "barbarian" conquest. The "eight-legged essay" had done more harm, he claimed, than the First Emperor's "burning of the books." To remedy this intellectual failure of the Chinese scholar class, Ku advocated the pursuit of knowledge "of practical use to society" (*ching-shih chih-yung*).

The "Han Learning." Ku Yen-wu's attack on the "Sung Learning" was by no means an attack on the classics. To the contrary, he advocated a closer approach to the classical wisdom through the commentaries of the Han scholars, who had been closer in time to the sages and lacked the metaphysical preconceptions of Neo-Confucianism. Thus Ku Yen-wu was the chief founder of the great Ch'ing school of "Han Learning," which sought to restudy the classical inheritance by going back to writings of the pre-Sung period. The "Sung Learning," as the established orthodoxy now under attack, gave ground only slowly, but the fresh ideas of the Ch'ing period came mainly from adherents of the new "Han Learning."

This new approach brought with it the use of the inductive method, assembling evidence from the broadest range of sources, not from a few selected texts, and making new hypotheses to test against the evidence. This new method was applied first in the field of phonetics (studying the rhymes of ancient poetry to determine the ancient pronunciations) and led into broader studies of philology, etymology and textual criticism. It was called the method of "empirical research" (*k'ao-chü* or *k'ao-cheng*, literally, "search for evidence") and greatly enlarged the subject matter of classical studies.

Studies of this sort made it possible to determine the authenticity of ancient texts. The great scholar Yen Jo-chü (1636–1704), for example, after studying the *Classic of Documents* (*Shu ching* or *Shang shu*) for thirty years, proved by textual analysis and historical reasoning that the so-called "old text" of this venerated classic, which had been accepted for over 1000 years and used in the official examinations, was really a forgery! Thus the "Han Learning," through the many scholars who came after Ku Yen-wu, achieved a new critical mastery of the great corpus of Chinese classical literature.

This scholarly work has been hailed by some as a growth in premodern China of the "scientific method," but if this term is used it must be understood to apply to the limited field of literary studies, not to the fields of natural science and material technology with which we usually associate the word "science." The many proto-scientific discoveries and inventions in China had been associated more with the nature-loving Taoists than with the scholarly Confucians. They had never been absorbed into an ongoing system of organized and verifiable knowledge, accumulated and transmitted accurately to successive generations. In short, the promising early beginnings of scientific lore in China had never been consciously rationalized and institutionalized like modern science in the West. The Ch'ing scholars continued to be entirely divorced from the practical inquiries and manipulations of the workshop and laboratory.

The Ch'ing reappraisal of Neo-Confucianism inevitably had its effect on formal philosophy, which came to fruition in the vigorous work of Tai Chen (or Tai Tung-yüan, 1724–1777). Tai attacked Chu Hsi's dualism, which consisted of the two elements of form (*li*) and material stuff or ether (*ch'i*), as based on a misreading of the classics. He accused the Sung philosophers of having been misled by Taoist and Buddhist concepts. Under this influence, they had accepted the *li* as transcendent and heaven-sent, superimposed on man's physical nature, and setting proper limits to his physical desires. Instead, Tai Chen asserted that *li* is the immanent, internal structure of things, inherent in the processes of life, including the desires. Tai denied the Neo-Confucian contention that one can grasp the *li* through introspective meditation and achieve sudden enlightenment. Instead, he argued that the *li* exists objectively and can be grasped only through study, by "wide learning, careful investigation, exact thinking, clear reasoning and sincere conduct."

In historical studies, one of the most vigorous Ch'ing thinkers was Chang Hsüeh-ch'eng (or Chang Shih-chai, 1738–1801), who advocated an all-inclusive use of historical evidence of all sorts so as to get at the broad moral significance behind events. Like so many scholars, Chang spent his life as a compiler of local gazetteers or director of academies, dependent on the patronage of official friends. His views on historical method remained in obscurity until recent decades.

Although these few words cannot do justice to Ch'ing philosophy, it is plain that systematic thinkers like Tai Chen were making constructive additions to Chinese thought. But they were modifying and continuing the great Sung tradition, not subverting or denying it. Their contribution was still "change within tradition."

THE OFFICIAL DOMINATION OF LEARNING

Much of the intellectual activity of the early Ch'ing period was carried on within the official system, often in the shadow of the imperial institution. Yung-cheng had promoted and subsidized the growth of academies (*shu-yüan*) to give employment to scholars all over the empire. Ch'ien-lung early in his reign had arranged for an edition of the twenty-one dynastic histories (which were soon increased to twenty-four). By the

IMPERIAL PATRONAGE OF LEARNING

Ideally, academies were situated in beautiful surroundings where scholars could pursue learning in close communion with nature. This illustration is described in Nan-hsün sheng-tien, *the work commemorating Ch'ien-lung's tours to the south, as follows: "The Fu-wen Academy, located between a lake and a river, on the imposing Peak of Myriad Pines in the Phoenix Mountains in Chekiang, was given special funds by Emperor Yung-cheng in 1733 to support the scholars, and a director was invited to give instruction. The talented scholars who were collected from the whole province studied morning and evening. Honoring scholarship, the Ch'ien-lung Emperor on his fourth southern tour graced the academy with his presence. He composed poems and had the scholars match them with similar compositions so as to promote the spread of culture. Thus the achievements in the cultivation of human talent reached high into the clouds."*

end of his sixty-three years in power, he had sponsored some fifty-seven large publications compiled by a host of learned editors. Ch'ien-lung also outdid K'ang-hsi in his personal literary production. In addition to state papers, his prose writings fill many volumes, and more than 42,000 poems are attributed to him — truly an august example for the scholar class.

It was typical of Ch'ing scholarship that it interpenetrated and was closely dependent upon official life. Tai Chen, for example, the son of a cloth merchant, found his livelihood mainly as tutor or editor in the homes of leading officials. After failing five times in the metropolitan examinations, he finally received an imperial appointment as a compiler, four years before his death.

Ch'ien-lung's "Four Treasuries." Tai Chen was one of a number of leading scholars who were appointed by Ch'ien-lung in 1773 to compile a great imperial manuscript library called the *Ssu-k'u ch'üan-shu, The Complete Library of the Four Treasuries,* that is, the four branches of literature — the classics (*ching*), history (*shih*), philosophy (*tzu*), and belles-lettres (*chi*). This ambitious project marked a high point in the great tradition of bringing together a number of works previously produced, sometimes on a common theme, and republishing them as a collection (or *ts'ung-shu*), a practice that has preserved or given greater accessibility to scattered Chinese works on an infinite variety of subjects.

The compiling of Ch'ien-lung's super-collection of the *Four Treasuries* employed as many as 15,000 copyists and lasted nearly twenty years. It involved a review of all the rare works in the palace and other libraries, selection of certain works to be copied in their entirety and others only to be commented upon, and the transcription of all the materials so selected into uniform, bound volumes. As might be expected, the compilers began by copying at least 365 rare works from the great Ming encyclopedia, *Yung-lo ta-tien,* only about three-fourths of one set of which was still available (see page 308). Where the Yung-lo collection had produced 11,095 manuscript volumes, the Ch'ien-lung emperor's *Four Treasuries* now comprised more than 36,000 volumes, containing about 3450 complete works. Seven manuscript sets were made. In addition, a great printed catalogue was compiled with comments on a total of about 10,230 titles, including those which had been copied — making the most complete single bibliography of Chinese literature. By collecting complete works, instead of quoting selected passages as earlier encyclopedias had generally done, the *Four Treasuries* met the more critical demands of Ch'ing scholarship. Moreover, the critical comments expressed by the editors in the printed catalogue of the *Four Treasuries* crystallized the anti-Chu Hsi views of the Ch'ing school of "Han Learning" and had wide influence.

The seven original manuscript sets of the *Four Treasuries* library had a varied history. Those deposited at Yangchow and Chinkiang in the Lower Yangtze region were destroyed during the mid-nineteenth-century Taiping Rebellion, and the one at Hangchow partially so. The set deposited at the Old Summer Palace (Yüan Ming Yüan) outside Peking was destroyed when the Anglo-French expedition burned it in 1860. Two sets were preserved at Peking, however, and one at Mukden, so that Ch'ien-lung's great collection fared better than that of Yung-lo, and some parts of it have now been printed.

The Literary Inquisition. The Ch'ien-lung emperor's domination of the Chinese learned world was demonstrated in the literary inquisition which for some fifteen years paralleled the compilation of the *Four Treasuries*. The searching out and reviewing of all major writings afforded an opportunity to suppress objectionable works. Some 2300 works were listed for total suppression and another 350 for partial suppression, as works containing seditious or abusive language. "None may remain to after generations," declared Ch'ien-lung, "in order to cleanse our speech and make straight the hearts of men." All available copies of such works were ordered collected in the provinces under heavy penalties. This was done sometimes by a house-to-house canvass as well as by offering high prices. In the end, many hundreds of works were wiped out.

The emperor's highly practical and totalitarian aim was to destroy writings that were anti-Ch'ing or rebellious, that insulted previous "barbarian" dynasties, or that dealt with frontier or defense problems. All the works of certain authors, and even inscriptions by them on monuments, were also destroyed, as were works that seemed heterodox in general, or merely unliterary. "Although there is nothing that shows evidence of treason in this work," wrote the censors in one case, "still the words are in many cases lying nonsense, fishing for praise. It should be burned." Of another book the Hunan governor wrote, "This belongs in the class of fiction. Its words are very confused. It ought to be destroyed."

The operation of this literary despotism may be illustrated by one case among many, that of the unfortunate dictionary-maker, Wang Hsi-hou, who not only treasonably criticized the *K'ang-hsi Dictionary* but in his own work disrespectfully printed in full the forbidden characters for the personal names of Confucius and the Ch'ing emperors, contrary to the rule that all such characters, if reproduced at all, should be printed without their final brush strokes or be altered in some other way. "My hair stood on end," wrote Ch'ien-lung, "at this revelation of rebellion and lawlessness." Wang and twenty-one members of his family were arrested and sent to Peking. His property was confiscated and all his works destroyed. Wang was executed; two sons and three grandsons were sent into slavery.

Ch'ing Encyclopedias. One monument illustrative of the official compilation work under Ch'ien-lung was the series of encyclopedias on government, which formed supplements to four such works inherited from earlier dynasties, namely, the *T'ung-tien* from the T'ang, the *T'ung-chih* from the Sung and the *Wen-hsien t'ung-k'ao* from the Yüan, together with a supplement to the last compiled in the Ming. (Translations of these titles would hardly be meaningful. Each is intended to be a comprehensive summary, with copious quotations, of the major institutions of Chinese life, particularly of the state system — official structure, fiscal and other economic arrangements, laws, examinations, military and border affairs, rites, philology, etc.) Under Ch'ien-lung six massive new compendiums were now produced, three of them to continue the above-mentioned encyclopedias down to the end of the Ming and three more to continue them for the early Ch'ing period.

All these reference works, as well as the imperial publications on the official structure (*Ta-Ch'ing hui-tien*, or *Collected Statutes*), the laws, administrative geography, and a host of other subjects, centered about the institutions of government. Their compilation gave employment to those scholars who were not active officials and gave guidance to those who were. Thus, through the examination system and the activities of officially sponsored compilation, Chinese of ambition and intellectual capacity were drawn into the service, and the study, of the Confucian state and culture.

CHINESE CULTURE IN THE MING AND CH'ING PERIODS

In pre-empting intellectual talent for official projects, the Ming and Ch'ing governments were drawing upon the human resources of the "gentry" class. The common people who formed the mass of Chinese society did not bulk large in the cultural record, which has come down to us chiefly from the brushes of scholar-officials. Most Chinese were neither scholars nor Confucian gentlemen, and had very little, if anything, to do with officialdom. For the common people, Taoism and Buddhism still supplied the principal explanations of the cosmos, and the family and village still were the focus of everyday living. But it is not yet possible to reconstruct with verisimilitude the daily life of the average Chinese villager in the pre-modern centuries. What we know most about is the educated, urban upper class, who had the means and leisure to enjoy their own private gardens or collections of *objets d'art*, practice their own calligraphy and painting, and who also, without boasting about it, read novels and joined the city crowd at the theater.

The sophisticated interests of these inheritors of the great cultural tradition made them first of all collectors, connoisseurs and critics. Many formed their own private collections, with a strong antiquarian interest. Not only finely printed and illustrated books (some with color prints), but works of calligraphy and painting, rubbings of famous inscriptions and stone bas-reliefs, and ceramics and ancient bronzes were brought together, appreciated and studied by amateurs who were themselves at the same time often writers or artists. This amateur ideal of the cultivated man was a natural result of his classical education. Neither in his formal studies nor in his aesthetic interests did he seek to be a highly specialized technician aiming at utilitarian goals. His purpose was humanistic, to perceive the principles and proper values of the inherited tradition.

This life of culture, though widespread over the empire, centered in the commercial cities of the Lower Yangtze delta, which had remained largely intact in direct descent from the Southern Sung. Hangchow was famous for its beautiful natural setting on the West Lake with its wooded hills and many temples. Soochow women were reputed the empire's most beautiful. The proverb went, "Above is paradise; here below, Soochow and Hangchow."

THE EMPEROR VISITS HANGCHOW

Like his grandfather K'ang-hsi, the Ch'ien-lung Emperor toured the southern provinces. This picture from the commemorative volume Nan-hsün sheng-tien *records his visit to Hangchow early in 1765. On the left, the Ch'ien-t'ang River; center foreground, the walled city; above it on the right, the West Lake. The small captions mark temples on the pine-clad peaks and other famous beauty spots. The emperor's route is indicated by the broken lines. His itinerary is summarized in the inscription across the top.*

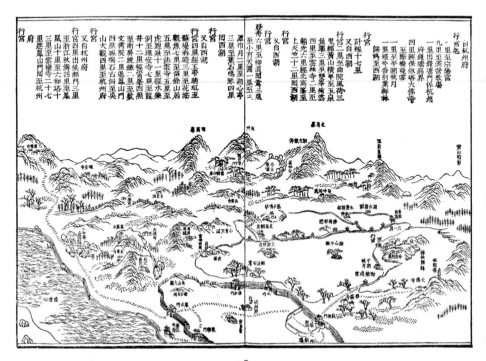

Painting. One major avocation of cultivated men was painting, and the names of over 1000 Ming painters have come down to us. Most of the Ming emperors patronized artists, and Hsüan-te (who ruled from 1426 to 1435) was a talented painter. (See Plate 34). One major conservative style, that of the Chekiang School, followed the landscape painting of the Southern Sung, with the misty distances, the angular pine trees and broken cliffs of masters like Ma Yüan and Hsia Kuei. Another major group of scholar-artists centered at Soochow and so are known as the Wu School from the state that existed in this region in Chou times. In general they set high standards of technique in their command of brush strokes and styles and used a somewhat greater degree of realistic detail, though always deriving inspiration from Yüan and Sung masters. (See Plate 35.)

The amateur ideal of these scholar-gentlemen-artists was expressed by Tung Ch'i-ch'ang (1555–1636) of Sungkiang, near Soochow, who summed up the view that painting together with poetry and calligraphy were the highest expressions of the human spirit. The creation of scholarly amateurs, this "literati-painting" (*wen-jen-hua*) reflected the cultivated man's communion with the forces of nature. For this purpose his mastery of technique and avoidance of the vulgar or sentimental were essential. Both had to be gained through close study of the old masters. Through the general acceptance of this view, the appreciation of nature was combined with the study of tradition. The artist paid minute attention to method. The famous *Mustard Seed Garden Painting Manual* (*Chieh-tzu yüan hua-chuan*) of the seventeenth century described and illustrated the painter's vocabulary of techniques. (See illustration, page 290.)

Tung Ch'i-ch'ang and his fellow-critics appraised and classified the whole inheritance of Chinese painting. Following the seventh-century division of Ch'an (Zen) Buddhism into two schools, Northern and Southern, they grouped all painters, without reference to actual geography, into Northern and Southern traditions. In general, the Northern School was closer to the court, more formal, superficial and decorative, while the Southern School was closer to the spirit of Ch'an (Zen). It sought to be more spontaneously and profoundly expressive of the inner realities of the spirit. The Southern School included most of the great masters.

Painting under the Ch'ing continued along the lines laid down by Tung Ch'i-ch'ang, with steady development of schools and further study of the examples of the past. Private collections were absorbed into the palace at Peking, where Ch'ien-lung, with great zeal if not taste, eventually brought together an imperial collection of some 8000 paintings. He himself painted in the style of Tung Ch'i-ch'ang.

Chinese painting is only the most obvious of the humanistic arts that embody the spirit of Taoism and Buddhism rather than that of Confucianism. The same spirit pervades many forms of literature. This may serve to remind us that the institutions of political and economic organization, so heavily stressed in this volume, formed the framework of Chinese life but by no means summed it up. The public scene was dominated by the Sage, to be sure, but not the private thoughts of most individuals. Consequently, the day-to-day values and feelings of the members of the literate upper class may be approached more closely through some of the books they read for amusement than through their own scholarly productions.

Popular Literature. One widely read work, published in the eighteenth century, was *Liao-chai chih-i* (translated as *Strange Stories from a Chinese Studio*), by P'u Sung-ling (1640–1715). This collection of 431 short stories continued the T'ang tradition of tales of the marvelous and supernatural (*ch'uan-ch'i*), with an abundance of fairies, ghosts, charms and contacts with the spirit world, and not a little wish-fulfillment which might now be called "escapism."

Consider, for example, the typical story of a lonely young man visited alternately by two beautiful girls, each more eager than the other to please him in every way, who turn out, after he is nearly dead from exhaustion, to be actually a ghost in human form and a fox-fairy (fox-fairies are mischievous creatures who live as foxes in their holes but often appear among mankind in the form of beautiful women). In such a story neither the situation nor the action is in the Confucian vein, to say nothing of the actors. But since the author wrote in a classical style with a wealth of literary allusions, it was intelligible only to the educated elite, with whom it was actually very popular.

For a broader public, including the barely literate in addition to the well-educated, the vernacular novels supplied a great wealth of fiction, romantic in theme and realistic in detail. The plots derived in part from the late Sung and Yüan, as we have already noted briefly on pages 287–289. However, most of the great novels were written in their modern form during the Ming period. One of the most popular, *Shui-hu chuan* (translated as *All Men Are Brothers* and as *Water Margin*), originated in legends concerning a minor bandit (named Sung Chiang) who actually lived in the Sung period about 1121. With thirty-six companions he probably had his lair in a great marsh (Liang-shan-po) in western Shantung near the juncture of the Yellow River and the Grand Canal. During the late Sung period, professional storytellers developed the exploits of this band in a type of narrative interspersed with verses to be sung by the raconteur. Playwrights of the Yüan period also used these themes in creating some of their dramas. Several story sequences were recorded about 1300 in a summary- or prompt-book by members of the storytellers' guild. By this time the bandits of the Liang-shan marsh had become "faithful and just" heroes, champions of the oppressed common people, who were victimized by evil and corrupt officials. Their number had grown to 108, with a corresponding expansion of incident and locale.

Shui-hu chuan in its final written form was the work of several authors in succession, who gave the story more shape and subtlety — a retired scholar-official (Shih Nai-an) and a novelist-playwright (Lo Kuan-chung) who collaborated at the end of the Yüan period; a prosperous bookseller (Yü Hsiang-tou) of the late sixteenth century, who published a popular abridgment with illustrations; an iconoclastic, egalitarian scholar (Li Chih) who produced the most complete version in 120 chapters about 1600; and a rebellious commentator (Chin Sheng-t'an) who brought out a truncated but attractive version in 70 chapters in 1644, which has remained the dominant one ever since. Thus *Shui-hu chuan* is a truly popular work, developed gradually in response to public taste during several centuries — an example of the extensive literature of protest which the Confucian system called forth but tried to ignore.

Another very popular adventure tale, also derived from the long tradition of Buddhist stories of the supernatural, was *Hsi-yu-chi* (*Record of a Journey to the West*, also translated as *Monkey*). This lively story was the work of a single, though for long anonymous, scholarly author (Wu Ch'eng-en, c. 1500–1580). It narrates the colorful exploits of an omnicompetent monkey who overcomes superhuman obstacles in escorting the Buddhist priest Hsüan-tsang on a journey to the Western Paradise. Starting with the historical fact of the real Hsüan-tsang's pilgrimage to India in the seventh century, the story draws on the traditional motifs of the marvelous and ultramundane with great imagination, while from time to time it pokes fun at its subjects with such a sense of humor that it retains its vitality even today.

The first great realistic novel, created by a single (although still unknown) author, was *Chin P'ing Mei* (translated as *Golden Lotus*), written in the late Ming period. It marks a new departure in many ways. The story of its central character, Hsi-men Ch'ing, and his pursuit of pleasure in an everyday urban life, avoids overtones of popular legend, heroic adventure or the supernatural. *Chin P'ing Mei* is also the first novel to treat its women characters convincingly as individuals. Its value as a reflection of social manners and family life should not be obscured by the fact that it is also pornographic. The moralistic purpose alleged by the author is, of course, in the usual tradition of pornographic works. But *Chin P'ing Mei* has its proper historical value as a picture of a very non-Confucian mode of life in the late Ming period.

The most sophisticated and satirical attack on the official system was the novel *Ju-lin wai-shih* (*An Unofficial History of the Literati*), by Wu Ching-tzu (1701–1754). A gifted writer who failed to get beyond the bachelor's degree (*hsiu-ts'ai*), Wu became a lifelong enemy of the examination system and of writers of "eight-legged essays," who, he felt, prostituted their talents for worldly advancement. A failure himself, poor and disillusioned, he exposed in realistic detail the intellectual shallowness of worldly scholars who made their way by flattery, favoritism, bribery and corruption. These ignorant and greedy opportunists are contrasted in Wu's rambling chapters with upright individuals, filial and generous, who exemplify the ancient virtues but seldom get on in the world.

The Chinese family system has its greatest monument in *The Dream of the Red Chamber* (*Hung-lou meng*), by Ts'ao Hsüeh-ch'in, whose family history is obviously reflected in the novel. Ts'ao's forebears had grown rich in the service of the Manchus. The founder of the family had joined the Ch'ing cause in Manchuria and became a Chinese bannerman under the imperial household. His descendants held lucrative posts, principally in charge of the imperial textile factory at Nanking. Thus Ts'ao Hsüeh-ch'in's grandfather was wealthy enough to play host to K'ang-hsi on four of his southern tours. He was both a cultivated man — a calligrapher and writer of plays and verse, with an excellent library — and also a patron of literature who printed fine imperial editions of T'ang poetry and various dictionaries. Small wonder that his debts survived him! The Yung-cheng emperor collected some of these debts owed to the imperial court by confiscating the family property in 1728. At the time the household comprised 114 persons, including servants, with some thirteen residences in Nanking and 2000 *mou* (about 300 acres) of land.

Ts'ao Hsüeh-ch'in lived meagerly with his early memories of this vanished household. He portrayed in his novel, written mainly in the 1750's, the varieties of personality and of incident, the strengths and weaknesses of character, which attended the gradual decline and collapse of a well-to-do "gentry" family. In this setting the frustrated love story of two cousins, Pao-yü and the beautiful Black Jade, forms only the most tragic of several interwoven themes. Another writer (Kao E) added forty chapters to Ts'aos original eighty to make the 120-chapter work published in 1792.

Drama. While the professional storytellers' tales in the market place had gradually been developed through the work of talented writers into the vernacular (*pai-hua*) novels, the drama remained somewhat less developed and less widely read as literature. Possibly this was because of its spoken character, which was part of its broad appeal to city artisans and shopkeepers. Its combination of singing, dancing, violent action and earthy humor left little chance for the few spoken lines of the libretto to develop into a literary form of interest to the scholar class. Nevertheless, a great many plays were produced and a considerable development occurred within the tradition.

In the late Ming the most popular type of drama became the *K'un-ch'ü*, named for the city of K'un-shan (Quinsan) near Soochow, the great economic and cultural center of the Lower Yangtze region. The music of the *K'un-chü* (literally, "K'un tunes") was more melodious than that of the Northern four-act drama inherited from the Yüan, and its structure was less rigid.

Even though its actors used the local Wu dialect of the Yangtze delta, its popularity spread widely from the Soochow area. During the seventeenth and eighteenth centuries the *K'un-ch'ü* attracted more interest from scholars and became more elegant and literary and less popular in its appeal, but it prospered under enthusiastic imperial patronage until the rise of the Peking opera in the nineteenth century.

Present-day impressions of the culture of the Ming and Ch'ing periods will no doubt be greatly modified as modern studies of these five and one-half centuries gradually approach the thoroughness and detail already achieved in studies of the same centuries in Japan. In the broad terrain of Chinese civilization we may expect to find plentiful variety and continued vigor, both in artistic concept and in fineness of execution. Yet our over-all impression of the Ming and Ch'ing is of a rich and sophisticated culture so firmly imbedded in its inherited tradition that it is more critical than creative and, in some cases, even repetitive and decadent.

In architecture, for example, the grandeur of the palace buildings at Peking derives from an ancient and well-proved formula — white marble terraces, red pillars and beams supporting massive gold-tiled roofs. Under the broad eaves the beams are brilliantly colored, yet their construction betrays the decadence of the architectural style. T'ang and Sung buildings had carried the weight of the heavy tiled roof down to the pillars through a complex series of large wooden brackets. The large, twin-armed brackets of the T'ang style, visible in the temples at the contemporary Japanese capital at Nara, were thus both functional and decorative, lending rhythm and grace to the wooden construction by which an imposing roof was supported on a few columns. By Ming and Ch'ing times, however, the brackets had become smaller and more numerous, set in a continuous series and performing no more function than a cornice — in short, vestigial ornaments instead of important structural members. (See Plates 41 and 50, and illustration on page 180.)

THE BEGINNING OF DYNASTIC DECLINE

The end of the eighteenth century saw certain changes which fit rather neatly into a pattern of cyclical dynastic decline, even though further research may stress the extent to which this period also saw long-term, non-recurring, that is, secular, changes.

"Cyclical" and "secular" are not precise terms of social science. The historian uses them only descriptively, to suggest a degree of similarity or dissimilarity between one period and other periods. Thus the problems of China in 1800 were cyclically reminiscent of certain periods in the past, whereas the China of 1850 faced additional problems which were wholly unprecedented. Again, the human factors of leadership or bureaucratic morale may seem to wax and wane, while, on the other hand, technological and institutional factors pursue a continuous development. In the end, the Ch'ing dynasty collapsed for both cyclical and secular reasons. The Western impact in the nineteenth century was a new phenomenon quite outside any previous pattern. Yet this foreign impact was more disastrous, we may assume, because a cyclical domestic decline of the ruling dynasty was already under way.

By 1800 symptoms of decline had appeared which we may assume reflected a general deterioration in the administrative, fiscal and psychological conditions of the imperial government. The full-scale process of dynastic decline did not get under way until the middle decades of the nineteenth century, when flood, famine, corruption, rebellion, invasion and fiscal bankruptcy all but destroyed the Ch'ing regime. Here let us take note of certain preliminary signs of decline which had appeared by 1800 in at least three forms — military ineffectiveness of the banner forces, corruption at the top of the bureaucracy, and difficulties of livelihood among a greatly increased population.

Military Exploits. The decline of the banner forces came only after they had dominated continental East Asia for almost two centuries. We have already seen their success in establishing Ch'ing control over China, Mongolia, Turkestan and Tibet down to about 1750. The imperial military exploits under Ch'ien-lung, the "Ten Great Campaigns," were much celebrated in the official annals, yet most of them shared certain characteristics that put them in a different category from the early Manchu conquests. The "Ten Great Campaigns" included three already mentioned — two against the Dzungars and the pacification of Turkestan, all of them strategic achievements of the 1750's which enlarged the area of Ch'ing control in Central Asia. But the other seven campaigns were more in the nature of police actions on the frontiers already established — two wars to suppress the Chin-ch'uan rebels in Szechwan, another to suppress rebels in Taiwan (1787-1788), and four expeditions abroad to chastise the Burmese (1766–1770), the Vietnamese (1788–1789) and the warlike Gurkhas in Nepal on the border between Tibet and India (1790–1792), the last counting as two. All these campaigns had certain common features: they took place on the periphery of the empire, they were conducted by a group of professional Manchu generals, and they required large expenditures of funds, often through the hands of these generals.

The Chin-ch'uan rebels, for example, were aborigines in the mountains on the Szechwan-Yunnan border on the Upper Yangtze (called here the "River of Golden Sand," Chin-sha-chiang). Their local expansion brought imperial armies against them in 1747–1749 and again in 1771–1776. The mountaineers, although they totaled fewer than 30,000 households, built thousands of stone forts in the rocky defiles of their homeland and were eventually dislodged only with cannon. The second campaign against them took five years and seventy million taels of silver, equal to more than two years of the cash revenues normally received at Peking.

Ch'ien-lung's generals, almost all Manchus, led busy lives. A-kuei (1717–1797), for example, qualified as a civil official and became a Grand Councilor, but he also participated successively in the campaigns in Szechwan, Ili, Turkestan (twice), Burma, Szechwan again, and Kansu (twice). A more famous commander but less scrupulous official was Fu-k'ang-an (died 1796), who led forces in Szechwan, Kansu, Taiwan, and against the Gurkhas. To fight the Gurkhas, who had invaded Tibet, he led an army over a thousand miles across the roof of the world in 1792 and drove the invaders back through the Himalayan passes into their homeland of Nepal, which thereafter sent tribute to Peking every five years until 1908.

Until the mid-Ch'ing campaigns are thoroughly studied, we can only speculate as to the corrupt pecuniary motives that may have played a part, though only a part, in their origin and prosecution. The large allocations of imperial funds necessary in each case seem to have created a vested interest in the expansion or, more commonly, the prolongation of operations. Fu-k'ang-an, for example, was a leading official of the empire, a governor-general over various provinces continuously from 1780 to 1795 and eventually a prince, though not a member of the imperial family. This was during the very period when large-scale corruption became entrenched within Ch'ien-lung's court. Fu-k'ang-an was in fact a henchman of a notoriously corrupt courtier named Ho-shen (1750–1799).

Official Corruption. Ho-shen was the classic type of evil courtier, whose malign influence is reminiscent of infamous eunuchs of earlier times. His rise was a symptom of the emperor's senescence. With great prudence and foresight the Manchu regime had succeeded in forestalling the rise of most of the evils which had beset the leadership of earlier dynasties. Imperial princes, military commanders on the frontier, new barbarian invaders, great landed families entrenched in the provinces, eunuchs at the court, empresses and their relatives, even factionalism among the officials — all had been sedulously guarded against, so that the centralized power of the state might remain undiminished in the emperor's hands. The one thing that could not be prevented was the aging of the emperor himself, the infirmity of judgment at the very core of the imperial structure.

When Ch'ien-lung was sixty-five he became much impressed by a handsome twenty-five-year-old bodyguard, an intelligent, able, clever and unscrupulous Manchu who became his favorite and chief minister and plundered the state for the next twenty years. This was Ho-shen, a sycophant and manipulator extraordinary, who rose like a meteor in one year from the fifth rank to be a Grand Councilor and minister of the imperial household. Thereafter he got his hands on the principal posts in charge of revenue and personnel, betrothed his son to the emperor's youngest daughter, and entrenched himself in as many as twenty different positions at a time. Having the emperor's ear, he built up his clique of similarly corrupt henchmen all over the empire and levied a squeeze upon the whole officialdom. The private wealth attributed to him by his enemies after his fall included 60 million ounces of silver, 75 pawnshops, 70,000 furs, a gold table service of 4288 pieces and other items, alleged to be worth a total of 900 million taels or, say, one and a half billion dollars — an incredible sum, the size of which in the official record no doubt indicates the degree of enmity he had created against himself.

With Ho-shen leading the way at Peking, we can more easily understand how military corruption went hand-in-hand with its civilian counterpart. The banner forces became gradually ill-supplied, poorly trained and demoralized. When the White Lotus Rebellion broke out in 1795 in the poverty-stricken Szechwan-Hupei-Shensi border region, the first large Chinese uprising against the Ch'ing in over a century, the banner armies proved at first incapable of suppressing it. Ch'ien-lung formally retired in 1796 so that his reign would not be as long as the sixty-one years of that of his grandfather K'ang-hsi, but actually he continued to rule, through Ho-shen, until his death in 1799. Only then could his successor, Chia-ch'ing, destroy Ho-shen and try to revitalize the administration and the army. The White Lotus Rebellion was finally suppressed in 1804, but already it had signalized the downward turn in the Ch'ing fortunes.

The Growth of Population. Behind this popular rising at the turn of the century lay an era of unparalleled domestic peace, prosperity and population increase. The growth of numbers, however, eventually like a cancer destroyed both the prosperity and the peace which had made it possible. Literary records afford some evidence that the Chinese standard of living was already declining by 1800. The official population estimates, on the other hand, show a year-by-year increase from 142 million in 1741 to 432 million in 1851. If true, this would be a tripling of numbers in 110 years, not unusual for a modern country undergoing industrial expansion but most remarkable for a huge tradition-bound, agrarian country like China.

The official Ch'ing estimates of population, however, cannot be accepted at face value, for they were not based on real censuses of a modern type. The figures were a product of complex administrative arrangements, originally intended to show taxable units, and must be discounted. Probably the growth was not the 290 million recorded, because the figure of 142 million in 1741 was a serious underestimate, and the huge total of 432 million in the mid-nineteenth century may have been an overestimate. Yet we must accept as a fact some considerable growth of the Chinese people during the eighteenth century, before the impact of industrialization.

A principal explanation for such growth lies in the increase of food supply made possible by the opening of new land to cultivation, often under imperial encouragement, and by the use of new food crops. Maize, sweet potatoes, tobacco and peanuts all were introduced into China from the Americas in the sixteenth or early seventeenth century. The sweet potato became the poor man's food of South China, for it could be grown on sandy soil, useless for rice, and provided more food energy per unit of land than most crops. Earlier-ripening varieties of rice were also continually being developed in China, with a consequent greater efficiency in land use.

Other factors in population growth presumably lay in the area of hygienic practices affecting public health, in the increase of foreign trade and of handicraft production and trade attending it, and in other domestic economic developments as yet unexplored.

Whatever the causes of China's demographic growth, it was not paralleled by comparable growth of the Ch'ing administration. The populace may have doubled, but not the official class and its services for the people, nor the military forces which maintained peace and order. On the contrary, the Ch'ing government in all its aspects seems to have grown less effective just at a time when its domestic problems were increasing. The two developments were of course interrelated. Bad government and unsolved problems exacerbated each other in a vicious downward spiral, such as China's long history had seen so often before. This time, however, because of new factors from abroad, the process culminated during the late nineteenth and early twentieth centuries in an unprecedented collapse of the whole traditional system of government and society.

10

Traditional Korea: A Variant

of the Chinese Cultural Pattern

THE PLACE OF KOREA IN
EAST ASIAN CIVILIZATION

One of the difficulties in the study of East Asia is the comprehensive extent of China and the consequent paucity of significant variants from the Chinese pattern within East Asian civilization. China, unlike Rome, remained a solid political unit, encompassing the greater part of its whole zone of civilization. We would have a comparable situation in the West if all Europe, except, for example, Scandinavia and Russia, had been absorbed into a homogeneous, indestructible Roman Empire.

The size of the Chinese unit has precluded anything like the rich diversity of historical experience that has characterized Western civilization, with its national segments varying from Greece to Ireland and its center of gravity shifting from the Mediterranean to northwestern Europe and, in recent centuries, to even more distant areas. There have been few other political units within East Asian civilization with which China can be compared, and there has been none of similar extent or age. As a result, the Chinese have tended to view their history as entirely unique, with comparisons possible only between different periods within it. The other peoples of East Asia have either looked upon themselves as such exact reflections of China that no significant comparisons emerged or else have viewed their own histories as being unique. Such assumptions of uniqueness are characteristic of most pre-modern societies, but today it is generally recognized that both China and these various other countries can be better understood if we try to discover the true parallels and important contrasts in their historical experience. Their resemblances to one another and, still more, their differences help illustrate the basic characteristics of East Asian civilization.

The Peripheral Areas of East Asian Civilization. We have seen how the steppes and deserts to the north of China and the cold Tibetan Plateau to the west prevented the spread of China's agricultural civilization in these directions. This wall was never breached except where it lacked firm climatic foundations — that is, at the points where agriculture was in fact possible, as on the well-watered plains of Manchuria, the border regions of Inner Mongolia, the oases of Chinese Turkestan, and the lower valleys of eastern Tibet. In time Chinese farmers moved into most of these areas, carrying with them their whole civilization and a strong sense of participation in the Chinese political unit. But the steppes, deserts, and high plateaus still support only a pastoral economy, and their inhabitants therefore remain culturally distinct, even if not politically separate, from the rest of East Asia.

Chinese civilization never encountered any climatic barrier in its spread southward and thus rolled steadily onward. The peoples of Central and South China, who linguistically and culturally were closely related to the ancient Chinese, were not only absorbed into the civilization but were brought into the close-knit Chinese Empire. Only in Vietnam did the culture outpace the political unit. The Vietnamese speak a Sinitic language related to Chinese; they derived their higher culture largely from China; and they were for long periods under Chinese rule. Yet eventually they managed to establish their national identity as an independent country within East Asian civilization.

Beyond Vietnam, the forward-rolling wave of East Asian civilization encountered crosscurrents from India and the West — which explains why the rest of Southeast Asia, although climatically suited to rice culture and therefore readily adaptable to Chinese agricultural civilization, has never been absorbed into either the East Asian cultural zone or the Chinese Empire. In early times this area derived its higher civilization from Hindu and Buddhist India. Subsequently, Islam spread over Malaya and Indonesia, and Christianity eventually came to the Philippines. Despite the emigration during recent centuries of great numbers of Chinese to all the countries of Southeast Asia, their settlements have remained isolated cultural islands in essentially foreign civilizations.

To the east, Chinese civilization encountered neither climatic nor cultural barriers. Korea and Japan were suitable for an agricultural civilization, and specifically for intensive rice culture. The ancient inhabitants of these areas were linguistically and culturally very different from the early Chinese, but they remained untouched by any other higher civilization, except as Buddhism from India and other elements of the civilizations of South and West Asia were transmitted through China itself. As a result, they were completely absorbed into East Asian civilization, becoming its two most interesting variants.

For more than a thousand years the higher cultures of Korea and Japan resembled that of China so closely that in many respects they seemed virtually identical with it. Much of the finest artistic output of these two countries is hardly to be distinguished from Chinese prototypes; many of their religious, philosophical, and even strictly literary books might for all practical purposes have been the work of Chinese writers. This is especially true of Korea, where the bulk of literary production is almost indistinguishable from the writings of Chinese authors. In political institutions, in religious and ethical concepts, and in arts and letters, Korea and Japan have long been full-fledged participants in East Asian civilization.

Korea in particular has become so closely identified with Chinese civilization that even its proper names are patterned on Chinese models. Most Korean place names, when written with Chinese characters, cannot be distinguished from Chinese place names, even though they are pronounced somewhat differently. Similarly, all personal names in Korea are virtually identical with names used in China, being made up typically of a one-character family name followed by a two-character given name. (As in China, there are some two-character surnames and quite a few people with one-character given names.) On the other hand, some of the commonest Korean surnames happen to be unusual in China. For instance, Kim, meaning "gold" (*chin* in Chinese), which accounts for about a fifth of the families in Korea, is rare as a surname in China.

The Cultural Distinctiveness of Korea and Japan. Japan's heavy cultural debt to China, and Korea's even closer cultural similarity with its great neighbor, can scarcely be overemphasized. But there has never been any danger that Korea or Japan would be entirely absorbed into the Chinese political unit, as were the Yangtze Valley and South China. They have always, for various reasons, remained clearly separate.

In comparison with peoples from other zones of civilization, the Chinese, Koreans, and Japanese are all unmistakably East Asian in temperament. Yet they have developed sharply contrasting national personalities. All appear to have a stronger aesthetic bent than do the peoples of most other parts of the world, but when compared with one another the Koreans seem somewhat volatile in contrast to the relaxed but persistent Chinese and the more tensely controlled Japanese.

Even in their habits of daily life, the Chinese, Koreans, and Japanese have developed entirely different patterns, far more distinctive than those of the various national units of Europe. Their styles of clothing have all been derived at least in part from early Chinese costumes. But before the invasion of Western clothing in recent years, Chinese, Korean, and Japanese costumes differed radically from one another at almost every social and professional level and not merely among the peasantry, as was the case in early modern Europe. The long-sleeved, flowing robes of the Japanese contrast sharply with the slim trousers and close-cut robes of the Chinese, and neither costume resembles the baggy trousers of the Korean men and the full skirts and short, separate bodices of the Korean women. The traditional white color of Korean clothing also contrasts with the many-hued costumes of the Japanese and the sober black or dark blue worn by most Chinese. The turned-up toes and boot-like shape of Korean footgear (see Plate 48) are markedly different from the cloth slippers worn by the Chinese, and both contrast sharply with the split-toe socks and wooden clogs of the Japanese.

Similarly, Chinese, Korean, and Japanese homes are entirely different from one another. The usual brick-walled houses of China give place in Korea to mud-walled homes with mushroom-shaped thatched roofs in the countryside and tile roofs with sagging ridgepoles and upturned edges in the towns. Still more distinctive are the light wooden homes of Japan, with their high, thick-thatched roofs in the countryside and straight-lined tile roofs in the towns. Inside their houses the Chinese sit on chairs and stools, the Koreans and Japanese on pads on the floor. Chinese homes have brick or clay floors and in North China the people sleep on raised, heated beds made of brick or clay; in Korea the floors are made of clay covered with oil paper and heated by flues from a fire fed from outside the house; Japanese floors, raised a few feet off the ground, are covered with thick, soft rush mats, and the only heating is provided by charcoal braziers.

The differences carry over to the cuisine, too. Although many of the main elements, such as rice, noodles, soy sauce, and bean curd, are the same, nothing could be less alike than the rich mixed dishes of the Chinese, with their many ingredients and flavors, and the attractively arranged but plain (and, according to Western tastes, sometimes insipid) small dishes of the Japanese. Korean cooking stands between these two extremes yet for the most part is still clearly distinct. In particular, its characteristic peppery *kimch'i* pickles, made of such things as fermented Chinese cabbage and red peppers, are not likely to be confused with either Chinese or Japanese food.

One can conclude that, although the national units within East Asian civilization are few in number, the distinctions between them seem much greater than the distinctions between the more numerous national units of the West. Why this should be so is not easy to determine. One reason may be that Korea and Japan, as we shall see, inherited a primitive cultural substructure which was quite different from that of ancient China. Another and more obvious reason is the sharp linguistic cleavage between China on the one hand and Korea and Japan on the other.

The Languages of Korea and Japan. The strong structural similarities between Korean, Japanese, and the Altaic languages of North Asia make it seem probable that both Korean and Japanese are at least close relatives if not full members of this wide-flung family of languages. It should be noted, however, that scholars thus far have not discovered such close vocabulary parallels between Japanese, Korean, and the definitely Altaic languages as are found throughout the Indo-European languages.

In any case, Korean and Japanese, like the definitely Altaic tongues, are agglutinative in type and as such contrast sharply with Chinese and the other Sinitic languages. The latter are characterized by tonal, uninflected, and often monosyllabic words and by simple staccato sentences in which the relationship between words depends entirely on their relative positions, as in the English sentences, "The man ate the lion," and "The lion ate the man." By contrast, the agglutinative languages are characterized by polysyllabic but toneless words which are highly inflected. The role of the noun in a sentence is indicated not so much by position as by inflected endings or by independent postpositions (small words coming after another word, much as prepositions precede English words). In the case of Korean and Japanese verbs and adjectives, one inflection can be added after another to indicate such things as tense, mood, voice, and the degree of politeness or formality. Sentences in the agglutinative languages, unlike the direct terse statements of Chinese, are usually made up of a series of closely interdependent clauses, sometimes in apparently unending succession.

All in all, there is no greater linguistic contrast in the world than that between the Sinitic and the agglutinative languages. Although the Koreans and Japanese borrowed the Chinese writing system and with it thousands of Chinese words and terms, their languages today remain fundamentally and irreconcilably different from Chinese, contrasting with it far more sharply than does English with ancient Greek, or Russian with Hindi and the other North Indian languages.

Korea's Medial Geographical Position. Another reason for the cultural distinctiveness of Korea and Japan is their geographical separation from China. On this point, however, one should note the sharp contrast between the two. Japan, separated by five hundred miles of open sea from the nearest point in China, was far more isolated from China than was Korea and, therefore, remained very much more distinctive. On the other hand, Korea, connected by land with China through Manchuria, was repeatedly invaded by Chinese armies and sometimes joined to the Chinese political unit. Not unnaturally, its social and political institutions and its history became more and more like those of China. Korean culture and experience seem like variations on Chinese themes. Japanese culture and experience show what very different tunes can be played with the same set of instruments.

China, Korea, and Japan thus represent a rich field for comparative studies within East Asian civilization, with Korea occupying the medial position. Its close linguistic parallels and similarities in early culture with Japan highlight the distinctive historical development of Japan. Its close parallels in more modern times with China, and still more its points of significant difference, highlight equally the nature of Chinese civilization.

Korea in its central geographical position served as the bridge over which in early times higher civilization passed from China to Japan. Throughout history it has been a meeting ground for influences and pressures not only from China and Japan but also from the areas to the north. In the early period, the northern influences came from the far-ranging Altaic-speaking nomads — the Mongols and the Tungusic Jürched, Khitan and Manchus; in the modern period, from Imperial and then Communist Russia. The clash of the cultural, political, and military forces from these three larger areas have made Korea a strategic zone of contact in East Asian history.

Thus Korean history and culture offer a particularly significant field of study, though, unfortunately, one which has been little explored. There seem to be several reasons for this. In the past, the Koreans themselves often tended to ignore their own culture and history in their enthusiasm for Chinese civilization. They also kept the West at arm's length, while Westerners themselves, fascinated by the size and age of China, usually overlooked the interesting Korean variant of East Asian civilization which nestled in China's shadow. Then, in more recent years, the Japanese erected around their Korean colony the first of the modern bamboo curtains. All foreign contact with Korea was systematically discouraged, and, as a result, the West remained largely oblivious of Korea's existence until Korea was suddenly liberated from Japanese rule in 1945.

Whatever the causes of our ignorance of Korea, there can be no doubt that the modern world has much less understanding of Korean history and culture than of Japanese or even of Chinese history and culture. This is not to say that we lack facts about Korea's past. The historical record in Korea happens to be unusually extensive, particularly for the past five or six centuries, but these materials have been little studied in either East Asia or the West. For this reason the treatment of Korea in this volume is briefer than it deserves to be, and the interpretations set forth here are presented with less assurance than in the case of Japan and China.

THE BEGINNINGS OF KOREAN HISTORY

The Geographical Setting. Though dwarfed by China, Korea is actually a country of average size and of larger than average population. One can emphasize its smallness by saying that it is scarcely larger than the single state of Minnesota, but it would be more meaningful to say that it is not much smaller than the combined areas of England, Scotland, and Wales. Its present population of around 30,000,000 is comparable to that of Spain.

The climate is much like that of North China — hot and humid in summer but very dry and cold in winter. Only along the southern coast are the winters relatively mild, as in Central China and most of Japan.

Nearly all of Korea is mountainous; only a fifth of the land is suitable for cultivation. A big mountain barrier along the northern frontier effectively divides Korea from Manchuria, and a great north-and-south chain protrudes from this mass southward along the east coast, forming the spiny backbone of the country. The remote higher mountains are still densely wooded; the more accessible lower mountains, now denuded of their tree cover, are barren, jaggedly eroded masses of granite. Most of the terrain is rugged, and there are many places of great beauty, such as the fantastically shaped Diamond Mountains near the east coast, northeast of Seoul.

The coastal strip to the east of the mountainous backbone of Korea is narrow and has few good harbors. To the west, however, the land slopes more gradually down to the deeply indented west and south coasts. Here there are numerous good harbors despite a phenomenally high tide, comparable to the tides of the Bay of Fundy. The broader river valleys and wider coastal plains are found along the western and southern coasts, and the bulk of the agricultural yield comes from these areas. Two harvests a year can be produced in much of the south, and the vital rice crop is grown largely in this part of the country. The greater agricultural productivity of southern and western Korea, together with their greater accessibility to China and also to Japan, has made these regions the dominant parts of the peninsula throughout history.

Early Cultures. There is no clear evidence of human occupation of Korea in Paleolithic times, but by the third millenium B.C. numerous small tribal groups had drifted into Korea across its northern land frontier. The early Korean tribes may have been of diverse origins, but probably North Asian strains were already dominant, and the movement of people into Korea from the north continued well into historic times. The Koreans of today are physically much like the other Mongoloid peoples of northeast Asia, being somewhat taller than the Japanese and South Chinese and having on the whole more prominent cheek bones. Their language, too, as we have seen, is probably related to that of the Altaic-speaking peoples. Thus Korea, unlike China, which received only periodic cultural and racial infusions from the nomadic and forest tribes to the north, seems to have been peopled largely by tribes from this area.

The shell mounds and camp sites of the early Koreans indicate that they lived by fishing and hunting, and their pottery shows connections with the prehistoric wares of Manchuria and Siberia, Mongolia, and North China. Among the Neolithic remains of Korea are pottery with comb markings, and dolmens (tomb-like chambers or altar-like structures made of large stones). Though common throughout North Asia, the comb pattern is rare in China and dolmens are unknown.

We know very little about the social and political organization of the early Korean tribes, but, like most other North Asian peoples and like certain early tribes that moved on from Korea to Japan, they seem to have been ruled by aristocratic hereditary leaders. As in Japan, there may originally have been a matriarchy (feminine rule has appeared sporadically in historic times).

The underlying shamanistic demon worship of later Korean religion, which is much like the shamanism of all the tribal peoples of North Asia, may stem from these first inhabitants of the peninsula as well as from later invaders from the north. The early Koreans, like the Japanese, considered the more impressive phenomena of nature to be deities and also attributed divinity to their own ancestors, who were sometimes considered to be totemic animals. Unlike the nature divinities of Japan, those of Korea came in time to be regarded for the most part as malevolent spirits. These, it was believed, required propitiation through the agency of shamanistic mediums, who, as in ancient Japan, were usually women. Despite later overlays of Buddhism and Confucianism, this shamanistic demon worship has remained strong among the common people, and in rural areas the female sorceress (*mudang*) is still frequently called upon in times of sickness or death.

Chinese Influence: the State of Chosŏn. Around the fourth century B.C. the pre-agricultural, Neolithic, and tribal culture of early Korea was upset by new waves of influence coming into the peninsula across its land frontier. From the west the expanding power of the Hsiung-nu tribes of Mongolia pressed on the Tungusic peoples of Manchuria, and some of these Tungusic tribes moved eastward and southward into Korea, bringing with them a knowledge of both iron and bronze.

The expanding civilization of China began to have an even more direct and pervasive impact. By the third century the state of Yen in northeast China had incorporated parts of South Manchuria into its realm and was exercising direct political and cultural influence over northwestern Korea. By this time, if not already a century or two earlier, agriculture began to seep in from China. Both agriculture and the use of metals spread slowly and irregularly through the peninsula, and for several centuries cultural backwaters persisted where stone implements were used and agriculture had not yet displaced the hunting economy.

In northwest Korea, however, Chinese cultural influences were strong, and it was here that the first true state took shape by the third century B.C. This principality was known as Chosŏn (Ch'ao-hsien in Chinese), a name which was to be applied to all of Korea at various times in its history and, in its Japanese pronunciation of Chōsen, was used for the whole country during the recent period of Japanese colonial rule.

Chinese influence in Korea may have been heightened by an influx of refugees from the series of wars that preceded the unification of China under the Ch'in and the subsequent founding of the Han. In any case, a man named Wiman (Wei Man in Chinese), who was either a Chinese or a Korean in Chinese service, usurped the throne of Chosŏn around 190 B.C. Establishing his capital at the modern P'yŏngyang on the Taedong River, he created a much stronger state than had existed before and apparently exercised some political control over much of the peninsula.

Foundation Myths. Chosŏn, as a semi-Sinicized state, even at this early time illustrated Korea's double cultural heritage from China and from North Asia. This dual heritage has given rise to two contrasting foundation myths. One concerns the son of the divine creator, who, like the progenitor of the Japanese imperial line, descended to earth with his followers. The date of 2333 B.C. alleged for this event looks suspiciously like an effort to approximate the supposed founding of the Hsia, traditionally the first Chinese dynasty, and thus to claim an equal antiquity for Korea. The rest of the legend involves a bear, which is an animal that is worshiped throughout northeast Asia and by the Ainu of North Japan, and a tiger, an animal that figures prominently in the folklore and art of Korea. These two beasts entered a cave for a twenty-one-day period during which they were to be transformed into human beings. Only the bear persisted, emerging as a damsel, and a son called Tan'gun was born of the union of this metamorphosed creature with the son of the divine creator. Tan'gun became the founder of Korea, ruling over the nine wild tribes of the peninsula and teaching them the arts of civilization. Although the earliest remaining written account of this legend dates only from the thirteenth century A.D., it obviously reflects early Korean mythology and primitive North Asian concepts.

The other foundation myth illustrates the cultural debt of Korea to China. It concerns Kija (Chi-tzu in Chinese), who was supposedly a scion of the royal line of the Shang. When his dynasty was supplanted by the Chou in 1122 B.C., Kija is said to have refused to serve the new dynasty and migrated with 5000 followers to southern Manchuria, where he founded the state of Chosŏn. This is a much more sophisticated legend than the Tan'gun myth and closely parallels the Occidental story of Aeneas' flight from Troy to found Rome. It also has some historical substance in that it relates to the definitely Sinicized kingdom of Chosŏn. It was recorded in the first century B.C. in the *Historical Records*, the great work of the Chinese historian Ssu-ma Ch'ien (see pages 111–113).

The Chinese Colonies: Lo-lang. Chinese influence was intensified by Han Wu Ti's conquest of Korea. As we have seen (pages 97–101), Wu Ti was determined to break the power of the Hsiung-nu nomads to the north and for this purpose wished to outflank them in Korea and prevent any alliance between them and the state of Chosŏn. He may also have wished to control the trade routes to the more easterly regions. In any case, he launched an invasion by land and sea in 109 B.C. and by 108 had destroyed Chosŏn. He then set up four large commanderies, subdivided into prefectures, like the administrative units into which China itself was divided. These commanderies covered most of northern and central Korea, but, in the face of the continuing hostility of the native population, the Chinese conquerors soon found themselves overextended. By 75 B.C. the original four commanderies had been reduced to the single one of Lo-lang (Nangnang in Korean), which had its capital at P'yŏngyang and occupied the northwestern corner of the peninsula.

Though reduced in size, the Chinese colonies remained a rich and prosperous outpost of Han civilization. The Lo-lang commandery was divided into twenty-five prefectures and had an officially recorded population of around 400,000. Probably one of the reasons for Lo-lang's prosperity was the trade that flowed through it between China and the rest of Korea and also to and from Japan. The ruling class of Lo-lang was made up largely of Chinese immigrants, and the tombs that they left in the environs of P'yŏngyang contain some of the finest remains of Han times, including beautiful gold filigree work and many superb pieces of lacquer. (See Plate 11.)

The Chinese colonies in Korea lasted for more than four centuries, despite several changes of dynasty at home and the gradual collapse of the centralized Chinese state. As the Han Empire faltered, Lo-lang declined somewhat in population and prosperity, but the Chinese were still strong enough in the early third century A.D. to set up the separate commandery of Tai-fang on the west coast of central Korea. It was not until after the northern "barbarians" had swept over North China in the early fourth century, breaking the contact between the Chinese in Korea and their homeland, that Lo-lang was finally overwhelmed by the Koreans in 313 A.D. and Tai-fang probably soon thereafter.

The historical role of the Chinese commanderies in Korea was much like that of the contemporary Roman colonies in Britain. Although the later kingdoms of Korea were not the direct political heirs of these foreign colonies, they derived much of their culture from contact with these outposts of Chinese civilization. In fact, the cultural continuity between the Han colonies and later Korean states was much greater than that between Roman Britain and Anglo-Saxon England. This may be one of the chief reasons why the Koreans were able to create a well-organized and unified national state much earlier than did the post-Roman inhabitants of the British Isles.

THE THREE KINGDOMS

Although the natives in the Chinese commanderies probably had been a suppressed and exploited class, the local peoples in the rest of Korea were greatly stimulated by their long and close contact with Chinese civilization through its outposts at Lo-lang and Tai-fang. They grew steadily in wealth and in strength, and in time some of them began to form fairly large and well-organized political units.

The Emergence of the Three Kingdoms. Koguryŏ was the first purely native state to make its appearance in Korea. The Koguryŏ people, whose economy was based largely on hunting, were a branch of the Tungusic Puyŏ tribes (Fu-yü in Chinese) of northern Manchuria. They had moved down into the mountainous upper reaches of the Yalu River around the second century B.C. When the Chinese drew back to Lo-lang a quarter of a century after Wu Ti's conquest of Korea, the Koguryŏ tribes asserted their independence, and their leader adopted the title of king. The Koguryŏ people soon established control over the related tribes who lived on the east coast, and during the second half of the first century B.C. they extended their conquests deep into southern Manchuria, enriching themselves with tribute in grain and treasure from their conquered territories. Naturally they came into conflict with the Han Empire, but repeated Chinese expeditions failed to crush the elusive warriors of Koguryŏ, who were very mobile because of their hunting economy, besides having excellent protection in their mountainous habitat.

Chinese records of the third century A.D. describe the people of Koguryŏ as aristocratic tribal warriors. There had originally been five tribes, but the chieftains of one of these had established their hereditary right to the kingship. Under the aristocratic tribal chieftains was a large class of warriors, and under them a mass of serfs and slaves, mainly the peoples of conquered tribes. The aristocratic nature of Koguryŏ society was reflected in the impressive tombs of their leaders. At first these were large stone chambers furnished with stone replicas of metal weapons and mirrors, but in the first or second century A.D. the stone tombs were supplanted by huge earthen mounds containing a wealth of rich funerary ornaments.

The southern half of Korea was occupied by a tribal people called the Han, from whose name the official title of the present South Korean government has been derived.[1] By the first century A.D. agriculture had penetrated this area, and the iron deposits of the southeastern corner of the peninsula were the basis for a flourishing trade with the Chinese colonies, the other Korean tribes, and Japan. As a consequence, the population in the south was much greater than in the Koguryŏ area, but the Han tribes made slow progress in political development. They were divided into three major groups, possibly on ethnic lines, and these groups were each subdivided into a large number of tribal units. The Ma-han group occupied the southwestern part of the peninsula; the Pyŏn-han group is, according to different authorities, identified as having been either on the central stretch of the south coast or in the southeastern corner; and the Chin-han group occupied either the southeast or central Korea.

While the Han peoples of the southeast apparently had strong class distinctions like those of Koguryŏ, the more numerous tribes of the southwest, where Chinese influence was particularly strong, seem to have had these distinctions blurred by their contact with the Chinese. What authority their petty leaders exercised apparently was derived in large part from the titles and official seals given them by the Chinese officials of Lo-lang and Tai-fang. It was not until the fourth century A.D. that the Han tribes of the south had established large enough political units to be capable of building for their dead leaders large stone-chambered tombs like those of Koguryŏ.

As we have seen, after the "barbarian" invasion of North China at

---

[1] This Han is written with a different character from that for the Han River of Korea and the Han dynasty of China.

the start of the fourth century the native Korean states took advantage of the collapse of Chinese power to wipe out the Chinese colonies in Korea and divide the peninsula among themselves. Koguryŏ, after conquering the Chinese holdings in southeastern Manchuria, destroyed Lolang in 313 and annexed its territory. Within a few decades Tai-fang had been similarly submerged and divided between Koguryŏ and the state of Paekche, which had arisen in the Han River valley and had unified the whole Ma-han area in the southwest. The rulers of Paekche probably were themselves conquerors from the north, for they boasted of their descent from the Puyŏ of Manchuria.

In the meantime, another small tribal unit, Silla, had similarly unified the tribes of southeastern Korea (in what is variously said to be the Pyŏn-han or the Chin-han area). But the central zone along the south coast between Paekche and Silla was not incorporated at this time into either state, nor did it consolidate into a single monarchy. This area was known as Kaya, or as Karak after its largest single unit, and was called Mimana by the Japanese. It became loosely allied with the slowly rising state of Japan, perhaps as the result of trade ties, which invited Japanese intervention, or possibly because the people of Kaya were closely related to tribes that had crossed over to Japan not long before and therefore naturally sought aid from the islanders in feuds with their immediate neighbors. The traditional but obviously unreliable dates for the founding of the various Korean states are 57 B.C. for Silla, 37 B.C. for Koguryŏ, 18 B.C. for Paekche, and 42 A.D. for Karak.

During the three and a half centuries following the destruction of the Chinese colonies in the fourth century A.D., the bulk of Korea was divided among the three states of Koguryŏ in the north, Paekche in the southwest, and Silla in the southeast. These are known as the Three Kingdoms, in obvious imitation of the name for the tripartite division of China during the third century.

The Sinification of Koguryŏ. The elimination of the Chinese colonies from Korea did not diminish China's cultural influence. The incorporation of the Sinicized populations of southern Manchuria and Lolang into Koguryŏ naturally had a profound effect, and a wave of new influences also poured into Korea from semi-"barbarianized" North China. Around 342 Koguryŏ was temporarily overrun by the Hsienpei tribe, which was soon to found the Earlier Yen dynasty of northeastern China (see pages 149–151), and thereafter it usually gave tribute to one or another of the Chinese states. Buddhism was officially introduced to Koguryŏ from China a few years later in 372. At about the same time, Koguryŏ drew up a law code on the Chinese model, founded a "university" for the teaching of Confucianism and Chinese history, and officially adopted much of the scholarly lore and scientific

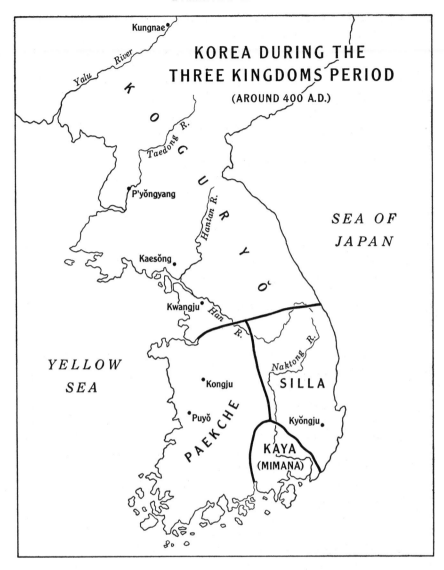

knowledge of the Chinese. A further step in the Sinification of the state was the moving of the capital in 427 from Kungnae on the middle stretches of the Yalu River down to P'yŏngyang, the former headquarters of the Lo-lang commandery.

As a result of all these changes, Koguryŏ came to depend heavily on Chinese-type agricultural taxes and *corvée* services provided by the Sinicized population it had conquered. It also developed a more Sinicized form of government, with complex hierarchies of bureaucratic officials and organized garrisons of soldiers ruling over the subject peoples. The old tribal cults of ancestor worship were largely replaced by a unified state cult and by Buddhism. While the old tribal forms of organization naturally started to degenerate, the state as a whole prospered greatly. The great stone tombs of the kings and nobles around Kungnae and P'yŏngyang attest Koguryŏ's prosperity, and the Chinese-style paintings on the walls of some of these tombs are among the finest East Asian works of art of the fourth and fifth centuries. (See Plate 43.)

Under the leadership of a strong warrior king, Kwanggaet'o (392–413), Koguryŏ expanded in all directions, but especially toward the south. For the next two centuries, it was the paramount power in Korea, ruling over the greater part of the peninsula. It waged frequent wars against the southern states and often exercised suzerainty over them. The chief object of these wars was to capture more subject peoples, for these were the major source of wealth. A great stone stele, erected in 414 on the Manchurian side of the Yalu River in the old capital region of Koguryŏ, records the successful wars of Kwanggaet'o, including his campaigns against the Kaya states and their Japanese allies in the south.

The Development of Paekche. Paekche, which appeared in southwestern Korea in the late third century, was also a prosperous state, for it occupied the most heavily populated and agriculturally the richest part of the country. Cut off from North China by Koguryŏ, it maintained close maritime contact with the dynasties of South China and usually recognized their suzerainty. Many cultural elements came to Paekche from South China, and in 384 Buddhism was first introduced to the court by a monk from China. Few remains have been found of the Paekche state, but some beautiful tiles suggest that the arts and crafts of the area were highly developed. This conclusion is borne out by the fact that Paekche played a large role in the successful transmission of Buddhism and Chinese culture to Japan.

Despite its prosperity, Paekche was never well organized or militarily strong. The original political divisiveness of the Ma-han area had been overcome only by conquerors from the north, and the latter perhaps never won the full support of their subject peoples. In any case, Paekche was usually the loser in its repeated wars with Koguryŏ and, in later years, with the rising power of Silla. In 475 it was forced to move its capital southward from the site of the modern town of Kwangju, a little south of the Han River, to the modern Kongju and in 538 still farther south to Puyŏ (the same name as the Manchurian tribe). Frequently Paekche adopted Silla or Japan as an ally against its dangerous northern neighbor, and early in the sixth century it divided its territory and population into five large units in an effort, only partially successful, to bolster its defenses.

The Growth of Silla. Silla, which appeared in the fourth century, was at first a weak and backward state, for it was located in the southeastern corner of Korea, which had never been occupied by Chinese armies or subjected to strong Chinese influence. Its capital district was near the modern Kyŏngju, in the extreme southeast. At first Silla was hard pressed to maintain itself against Paekche and Japanese marauders from Kaya. In the long run, however, the strong leadership provided by its traditional tribal organization and class structure seem to have given it greater cohesiveness and lasting power than the more Sinicized populations of Paekche and Koguryŏ derived from Chinese institutions.

Silla consisted of a confederation of tribes — six, according to tradition — which had established their rule over a number of other tribal units. A council of all the leaders of the ruling tribes chose the supreme leader and decided other important matters. The peoples of these tribes as well as of the subordinate units were strictly divided into hereditary classes, appropriately called "Bone Ranks," that is, ranks determined by heredity. These fixed the status and function of each individual. Only members of families of the first and second "Bone Ranks" were eligible to lead the confederacy or occupy high posts. Younger members of this nobility served as leaders of bands (known as Hwarang) consisting of several hundred youthful warriors. These Hwarang groups, which at their height in the seventh century numbered several hundred, emphasized moral and physical training, military skills, and comradeship. They served as the core of Silla's armies and a training ground for future national leaders.

The gold bracelets, ear pendants, and crowns found in the burial mounds of the rulers and nobles of early Silla have a certain barbaric grandeur that indicates the relative weakness of Chinese influence in this corner of Korea. In particular, the antler-like crowns covered with pendant decorations suggest that the wearers were leaders in the primitive shamanistic cults of Silla. Close cultural connections with early Japan are also indicated by the curved stone pendants themselves, the design of which is identical with the *magatama*, or "curved jewel," which is one of the three symbols of the authority of the Japanese imperial line and a common feature of Japanese archaeological sites. (See Plate 44.)

Chinese culture and ideas, however, gradually penetrated even to remote Silla. It was possibly under Chinese influence that by the fifth century leadership of the confederacy had become hereditary in the Kim family. A number of reforms carried out in the early sixth century were clearly inspired by China. In 503 the Chinese term for king (*wang*) was at last adopted, though it should be noted that the kings of this and later Korean dynasties were never granted the unique status in society of the Chinese emperors. During the next four decades Silla created a Chinese type of legal code, borrowed Chinese titles for high government posts, and adopted the Chinese system of using "year periods" to count time. In 528 the Silla court accepted Buddhism as an officially favored religion.

This synthesis of Chinese civilization with native Korean traditions seems to have produced a sudden burst of energy. By 562 Silla and Paekche between them had overwhelmed the Kaya area, which the Japanese had used as a foothold on the peninsula. At much the same time Silla also conquered northward up the east coast of Korea and then across the peninsula to the west coast in the region of the Han River, thus separating Paekche from Koguryŏ and winning for itself direct access to China across the Yellow Sea. Silla was now in a position to challenge Koguryŏ for military supremacy in Korea.

The reunification of China in 589 by the Sui dynasty had a profound effect on the strategic situation in Korea. For more than three centuries China had been so disunited and overrun by "barbarians" that it had exercised little direct military influence on the peninsula. Now a reunified Chinese Empire returned to the old Han policy of attempting to outflank the northern nomads — this time the Turks rather than the Hsiung-nu — by extending its control over Korea.

The Korean kingdoms, however, were immeasurably stronger by the sixth century than the state of Chosŏn had been when Wu Ti of the Han overran it in 108 B.C. In 598 Koguryŏ repulsed a large-scale attack by Wen Ti of the Sui, and Yang Ti's three expeditions against Koguryŏ between 612 and 614, the first reportedly with an army of more than a million, ended so disastrously that they contributed to the early demise of the dynasty. T'ai Tsung, the leading spirit in the founding of the T'ang, was no more successful in the three expeditions he launched against Koguryŏ between 644 and 646, and Kao Tsung's first attacks, in 658 and 659, also failed.

A change of strategy finally brought success to the Chinese forces. A naval expedition was dispatched in 660 against Paekche, and with the aid of Silla it destroyed this kingdom. A fleet sent to Paekche's aid by its Japanese allies was repulsed in 663. Meanwhile, the combined forces of T'ang and Silla had turned on Koguryŏ and in 668 put an end to that kingdom, which had prospered for more than seven centuries.

The T'ang rulers had expected to incorporate their Korean conquests into their empire, as had the Han, but Silla naturally had different ideas. Soon after the surrender of Koguryŏ, fighting broke out between the Chinese and Silla forces, and the latter were supported by outbreaks on the part of the conquered peoples of Koguryŏ and Paekche. Within a decade the T'ang armies had been forced to withdraw from all but the northern fringes of the peninsula, and China had to accept Silla as a tributary but autonomous state, ruling over all Korea south of the Taedong River. A second long period of Chinese colonialism was averted, and Korea firmly established itself as a virtually independent nation.

SILLA RULES A UNIFIED KOREA

The destruction of Koguryŏ in 668 and the subsequent expulsion of the Chinese mark the first political unification of Korea. It was to prove a lasting unification, for Korea thereafter was always a united country, except for relatively brief transitional periods of division. In fact, Korea was one of the earliest of the present-day nations of the world to emerge and remain clearly on the map of history. By the end of the seventh century it was essentially the same country it is today, in population, underlying culture, language, and general geographical extent. In East Asia only China is clearly older. Certainly none of the countries of Western Europe achieved both its modern boundaries and its present ethnic composition until well after Korea.

The Adoption of Chinese Political Institutions. The incorporation into Silla of the more Sinicized populations of Paekche and southern Koguryŏ and the increased direct contact between Silla and the T'ang resulted in a wholesale borrowing of Chinese culture and institutions during the first half century following the unification of Korea. Annual embassies and tribute were sent from Silla to the T'ang capital, and large numbers of Korean Buddhist monks and lay students spent long periods of study in China. As a consequence, Silla was virtually remade into a little T'ang — perhaps the most exact and faithful of the many replicas in miniature of the great Chinese Empire that came to surround the T'ang on all sides.

The government of Silla was reorganized along Chinese lines, and as a result a great complex of ministries, bureaus, and directorates came into being. The officials of these government agencies were given fixed salaries measured in grain or the yield of specific pieces of land. The country was also divided into nine provinces, in imitation of the supposed ninefold division of China in antiquity. These provinces in turn were subdivided into prefectures, subprefectures, and smaller units, all of which were given Chinese-type names in 757. Five subcapitals were set up in addition to the main capital at Kyŏngju, and military garrisons were scattered throughout the country. Agricultural lands are said to have been assigned to peasants in 722, in accordance with the early T'ang system of landholding, though we cannot be sure how far this reform was actually carried out.

The adoption of these Chinese political and economic institutions had perhaps been necessitated by the gradual decline of the older social order and the resulting loss of political cohesiveness. The growing wealth of individual family units had shown signs of disrupting the solidarity of the larger tribal groupings of Silla even before the unification of Korea. Generous grants of land and serfs to these aristocratic families after Silla's victory, together with the incorporation of the Paekche and Koguryŏ nobility in the ruling group, may have further weakened the old system.

The aristocratic nature of Silla society persisted, however, greatly modifying the Chinese-type political institutions that were created in Korea. It was at this time that the examination system began to be a determining feature of both government and society in China, but Silla made little effort to utilize this institution for the broad recruitment of leadership. Instead, it maintained its old tradition of determining status and function by birth. High government posts remained the monopoly of families of the top "Bone Ranks," and lesser positions went, in descending order, to men from the lower "Bone Ranks."

Moreover, the government of Silla, despite its Chinese trappings, did not become a broadly based administration, like that of China, but remained much more the personal household government of the ruling family. For instance, its various departments for the production of fine industrial and art goods for palace use, while modeled on those of the Chinese court, came close to monopolizing the whole production of such things in Korea. And the efforts to create a tax-paying free peasantry and a salaried bureaucratic class in accordance with the Chinese model did not really affect the status of the Korean peasants as virtual serfs whose labors went to the personal enrichment of the hereditary aristocracy.

The Appeal of Buddhism. Confucianism naturally accompanied Chinese political institutions to Silla, but the Koreans showed little interest in it during this period. For one thing, Confucianism was too closely associated with the examination system to have much appeal for the aristocratic Silla leaders. Moreover, it was at this time relatively weak in China, which was still in its Buddhist age. It is not surprising, therefore, that the people of Silla were more enthusiastic about Buddhism than they were about any other feature of Chinese civilization.

This same predominant interest in Buddhism characterized the Japanese, and also, apparently, the peoples of Paekche and Koguryŏ, in their borrowing of Chinese civilization. The optimistic philosophy of Mahayana naturally appealed more to these comparatively unsophisticated peoples on the eastern fringes of the Chinese world than did the pessimistic premises of early Indian Buddhism, and Buddhism's apparent magical strength had an even stronger attraction than did any of its doctrines. Coming with the prestige of Chinese civilization behind it, Buddhism appeared to offer greater protective powers to the state, as well as richer promise of worldly rewards to the individual, than did the old native cults. The beautiful art that accompanied Buddhism also made a direct appeal to these eastern peoples, who throughout their history have shown a strong aesthetic bent. Both in Korea and in Japan the immediate and complete success of the new converts in mastering the art forms of Buddhism contrasts sharply with the slow and painful efforts during these same centuries in the West, where the Christianized peoples of northern Europe strove with only modest success to imitate the classic Mediterranean art that had become fused with early Christianity.

The Silla kings expended great sums to erect beautiful Buddhist monasteries around their Kyŏngju capital and throughout the land, and several government bureaus, headed by officers of the first and second "Bone Ranks," were created for the express purpose of maintaining and repairing these temples. The government also appointed clerical officers in each province and in each smaller administrative unit to supervise the church. In the latter part of the dynasty, monasteries were often erected in the high mountains at points where their location was supposed to have a beneficial influence on the surrounding terrain. Such ideas were based on the Chinese concept of geomancy, which, becoming mixed with Buddhism at this time, continued to influence Korean thinking until recent years. By the ninth century many monasteries had become so rich and powerful through gifts from the kings and from private individuals that the government was forced to put restrictions on their holdings.

Great monks appeared in large numbers during the Silla period. Many of them went to China to study and sometimes they traveled on to India. These pilgrims brought back to Korea all the sects that were then popular in China, but their religious and intellectual contributions did not compare with the artistic treasures of the Silla monasteries. Massive rectangular stone and brick pagodas of this period are scattered all over southern Korea, as are also large numbers of stone or bronze Buddhist images as fine as anything produced in T'ang China. One of the two small stone pagodas and the stone retaining walls of the Pulguksa, a monastery founded in 751 a few miles south of Kyŏngju, suggest Indian rather than Chinese prototypes. (See Plate 45.) On the other hand, the great Buddhist images of this monastery and the large stone Buddha and bas-reliefs of the Sŏkkuram grotto, high on a ridge behind the monastery and commanding a glorious view of the Japan Sea, are among the finest works of Buddhist art in the Chinese tradition. (See Plate 47.) A great bronze bell, eleven feet high and decorated with beautiful figures in low relief, now in the museum at Kyŏngju, is another outstanding relic of Silla Buddhism. (See page 394.)

The Use of Chinese Characters. The Chinese cultural influence on Silla, as well as on the earlier Korean states, was transmitted in large part through the Chinese writing system. The early Koreans knew no other form of writing than Chinese characters, but these, unfortunately, were entirely unadapted to writing their own inflected, agglutinative language. Consequently, at first the only writing the Koreans could do was in the foreign language. Despite this handicap, there was a great deal of literary activity in Silla. Historical records were compiled, though none of these has been preserved intact from this early date; Buddhist works were written; and the nobles enthusiastically composed poetry in Chinese.

In the late seventh century, a system of using Chinese characters for phonetic purposes was developed as an aid to recording the appropriate inflectional endings necessary for rendering Chinese texts into Korean. This system, called *idu*, which was first put to important use by a famous Confucian scholar named Sŏl Ch'ong, was also used for transcribing Korean names and native songs and was thus the beginning of a native writing system, though it was never extensively used.

The State of P'o-hai. When Silla was at its height, a very similar state rose to the north, in the forested eastern half of Manchuria. This was the country of P'o-hai (Parhae in Korean), made up of remnants of the Koguryŏ nation, their relatives the Puyŏ, and other Tungusic tribes. P'o-hai, which was founded in 713, was, like Silla, a tributary but autonomous state under the T'ang. Also, like Silla, it created a Chinese type of administration, built Buddhist monasteries in the T'ang style, and produced a literature written wholly in Chinese. Its people traded not only with China but also across the sea with Japan. Eventually occupying all of southern and eastern Manchuria and the northeastern corner of Korea, P'o-hai lasted for more than two centuries, until it was extinguished in 926 by the Khitan, who were soon to found the Liao dynasty on the northern borders of China.

The Decline and Fall of Silla. The century following the unification of Korea in 668 was a golden age for Silla both politically and in artistic creativeness, but thereafter a rapid degeneration set in. Since Silla's heyday and decline so closely paralleled in time the rise and fall of the T'ang, it is possible that conditions in China had some influence on Korea. It seems probable, however, that factors within Korea were more significant in determining the course of Silla's history.

The dynastic administrative cycle, which is so marked in Chinese history, seems to show up independently in Korea in the history of

Silla as well as in succeeding dynasties. In the case of Silla it may have been accentuated because the strongly aristocratic and hereditary social system inherited from earlier times formed an unsuitable foundation for the Chinese type of centralized, bureaucratic state, and the latter in turn proved disruptive to the indigenous social order. The old cohesiveness of Silla society had begun to disappear by the late eighth century. The Hwarang bands lost their fighting prowess and degenerated into groups of effeminate dilettantes. While the prestige of the old aristocracy remained, the "Bone Ranks" broke up into contending family groups, each struggling to maintain its own interests at the expense of the others. The Chinese type of examination system was at last adopted in 788, perhaps in a desperate effort to bolster the collapsing political order. The examinations did make possible some mobility in status between different "Bone Rank" levels, but they had little other effect, since the Koreans, because of their strong class feeling, let only aristocrats enter the examinations.

The turning point in Silla's fortunes came when, after a series of revolts, the king was killed in 780. With his death the direct line of royal descent from the man who had unified Korea in 668 came to an end. Later kings were selected from among a large number of rival aspirants from collateral lines, and during the remaining 155 years of its existence Silla had no fewer than twenty kings, the majority of whom met violent deaths in the general competition for the throne. Rebellions and *coups d'état* followed in rapid succession, as one group after another among the nobility placed its candidate on the throne and massacred those of its rivals it could lay hands on. Naturally the capital district was repeatedly despoiled, and the fighting occasionally spread to the provinces. For example, the governor of the area around Kongju, the old Paekche capital, founded a short-lived rival state there in 822, when his father failed to win the throne of Silla.

The collapse of the old social order was also marked by the growing resentment of the lower classes. As conditions deteriorated, serfs in increasing numbers absconded from the estates where they worked and sometimes turned to banditry. Certain groups from the lower classes developed into independent merchants, and by the ninth century Korean sailors and traders of humble origin had come to dominate the three-cornered trade in the East China Sea between China, Korea, and Japan. The Japanese pilgrim Ennin tells us of large numbers of Korean traders along the southern coast of the Shantung Peninsula and in the cities along the lower course of the Huai River, living in their own autonomous communities and worshiping at their own Korean Buddhist temples.

The most interesting product of the lower classes at this time was Chang Po-go, who rose to prominence as a leader of the Korean trade communities in China and became a virtual merchant prince at his head-quarters, which were strategically located on an island off the south-western corner of Korea. In 839 he was instrumental in putting one of the contending candidates on the Silla throne, but in 841, when he defied the prejudices of aristocratic Koreans by trying to marry his daughter to the king, he was assassinated, and his commercial empire collapsed.

Central authority had further deteriorated before the end of the ninth century. By 889 peasant uprisings had broken out in many regions, and the authority of the government was soon limited to the old capital district of Silla. One of the rebels in 892 founded a Later Paekche state in the old Paekche region.

Many of the rebel leaders came from the lower classes, but one of the most successful was the monk Kungye, the *déclassé* son of a Silla king by a concubine. Motivated by a burning personal hatred of Silla, Kungye in 901 set up the rival state of Later Koguryŏ in north-central Korea. He made the government of his state a replica of that of Silla, but in his later years he turned into a crazed tyrant.

Wang Kŏn, one of Kungye's officers, supplanted his master in 918 and made his capital at Kaesŏng (also known as Songdo) on the west coast. Wang Kŏn, shortening the ancient name Koguryŏ, called his state Koryŏ, from which we have derived the Western name for Korea. In 935, after the Silla capital had been overrun by the Later Paekche, the enfeebled king of Silla came meekly to surrender to Wang Kŏn. Wang Kŏn paid him every possible respect, accepting his submission with an outward show of reluctance. He gave the former king his eldest daughter in marriage and re-established him in a supervisory capacity in the old capital district of Silla. Thus the remains of the Silla administration were peacefully incorporated into the new state of Koryŏ. In 936 Wang Kŏn finally destroyed the Later Paekche, reuniting Korea again under a single government.

THE KORYŎ DYNASTY

The Koryŏ dynasty founded by Wang Kŏn lasted from 918 to 1392. During this period Korean society and historical experience seem to have diverged more from the contemporaneous Chinese pattern than they had during the latter part of the Silla dynasty. This may have been because of the comparative weakness of Sung China and the existence between it and Korea of the powerful Liao and Chin empires, both of non-Chinese origin.

In the externals of political administration, however, the triumph of Koryŏ marked a significant step forward in the Sinification of the government. Since the "Bone Rank" system and the whole tribal social order had disappeared during the constant civil wars of the later Silla period, Wang Kŏn and his successors were able to create a political administration that was a much closer imitation of that of China than the Silla government had ever been. The posthumous titles by which we know the Koryŏ kings are symbolic of this change. Wang Kŏn, for example, is known as T'aejo, the Korean form of T'ai Tsu ("Grand Progenitor"), which was also the posthumous title of the roughly contemporary first emperor of the Sung. The institution of kingship, however, remained relatively weak, as it had been during the Silla dynasty.

The capital at Kaesŏng was a magnificent city even by Chinese standards, laid out in checkerboard fashion in the manner of Ch'ang-an and dominated by a great palace. Here, during the first few decades of Koryŏ rule, was established an elaborate bureaucratic government, closely patterned on that of the T'ang, with six ministries, nine courts, and a host of lesser administrative organs. P'yŏngyang, Kyŏngju, and the modern Seoul were made, respectively, subsidiary Western, Eastern, and Southern capitals, and the rest of the nation was divided into provinces, prefectures, subprefectures, districts, and smaller administrative units.[2] The whole country was centrally governed by a salaried bureaucracy, and in 958 the Chinese examination system was adopted as a means of selecting officials.

Class Distinctions. Beneath this imposing political superstructure, however, Korea had a very different social and economic system from that of contemporary Sung China. It was perhaps more like the early T'ang before the great transformation that had started in the eighth century, but there were certain characteristics that distinguished it even from this earlier and more aristocratic China.

For one thing, class lines were more sharply drawn in Korea than they had been even in pre-eighth-century China. The "Bone Ranks" had disappeared, but a new closed, hereditary aristocracy had risen to take their place. This consisted of the associates of Wang Kŏn, the various local strong men who had submitted to him, and the remnants of the Silla ruling class. Though this new aristocracy formed a larger group than the old first and second "Bone Ranks," its monopoly of high official posts was equally complete. The government examinations theoretically were open to commoners, in accordance with Chinese tradition, but the commoners' lack of time for continued Chinese classical studies, their exclusion from many of the government schools, and a number of petty restrictions inspired by class prejudice prevented

[2] The Korean word for province, *to* or *do*, was derived from the Chinese *tao*; *chu* or *ju* for prefecture from the Chinese *chou*; *kun* or *gun* for subprefecture from the Chinese *chün* (commandery); and *hyŏn* for district from the Chinese *hsien*.

them from taking any real advantage of this theoretical opportunity.

The aristocratic bureaucrats were for the most part concentrated at the capital where they, together with the petty civil and military underlings, lived on the official salaries assigned them. Salaries were usually defined as the produce of specific pieces of land. In addition, many officials received hereditary tracts of land as rewards for services of special merit performed for the royal line. The rest of the land was, at least in theory, state-owned, but in time much of this taxpaying public domain also gravitated into private hands. Such privately owned pieces of land gradually evolved into large, well-organized estates which presented their surplus produce directly to their noble owners rather than to the central government. The owners, however, did not themselves live on these estates or attempt to operate them.

Both the aristocracy and the lower classes were divided into very large kinship units. Although similar to the extended family system extolled by Chinese Confucianists, these kinship units were probably more the outgrowth of native social institutions than the result of Chinese influence. All relationships tended to be expressed in family terms. Even slaves were considered to be part of their master's family organization. As in China, the large kinship units of the aristocracy were in keen competition with one another for power and wealth. The great nobles strove to win places for their daughters as consorts of the kings and, if successful, would attempt to take advantage of such unions with the royal line to monopolize the high posts of government and obtain more land for themselves.

A vast gulf divided Koryŏ officialdom from the rest of the nation. As in China, the officials deputed from the central government went no lower than the district level. Moreover, higher officials took posts in the provinces only rarely and with reluctance. Banishment from the court was considered one of the severest punishments for an aristocrat.

The majority of the population consisted of commoners (*yangmin*, literally "good people"), whose taxes and *corvée* labor supported the government and the aristocracy. Some 30,000 peasants were constantly under arms as capital guards, and in time of war armies of hundreds of thousands might be mobilized. Certain descendants of the old local aristocracy were designated to be the petty officers in the units of local government, and on them fell the duty of collecting the taxes and providing the *corvée* labor for the ruling aristocracy. Although the whole government depended on the faithful services of these former local aristocrats, they were not considered part of officialdom. Members of their families were kept at the capital as hostages, and they themselves were supervised by officials from the central government. In time it became the rule that these central government officials should be in no way related to the local people.

Below the commoners was a large class known as the "lowborn" (*ch'ŏnmin*). These included outright slaves, who seem to have been more numerous than in Silla times. Besides the privately owned slaves, who could be bought and sold, there were large numbers of government slaves, many of whom were assigned as attendants to the high officials. The "lowborn" also included government workers in mines, porcelain factories, and other official industries, as well as the workers at post stations and similar government agencies in the provinces. Sometimes the whole peasant population of a particular administrative area, embracing perhaps dozens of villages, was classed as "lowborn." Such hereditary groups of inferior social status had existed in the Silla period but apparently they were even more widespread under the Koryŏ dynasty.

The Backward Economy. Besides the sharpness of class lines in Korea, another major difference from Sung China, or even from the early T'ang, was the backwardness of the Korean economy. In the ninth century Korean merchants had been important in the international trade of East Asia, but subsequently they sank into insignificance, and even at home the commercial classes had only a negligible role during the Koryŏ period. There were virtually no shops, only peddlers, except at the capital. Trade took place largely at periodic markets, where exchanges were made by barter rather than through the use of money.

Still another contrast was the great concentration of wealth and power at the capital — greater than had ever been known even in highly centralized China. The wealth of the nation was collected at Kaesŏng through government taxation or through the direct support given by agricultural estates to their noble owners, who were residents of the capital. This concentration of wealth and power may have reflected the sharp distinctions of class and the superimposition of the centralized Chinese form of government on a country with a less advanced economy. It may also have been a natural result of the process of acculturation, in which strong foreign influence at the capital made this one advanced area contrast all the more sharply with the rest of the country. A similar situation existed in early Japan, and somewhat analogous conditions have appeared in various Asian countries during the past century of strong Western influence.

The size of the peninsula may have been another reason for the concentration of power and wealth at the capital. Complete centralization was easier in a relatively small country like Korea, which is comparable in size to a single Chinese province, than it was in the vast, sprawling Chinese Empire. In any case, envoys to Koryŏ from the Sung commented on the contrast between the palaces and great homes of the capital and the wretched hovels throughout the rest of Korea.

Koryŏ Culture. Despite Korea's adoption of the Chinese examination system, Buddhism was at its height during the Koryŏ period. T'aejo, in the "Ten Injunctions" he left his heirs, clearly stated that the success of his dynasty depended entirely on the Buddha's protection. Most of his successors proved equally ardent in their patronage of the church. In return, the monasteries provided religious ceremonies on the birthdays of the kings and on other national festivals.

Buddhism by this time had achieved popularity among all social classes. Nobles who became monks occupied the high clerical posts, as in medieval Europe. The nobility frequented monasteries as places of beauty where they could pursue their amusements. Members of the humbler classes flocked so eagerly into the tax-exempt lower clerical positions that restrictions had to be placed on their numbers. Many of the monasteries were richly endowed with lands and in some cases built up their own military power to protect their holdings. Occasionally they also engaged in moneylending and banking functions, as was common among the Buddhist institutions of that period in both China and Japan.

The Buddhist monasteries were also major centers of learning and art during the Koryŏ period. By the thirteenth century Zen (Sŏn in Korean) and T'ien-t'ai (Ch'ŏndae) were established as the leading sects. The intellectual vigor of Koryŏ Buddhism is attested by a huge collection of 81,137 printing blocks, each measuring eight by twenty-seven inches, carved in the thirteenth century for the printing of the Buddhist Tripitaka. These, together with 4745 blocks of Silla date, are still preserved in the Haeinsa, a monastery high on beautiful Mount Kaya in southern Korea. They form a collection of early printing materials unique in the world.

Koryŏ Buddhism, however, was highly adulterated by other beliefs. T'aejo's "Ten Injunctions" show that Taoistic concepts of geomancy strongly influenced the location of monasteries and that, although an ardent believer, he felt that the ancient native cults should be maintained alongside the newer Buddhist rituals. In fact, Buddhism had become so mixed with other ideas — older native beliefs as well as Chinese geomancy and cosmological concepts — that it was beginning to lose its identity. This, together with the decline of Buddhism in China, may help to account for the rapid degeneration of Buddhism after the fall of Koryŏ. Although Korea has been nominally a Buddhist country for a millennium and a half, it is perhaps not inappropriate that the flag of the present South Korean government shows only symbols of pre-Buddhist Chinese origin — the two entwined "commas" of the complementary dualism of *yin* and *yang* surrounded by four of the eight trigrams of the *Classic of Changes*. (See page 53.)

One would expect that the chief artistic remains of so Buddhistic an age as Koryŏ would be Buddhist statues and icons, but such is not the case. Perhaps the declining vigor of Buddhism in China had already affected Buddhist art in Korea. At any rate, Buddhist sculpture seems to have degenerated rapidly during Koryŏ times, and more secular arts took its place. Landscape painting is said to have flourished under Sung and Yüan influences, though few authentic works remain from this period. A quantity of fine ceramic ware, however, has been preserved. The pale green Koryŏ celadons, with their graceful modeling and lovely designs executed in inlaid clays of white or grey color, were very different from the celadons of the Sung that had inspired them. They were much admired even in China and constitute one of the greatest triumphs of the potter's art. (See Plate 46.)

The greatest literary works of the Koryŏ period were also secular rather than Buddhistic. The most important piece of scholarship was the *Samguk sagi* (*History of the Three Kingdoms*), compiled in 1145 in Chinese by Kim Pu-sik on the model of Ssu-ma Ch'ien's *Historical Records*. This work is the chief source of our knowledge of early Korean history and is supplemented only in minor details by the *Samguk yusa* (*Memorabilia of the Three Kingdoms*), compiled by a thirteenth-century monk.

INTERNAL DECLINE AND FOREIGN PRESSURES IN THE LATER KORYŎ PERIOD

Much of the Koryŏ aristocracy was a parasitic class, living in great luxury and addicted to literary and artistic diversions. But this did not preclude intense rivalry over honors and rewards at court. The capital was repeatedly disturbed by palace wars, and many of the Koryŏ kings met untimely ends. During the middle decades of the eleventh century a certain noble Kim family established its supremacy at court through intermarriage with the kings. The Koryŏ kings, like the Silla rulers before them, frequently married their own close relatives in order to consolidate the ruling family; thus the Kim family was thoroughly intermarried with the Wang royal line. Subsequently the Kim lost their power in the same way to a family with the almost equally common surname of Yi.

In the twelfth century, after the dynasty had occupied the throne for about two centuries, conditions began to deteriorate seriously, once again suggesting the operation of the dynastic cycle. A member of the Yi family, hoping to usurp the throne, burned the palace in 1126 but was destroyed by one of his own henchmen, and the power of the Yi family crumbled. Subsequently a Buddhist monk named Myoch'ŏng won great influence as an expert on geomancy and *yin* and *yang*. He revolted in 1135 when his plan to move the capital to P'yŏngyang was blocked, but he was soon destroyed by one of his followers, who in turn was destroyed by the statesman-historian Kim Pu-sik.

Meanwhile, signs of more basic trouble had become apparent. The greed of the aristocracy was cutting into the state's revenues, and there were serious signs of disloyalty among the military officials, who had been less favored than the civil bureaucrats and systematically subordinated to them. Relying on their own armored bands of personal retainers, the military officers sometimes made direct bids for power. The resulting turmoil inspired uprisings by the peasant levies, made desperate by the miserable poverty of the lower classes from which they were drawn. The disruption caused by these popular revolts in turn helped the military officials to assert their power at court.

Although an unsuccessful revolt of the military officers had occurred as early as 1014, the situation did not become acute until the twelfth century. In 1170 the palace guards, led by Chŏng Chung-bu, massacred the civil officials at court and placed a new king on the throne. An attempt in 1173 to dislodge Chŏng resulted in a second great massacre of civil officials and the complete elimination of this group from power.

The following three decades were a period of incessant civil warfare. Civil officials continued the fight in parts of the north, while uprisings of the lower classes broke out in many parts of the country, particularly in the south. There were revolts by *ch'ŏnmin* ("lowborn") groups in government factories, by slaves at the capital, and by monks as well as by commoners. Often these outbreaks were acts of desperation aimed at throwing off some of the economic burden and social stigma under which the lower classes labored.

The Dominance of the Ch'oe Family. The military officials, who now dominated the capital, were by no means united among themselves. Chŏng Chung-bu was killed by rivals in 1179, and *coups d'état* followed in quick succession until one of the generals, Ch'oe Ch'ung-hŏn, established his supremacy at the capital in 1196 by ruthlessly destroying his rivals. The next year he showed his mettle by setting aside the king and putting his own candidate on the throne. By 1203 he had stamped out the last of the major uprisings.

When Ch'oe Ch'ung-hŏn died in 1219, he passed on his power to his son, Ch'oe U, who with his heirs maintained the family's supremacy until 1258. Ch'oe U, in fact, set up "administrative quarters" in his own palace which served as the real government of Korea.

The power of the Ch'oe family was based primarily on its own private army. This consisted of an elite band of warrior-retainers, said to have numbered 3000, and a mass of virtual slaves, a few of whom were allowed to rise under the patronage of the Ch'oe to the status of retainers or government officials. This group of retainers was reminiscent of the old tribal warrior bands of earlier days. Moreover, the similar but smaller private groups of lesser military officials were often bound to the Ch'oe family through ties of blood and marriage in the old tribal manner.

The domination of the Koryŏ dynasty by the Ch'oe strongly resembles the prelude to feudalism in Japan, where warrior bands seized power in the twelfth century. In fact, the Ch'oe rulers in some ways resembled the Japanese feudal shoguns, who like them monopolized power without actually usurping the throne. But their rule had one essential point of difference both with Japan and with the proto-feudal Europe of a few centuries earlier. The Ch'oe family and the other military groups were not closely linked to the land and the agricultural population. They owned great estates and assigned themselves the tax yield of even larger areas, but they neither managed these lands themselves nor drew their military forces directly from them. For all their pseudo-tribal organization, they were divorced from the land and remained essentially private military pressure groups within a degenerated bureaucracy.

Invasions from the North: the Mongol Domination. Another great difference from Japan was that Korea remained constantly under a heavy military threat from abroad, and so needed a more effective centralization of military power than would normally have been provided by a fragmented feudal system. As we have seen, Koryŏ was not under military pressure from the Chinese, though it recognized its tributary status first to the successive Five Dynasties and then to the Sung. The rise of Khitan power in Manchuria, however, changed the situation. Although Koryŏ as early as 994 acknowledged the suzerainty of the Khitan and their Liao dynasty, it was repeatedly subjected to raids by these nomadic neighbors, and in 1011 even the capital was captured. After the Jürched replaced the Khitan in Manchuria, the Koreans attacked them in 1108, but the Jürched soon struck back, invading Korea. After the Jürched had conquered North China in 1127, Koryŏ became tributary to their Chin Empire, as well as to the Southern Sung.

The subsequent rise of the Mongols posed an even greater threat to Korea than the Khitan or the Jürched had ever been. In 1231 the Mongol hordes poured across the Yalu River, which by this time had become established as Korea's northern frontier, and laid siege to the capital. The Korean court then submitted to the Mongols. However, when the invaders had withdrawn, the Koreans moved the capital to Kanghwa Island off the west coast for purposes of more effective defense against the formidable Mongol cavalry. The Mongols regarded this an act of revolt and during the next two and a half decades repeatedly overran Korea, despoiling the country. They reportedly took away 206,800 male captives in their incursion of 1254 alone.

The Mongols could not capture Kanghwa, however, and the Korean court continued to maintain itself there in comparative luxury. It was during this period that the wood blocks for the Buddhist Tripitaka, now preserved at the Haeinsa, were carved in an effort to win divine protection against the invaders. The recording of the Tan'gun myth about the origins of Korea in the *Samguk yusa*, which was a product of this century, may also reflect a stirring of nationalistic feeling as a reaction to the Mongol menace.

The Koryŏ court, however, did not hold out for long. In 1258 the last of the Ch'oe dictators was assassinated, and Korea surrendered completely to the Mongols. There followed a century of more complete domination from abroad than Korea experienced at any other time before the twentieth century. The central government's power was re-established over the country, but at the price of complete subservience to the Mongols. The direct annexation by the Mongols of the northern part of the peninsula was accepted with little protest; the Koryŏ kings were no longer given pretentious posthumous titles that suggested equality with the emperors of China, and the word "loyal" was included in all their titles; they were married generation after generation to Mongol princesses, becoming in time nothing more than a branch of the Mongol ruling family; their Mongol consorts exercised great power; the royal family often resided in Peking rather than in Korea; Mongol officials directly supervised the administration; and the customs of the ruling class became strongly Mongolized.

Some of the heaviest burdens imposed by the Mongols on Korea resulted from the two unsuccessful Mongol invasions of Japan in 1274 and 1281. Both times the Koreans were called upon to provide vast quantities of provisions and 900 ships, though Korean soldiers constituted only 5000 of the total force of 25,000 in 1274 and 10,000 of the huge army of 140,000 seven years later.

Dynastic Decline and Collapse. The strong hand of Mongol overlords had served to revive temporarily the control of the Koryŏ dynasty over the peninsula, but beneath the surface the foundations of its power were disintegrating. This process could be seen most clearly in the steady transfer of lands from the public domain into privately owned estates. Though some of these estates were managed by the government in behalf of their owners, others came to be operated by the owners' own henchmen and worked by their slaves. Most of the estates were owned by the great officials, and income derived from the land gradually replaced government salaries as the chief source of revenue for the aristocracy. This changed source of revenue made no great difference to the ruling class, but the rise of estates seriously affected the government, cutting into its income and undermining its ability to pay adequate salaries. One result of this situation was that toward the end of the dynasty there were repeated demands on the part of the landless lesser bureaucrats and petty government functionaries for a share of the lands monopolized by the great officials.

During the long periods of civil war and foreign invasion in the twelfth and thirteenth centuries, there was some reshuffling of classes. In the confusion, enterprising members of the *ch'ŏnmin* or "lowborn" class managed to win acceptance as commoners, and a few able individuals, through the favor of their masters, worked their way up into the ruling class. Still larger numbers of commoners, however, slipped down into *ch'ŏnmin* status. Some in desperation sold themselves or their children into slavery. Many more entered estates and were reclassified as slaves or serfs, either at their own or the owners' wish, in order to escape taxation.

Another disruptive factor in the last century and a half of the Koryŏ dynasty was the rise of the Japanese piratical attacks, which resembled the depredations of the Norsemen at a somewhat earlier period in Europe. These attacks started in the thirteenth century and mounted to very serious proportions by the middle of the fourteenth century. Japanese pirates not only despoiled the coastal districts and towns of Korea but prevented the vital transportation of grain taxes by sea. The only effective response of the harried coastal people was to retreat inland, thereby abandoning some of the richest sections of Korea, or to take to piracy themselves, either in cooperation with the Japanese or on their own.

The Koryŏ dynasty had come to rely so heavily on Mongol power and prestige that it could not long survive the collapse of the Mongol Empire in the middle of the fourteenth century. Although the Mongols levied Korean troops to help them maintain their hold on China, Chinese rebel bands penetrated all the way to northern Korea. Koryŏ took advantage of the situation to regain control over the northern part of the peninsula.

In 1370, only two years after the founding of the Ming, Koryŏ tacitly acknowledged this new dynasty's suzerainty by adopting its "year periods." But a bitter debate broke out at the Korean court between the advocates of an alliance with the Ming and those who wished to maintain the old ties with the Mongols, even after the Mongols had retreated northward. The pro-Mongol faction eventually won out and embarked upon a campaign against the Ming armies in southern Manchuria. However, one of the leading generals, Yi Sŏnggye, realizing the folly of the undertaking, revolted. Marching back from the Yalu River, he seized the capital in 1388, put his own puppet king on the throne, and assumed complete control of the government. In 1392 he usurped the throne, bringing the Koryŏ dynasty to an end after 474 years of rule.

THE SOCIAL AND POLITICAL ORGANIZATION
OF THE YI DYNASTY

Yi Sŏng-gye immediately entered into tributary relations with the Ming. With Chinese permission, he adopted the ancient name of Chosŏn for his regime, though it has usually been called, after his surname, the Yi dynasty.[3] It was to remain in existence for 518 years, from 1392 to 1910, almost twice as long as any of the dynasties of imperial China.

Until the last few years of this period, Korea was in close tributary relationship with her great neighbor, and Chinese cultural influences were overwhelming. Yi Korea became a far more perfect replica of Ming China than Silla had ever been of the T'ang. In fact, Korea during this phase of its history seemed at times even more Confucian and traditionally Chinese than China itself. But beneath the political and intellectual surface, the social and cultural substructure was in many ways quite different, and Korea, for all its Sinification, remained a distinctive variant of the Chinese pattern.

Yi Sŏng-gye was a military man who had first distinguished himself by repulsing Jürched raiders in the northeast and Japanese pirates in the south, but he also proved to be a statesman of unusual ability. Even before he usurped the throne, he carried out a complete reform of the landholding system, sweeping the slate clean in the traditional manner of dynastic founders in earlier Chinese history.

The Landholding System. Great confusion had grown up over land titles. Moreover, the landless lesser bureaucracy greatly resented the monopoly by the high officials of the estates into which the country had become divided. In 1390 Yi Sŏng-gye confiscated all these estates in a dramatic burning of the land registers, reportedly while the last of the Koryŏ kings wept at the loss of ancestral lands. The next year Yi Sŏng-gye carried out a new distribution of the land.

The new land distribution was consciously aimed at the creation of a strong bureaucratic central power. Lands in Kyŏnggi Province, the area around the new capital, Seoul, were used to support the central bureaucracy and to reward those who had rendered service of exceptional merit to the throne. Lands in the other provinces were assigned largely to the support of the military establishment. The purpose of this was to concentrate the economic interests of the military groups in the peripheral provinces, so that they would be personally concerned in the defense of these outer bulwarks of the state.

---

[3] The family name of Yi is sometimes Romanized Li or Lee, in correspondence with the Chinese pronunciation of the character with which it is written, or Ri or Rhee (which happens to be the Japanese pronunciation).

Yi Sŏng-gye also elevated a few dozen men who had been closest to him in his work of founding the dynasty, making them a special category of "Merit Subjects" (*Kongsin*), to whom he gave large outright grants of land and slaves and important special privileges. A larger category of "Minor Merit Subjects" (*Wŏnjong kongsin*) received lesser awards. His successors on the throne, especially after succession disputes, commonly followed his example in creating additional groups of Merit Subjects and Minor Merit Subjects. In these ways the late Koryŏ pattern of concentration of land in the hands of a few high bureaucrats was changed, and the new regime won the support of a much wider group of landowning officials.

Yi Sŏng-gye's reforms were to some degree a revival of the old T'ang system utilized in the early Koryŏ period, by which the income of specific pieces of land was assigned to individual officials, but there were some important differences. From the start it was recognized that the lands assigned Merit Subjects were hereditary property and might be confiscated later only as punishment for very serious crimes. Moreover, unlike the T'ang and the Koryŏ holdings, most of the newly assigned lands were taxable. In these two ways the landholding system in Korea became more like the landlordism of modern China.

Landlordism of this sort was not entirely new in Korea, nor did Yi Sŏng-gye's reform mark the end of great tax-free estates. In late Koryŏ times some provincial men of wealth, not connected with the court, had been able to establish their own private holdings, and these owners came to be the pattern for the new landlordism. Furthermore, overly generous grants to the Merit Subjects and Minor Merit Subjects and the enterprise of some of the leading families soon led to the reappearance under the Yi of large estates owned by the aristocrats in the capital. As early as the fifteenth century, the new dynasty was already seriously embarrassed by the inadequacy of lands for assignment to new officials or for use as rewards. Some aspects of the landholding pattern of Koryŏ days thus reappeared, but more modest landlord holdings continued to be the rule, and the landowning class remained a very much larger group than had been the case before.

Class Structure. Another great difference from the past was the close identification of many landlords with their holdings. Although this was not true of the chief families in the capital aristocracy, many others who aspired to official posts at the capital left part of their families on their agricultural lands and themselves returned to them when out of office. In this way they began to approximate the "gentry" class of early modern China in combining the functions of provincial landlords and those of central government officials.

The identification of officialdom with landownership grew even more marked in Korea than in China. Because of the much stronger class consciousness of the Koreans, important official positions were in effect limited to the landowning class, or, to put it more correctly, landowner-ship was for all practical purposes limited to the official class. This class came in time to be known as the *yangban*, a term meaning literally the "two groups" — that is, the civil and military branches of the bureaucracy — but designating the whole landowner-official class.

Other important differences from China were the sharp social cleav-age between the *yangban* and their fellow Koreans and the complicated structure of the lower classes. In Korea as in China, the examination system had become the chief road to high official position, but com-petition in the examinations was normally limited to members of *yang-ban* families, and there was virtually no movement into or out of this class.

Below the *yangban* class a small group, known as the *chungin* or "middle people," served as petty government functionaries and special-ists in medicine, scientific knowledge, and foreign languages. But despite their importance in government administration, these "middle people" only occasionally succeeded in rising socially through the examina-tion system.

The vast bulk of society was made up of commoners (*yangmin*), who carried the main load of both production and taxation. Unlike the peasants of China, who by Sung times were already beginning to shake off their serf-like status, Korean commoners were more closely bound to the soil during the Yi dynasty than they had been before. On the other hand, the government guaranteed their right to the lands they farmed and a share of its produce, thus giving them, initially at least, some degree of protection from exploitation by the landowners.

At the bottom of society there was still a large *ch'ŏnmin* or "low-born" class. Although the old administrative areas peopled entirely by *ch'ŏnmin* peasants had disappeared, many of the workers on the large private and government estates were *ch'ŏnmin* slaves, and the workers in government industries and the lesser government employees also belonged to this class. Large numbers of government and private slaves were employed as servants, while certain professions, such as those of actors, shamans, *kisaeng* (female entertainers comparable to the Japanese geishas), and butchers, carried with them *ch'ŏnmin* status.

The Organs of Government. The basic political structure of the Yi dynasty was established during its first quarter-century of rule, but important additions were made for another half-century. The two chief designers of the new administration were Yi Sŏng-gye himself, who is known to history as T'aejo ("Grand Progenitor"), the traditional title for a dynastic founder, and his son, the third ruler, T'aejong

("Grand Ancestor," T'ai Tsung in Chinese), who ruled from 1400 to 1418. The capital was first established at Seoul[4] in 1394 and has remained there permanently ever since 1405. (See Plate 42.)

The major organs of central government were a State Council (*Ŭijŏngbu*), a Royal Secretariat (*Sŭngjŏngwŏn*), and the Six Ministries, or Boards of Personnel, Revenue, Rituals, War, Justice, and Public Works, named after the Six Ministries of the T'ang. The Six Ministries were at first subordinate to the State Council but later became independent of it.

There were also two Boards of Censors (*Sahŏnbu* and *Saganwŏn*), the first in theory designed to scrutinize and criticize government policy and the actions of the officials, the second to do the same for the king himself. These two censoring organs were subsequently joined by a third, the Office of Special Counselors (*Hongmun'gwan*). Mention should also be made of the Office of the Royal Lectures (*Kyŏngyŏn*). The staff of this office, which was made up largely of high bureaucrats and members of the censoring organs, met as often as three times a day, ostensibly for the purpose of delivering lectures on Confucian texts to the king. Actually this institution evolved into a forum for general debate and criticism of high policy and the actions of the king and his officials.

The concept of a censoring branch of government specifically designated to ferret out dishonesty and maladministration in the bureaucracy and to offer criticism of the sovereign was, of course, of Chinese origin, but these censoring offices flourished under the Yi in a way they never did in China. No doubt the reason for this was the fundamental weakness of the institution of monarchy in Korea and the corresponding strength of the aristocracy. Lacking the semi-religious aura of the Son of Heaven, the Silla, Koryŏ, and Yi kings were never accorded the unique status of the Chinese emperors; and, though a wide gulf separated the *yangban* from the lower classes, there was no corresponding gulf between the *yangban* and the king, who was regarded as little more than *primus inter pares*.

The creation by Yi Sŏng-gye and his successors of Merit Subjects reflected the weakness of the kings' position and their need to build up groups of strong families whose own fortunes would depend on the continuation of the Yi line of rulers. But in a way the Merit-Subject system weakened the kings' position by increasing the wealth and prestige of certain members of the aristocracy. Another sign of the relative weakness of the kings was the frequency with which lesser bureaucrats made direct appeals to the king. The third and clearest sign of the feebleness of the royal institution was the extraordinary

[4] Seoul simply means "Capital." A more formal modern name for the city is Kyŏngsŏng, which is rendered as Keijō in Japanese.

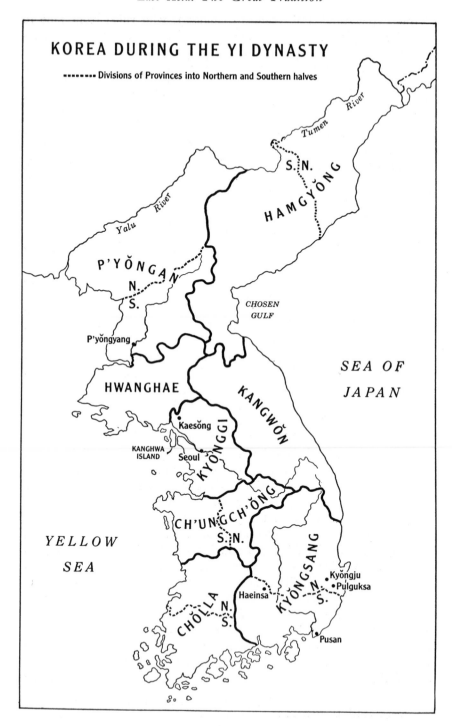

KOREA DURING THE YI DYNASTY

-------- Divisions of Provinces into Northern and Southern halves

temerity with which even very junior officials in the censoring organs criticized both the king and his chief officers.

Under the Yi dynasty local government was based as much on the Chinese pattern as was the government at the capital. In 1413 the old Koryŏ division of the country into a capital district, five provinces, and two northern border zones was revised into a uniform pattern of eight provinces: Kyŏnggi around the capital, surrounded by the three provinces of Hwanghae, Kangwŏn, and Ch'ungch'ŏng, with Chŏlla and Kyŏngsang in the southwest and southeast, and P'yŏngan and Hamgyŏng in the northwest and northeast respectively.[5] These eight provinces remained the major administrative divisions of Korea until the late nineteenth century, when the four peripheral provinces and Ch'ungch'ŏng were each divided into northern and southern halves, making the thirteen provinces of recent decades.

The provinces were divided into a variety of mutually independent administrative units, the most common of which might be called districts or counties (the *hsien* of the Chinese system). As in China and during the Koryŏ dynasty, central government officials were not appointed to posts below the district level. The officers of the still smaller administrative units were drawn from the richer local commoners. To prevent any local group from challenging the authority of the central government, minor local officers, whose posts were commonly hereditary, were forced to keep their sons in service at the capital, where they were practically hostages, as had been the custom ever since Silla times. Moreover, central government officials, as in post-Sung China, were never assigned to posts in their home districts.

The Examination System. The government depended on a large bureaucracy which, as in China, was recruited in part through the examination system. This system had taken on increasing importance during the Koryŏ period despite political and military troubles, and Yi Sŏng-gye reinstituted and perfected it the year after his usurpation. The examination techniques were closely patterned on those of China, and the subject matter consisted almost entirely of the Chinese classics, histories, and belles-lettres. The one great difference from Chinese precedent lay in the effective limitation of the system to the *yangban* class. Every three years 700 candidates each for a degree in the classics and for the more coveted *chinsa* degree (the *chin-shih* of China) were selected through provincial examinations, and the next year, after final examinations held in Seoul, 100 aspirants were awarded each of these degrees. The degrees qualified the holders to be part of officialdom, but the real elite of government and society was chosen by a further test. From among the degree holders and a few other

[5] Hwanghae and Hamgyŏng were not the original names for these two provinces.

specially privileged persons, 33 men were selected at the triennial national examinations for immediate assignment to court rank and government posts in general correspondence with their examination grades. In time such national final examinations came to be held much more frequently than every third year. A sequence of military examinations for military officers paralleled the civil examinations.

The examination system in Korea displayed many of the same virtues and faults that it had in China. It produced a bureaucracy chosen in terms of personal merit more than inheritance, though the class base was much narrower in Korea than in China. It made government service the great ideal of the upper class, though, as in China, high government office was recognized as the surest means to personal enrichment. It placed men of intellectual inclination and philosophical training in charge of the mechanisms of government but at the same time excessively emphasized the scholarly and literary skills and antiquarian and historical interests. This tendency may have been even more limiting to intellectual originality in Korea than in China, since scholarship had to be demonstrated in a foreign language and the historical orientation was toward a foreign country. Despite these weaknesses, however, the examination system produced a bureaucratic form of government which continued without significant break or modification for about five centuries, constituting probably the longest administrative cycle in world history.

The Culture of Yi-Dynasty Korea

In general, the Yi followed the dynastic cycle made familiar to us by Chinese history. The fifteenth century, the first century of Yi rule, was the time of greatest strength, prosperity, and cultural brilliance. There was a considerable expansion of land under cultivation. A marked increase in population brought about the migration of large numbers of people from the heavily populated south to the relatively empty north. Such mass migrations, which for the most part were forced on the participants by the government, firmly established the hold of the Korean people on the whole peninsula up to the Yalu River on the northwest and the Tumen River in the northeast.

Confucianism. The strengthening of the examination system during the early Yi dynasty naturally brought about a new emphasis on Confucian philosophy, which was so inextricably connected with the system in China. With the founding of the Yi dynasty, the Confucian age of Korean history really begins.

For all their close contact with the Chinese, the Koreans had shown relatively little interest in Confucianism until the latter part of the

Koryŏ dynasty. This was no doubt partly the result of the low fortunes of Confucianism in its homeland during the era of Korea's first important contact with China in the Three Kingdoms and Silla periods. Another factor may have been that Buddhism, facing less challenge in Korea from local religious and philosophical concepts, became more solidly entrenched there than in China. Still another factor may have been the more aristocratic social organization and attitudes of the Korean upper class, which made Confucian concepts less intelligible or appealing to its members than to the Chinese in similar circumstances.

During the last century of Koryŏ rule, however, there had been a marked increase in Korean interest in Confucianism. This presumably reflected the perfection of Neo-Confucianism at the hands of Chu Hsi a century earlier (see pages 235–241), as well as the extremely close contact between Korea and China resulting from the virtual incorporation of Korea into the Mongol Empire ruled from Peking.

By the time of Yi Sŏng-gye's usurpation, Confucian ideas had won a firm hold among the educated classes. Officials who failed to reconcile themselves to the change of dynasty retired to pursue Confucian studies, regarding themselves as loyalists in the best Confucian tradition. Since they lived away from the court, such men have come to be known as the "Mountain and Forest" (Sallim) scholars. Even Yi Sŏng-gye, though himself a Buddhist, was much influenced by his Confucianist followers, and he adopted Confucian concepts useful in government, including the Chinese theory of the Mandate of Heaven as a means of emphasizing the legitimacy of his dynasty. On the whole, his successors were even more Confucianist. T'aejong seems to have taken the Mandate of Heaven theory so literally that he abdicated in favor of his son in 1418, when he thought that natural disasters indicated he had lost Heaven's favor.

The complete triumph of the examination system under the Yi dynasty insured the lasting hold of Confucianism. Henceforth, the way to fame and success clearly lay through the mastery of Confucian scholarship and philosophy. Eventually the Chu Hsi school of Neo-Confucianism became established as the only acceptable interpretation of the classics. All ambitious boys of the upper class eagerly sought a Confucian education, and the indoctrination became stronger with each generation. Perhaps because it was a borrowed ideology without old native roots, Korean Confucianism became in time even more dogmatic and more rigidly bound by a narrow orthodoxy than it was in China.

The new emphasis on Confucianism and the examination system under the Yi dynasty was accompanied by a great development of schools. The curriculum of these schools was limited to the Chinese language and the type of texts that a candidate needed to know for the examinations. As we have seen, the literary bias of Chinese civilization resulted in a greater emphasis on formal education in East Asia than in the other major zones of civilization. Within East Asia, however, the Koreans seem to have emphasized formal education even more than the Chinese. Such an emphasis was obviously necessary when the whole subject matter of education was of foreign origin.

At the bottom of the educational scale were the private elementary schools, which were to be found in almost every village. These were supported by either private teachers, individual families, larger social groups, or the whole village. Above the elementary schools were the government schools in each district, dating from Koryŏ times. These maintained their own Confucian shrines and prepared students for the degree examinations. On the same level as the district government schools were the Four Schools (*Sahak*) at the capital. Each of these took one hundred students a year, almost exclusively from the *yangban* residents of Seoul, and prepared them for the degree examinations and entrance into the Sŏnggyun'gwan, the capital university. The two hundred students accepted in this institution were a privileged elite whose object was to prepare for the triennial national examinations or for direct appointment to government posts.

The rise of Confucianism meant a corresponding fall of Buddhism. The decline had become apparent in the increasing corruption of Buddhist monasteries in the late Koryŏ period and the lessening intellectual vigor of the church. With the removal of official sponsorship under the Yi dynasty, this decline became precipitous. Yi Sŏng-gye (T'aejo) withdrew the tax exemptions of the Buddhist church, banned new buildings and even the repairing of temples, and required monks to have government licenses; T'aejong destroyed all but about 250 temples, confiscating the lands and slaves of the remainder; his son Sejong (Shih Tsung in Chinese; 1418–1450) banned monks from Seoul, forced the existing seven sects to combine into two, and eliminated all but thirty-six temples with a total of 3700 resident monks. In this way the wealth and power of the Buddhist church were drastically reduced, and Korean Buddhism rapidly sank to the sad state of theological confusion and low social esteem which it occupies today.

Scholarship, Printing, and Han'gŭl. The fifteenth century was one of the greatest periods of scholarship and literary activity in all Korean history. A host of important works appeared, most of them, naturally, in the Chinese language. There were great encyclopedias, geographies, commentaries on the Confucian classics and philosophy, legal compendiums, and, of course, histories. Among the latter special mention should be made of the *Koryŏ sa*, the *"History of Koryŏ,"* completed in 1451, a work compiled in the best tradition of Chinese scholarship to establish the official account of the preceding dynasty.

Accompanying all this scholarly work was a tremendous amount of activity in the field of printing, which was motivated primarily by the desire to make Confucian texts more widely available to the scholar class. Much of the printing was done with movable type. The latter may have been a Chinese invention, but it was in Korea in the early fifteenth century that movable type was first put to extensive use anywhere in the world. Between 1403 and 1484 eight large-scale printing projects in movable type were undertaken by the Korean court.

Among other technological achievements of the same period were a rain gauge and certain astronomical instruments, but the most remarkable intellectual accomplishment of the era was the invention of an excellent phonetic system for writing the Korean language. This system, known today as *han'gŭl* (meaning "Korean letters" but formerly called *ŏnmun* or "vernacular writing"), was developed by the fourth Yi ruler, Sejong, and was officially adopted by royal decree in 1446.

Han'gŭl is perhaps the most scientific system of writing in general use in any country. The basic vowels are indicated by vertical or

HAN'GŬL CHART

Vowel pairs: ├ a ╞ ya, ┤ ŏ ╡ yŏ, ┴ o ╨ yo, ┬ u
┬┬ yu, — ŭ │ i.

Some consonant pairs: ㄱ k ㅋ k', ㄷ t ㅌ t', ㅂ p ㅍ p',
ㅈ ch ㅊ ch'.

Some other consonants: ㅅ s, ㄴ n, ㅁ m, ㅇ ng.

Syllables:* Chosŏn 조 선   Taedong 대 동

ch'ŏnmin 천 민   T'aejong 태 종

Puyŏ 부 여   *yangban* 양 반

P'yŏngyang 평 양

* *K, t, p* and *ch* are voiced (*g, d, b* and *j*) when occurring between vowels. The symbol ㅇ is used both for a final *ng* and to indicate the absence of an initial consonant. *Ae* is written ╫ (*ai*).

horizontal straight lines, modified by short lines on one side or the other, a single short line for a simple vowel and two if it includes the *y* sound. Consonants are represented by curved or angled lines, originally designed to suggest mouth positions used in forming the respective sounds. Unaspirated and aspirated pairs (e.g., *k* and *k'*) are indicated by related symbols, the aspirated form usually being shown by the addition of an extra line. Finally, the advantages of an alphabetic script and a syllabary (in which each symbol represents a whole syllable) are combined by bunching the individual letters into syllabic groups.

Although *han'gŭl* was a simple and almost perfect system for writing the native Korean language, Sejong's invention was little used by men of scholarship during the next five centuries. The emphasis on the Chinese written language and Confucian literature continued to such an extent that the use of *han'gŭl* was limited mainly to technical linguistic works, books designed to instruct the lower classes, or correspondence between women and other persons of little education. It was not until after the liberation of Korea from Japanese rule in 1945 that *han'gŭl* came into its own as the primary method of writing in Korea. It proved to be as excellent a system for transcribing the spoken language in the twentieth century as it had been when first invented.

The Fine Arts. The predominance of Confucianism during the Yi dynasty was reflected even in the field of art. Naturally, there was no Buddhist art of any great distinction. Painting, which in China was so closely associated with calligraphy and the literary tradition, became the great art form of the day. In subject matter and style Korean painting closely paralleled the various schools and artistic currents in China. Though much of it was obviously imitative, Korean painters did produce many works of considerable merit.

Typically, the Korean artists fell into two distinct social groups. The scholar-officials, for whom calligraphy and painting represented socially approved skills, tended to be academic in their interests and closely bound to Chinese models. They also insisted fiercely on their amateurism. The professionals of the Office of Arts, on the other hand, from the "middle people" class, were employed primarily to paint ancestral portraits. It was their interest in genre subjects that infused new life into Korean painting during the latter part of the dynasty. (See Plate 48.)

The Yi dynasty maintained a government kiln, but the great period of Korean celadons came to an end with the disappearance of the Koryŏ government kilns which had produced them. Instead, the potter's art became more widespread among the common people. Pottery of the Yi dynasty tends to be simpler and rougher, yet more spontaneous and original, than the highly refined Koryŏ celadons.

FACTIONALISM DISRUPTS THE YI GOVERNMENT

After its brilliant first century, the Yi, in typical dynastic fashion, declined in administrative efficiency and effective unity. The turn of the dynastic cycle manifested itself not by rebellions and uprisings, as it had during the Koryŏ dynasty and in China, but rather by disruptive factional conflicts within the central officialdom. Such bureaucratic factionalism characterized some of the later Chinese dynasties, and its appearance at this time in Korea suggests that Korea had at last come to approximate China in its state of political organization. In fact, bureaucratic factionalism went to even greater extremes in Yi-dynasty Korea than it ever reached in either the Sung or the late Ming, when Chinese factionalism was probably at its worst.

Factionalism seems to have been a problem inherent in the Chinese bureaucratic state, once the officials serving a new dynasty had lost their initial unity and *esprit de corps*. The examination system was an admirably fair way of providing candidates for official positions, but the actual appointment to office and subsequent promotions frequently came to depend on the patronage of high officials, who were themselves often in competition with one another for the confidence and favor of the ruler.

Certain ideological factors intensified the resulting power struggles within the bureaucratic hierarchy. Inevitably a gap existed between the ideal pattern of Confucian conduct and the realities of bureaucratic life, and there was a similar disparity between the Confucian ideal of the scholar-official's responsibility to advise the ruler on his administration of affairs and the frustrating fact that rulers were fallible and often capricious human beings, unable in any case to accept every official's advice. The result was that the classical ideals of Confucian conduct and administration could always be invoked to criticize officials high and low, and even the sovereign himself. Moreover, such criticism was not made in legal terms, according to clearly defined rights and duties, so much as in moral terms, according to rather vague and abstract principles. Thus moralistic criticism and denunciation became one medium through which rival groups strove for power, filling the historical record with self-righteous attacks and counterattacks that often obscure the other factors involved in such struggles.

Unlike the party system in British or American democracy, factionalism in the Chinese type of bureaucratic state was seriously disruptive, because there was no mechanism for reconciling policy differences if the throne failed to settle them through strong leadership.

Because of the Confucian emphasis on ethics as the basis of good government, opposing policies could not be accepted as the product of honest differences of opinion but were commonly regarded as signs of the depravity of one's opponents. Moreover, with good government considered to be the natural product of sound ethical standards, majority decisions would not suffice; unanimity was necessary. The democratic balance of our own partisan politics would have been unthinkable. Any opposition represented a disloyalty tantamount to both treason and moral turpitude. Such an attitude helps to account for the ferocity of the factional struggles, which led to numerous executions and the purging of hundreds of officials at a time.

Factional Disputes of the Yi Dynasty. The weakness of the royal institution in Korea made the problem of bureaucratic factionalism more severe under the Yi dynasty than during any dynasty in China. Not only did the kings exercise much less control over their bureaucrats than did most Chinese emperors, but the lesser officials, as members of the privileged *yangban* class, stood less in awe of the high officers than was the case in China. The direct access of petty bureaucrats to the king, the strong position of the various censoring organs, and the institution of the Royal Lectures described in the preceding section all invited factional disputes and created ideal conditions for their growth.

The great factional outbursts of Korea as well as of China were struggles for power, but they usually arose over policy differences and only subsequently degenerated into fights centering around personalities rather than ideas. The famous factional divisions of Sung China arose over major economic and foreign policies (see pages 205–209). The great factional dispute that started in Korea in the late fifteenth century began over the question of the role of the censoring organs in government. Junior officials tried to expand the role of these organs, while senior officers endeavored to curb their power and maintain the traditional administrative chain of command.[6]

This was the underlying issue in Korea, but the arguments usually centered around less fundamental problems. Accusations of personal incompetence for office, immorality, or even lese majesty were freely exchanged; squabbles arose over points of Confucian ritual, such as the proper period of mourning; and by the seventeenth century even points of Confucian philosophical doctrine had become involved. But all these were more occasions than real causes of conflict. Eventually, after the factional disputes had continued for two or three generations, their original causes became submerged in the personal animosities aroused

[6] This and the following paragraphs on Korean factionalism are based primarily on a forthcoming work by Edward W. Wagner.

by repeated purges and counter-purges. Once fully launched, factional disputes thus became self-perpetuating.

Factions had existed from the very outset of the Yi dynasty, but at first these were merely ephemeral groupings occasioned by succession disputes. It was only in the reign of Sŏngjong (1469–1494) that factionalism began to be a serious problem. Sŏngjong had been raised to the throne when still a child, and, as a result, he was subjected to heavy indoctrination regarding the Confucian duty of a ruler to heed his advisors. Perhaps for this reason he proved to be unusually tolerant of criticism from his officials.

Moreover, recent alterations of the administrative structure had stripped the State Council of its function of general review and control of governmental operations, leaving a power vacuum into which the censoring organs hastened to move. The relatively young men in these latter offices, perhaps more thoroughly indoctrinated in Confucian theory than their elders, and certainly less experienced in administration, tended to be idealistic but doctrinaire Confucianists. Given full rein by Sŏngjong, they soon drove many of the long-entrenched older officials out of office. In fact, the officials of the censoring groups, who themselves lacked administrative responsibility, made strong leadership in government all but impossible by their unrestrained criticism of each man and each act.

The Great Purges. A showdown between the older officials and the young zealots came in the reign of Sŏngjong's son, Yŏnsan'gun (1494–1506), who, largely on account of his role in factional disputes, was subsequently denied the usual laudatory posthumous title. A man of different outlook from his father, Yŏnsan'gun gradually sided with the older, responsible officials. For a few years he tolerated the presumption and insolence of the censoring organs, but finally in 1498 he turned on them, executing, banishing, or discharging from office some forty or fifty men, many of whom had won fame for vigor and fearlessness in their roles as censors. The purged group consisted mainly of disciples and associates of Kim Chong-jik (1431–1492), a famed scholar-official in the direct "Mountain and Forest" tradition.

Yŏnsan'gun seems later to have developed paranoiac tendencies. In any case, in 1504 he started a broad attack on the whole concept that royal decisions and governmental processes should be subject to review. From his father's reign as well as his own, he picked out a wide variety of issues on which the censoring organs had "presumptuously" offered their opinions, broadening the attack to other persons who had been involved in policy decisions. For two years he carried on a reign of terror unmatched in the annals of Korean history, executing or banishing hundreds of hapless officials.

Yŏnsan'gun at length was deposed by the remaining officials of his court, and under his successor, Chungjong (1506–1544), the censoring organs were again emphasized as a means of inhibiting the despotic exercise of power.

But the fight between responsible administrative officers and the younger censoring officials soon broke out again. Chungjong had been set upon the throne by certain prominent officials and had rewarded them by enrollment as Merit Subjects. Within a decade, however, he fell under the influence of an idealistic Confucianist, Cho Kwang-jo. Cho Kwang-jo gathered to his standard a number of similarly dedicated younger men, who, basing themselves on the censoring organs, started a furious attack upon existing institutions and high officials in an effort to recreate the hypothetical, ideal Confucian state of Chinese antiquity. In the process they incurred the enmity of the senior officials and even alarmed Chungjong by their obvious threat to strong administrative leadership. Consequently Chungjong gave his blessing in 1519 to Cho's opponents, who filled the censoring organs with their own adherents and then used these organs to have Cho and his supporters executed, banished, or dismissed from office.

The pattern had now been set for successive strong men or bureaucratic groups to utilize the censoring organs as the base of power from which to destroy their opponents. In 1531 Kim Al-lo rose to power with the support of a cooperative group of censors and through his connection by marriage with the royal family, but he was destroyed in turn when the king himself made use of the censoring organs to get rid of him.

The court then became split by the rival ambitions of the families of Chungjong's first and second queens. Chungjong's death in 1544 precipitated a purge in 1545 manipulated through the censoring organs by the second queen's faction against that of the first queen, which included remnants of Cho Kwang-jo's group (purged earlier, in 1519). For the next twenty years the victorious faction continued to use the censoring organs to eliminate rivals, forestalling the efforts of its opponents to turn these powerful institutions against itself.

Later Factionalism. By this time the original dispute over the proper role of the censoring organs had been resolved by a general acknowledgment of their pivotal importance in government. Indeed, these organs had become the chief weapons employed by rival power groups, even though they actually began to lose some of their former influence at about this time. In any case, personal and family animosities were becoming more important than issues, and factional divisions were beginning to harden along almost hereditary lines.

During the sixteenth century regional differences also became increasingly important in the development of bureaucratic cliques. The bulk of the lesser scholar-bureaucrats now lived on their agricultural holdings. There the more outstanding men gathered around themselves large numbers of relatives and disciples who had supported them when they were in office at the capital and had rallied round them when they returned in defeat to their rural homes. Such local groupings often perpetuated themselves for many generations. The bureaucratic factions thus came to have secure geographical bases. Instead of remaining ephemeral groupings centering around individual personalities and passing issues, as they had been in earlier periods, they became semi-permanent.

The intensification of factional division was also related to a significant change in the educational system that began in the sixteenth century. This was the appearance of private academies, or *sŏwŏn*, named and patterned after the *shu-yüan* of Sung China. The first *sŏwŏn* was founded in 1543. The *sŏwŏn* were usually located at rural sites associated with some famous scholar and were commonly endowed by the government. Gradually they replaced the local government schools and even those at the capital as the chief educational institutions of the land.

In their early years the *sŏwŏn* contributed to a great reinvigoration of Confucian scholarship throughout Korea. But soon, by dividing education among family and factional units, they also accentuated the growing factionalism of the bureaucracy. Thus they helped to involve the whole scholar-official class, from the highest officials down to the lowliest student candidates, in the controversies that divided the court.

In the latter part of the sixteenth century much of the bureaucracy became divided into two great factions, known as the "Easterners" and the "Westerners" after the locations of the residences at the capital of their respective leaders. The "Easterners," who may have derived in part from the "Mountain and Forest" tradition, were led by Kim Hyo-wŏn, the "Westerners" by Sim Ŭi-gyŏm. The "Easterners" eventually emerged victorious, but in 1591 split into "Northerners" and "Southerners," with first the latter and then the former in the ascendancy. The victorious "Northerners" then divided into "Great" and "Small" factions. In 1623 they were replaced in power at court by the long quiescent "Westerners." The "Westerners" in turn broke up into several factions, out of which two major groups emerged, the "Old Doctrine" and the "Young Doctrine." Thus the factional pot boiled on, with successful groups constantly splitting apart and defeated groups recouping their strength in retirement.

By the late seventeenth century, however, the factional division had achieved a certain balance among four major groups — a balance which remained fairly constant for the remainder of the dynasty. These four, known as the "Four Colors" (*Sasaek*) — they actually came to wear different-colored clothes — were the "Old Doctrine," the "Young Doctrine," the "Northerners," and the "Southerners." These hardened into hereditary groupings which refused to intermarry and which worked out among themselves a rough apportionment of the numbers of persons who were to pass the official examinations and receive government posts.

ABRIDGED CHART OF YI-DYNASTY FACTIONS

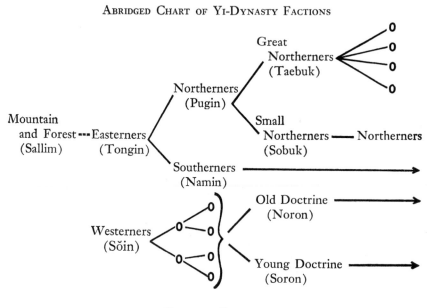

FOREIGN INVASIONS

While the factional struggles were mounting in intensity during the late sixteenth century, disaster struck Korea from abroad in the form of a massive invasion by the Japanese. Until then the Yi dynasty had been relatively free from foreign encroachments. The Ashikaga shoguns, who had established some degree of authority throughout feudal Japan in 1392, the very year that the Yi dynasty was founded, had managed to keep the Japanese pirates somewhat under control. In return, the Koreans had permitted Japanese traders and fishermen to use Pusan and two other southeastern ports as bases for their peaceful activities. Even after the collapse of Ashikaga authority in the late fifteenth century, there were only sporadic conflicts between the overseas Japanese adventurers and the Koreans. For example, there was an outbreak among the Japanese residents in the three open ports in 1510, and this was followed by occasional large-scale piratical attacks on the Korean coast.

In the late sixteenth century centralized control was restored to Japan more thoroughly than ever before, but this time the results for Korea were far different. Hideyoshi, who established his mastery over all Japan in 1590, had the Alexandrian desire for more worlds to conquer. He invited Korea to join him in the conquest of China or to give him free passage. When the Koreans refused, Hideyoshi in 1592 dispatched an army of about 160,000 men to conquer the peninsula as the first step in the achievement of his great plan. The Japanese met with little effective resistance because of the disruption of leadership in Korea, the failure of the Korean government to prepare for the invasion, and the inability of the Korean troops to stand up against the firearms which the Japanese used. Within a month the Japanese had captured the capital. They then fanned out to cover the whole country, except for the extreme southwest. One force even crossed the Tumen River, in the far north, into what is now Manchuria.

The Ming dynasty, however, soon came to the aid of its tributary state, putting heavy military pressure on the Japanese from the north. An even more serious threat to the Japanese was posed by the Korean admiral Yi Sun-sin, a master naval tactician who repeatedly defeated the Japanese naval forces and disrupted their line of supply. His heavier vessels, which because of their ironclad superstructures were known as "turtle ships," are claimed by some to be the world's first armored warships. Guerrilla outbreaks also undermined the Japanese hold on the peninsula. Under these multiple pressures, the Japanese entered into truce talks with the Chinese and before the end of 1593 withdrew to a foothold in the extreme south.

The peace parleys dragged on for three years but without hope of success, since the Japanese assumption that they were the victors in the struggle and the Chinese insistence that Japan must admit vassalage to the Ming prevented any agreement. Hideyoshi, partly because of pique at the condescending tone of communications from China, reopened the war early in 1597, sending a fresh army of about 140,000 men. This time the Japanese met much stronger opposition. Winter had set in before they reached the environs of the capital, and they were forced to withdraw southward again in the face of the elements. The Ming dispatched strong new forces to Korea, but Hideyoshi died just at this juncture, and the Japanese expeditionary force hastily returned home. The Tokugawa shoguns, who came to power in Japan in 1600, restored amicable relations with Korea in 1606, and these continued without a break until the second half of the nineteenth century.

Hideyoshi's great invasions of Korea left little lasting mark on Japan, but their effects on the two other participants were disastrous. These wars seriously strained the faltering Ming and by denuding Manchuria of its garrisons helped to pave the way for the rise of the Manchus. For Korea the invasions were an unmitigated tragedy. The Japanese armies ravaged and despoiled the whole land, and the Chinese armies that came to Korea's aid were not much better. For six years the whole administration and economy were entirely disrupted. The Yi dynasty never fully recovered from the blow.

Recovery was made the more difficult not only by the old problem of factionalism but also by a series of new invasions from a different quarter. Factional disputes, which had temporarily subsided in the face of the Japanese invaders, now revived with renewed intensity. A disaffected member of the "Westerners" faction, who considered that he had been inadequately rewarded for his services in bringing his clique back to power, led a military uprising that swept the northern half of the peninsula in 1624.

The Koreans, as vassals of the Ming, also became embroiled in the Ming wars with the rising Manchu power on the northern frontiers of Korea. In order to secure their flank, the Manchus in 1627 overran northwestern Korea and forced the government into reluctant neutrality. Complete subjugation soon followed. Late in 1636 the Manchu emperor led an army of some 100,000 men across the Yalu. Early in the next year he forced the Koreans to renounce their allegiance to the Ming and become a vassal state of the Ch'ing; but loyalty to the Ming continued strong in Korean hearts for many years.

THE LATER YEARS OF YI RULE

A characteristic feature of the Chinese bureaucratic state had been its need for periodical rejuvenation through a new dynastic start. Korea in the early seventeenth century was in obvious need of such a fresh beginning, but, unfortunately, no new dynasty came to power. The Yi administration dragged on for another three centuries in the conditions of near collapse in which it found itself after the Japanese and Manchu invasions. In fact, instead of improving, conditions tended to deteriorate.

The Long Survival of the Yi Dynasty. Looking at the Yi dynasty from the vantage point of Chinese history, it seems strange that it could have lasted so long. One reason for Korea's clear departure at this time from the normal Chinese dynastic cycle may have been that a badly degenerated bureaucratic state could be maintained longer in a small country like Korea than in a sprawling empire like China. Another reason may have been the fanatical adherence of the Koreans to the borrowed Confucian concepts of loyalty, which made them cling to a dynasty, once it was established, even more faithfully than the Chinese.

A still more fundamental reason for the long survival of the Yi dynasty was probably that the Manchus were content to accept the Yi as a vassal state, thereby providing it with a firm new external prop, whereas, by the very nature of their ambitions, they were committed to destroying the Ming. Perhaps the later Chinese dynasties too would have survived in almost endless decrepitude if it had not been for the ebb and flow of power between foreign invaders and native rulers. The Sung and Ming were both given the *coup de grâce* by alien invaders at a time when their hold over their own populations remained relatively secure. In this sense, paradoxically, it may have been the misfortune of the Koreans that no foreign conquerors hungered for their throne.

In any case, the Yi dynasty was in a sorry state by the seventeenth century, and during the rest of its history never significantly recouped its power. Even the long and relatively strong reigns of Yŏngjo (1724–1776) and his grandson Chŏngjo (1776–1800) saw little, if any, real improvement in the situation. It is true that during this period the officially recorded population climbed to 7,238,522 in 1777 and to a high of 7,561,403 by 1807. Factionalism also subsided somewhat, because the "Old Doctrine" group won a lasting victory over their chief rivals, the "Young Doctrine" faction, and because Yŏngjo and Chŏngjo made strong efforts toward reconciliation. This was also a period of outstanding achievements in literature and scholarship. On the other hand, there was no diminution of social decay and administrative weakness during Yŏngjo's reign.

Economic Decline and Social Discontent. The seriousness of the situation following the Japanese invasions of the 1590's is indicated by the figures on registered taxpaying lands before and after this period. The decline was more than two-thirds during these few years. This was only in part a reflection of loss of life and property during the wars. A more important reason for the drastic decline in taxpaying lands was their illegal transfer, after the Japanese had destroyed the records, into the hands of powerful tax-free landowners. Despite strenuous efforts by the government to regain control of lands lost in this way, tax lands continued to be incorporated into tax-free estates through the machinations of a corrupt bureaucracy.

Such a drastic curtailment of normal tax income necessitated the raising of new types of revenue. This was achieved primarily by establishing new forms of taxation on the remaining public lands. Local tribute, which had once consisted of specialized local products presented to the court, was developed into a heavy grain tax levied in addition to the standard land taxes. Similarly, the old *corvée* services were commuted into a heavy tax levied in textiles, in some cases without actually eliminating the *corvée* services themselves. Since the powerful landowners were able to prevent the application of these new taxes to the slaves and other *ch'ŏnmin* who farmed their estates, the burden was all the more crushing on the remaining peasants who did pay taxes.

Despite these new efforts, the income of the government continued to decline dangerously, with the result that adequate salaries could no longer be paid to government officials and soldiers, and many normal government services were abandoned. Such conditions naturally encouraged corruption and misgovernment on the part of the officials, who increasingly were driven to extort their living from the people over whom they ruled. The central bureaus attempted to check excesses through the use of spies commissioned to ferret out cases of flagrant misgovernment, but their efforts were nullified by the factional divisions within the bureaucracy itself. Factionalism was naturally aggravated by the increasing corruption of government.

An additional sign of political decay was the growing discontent within the official class, resulting primarily from the inadequate pay of its lesser members and the injustices of a corrupt system. The poorer, less powerful members of the class resented the extreme wealth of the top bureaucrats and the royal family. Those who failed in the examinations or did not receive appointment after gaining their degrees resented the success of their more fortunate competitors. The sons of *yangban* fathers born to concubines resented the extreme social and political discrimination which they suffered in strongly class-conscious Korea.

The discontent and misery of the lower classes was, of course, much greater. Ground into hopeless poverty by the exploitation of the government tax collectors or by their own landlords, the common people were the prey of usurious moneylenders, including those of the government. In the stranglehold of a landowner officialdom, the economy remained extraordinarily backward as compared with contemporaneous China or Japan. Most finer manufactured goods continued to be produced by government slaves, and trade was largely oriented toward the needs of the narrow ruling class. Among the people, commerce remained largely restricted to peddlers and market places, where the barest necessities of life could be exchanged by barter.

Worst of all, the inefficient and bankrupt government provided the nation with no protection against bad harvests. As a result, famine was endemic throughout these centuries, and pestilence and disorder followed in the wake of famine. In the single year of 1671 more Koreans are said to have died from famine and disease than during the whole of the Japanese invasions. In 1748, during Yŏngjo's more stable reign, famine reportedly carried off a half million people, and the loss of lives in 1812 was very much greater.

At the same time, civil disorders were growing in frequency and size. Banditry became widespread, and during Yŏngjo's reign there appeared better organized groups of brigands who concentrated on robbing government storehouses. In 1811 the misery of the peasantry and the discontent of the lesser officials coalesced in a great organized revolt that briefly swept northwestern Korea. Again in 1862 large-scale uprisings broke out in rapid succession in both the north and the south.

Christianity and Pressures from the Occident. None of these outbreaks seriously threatened the regime, but a more fundamental challenge had emerged from a new quarter. This was Christianity, which the Koreans called the "Western Learning" (*Sŏhak*). Orthodox Confucianists in Korea naturally looked upon Christianity as subversive, because it brought into question the whole Confucian system of loyalties and ancestor worship on which the state rested.

Roman Catholic doctrines began to penetrate Korea on a significant scale in the second half of the eighteenth century, brought back from Peking by the annual Korean tribute envoys to the Ch'ing. Subsequently Catholicism was spread by Chinese, and later French, missionaries. Many of the discontented lower officials were ready to embrace the new religion. Even some leading Confucian scholars showed interest in Christianity, attracted by the Occidental scientific knowledge that accompanied it. These scholars tended to be men of the disfavored "Southerners" faction, who were also identified with the "Practical Learning" (*Sirhak*) school of Confucian thought. This school had risen in the eighteenth century under the influence of the more realistic "Han Learning," or school of "empirical research," of the Ch'ing, and was fostered by the desire of some scholars to find better answers to the problems of the day than those provided by the fossilized doctrines of Chu Hsi. Such was the specific background of Chŏng Tasan (1762–1836), a leading scholar who showed a keen interest in Christianity and possibly was even a convert.

The intensely conservative government naturally attempted to stop the spread of Christianity. The bringing back of "subversive" books from Peking was proscribed as early as 1786. In 1801 there was a serious persecution in which the leading Chinese missionary was executed and Chŏng Tasan was exiled in disgrace from the court. Other severe persecutions followed in 1839 and 1866. Christianity was forced underground, but it continued to spread.

In the meantime, a new threat had materialized from the Western world. Because Korea was off the main oceanic trade routes and the economy was relatively backward, it had been spared the direct pressure of the Occident that many other Asian countries had felt much earlier. In the late eighteenth century, however, French and English ships began to frequent the Korean coast. By the middle decades of the nineteenth century, Western demands for trade and diplomatic relations were becoming insistent, and coastal incidents involving European or American ships had become an almost annual occurrence.

Korean Resistance to Change. The Koreans, however, seem to have remained on the whole strangely unmoved and unchanging despite these foreign pressures and the long centuries of inefficient government and social disruption. In many ways Korea in the nineteenth century was little different from what it had been two centuries earlier. The continuing erosion of the government and the social order had been a slow, hardly perceptible process, and on the surface government, society, and the economy remained seemingly unchanged. The meager lives of the common people and the cultural activities of the scholar-bureaucrats followed the timeworn paths established by their ancestors. The scholars in the "Practical Learning" tradition showed refreshing interest in native Korean studies, but otherwise literary and scholarly activity, mostly in the Chinese language, was hardly distinguishable from that of earlier centuries, while the arts and crafts generally held to age-old patterns.

We have already noted the greatly increased social and cultural stability of China between the fifteenth and nineteenth centuries and the slackened pace of institutional change during this period. Yi-dynasty Korea thus followed the Chinese pattern, but here again the Koreans showed this characteristic of early-modern Chinese civilization in extreme form. In China stability and the slowness of change were associated with political strength and social harmony. In Korea there seems to have been less strength and social harmony and greater economic stagnation, political corruption, and, perhaps, even cultural sterility.

The question arises why the extraordinary stability of early-modern Chinese civilization should have been carried to these less desirable extremes in Korea. It would be useless to allege racial or national characteristics as causes of this difference. The dynamism of the Koreans in their earlier history, as well as the conclusions of modern anthropology in general, suggest how meaningless would be any explanation based on racial factors.

A more valid answer might be found in the relative sizes of Korea and China. When applied to a small and culturally uniform country, the highly organized but possibly too rigid Chinese philosophical and political system produced a deadening degree of uniformity, which China was spared because of its greater size, its greater geographical, linguistic, and cultural diversity, and the more rapid change of dynasties resulting from "barbarian" incursions.

A still more important reason for the difference between Korea and China may have been that Confucian philosophy and the Chinese political system had originated with the Chinese but had only been borrowed by the Koreans. The Chinese, as the originators of the whole system, may have retained more capacity for adjustment and innovation. Perhaps they also maintained a clearer realization that basic principles take precedence over external forms. The Koreans, as the borrowers of a ready-made system, seem to have adhered ever more rigidly to the external minutiae. While maintaining strict social cleavages that were the antithesis of Confucian egalitarian doctrines, they adopted Confucian ritual forms with a literalness that far surpassed the Chinese. This literal and sometimes blind acceptance of Chinese ideas naturally proved stultifying to intellectual development. It took even greater courage to be an innovator or iconoclast in Korea than in China itself. Possibly this also applied in some degree to the arts.

Another important factor may have been the orientation of all Confucian thought and, with it, all Korean education toward China and its classical language, rather than toward Korea and the native language. As a result, most Korean minds tended to be drawn away from immediate realities. Even for Chinese minds, the gap between an ideal classical tradition and the facts of an imperfect present must have been hard to bridge; for Koreans, the much greater chasm between the homeland which they saw around them and China's past which they had studied in books proved uncrossable for all but the hardiest intellects. The Koreans had proved brilliantly creative in adapting Chinese civilization in earlier centuries, but in the late Yi dynasty the dead weight of the Chinese language and the heavy hand of China's classical tradition seem to have inhibited all creative endeavor in Korea.

Whatever the reasons, it appears that by the nineteenth century the cultural and political stagnation of the Chinese-type system was much more marked in Korea than in China. Korea stood in much greater need of rejuvenation than its neighbors; and yet for this very reason it was less prepared to undertake changes. Its economy was much more backward; political efficiency was far more eroded; society was more stagnant; and, worst of all, Korean intellectual and cultural creativeness was more dormant. China had achieved a high degree of immobility through inner strength; Korea had become even more immobile, but through inner weakness. The stage had been set for a very bitter century in Korean history.

11

Early Japan: The Absorption
of Chinese Civilization

The Geographical Foundations
of Japanese History

The early history of Japan paralleled that of Korea in many respects, but thereafter the two diverged. While Korea became an interesting variant of the Chinese pattern, Japan became a country which had much in common culturally with China and Korea but contrasted sharply with them in social and political structure as well as historical experience.

These differences between Japan and the other members of East Asian civilization reveal the richness and variety within the cultural area. They are also significant in world history. Many points of contrast between Japan and China happen to be points of resemblance between Japan and the West. Feudalism in Japan is an outstanding example of this. So also is Japan's more rapid modernization during the past century, which has produced closer parallels to the political, economic and social phenomena of the contemporary Occident than are to be found in China or anywhere else in Asia.

Thus, Japanese history offers the most significant variant within East Asian civilization and at the same time provides a fruitful field for comparison with the West. The reasons for these historical parallels with the Occident will be considered in later chapters. It should be noted, however, that they are not unrelated to the reasons for the cultural and historical divergence of Japan from its neighbors.

The Japanese themselves often explain their distinctiveness within East Asia as due to a unique national character, but this actually tells us nothing. It is tantamount to saying that the Japanese are different because they are different. Moreover, there is no reason to believe that the ancient Japanese were any more distinct from the Chinese than were the ancient Koreans. Probably both owed the preservation of their cultural identity, in the sea of Chinese civilization that inundated them, to two main factors: their early cultural substructures, which were very different from that of China, and their agglutinative languages, which were entirely unassimilable by the Chinese language. The greater departure of the Japanese from Chinese norms in later times, however, is explained by factors that do not apply equally well to Korea.

The Influence of Isolation. One chief point of difference between Korea and Japan lies in their respective geographical locations. Japan's position as a relatively remote island country may best explain its distinctive role in East Asian history. The parallels with the British Isles, at the opposite end of the Eurasian land mass, are striking. But the historical isolation of Japan has been considerably greater than that of England. The widths of the straits separating each of these two island nations from the continent, about 115 miles for Japan and only 21 miles for England, offer a good measure of the influence of geographical isolation on their respective histories.

Chinese culture of course influenced Japan less than Korea because of Japan's greater distance from China and the open seas that intervened. Whereas Chinese armies had set up colonies in Korea as early as 108 B.C., Chinese military power and political control never extended to Japan. Whatever cultural influences reached Japan from China naturally came more slowly than to Korea, and usually in more diluted form. As a consequence, the primitive cultural substructure of Japan was less modified and so may have remained more dominant in the later stages of civilization than in Korea.

The surrounding seas also gave Japan comparative freedom from the military pressures that swept the continent. Before their recent defeat at the hands of the United States, the Japanese had only once before in historic times been seriously threatened by foreign invasion, and that was during the thirteenth century. Thus, until the nineteenth century, external pressures penetrated to the islands only sporadically and, for the most part, rather weakly. Japan did not experience the catharsis of foreign conquest and was only rarely stimulated to vigorous response by a foreign challenge. Change came relatively slowly and resulted primarily from internal evolution rather than from external pressure.

Another interesting result of isolation has been the Japanese tendency toward cultural conservation. The old and outmoded were not brushed away by foreign pressures or discarded in the struggle for survival, but could be lovingly preserved alongside the new. This does not mean that the Japanese have been particularly conservative in temperament; they have usually been as interested as most other peoples in innovations and in keeping abreast of styles. But they have, at the same time, shown an amazing capacity for holding on to the old, even when the old was clearly outdated. For example, all the stages of the various religious movements that Japan has known throughout its history appear to be preserved there in one form or another, and at least three major historical phases of the theater exist side by side. Perhaps the most spectacular example of such cultural conservation is the maintenance of a "ruling" family for a millennium after its having relinquished almost all semblance of ruling. It is hard to imagine this happening in a country more subject to foreign pressures.

Still another significant result of Japan's isolation has been an unusual awareness of the historic fact of cultural borrowing. Foreign influences, arriving as they did by ship, could be more easily identified and labeled as such in Japan than in countries into which they seeped less perceptibly across land frontiers. The Japanese developed a strong consciousness of what in their culture had come in historic times from abroad, as opposed to those elements, considered "native," which characterized Japan even at the dawn of recorded history. The result has been a much greater emphasis than in most other countries on the primitive and therefore supposedly "native" elements in the culture. The consciousness of borrowing from abroad has also fostered the myth, both in Japan and elsewhere, that the Japanese, in contrast to other peoples, have been a nation of borrowers, although the truth seems to be that, just because of their isolation, they have independently created a larger part of their own culture than has any other nation of comparable size and cultural development.

Size and Terrain. Japan's geography has been almost as important as its isolation in determining the country's history. Japan is commonly described as a small country, in contrast to China or the United States, corresponding in size as it does to the single state of Montana. A fairer comparison in terms of terrain, climate and productive capacity, however, would be with the combined states of New York, Pennsylvania, Maryland and Virginia. An even better comparison would be with the lands of Western Europe. Japan is smaller than France but slightly larger than the combined Eastern and Western zones of Germany and considerably larger than the British Isles or Italy.

In terms of population Japan has been a relatively large country for

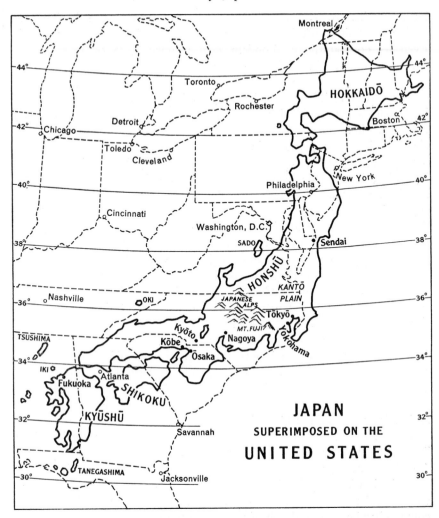

JAPAN
SUPERIMPOSED ON THE
UNITED STATES

many centuries. Its present population of more than ninety million places it fifth in the national groupings of the world. It probably ranked even higher early in the eighteenth century, when it seems to have first reached the thirty-million mark.

Japan's heavy population is all the more remarkable in view of the scarcity of level terrain and natural resources. Most of Japan is composed of rugged mountains, which rise in the central part of Honshū, the main island, to the 10,000-foot peaks of the Japanese Alps and the perfect volcanic cone of Fuji soaring majestically to 12,365 feet above the Pacific. Such mountainous terrain makes Japan a land of great natural beauty but leaves less than a fifth of the area available for agriculture. The soil of Japan, moreover, is relatively infertile and its mountains are poor in minerals. Japan possesses few subsoil riches, having very little oil, iron ore, or other industrially important metals. Even its comparatively abundant coal resources are of poor quality and are found in thin and broken seams.

The Climate. The great size of Japan's population on so small and inadequate a geographical base can be explained only by the extremely favorable climate for agriculture and the intensive nature of East Asian rice farming (see pages 24–25). Plentiful rainfall, a hot sun and a long growing season, together with extraordinary human industry and ingenuity, have made Japan the most productive land per cultivated acre in the world.

Japan's climate closely resembles that of the east coast of the United States, since both lie at the eastern fringe of a great continent. The resemblance extends even to such particulars as Japan's late-summer and early-autumn typhoon season, which is a somewhat more destructive counterpart of the hurricane season in the United States. Similarly, the Japan Current (or Black Current, Kuroshio), which flows northward from the tropics past Japan, corresponds to the Gulf Stream, which flows past the American east coast.

If laid out at the same latitude along the east coast of North America, Japan would stretch from Montreal almost to the Gulf of Mexico. The northern island of Hokkaidō corresponds in latitude and climate to Vermont and New Hampshire, Northern Honshū to Connecticut, New Jersey and Maryland, and the southern two-thirds of the country to the region from Virginia to Georgia.

Because of the surrounding seas, temperatures in Japan tend to be a little more moderate both in winter and in summer than at corresponding American latitudes, and rainfall and humidity are considerably higher. Precipitation is heavy in all seasons, except in the late autumn and early winter, and the snows in the mountainous areas of the northwest coast commonly pile up to a depth of more than ten feet.

Japan's abundant water resources are made even more effective for agriculture by irrigation wherever the terrain permits. Rice is grown in these irrigated areas, and double cropping is practiced wherever the growing season is long enough and the paddy fields can be adequately drained in the autumn for planting. Such double cropping is the rule as far north as the thirty-sixth degree of latitude, a little above Tōkyō.

Heavy rainfall also gives the mountains of Japan a dense cover of timber — a great boon to the Japanese economy. Rainfall and mountains together provide abundant hydroelectric resources, which the Japanese have intensively exploited.

One other advantage to the economy that cannot be measured in terms of land area is the richness of the surrounding seas. A combination of the warm Japan Current with cold currents from the north have made Japanese waters prime fishing grounds, and they are also rich in shellfish and edible seaweeds. Since prehistoric times the Japanese have relied on the sea as the chief source of proteins in their diet. Today Japan's far-ranging fishing fleet has made it the greatest fishing nation in the world.

The Dominance of the Southern Coastal Area. The southwestern half of Japan, where double cropping is possible — and particularly the sunnier, warmer southeastern side of this area facing the Pacific Ocean — has always been the most productive part of the country and, therefore, the center of population and of cultural and political life. A further advantage of this area is the proximity of its western end to the continent, which was the source of most major technological innovations in early times. The predominance of this region has also been heightened by certain features of the local terrain which permitted greater concentrations of agricultural production and closer communications than were possible in the rest of the land.

Japan is made up chiefly of narrow river valleys and small alluvial coastal plains around river mouths, separated from one another by stretches of rugged hills. To go from one of these relatively isolated pieces of agricultural land to another, one must cross mountain passes or make often hazardous coastal journeys around precipitous headlands. Rivers, being for the most part shallow and unnavigable, have played only a minor part in communications. This marked contrast with the broad plains and great navigable rivers of China and the other Asian centers of civilization may help to account for the Japanese divergence from the pattern of centralized rule that has characterized so much of Asia.

Only on the southern side of southwestern Japan are there relatively large areas of agricultural land in fairly easy communication with one another. The Inland Sea, lying between Honshū and the smaller islands of Kyūshū and Shikoku, provides a safe water route between the plains of North Kyūshū, those along the shores of the Inland Sea, and finally the plains of the Kinki, or old capital region, at its eastern end, where the cities of Ōsaka, Kyōto and Kōbe now stand. It was this area from North Kyūshū to the Kinki region that was the central zone of early Japanese history.

A single low mountain pass leads from the Kyōto area to the extensive plain around Lake Biwa and another from there to the even broader plains surrounding the modern city of Nagoya. From there eastward along the coast the terrain becomes more difficult until one reaches the Kantō Plain (Kantō means "East of the Pass"), the largest stretch of agricultural land in Japan. This region, the site of the modern cities of

Tōkyō and Yokohama, became an eastern extension of the central zone of Japan's historical development. Along a fairly narrow line between the Kantō Plain and North Kyūshū lie all of Japan's historic capitals, its six largest modern cities, well over half of its other cities of more than 100,000 population, and a very high proportion of its agricultural and industrial areas.

THE ORIGINS OF THE
JAPANESE AND THEIR CULTURE

Because of their emphasis on the primitive, "native" elements in their civilization, questions of racial origins and prehistoric cultures seem vastly more important to the Japanese than to most other peoples. The average Englishman, for example, might be only mildly interested in the exact mixture of Celts and Teutons in the English population or the nature of the early druidic and Teutonic societies of the British Isles, but to the Japanese the original racial composition and primitive society of Japan loom as subjects of major historical significance.

Our knowledge of the origins of the Japanese, however, is still quite shaky. It is derived from a variety of conflicting sources: the archaeological record, Japanese mythology and historical traditions, early Chinese and, to a lesser extent, Korean accounts of Japan, and such inferences as can be drawn from physical anthropology, ethnological studies and comparative linguistics. The combination of evidence from these various sources produces only a vague and confused picture. Not until the early fifth century A.D. does it begin to come into clear focus, and not until the sixth or seventh century can we see Japan in the full light of recorded history.

Jōmon Culture. Archaeology reveals a series of successive cultures in prehistoric Japan. Recent discoveries suggest that men who still lacked a knowledge of pottery, but whose stone implements resembled those found elsewhere in Northeast Asia, roamed the islands perhaps 6000 or 7000 years ago. The first major Japanese culture, however, spread over the islands about the third millennium B.C. This culture is known as Jōmon and in its earlier stages is classed as Mesolithic (intermediate between Paleolithic and Neolithic), since the Jōmon people made pottery but did not yet practice agriculture. It was closely related to other early cultures which extended throughout the northern woodlands of the world from Finland across Siberia to the northeastern part of the United States. The Jōmon people lived in sunken-pit dwellings and, lacking agriculture, subsisted by hunting and gathering roots, nuts and shellfish. The refuse from the shellfish has left innumerable shell mounds around Jōmon dwelling sites.

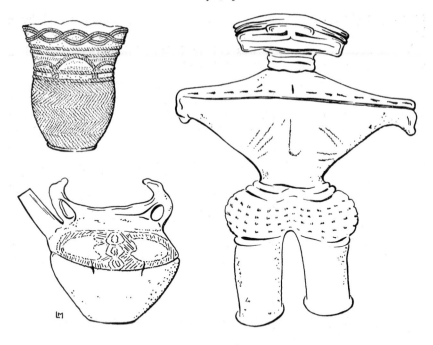

JŌMON CULTURE

The pot in the upper left-hand corner is decorated with a cord design and comb markings. The other two pieces of pottery indicate the imaginativeness of Jōmon designs.

The name Jōmon is derived from the "cord pattern" commonly pressed into the external surface of the pottery that is distinctive to this culture. This pottery was not made on a potter's wheel, but it reveals, particularly in its later phases, great artistic skill and imagination and richness of design unsurpassed by any other Stone Age pottery in the world. The pottery and other artifacts of Jōmon culture show considerable regional variation, particularly between the general eastern and western zones which meet in the mountains between the Kantō Plain and the Kinki region. Jōmon remains are most plentiful in eastern and northern Japan, since the culture lasted longer in these areas.

Yayoi Culture. In about the third or second century B.C. a new culture developed in West Japan, clearly under influences from the continent, and spread rapidly from Kyūshū to the Kantō Plain, displacing the older Jōmon culture. This new culture, named Yayoi after a type site in the city of Tōkyō, is characterized by a more delicately modeled, wheel-made pottery which lacks the rich surface designs of the Jōmon ware. More important, it was distinguished by the presence of agriculture alongside the old hunting and shell-gathering economy and by a knowledge of both bronze and iron.

Yayoi agriculture, which was chiefly irrigated-field rice cultivation, was of Chinese origin. The knowledge of metals too probably stemmed from China, since the earliest metal objects in Yayoi sites seem to be Chinese bronze mirrors and coins of Han date. However, bronze mirrors, swords, spears, halberds and bells were soon being cast in Japan. The bells, known as *dōtaku*, are sometimes four or five feet high and are covered with geometric designs, scenes and figures (they are too thin to have been effectively rung). A few traces of iron implements and weapons and the fact that the bronze weapons were merely ceremonial, since they were too fragile for practical use, indicate that iron came in at about the same time as bronze and, therefore, that Japan had no true Bronze Age.

The Yayoi pottery bears resemblances to some of the prehistoric or early historic pottery in both China and Korea. The practice of agricul-

YAYOI CULTURE

Two typical Yayoi pottery shapes and, on the right, a dōtaku, *or bronze bell, found in Yamato.*

ture and bronze- and iron-working also shows strong continental influence. The culture, however, cannot as yet be attributed to any specific point or points of origin on the continent. Nor is the history of its spread and development within Japan entirely clear. The pottery falls into two principal eastern and western types, which meet in the middle stretches of the Inland Sea. The bronzes divide Yayoi culture into three major areas: a western zone, centering around North Kyūshū, where bronze weapons are common but bronze bells are lacking; a central zone, around the Kinki region and overlapping the western zone in the middle stretches of the Inland Sea, where bronze bells are common; and the Kantō area, which is almost entirely lacking in either bronze bells or weapons.

Although the exact continental provenance of the various elements in Yayoi culture is not known, the place of Yayoi in the continuous stream of Japanese culture is clear enough. Its shell mounds and pit dwellings show a close link with the Jōmon culture. On the other hand, the thatched roofs of these dwellings, as portrayed on the bronze bells, have a shape that is still current in Japan. Even more striking is the identity of the basic Yayoi methods of rice cultivation with those still practiced today. Thus the prehistoric Yayoi culture already displayed certain characteristics of modern Japan.

The Tomb Culture. A new culture was superimposed on the Yayoi around the middle of the third century A.D., but it did not greatly change the agricultural life of the mass of the people. This is called the Tomb culture, because of the huge earthen tumuli and, in its later phases, the large stone burial chambers which typify it. These tombs and most of the other new features of the culture are strongly reminiscent of ancient Korea and its Northeast Asian hinterland. There can be no doubt that the Tomb culture represents new cultural influences from Korea, if not necessarily a wave of new conquerors from the continent; but many features of this culture were probably developed locally. For example, although stone coffins had already come into use in North Kyūshū, opposite Korea, in Yayoi times, real tumuli appeared first in the Kinki region, far eastward from Korea. Only subsequently did they spread to North Kyūshū and still later to the Kantō Plain.

The tombs, as in Korea, indicate a highly aristocratic society, for the men buried in them must have had a large number of workers at their command. The largest of the great earthen mounds are as much as 1500 feet long and 120 feet high, and are surrounded by moats. Some are round or square, but others have a peculiar keyhole shape, square in front and round behind. On many of these mounds are found concentric circles made up of pottery cylinders, known as *haniwa*, some of which are surmounted by figures of men, animals or houses.

The *haniwa* figures, together with the artifacts inside the tombs, reveal a culture marked increasingly by continental traits. The ruling aristocrats were obviously horse-riding warriors, wearing helmets and armor and carrying swords and other iron weapons. Iron tips for plows and other agricultural instruments indicate how extensively iron was used. The hard-fired pottery of this culture is much like that of southern Korea in the same era. The *magatama* or curved jewels found in the tombs are identical with those which decorate the golden crowns of Silla. In fact, the latter may have been imports from Japan and thus may indicate a flow of cultural influences in both directions.

Tomb Culture

Figure a shows a contour sketch above a silhouette of a typical keyhole-shaped tumulus of the early Tomb-culture period. Figure b is a typical pottery shape, not very different from some of the Yayoi period. Figures c and d are haniwa *figures of a saddled horse and an armored man, unearthed in the Kantō area of eastern Honshū.*

a

b

c

d

Although the close contact of the Tomb culture with Korea is beyond dispute, that culture also clearly belongs in the stream of Japanese cultures. In many ways merely a late and more developed phase of the Yayoi, it lasted into the seventh century A.D., thus growing into fully historical Japanese civilization. The greatest concentration of large tombs is in the capital district, at the eastern end of the Inland Sea, and many of the most magnificent tombs are identified, perhaps with good reason, as the tombs of emperors whose names appear in the historic tradition. The present Japanese imperial line undoubtedly dates back to the Tomb-culture rulers, if not to earlier times.

Racial Strains. We know much more about the artifacts of the early Japanese cultures than about the racial composition of the people who created them. It was once assumed that the Yayoi people were the ancestors of the modern Japanese and the Jōmon people the ancestors of the Ainu, a people living at present in isolated regions in Hokkaidō and the islands to the north. The Ainu are of particular interest because their abundant facial and body hair indicates either a proto-Caucasian element in their blood or, more probably, the survival of a primitive human type with a mixture of racial characteristics. Since the historical "barbarians" in North Honshū of the eighth and ninth centuries A.D. were obviously the survivors of people of Jōmon culture and the present Ainu appear to be descended at least in part from these "barbarians," there is some justification for this simple theory. The actual story, however, seems to have been much more complicated.

Physical anthropology raises certain problems. The Jōmon skeletal materials differ from both the modern Japanese and the Ainu. Only in later archaeological levels do the human remains begin to resemble either type very closely. Apparently the modern Japanese and the Ainu evolved only after later racial admixtures, and possibly after certain bodily changes that resulted from altered conditions of life. Furthermore, there was undoubtedly a great deal of intermixture between the two strains.

Ainu blood probably explains why the Japanese usually have more facial and body hair than other Mongoloids, but it does not necessarily explain why they are smaller and somewhat darker than the Northeast Asians to whom they seem most closely tied by archaeological and linguistic evidence. These characteristics point to a Southeast Asian strain in their blood. Ethnographic evidence, based on archaeology and the early Chinese and Japanese records, also suggests that certain of the early Japanese cultural traits may have Southeast Asian rather than Northeast Asian affiliations. And some linguists feel that elements in the Japanese vocabulary show affinities to the languages of Southeast Asia.

Thus we may reasonably assume the existence of a "southern" as well as a "northern" strain in Japan's early racial and cultural composition. But this does not justify the popular theory of migrations conveniently borne by the Japan Current from Indonesia or the Philippines to Japan. Archaeology speaks strongly against this concept. Much more probable was a diffusion of cultural and racial elements from East and South China to two other areas, eastward to Japan and southward to Southeast Asia. But, even assuming the existence of these "southern" traits in primitive Japan, we do not know when or by what route they came there.

Moreover, it should not be forgotten that archaeology points overwhelmingly to a Northeast Asian origin for the various levels of prehistoric culture in Japan and that linguistic evidence indicates that the Japanese language is closely related to Korean and the Altaic languages of North Asia. The Ainu language also seems to have closer affinities to Japanese and the Altaic languages than was at first assumed.

Our confused and conflicting evidence does not allow any very precise hypothesis. All we can say is that the early Japanese, like their prehistoric cultures, were clearly of mixed origins. The early inhabitants of the islands may have included peoples related to those of Southeast Asia; others of Ainu type probably formed at least part of the Jōmon people; and both these strains were probably absorbed for the most part into the later Japanese stock. No doubt Mongoloids from Northeast Asia also inhabited Japan at least by Jōmon times. It seems likely that more people of this type continued to drift into the islands, primarily from Korea, during the Yayoi and early Tomb culture periods, and there is indisputable evidence of migrations of this sort in early historic times. Eventually these Northeast Asians became the predominant stream among the Japanese, if they had not been so from the start, just as Northeast Asian cultural influences gradually predominated and an Altaic type of language became the basis for the historic Japanese language.

Much more important than these vague speculations about racial and cultural origins, however, is the indubitable fact that by historic times the greater part of Japan was inhabited by a racially homogeneous people unified by a common language and culture.

THE FORMATION OF THE JAPANESE STATE

Early Chinese Accounts of the Wa. The early Chinese records add many interesting facts about social and political organization in ancient Japan which could not even be guessed at from the archaeological evidence. The most important of these accounts is found in the *Wei chih*, the section dealing with the Wei dynasty in the official *Account of the Three Kingdoms (San-kuo chih)*, compiled before 297 A.D. Among the sections on peripheral peoples appended at the end of the "Biographies" in this work is a detailed essay on the inhabitants of the Japanese Islands, whom the Chinese then called the Wa,[1] a term which may have had the pejorative connotation of "dwarf."

The *Wei chih* account, which carefully describes the route from the Chinese colonies in Korea by way of the islands of Tsushima and Iki to North Kyūshū, was obviously based on the factual reports of officials or traders who had actually made the journey and seen Japan at first hand. Some of the place names it mentions in West Japan are still in use, and the whole document appears to be highly reliable. Referring to the time of transition between the Yayoi and Tomb cultures, it describes a law-abiding people, fond of liquor, familiar with agriculture, versed in spinning and weaving and expert at fishing, living in a society of strict social differences which were indicated in part by tattooing or other facial and body markings. This last point is apparently corroborated by markings on some of the *haniwa* figures.

The *Wei chih* credits the Wa with a considerable degree of political organization. They are said to have originally been divided into 100 countries, or, as we would call them, tribes. These units reportedly varied in size from 1000 to 70,000 households. Some were ruled over by hereditary kings, others by queens — perhaps indicating a transitional stage from matriarchy to patriarchy.

The "countries" of West Japan are said to have been under the suzerainty of an unmarried queen named Himiko who ruled in Yamatai, but the more distant "countries" beyond Yamatai were independent. Yamatai looks as if it might be a rendition of Yamato, the old capital district of the Japanese emperors, and Himiko probably means "Sun Princess," an appropriate name for a member of a line of rulers who, as we shall see, claimed descent from a Sun Goddess. Unfortunately the distances and directions within the Japanese Islands are obviously incorrect as recorded by the *Wei chih*, and consequently we do not know exactly where Yamatai was located or if Himiko actually was an early Yamato ruler. The stationing of a chief lieutenant of the queen in North Kyūshū, however, checks with the early Japanese records, and the great mound said to have been erected over Himiko's grave corresponds with the tumuli that remain from this period. Her status as a sort of high priestess and the other indications of shamanistic practices among the Wa also fit with what we know from other sources about the early Yamato state.

The *Wei chih* and other Chinese histories indicate that there was a good deal of official intercourse between the ancient Japanese and Chinese. An envoy from the Wa state of Nu is reported to have visited

---

[1] Wo in Chinese. This and the other names from the early Chinese histories are given according to the traditional Japanese phonetic readings of the characters with which they are written.

the Han court in 57 A.D., and a golden seal found in 1789 in North Kyūshū, which seems to read "King of Nu of Wa, [Vassal of] Han," may be the very seal which the Chinese records say was given to this man. The *Wei chih* claims that thirty Wa "countries" were in communication with China and describes in some detail several exchanges of envoys between Himiko and the Wei court between 238 and 247.

The *Sung shu* (*Sung History*), the official account of the Liu Sung dynasty (420–479) of South China, compiled shortly after its fall, describes several embassies that came to the Sung court from what was obviously the emerging Yamato state centered in the Kinki region. The Wa kings mentioned in this *Sung History* seem to be identifiable as specific emperors in the Japanese tradition. They are described as having subjugated to the east fifty-five "countries" of hairy men (presumably Ainu), sixty-six "countries" to the west, and ninety-five across the sea to the north, meaning southern Korea. This is a good indication of the extent of Japanese rule at that time.

The "Kojiki" and "Nihon Shoki." The most important materials bearing on Japanese origins and on the formation of the Japanese state are the early native records, but this is not for reasons of accuracy. The *Kojiki* (*Record of Ancient Matters*) was compiled only in 712 and the *Nihon shoki* (*History of Japan*, also known as the *Nihongi*) in 720. Influenced by eighth-century concepts, the authors of these works obviously reshaped Japanese mythology and historical traditions to enhance the prestige and power of the ruling family and to create a false picture of long centralized rule and a respectable antiquity comparable to that of China. Although reasonably reliable on the later periods, their accounts of the early centuries are almost worthless as history. They are, nonetheless, of immense importance to the student of Japan, not only for their mythological content, but still more because their accounts of the beginning of Japan were accepted as sober fact throughout most of Japanese history — in fact, until quite recently.

The accounts of early history in the *Kojiki* and *Nihon shoki* were woven together out of a variety of myths, legends, genealogies, vague historical memories, and borrowings from Chinese philosophy and history. Frequently the two books flatly contradict each other, or the *Nihon shoki* offers a series of variants of a myth or tradition.

The Japanese creation myths, which are reminiscent of those of Polynesia, seem naïvely crude by modern standards. They concern largely the procreation of the ubiquitous nature deities of ancient Japan. Many of these deities are still worshiped, and some are identified by the ancient records as the ancestors of families prominent in the early historic period.

Among the first deities to emerge were a sister and brother, Izanami and Izanagi, who, descending to earth, gave birth to the islands of Japan and a number of other deities. Izanami died when bearing the Fire God and descended to the lower world, where Izanagi visited her, only to be driven away because of Izanami's mortification at being seen in her putrified state.

A whole new series of deities generated from the clothes Izanagi then discarded and the parts of his body he washed to purify himself after this episode. Among these were a Sun Goddess called Amaterasu, a Moon God, and another deity, named Susa-no-o, who seems to have embodied the destructive forces of nature. Mounting to the Plain of High Heaven, Amaterasu and Susa-no-o together produced another series of divinities.

When Susa-no-o subsequently damaged the rice fields of his sister, the Sun Goddess, and fouled her residence with excrement, she hid in a cave, darkening the world. The myriad deities eventually lured her forth by the sound of merriment and a lewd dance performed by one of the feminine deities. This whole episode is obviously a solar eclipse myth. The assembled deities then banished Susa-no-o to earth, where he became the progenitor of the rulers of Izumo on the north coast of West Honshū. The story of Susa-no-o going to Korea and of his finding there a sword in the tail of a dragon may reflect the early introduction of iron weapons to this region, which lies opposite the coast of Korea.

Although archaeology does not indicate that Izumo was a major cultural center, the Great Shrine of Izumo, the second most important shrine in Japan, may be the survival of a major political center there, and the cycle of legends centering around Susa-no-o and his descendants the remnants of the myths of its rulers. The importance of the Izumo rulers at some time in the shadowy past is suggested by the care with which the early Japanese records establish intermarriages between the Izumo line and that descending from the Sun Goddess, the surrender of the former to the latter, and the subsequent establishment of the worship of the Izumo gods by the sun line.

The Founding of Japan by the Sun Line. The sun line was founded by Ninigi, a grandson of the Sun Goddess, who descended from heaven to Kyūshū. The cycle of myths about him and his descendants deals in part with North Kyūshū, which we know from archaeology was a major cultural center and the chief point of contact with the continent, but most of the legends are localized in Hyūga in southeastern Kyūshū. This region does have some early tumuli, but, since it faces eastward and its name means "Facing the Sun," it may have entered the mythology as a cult spot for these sun-worshiping people rather than as a major political center.

Ninigi is said to have brought with him to earth the Three Imperial

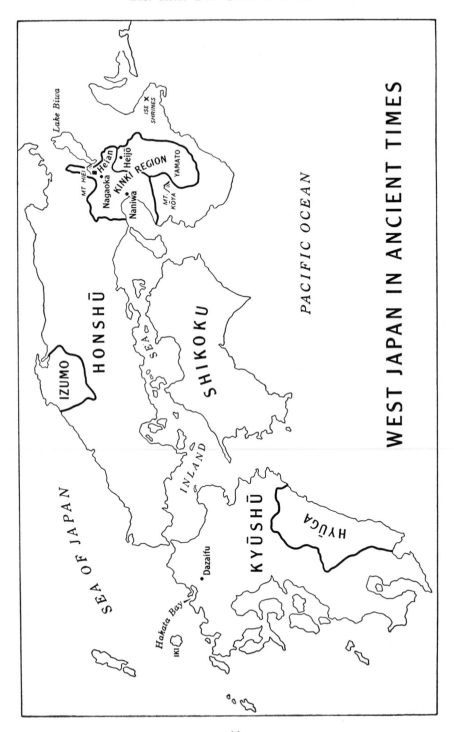

WEST JAPAN IN ANCIENT TIMES

Regalia, which are still the symbols of imperial authority in Japan. These are a bronze mirror (the symbol of the Sun Goddess), Susa-no-o's iron sword, and a curved jewel (*magatama*). It is worth noting that these three symbols, all of which we know from archaeology were of Chinese or Northeast Asian origin, are plentiful in the remains of the Tomb culture and are found even in Yayoi sites.

According to mythology Ninigi's great-grandson moved with a large force from Kyūshū up the Inland Sea to the Kinki region, where, after conquering the local deities, he founded the Japanese state in 660 B.C in Yamato, the area centering around the Nara Plain a short distance inland from Ōsaka. He and the "emperors" who followed him appear in the early records under long Japanese names, but they are best known to history under the Chinese type of posthumous titles later assigned to them. The title for this legendary founder of the imperial line is Jimmu ("Divine Warrior").

There may be some historical validity in the genealogy of the imperial line extending all the way back to Jimmu. Many peoples have maintained accurate genealogies by oral tradition over many generations. The dates assigned to the early Japanese rulers, however, are entirely fictitious. It seems probable that the date of 660 B.C. was arbitrarily selected in about 601 A.D. by counting back 1260 years — a period which, according to Chinese concepts, constituted a major cycle of history. The first seventeen rulers (including the feminine regent, Jingō) reportedly spanned 1060 years, and three are credited with reigns of 100 years or more. By way of contrast the next seventeen rulers, who for the most part appear to have been historical, covered only 126 years.

The events attributed to the reigns of these early rulers are almost equally suspect. Much of the detail merely establishes the descent of prominent families of early Japan from the imperial line, perhaps in an effort to insure their loyalty. Very few events are recorded under the reigns of the first nine rulers, except for Jimmu himself. Thereafter the record becomes fuller, but not much more plausible. Apparently certain events of the fourth or early fifth century A.D. appear in the Japanese chronicles predated by 120 years, that is, by two small Chinese cycles of sixty years. Not until about 400 A.D. can much credence be given to either the dates or the events in the Japanese records.

The Expansion of the Yamato State. The story of Jimmu's conquest eastward, together with an account of a similar conquest dated in the third century A.D., may reflect dim memories of a movement of conquering peoples from Kyūshū up the Inland Sea, which would be perfectly consistent with the archaeological record. The legends of conquest outward from Yamato, however, probably have more historical validity. There are several stories of the conquest of the "barbarians" of

Kyūshū. We know that the peoples of South Kyūshū were still considered semi-"barbarian" as late as the seventh century, although archaeology gives no indication that they were racially or even culturally very distinct from the other early Japanese.

The most interesting conquest legends center around Prince Yamato-takeru, who, after subduing the Kyūshū "barbarians," supposedly around 100 A.D., also subjugated the "barbarians" of the Kantō Plain. The *Sung shu* confirms that conquests like his had definitely taken place by the middle of the fifth century, and the *Wei chih* indicates that some of these conquests may date back at least two centuries earlier. It is not clear, however, why a group centered on Yamato won out over comparable groups in other parts of Japan, unless it was because of Yamato's strategic central location, together with the relatively large size of the plains of the Kinki region and their easy adaptability to rice cultivation.

The sun-worshiping descendants of the Sun Goddess located their chief shrine, dedicated to her, at Ise on a promontory east of Yamato looking eastward out to sea. The Great Shrine at Ise is still the most important shrine in all Japan. According to tradition, the sacred mirror was removed from the court and installed at Ise in 5 B.C. under the supervision of a princess appointed as High Priestess. However, if the Himiko of the *Wei chih* really was one of the Yamato rulers, as seems quite possible, this partial separation of the religious and political functions of the ruling line probably came after her time.

The Japanese records have an Empress Jingō serving as regent from 200 to 269 A.D. We cannot identify Jingō with Himiko, as many have done, since we cannot be sure that Himiko was a Yamato ruler. But the prominence of an empress in the native tradition, the feminine origin of the ruling line, and the presence of a High Priestess at the leading national shrine all corroborate the *Wei chih* account of early feminine rule in Japan.

The legend that Jingō conquered Korea in the first year of her regency seems to reflect some historical fact. The Korean histories indicate that in the fourth century the Japanese actually did have a foothold in Kaya (or Mimana) on the south coast, and the Koguryŏ stele of 414 can be interpreted as proof of their activity in South Korea at that time. Possibly the people of Kaya were culturally close to the ruling groups in Japan, who may themselves have migrated to Japan from Korea not long before. The Kaya people thus may have recognized Japanese suzerainty in order to obtain the support of their Japanese kinsmen in their conflicts with the three larger states that were then rising in the peninsula. In any case, the Japanese foothold in Korea was maintained until clearly historical times. Narrowed by revolts and depredations by its neighbors in the late fifth and early sixth centuries, this holding was not totally destroyed by Silla until 562. The Japanese kept on attempting to restore it until their defeat in 663 at the hands of a T'ang force in Korea, and the subsequent unification of the peninsula by Silla after 668.

Scribes from the Korean state of Paekche seem to have been installed at the Japanese court about 400 A.D. to keep records in Chinese. As a result, the chronology and records achieve a degree of credibility from about that time, and the whole historical picture begins to come into focus. The Yamato "emperors" of the *Kojiki* and *Nihon shoki* are clearly the fifth-century Wa rulers described in the *Sung shu* as exercising political control from the Kantō area to south Korea, and the great tumuli of the Kinki region are undoubtedly their tombs. Since their direct lineal descendants still occupy the Japanese throne, the Japanese imperial family, which emerged into the light of history in the fifth century, is by far the oldest ruling line on earth.

The Japanese rulers of the fifth and sixth centuries were apparently a lusty, brawling lot, and succession wars seem to have been the rule rather than the exception. This state of affairs can be explained by the lack of any clear system of inheritance among the many offspring of the polygamous rulers, and also by the custom of passing the throne from brother to brother. As a result, the reigns of these centuries averaged only about seven years in length, though erroneous repetition of some of the rulers' names in the records may partly account for their apparently excessive number and short reigns.

THE UJI SYSTEM

Although the Yamato rulers exercised some authority all the way from the Kantō Plain to South Korea, it would be a mistake to think of them as ruling over a centralized state. Japan at this time consisted of a large number of semi-autonomous units called *uji*. These have sometimes been compared to the Scottish clans, though they did not resemble "clans" in the sociological sense of exogamous sub-groups of a tribe. The Japanese *uji* were probably the outgrowth of the sub-units which comprised the old tribal "countries" described in the *Wei chih*. The members of each *uji* considered themselves to be of common descent, and, under their *uji* chief they worshiped a common *uji* deity, who in some cases, as in the imperial line, was considered to be the original ancestor.

As the *uji* grew in size and complexity, some developed subsidiary units, comparable to the "corporations" of late Roman times, to perform specific economic functions or other services. These units, usually called *be* (or *tomo*, "attendants"), were also hereditary groups, organized like *uji* under their own chiefs, even though they were made up of persons with no blood relationship. At the bottom of *uji* society were a few slaves, but these were of little economic importance compared with the "corporations."

The Yamato rulers were simply the chiefs of the Yamato *uji*, which had extended its control by conquest over the others. If Himiko was a ruler of this line, the process of conquest had already started by the third century. The *Sung shu* shows that by the fifth century the Yamato rulers claimed suzerainty over 121 units in Japan alone.

The extension of Yamato power seems to have been achieved largely by the incorporation of many lesser *uji* into the Yamato group and by the creation of a great number of subsidiary "corporations." For example, the Yamato group included the two prominent military *uji* of the Ōtomo ("Great Attendants") and the Mononobe ("Corporation of Arms"), as well as certain groups with religious functions, such as the Nakatomi ("Medium Ministers"), the Imibe ("Corporation of Abstainers"), and the Urabe ("Corporation of Diviners"). There were also many other lesser economic or service groupings, such as the Oribe ("Corporation of Weavers") and the Kataribe ("Corporation of Reciters"). All such units were agriculturally self-supporting, whatever the nature of their service to the throne. In addition, the many corporations of purely agricultural workers — usually created in memory of a member of the imperial family — helped extend the direct agricultural holdings of the Yamato rulers, often at the expense of the local *uji*. Since at this time land was more plentiful than people, wealth was measured by the number of such workers under one's control rather than by the extent of land owned.

With the passing of time the system became both more complex and more confused. Various traditional titles used by the chiefs of the *uji* and the "corporations" came to represent strictly graded ranks of nobility, which the ruler could confer or withdraw. These titles were known as *kabane*, a word probably related to the "bone" in the "Bone Ranks" of Silla. In this emerging nobility, the *uji* and the "corporations" belonging to the Yamato group, being close to the source of political authority, naturally outranked the others. Those among the sub-units of the Yamato group which could claim to be offshoots of the imperial line usually sported the title of *Omi*, while *Muraji* was used for the most important sub-units that had been of independent origin and, therefore, claimed to be the descendants of heavenly gods who had joined the sun line in its conquest of Yamato or the descendants of earth gods who had submitted to Jimmu. There were other *kabane* in common use among the less important sub-units of the Yamato group and similar titles for the leaders of the various local *uji*.

By the fifth century the central regime had become so complex that in each reign a leading *Omi* and a leading *Muraji* were appointed as Great *Omi* (*Ō-omi*) and Great *Muraji* (*Ō-muraji*) to supervise the other members of their respective categories. The chiefs of the military *uji* of the Ōtomo and the Mononobe monopolized the post of Great *Muraji*, and in the sixth century the post of Great *Omi* fell into the hands of the Soga family.

These powerful *uji* overshadowed the imperial line itself, and the rivalries between them came to dominate the court. In fact, by the sixth century the Yamato "emperors" had become to some extent the symbolic source of legitimate authority rather than actual rulers. This characteristic of the Japanese throne grew more marked in later periods. Undoubtedly the tradition of emperors who reigned but did not rule helps account for the survival of the imperial line.

Immigrants from Korea. One important reason for the growth of the Yamato state and for its political and cultural development during the fifth and sixth centuries was the steady immigration from the Korean peninsula to the capital district. Many of the people came as large and well organized groups, whose leaders took a prominent place in the Yamato aristocracy since they possessed skills and knowledge which were highly prized in relatively backward Japan. This flow of immigrants no doubt was facilitated by the Japanese foothold in south Korea and was further stimulated by the great wars in the seventh century that led to the unification of Korea. It continued on a significant scale until the early ninth century.

A high percentage of these Korean immigrants boasted Chinese rather than Korean ancestry, by which they probably meant to claim ultimate descent from the Chinese of the Han colonies in Korea. For example, the great Hata *uji* of weavers, who came originally from Korea, had a name which literally means "loom" but was written with the character for the Ch'in dynasty of China. The great importance of the Korean immigrants in the Yamato aristocracy is indicated by a book of noble genealogies compiled in 815 (the *Shinsen shōjiroku* or *New Compilation of the Register of Families*), which attributes foreign origins to more than a third of the 1182 families of the central nobility of the period.

Primitive Shintō. The Japanese records make clear that the early Japanese "emperors," like Himiko of the *Wei chih* account, served a dual function — as high priest and as secular ruler. In fact, there was little distinction between the performance of the *uji* chief's ritualistic, religious activities and his rule over his people. The early Japanese word for government, *matsurigoto*, literally means "worship"; and *miya* means both "palace" and "shrine." Despite the sharing of religious functions with the High Priestess of Ise sometime in the shadowy past, the Yamato ruler retained a major sacerdotal role as the high priest of what grew from an *uji* cult into a national cult. His present successor on the Japanese throne still retains these ancient priestly functions.

The religion of the primitive Japanese was at first nameless, but later it came to be called Shintō to distinguish it from Buddhism and from Chinese religious ideas. Shintō is a name of Chinese origin which means the "Way of the Gods." In the early Japanese records Shintō appears primarily as a conglomeration of local cults skillfully integrated through the official mythology to establish the supremacy of the Yamato cult of the Sun Goddess and the subordinate relationship of the cults and chieftains of the other *uji* to those of Yamato. The formal organization of these many local cults had spread so far by the eighth century that of the more than 3000 officially recognized and graded local shrines about one-fourth were supported by the government. This system of official ranking of the many Shintō shrines was continued in one form or another until the end of the Second World War.

Beneath this officially organized series of cults, however, lay a much broader and deeper religious current. Shintō was basically a simple nature worship, of which the organized mythology and officially recognized cults were merely a surface manifestation. In the face of the wonders of nature, the early Japanese attributed deity to all its more awesome manifestations, whether such manifestations happened to be waterfalls, mountains, great trees, unusual rocks or even pestiferous vermin. Even today a freshly built box-like shrine on a mountaintop or a sacred straw rope around the trunk of a giant tree shows that this elementary Shintō concept is still very much alive. The fertility of nature in particular attracted worship. A number of fertility festivals are among the most important in the Shintō calendar; the shrines to Inari, the God of Rice, symbolized by his messenger, the fox, are the most numerous throughout the land; and signs of phallic worship are still sometimes to be found.

Shintō deities of all types were called *kami*, a word which in origin means nothing more than "superior." *Kami*, only rarely represented in human form, are usually symbolized by such objects as mirrors, swords or *magatama*, whenever the original object of worship, such as a tree or a waterfall, is not present.

Moreover, as we have seen, the mythology identified many of the deities with progenitors of the *uji*; in time other mythological or historical figures joined their ranks. With the rising prestige of the imperial line, the emperors themselves came to be regarded as *kami*, and some early emperors, as well as certain fully historical personages of more humble origin, eventually became prominent members of the pantheon. Thus the so-called divinity of the Japanese emperors amounts to only a faint echo of what the Western or Islamic worlds mean by that term.

Despite the involved mythology associated with it, Shintō had no organized philosophical system, nor even a clear moral code. It stressed ritual purity rather than ethical virtue. Ritual impurity, caused by such things as physical dirtiness, sexual intercourse, menstruation, childbirth, wounds and death, was to be overcome by exorcism, cleansing ceremonies or ritual abstention. Members of the priestly class who performed the various rites or served as mediums and diviners probably represented the Japanese variant of the shamans of Korea and Northeast Asia. The modern Japanese fondness for cleanliness seems to hark back to these primitive concepts of ritual purity, which may have led to the development of the hot-spring bathing and deep-tub hot baths which are among the pleasantest features of modern Japanese culture.

Shintō, lacking any moral sense of guilt or sin, is an essentially cheerful, sunny religion. Unlike the Koreans, who came to concentrate on the menacing aspects of nature, the Japanese emphasized its beauty and bountifulness. The major historical shrines are often situated in places of great natural beauty or stand in man-made forests of magnificent trees. Some, like the great shrine at Ise, though constantly rebuilt, still reflect the clean, simple lines of primitive Japanese architecture of about the sixth century. (See Plate 49.) Even the countless small village shrines, under their towering trees, are usually places of quiet charm. The *torii*, a gateway consisting merely of two uprights and one or two crossbeams, stands in front of all shrines, both great and small. (See page 450.)

Worship at Shintō shrines has always been simple, usually amounting to no more than clapping the hands, bowing and making a small offering. Offerings consist of food, sake (the fermented rice wine of Japan), cloth, strips of paper (usually tied to sacred branches), or, in more modern times, money. The local shrine festival is a gay carnival. Food and amusement booths are set up on the approaches to the shrine, sake flows freely, and the young men of the community, often in boisterous intoxication, take the local deity for an outing in a portable shrine carried on their shoulders to visit and purify the individual homes in the neighborhood.

Shintō unquestionably is a primitive religion when compared with the great faiths of Asia and Europe. Its beliefs, attitudes and practices, however, have remained a major ingredient of Japanese culture until modern times. Shintō together with strong patterns of hereditary, aristocratic social organization were basic elements of fifth and sixth century Japanese society that survived the subsequent cultural inundation from the continent to help shape the Japan of later days.

The Adoption of the Chinese Pattern

As archaeology reveals in the bronze mirrors and coins found in the Yayoi sites, Chinese culture began to influence Japan even in the prehistoric period. The Chinese histories prove that there was direct contact between Japan and China as early as the first century A.D., and the steady flow of people into the islands from Korea, an area permeated with Chinese influence, did a great deal to spread the higher continental civilization. The Chinese writing system was known to the Japanese at least by the fifth century, and the very formation of the Yamato state may have been inspired by the example of the centralized empire of China.

Slow cultural borrowing thus had gone on for a long time, but in the middle of the sixth century the Japanese began to be consciously aware of the process. By the early seventh century the volume of borrowing had become so great as to mark the start of a new age in Japanese history.

Probably there were several reasons for this rather sudden change. The Japanese by this time seem to have attained a cultural level that made them capable of adopting sophisticated Chinese civilization more easily and thoroughly than before. Another reason may have been the increasing inadequacy of Japan's loose and confused *uji* system of political organization. According to this system, the Yamato ruler was merely a *primus inter pares*, and the central state exercised only a tenuous control over its own sub-units, to say nothing of the more distant *uji*. For example, a powerful magistrate in North Kyūshū, which the tumuli show was a major center of power, succeeded in about 527 in blocking a Yamato army dispatched to Korea, and the court was constantly torn by conflicts between the more powerful *uji* within the Yamato group. Obviously, a more efficient and centralized system of government was needed.

The political situation within China itself may have been another important factor. As we have seen, the Sui reunited the empire in 589 and in 618 the vigorous T'ang dynasty began its rule. A united, successful imperial China exercised much greater powers of attraction than had the divided and semi-"barbarian" China that had preceded the Sui.

Buddhism. The first element in Chinese civilization to be consciously borrowed by the Japanese was Buddhism. This may have been because the sixth-century Japanese could readily understand the supposed magical qualities of Buddhism as a cult even more powerful than those of the native deities, though its philosophy remained beyond them. In any case, the presentation by Paekche of a gilt-bronze image and sutras, in an effort to win Japanese support against Silla, started a debate at the Yamato court over the desirability of admitting the foreign religion. (The traditional date for this incident, given as 552 in the *Nihon shoki*, should probably be revised to 538.)

The Nakatomi, as might be expected of an *uji* of Shintō ritualists, opposed Buddhism. The Mononobe *uji* of warriors joined them in this conservative stand, but the Soga, who were the Mononobe's rivals both for power at court and as the champions of a strong policy against Silla in Korea, supported the new religion. The Soga were allowed to worship the image privately, but when an epidemic subsequently broke out the image was judged to be the cause and was cast into a canal. This story, even to the casting of images into a canal, was repeated around 585, when the Great *Omi*, Soga no Umako,[2] carried out a larger experiment in Buddhist worship with monks and nuns of Korean origin.

Despite this second failure, however, Buddhism was soon officially adopted by the court. The emperor, who was Umako's nephew, became a convert just before his death in 587. In the subsequent war of succession, the Soga, supported by the military Ōtomo *uji*, destroyed the power of the Mononobe and the Nakatomi. The victory was attributed to the superior efficacy of Buddhism, and thenceforth the new faith was unchallenged at court, even though the Japanese neither then nor later felt any need to abandon their native cults just because a foreign religion had been adopted.

The Soga and Prince Shōtoku. The victory of 587 also made the Soga supreme. For the next half century they completely dominated the central government of Japan and saw to it that the throne was occupied by members of the imperial family born of Soga mothers. Umako placed another of his nephews on the throne, but he fell out with this puppet and had him murdered in 592. He then enthroned his niece as the Empress Suiko. Suiko's nephew, Prince Shōtoku, who was half of Soga blood and married to a Soga lady, served as regent (*sesshō*) for his aunt and apparently exercised even greater authority than Umako.

The triumph of the pro-Buddhist faction at court and the conscious adoption of such an important aspect of continental civilization seems to have opened the floodgates to further borrowing under the vigorous leadership of Prince Shōtoku, who was not only an extremely able man but also a devout Buddhist with a real understanding of Buddhist philosophy. In addition, he was well versed in other aspects of Chinese civilization and apparently was determined to transplant the Chinese political system to Japan as rapidly as the backward island country could absorb it.

In 604 Prince Shōtoku issued what is known as the "Seventeen-Article Constitution."[3] Actually this amounted to nothing more than

[2] In Japan, as in China and Korea, the given name follows the surname, but in ancient times the given name was bound to the surname by the genitive postposition *no*. Thus Soga no Umako would correspond to Umako of Soga.

[3] Even if this document is a later forgery, as some claim, it appears to represent Shōtoku's ideas.

a set of precepts for the ruling class, but nonetheless it contained revolutionary doctrines of the greatest importance in Japanese history. In place of the strictly hereditary and divided *uji* system, it set up Confucian ethical concepts and the centralized political institutions of China as the ideal in government.

One article in Shōtoku's "Seventeen-Article Constitution" enjoins reverence for the "three treasures" of Buddhism: the Buddha, the "law" and the monastic communities. The other articles, however, read like a Confucian tract. The unique supremacy of the emperor is made clear: "A country does not have two lords; the people do not have two masters." Local leaders are specifically denied the right to levy taxes or exact *corvée* services. The ideal of a bureaucratic hierarchy of meritorious officials is extolled together with such Confucian virtues as harmony, decorum (*li*), sincerity, diligence, justice and public service.

In 604 Shōtoku also adopted the Chinese calendar, an important political act by Chinese standards, and about this time, as we have seen, the year 660 B.C. was chosen as the date when the Japanese state had been founded. A more important innovation was the institution of a system of twelve ranks for court officials in 603. Named after the Confucian virtues and identified by the colors of caps to be worn, these ranks constituted a revolutionary departure from the old system of purely hereditary posts and honors, for they implied a bureaucracy of merit appointed by the ruler.

The court rank system, in fact, became a major feature of the Chinese type of bureaucratic government that the Japanese developed during the course of the following century. It was repeatedly revised after Shōtoku's death but early in the eighth century finally achieved the form it was to maintain until modern times. All officials were divided into eight numbered ranks; these were further divided into "senior" and "junior" classes, while the classes from the fourth rank on down were still further divided into "upper" and "lower" grades. Every post in the government was made to correspond with one of these ranks, from the "Senior First Rank" down to the "Junior Eighth Rank Lower Grade." In addition, there was a separate set of imperial ranks for members of the ruling family. The precedence of court ranks over the old hereditary *kabane* titles was assured in 684 by the adoption of a new system of titles assigned by the court, in which *Omi* and *Muraji*, originally the highest titles, ranked sixth and seventh out of eight.

Embassies to China. Another of Shōtoku's major innovations was the sending of an embassy to the Sui in 607, the first Japanese mission to China since the fifth century embassies recorded in the *Sung shu*. After returning the next year accompanied by a Chinese ambassador, the Japanese envoy went again to China in 608, and Shōtoku dispatched still a third mission to the Sui in 614. After the T'ang supplanted the Sui, the Japanese continued to send embassies, and thirteen more succeeded in reaching China between 630 and 838.

In the messages which Shōtoku sent to the Chinese emperor he revealed his ambition to make Japan into a centralized empire like China. The first message he addressed from "the Son of Heaven in the land where the sun rises" to "the Son of Heaven in the land where the sun sets." His second was from "the Emperor of the East" to "the Emperor of the West." The Chinese, of course, refused to tolerate such presumptuous claims of equality by the eastern "barbarians." It should be noted, however, that about a century later their somewhat contemptuous name of Wa for the Japanese began to go out of use, to be replaced by a term that reflected the country's geographical location and perhaps the sun worship of its ruling line. This name was Nihon or Nippon, "the Source of the Sun," which in its Chinese form of Jih-pen gave rise to our word Japan.

The importance to the early Japanese of their embassies to China can be judged from the cost and size of these expeditions and the extreme perils they braved. By the eighth century it had become customary to provide each embassy with four newly constructed ships, and perhaps 500 or 600 men at a time set sail in the later of these diplomatic armadas. The trip to China was at best dangerous in the stormy northern seas, and especially so at a time of still primitive navigation, before the invention of the compass. The worsening of relations with Silla increased the difficulties. Silla had earlier accepted a position of inferiority in her diplomatic contact with Japan but in the eighth century began to insist on a status of equality. Quarrels resulted, and Korean waters became unsafe for Japanese ships. As a result, the Japanese embassies early in the eighth century began to avoid Korea and sail directly to China, 500 miles across the open sea. No embassy made this hazardous round trip without serious losses. The clerical diarist Ennin, who accompanied the last embassy to the T'ang, gives us a graphic and detailed picture of the hardships and shipwrecks he encountered on this journey.

The value of these missions, however, made the undertakings worthwhile despite their great cost and peril. This value lay neither in diplomatic accomplishments nor in the resulting incidental trade, but, rather, in the cultural and technological advances that were brought about by the missions. All sorts of students accompanied the embassies — young Buddhist monks, scholars of the Chinese classics, painters, musicians, junior government officials, and the like. These men, after studying in China during the year of the embassy's stay there — or possibly for many years longer — returned to Japan to become the major exponents of Chinese culture and technology. How well they fulfilled their task is clearly illustrated in the field of music: the orchestral music of T'ang China has been preserved by the Japanese court musicians, though it has been entirely lost in China itself.

The students who went with the embassies to China were joined in this cultural work by others, who made the trip in private merchant ships. Immigrant Koreans and a few Chinese Buddhist missionaries also played a part. Frequent diplomatic contact continued between Japan and Korea until the ninth century, and no fewer than thirty-three trade missions arrived in Japan between the years 727 and 927 from the state of P'o-hai in Manchuria. The embassies to China, however, remained the chief source of knowledge of Chinese civilization, and the years 607 to 838, during which sixteen missions went to China, constitute a major epoch in Japanese history.

The Taika Reforms. Shōtoku during his lifetime set up the ideal of Chinese centralized rule and laid the foundations for its achievement, but after his death in 622 the Soga did little to complete his work. Soga no Emishi, who succeeded his father as Great *Omi* in 626, became all-powerful at court, and he and his son Iruka began to assume imperial prerogatives for themselves, thus indicating possible designs on the throne. In 643 Iruka even destroyed Prince Shōtoku's heir as a possible threat to his own ambitions.

Such highhanded conduct, however, built up opposition to the Soga. The lead was taken by Nakatomi no Kamatari and an imperial prince (Naka-no-ōe) who was later to reign as the Emperor Tenchi (661–671). These two in 645 eliminated Iruka and Emishi in a *coup d'état* and took over control of the government themselves. Kamatari, as a reward for his services, was given the new surname of Fujiwara, becoming the progenitor of a line of nobles that was later to dominate the court completely.

Kamatari and Tenchi at once embarked upon a second great attempt to adopt Chinese forms of government. This effort, based as it was on Shōtoku's preparatory work, was able to go far beyond his achievements. Students who had returned from the Chinese embassies that Shōtoku had instituted played a large role in these reforms. Tenchi and Kamatari themselves sent five embassies to China between 653 and 669. The very fact that the head of the Nakatomi *uji* of Shintō ritualists, which had opposed Buddhism so bitterly in 587, was now the leader in this new attempt to Sinicize the government indicates how great a change in attitudes had taken place in a mere half century as a result of Shōtoku's pioneering work.

The great reforms of Kamatari and Tenchi are known as the Reforms of Taika (*Taika no kaishin*), from the name of the Chinese-type "year period," Taika or "Great Change," which they adopted. The Chinese practice of counting time by arbitrary "year periods" (*nengō* in Japanese) had already been imitated a few times in the preceding half century, but it did not become firmly established in Japan until 701.

In 646 the new leaders issued an imperial edict abolishing all the great private holdings of land and of agricultural workers and establishing in their place various aspects of the early T'ang system of landholding and government. The major innovations were provincial administrations under appointees of the central government, the allotment of land to peasants in accordance with carefully kept census records, a nation-wide system of government roads provided with post stations and controlled at barriers, and a uniform system of taxes (see pages 158–161 and 167).

Naturally, all these great reforms could not be achieved overnight. In fact, the edict of 646 probably amounted to a sort of "fifty-year plan," and it was carried out bit by bit over the next several decades, and only after many compromises with native institutions and ideas. But Japan was now definitely committed to the Chinese political and economic pattern, and there was no turning back. The government was gradually transformed into a small and not entirely imperfect replica of the T'ang.

THE GOVERNMENT OF THE NARA PERIOD

We do not know all the steps by which the Taika Reforms were achieved, no doubt against considerable opposition from the conservative forces. It was not until the beginning of the eighth century that the resulting Chinese type of government took definite shape. During the following century the borrowed institutions seem to have operated with their greatest efficiency, and consequently the so-called Nara period, 710 to 784, when the capital was located in what is now the city of Nara in Yamato, is considered the height of the epoch of Sinicization in Japanese history.

The Nara and Heian (Kyōto) Capitals. The very establishment of the capital at Nara represented a major step toward the creation of the new pattern. Hitherto both the economy and the political administration had been so simple as to require no true capital city. Imperial princes had lived on their own agricultural estates. When one of them was selected to be emperor, he normally made his own residence the capital, in place of that of his predecessor. Such constant shifts of the center of government may also have been encouraged by Shintō concepts of ritual impurity, according to which the death of a ruler defiled his residence. The primitive and impermanent nature of Japanese architecture at that time may have been another factor. In any case, the capital had been moved freely from reign to reign over the whole capital district, from the southern shores of Lake Biwa to the port of Naniwa at the head of the Inland Sea.

Thus the establishment in 710 of the capital of Nara, or Heijō as it was then called, symbolized the adoption of Chinese centralized rule. The city was laid out at the northern end of the Nara Plain in regular, checkerboard fashion, with the palace at the northern end, in close imitation of peerless Ch'ang-an (see pages 168–170). Its size, roughly two and two-thirds by three miles, was much smaller than that of the Chinese capital (which was about five by six miles) but appeared grandiose by Japanese standards and needs. No city walls were ever erected, since there were no foreign enemies to ward off, and the western half of the city was not built up. After the capital moved from Heijō, the city withered away. The modern city of Nara had its origin in a medieval town which grew up around the ancient Buddhist monasteries and Shintō shrines that were located along the edge of the hills east of Heijō.

In 784 Kammu (781–806), the strongest emperor of these centuries, decided to leave Heijō, largely, it seems, to escape what had become the oppressive influence of the great Buddhist monasteries and temples that ringed the city. He moved his capital to Nagaoka, a few miles north in the Kyōto Plain. The murder in 785 of the official who was building the new capital slowed the work and resulted in the banishment of Kammu's brother, the crown prince, and his subsequent death from starvation. Since this prince's malevolent spirit was felt to have put a curse on Nagaoka, a new site, named Heian, was chosen at the northern end of the Kyōto Plain, and Kammu established himself in the new Heian capital in 794.

Kammu laid out the plan of Heian on a still grander scale than Heijō, roughly three by three and one-third miles, and again in close imitation of Ch'ang-an. As in the case of Heijō, no real city walls were constructed, the western half of the city was not built up, and the whole metropolis gradually gravitated toward the hills to the east, where great shrines and temples had been located. Heian, however, never disappeared. It became the modern city of Kyōto, in which the checkerboard pattern is still clear and the main east and west avenues still bear the numbers from one to nine assigned them in the original plan.

After its founding, Kyōto remained the capital for more than a thousand years. In fact, the Heian period could be said to have lasted until 1867, but it is customary to use the term only for the first four centuries during which Kyōto served as capital (794–1185), and especially for the first century of this period.

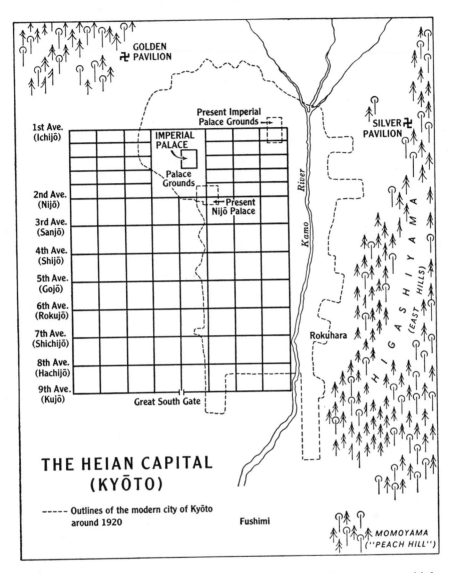

GOLDEN 卍 PAVILION

Present Imperial
Palace Grounds →

1st Ave.
(Ichijō)

IMPERIAL
PALACE

SILVER 卍
PAVILION

Palace
Grounds

2nd Ave.
(Nijō)

← Present
Nijō Palace

3rd Ave.
(Sanjō)

4th Ave.
(Shijō)

5th Ave.
(Gojō)

6th Ave.
(Rokujō)

7th Ave.
(Shichijō)

8th Ave.
(Hachijō)

9th Ave.
(Kujō)

Great South Gate

Kamo River

Rokuhara

HIGASHIYAMA ("EAST HILLS")

THE HEIAN CAPITAL
(KYŌTO)

----- Outlines of the modern city of Kyōto
around 1920

Fushimi

MOMOYAMA
("PEACH HILL")

The Law Codes. The details of the administrative system which the Japanese borrowed from China can best be learned from the law codes they compiled on the basis of Chinese models and sometimes as verbatim copies of the Chinese laws. The very concept of law was a new idea. Hitherto, the Japanese had had only the unwritten precepts of the Shintō religion, which had been transformed into a vague approximation of law by the supremacy of the Yamato rulers and their assessment of fines for offenses against this religious tradition. Now, detailed law codes were enacted. These were divided into the customary categories of the T'ang codes: penal laws (*ritsu*), administrative laws (*ryō*), and various later supplementary regulations (*kyaku* and *shiki*).[4] The first code seems to have been compiled under Tenchi, but the most famous was the Taihō Code of 701. A slightly revised form of this code, dating from 718 (the Yōrō Code), has been preserved through later commentaries (the *Ryō no gige* of 833 and the *Ryō no shuge* of the early tenth century).

Local Government and the Tax System. As we have seen, the first concern of the Taika reformers was to establish a firm, uniform control over all parts of Japan and its agricultural produce. The islands were divided into "countries" (*kuni*), which are normally translated "provinces," though in size they might be compared more with a Chinese subprefecture than with a province. These *kuni* were subdivided into districts (*gun*, from the Han word for "commandery"), and the districts in turn into village units, each unit consisting of about three natural villages. The peasants were further organized into units of five families that were mutually responsible for one another's taxes and good conduct. This ancient Chinese system of mutual guarantee was to continue in Japan, in one form or another, until recent years.

The provinces, which were all given two-character names in the Chinese manner, by the early ninth century numbered 66, and the districts, 592. The division of Kyūshū into nine provinces and Shikoku into four gave rise to the names by which these islands are still known, for they mean "Nine Provinces" and "Four Countries" respectively.

Except for the provinces around the capital, which constituted a separate category (Kinai, now called Kinki), the provinces were grouped together by circuits (*dō*; in Chinese, *tao*), according to the routes by which they could be reached from the capital, and supervisory officials were assigned to these circuits. The most famous of the circuits was the Tōkaidō, the "Eastern Sea Route," comprising the provinces along the Pacific coast from the capital to, and including most of, the Kantō Plain. A special government center located at Dazaifu, a few miles inland from Hakata Bay in North Kyūshū, exercised some control over all of Kyūshū. It was in charge of the defense of this key area and supervised contact with the continent.

The governors of the provinces were central government officials, but were usually officers of only middle rank. Such provincial posts were prized more for the chance they provided for self-enrichment through control of government granaries and a percentage of the tax returns than for their prestige or power in the government hierarchy. Not infre-

4 The *lü, ling, ko,* and *shih* of the T'ang. See page 167.

PLATE 46. Koryŏ celadon wine cup and stand with inlaid design, dating from the twelfth or thirteenth century.

PLATE 47. Eighth-century stone reliefs of Bodhisattvas in the Sŏkkuram grotto above the Pulguksa near Kyŏngju.

PLATE 48. A girl selling wine, painted by Sin Yun-bok (born 1758), with a poem to wine in Chinese. Note the turned-up slippers and stiff horsehair hats, characteristic of Korean dress.

PLATE 49. Main building of the Inner Shrine (Naikū) at Ise. Although rebuilt every few years, the shrine buildings reflect an early architectural style.

PLATE 50. Lecture Hall of the Tōshō-daiji ("Temple Brought from the T'ang") near Nara, dating from the eighth century.

PLATE 51. Wooden figure of a Bodhisattva, dating from the late seventh century, preserved at the Chūgūji (a nunnery attached to the Hōryūji) near Nara.

PLATE 52. The "Paekche Kannon" (Kudara Kannon), a wooden figure of a Bodhisattva, dating from the early seventh century and preserved at the Hōryūji.

PLATE 53. Eighth-century bronze Yakushi trinity (the "Buddha of Medicine" and his attendant deities) in the Golden Hall of the Yakushiji ("Temple of the Buddha of Medicine") near Nara.

PLATE 54. Eighth-century lacquer statue of the blind Chinese missionary priest Chien-chen (Ganjin), preserved in the Tōshōdaiji.

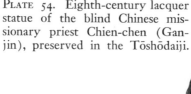

PLATE 55. Detail of a wall painting showing the Bodhisattva Kannon, in the Golden Hall of the Hōryūji, from the eighth century.

PLATE 56. Taizōkai Mandara, a ninth-century painting on silk, preserved at the Kyōōgokokuji in Kyōto.

quently governors sought to obtain these benefits in absentia, and the district magistrates thus became the effective local officials. From the start, the district officials were selected from the old local aristocracy, and in time they were able to make their posts hereditary. Thus the shift in local leadership existed more on paper than in reality.

The chief motive in attempting to extend the control of the central government to all parts of the country was the hope of increasing and regularizing government income from agricultural produce through adoption of the Chinese tax system. In fact, the most amazing part of the whole reform was this adoption of the highly complicated land-holding and tax system of the early T'ang (see pages 158–161), which called for the compilation of registers recording in detail the age and status of each individual and the use of each piece of agricultural land. In theory, the government was to see to the periodical redistribution of the land so that each peasant family could be allotted a specific area in conformity with the number of its members and their ages and sex. This complex system was necessary because taxes were assigned principally by head rather than by the amount of land farmed. The major taxes, as in China, were the agricultural produce tax, the textile produce tax, the *corvée*, the *corvée* commuted into produce, and military service in lieu of other taxes.

Such a cumbersome system obviously could not be applied easily or quickly in a country accustomed to the highly decentralized *uji* system. There can be no doubt, however, that it was at least partially en-forced and with considerable success. Land and population registers, dating largely from the eighth century, show that these were indeed maintained with meticulous care and in close imitation of the Chinese models. Moreover, the greatly increased scale and magnificence of the imperial court during this period and the very existence of large and imposing capital cities indicate the reformers' success in bringing much of the wealth of the country into the hands of the central government.

The system does not seem to have been enforced with the same rigor in all parts of the country. As in China, untaxed or only partially taxed lands were assigned to government officials and certain other categories of persons because of their court ranks and official posts, or for other reasons. Thus both the court aristocracy and the former local *uji* chiefs may have retained the greater part of their hereditary holdings or equivalent lands free of the tax collector. In fact, the new tax system probably served primarily to regularize and increase the income to the government from the lands which were already under direct imperial control. In some parts of the country the national-ization of the land and the new tax system may have amounted to little more than paper reforms.

Nor should one suppose that even the tremendous economic advances resulting from the adoption of the Chinese system brought Japan economically abreast of the T'ang. Unlike China, Japan did not witness the growth of commercial cities or the development of an advanced money economy at this time. Except for the capital, Japan had no cities, and the attempt to develop a money economy was a failure. Copper cash were coined in 708 and at several other times during this period, but despite government efforts to popularize their use they remained more a curiosity than an effective currency, and barter continued to be the rule.

The Central Government. On the whole, the reformers were more successful in creating the central organs of the Chinese political system than they were in the case of the local administrations. Perhaps this was because there were fewer entrenched interests to contend with at the capital. The capital city itself symbolized the reformers' success, and there, from the emperor on down, all the institutions of government were recast in the Chinese mold.

The reformers adopted the Chinese concept of an omnipotent emperor, now called *Tennō* ("Heavenly Emperor," a Chinese type of title), ruling uniformly over every part of the land. At the same time, however, they continued to regard their rulers as supreme cult leaders of divine origin. Thus the Japanese throne acquired dual attributes, which it has retained ever since.

Despite the borrowed Chinese theory of sovereignty, the actual emperors possessed no more personal power than they had had before. Most of them were dominated and manipulated by the great court families, just as they had been during the period of Soga supremacy. In fact, the emperor's heavy ceremonial functions, made doubly onerous by the dual political-religious nature of his office, gave rise at this time to the practice of abdication whenever an emperor's heir was old enough to take over the formal imperial duties. Early abdications had become the rule by the eighth century and remained so until the nineteenth.

The Chinese pattern may have helped induce the Japanese to eliminate women from the succession. Between 592 and 770, half the rulers were women, but since then there have been only two, one each in the seventeenth and eighteenth centuries. This abrupt change in practice after 770 was probably occasioned by the unfortunate incidents of the reign of the empress who died in that year. Twice on the throne herself (as Kōken, 749-758, and as Shōtoku, 764-770), she had ruled through a Buddhist priest, Dōkyō, who seems to have been her lover and to have aspired to the throne himself. Dōkyō survived a revolt in 764 by his chief rival at court, who was Kamatari's great-grandson, but he fell from power when his imperial patroness died. The officials then saw to it that a threat of this sort to the throne should never be repeated.

Under the emperor was a Grand Council of State (*Daijōkan*), composed of a Grand Minister of State (*Daijō Daijin*),[5] Ministers of the Left (*Sadaijin*) and Right (*Udaijin*), and other high officials. The Minister of the Left, or the Minister of the Right acting in his place, served as the chief administrative officer and therefore corresponded in function more to a modern prime minister than did the Grand Minister of State. The latter, in fact, acted merely as a sort of moral preceptor for the emperor, and consequently the post could often be left vacant.

Under the Grand Council of State were eight ministries (*shō*) and various lesser offices. The ministries of Ceremonial, Civil Affairs, Popular Affairs, War, Justice, and the Treasury corresponded to the six T'ang ministries of Rites, Personnel, Public Works, War, Justice, and Revenue (see page 168). In addition, there were also a Ministry of Central Administration, which was a sort of central secretariat, and a Ministry of the Imperial Household. The ministries that concerned themselves with court matters had much more prestige than those primarily concerned with the affairs of the people.

The rituals and ceremonies of government, largely of Chinese origin, were carefully prescribed and meticulously observed. Orchestral music and accompanying stately dances were borrowed from China to enhance court ceremonials. Combining diverse influences from India and Central Asia, this T'ang music (known in Japan as *gagaku*), together with its accompanying dances, has been maintained until today at the Japanese imperial court — apparently without change. Thus *gagaku* probably constitutes the oldest fully authenticated musical and dance tradition in the world.

In general, the Japanese structure of government was simpler and more logical than its T'ang prototype, as might be expected of a system designed after a model instead of having gradually evolved. There was also one striking departure from the Chinese pattern, which reflected the traditional sacerdotal nature of Japanese government. This was the creation on a level with the Grand Council of State of an Office of Deities (*Jingikan*), which was in charge of the Shintō rituals of the court.

Further modifications occurred in the borrowed military system. The Japanese took over the Chinese system of drafting peasants for the army as part of their tax service, and at first these stints of military service, at the draftees' own expense, were considered among the most onerous aspects of the whole tax structure. Japan, however, had no need for the large armies which this system produced. Except in special defense areas on the coast of Kyūshū and along the border against the Ainu in North Honshū, the draft armies soon degenerated into a sort of labor corps.

[5] Pronounced *Dajōkan* and *Dajō Daijin* in more modern times.

Great capital guard armies had also been a feature of the Chinese system, and the Japanese dutifully created eight palace guard groups, but these too had little military significance. Officered by court aristocrats, they became an important part of the pomp and splendor of the court but contributed little to its military security.

Modifications of the Chinese System. On the whole, the Japanese government of the eighth century presented an amazingly faithful reproduction of the T'ang system, but, as we have seen, there were some significant differences. For the most part these were not the result of Japanese ignorance or misunderstanding of the Chinese government. For example, the Office of Deities was obviously a deliberate modification of the pattern, and the continuing local authority of the descendants of the old *uji* chiefs probably reflected the simple impossibility of eliminating the traditional authority of this group.

Another crucial modification of the Chinese pattern perhaps resulted both from choice and from necessity. This was the absence of a real bureaucracy to carry on the bureaucratic type of state administration that had been borrowed. The Japanese did not accept the examination system, which was becoming a dominant feature of Chinese government and society just at this time. Their feeling for hereditary authority was so strong that they had no desire to create a system in which status and power would be determined more by literary skill and administrative ability than by birth. Nor would the great families of the capital aristocracy have tolerated any such drastic innovation.

The central university, which existed primarily to give the court aristocracy the technical skills and polish needed to carry on the Chinese type of administration, did not serve as the normal path to political leadership. Instead, high court rank and government posts were for the most part reserved for those of high birth. Very soon the aristocracy fell into clear-cut hereditary strata, and government posts came to be assigned largely on a hereditary basis, as in earlier times. The greatest noble families, which could achieve the three highest court ranks, stood at the top; next came the bulk of the courtiers, who normally could not rise above the fourth or fifth ranks; then the petty government officers of the lower ranks; and, finally, the local aristocracy, which controlled the district administrations.

Only rarely did men of exceptional ability rise to a higher status than that to which their birth entitled them. One of the few exceptions was Kibi no Mabi (or Makibi, 693–775), who accompanied an embassy to China as a student in 717 and returned home in 735 with the next embassy. He became an important transmitter of Chinese culture, served as a vice-ambassador to China in 752, and eventually in 766 achieved the high post of Minister of the Right.

Below the aristocracy were the common people, called the "good people" (*ryōmin*), and below these was a smaller group of "lowborn" (*semmin*), which included slaves and may have constituted about a tenth of the total population. Social stratification thus very much resembled that of Korea at about the same time.

The Lasting Influence of the Chinese System. Most historians emphasize the ultimate failure of the Chinese system of government in Japan, apparently on the assumption that, once established, it should have gone on almost indefinitely. They point out that the system showed signs of faltering even before the end of the Nara period, and that in the course of the ninth century it lost most of its effectiveness as a means of controlling the whole country and providing the government with an adequate income through taxation.

The rise and fall of the system in a two-century cycle is scarcely surprising, however, when one remembers that a similar cycle was common in China itself. The Japanese, of course, faced a problem of much smaller geographical extent than did the Chinese; but otherwise their task was much harder. They started with a country economically, politically and culturally quite backward as compared with T'ang China. Its strong habits of hereditary, aristocratic rule, both at court and in the provinces, provided infertile soil for the successful growth of bureaucratic institutions. The considerable success of the experiment for a century or more, and the lasting influence it left on Japan, are far more remarkable than its ultimate collapse.

As a result of the borrowed Chinese institutions, Japan made truly astounding advances from the seventh to the ninth century. A country which had never had a city of any sort came to boast a capital whose population numbered in the tens of thousands and which was one of the world's great cities at that time. A land which had had no permanent architecture was now graced with many beautiful temples and palaces, and some of the artistic works that they housed still remain among the great art treasures of all time.

Japan on the whole became much more orderly and peaceful than in earlier periods. Wars of succession and rebellions, though not entirely eliminated, became much less dominant features of its history. The succession war of 672 (*Jinshin-no-ran*) was the last major one. After the revolt against Dōkyō in 764, for almost five centuries there was no civil disturbance on a scale large enough to present any serious threat to the central government.

Moreover, the area under cultivation was greatly increased, and, despite the government's military weakness, the frontiers were significantly expanded. In the course of the eighth century, South Kyūshū was fully incorporated into the Japanese state. In a series of campaigns during the late eighth and early ninth centuries the Japanese general Sakanoue no Tamuramaro broke the power of the recalcitrant Ainu, with whom Japanese settlers had become intermingled, in the area north of Sendai in North Honshū.

Even when the borrowed Chinese system started to fade, Japan did not revert to its earlier, more primitive conditions. The aristocratic *uji* system may have proved unassimilable to Chinese bureaucratic institutions, but it did not itself survive intact. While aristocratic, hereditary traditions continued strong, the *uji* began to disintegrate into smaller family units. Perhaps this was because, under the system borrowed from China, land was assigned by families and taxation by individuals. Most of the cultural and economic gains achieved during these centuries were never lost, even though elements in the government structure did atrophy. Japan remained, ever after, a part of the world of advanced culture and a full-fledged member of East Asian civilization.

Buddhist Art and Philosophy

The political and economic advances of the seventh to ninth centuries in Japan were remarkable enough, but they were overshadowed by achievements in the cultural field. Japan's rapid progress in these areas of human endeavor is all the more surprising when one remembers that it was made without the stimulus of conquest from abroad and with only tenuous contact with the source of inspiration across a wide expanse of open sea.

In view of these handicaps, the achievements of the early Japanese were even more amazing than those of the Koreans and the other peoples peripheral to the Chinese Empire, who were similarly adopting the T'ang pattern. The contrast with the peoples of North Europe was still greater, for the latter managed to destroy more of Mediterranean civilization than they were able to absorb. In the era when the transfer of elements of Greek and Roman culture to North Europe was proceeding at a snail's pace, the Japanese, after only a few decades of effort, were able to produce in their remote islands artistic masterpieces that equaled the best products of China and even scholarly and literary works not far inferior to their Chinese models. Part of this difference from North Europe no doubt can be explained by the fact that Japan's cultural model was still in full vigor, while the Roman model had sunk into sad decay.

We have seen that Buddhism was an aspect of Chinese civilization that immediately appealed to the Japanese. Naturally the arts which were intimately associated with this foreign religion were also prominent among the early borrowings. The visible and tangible aspects of Chinese civilization — sculpture, architecture, painting, and the crafts

—were, no doubt, easier for the Japanese to absorb than were the philosophical, intellectual, or institutional aspects, which had to cross a difficult language barrier between Chinese and Japanese. The great and immediate success of the Japanese in the artistic field might also be attributed to the high aesthetic gifts they have always demonstrated. (See, for example, Plate 51.) In any case, there are still preserved in Japan many fine works of art in the continental tradition dating as far back as Shōtoku's time. By the eighth century the artistic output had become prodigious.

Many of the earlier Buddhist works of art were obviously imported from Korea or were the products of immigrant Korean artists. The somewhat stiff and angular Japanese images of the early seventh century are almost identical with those of Korea, and some of the finest bear names like "the Paekche Kannon" (Kudara Kannon). (See Plate 52.) By the eighth century, however, Japan was drawing its inspiration directly from China, and the Buddhist images and realistic portrait statues of the Nara period show the same round, full-bodied figures covered by draperies — the latter stylistically traceable to the Hellenic world — that were popular during the T'ang. (See Plate 53.) Japanese sculptors, unlike the Chinese and Koreans, made little use of stone, but skillfully employed bronze, wood, clay and lacquer. By the Nara period the Japanese had demonstrated not only a complete mastery of the borrowed artistic techniques and styles but even an ability to use them in successful innovations.[6]

The Buddhist temples and monasteries built in Japan during these centuries are our best remaining examples of classic Sui and T'ang architecture, since very few wooden buildings remain from this period in China. The Golden Hall, the pagoda, and some other parts of the Hōryūji, originally founded by Prince Shōtoku on the western edge of the Nara Plain but apparently rebuilt a few decades later, appear to be the oldest wooden buildings in the world. The Golden Hall is crowded with beautiful images from Shōtoku's time, and its walls were covered by frescoes reminiscent of the paintings of the Buddhist caves of Ajanta in India. (See Plate 55.) Until recently these frescoes constituted the finest remaining examples of the East Asian religious painting of this period, but in 1949 they were seriously damaged by a fire resulting from faulty electrical wiring.

The Nara capital was graced by a number of great temples with stately tile-roofed halls and towering pagodas, many of which are still standing. (See Plates 17 and 50.) The Tōdaiji ("Great Eastern Tem-

---

[6] Japanese art historians tend to use period names quite different from those employed by other historians. Some in common use are Asuka (552–645), Hakuhō (645–724), Tempyō (724–794), and Kōnin (794–897). The last three are all named after "year periods."

ple") and the Kōfukuji, which became the family temple of the Fujiwara descendants of Kamatari, were erected on the fringes of the hills to the east of the city. Scattered about the capital itself were other great temples, in some cases moved from earlier sites. Among these were the Saidaiji ("Great Western Temple"), the Tōshōdaiji ("Temple Brought from the T'ang"), and the Yakushiji ("Temple of the Buddha of Medicine").

The Six Nara Sects. The Japanese mastered the philosophy of Buddhism more slowly than they borrowed its art and ceremonials, and their original contributions on the philosophical side were never so great as in art. Their chief interests obviously lay elsewhere. But even in the early seventh century Prince Shōtoku had shown himself so deeply versed in the new religion as to be able to compose in good Chinese (though probably with the aid of Korean clerics) three commentaries on Buddhist texts. All three have been preserved, the one on the *Lotus Sutra* apparently in his own bold handwriting. During the next several decades the major philosophical schools of Buddhism that had been transmitted from India to early T'ang China were introduced to Japan. The Japanese, following the Chinese in their love for classification, have labeled these the Six Nara Sects.

The first of the Nara sects, Sanron, introduced by a Koguryŏ monk in 625, was an extremely idealistic philosophy emphasizing the unreality of worldly phenomena. The Hossō sect, which the great Chinese pilgrim Hsüan-tsang had brought back to China in 645, was introduced to Japan by a student monk within a decade (see pages 146 and 170). Its alternate name, Yuishiki ("Only Consciousness") reflects its insistence that the only reality is man's own consciousness. Two other so-called sects, Jōjitsu and Kusha, may never have had an independent sectarian existence. The fifth, Kegon (based on the *Kegon* or *Avatamsaka sutra*), was introduced by a Chinese monk in 736. It taught a cosmological harmony under the universal Buddha, Vairocana (Roshana in Japanese), of whom even the historical Buddha was only a manifestation.

The sixth sect was not a philosophical school, but emphasized the rules (*ritsu* in Japanese, *vinaya* in Sanskrit) of the clergy and was therefore called the Ritsu sect. It insisted that the clergy receive their ordination on specially designated ordination platforms, three of which were established in Japan. The chief introducer of this sect was the Chinese missionary monk Chien-chen (Ganjin in Japanese). He started out from his homeland in 742, but his first five attempts to reach Japan were frustrated by pirates, storms, shipwreck and the Chinese authorities. He had lost his eyesight before he finally reached the Japanese court in 754. (See Plate 54.)

Buddhism completely dominated the Japanese court by this time. The native cults, of course, had not been abandoned, but the rulers usually were ardent believers in and patrons of the new religion. The emperor placed on the throne by the Taika reformers in 645 is said to have "despised" Shintō. The Empress Shōtoku, less fondly remembered for her clerical lover, is also renowned for printing a million Buddhist charms, many of which remain as the earliest examples of printing in the world.

Shōmu (reigned 724–749, died 756) was perhaps the most outstanding of all the imperial patrons of Buddhism. He set out to create a state cult of Buddhism that would parallel the centralized civil government and extend adequate spiritual protection to the whole country. It had already become customary for the government to assign clerical ranks to the clergy and to appoint bishops. Now Shōmu attempted to create a still more fully organized system. In 741 he ordered the erection of an official "branch monastery" (*kokubunji*) and nunnery in each province, with fixed numbers of monks and nuns and with lands assigned for the support of each institution, after the T'ang manner.

In 743 Shōmu decided to cast a heroic bronze image of Vairocana at the capital and make it the religious counterpart and protector of the central government. Completed in 749, this seated figure, 53 feet high, consumed about a million pounds of copper, tin and lead and 500 pounds of gold for gilding — a tremendous financial outlay for any country at that time. Marred by later repairs, the image is not a great work of art, but it and the thirteenth-century Great Buddha (Daibutsu) of Kamakura are the two largest bronze figures in the world. The Great Hall in the Tōdaiji, where it was housed, measured 284 by 166 feet and stood 152 feet high. The present structure, rebuilt nine centuries later on a smaller scale, is still the largest wooden building in the world.

The Great Buddha of Nara was dedicated in 752 in a magnificent ceremony presided over by an Indian monk. The ritual objects used in this ceremony, together with Shōmu's personal belongings, were after his death placed in the Shōsōin, a large imperial storehouse built of great logs, where they still remain in virtually perfect preservation. Consisting of ornaments, musical instruments, painted screens, textiles, pictures, weapons, manuscripts (including land and population registers), and a great number of other things, they form a unique treasure-trove of eighth-century civilization. Many of the art objects in the Shōsōin were undoubtedly imported from China, and some appear to have come from as far afield as West Asia.

The Shingon and Tendai Sects. Four of the Nara sects still exist as separate entities in Japan, but they were all soon overshadowed by two new sects which arose early in the ninth century to become the chief religious protectors of the state. In part their triumph may have been the result of the desire of the court, which had just moved from Nara to Kyōto, to find some institutional counterweights to the oppressive influence of the great temples around the old capital. A more fundamental reason lay in the nature of the new sects. Stemming from the type of Buddhism that became popular in China during the middle of the T'ang period, they represented aspects of the Buddhist religion that held a greater appeal for East Asians — Japanese as well as Chinese — than had the Indian philosophical schools.

The two new sects were both introduced by Japanese monks who had accompanied the embassy of 804 to the T'ang. Returning to his homeland in 806, Kūkai, who is best known by his posthumous title of Kōbō Daishi (*Daishi* means "Great Teacher"), founded the Shingon sect ("True Word"; Chen-yen in Chinese), which like Kegon centered around the cult of Vairocana. The Shingon emphasis on incantations, magic formulas, ceremonials, and masses for the dead proved as popular in Japan as in China. The influence of this sect on religious art was overwhelming during the next two centuries. A large proportion of the many Buddhist paintings and images that remain from the ninth century show the complicated iconography of the many-armed deities of Shingon. Its two *mandara*, the schematic drawings of Shingon philosophical ideas, also became an important art subject. (See Plates 56 and 57.)

Kūkai, breaking with the tradition of city temples, in 816 founded his monastic headquarters on top of Mount Kōya, south of the Nara Plain, where it still remains Japan's most impressive religious center. Personally he must have been a man of extraordinary genius, for he was a poet, artist, and great calligrapher as well as a philosopher, religious leader, and prodigious writer of Buddhist texts. A great number of miracles and cultural innovations have become attached to his name. All in all, he is probably Japan's most beloved and best known Buddhist saint.

The other student monk of 804, Saichō, returning with the embassy the next year, introduced the Tendai sect (T'ien-t'ai in Chinese) which was then extremely popular in China. Its typically East Asian eclecticism and its classification of various conflicting doctrines of Buddhism as different levels of truth, each valid in its own way, appealed as much to the Japanese as it had to the Chinese. Out of its syncretic diversity were to emerge most of the great sectarian movements of later periods.

Saichō founded his monastic center, the Enryakuji, near the summit of Mount Hiei. Here he formulated strict rules for his disciple monks, and in 827 his successors were permitted to set up an ordination platform in rivalry with those of the older sects. Located a few miles northeast of the new Kyōto capital — the direction of magical danger according to Chinese concepts — the Enryakuji came to be regarded as the spiritual protector of the city.

The new sects were bitterly opposed by their older rivals, and at first their supremacy was by no means assured. It was not until the time of the third abbot of the Enryakuji that Tendai won out at the court. This cleric was the great traveler and diarist, Ennin. Returning from China in 847, he added to the traditional Tendai teachings the esoteric, magical doctrines and rituals of Shingon, which greatly increased the sect's popularity. A measure of Ennin's success is the fact that the bestowal by the court in 866 of the posthumous title of Jikaku Daishi on him and that of Dengyō Daishi on his master, Saichō, marks the beginning of this custom in Japan.

The Spread of Buddhist Influence. Buddhism, as it grew more powerful in Japan, tended to absorb the older native cults, as it had elsewhere in its spread through Asia. For example, the Shintō "God of War," Hachiman, usually identified with an early emperor, came to be known as Hachiman Bosatsu, or the Bodhisattva Hachiman. When this deity, upon due request, was moved in 749 to the capital from his chief shrine in North Kyūshū, 5000 Buddhist monks participated in the ceremony, and Hachiman was raised to the first imperial rank (Shintō *kami* being included in the rank system). This incident shows how fully Buddhist, Shintō, and secular Chinese traditions had merged.

At first Buddhism was heavily centered in the capital district, but the founding of provincial monasteries in the eighth and ninth centuries, notably in Kyūshū, the Kantō area, and even in North Honshū, marked its spread as a missionary religion throughout the country. It also indicated the spread of continental culture and technology, for the Buddhist clergy of this period was closely associated not only with education in the Chinese language but also with bridge-building, road-laying and other practical activities.

Even at this early date the spread of Buddhism began to affect the life of the Japanese in fields outside of art and religion. For example, Buddhist ideas of an afterlife had brought an end in the seventh century to the elaborate tumuli and stone-tomb burials in the capital district, and the Japanese began to adopt the Indian custom of cremation, which still prevails in Japan. Buddhist injunctions against the taking of life, animal as well as human, had also begun to have an effect. Execution was for the most part dropped in favor of banishment, though a high incidence of violent deaths among those banished suggests that banishment at first may have sometimes been a pious subterfuge. Japanese life as a whole, however, seems to have become decidedly less cruel and warlike. The Indian prejudice against killing animals also began to affect eating habits. Strengthened by the scarcity of grazing land and farm animals in Japan, this prejudice was eventually to result in a virtual prohibition against meat eating, though the Japanese, except for the Buddhist clergy, never extended this ban to the creatures of the sea, which have always been their chief source of proteins.

CHINESE WRITING AND SCHOLARSHIP

The adoption of the Chinese pattern of course meant the borrowing of the Chinese writing system, around which the whole civilization centered. This was no easy task. The pictographic and ideographic characters of Chinese were ill adapted to writing other languages, particularly the polysyllabic and highly inflected languages of Japan, Korea and North Asia. It was a major historical tragedy for both the Japanese and the Koreans that, because they were so far removed from the other centers of early writing, they did not learn about phonetic systems of transcription until after the use of Chinese characters had become firmly established.

Each Chinese character stood for a Chinese word, with its specific meaning and sound. It could be borrowed as a whole — character, meaning, and sound. In fact, thousands of Chinese words were gradually incorporated into the Japanese language in this way. However, because these borrowed characters and words reached Japan at different times and by different routes from various parts of China, in Japan they came to have more than one pronunciation derived from the Chinese. One early category of pronunciations, known as the "Han sounds" (*kan-on*), was associated with Confucian and secular texts; another category, called the "Wu sounds" (*go-on*), was used primarily in Buddhism; and in some cases still other pronunciations were adopted for more recent Chinese names or words. Thus, the character for *ch'ing* ("pure"), by which the Ch'ing dynasty is known, is read *sei* in *kan-on*, *shō* in *go-on*, and *Shin* when referring to the dynasty itself.

The use of Chinese characters for words borrowed from China thus had its complexities, but these were simple compared to the problems of using the Chinese writing system for native Japanese words. There was no way to indicate the absolutely essential inflected endings of verbs and adjectives, nor was there always a one-to-one correlation between Japanese and Chinese words. In short, Japanese could not be adequately written with Chinese characters.

The Japanese, like the Koreans, solved the problem at first by writing primarily in the Chinese language, and it is a tribute to their diligence and intellectual ability that the great transformation of the seventh to ninth centuries was carried out in the main through a foreign language not only quite unrelated to their own but also encumbered by an intensely difficult writing system.

The importation of Buddhist, Confucian and secular texts, all written in Chinese, and the dutiful copying of such texts in Japan constituted major activities during these centuries. All the books by Japanese Buddhist monks were written in pure Chinese, as were also the records of the government and practically all other literary works. The great diary of Ennin, for example, was composed in a combination of classical and medieval colloquial Chinese only slightly marred by errors attributable to the author's Japanese background. Korean immigrants and their descendants, who were well versed in Chinese, played a large role in clerical and scholarly activities, as well as in Buddhism and the arts.

With the Chinese writing system, the Japanese naturally adopted Chinese ways of thinking. Among these, Buddhism and the Chinese concept of centralized government have already been discussed. There were also the Confucian ethics, which henceforth constituted Japan's own moral system. The Japanese also adopted the complex Chinese omen lore and the pseudo-scientific ideas centering around *yin* and *yang* and the "five elements," which had been dominant in "Confucian" thought during the preceding few centuries. In fact, the Japanese seem to have put more stress at this time on the concept of a cosmic order which magically controlled human society than on the original Confucian ethical system itself. An important government office, the Bureau of Yin and Yang (*Ommyō-ryō*), was devoted to the study of natural phenomena as an aid in deciding government policy. Mixed together with native superstitions, these pseudo-scientific Chinese ideas developed into a complex system of portents, divination and calendrical lore which has lasted until modern times.

The Writing of History. The Japanese also acquired Chinese attitudes toward scholarship and literature. Gradually, literary skills in Chinese and a distinguished hand became the coveted marks of the man of breeding. Furthermore, the Japanese adopted the Chinese emphasis on keeping an accurate record of the past, and the writing of history became one of the important duties of the court. As early as 620, Prince Shōtoku ordered the compilation of a history, since lost. About a century later a revival of historiographic activity resulted in the appearance of the *Kojiki* in 712 and the *Nihon shoki* in 720.

Possibly the *Kojiki* was only one of several drafts drawn up in preparation for the official history eventually completed under the title of *Nihon shoki*. In any case, it is a much more faithful effort to commit to writing the native oral traditions and mythology. It is written partly in Chinese, partly in Chinese characters used phoentically to represent individual syllables of Japanese names or words, and partly in Chinese characters used to express the meaning of whole Japanese words. The result, naturally, is extremely difficult to read. The *Kojiki* deals largely with the early myths and legends and dwindles to little more than genealogies for the rulers traditionally dated between 488 and 628.

The *Nihon shoki*, by contrast, is written in pure Chinese and becomes increasingly more detailed as it approaches its terminal date of 689. It was followed by the *Shoku Nihongi* (*History of Japan Continued*), which extended the record to 791. This in turn was followed by four other official court histories, not preserved in toto, which take the record up to 887. These six histories written in Chinese are known collectively as the "Six National Histories" (Rikkokushi). They are often said to be modeled on the dynastic histories of China, but actually they are strictly chronological presentations patterned after the Chinese court records that were used as a prime source for the subsequent dynastic histories.

The early introduction of the Japanese to historical writing had its disadvantages as well as its advantages. It has given us a fuller record of their history and society than exists for any other major people at a comparable level of cultural development. On the other hand, Japanese myths and traditions have been preserved in relatively primitive form. Since the Japanese, in compensation for their hyper-consciousness of having acquired much of their higher culture from abroad, have emphasized their supposedly "native" beginnings, these primitive myths and traditions often had wide and sometimes pernicious influence in later ages. Other civilized peoples have usually had the good fortune to come to the arts of literacy and history writing so slowly that they have preserved their early myths and traditions only in relatively late and therefore more sophisticated form.

History writing was not the only secular literary activity. Mention has already been made of the *Shinsen shōjiroku*, a compilation made in 815 of the genealogies of the aristocratic families. In the eighth century, records (called *fudoki*) of the geography, products, governmental institutions, and legends of each province were compiled by imperial order, and some of these remain.

Poetry: the "Man'yōshū." Because of the great importance of poetry in the Chinese literary tradition, Japanese monks and aristocrats also attempted to write Chinese verse. The *Kaifūsō*, an anthology of 120 poems in Chinese composed during the Nara period, has been preserved, and three more collections were made by imperial command early in the ninth century.

Perhaps interest in Chinese poetry helped spur the brilliant development of native poetry that took place at this time amidst the inundation of Chinese literary forms. The *Kojiki* and *Nihon shoki* contain a number of rather primitive Japanese poems, some spuriously attributed to great antiquity. A much more sophisticated poetic level is represented by the 4516 poems, dating from the century before 760, collected in a great anthology called the *Man'yōshū* (*Collection of Myriad Leaves*, probably implying "Myriad Generations"). The poems are all laboriously spelled out in Chinese characters, used phonetically in most cases, and many of the images and sentiments indicate strong Chinese influence. However, the *Man'yōshū* represents an essentially original expression of poetic feeling on the part of the court aristocracy. We know from other sources that during this and subsequent centuries it was taken for granted that any person of breeding could on the spur of the moment compose a poem appropriate to almost any occasion.

Some 4000 of the poems of the *Man'yōshū* are *tanka*, or "short poems." Still the favorite poetic form in Japan, the *tanka* consists of 31 syllables divided into phrases of 5-7-5-7-7 syllables. The polysyllabic nature of Japanese limits the 31-syllable *tanka* to fewer words than we can cram into a 34-syllable limerick. It is thus an exceedingly restricted literary medium, but the Japanese *tanka* poet, with delicate sensibility, manages to suggest a natural scene, then, through a deft turn, transforms it into an emotional feeling. The result is a type of impressionism that seems quite modern to the Occidental reader.

Constant use of this limited literary medium ever since the eighth century has made much of the later production stereotyped, repetitive, and dependent for new interest on plays on words or on intricate allusions. But the *tanka* of the *Man'yōshū* display great freshness of inspiration. For the most part they cannot be translated both artistically and accurately at the same time. The following *tanka*, however, dating from about a century later, is so simple and straightforward that it can be literally translated, and, even though its simplicity may make it atypical, it will give some understanding of the quality of a *tanka* in the original:

Haru tateba	When spring comes
Kiyuru koori no	the melting ice
nokori naku	leaves no trace;
Kimi ga kokoro mo	Would that your heart too
ware ni tokenan	melted thus toward me.

THE MODIFICATION OF CHINESE INSTITUTIONS

As we have seen, the complicated early T'ang system of landownership and taxation which the Japanese had borrowed tended to collapse even in China after a century or two of use, and not infrequently brought down with it the superstructure of centralized government. It is not surprising, therefore, that the system also degenerated in Japan. Probably it had never been fully applied in the more remote parts of the country, and even in the areas under close control by the central government the lack of administrative experience and a strong sense of hereditary authority had provided weak foundations for the system from the start. The end results of the failure of the Chinese system in Japan, however, were quite different from what happened periodically in China. A prolonged and severe degeneration of the fiscal basis of centralized government did not lead to conquest by foreign peoples or to a revolutionary change in dynasty.

This contrast with China resulted from fundamental differences in geographical environment and cultural substructure. Isolated, Japan had no dangerous neighbors who could threaten even an enfeebled government and, consequently, no great generals of border armies who might overthrow the reigning dynasty. Moreover, uncultivated land was more available in Japan than in China, easing the pressure on the overtaxed peasants and allowing the government — for a while — to develop new tax resources when the old failed. Although the lack of a real bureaucracy meant that there were few defenders of the old system when it started to collapse, the emphasis on hereditary authority prevented any usurpers from seizing the throne for themselves. It also maintained the prestige and, to some extent, the authority of the emperors long after the court had lost the strength to enforce its decisions.

In spite of these differences in outcome from China, the process of fiscal collapse was similar. As in China, the costs of government steadily increased, though this was due primarily to extravagances at court, like the casting of the Great Buddha of Nara, rather than to foreign wars and border defenses like those that often strained Chinese finances. Also, as in China, tax income failed to keep up with expenditures and presently began to decline.

The Rise of Estates and Decline of Taxes. From the start, many tax-free agricultural lands had been assigned to the aristocrats as their due, in view of the court ranks and government positions they held or as special imperial rewards or gifts. Government offices were supported by other tracts of land, and the officially recognized Shintō shrines and Buddhist temples had similar tax-free holdings for their maintenance. These favored families and religious institutions tended to add to their private holdings by developing new agricultural lands, and pious believers, including emperors, commonly made donations of land to the Buddhist institutions. Since the powerful nobles and the clergy were usually able to make their new acquisitions tax-free, the government lost the income it might otherwise have obtained. The situation had become so severe by the early eighth century that specific prohibitions of these practices were issued.

On the other hand, a rising population and expanding court expenses required the development of new agricultural lands, and, since the government proved unequal to the task, encouragement had to be given to others to perform this function. Temporary tax exemptions were allowed those who brought new lands into cultivation, and in 723 such individuals were permitted to retain their lands for three generations. By 743 it had become recognized that this tenure really amounted to permanent possession, and in 772 all restrictions were removed on the incorporation of wastelands into private holdings. Since even small peasant holdings, too, tended, as in China, to be retained permanently in a family and redistribution of land was not actually practiced, the whole system of equal distribution of public land among an equally taxed peasantry had become a dead letter by the end of the eighth century. At the same time, the larger holdings were beginning to develop into the private estates or manors (*shō* or *shōen*) which were to characterize Japan's agricultural economy for the next six or seven centuries.

If taxation had been adequately maintained on the increasing percentage of privately owned land, the government could have financed itself in the manner of Chinese dynasties after the late T'ang period, but an increase in tax exemption and evasion accompanied the growth of private property. Only the wealthy had the capital to open up new land, which in the case of irrigated paddy fields is a big undertaking. Consequently the new lands remained mainly in the hands of wealthy families and large Buddhist institutions. The latter, which were especially favored by the strongly pro-Buddhist court, led the way in winning tax exemption for their property and were soon followed in this by the noble families which dominated the government.

During the ninth and tenth centuries it became common for ambitious members of the central aristocracy to seek appointment as provincial governors, or even to buy such posts, specifically for the purpose of building up their own fortunes. Many governors pilfered the public domain by misappropriating the income or reserve stocks of the local governments. It was also common for governors to accept the financial perquisites of these posts without leaving the capital to perform their duties. The appointment of members of the imperial family and other powerful persons to governorships became accepted as simply a means of providing them with extra income. Consequently the actual control of local tax registers usually lay in the hands of greedy self-seekers or local aristocrats. These men, anxious to build up their own tax-free holdings, were open to bribery, and thus tax exemption was not hard to win from the local authorities.

Naturally the central government fought against such malpractices, and therefore tax exemption was harder to obtain from the central authorities. Government inspectors were assigned to prevent the outflow of taxable lands, and provincial authorities were required to secure official approval for their acts, both from their successors and from the central government inspectors, before they could relinquish their posts. But these other men were themselves not above collusion, and they might also be deceived or frustrated by the supposedly accidental burning of records.

The tax situation continued to deteriorate rapidly during the ninth century. A determined effort to abolish these abuses and restore centralized control was made under the Emperor Uda (reigned 887–897, died 931) and his chief minister, Fujiwara no Tokihira (871–909), but little was actually accomplished. One result of this effort, however, was the compilation in 927 of the *Engi shiki*, an elaboration of the old law codes. A few later attempts were also made to check the fiscal collapse, but these proved to be no more than empty gestures.

One major reason for the central government's inability to stem this financial ebb tide was that the chief offenders included the great officials themselves. During the ninth century, income from their estates became more important to them than their government salaries and perquisites. Being influential at court, they could find ways to obtain tax exemption for their own lands from the central government. Quite naturally, lesser estate owners commonly sought, through the powerful court families or the temples of the capital region, to win similar exemptions for their own lands. They would accept the court families or temples as their legal protectors (known as *honke*, "main family"), assigning a portion of the income from their estates to these families or institutions — provided that the promised protection from taxes actually took effect.

The drift of land away from the tax registers naturally increased the burdens on the remaining taxpaying peasants, as normally happened in China. As early as the beginning of the eighth century we hear of peasants escaping to the Kantō or North Honshū. Subsequently it became common for Japanese peasants, like poor householders in China, to seek refuge from the tax collector by putting themselves under the protection of large private, tax-free estates, where the dues collected by the owners were less burdensome than the government taxes and levies. Thus vagrant peasants might, through benefice, be assigned fields to cultivate by some great estate owner for a percentage of the yield; or small proprietors might, through commendation, deliver their holdings to a more powerful estate owner to obtain tax exemption and thereafter share the crop with him.

By the tenth century a majority of the peasants and most of the agricultural land had become distributed among tax-free and virtually autonomous estates, and as a result the tax system had largely withered away. This in turn meant the gradual starvation of the government and also the atrophy of many of its organs, because now little public domain and few taxpaying citizens remained for it to administer.

The Modification of the Central Government. This was a sorry state of decline for the central government, but one should not assume that it meant a general decline for all Japan. On the contrary, rapid economic and geographical growth had been one of the chief reasons for the collapse of the borrowed Chinese institutions, and the opening of new agricultural lands had been a key feature in the development of tax-free estates. The rise in population and wealth of distant areas like the Kantō, over which the central government had probably never exercised close control, and the incorporation into the Japanese political unit of North Honshū, to which the Chinese system had never extended, may also have helped disrupt the old methods of government.

It should be borne in mind that while the income of the central government gradually disappeared the income of the aristocratic court families, derived from the estates they owned or protected, grew greater than ever. Through this affluent, self-supporting aristocracy, therefore, the court itself could be maintained after a fashion. But the central government had little to do besides conducting court ceremonials. What administrative coordination there was among different parts of Japan became largely the function of the family administrations (known as *mandokoro,* "administrative boards") of the court nobles who owned estates in many places.

This did not mean that the organs of central government disappeared, as they might have done in a country more subject to foreign pressures. Almost all the posts of the old Chinese-type system were preserved as honorary titles, even after the functions associated with them had come to an end. In fact, these posts survived, at least in name, until the nineteenth century. Even during the Nara period there had been a tendency to allow government posts to become hereditary, and as they gradually lost their administrative significance during the ninth and tenth centuries the tendency was greatly strengthened. Eventually, what had been valid governmental posts in the eighth century degenerated into purely honorary hereditary titles awarded regardless of the incumbents' age or ability, and subsequently some of these titles degenerated to mere surnames or personal names of those who had inherited them.

Since the capital aristocrats received ample income from their estates, they could preserve not only the old government titles but also the court ceremonials, and this they did with meticulous attention to precedent. But the dwindling of the other functions of government made it unnecessary to maintain the elaborate organs of centralized rule, however much the titles and ceremonials of these offices might be esteemed.

Gradually a much simplified central government structure replaced the older institutions to administer the greatly reduced functions of centralized control. For example, the Audit Officers (*Kageyushi*), first appointed in about 790 to audit the accounts of retiring local administrators, became in time the only even partially effective channel of control between the central administration and the provinces. This group also came to handle what little tax income the central government still received. Similarly, the Bureau of Archivists (*Kurōdo-dokoro*), established in 810, had by the end of the century become the chief organ for drafting imperial decrees and transmitting petitions to the throne. In addition, the Examiners of Misdeeds (*Kebiishi*) — in other words, Police Commissioners — who were first appointed around 820 in the capital and a few decades later in other parts of the country, soon grew into the only effective force to maintain law and order. The Police Commissioners administered a type of customary law that had grown up outside the official law codes. Chosen from among the militarily more competent members of the decorative palace guard groups, the Police Commissioners supplanted both these and the original draft army as the only remnant of military power under government control. They also took over the functions of the Ministry of Justice and the courts. Thus, three relatively small and simply organized groups, the Audit Officers, the Bureau of Archivists, and the Police Commissioners, became during the course of the tenth century the only effective operational organs of what had once been a complex and well-organized central administration.

THE FUJIWARA PERIOD

While these great changes were taking place in the central government and its financial foundations, the Fujiwara family, descended from Kamatari, was taking over most of the power and much of the prestige that had once belonged to the emperors. Kamatari's son, Fuhito (659–720), had been a leading statesman in his day, and the Emperor Shōmu was his grandson, but the family's fortunes received a sudden check when Fuhito's four sons died in a smallpox epidemic in 737. However, their sons and grandsons, who constituted four rival branch families, proved very successful in the competition for high posts at court. By the ninth century the Fujiwara had secured an inordinate share of the higher offices and were gaining considerable influence over the imperial family by giving their daughters to it as empresses or imperial concubines. This strong position at court was solidly based on the family's economic strength as the owner of many estates throughout the country.

The Supremacy of the Fujiwara Family. By the middle of the ninth century the Northern Branch (Hokke) of the Fujiwara family had outstripped the others and had established complete supremacy over the court. In 857 the head of this line, Yoshifusa, a descendant of Kamatari in the sixth generation, became Grand Minister of State — the first Grand

Minister appointed since the monk Dōkyō. In the next year he had himself assigned regent for his nine-year-old grandson, whom he had placed on the throne. This was the first instance of a small child being made emperor, as well as the first instance of anyone outside the imperial line serving as regent.

Yoshifusa was succeeded in the headship of the family in 872 by his nephew and adopted son, Mototsune, who in turn became the regent of another minor in 876. Two successive adults came to the throne in 884 and 887, but Mototsune went on acting in effect as regent. Thereafter the post of regent for an adult emperor came to be known as *kampaku*.

Once Yoshifusa had established the supremacy of the Fujiwara, members of his family continued to occupy nearly all the top posts in the government, to supply almost all the empresses and most of the imperial concubines, and to place sons of Fujiwara mothers on the throne. In fact, they so dominated the central government that the three centuries from about 857 to 1160 are commonly called the Fujiwara period.

Actually the Fujiwara remained dominant at the Kyōto court most of the time from the ninth century until the nineteenth. From time to time vigorous emperors or newly risen families briefly challenged their authority, but, except for a few breaks, particularly between 891 and 1015, Yoshifusa's descendants occupied the post of regent for minors or that of *kampaku* for adult emperors until 1867. Moreover, they squeezed out most of the other noble families, with the result that the court aristocracy of later periods was almost entirely of Fujiwara origin.

By the thirteenth century the Fujiwara had so proliferated that they began to be known by branch names, which were usually derived from the streets where their palaces were located or from some inherited titular post. Until the nineteenth century, regents and *kampaku* were almost always chosen from the five chief branch families (*gosekke*). These were the Konoe ("Imperial Guards"), Kujō ("Ninth Avenue"), Nijō ("Second Avenue"), Ichijō ("First Avenue"), and Takatsukasa ("Falcon Office"). A Konoe was to serve as prime minister even in the modernized government of the twentieth century. The present descendants of the Fujiwara, tracing their line in great detail and with complete historical accuracy back to Kamatari and even a century or two before him, constitute, together with the various offshoots of the imperial line, the most ancient fully pedigreed aristocracy in the world.

Although the Fujiwara, as the chief owners of estates, were the richest and most powerful family in the whole country and completely dominated the emperors and the remaining machinery of central government, they never made the slightest move to usurp the throne. Even when the emperors were clearly recognized to be their puppets and were entirely overshadowed in prestige and magnificence by their Fujiwara regents and *kampaku*, the family remained content with their theoretically secondary position. Concepts of hereditary authority and the special religious aura of the imperial line were simply too strong to be disregarded even by this all-powerful family. The tendency for the actual controller of power to operate through a figurehead, a trend which had been apparent since the time of the Soga and Prince Shōtoku, became a firmly entrenched custom under the Fujiwara and remained ever after a dominant characteristic of Japanese political life. The establishment at this time of the concept that the emperors should continue to reign even though others ruled helped to preserve the Japanese monarchy through still more serious vicissitudes in later centuries.

The Emperor Uda, who did not happen to be born of a Fujiwara mother, challenged the Fujiwara supremacy during his reign (887–897) and thereafter as retired emperor. He refused to appoint a regent or *kampaku* after Mototsune's death in 891, and he attempted to break the Fujiwara monopoly on the high posts of government. In 899 he succeeded in having Sugawara no Michizane, a lesser aristocrat but a renowned scholar, made Minister of the Right; but in 901 Tokihira, the head of the Fujiwara family, managed to have his rival sent off into virtual exile as Provisional Governor of Dazaifu in Kyūshū, where Michizane died two years later. Apparently he proved more successful in opposing the Fujiwara as a vindictive spirit than he had as a living man. In order to propitiate him, he was enshrined in 987 at the Kitano shrine in Kyōto as the deity of letters.

Tokihira's younger brother, Tadahira, revived the posts of regent and *kampaku* in 930 and 941 respectively. The height of Fujiwara power and glory was achieved under Tadahira's great-grandson, Michinaga, who dominated the court from 995 until his death in 1027. Michinaga set a brilliant example for later ages. The extent of his control over the imperial family can be seen from the fact that four emperors married his daughters, two were his nephews, and three his grandsons. His family administration (*mandokoro*), rather than the remaining organs of central government, was the real center of power at the capital.

The Decline of the Fujiwara and the Rise of the Retired Emperors. Michinaga's son and successor, Yorimichi, who acted as regent and *kampaku* between 1017 and 1067, continued the supremacy of the family, but by his later years Fujiwara power was beginning to falter. One reason for its gradual fading was the declining vigor of the whole central government. With the disappearance of effective control over the provinces, lawlessness and warfare were becoming prevalent everywhere, and even Kyōto found itself plagued with robbers and outlaws. In order to protect themselves, the great monasteries in the capital area had built up their own armed forces, and these, too, frequently disturbed the peace of the capital. Almost bereft of financial resources, the government had begun to allow the palace and public buildings to fall into decay. Fires, some of incendiary origin, took a heavy toll. An air of foreboding and gloom hung over the once brilliant capital and the polished but effete courtiers who inhabited it.

Fujiwara decline was also caused by the violence of the rivalries among the various branches into which the family had further divided. This enervating divisiveness permitted the emperors to return to the fore politically. As the theoretical source of the authority that the Fujiwara had exercised for so long, the imperial family remained the one group within the court aristocracy capable of challenging Fujiwara supremacy. When the Fujiwara relaxed their grip on the government, certain strong emperors reasserted their authority and won back much of what remained of the drastically shrunken powers of the central government.

The Emperor Go-Sanjō [7] (1068–1072), who happened not to have a Fujiwara mother, was the first to try to re-establish imperial control over the country. In 1069 he formed a Records Office (*Kirokujo*) and ordered the confiscation of all estates formed since 1045 and earlier ones lacking valid legal documents. The retired *kampaku* Yorimichi, however, frustrated this bold attempt simply by ignoring it.

Go-Sanjō's son and successor, Shirakawa, followed his father's lead in reasserting his authority at the capital. After abdicating in 1086, he made his headquarters the real center of power in the government, despite the continuance of a reigning emperor and the emperor's regent in their own separate palaces. Since he ruled from the "rear quarters" (*goin*) of a retired emperor, his administration was called *insei* or "(rear) quarters government." To offset the power of the Fujiwara, Shirakawa employed in his *insei* administration minor scholar-aristocrats and members of the lesser court aristocracy who had made their fortunes in provincial posts.

For about a century after Shirakawa's death in 1129 other retired emperors, who usually had taken Buddhist orders, maintained this *insei* form of government, and it was sporadically revived for another century after that. But while this struggle was going on between retired emperors and Fujiwara regents and *kampaku* in Kyōto, the position of the imperial court was deteriorating still further, until it finally lost its last shreds of actual power.

THE NATURALIZATION OF BUDDHISM AND ART

The Fujiwara period, as a time of steadily ebbing central government authority, is usually regarded as a time of general decline, but this was true only in the realm of the centralized political institutions borrowed

---

[7] *Go* means "Later." After the eleventh century, posthumous imperial titles were commonly repeated in this way.

from China. In other fields it was an age of great growth. The development of the manorial system brought about a considerable increase in land under cultivation. Particularly in the Kantō region and North Honshū there seems to have been an increase of population and production. Moreover, the higher culture, which had been heavily concentrated at the court, began to spread geographically throughout the country and socially down to the lower strata of society.

In other words, the political decline at the capital did not mean cultural stagnation. The Fujiwara period was culturally one of the most brilliant in all Japanese history. Centralized government might be disintegrating, but the estate system maintained a wealthy and sophisticated society of high aesthetic sensibility and great artistic and literary creativeness. More important, the culture of this society was no longer a borrowed one; it had become thoroughly Japanese. In the Nara period nearly all aspects of higher civilization, except for the Shintō cults and the poetry of the *Man'yōshū*, had been closely patterned on Chinese models, but the higher culture of the Fujiwara demonstrated a complete and natural blend of now thoroughly assimilated Chinese elements and earlier native tendencies, from which grew distinctive new trends in the fine arts and literature and a uniquely Japanese art of living.

The Decline in Borrowing from China. A major difference between the Fujiwara age and the period that had preceded it lay in the rapid decline in cultural borrowing from China. Most of the major elements of Chinese civilization had already been borrowed and were now undergoing such profound modifications that new borrowings seemed uncalled for. There was less reason to copy minor aspects of Chinese culture when its more important aspects, already known in Japan, were being discarded or changed almost beyond recognition.

The early ninth century had probably seen the high point of Chinese cultural influence. The continued compilation of histories, anthologies of Chinese verse, encyclopedias, law commentaries, and the like, all in good Chinese, indicates how strong Chinese scholarship remained for another century or more. However, a decided swing away from Chinese models had already set in. The Japanese aristocrats, completely at home in the culture acquired over the previous three centuries, now felt free to depart from Chinese norms and innovate wherever they wished. There were many signs of this new attitude. For example, by the beginning of the tenth century the posthumous titles of emperors had shifted from Chinese-type descriptive names (Tenchi, "Heavenly Wisdom"; Kōtoku, "Filial Virtue") to local place names associated with their palaces or graves (Sanjō, "Third Avenue"; Shirakawa, "White River").

Another sign of the change in attitudes was the ending of official embassies to China. None was proposed for over fifty years after the last embassy of 838. Finally, when the Emperor Uda appointed his favorite, Sugawara no Michizane, as ambassador to China in 894, the latter begged off on the grounds of the dynastic collapse already obvious in T'ang China and the hazards of the trip. More basic reasons, however, were the impoverishment of the central government and the largely subconscious feeling of the Japanese that they no longer needed the cultural inspiration that had been the chief fruit of these embassies.

No imperial embassies were to go to China again until modern times, but this does not mean that the Japanese broke off relations with the continent. On the contrary, contacts were actually becoming more frequent. Mention has already been made of the Korean traders who dominated commerce between China, Korea and Japan during the middle of the ninth century. Subsequently, Chinese ships gained control of the growing private commerce in these waters. In fact, the growth of private trade contacts was probably one reason for abandoning expensive embassies. Japanese monks continued to go to China on private ships (one of them, Jōjin, who went in 1072, left a very detailed diary of his travels), but by the tenth century the slackening of interest in learning from China had robbed such contacts of much of their original significance.

The Further Assimilation of Buddhism. One of the major ways in which Japanese culture began to depart from Chinese patterns was in the continuing development of Buddhism. During this same period in China, the revival of native philosophical ideas had begun to relegate Buddhism to a secondary position. In Japan, however, where the Chinese type of centralized government was disintegrating, Confucian philosophy offered no challenge to Buddhism; nor did primitive Shintō beliefs seriously threaten its supremacy. Japan therefore remained a thoroughly Buddhist country until modern times, while the Indian religion was steadily decaying in both China and Korea.

During the Fujiwara period Buddhism in Japan developed into Japanese Buddhism. Hitherto it had derived its chief inspiration from successive borrowings from abroad; now it became thoroughly naturalized, in more ways than one. For example, the almost exclusive emphasis on magical prayers, elaborate ritual, and beautiful works of art which characterized the Buddhism of the Fujiwara court aristocracy — at the expense of deeper religious or philosophical content — was a natural development in a society in which government too had become largely an empty ritual.

Still another aspect of the complete assimilation of Buddhism was the further correlation of Shintō *kami* with Buddhist deities. This process had started in the eighth century, but now elaborate systems were worked out identifying all the Shintō deities as the local manifestations of universal Buddhist gods. For example, the idea grew up that the Sun Goddess, as the supreme Japanese deity, was a local manifestation of Vairocana, the supreme and universal Buddha (the latter's alternate name, Dainichi or "Great Sun," obviously fitted this concept). Moreover, many Shintō shrines and Buddhist temples began to be administratively connected with one another. The virtual incorporation of Shintō into Buddhism and its resultant recasting as a local phase of universal Buddhist truth had by the twelfth century become systematized by Shingon priests under the name of Dual Shintō (Ryōbu Shintō). Subsequently the other sects developed similar synthetic systems. Not until the nineteenth century was Shintō divorced from Buddhism and made fully independent again.

A still more important development was the growing popularization of Buddhism throughout Japanese society. During this period it seems to have spread its influence to the lower classes more rapidly than ever before. In doing so it became progressively less like the religion which had originally been borrowed from China to serve as the magical protector of the state. This new and more popular Buddhism was based on the Pure Land doctrines introduced from China by Ennin and others, but these doctrines now underwent a spectacular development at the hands of native monks not directly influenced by Chinese Buddhism.

The new tendencies were illustrated by the monk Kūya (died 972), who went dancing through the streets preaching the simple doctrine of salvation through faith. The most important figure in the new Buddhism was Genshin (also known as Bishop Eshin, 942–1017), a scholarly monk from Mount Hiei. His work, the *Essentials of Salvation* (*Ōjō yōshū*), was extremely popular and had been put into print by the early thirteenth century (if not before). In this book he emphasized the concept of *mappō*, that is, the degenerate "latter period of the 'law,' " when simpler doctrines and methods of salvation would take the place of the more austere original Buddhist teachings. The *mappō* idea seemed to fit a period of growing political confusion, and the optimistic concept of easy salvation was well adapted to the naturally cheerful inclinations of the Japanese. It was thought that rebirth into Amida's Pure Land, the Western Paradise, could now be best achieved not by one's own strength (*jiriki*) but by the strength of others (*tariki*) and, in particular, by calling on the Buddha's name (*nembutsu*) through such chants as "Hail to the Buddha Amida" (*Namu Amida Butsu*), since it was Amida who had made the "original vow" to save all creatures. Much of Genshin's book was devoted to detailed descriptions of the horrors of hell and pleasures of Paradise. A variant on Genshin's beliefs was taught by the singing monk Ryōnin (1072–1132), who propagated the doctrine of "circulating *nembutsu*," according to which one man's calling on the name of the Buddha would benefit others.

Genshin's ideas and vivid portrayals of heaven and hell were to remain dominant during the next several centuries and become the main stream of later Japanese Buddhism. Even in his own day they had become very popular, and on their deathbeds many people, including the great Michinaga, held in their hands threads attached to a figure of Amida to obtain his help in passing into Paradise.

Sectarian Divisions. The incorporation of the Buddhist church into the aristocratic society and family-divided economy of the Fujiwara period was another important aspect of its assimilation. Temples, as we have seen, came to own some of the greatest estates and in time built up their own military units, composed of estate workers and armed monks, to protect their lands and prerogatives. In the course of the ninth century the government also gave up its earlier efforts to regulate ordinations and limit the number of the clergy. Consequently, religious establishments began to grow as rapidly as their economic foundations permitted.

Growing cleavages among the sects paralleled the strict family divisions of secular society. In China, and even in Nara Japan, sectarian divisions had been rather vague and primarily philosophical, but now they hardened into clearly separate administrative entities. Relations among temples and monasteries fell into strict hierarchic patterns, and the larger sects divided into priestly lines of authority which resembled the hereditary families of the secular world. These well organized religious units gave a chance for ambitious commoners to rise to prominence through their abilities, even though rapid promotion in the clerical ranks was more likely to come to the born aristocrat than to the man of humble origin.

The sectarian divisions and subdivisions naturally fell into bitter disputes with one another or with the government authorities over land ownership, as well as over religious duties and rights. By the late tenth century they even began to engage in military encounters. During the period from the late eleventh century until the sixteenth, priestly armies repeatedly descended on Kyōto, armed with sacred Shintō symbols as well as with their weapons, so as to overawe the court into making desired concessions or judgments in their favor. The monks of both the Kōfukuji and the Tōdaiji of Nara were particularly noted for turbulence, but the most famous and most destructive clerical feud was that between the Sammon or Mountain branch of the Tendai sect, stemming from Ennin and ensconced at the Enryakuji on Mount Hiei, and the Jimon or Temple branch of the sect, centered at the Miidera (or Onjōji) at the foot of the mountain near Lake Biwa. These two groups repeatedly attacked and burned each other's establishments.

The seriousness of such clerical wars is illustrated by Retired Emperor Shirakawa's quip that the only things he could not control were the Kamo

River (which flowed through the capital), the fall of the dice and the monastic armies. While the military strength and political insubordination of the monasteries clearly indicated the sorry decline of the central government, they also illustrated an even more important trend — the rise of new focuses of military power outside the central government.

The Naturalization of Art. The thorough assimilation and modification of Chinese culture during the Fujiwara period was as obvious in art as in religion. In architecture, a distinctive style of palace building developed from the balanced architecture of the T'ang to become the ancestor of later styles of domestic architecture in Japan. This Fujiwara style was characterized by light, airy pavilions connected by covered passageways and placed in an artfully natural setting of gardens and ponds. The ornate Byōdōin, built in 1053 a few miles south of Kyōto, indicates how greatly temple architecture had departed from its classic T'ang prototypes.

On the whole, Buddhist sculpture and painting continued in earlier forms, but the growing gentleness and femininity of even the fiercer deities and the increasing use of gold leaf to decorate paintings were distinctive Japanese characteristics. The popularity of pictures of Amida greeting the dying believer (some of which are attributed to Genshin himself) reflected the growing belief in salvation through faith.

Secular painting showed the greatest and most important departure from Chinese models. There developed a style of simple, flowing lines and flat colored surfaces, quite unlike anything in contemporary or

Toba Sōjō Scroll

This small section shows a frog as an image of the Buddha, a monkey, fox and rabbit dressed in Buddhist clerical garb, a fox as an aristocratic lady with her attendants in the background, and a rabbit on the right in a layman's black hat. The seals read "Kōzanji," a monastery which once owned the scroll, and are placed where different sheets of paper overlap.

earlier Chinese painting, which was fittingly called *Yamato-e* or "Yamato pictures." A popular form of *Yamato-e* painting was the picture scroll (*e-makimono*), a largely Japanese development of the Chinese convention of telling a story pictorially in a continuous drawing or series of pictures on a single long scroll of paper. The earliest remaining examples are the illustrations in scroll form of the famous early-eleventh-century novel, *The Tale of Genji*. One delightful variant of the picture scrolls is attributed, though dubiously, to Toba Sōjō (the Toba Bishop, 1053–1140). This work portrays in masterful line drawings a series of frogs, foxes, rabbits, monkeys and other animals decked out as solemn Buddhas, rascally monks, or timid court ladies, acting out an obscure but amusing-looking plot.

The appearance at this time of hereditary families of artists, their continuity usually maintained by the common Japanese practice of adoption, provides another illustration of the modification of continental culture. In fact, the hereditary principle, on which the political organization was now completely based, came to dominate almost all aspects of the culture. The various branches of scholarship, medicine, calendrical lore, calligraphy, music, and the like became, as a rule, the property of hereditary schools, which jealously guarded their secret family traditions.

THE DEVELOPMENT OF A JAPANESE WRITING SYSTEM AND LITERATURE

In the process of naturalizing Chinese culture, the Japanese also developed new methods of writing and new types of literature. In the ninth and tenth centuries it became customary to read Chinese texts according to Japanese word order and with native Japanese words that corresponded in meaning to the Chinese characters. The changed word order necessitated the use of symbols (now called *kaeriten* or "return points") showing the grammatically correct sequence of words in Japanese, which was very different from that of the original Chinese. This development was in part a sign of declining competence in Chinese, which may also have been a reason for the appearance of several dictionaries at this time. In any case, much of the Chinese composed in Japan from the tenth century onward was so heavily Japanized that it is unintelligible to a Chinese. Known as *Kambun* ("Han writing"), much of this Japanese–Chinese is a peculiar language that can be read only by persons who know both Chinese and Japanese.

The Kana Syllabaries. A much more important development was the appearance of purely phonetic scripts for writing Japanese itself. Parts of the *Kojiki* and most of the *Man'yōshū* had been written in Chinese characters used phonetically to represent individual syllables in Japanese. Characters used in this way in the *Man'yōshū* are called *Man'yō-gana*

JAPANESE TEXT　　　　　KAMBUN TEXT

以粟易械器者、不為厲
陶冶。陶冶亦以其械器
易粟者、豈為厲農夫哉。

粟を以て械器に易ふる者は、陶冶を厲ましむと為さず。陶冶も亦其の械器を以て粟に易ふる者は、豈農夫を厲ましむと為んや。

The Kambun *text on the right is a passage from the* Mencius *in the original Chinese but with* kaeriten *added on the left-hand side of each column to indicate the sequence in which the characters should be read to turn the passage into Japanese. Among the* kaeriten, *the one that looks like a check mark indicates that the two characters between which it appears should be read in reverse order, and the double line (meaning "two") indicates that the character directly above it should be read after the characters that are followed by a single line (meaning "one"). The circles are periods. The same text is transcribed into Japanese on the left in the usual mixed style of writing, with* hiragana *written between the characters to indicate the necessary verbal inflections and postpositions. In this particular text small* hiragana *have also been added beside each character to indicate how it should be pronounced in Japanese. A literal English translation in almost the exact word order of the original Chinese text would read: "If one were to take grain and exchange it for implements, this would not be oppressive to the potter or founder. If the potter and founder also were to take their wares (implements) and exchange them for grain, how would this be oppressive to farmers?" The first sentence in Chinese transcribed into our alphabet reads: "I su i hsieh-ch'i che, pu wei li t'ao yeh." In Japanese this reads: "Zoku o motte kaiki ni kauru mono wa, tōya o yamashimu to nasazu."*

EXAMPLES OF THE DERIVATION OF *KANA*

Chinese character	安	以	加	多	奴	保
Original meaning	peace	take	add	many	slave	protect
Chinese pronunciation	*an*	*i*	*chia*	*to*	*nu*	*pao*
Katakana			カ	タ	ヌ	ホ
Hiragana	あ	い	か		ぬ	ほ
Phonetic value in Japanese	*a*	*i*	*ka*	*ta*	*nu*	*ho*

("the Man'yō syllabary"). During the course of the ninth century these characters evolved into two purely phonetic systems of writing, called *kana*, which are both popularly attributed to Kōbō Daishi. Whole Chinese characters written cursively in abbreviated form became *hiragana*, while elements selected from characters to represent their phonetic values developed into *katakana*.

The development of the *kana* was no doubt influenced by the Sanskrit studies of Buddhist monks and their knowledge of the alphabets of India. The *kana*, however, did not constitute alphabets but were syllabaries, in which the symbols represented whole Japanese syllables, which at that time invariably consisted of one of the five vowels, *a, i, u, e, o,* usually preceded but never followed by a consonant. They thus required a minimum of forty-seven different symbols, instead of the fourteen that would have sufficed to write tenth-century Japanese with an alphabet. Moreover, both *hiragana* and *katakana* included many variant forms. In fact, the two systems were not fully standardized until the nineteenth century, and variant forms are still used in daily correspondence. Thus, *hiragana* and *katakana* constituted a less simple and flexible system than an alphabet would have provided; nonetheless they did provide efficient systems for writing tenth-century Japanese.

The Mixed System of Writing. The solution that *kana* provided for the writing problem during the ninth and tenth centuries proved only temporary. For one thing, Japanese continued to develop phonetically and came to include a great number of long vowels and doubled consonants that could not be represented clearly in *kana*. Thus, while tenth-century Japanese could be written with full clarity in *kana*, a modern text in pure *kana* can be extremely confusing.

A greater problem was created by the heavy vocabulary borrowings from Chinese and the continued prestige of Chinese learning, both of which brought characters back into texts written in Japanese. The use of characters for borrowed Chinese words, which invariably entered the language as uninflected nouns, was reasonable enough. In fact, it was quite necessary for the less familiar or more technical terms, because many different Chinese words, as incorporated into the much simpler Japanese phonetic system, were pronounced alike. Thus, characters pronounced variously in Chinese as *chiao, ch'iao, hao, hou, hsiang, hsiao, hsing, hung, kang, k'ang, kao, k'ao, keng, k'eng, kou, k'ou, kuang, k'uang, kung,* and *k'ung,* each theoretically pronounced in four different tones — constituting thus eighty distinct sounds in Chinese — boil down to the single sound *kō* in Japanese. Consequently, the number of homophones (words of identical sound but different meanings) is staggering, even among compound terms composed of two or more characters. A simple modern abridged dictionary lists twenty-five words of Chinese origin pronounced *kōka,* including such common terms as "costliness," "elevated," "efficacy," "descent," "gelatination," "hardening," and "engineering department." An unabridged dictionary lists well over a hundred words pronounced *kōka.* If most of these words are to be read intelligibly in Japanese, obviously they must be written in characters.

The use of Chinese characters for native Japanese words, particularly for inflected verbs and adjectives, was less justified. Japanese and Chinese words did not necessarily correspond in meaning. For instance, the various meanings or connotations of a single Chinese character might be divided among several different words in Japanese. The character for the *shang* of Shanghai or of Shang Ti (the "Supreme Ti" of Chinese antiquity), for example, has been borrowed as *jō* into Japanese, but it is also interpreted as corresponding to the native Japanese words *ue* (top), *kami* (upper), *noboru* (to climb), *agaru* (to rise, to ascend), and *ageru* (to raise, to present). Moreover, semantic developments in China and Japan were often quite different. A Japanese word which in earlier times was equated with a Chinese word through the latter's written character might subsequently evolve in meaning in one direction and the Chinese word in another. And, in any case, Chinese characters could not indicate the essential inflections of verbs and adjectives or the postpositions used with nouns.

A mixed style of writing in both *kana* and characters had already appeared by the eleventh century through the addition of *kana* to texts written in incredibly bad and heavily Japanized Chinese or through the insertion of characters into texts written in Japanese. From then until the nineteenth century, three writing systems competed with one another in Japan: straight Chinese characters for texts in Chinese, or in what the Japanese thought was Chinese; pure *kana* for poems and some prose texts in Japanese; and mixed characters and *kana* for other Japanese texts, with most of the nouns and the roots of many verbs and adjectives represented by characters and with *kana* used for all inflections and postpositions. Eventually this third style won out and became modern written Japanese.

Most of the many characters used in modern Japanese can represent more than one Chinese-derived pronunciation and often a number of native words. Therefore it requires close attention to the context to determine how a character should be pronounced in each instance. Moreover, all the sometimes contradictory semantic developments of the respective Chinese and Japanese words can be represented by the characters used to write them. Consequently, even the interpretation of characters often presents something of a puzzle. All in all, the modern Japanese writing system is probably the least efficient in wide use anywhere in the world.

The reform of the Japanese writing system, however, would be no easy task. Great progress has been made in recent decades in limiting the number of characters, simplifying their composition, and standardizing their meanings and pronunciations. But the system remains discouragingly complex. Only the total elimination of Chinese characters would really solve the problem. But this could not be achieved without a drastic pruning of the huge number of Chinese-derived homophones now in use in written Japanese. Actually this problem is not so difficult as it appears, for the spoken language does produce such a pruning, inasmuch as spoken Japanese must remain aurally intelligible. If the Japanese ever do make the shift back to a purely phonetic writing of their language, however, they will probably not return to *kana*, which is so inadequate for writing modern Japanese. The contemporary language can in fact be written far more easily and accurately with seventeen of the letters of the Roman alphabet (*Rōmaji* in Japanese), plus two diacritical marks, than by either of the present forty-eight-symbol *kana* syllabaries, with their two diacritical marks.

Literature: the "Kokinshū" and "The Tale of Genji." The development of syllabaries in the ninth century made possible the easy writing of poems in Japanese and the rapid growth of a native prose literature. But the motivation for this development probably worked the other way around. It was the urge to write more in the native language that gave rise to the development of the syllabaries.

The emphasis at court on the composition of poetry continued in the Fujiwara period and resulted in the compilation in 905, on imperial order, of an anthology of about 1100 poems, almost all *tanka* ("short poems"), composed since the time of the *Man'yōshū*. This work, the *Kokinshū* (*Ancient and Modern Collection*), became the model for twenty other imperial anthologies of poetry, the last completed in 1439, after which time the court became too impoverished for even this sort of innocuous undertaking.

In addition to a preface in Chinese, the *Kokinshū* contains another, in Japanese, by Ki no Tsurayuki, one of the compilers of the work. This second preface, which treats the nature of Japanese poetry, is one of the earliest examples of Japanese prose writing. Tsurayuki a few years later wrote another work in Japanese, the *Tosa nikki* (*Tosa Diary*), which is the brief account of a journey, studded with poems composed by the author during his trip. It became the model for a number of later poetic travel diaries. Other types of diaries were also written in Japanese or Chinese, many concerned with the annual round of rituals performed by the court aristocracy. Ever since the Fujiwara period, in fact, the Japanese have shown themselves to be the most enthusiastic diary writers in the world.

Even in the ninth century several simple, unsophisticated stories had also appeared in Japanese. These were followed in the tenth century by more ambitious works, such as the *Ise monogatari* (*Tales of Ise*), a series of 125 episodes, each centering around one or more poems. Then, in the early eleventh century, during the time of Michinaga, the greatest of the Fujiwara leaders, Japanese prose had a sudden flowering that is one of the most remarkable phenomena in the history of world literature. A group of sophisticated ladies turned their considerable talents to writing diaries and novels that brilliantly portrayed the court life they knew. One of the notable works of this period was the *Makura no sōshi* (*Pillow Book*), a miscellany of witty and sometimes caustic comments and observations by a court lady known by her cognomen of Sei Shōnagon. The dominance of court ladies in the Japanese prose literature of the time is probably to be attributed to the relative freedom of women in Fujiwara court society and to the preference on the part of most men of education for writing in Chinese.

The outstanding literary product of the early eleventh century — in fact the greatest work in all Japanese literature — is the *Genji monogatari* (*The Tale of Genji*), by a court lady with the cognomen of Murasaki Shikibu. A tremendously long account of the amorous adventures of the peerless Prince Genji, it is told with much charm and humor and with a psychological sublety and aesthetic sensitivity that has characterized the best of Japanese literature ever since. Its prevailing mood of sweet melancholy and nostalgia also became typical of many later works. All in all, *The Tale of Genji* has exerted immeasurable influence in Japan and, in its extremely free but masterly translation into English by Arthur Waley, has had considerable impact even in the Occident in recent years.

The life portrayed by Murasaki and her contemporaries should not be interpreted as a full picture of the Fujiwara court, much less of the society as a whole; but it is nonetheless a vivid portrayal of one aspect of Japanese life at this time. The court aristocrats were well supported by the estates they owned, but, with the decline of the central government, they had few duties to perform other than various ceremonies. Their lives tended to be luxurious but shallow, centering about symbols rather than realities. The emphasis was strongly aesthetic; what counted was the proper costume, the right ceremonial act, and the successful expression of an emotion in a poem. The courtiers occupied themselves with an endless round of annual ritual observances and dilettantish pastimes, such as judging the relative merits of poems or of flowers, shells, and the like, or composing poems as a wine cup floated to each person in turn among a company seated along a specially constructed miniature "winding waterway." Morals were dissolute by most standards. The institution of marriage was not clearly defined, and the courtiers and ladies freely followed their whims in sexual matters. The writings of the court ladies do not show the slightest shadow of the stern asceticism and military virtues which were to characterize later Japanese history. Fujiwara culture, in contrast to that of later Japan, tended to be both effete and effeminate. Yet one major strain has continued without interruption from the Fujiwara period until the present day. This is the extreme sensibility of the Japanese to beauty in all its forms.

Although the literature written in Japanese in the later Fujiwara period was in large part imitative of Murasaki and her contemporaries, there were some new developments, including a comparatively popular type of narrative writing. The *Konjaku monogatari* of the late eleventh century, which is a compilation of Buddhist and historical stories from India, China, and Japan, written in mixed characters and *kana* in a heavy style much influenced by Chinese, became the model for several later compilations of historical and Buddhistic stories.

About the same time appeared a new type of history written in Japanese. Evidently the end in 887 of the official histories compiled in Chinese had not resulted entirely from the decline of the central government but was partly the product of changing interests and attitudes. The *Eiga monogatari* (*Tale of Splendor*) of the late eleventh century presents a romanticized and somewhat imaginative chronological account of the glories of the Fujiwara between 889 and 1092. The *Ōkagami* (*Great Mirror*) of the early twelfth century covers the same story in biographical style for the period from 850 to 1025. These two works, which center on the incomparable Michinaga, became the prototypes for a whole series of somewhat fanciful historical records in *kana* or in mixed *kana* and characters.

These romanticized histories, like the diaries and novels of the court ladies, the beautiful picture scrolls, and the aesthetic life at court which they all portrayed, were very different from anything in China. A successful adaptation of Chinese themes had characterized the higher culture of the Nara period. Under the Fujiwara this had given place to a distinctive Japanese culture that owed to China only a somewhat remote heritage. The backward country which a few centuries earlier had so successfully imitated China was now a culturally advanced nation, capable of making its own contributions to world civilization.

12

Feudal Japan: A Departure

from the Chinese Pattern

The Rise of a Semi-Feudal Society

For all its cultural brilliance, Fujiwara court society was not the direct ancestor of later Japanese society and culture. In its long isolation from the realities of life, it had grown too effete to continue in a creative role. Instead, it served as the transmitter of the now fully assimilated residue of T'ang civilization to more vigorous groups, in whose hands the future of Japan was to lie. By the twelfth century the focus of our attention shifts from the increasingly stagnant life in Kyōto to the less refined but more dynamic society in the provinces.

This change in leadership reflected the rising status of peripheral areas. By 1100 the once great gap in cultural levels between the capital and the rest of the country had been appreciably reduced through the declining fortunes of the court and the growing wealth and culture of rural Japan. As we have seen, the acreage under cultivation had been expanded greatly under the estate system. The need to transport some of the yield of these estates from the provinces to the capital district, where their owners resided, was also developing a more efficient system of roads and waterways than had existed under the relatively centralized political order of the Nara period. As a result, the movement of both goods and people throughout Japan was considerably greater in the twelfth century than it had been in the eighth. Centers of industries such as paper making, iron casting, and pottery making were also beginning to appear in various localities, showing the spread of technological skills. There was a considerable growth in foreign trade which affected not just the capital, as in the early days, but the whole country. Chinese merchant vessels frequented the ports of Japan in increasing numbers, and Japanese traders had started to venture abroad.

Most of the economic and cultural rise of the provinces can only be inferred from fragmentary evidence, but one clear piece of proof remains. There is a small building at Hiraizumi in North Honshū, some fifty miles north of Sendai, which was erected in 1124 by a locally powerful branch of the Fujiwara family as part of a great temple called the Chūsonji. This building, one of the most beautiful examples of the sumptuously decorated architecture of the Fujiwara period, indicates how rich this provincial family must have been and how high the cultural level had become even in such a remote part of the country.

The Estate System. Life in the provinces, though characterized by the same strong emphasis on class and hereditary status as at the capital, differed considerably in other respects, since it centered around private agricultural estates or manors (*shōen*). These estates varied greatly in their historical origins, organization, and size. Some were no more than large farms; others comprised thousands of acres of paddy fields spread over more than one province. Unlike the manors of feudal Europe, which usually conformed to village units and included large tracts of common pasture land, the chief components of the Japanese estates were the irrigated paddy fields, which might be widely scattered. Moreover, the estates owned by a single family were commonly located in different parts of the country.

The division of most of Japan into private agricultural estates in some ways resembled the earlier division of the country into autonomous local *uji* units. There was, however, one big difference. These estates were not owned and operated by cohesive kinship or pseudo-kinship groups. The borrowed Chinese land system had left a complex legacy of legal rights, and the income from an individual estate might be divided among a number of groups which lacked any actual or theoretical blood ties.

The people connected with each estate usually fell into three or sometimes four distinct social levels determined by their functional relationship to the estate. The lowest level consisted of the actual cultivators, themselves divided into various sub-categories, with hired hands at the bottom. This stratum of cultivators was made up chiefly of the old free peasants, but it also included many former slaves and other "lowborn" groups, since the distinction between "good people" and the "lowborn" had lost most of its meaning.

Above the cultivators were the managers of the estates — either representatives of absentee owners sent to administer the land or the descendants of old local aristocrats who, for mutual protection, had merged their holdings into larger estates. These managers, who were divided into several different categories according to their specific functions, all received their income in the form of the yield from specific areas of land.

Above the managers, in turn, were the owners (*ryōke* or *ryōshu*) — powerful local families, court aristocrats and influential religious institutions. If the owner himself were not strong enough at court to insure the protection of his estate from the tax collector, then above him would be still another category, that of the legal protectors (*honke* or *honjo*).

These groups all had their respective legal rights, called *shiki* (originally meaning "function"), which entitled them to a fixed proportion of the produce of the whole estate or, more commonly, to all the produce from certain fields within the estate. These *shiki*, which were usually specified in written documents and supported by customary law, could be inherited by women as well as men and also could be freely divided, since no rule of primogeniture existed. There were many sub-types among the major categories of *shiki*, and a man might hold *shiki* of more than one type in more than one estate. Obviously, this could lead to a great confusion of individual relationships, with one man being another's superior on one piece of land but his equal or even his inferior on another.

The resemblance of the *shiki* system to the system of multiple rights attached to a single piece of land in feudal Europe is striking but perhaps not surprising. Both were the outgrowth of simpler, more uniform legal systems — Roman law in Europe and the borrowed T'ang codes in Japan — after the effective power of the central government had disappeared.

Local Leadership: the Minamoto and the Taira. In the evolving provincial society the most important group proved to be neither the cultivators at the bottom nor the absentee owners and legal protectors at the top, but those in actual control of the estates, that is, the owners who lived in the provinces and the various types of estate managers. These local leaders were probably descended in large part from the old provincial *uji* aristocrats. The latter had been transformed by the borrowed T'ang system into local officials, who, apparently, retained a large measure of control in the provinces. Now the stronger of these descendants of the *uji* had become estate owners, and the weaker had fitted into managerial positions on estates owned by others.

Another important element in the new provincial leadership came from offshoots of the capital aristocracy. In the ninth and tenth centuries lesser members of the Fujiwara and other noble families in Kyōto, as well as collateral descendants of the emperors, often went to provincial posts to build up their fortunes. Supported by the remaining authority of the central government and aided by the armed retainers they usually brought with them from the capital, these men were often able to acquire considerable property and therefore sometimes found it more attractive to settle permanently on their provincial estates, instead of returning to relatively humble positions at the capital. Since they enjoyed the prestige of noble or even imperial descent, which meant a great deal in class-conscious Japan, such transplanted aristocrats often became the cream of the local aristocracy. In fact, so great was the prestige of their Kyōto heritage that by the twelfth century virtually all of the other prominent families of rural Japan claimed a similar descent for themselves.

The members of the imperial line who established themselves in the provinces were no longer considered princes but headed independent families. As the imperial line proliferated and government finances declined, it became necessary to cut off these collateral branches by giving them their own surnames (the imperial line had none) and by providing means for them to earn their own living as officials in the central government or in the provinces. Minamoto and Taira were the two family names given the sons and grandsons whose connection with the imperial line had been severed. Minamoto is also known by its Sinicized pronunciation as Genji ("the Minamoto Family") and Taira as Heike ("the House of Taira"). The Minamoto name was first given in 814 by the Emperor Saga to some of his sons and brothers, and the name of Taira was first given a decade or two later to a grandson of the Emperor Kammu. Both names were also assigned at various later times to other groups of princes. The most famous of the several Minamoto families traced its descent to the Emperor Seiwa (858–876) and therefore was known as the Seiwa Genji.

The Development of a Rural Military Aristocracy. As the central government gradually withered, the local leaders, descended from offshoots of the imperial family and the court nobility as well as from the old local aristocracy, took over actual control of their respective regions. They ran the estates into which Japan had become divided, even though most of these estates were owned or legally protected by court aristocrats or religious institutions in the capital region. The distant owners and protectors drew a fixed income from their estates, but their control was at best indirect. In particular, matters of military defense and the preservation of order during this time of growing lawlessness fell entirely on the shoulders of the local leaders. Consequently, the latter became basically a military class.

As early as the eleventh century, the leaders in rural Japan had become clearly a warrior aristocracy. This, however, may not have been an entirely new development. The *uji* leaders of the Tumulus period, we know from archaeology, were mounted and armored warriors. The *uji* had been supplanted, at least according to the law books, by a drafted peasant army and elite capital guard units, but the provincial leaders, unlike the court aristocracy, seem never to have lost their military prowess. When the borrowed Chinese-type military institutions proved ineffective, the rural aristocracy emerged again in its old military role. The conscripted army was abandoned entirely in 792 in favor of small bodies of volunteer militia drawn from the provincial aristocracy, and during the ninth century the functions of the capital guards were taken over by the Police Commissioners, who were recruited to a large extent from among these same provincial leaders. (See page 502.)

Thus the armored knight who emerged fully onto the stage of history in the twelfth century seems to have been a direct descendant, functionally if not always biologically, of the mounted warrior-aristocrat of the *uji* period. The considerable cost of his fine mount and equipment meant that he, like his ancient predecessor, had to be a man of wealth. Only the aristocrats of rural society could be knights.

Here we see another close resemblance to feudal European society. The aristocratic mounted knight of twelfth-century Japan, supported by a few attendants on foot, constituted the basis of military power. In fact, in battle he tended to act as an entirely independent military unit, seeking out a corresponding enemy knight and dealing with him individually. His fighting equipment differed from that of the European knight, but in some ways it was better. He used no lance or mace but relied instead on his bow and arrows, used from horseback, and on his curved sword, which had become the best in the world — a highly tempered piece of steel with an incomparable cutting edge. His light and flexible armor, made of small strips of steel held together by brightly colored thongs, might look flimsy when compared with that of a European knight, but, because of the greater mobility it gave him, was probably much more practical than the heavy European armor. (See Plates 59–62.)

Warrior Cliques: the Beginnings of Feudalism. Despite his military resemblance to the old *uji* aristocrat, the knight of medieval Japan lived in a very different type of society. As the owner or manager of an estate, he was thrown into close legal contact with non-related groups, and his military organization did not depend primarily on kinship. The smallest and most fundamental defense grouping probably consisted of the fighting men from a single estate, drawn from among the managers and the more warlike and prosperous of the cultivators. Larger groupings were probably based as much on geographical as on family relationships. Fighting men from estates close to one another might join forces for mutual protection, or those from scattered estates owned or managed by related persons might band together. Many warriors joined successful groups, attracted simply by the renown or personality of certain leaders.

Once formed, the relationship between a leader and his retainers or samurai (the term literally meant "servant") might be continued for generations. The leader rewarded his followers with land or with positions of honor and wealth; in return, his followers were supposed to serve him with absolute loyalty. In origin the bond was clearly one of mutual benefit, but it tended to become idealized as an ethical rather than a contractual or legal relationship. In this sense it approximated kinship and to this extent represented a revival of the old *uji* type of organization, although most of the fighting men in the larger warrior cliques had no real or fancied blood ties.

The bond of loyalty that united members of the warrior cliques of Japan is another point of close resemblance to feudal Europe. In fact, the whole development of these warrior cliques, from the tribal *uji* unit of Japan, through the local defense group, to the proto-feudal association between leader and samurai of the twelfth century, strikingly resembles the development of European feudalism, from the Germanic tribal war bands and the local defense groups of late Roman times to the lord-and-vassal relationship of medieval Europe. Both were in a sense the continuation of tribal attitudes, after the disappearance of the tribe itself, in the more complex type of society derived from a disintegrating centralized state.

These similarities between the origins of feudalism in Japan and in Europe suggest that feudalism in both areas may have been the product of a specific mixture of a tribal society and a more highly integrated and centralized political and social order. The methods of mixture were quite different in Japan and in Europe, but the basic ingredients seem to have been much the same. Because of the scarcity of similar fully developed feudal societies in other parts of the world and at other periods of history, one might conclude that it takes a very special combination of these two not uncommon basic ingredients to produce a definitely feudal society. Repeated eruptions of nomadic tribal peoples into the Chinese Empire and into the other highly organized centers of agricultural civilization throughout the rest of Asia produced no fully developed feudal systems comparable to those of Europe or Japan.

In other words, feudalism appears to have been an unusual phenomenon in history, rather than an inevitable stage of historical development, as it is pictured in Marxism and certain other Occidental historical theories.

THE TRIUMPH OF THE PROVINCIAL MILITARY CLASS

We have only fragmentary glimpses of the development of the local Japanese defense groups composed of provincial aristocratic warriors (*bushi*). Because of the importance of hereditary prestige, the largest and most effective cliques seem to have gathered around the provincial offshoots of the imperial family and court nobility, but even these groups were mentioned in the Kyōto chronicles only when their activities were of direct interest to court society. Only the greatest of their wars received much notice in the capital. These were usually described as occurring between rebels and imperial forces, since one side or the other might have been given the court's blessing, but the encounters were in fact private wars between local power groups.

The first large-scale local disturbances that we hear about came in East and West Japan at almost exactly the same time. A certain Taira no Masakado, who in a series of battles had made himself the master of much of the Kantō, was eliminated by a local Fujiwara rival in 940. The next year, Fujiwara no Sumitomo, who had originally been dispatched from Kyōto to help suppress piracy in the Inland Sea but had turned pirate himself, was destroyed after dominating these waters for five years.

In 1028 another Taira plunged the Kantō into war but was finally crushed in 1031 by Yorinobu, a member of the Seiwa Genji, that is, the Seiwa branch of the Minamoto. Yorinobu's son, Yoriyoshi, between 1051 and 1062 eliminated the Abe, a powerful family of local origin in North Honshū. Since periods of truce reduced the years of actual fighting to nine, this protracted series of campaigns is known as the Earlier Nine Years' War. Between 1083 and 1087 Yoriyoshi's son, Yoshiie, conducted a similar series of campaigns, called the Later Three Years' War, to eliminate another great northern family, the Kiyowara.

Through wars of this sort the more successful warrior bands gained prestige throughout the country and greatly increased their following. The development of the Seiwa Genji, the greatest of the early cliques, in the Kantō and North Honshū may have been occasioned by the stronger survival of the tribal spirit in such relatively backward parts of Japan. The large amount of fighting in North Honshū in particular may also have reflected the maintenance of a more vigorous martial tradition in this border area. In any case, such wars indicated the complete incorporation of this region into the Japanese political unit.

These distant wars had little effect on the court, except to stop temporarily the flow of income from the estates involved or, in extreme cases, to deprive the distant owners of title to their estates because of the confusion resulting from war. The provincial military groups, however, had meanwhile appeared in force at the capital. Individual warriors had long been active as Police Commissioners, and by the eleventh century organized groups of provincial aristocrats were being called in to Kyōto to lend military power to the local civil authorities.

The Rivalry of the Taira and the Minamoto. A close association grew up between certain court families and some of the more powerful military cliques connected with them through the estate system or in other ways. Michinaga relied primarily on the Seiwa Genji, and this formidable military band, which was winning great prestige in its successive wars in North Honshū, came to be known as "the claws and teeth" of the Fujiwara. His successors and subsequently the retired emperors too came to rely on such military groups from the provinces to protect them from their enemies and from the armed monks of Mount Hiei and other monasteries.

In the middle of the twelfth century the warrior bands active at the capital were forced into conflict with one another to support the intrigues of their imperial and Fujiwara patrons. One group was led by a branch of the Taira family which was descended from the Emperor Kammu but, being more recently from the province of Ise, was known as the Ise Heike. This family had risen to prominence in Kyōto after its leader, Masamori, in 1108 had eliminated a prominent member of the Seiwa Genji, Yoshichika, whose wars had for some years disturbed western Japan. After this victory, the Ise Heike established themselves as the chief power in the Inland Sea area, and under Masamori's son,

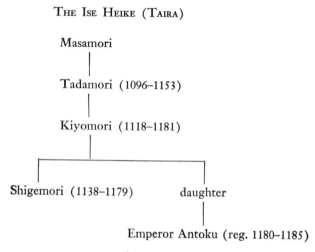

THE ISE HEIKE (TAIRA)

Masamori

Tadamori (1096–1153)

Kiyomori (1118–1181)

Shigemori (1138–1179)   daughter

Emperor Antoku (reg. 1180–1185)

Tadamori, and his grandson, Kiyomori, they became the main military support of the retired emperors at the capital.

The other group was headed by Minamoto no Tameyoshi, the son of Yoshichika and a descendant of the great Minamoto leaders of the earlier wars in the Kantō and North Japan. By eliminating his family rivals, Tameyoshi had won the headship of the Seiwa Genji, now firmly established in the Kantō region, but he was disgruntled by his failure to obtain high court appointments.

THE SEIWA GENJI (MINAMOTO)

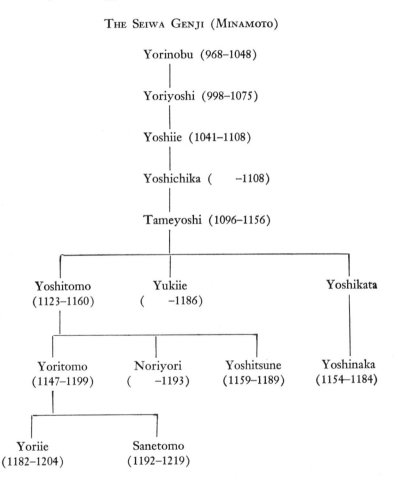

Yorinobu (968–1048)

Yoriyoshi (998–1075)

Yoshiie (1041–1108)

Yoshichika (–1108)

Tameyoshi (1096–1156)

Yoshitomo (1123–1160)   Yukiie (–1186)   Yoshikata

Yoritomo (1147–1199)   Noriyori (–1193)   Yoshitsune (1159–1189)   Yoshinaka (1154–1184)

Yoriie (1182–1204)   Sanetomo (1192–1219)

When the Retired Emperor Toba died in 1156, two of his sons, the Retired Emperor Sutoku and the reigning Emperor Go-Shirakawa, came into sharp conflict over control of the court. The *kampaku*, who was the titular head of the Fujiwara family, supported Go-Shirakawa, but his jealous younger brother took Sutoku's side. Sutoku's group resolved to resort to a *coup d'état* with the aid of whatever military forces they could muster. They obtained the support of a mixed group of Minamoto and Taira warriors, headed by Minamoto no Tameyoshi, but Tameyoshi's son and heir, Yoshitomo, joined the opposing band headed by Taira no Kiyomori.

Kiyomori emerged victorious in the ensuing conflict. Tameyoshi and his forces were crushed, and he and most of the other major military participants on the losing side were executed, since these warriors had none of the prejudices against taking life that had characterized the court for some centuries. The Retired Emperor Sutoku was sent into exile, and Go-Shirakawa, abdicating in 1158, took control of the *insei* government, remaining the dominant member of the imperial family until his death in 1192.

The warriors on the winning side, however, soon fell out. Yoshitomo, the chief Minamoto on this side, became jealous of the greater rewards bestowed on the Taira leader, Kiyomori. Each received support from ambitious Fujiwara of minor collateral lines. Eventually, in the winter of 1159–60, Yoshitomo and his allies seized power in another *coup d'état*, while Kiyomori was away from Kyōto on a pilgrimage. But Kiyomori quickly returned to defeat his opponents, hunt them down and butcher them. Named for the "year period" when each occurred, the brief struggle of 1159–60 is known as the Heiji War and that of 1156 as the Hōgen War. (See Plates 60–62.)

The Rule of the Taira. These two small wars, by eliminating all military rivals to Kiyomori and his henchmen at court, left him the unchallenged military master of Kyōto and, probably to his own surprise, in virtual control of the remnants of the central government. For the next two decades he in effect ruled the court from his palace at Rokuhara on the southeastern edge of the city or from his estate at Fukuhara (the modern seaport of Kōbe), to which he even moved the capital briefly in 1180.

As an offshoot of the imperial line and a man who had long been prominent in the central government, Kiyomori easily settled down to the now time-honored practice of dominating titular superiors without supplanting them. Emperors, retired emperors, and Fujiwara regents and *kampaku* continued to maintain their respective pretences of authority, but Kiyomori was the real source of power. He left most of the top government posts to the Fujiwara, though he did take the title of Grand Minister of State for himself for a few months in 1167, and he and his able son Shigemori (1138–1179) both served briefly as Inner Minister (*Naidaijin*), a high post dating back to the late tenth century. More important, Kiyomori followed Fujiwara precedent in marrying his daughters into the imperial line and also, for that matter, to the Fujiwara regents. In 1180 he finally had the satisfaction of placing his own infant grandson on the throne as the Emperor Antoku.

Many of the Fujiwara and some members of the imperial line resented the power of the upstart military band led by Kiyomori, but they could do little about it. The Ise Heike, however, were far from controlling the whole country. Kiyomori gained title from the court to extensive estates in the Inland Sea area and obtained governorships for many of his captains. Governorships were much coveted by the provincial warriors, because the prestige of such a post helped them to build up their land-holdings and personal following. But the Taira exerted little control over the great religious establishments of the capital region and still less over the remaining military cliques in more distant areas. In fact, the prestige of the Minamoto still remained strong in the Kantō, and the elevation of Kiyomori and his following from rural warrior-aristocrats to court nobles probably weakened rather than strengthened his personal hold over the warrior class as a whole.

The Triumph of the Minamoto. A plot in Kyōto against the Taira was severely dealt with in 1177, but three years later an aged Minamoto chieftain, who had survived by switching to the Taira side in 1160, persuaded a disappointed imperial prince to send out a call to arms to the remaining Minamoto of East Japan. Although the plotters were destroyed, some of the monasteries in the capital and many warriors in the eastland responded to their call.

Yoshitomo's third son, Yoritomo, had been spared in 1160 because of his youth and had been exiled to the Izu Peninsula. Now a mature man, he raised the standard of revolt against the Taira in 1180, gaining the support of many families of Taira as well as Minamoto descent in East Japan. He soon seized control of most of the Kantō, defeating local rivals in addition to the forces sent against him from Kyōto. A cousin, Yoshinaka, similarly rose in the province of Shinano in the central mountains. By 1182 Yoshinaka had seized large areas along the west coast of Honshū, and the next year he descended on Kyōto from the north. The Taira leaders (Kiyomori had died in 1181) fled the capital with the infant Emperor Antoku and established themselves at Yashima on the north coast of Shikoku, in the Inland Sea area that had for long been their base of power.

Yoritomo, who meanwhile had been strengthening his hold on the Kantō, was not pleased by Yoshinaka's more spectacular success and dispatched a large force to deal with him. The leaders of this expedition were Yoritomo's two younger brothers, Noriyori and Yoshitsune. Yoshitsune had been only an infant at the time of his father's destruction. Consigned to a religious life, he had escaped from his monastery near Kyōto in 1174 at the age of fifteen and had fled to North Honshū. Despite his youth, he proved to be a soldier of genius, and in 1184 he quickly destroyed even the able campaigner Yoshinaka.

Yoshitsune then moved on against the Taira, who in the meantime

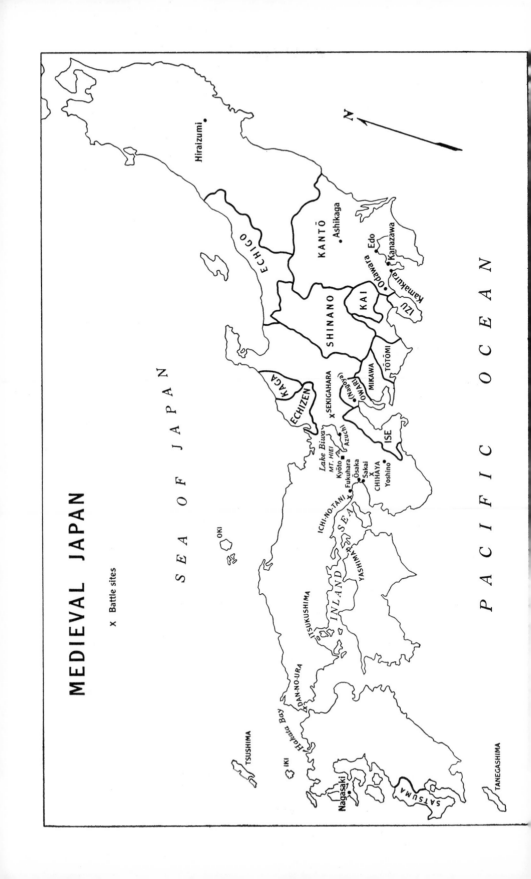

MEDIEVAL JAPAN

x Battle sites

S E A   O F   J A P A N

P A C I F I C   O C E A N

N

Hiraizumi

ECHIGO

KANTŌ

Ashikaga

Edo

Kanazawa

Odawara

Kamakura

IZU

SHINANO

KAI

TŌTŌMI

KAGA

ECHIZEN

x SEKIGAHARA

MIKAWA

OWARI

(OGAKI)

ISE

Lake Biwa

MT. HIEI

Azuchi

Kyōto

Fukuhara

Ōsaka

Sakai

x CHIHAYA

Yoshino

ICHI-NO-TANI

YASHIMA

INLAND

SEA

OKI

ITSUKUSHIMA

DAN-NO-URA

IKI

Hakata Bay

TSUSHIMA

Nagasaki

SATSUMA

TANEGASHIMA

had re-established their hold over all western Japan and had been worsting the Minamoto forces sent against them. He routed the Taira by a flanking cavalry attack down a precipitous gorge at Ichi-no-tani, a short distance west of the modern city of Kōbe, crossed over to Shikoku and destroyed their base at Yashima, pursued them down the Inland Sea, and finally, in the spring of 1185, annihilated them in a great naval battle. This famous encounter occurred at Dan-no-ura, at the eastern end of the narrow strait that separates Kyūshū from Honshū. The Emperor Antoku was drowned in the debacle, and the sword that was one of the Three Imperial Regalia was also lost to the waves.

THE EARLY FEUDAL SYSTEM

The series of wars between 1156 and 1185 had brought cliques of the provincial military class into firm control first of the capital and then of the whole country. Kiyomori by 1160 had become the military master of Kyōto as well as his own base of power in the Inland Sea area. By 1185 Yoritomo had achieved much more. The large-scale fighting which had swept Japan for five years from the Kantō in the east to Kyūshū in the west had spread the control of his personal band of warrior-followers throughout the greater part of the country, while building up its solidarity through unparalleled success. Where Kiyomori had been able to establish the power of his warrior band only within the withering imperial government, Yoritomo was in a position to extend the rule of his group over the whole country. His triumph in 1185 thus marked a much greater step toward feudalism than had Kiyomori's victory in 1160.

The triumph of the group from the Kantō cannot be dismissed merely as an accident of history. The Kantō Plain, by far the most extensive stretch of agricultural land in Japan, naturally supported the largest body of warriors; it was not surprising, therefore, that a Kantō clique could win control over the rest of the country.

The system of rule Yoritomo set up was based on one characteristic element of a feudal system — a hereditary military clique held together by the personal loyalty of the vassals to their lord. The warriors who swarmed out of the Kantō to conquer all central and western Japan considered themselves to be Yoritomo's retainers — his *gokenin* or "honorable house men." Warriors in other parts of the country, attracted by the success of this group or fearful for their own safety, eagerly enrolled themselves among his retainers. Thus, after the destruction of his Taira rivals, Yoritomo found himself the acknowledged master of the bulk of the provincial warriors of Japan, and the system he developed to control this group soon became the real government.

In two respects, however, Yoritomo's system of rule was not fully feudal, as the term is used in European history. He did not bestow fiefs upon his retainers, nor did his government completely replace the old civil administration. The latter continued to function, at least in theory, as the supreme government of the country, and Yoritomo's warriors continued to be owners or managers of estates which derived their titles from Kyōto rather than from him. The distinction, however, is a fine one. Yoritomo's government was in fact the only effective system of rule in Japan, and he saw to it that his men were rewarded with estates and managerial positions or confirmed in the possession of their lands and posts, even if title to the estates did not in theory derive from him. The Japanese, therefore, are justified in regarding the system he created as the first of the three successive stages of feudalism as it flourished in Japan.

Another non-feudal feature of Yoritomo's system was the continued ownership of many estates by court nobles, the imperial family, and religious institutions in the capital district. There was even a residue of public lands still paying taxes to the civil government. The great wars of the previous century and a half had brought many estates into the hands of the stronger provincial aristocrats or had induced property owners to commend their holdings to persons with sufficient local military power to protect them. Moreover, local military men often occupied the titular post of governor. It is, however, a measure of the slowness of change in isolated Japan that so much of the old land-ownership pattern survived the early feudal wars and that, for three centuries after the complete triumph of the provincial military class in the late twelfth century, the titles to some estates — and even a little income — remained in the hands of the long powerless court nobility.

The Steward and Protector System. Even before 1185 most of the estates of the Kantō region were either owned or managed by members of Yoritomo's clique. Now the destruction of the Taira permitted him to spread his men throughout most of central and western Japan. Confiscated Taira estates were given to his captains; Taira adherents were replaced as managers by his adherents; and hitherto neutral owners or managers were allowed to join his group. Yoritomo attempted to put some order into the system as early as 1185 by having one retainer named steward (*jitō*) in each estate, though opposition from the Kyōto court prevented him at this time from placing his men in some estates. The Taira had used the steward system to a limited extent, but Yoritomo's aim was to extend it to the whole nation.

A steward, who was supported by his own *shiki*, or share in the produce of the estate he controlled, served the primary function of seeing that the income from the estate was properly apportioned to the owner and the various other *shiki* holders. He also had the duty of maintaining peace and order on his estate, serving as the local judge, and performing the other offices of local government. He even collected a tax called "commissariat rice" (*hyōrōmai*), whether or not the estate had been exempted from taxes by Kyōto. Though only a small levy, about one-fiftieth of the yield, this tax symbolized the creation of a new government within the framework of the old.

The stewards, as members and appointees of a national military clique, exercised far greater powers than had the earlier estate managers, who had been appointees of the owners and therefore had operated more or less under the latter's control. This change in status of the man in immediate control of an estate showed how rapid had been the decline in authority of the older type of estate owner and the remaining organs of the civil government during the wars that had led to Yoritomo's triumph. The emergence of the steward as the key figure in provincial society marked a big step toward the complete feudalization of Japanese society. The position of steward, like almost every other position in twelfth-century Japan, was hereditary, and the estate which a steward and his descendants controlled naturally began to take on some of the aspects of a feudal fief, because they both controlled it economically and governed it, even though they did not in theory own it.

The stewards, being self-supporting, provided Yoritomo with a local administration and defense force at no cost to him. As his personal retainers, they could be called upon for military service at any time. As the effective controllers of the estates into which most of Japan had become divided, they actually governed the bulk of the people, besides controlling the income of the civil government and the court nobility. Thus, the stewards actually constituted both the military and the provincial administration of Yoritomo's government.

In order to give some integration to the extremely decentralized steward system, Yoritomo in 1185 appointed one retainer in each province to a supervisory post which came to be known as that of protector (*shugo*). These men had the responsibility for assigning the retainers in their areas to guard service, maintaining peace and order in their provinces, and serving as the captains of the local retainers in time of war. They also often bore the title of governor in the civil government, though this post now carried with it little more than prestige. The protector system was not entirely new, because temporary provincial military leaders had been appointed under one name or another in earlier times, but Yoritomo made it a uniform and permanent system, and the post of protector soon became hereditary.

There were, of course, many irregularities in both the protector system and the steward system. A few provinces had no protector, and some estates lacked stewards, while some protectors and stewards held a number of provinces or estates under their control. There was also considerable regional variation. The Kantō area, which formed the base of Yoritomo's power, and the region lying between it and the old capital district were more fully organized and much more closely controlled, at least during the early decades of Minamoto rule, than were North Honshū or the area west of Kyōto.

Government Organs at Kamakura. From the start of his rebellion, Yoritomo had made his headquarters in the Kantō at Kamakura, which is today a pleasant seaside resort south of Tōkyō. Even after the capture of Kyōto, he remained at Kamakura, close to his base of power, thus helping to keep his clique from being partially absorbed into the Kyōto aristocracy, as had happened to the Taira. In fact, Yoritomo's success, both in winning ascendancy over rival members of his own family and in establishing a more lasting political system than that of the Taira, probably resulted in large part from his stronger local base of power and his decision to keep the seat of his government in the East. He did not even seek high posts in the Kyōto administration but built up an essentially independent government at Kamakura.

Yoritomo's central organs of government were almost as simple as those he created in the provinces. Some men of learning from the lesser court nobility, such as Ōe no Hiromoto, came to Kamakura to help him organize his government, but it was derived largely from the institutions long in use in the family administrations of the great court nobles and the more important of the warrior families.

An Administrative Board (*Mandokoro*, so named in 1191), acted as a central policy-making body. The Board of Retainers (*Samurai-do-koro*), which Yoritomo set up in 1180 at the very beginning of his rebellion, administered the affairs of his retainers, allocating military duties and deciding on rewards and punishments. The Board of Inquiry (*Monchūjo*) constituted a final court of appeal, administering the customary family law that had grown up among the Minamoto. All these boards operated as committees, issuing only unanimous decisions — thus preventing any one member from becoming an independent source of authority and allowing all to be protected by the cloak of collective responsibility. Ever since this time the Japanese have shown a strong preference for collective leadership and great skill in its operation.

Theoretically the laws enforced by the Board of Inquiry applied only to members of the Minamoto family and the many retainers who had pledged their loyalty to it, but in fact these laws had become the only ones that counted in Japan, since only they were backed by effective power. As a result, court nobles and warriors alike came to Kamakura for justice, which the Board of Inquiry administered sternly but fairly, with careful attention to precedent and documentary evidence. Suits usually concerned the ownership and income of estates, since the system of *shiki* rights had grown extremely complex and much confused by the rapid military and social changes that had been taking place. Eventually, in 1232, the Minamoto family law was embodied in a written code drawn up by the Administrative Board. Called the Jōei Code (*Jōei shikimoku*) for the "year period" when it was compiled, it contained general maxims for the conduct of the warrior class. It was based on the administrative experience of the Kamakura government over the preceding four decades and soon became the accepted customary law of all Japan.

The Title of Shogun. Yoritomo was careful to obtain the sanction of the Kyōto government for any major action, but his organization really amounted to a purely private government which at first operated without so much as a theoretical connection with the old regime. Its central institutions consisted of the traditional organs of a family administration, and its control of the provinces depended entirely on the personal loyalty of a thin layer of family retainers.

It was not until 1192 that the position of this private government became theoretically justified through Yoritomo's appointment by the court as *Seii-tai-shōgun* or "Barbarian-Quelling Generalissimo," a post which had been assigned to leading generals intermittently ever since the Ainu wars of the late eighth century. Yoritomo had already been recognized as Steward General and Protector General of the system he had created, but the title of shogun now gave him clear status in the Kyōto government. As "generalissimo," he was recognized as having been delegated the emperor's military authority. Thus his private government became in a sense a provisional military government set up in behalf of the Kyōto administration.

The title of shogun became traditional for the hereditary military dictators who were to control Japan for most of the next seven centuries, and their military administrations, or shogunates, came to be known, in contrast to the civil government in Kyōto, as the *Bakufu* or "Tent Government." The government Yoritomo created is usually called the Kamakura shogunate or Kamakura *bakufu*, from its seat of rule.

THE KAMAKURA SHOGUNATE

Yoritomo's government, as we have seen, was a very simple organization, depending for its survival on the personal loyalty to the shogun of a large number of retainers spread throughout the whole country. But it must have met the needs of the time very well, for, despite various vicissitudes, it lasted for almost a century and a half, giving Japan more effective centralized government during this period than it may ever have had before.

The End of the Minamoto and the Rise of the Hōjō. The first serious problem the Kamakura shogunate faced was the early extinction of the shogunal line, on which its whole system of personal loyalties centered. The ability of the shogunate to survive this disaster shows how well Yoritomo and his colleagues had constructed their government. It also illustrates once again the Japanese capacity for rule through figureheads. The Minamoto shogunate could outlast the Minamoto themselves because power had passed to other hands even before they disappeared.

Yoritomo himself contributed as much to the demise of his family as he had to its triumph. He was extremely suspicious of his close relatives and particularly jealous of the military success of his brother, Yoshitsune. When the latter came to Kamakura to report after crushing the Taira, Yoritomo refused to see him. Yoshitsune was soon forced into rebellion and finally fled to North Honshū to the protection of the Fujiwara family that had built the Chūsonji at Hiraizumi. The new head of this house, however, fearing Yoritomo's wrath, in 1189 killed Yoshitsune. But this act of treachery did not save Hiraizumi as the last remaining major center of independent military power. In the same year, 1189, Yoritomo marched north and destroyed the Fujiwara of Hiraizumi, thus bringing all Japan for the first time under the control of a single military leader.

Meanwhile, in 1186, Yoritomo had done away with his one remaining uncle, Yukiie, who had played a prominent role in the wars against the Taira, and in 1193 he had his last brother, Noriyori, put to death. As a consequence, when he himself died in 1199 the only remaining members of the main Minamoto line were his two immature sons. (See page 527.)

The Kamakura administration, however, was maintained by Yoritomo's chief henchmen, though with repeated bloody quarrels, until one group was finally able to establish its unchallenged supremacy. The quarrels centered around Yoritomo's two heirs and the three sons of the older of them. The winners in this struggle for leadership within the shogunate were the Hōjō, a family of Taira descent from whom Yoritomo had taken his wife by elopement during his exile in Izu. Like many other families, the Hōjō had adopted a local place name as their distinctive surname. Three successive generations of the Hōjō family — Tokimasa, his daughter Masako (Yoritomo's wife) and his son Yoshitoki, and Yoshitoki's son Yasutoki — were chiefly responsible for consolidating the rule of Kamakura and making Yoritomo's system a lasting success.

The Hōjō Family

Tokimasa (1138–1215)

Masako	Yoshitoki	Tokifusa
(1157–1225)	(1163–1224)	(1174–1240)

Yasutoki
(1183–1242)

In 1203 Yoritomo's widow, Masako, and her father, Tokimasa, eliminated some of their chief rivals for power and forced Yoritomo's eldest son and successor, Yoriie, who had proved to be an unsatisfactory leader, to abdicate. Yoriie was assassinated the next year, apparently by Tokimasa's agents. Tokimasa, however, was ejected from power in 1205 by his own son Yoshitoki, who then proceeded to eliminate his other rivals. In 1219 the young shogun Sanetomo, Yoritomo's second son, was murdered at the instigation of his one remaining nephew, who of course was himself immediately destroyed, thus bringing Yoritomo's line to an end. The elimination of Yoshitoki's last rivals as a result of this incident left him with undisputed power, and his descendants were able to retain it for more than a century.

In 1203 Tokimasa had adopted the title of shogunal regent (*shikken*), and Yoshitoki followed his lead in this. Thus the Hōjō added one more step in the formal delegation of power. During the rest of the Kamakura period the Kyōto hierarchy consisted of an emperor, who had lost his power to a regent, who in turn had lost control of the court to a retired emperor, while the real power had been handed over to a shogun, who had now been supplanted by his Hōjō regent. In 1219 Yoshitoki brought an infant Fujiwara of high lineage to Kamakura, where he was made titular shogun of the warrior government in 1226. After 1252 the Hōjō regents chose imperial princes to serve as shogun, bringing the theoretical delegation of power, in a sense, full circle.

The Shōkyū War. The Kamakura shogunate faced a serious problem in the rebellion of disaffected groups. Mention has already been made of the destruction of the Fujiwara family of North Honshū in 1189. In 1204 a small uprising of Taira remnants in Ise was quelled. A much more serious challenge came a few years later from the imperial court.

Go-Toba, who had been placed on the throne by Yoshinaka in 1183 and had been the master of the *insei* government after his retirement in 1198, proved to be a vigorous man. He built up his own military force out of fighting men drawn from the imperial estates and, during the period of internecine struggles between the Hōjō and their rivals in Kamakura, came to exercise considerable power in the region around the capital. The end of the Minamoto line and the triumph of Yoshitoki in 1219 soon brought a showdown between the shogunal regent and the retired emperor, who was supported by some of the local warriors and Buddhist temples. In 1221 Go-Toba declared Yoshitoki a rebel. Yoshitoki at once dispatched a strong force, led by his brother Tokifusa and his eldest son, Yasutoki, and the Kamakura army quickly quelled the retired emperor's "rebellion."

This incident, known from the "year period" as the Shōkyū (or Jōkyū) War, turned out to be of great benefit to the shogunate. Henceforth it was clear who ruled Japan. Go-Toba and his two retired-emperor sons were sent into exile, and most of the other ringleaders were executed. The shogunal authorities assigned the *insei* administration to Go-Toba's brother, who thus became the controlling "retired emperor," even though he had never occupied the throne. Yasutoki and Tokifusa remained in Kyōto to oversee the court and also to serve as shogunal deputies for all West Japan, thereby strengthening the control exercised by the Kamakura government over that part of Japan. Since these two deputies were ensconced in the northern and southern palaces at Rokuhara, the old Taira headquarters on the southeastern outskirts of Kyōto, their posts came to be known as those of the Rokuhara deputies (*Rokuhara tandai*). Despite this close military control over Kyōto, however, the Hōjō always showed great respect for the throne as the source of all legitimate authority.

The Shōkyū War also allowed the Hōjō to take over either the actual ownership of or the position of steward in many estates owned by the court aristocracy which had hitherto remained outside the Kamakura system. Thus they extended their rule, besides acquiring means to reward their retainers with new honors and wealth. This latter asset was particularly important for the solidarity of the Kamakura regime, because a generation had elapsed since its original victory, and natural growth in the retainer class had left many members without adequate posts or income.

After the Shōkyū War the Hōjō ruled Japan sternly but justly for more than a century without interruption. Much of the credit for the lasting success of Hōjō rule should go to Yasutoki, who, succeeding his father, served as shogunal regent from 1224 to 1242. In 1225 he set up a Council of State (*Hyōjōshū*) as his chief administrative and advisory organ of government. In 1226, by forcing the Kōfukuji monastery of Nara to back down in a dispute, he taught the obstreperous monks of the great monasteries in the old capital district to respect Kamakura authority, and in 1232, as we have seen, he codified the shogunate laws.

When Yasutoki became shogunal regent in 1224, his uncle Tokifusa took the post of *rensho* or "co-signer," thus sharing with him the responsibility of leadership. Thereafter the two leading Hōjō usually occupied the posts of regent and co-signer in Kamakura, and two others, junior to them, the posts of Rokuhara deputies in Kyōto. Thus the Hōjō as a family demonstrated the same success at collective leadership that characterized the government boards through which they ruled.

The Mongol Invasions. The destruction in 1247 of the Miura, a powerful family in the shogunate, showed that Kamakura was still susceptible to internal feuds, but for a century after the Shōkyū War the only serious threat the Hōjō had to face came from outside Japan. Starting in 1266, Khubilai, the Mongol conqueror of the Southern Sung, sent repeated envoys to demand that the Japanese enter into a tributary relationship with him. The Kyōto court was terrified, but Tokimune, who acted as shogunal regent from 1268 to 1284, haughtily refused to bow to the Mongols.

Finally, in 1274, the Yüan emperor dispatched from Korean ports a mixed force of about 25,000 Mongols and Koreans. After wiping out the defenders on the islands of Tsushima and Iki, the Mongol army started to debark at Hakata Bay in North Kyūshū. The Kamakura government hastily dispatched forces, and its retainers in Kyūshū at once fell upon the invaders. Individually, the Japanese knights were formidable fighting men, with their excellent armor, skillful archery and superb swords, and their determination to defend their lands; but it is hard to say how well they would have stood up against the world-conquering Mongols if the latter had ever fully deployed ashore. It should be remembered that the Mongol troops were expert in massed cavalry tactics and could rely on the support of catapults that flung explosive missiles. The first encounter, however, was obviously not a clear-cut Mongol victory. That same night the invaders re-embarked and fled out to sea in the face of foul weather, returning to Korea with heavy losses suffered both from the storm and from Japanese swords.

After this first repulse, Khubilai repeated his demands that the Japanese acknowledge his suzerainty, but Tokimune twice executed the Mongol envoys. Kamakura energetically marshaled its forces to fend off another attack, and for five years the Kyūshū retainers were kept busy erecting a wall around Hakata Bay.

In the summer of 1281 the Mongols dispatched from Korea and China a second great force, made up of Chinese, Mongols and Koreans. Numbering about 140,000 men, this probably represented the largest overseas expedition in world history until recent centuries. But the Japanese were ready for it. Although the invaders seized various spots in North Kyūshū, the wall around Hakata Bay restricted their cavalry to a narrow beachhead in this most strategic area. Here the Mongols were held at bay for almost two months, and meanwhile the smaller Japanese boats played havoc with the junks of the invading fleet in the restricted waters of the bay. Then a typhoon struck, destroying much of the fleet and stranding the remaining invaders ashore, where they proved an easy prey for the Japanese. Probably less than half of the continental forces managed to return home, in complete defeat.

The Kamakura government maintained its defenses for the next two decades, but the Mongols never returned. These two attempted invasions of Japan were the first in recorded history, and they also proved to be the last until the twentieth century. It was fortunate for the Japanese that they came when they did, because a century or two earlier or later military disunity would have prevented the Japanese from meeting the onslaught so successfully. The Japanese themselves have usually ascribed their escape from Mongol conquest not to historical accident but to Japan's "uniqueness," attested by the *kamikaze* or "divine wind" that helped destroy the enemy. (The notion was still alive during the Second World War, when the name *kamikaze* was invoked in application to very modern forms of warfare.)

The memory of the Mongol invasions has been kept alive not only through literature but also by a wonderful pictorial account known as the Mongol Scroll. (See Plate 59.) This long and graphic scroll depicts in clear detail the Japanese knights, the unfamiliar Mongol soldiers, the ships of both sides, and even the Mongol bombs bursting in air. The scroll is so very accurate in its details that it must be the work either of an artist who himself saw the Mongols or of one who had eyewitnesses' drawings to refer to.

EARLY FEUDAL CULTURE

The Mongol invasions forcefully illustrated the growing closeness of relations with the continent. These contacts naturally brought new influences, but during this period Japanese culture, far from returning to the Chinese pattern, grew even more distinctly Japanese. This was because the warrior class, which had now come to the forefront, led a life still further removed from Chinese cultural norms than had the Fujiwara nobles.

Feudal Ethics. The ethos of the warrior class differed radically from that of either the Kyōto aristocracy or the Confucian bureaucracy of China. For these feudal fighting men, two ideals took precedence over all others — martial bravery and personal loyalty. They gloried in their military skills, making a fetish of their marvelous swords (a fetish which was still reflected during the Second World War, in the ancient swords which modern Japanese Army officers insisted on lugging into battle). The medieval fighter made an even greater fetish of his honor as a warrior and as a descendant of warriors. Before doing battle, he commonly called out his name and pedigree and taunted his enemies with his own and his ancestors' exploits. He took pride in his stoicism, in his disdain for petty profit, and, above all, in his physical bravery. He preferred death to capture or dishonor. The practice of suicide in defeat probably started as a practical measure to avoid torture and beheading, but in the wars of the late twelfth century it began to be institutionalized as *seppuku*, or disembowelment, a highly painful but much respected method of self-destruction that is known in the West by its more vulgar name, *harakiri*, or "belly slitting."

In feudal society personal loyalty to one's lord ranked as an even more essential virtue than bravery. The emphasis on loyalty may have been strengthened by Confucian teachings, which had originated in China in a period of strong personal loyalties, but it arose primarily from the needs of the time. Without personal loyalty, the whole feudal organization would collapse.

Although loyalty originally served to repay one's lord for his favors and protection, it was considered, as we have seen, primarily an ethical matter, not legal or contractual. The retainer owed his lord complete, unquestioning loyalty, even to death. Naturally great emphasis was also put on fidelity to one's word. But loyalty, coming into conflict as it often did with personal interests, inevitably proved the weakest link in the feudal chain. At certain times of stress treachery became almost as common. The bloody story of Yoritomo and the Minamoto family illustrates what little regard might sometimes be paid to the principle of loyalty even within a single family, just as the record of the Hōjō shows how strong and effective this bond could be.

The warrior clique behaved in some ways as a pseudo-family, and within the clique hereditary rights ranked all-important; yet one should note that from the beginning of Japanese feudalism extra-family bonds of loyalty took precedence over family ties. The vassal, if need be, was to sacrifice his own personal family, even his wife and children, for his lord; and very often he did. The contrast with China is marked. There, family interests usually took precedence over all others. Thus the family system of Japan, at least since early feudal days, has been very different from, and much less important than, the family system of China.

The code of the Japanese warrior, or *bushi*, which in more modern times was given the name of *Bushidō*, the "Way of the Warrior," showed points both of similarity and of contrast with the code of the European knight. *Bushidō* included, for example of contrast, no cult of chivalry toward women. Women had no special privileges, but neither were they relegated in the early feudal period to the inferior status they came to occupy in later times. They were expected to be as brave and loyal as their men, and they were allowed to inherit not only *shiki* rights but also positions in the Kamakura warrior clique. Some, like Masako, even played major political roles.

Though they might be inordinately proud of their fine steeds, brilliantly colored suits of armor and keen swords, the feudal warriors believed in a hard, Spartan life. A warrior was expected to be simple, frugal and austere. He was likely to be illiterate too, and boorish by court standards. But even in this age of the sword, the Japanese fighting man showed little of the contempt for book-learning that has sometimes characterized his European counterpart. The prestige of Chinese writing and learning exerted such an influence that military men took great pride in literary accomplishments if they could attain them.

Much of the feudal ethical code of twelfth- and thirteenth-century Japan survived intact through the nineteenth century, and some of it lingers on even today. While the world of the Fujiwara novels seems so remote from the life and thought of the modern Japanese that it might almost concern some alien civilization, the life and thought of the early feudal warrior is entirely understandable to them. Despite the large overlap in time and place between Fujiwara court society and early feudal society, the two contrasted sharply with each other. One was a survival of early Japan; the other was the beginning of the more modern Japan, which the West came to know first in the sixteenth century and again in the nineteenth.

Literary Trends. This same contrast can be clearly seen even in literature. Most of the writing of the age continued to follow the patterns of the Fujiwara period. There was, in fact, a revival of freshness in the overworked *tanka* form of poetry. The wandering monk Saigyō (1118–1190) proved to be one of Japan's finest poets. The greatest of the later imperial anthologies of poetry, the *Shin kokinshū* (*The New Ancient and Modern Collection*), was completed in 1205. Not merely a collection, this anthology was itself a sustained artistic work in which the poems selected were woven into intricate patterns of relationship. One of its compilers, Teika (or Sadaie), a member of a politically unimportant Fujiwara line noted for its poetic ability, is usually given credit for another small collection, aptly described by its title, the *Hyakunin isshu* (*One Poem Each by a Hundred Persons*). This work was so popular that it became the basis of a card game similar to our old-fashioned game of "Authors."

Although the tradition of novel writing gradually withered during the Kamakura period, collections of Buddhist and historical stories and romanticized court histories, similar to those of the Fujiwara period, still appeared. One famous miscellany, which in some ways can be compared with the *Pillow Book* of Lady Sei Shōnagon (though it is quite different in content), was the *Hōjōki* (*Record of a Ten-Foot-Square Hut*), attributed to Kamo no Chōmei (1151–1213) and describing his life as a recluse after he retired in disappointment from court society. The most famous poetic travel diary of the period, though close in style to Fujiwara writing, shows a very different society. Written by Abutsu, who was the widow, turned nun, of the heir of the great poet Teika, it tells of her trip to Kamakura in 1277 to seek title for her sons to the estates which she felt they should inherit from their father, together with his literary position.

Such works, though sometimes different in subject from those of the Fujiwara period, are otherwise quite similar to them in style and emotional attitudes. In sharp contrast, the tales of the exploits of the military class that began to appear at this time seem to come from a different world. They describe a drastically different life; they create an entirely different atmosphere. Whereas the works emanating from the Kyōto court society are refined almost to the point of sterility and are pervaded by a sense of melancholy, those dealing with the rising feudal society overflow with vigor and vitality. Even the language of the military works is different and seems much more modern, with many more borrowed Chinese words, and grammatical construction reflecting the influence of the Kantō dialect that later evolved into standard modern Japanese. Both in language and in ideas, the court writings of this period seem to come from a remote age; but the war tales sound almost as if they were composed yesterday. In fact, in only superficially modernized form they still sometimes achieve the rank of best sellers.

These war tales recount in well-organized and stirring fashion the series of struggles that led to the triumph first of the Taira and then of the Minamoto. Though historically accurate in broad outline, they are full of imaginative details. They became immensely popular with the warrior class and were often chanted to the accompaniment of the lute. The greatest of these works, dating probably from the early decades of Kamakura rule, is the *Heike monogatari* (*Tale of the House of Taira*). Two shorter works of about the same time, treating only limited parts of the story, are the *Hōgen monogatari* (*Tale of the Hōgen War*) and the *Heiji monogatari* (*Tale of the Heiji War*). In the middle of the thirteenth century the whole saga was reworked as the *Gempei seisuiki* (*Record of the Rise and Fall of the Minamoto and Taira*).

The exciting events recorded in these works helped set the attitudes and standards of conduct for the warrior class until the nineteenth century, and they so stirred the imagination of following generations that they became the favorite subjects of later writers. Many paintings also seem to have been based on these accounts, and three scrolls of illustrations of the *Tale of the Heiji War* still remain. These include a magnificent portrayal of an incident known as the "Burning of the Sanjō Palace," which is on display at the Boston Museum of Fine Arts. (See Plates 60–62.)

The war tales are by no means the most reliable historical sources for the events that led to the triumph of the Minamoto. The *Azuma kagami* (*Mirror of the Eastland*), based mainly on the official records of the Kamakura shogunate, provides a more sober and accurate account of the years 1180–1266, as the period appeared to the warrior class. Many diarists at the Kyōto court also kept records of events as seen from their own restricted points of view. The most important of these diaries, covering the years 1164–1200, is the voluminous *Gyokuyō* (*Leaves of Jade*), kept by Kanezane, the ancestor of the Kujō branch of the Fujiwara family, who served as Minister of the Right from 1166 to 1186 and then, with Yoritomo's support, as regent for the next ten years.

THE BUDDHIST REVIVAL OF THE KAMAKURA PERIOD

The early feudal period in Japan, as in Europe, was a time of ardent faith and high religious fervor. The military men of Japan were usually sincere believers in Buddhism, and many of them took holy orders in their later years. While Buddhism unquestionably imbued them with some pity and even mercy for their adversaries, they did not tend to identify their feudal ethics with their Buddhist faith, as the European knights often confused chivalry with Christianity. This may have been because Japan's few foreign enemies shared the Buddhist religion, whereas the Europeans looked upon such adversaries as the Saracens as religious foes.

The Buddhist fervor of the early feudal period seems to have sprung partly out of the constant warfare of the age, which made men long for salvation from this unhappy world. Certainly in court circles in Kyōto nostalgia for the good old days was mixed with a growing interest in religion. But this was by no means the whole story, since there also occurred a great upwelling of religious feeling of a positive, optimistic sort on the part of the hitherto suppressed lower classes. The religious revival of the Kamakura period thus represented a great popularization of Buddhism as a dynamic new force among the people as a whole and not merely the world-weary turning away from society of the aristocrats.

In the modern view, feudalism appears a repressive, hierarchic system, but in twelfth-century Japan it seems to have been accompanied by a degree of social liberation. Earlier Japanese society had been completely dominated at the top by a narrow court aristocracy. Feudalism, besides bringing the much larger and more widespread warrior class to the fore, also seems to have given the lower classes a more important and secure position in society than they had ever enjoyed in the Nara and Fujiwara periods. After the advent of feudalism, the lower classes as well as the new warrior aristocracy began to figure in Japanese culture as they never had before. Naturally the military man now figured prominently in both literature and art, and even the commoner began to make his appearance. The picture scrolls of the Kamakura period teem with intimate portrayals of the man in the street or the paddy field.

The religious revival of the early feudal period showed even more clearly the growing role of the warriors and the lower classes, for essentially it represented a revolt of these two social groups against the old aristocratic and hierarchic sects. There was a sudden new sectarian outburst, inspired in part by new influences from China, but growing even more out of the popular faith teachings of Genshin in his *Essentials of Salvation* (see page 508). The simplicity of these doctrines made them readily understandable to all, and a series of dedicated religious leaders further popularized them and energetically carried their message to the people.

Instead of being court aristocrats, these new religious leaders were chiefly of humble origin, the descendants of minor warriors or even commoners, and they loved to preach and minister to the lower classes. They often wrote in simple Japanese, rather than in classical Chinese, the traditional language of Japanese Buddhism, and they encouraged the translation of the scriptures into Japanese. They also manifested strong egalitarian tendencies, which contrasted sharply with the old aristocratic notions, and even with the strict social cleavages of feudal times. They emphasized the equality in Buddhism not only of laymen with the clergy but even of women with men.

The Pure Land Sect (Jōdo) and the True Sect (Shinshū). In 1175 Genkū (1133–1212), a monk from Mount Hiei who is better known as Hōnen Shōnin (Saint Hōnen), founded the Jōdo or Pure Land sect, which emphasized salvation through faith in the "Pure Land" or Paradise of the Buddha Amida. This sect was named after the Ching-t'u sect of China (see pages 171–172) but it had been inspired primarily by Genshin's teachings. Hōnen taught that salvation could be achieved simply by calling on the name (*nembutsu*) of the Buddha Amida. His type of Buddhism, which required no temples, priests or rituals, won adherents both at court and among the common people, but it stirred up strong opposition from the older sects, whose interests it undermined. The Kyōto court eventually decided against Hōnen. He was sent into temporary exile in 1207, and some of his followers were beheaded and others exiled. This persecution of Hōnen's movement marks the first appearance of severe intolerance among members of the Buddhist faith anywhere in East Asia.

One of his followers, Shinran (1173-1262), further popularized Hōnen's ideas and carried them to their logical conclusion. Shinran argued that a single sincere act of calling on the Buddha's name would be enough for salvation; thus, he frowned upon vain repetitions of the Buddha's name. He condemned self-conscious virtue as undermining simple faith and even went so far as to say, "If even a good man can be reborn in the Pure Land, how much more so a wicked man!" He all but ignored the historical Buddha, and his emphasis on Amida verged on monotheism. He discarded most of the scriptures and entirely repudiated the traditional monastic church organization. Since monastic life did not seem necessary for salvation, he had his priests marry and live normal lives and encouraged congregational groupings of priests and lay believers. The custom of marriage of the clergy in time spread from his followers to most other Buddhist groups in Japan. Shinran's branch of the Pure Land movement, in typical reformist style, came to be known as the True Pure Land sect or simply the True sect (Shinshū).

Other lesser branches in time emerged from the Pure Land movement. For example, there was the Jishū or Timely sect, founded by Ippen (1239-1289), a peripatetic dancing and singing monk. It emphasized the need to call on the name of Buddha at all times; hence its name. For a while it had a considerable following among the lower classes, and it still survives as a minor sect.

Because of their simple doctrines and egalitarian principles the Pure Land sects achieved immense popularity, but since they needed no strict hierarchic organization, they were at first only loosely organized. Eventually, however, they did grow into clear-cut religious communities. The True sect, centered in the great Eastern and Western Honganji (Temples of the Original Vow) in Kyōto, is now numerically the strongest in Japan, and the Pure Land sect comes second.

The Nichiren Sect. Another major branch of the popular faith movement was founded by Nichiren (1222-1282), a descendant of humble fisherfolk of East Japan. He stressed the Lotus Sutra rather than Amida as the source of salvation and taught his followers to chant "Hail to the Sutra of the Lotus of the Wonderful Law" (*Namu Myōhō-renge-kyō*). His sect, therefore, was named the Hokke or Lotus sect. Actually, however, it is usually called after him the Nichiren sect, indicating how dominant a personality he was. Indeed, he was more than that; he was a passionate, street-preaching revivalist and fanatic opponent of all other types of Buddhism. He minced no words in damning his religious rivals, certain that the natural calamities and social ills of his time occurred as the result of their baneful influence, and he predicted for-

PLATE 57. Ninth-century painting on silk of the Red Fudō, a Buddhist deity popular in the Shingon sect, preserved at the Myōō-in, one of the monastic establishments on Mount Kōya.

PLATE 58. Wooden guardian deity (Kongō Rikishi) at the Kōfukuji in Nara, dating from around 1200 and ascribed to Jōkei.

PLATE 59. Scene from the Mongol Scroll, depicting a Japanese armored knight, Takezaki Suenaga of Higo (central Kyūshū), battling Mongol bowmen in 1274. A Mongol bomb is bursting in mid-air. The scroll was painted around 1293 apparently to commemorate Takezaki's exploits.

PLATES 60, 61 and 62. Three scenes from the "Burning of the Sanjō Palace,"
one of three scrolls illustrating the *Tale of the Heiji War* (1159–60). The
attacking forces of Minamoto no Yoshitomo are shown above dashing out of
the burning palace, while court ladies leap into a well to escape the heat. On
the right, below, the attackers in armor and full battle array march away,
carrying on pikes two heads severed from fallen enemies. Plate 61, which shows
the end of the scroll and the beginning of the accompanying text, pictures the
van of the column, surrounding the carriage of the retired Emperor Go-
Shirakawa, who has been abducted from the palace. This great painting dates
from the thirteenth century.

PLATE 63. Autumn landscape in India ink on paper by Sesshū (1420–1506).

PLATE 64. Scene from "The Illustrated Biography of Saint Hōnen" (*Hōnen Shōnin e-den*), a fourteenth-century picture scroll, showing Hōnen and other monks invoking the Buddha Amida. The removal of the roof and walls to show an interior scene is a common Japanese artistic convention.

PLATE 65. Scene from the "Scroll of Hungry Spirits," dating from the Kamakura period. It depicts souls damned to perpetual hunger, surrounded by ordinary people. Two ladies on the left before a wayside shrine and a monk in the center carry rosaries.

eign invasions if their heretical doctrines were not suppressed. The Mongol invasions seemed to fulfill his prophecy, thereby contributing to his great success as a proselytizer, particularly in East Japan. The older sects naturally fought back, and once Nichiren was even condemned to execution.

One particularly significant aspect of Nichiren's teachings lay in their decided nationalistic coloring. He felt that Japan had become the center of the Buddhist faith, and he argued that his doctrines would benefit and protect the nation as a whole, not only the court, as the older type of Buddhism had done. The Mongol invasions may have contributed to his nationalistic bent, though he seems to have had it from the start, for his name, which means "Sun Lotus," can be interpreted as standing for "Japanese Buddhism."

While they stand in strong contrast to earlier Buddhism, the popular faith sects of the thirteenth century in many ways parallel the tendencies of Christianity in feudal and early post-feudal Europe. The reformist trends toward a simple, congregational type of organization, a married clergy, and the translation of the scriptures into the vernacular are all reminiscent of the Reformation in Europe. So also are the nationalistic tendencies displayed by Nichiren. The religious intolerance and persecutions arising from within medieval Japanese Buddhism, which have no precedent in earlier Buddhist history, find all too many medieval and modern parallels in the West. And the whole concept of salvation through faith and divine grace, the emphasis on Paradise, and the tendency toward an almost monotheistic concentration on a single Buddha brought the popular faith sects closer to Christianity in many respects than they were to the original ideas of Buddhism. Thus the striking social and political parallels between feudal Japan and Europe were reflected also in the field of religion.

The Zen Sects. There was another side to the religious revival in early feudal Japan, however, that differed greatly not only from European Christianity but also from the popular faith movement in Buddhism. This was Zen, the meditation school, which, as we have seen, had by Sung times become the dominant sect of the religion in China (see pages 172 and 237). Zen was introduced as a sectarian movement into Japan by monks returning from their studies in China. Eisai (1141–1215) brought the Rinzai sect of Zen back from China in 1191, and his disciple Dōgen (1200–1253), a scion of a noble court family, introduced the Sōtō sect from China in 1227.

Zen, as we have seen, stemmed from one of the earliest and most fundamental aspects of Indian Buddhism but had incorporated the Taoist emphasis on individual character and a close personal identification with the natural order, as well as Taoism's anti-intellectual and anti-textual bias. Zen stressed the direct, personal transmission of truth from master to disciple, apart from the scriptures; an individualistic independence of all authority; rigorous methods of meditation; a strict discipline of character; and salvation, in the more traditionally Buddhist form of enlightenment, through self-understanding and self-reliance. While its meditative practices made it seem quietistic, its discipline actually produced rugged individualists who could easily turn into men of action.

The Zen emphasis on personal character and discipline and on a simple life close to nature, as well as its rejection of scholasticism, all appealed to the medieval Japanese warrior because it fitted his need for inner stamina more than did the emotionalism and easy salvation of the popular faith sects. From Zen he could draw the strength required for his code of physical bravery and absolute loyalty. Zen, therefore, had an immediate success among the warrior class. Naturally many warriors embraced one or another of the popular faith sects, and some people from the lower classes took to Zen; but in general Zen held a special appeal for the warriors, and the faith sects for the lower strata of society.

On his return to Japan, Eisai made Kamakura, instead of Kyōto, the headquarters of his Rinzai sect and won the patronage of the shogunate through a policy of adaptation to its interests. One building of the Enkakuji, a Zen temple founded at Kamakura in 1282, remains as an example of the special style of Zen architecture, imported at this time from China, which flourished in the new military capital.

Eisai also brought tea back with him from China. Tea had been known in Japan for some time, but Eisai, by extolling its medicinal benefits, started it on its way to becoming the national drink. It is not surprising that the tea ceremony of later feudal times evolved at the hands of Zen aesthetes (see pages 565–566). Incidentally, the traditional form of tea in both China and Japan is green tea, which is never drunk with sugar, cream or lemon, and is a very different drink from the "red" or fired tea that was subsequently to become popular in the Occident.

Dōgen, a more characteristic Zen type of rugged individualist than Eisai, refused to compromise with any temporal authority. He made the remote west coast of Honshū his chief area of work. The techniques of meditation of his Sōtō sect also differed in emphasis from those of the Rinzai sect. Both used the method of *zazen*, or "sitting in meditation," and the *kōan*, an insoluble intellectual problem — or even a nonsense proposition — designed to help jar the meditator's mind into sudden intuitive enlightenment. The Rinzai sect, however, placed greater emphasis on *kōan*, while in the Sōtō sect the emphasis was more on *zazen*, through which a less sharply focused enlightenment was to be achieved by a slower, more gradual process. Both techniques are still very much alive today. In fact, Zen continues to appeal strongly to many who feel the need for self-discipline. The Rinzai and Sōtō sects today rank numerically next to the True and the Pure Land sects of Amida Buddhism.

Shintō and the Older Buddhist Sects. It should not be supposed that the new forms of Buddhism swept aside all the older religious movements. The traditional currents remained strong, in some cases showing a definite upsurge. The Shintō cults went on much as usual. The beautiful family shrine of the Ise Taira at Itsukushima (or Miyajima) in the Inland Sea and the Tsurugaoka Shrine at Kamakura, which was dedicated to Hachiman, the tutelary deity of the Minamoto, became famous cult spots. The older Buddhist sects also retained their vitality. Even the somewhat moribund Nara sects showed renewed life. The great old temples and monasteries of the capital area still owned a great deal of property, and the military activities at Kyōto in defense of their spiritual and worldly interests reached their height during the thirteenth century. Moreover, with the decline of the Kyōto court, Buddhist monasteries throughout Japan became increasingly important as centers of art and learning, just as the Christian monasteries came to play a comparable role in feudal Europe.

The revival of interest in Buddhism was clearly reflected in art, and the thirteenth century saw a second great flourishing of Buddhist sculpture. Unkei and other sculptors produced marvelously lifelike portrait statues, many of which still remain. (See Plate 58.) The religious fervor of the age was also manifested in the 1000 many-armed, identical images in the Sanjūsangendō, or "Hall of Thirty-Three Bays," in Kyōto and the beautiful fifty-two-foot bronze Great Buddha (Daibutsu) erected in Kamakura in the middle of the thirteenth century. Many temples were rebuilt. The towering main gate of the Tōdaiji in Nara, for example, demonstrates the influence of the multi-storied architectural style of Sung China, which was introduced to Japan at this time.

Most of the great temples came to have picture scrolls illustrating their histories, and other scrolls recounted the lives of great leaders, such as Hōnen, or illustrated popular religious ideas, such as the terrors of damnation. (See Plate 64.) All these afford wonderful pictorial data on the life, costumes and customs of early medieval times. (See Plate 65.)

THE COLLAPSE OF THE KAMAKURA SYSTEM

The view of the middle ages in Europe as a dark cultural trough between a glorious antiquity and an even more brilliant modern age has been generally abandoned. A similar interpretation of Japan's early feudal age as a period of decline is even less justified. The political system created by Yoritomo, though less centralized and less elaborately organized than the Nara government, probably gave Japan more effective rule, and certainly it possessed far greater military power. By the thirteenth century agricultural production had increased considerably, communications had improved, and trade and manufacturing had expanded greatly; in fact, the whole economy stood high above earlier levels. Cultural standards throughout the nation had risen appreciably higher than before, even if neither Kyōto nor Kamakura could match the brilliance of the imperial capital in earlier days. The artists and writers of the Kamakura period may have fallen short of their predecessors in some respects, but artistic, literary and scholarly production was now on a much larger scale and represented the activities of the whole nation, not just of a narrow group at court. Early feudal society thus reflected significant growth rather than any sort of decline, except that of the imperial court itself.

Rapid economic, political and cultural growth also characterized the remainder of the feudal period in Japan. In fact, the decentralization of control and the diversity of feudal society seem to have been more conducive to evolutionary development than was the more elaborately organized and more fully centralized system of political control that characterized Chinese history. On the other hand, the feudal political system, with its dependence on personal bonds of loyalty, was ill prepared to withstand the social and economic changes permitted by its loose organization. Political instability proved to be as characteristic of feudal Japan as of feudal Europe.

The Decline of the Shogunate. Although the Kamakura system met the challenge of change better than its successors, it had run into serious difficulties within a century of its founding. Its decline shows some of the characteristics of the Chinese dynastic cycle. The drive and cohesiveness of the founders of the system gradually dissipated in later generations. Justice was administered more slowly and less certainly, and feuds multiplied within the Hōjō family. The early emphasis of the Kantō warriors on simplicity and economy vanished, partly because of their increasing contact with the luxury of the Kyōto court. The stationing of warriors in Kyōto under the two Rokuhara deputies and, conversely, the settling in Kamakura of Fujiwara nobles and, later, of imperial princes to serve as shoguns, naturally mixed the two societies — to the detriment of the warriors, whose love for court luxuries tended to outstrip their income.

The chief reasons for the decline of the Kamakura shogunate, however, can be reduced simply to growth and the passage of time. The retainers' loyalty to Kamakura had withstood the shock of the disappearance of the Minamoto line, but it began to wear thin as the generations passed. The personal devotion of the members of Yoritomo's original warrior clique was hardly to be equaled by the loyalty of their descendants to his figurehead successors. In some cases these descendants of the original retainer group had been established for generations in an area remote from Kamakura. Usually they had had no direct contact with the Minamoto line, much less with the shoguns brought from Kyōto. What loyalty remained was seriously strained by the Mongol invasions, for the retainers of Kamakura were for years subjected to heavy military demands, and at the end there were no spoils in the form of new estates or stewardships to be divided among the victors, as there would have been in a domestic war.

The retainers' impoverishment presented an equally serious problem. During the century of internal peace following the brief Shōkyū War of 1221, the warrior class grew more rapidly than its income. Since Japanese feudalism had not yet adopted any system of primogeniture, patrimonies were often divided among a man's several sons, each of whom, however, inherited in full his father's duties of military service to Kamakura. The steward's *shiki* that provided an ample income for one of Yoritomo's original retainers was likely to prove inadequate when divided among several of his descendants. Many retainers thus found it difficult to support themselves during their periodical assignments to guard duty or even to afford the horse, armor and weapons which their status demanded. As a consequence, many fell into debt and were obliged to mortgage their *shiki* rights.

The shogunate repeatedly issued sumptuary regulations against extravagance on the part of its retainers, but these had little effect. Eventually the situation became so bad that in 1297 Kamakura issued what came to be known as an act of "virtuous administration" (*tokusei*), which amounted to a cancellation of the debts and mortgage payments owed by Kamakura retainers to those who were not members of the clique. This desperate measure, however, proved ineffective, because it made it difficult for impoverished retainers to borrow any more money. The decree therefore was rescinded the next year, and thereafter contracts of debt or mortgage commonly included clauses specifying that further acts of "virtuous administration" would not be applicable.

As the bonds of loyalty to Kamakura wore thin and the retainer class as a whole declined into poverty, certain more prosperous and stronger local warriors emerged as key figures on whom the lesser military men gradually became dependent economically or for protection and to whom they were beginning to transfer their loyalty. After four or five generations of growth the original Kamakura clique had simply become too large and too much diffused by time and space to continue effectively as a single group, and it was beginning to break up into a number of smaller, more cohesive local units.

Some of the new leaders had originally been mere stewards, but more commonly they were the hereditary provincial protectors appointed by Kamakura. As the only effective provincial authorities, these men were in a good position to strengthen themselves as the stewards sank into poverty and Kamakura's hold over them weakened. Such local leaders gradually came to form a new class of feudal lords that occupied an intermediary position between the shogun and his retainers, and thus they became the forerunners of the territorial lords who were later known as daimyo (*daimyō*), a term which literally means "great name" and was derived from the "name fields," one of the categories of private property in the make-up of the estates.

Go-Daigo's Attempted Imperial Restoration. In 1333 the weakening Kamakura system finally fell victim to men of this type, who had been its leading retainers. However, the war that brought the end of the shogunate actually started as a final challenge to feudal rule on the part of the old imperial court. In the late eleventh century the Emperors Go-Sanjō and Shirakawa had managed to regain control of the court from the Fujiwara, and in 1221 Go-Toba had made a disastrous effort to win back political leadership from Kamakura. Now Go-Daigo, who came to the throne in 1318 as a grown man of thirty, cherished the same antiquated belief that the emperor should rule.

A succession rivalry between two lines of the imperial family helped to complicate the situation. Two imperial brothers, Go-Fukakusa (1246–1259) and Kameyama (1259–1274), and their respective descendants fell into dispute over which branch should be regarded as the main line. The shogunate became involved and favored a policy of alternating the throne between the two lines. However, Go-Daigo, who was a grandson of Kameyama, was determined both to keep the succession in his branch of the family and to control the court as the reigning emperor. His ambitions involved him in plots against Kamakura as early as 1324. When the shogunate in 1331 attempted to force him to abdicate in favor of a member of the rival line, he launched a full-scale revolt (named the Genkō War after the "year period"). But Go-Daigo's uprising, far from accomplishing its objective, started a long period of warfare that was to wipe out most of the remaining wealth and prestige of the court, thus making any real imperial restoration quite unthinkable.

Go-Daigo, however, had considerable success at first. The great monasteries of the capital district backed him against the shogunate, and the adherence to his cause of certain locally prominent military men presaged the final breakup of the clique Yoritomo had founded. The forces sent down from the Kantō to suppress the revolt succeeded in capturing Go-Daigo and having him exiled to the remote island of Oki. However, they could not suppress all the rebels, particularly Kusunoki Masashige, one of the rising new local lords, who by turning traitor to Kamakura and espousing the imperial cause in 1331 won for himself the lasting reputation of being the greatest of loyalists to the throne. His defense of the fortress of Chihaya near Nara, which was typical of the mountaintop fortresses of this period, is one of the best-loved stories in Japanese history.

All over Japan others joined the revolt, probably attracted in most cases by the prospect of rewards for the victors. Early in 1333, Go-Daigo escaped from Oki, and the Kamakura general sent to recapture him suddenly changed sides, seizing Kyōto in Go-Daigo's name. This man was Ashikaga Takauji, who, as a descendant of a collateral line of the Seiwa branch of the Minamoto, hoped to destroy the Hōjō and seize the post of shogun for himself. Almost at once the Kantō too erupted into revolt. Nitta Yoshisada, another prominent descendant of the early Minamoto leaders, marched on Kamakura and completely destroyed the Hōjō and their government.

During the next three years Go-Daigo sought to restore imperial control over Japan, recreating some of the old civil organs of government and assigning the leading generals to governorships. This brave attempt (known from the "year period" as the Kemmu Restoration) has been made much of by traditional Japanese historians, but it was only an anachronistic interlude in Japanese feudal history. The clock could not be turned back to the Nara period, nor, as it happened, even to the age of Yoritomo. No one, least of all a non-military man, could control the many feudal factions into which Japan was disintegrating.

When Ashikaga Takauji and Nitta Yoshisada, the two chief destroyers of Hōjō power, fell into conflict in the Kantō in 1335 and the court sided with Yoshisada, Takauji turned against Go-Daigo. Eventually he eliminated Yoshisada and in 1336 seized Kyōto, setting up a new emperor from the rival line. He captured Go-Daigo on Mount Hiei, but Go-Daigo escaped to the protection of his supporters, who established Yoshino in the mountains south of Nara as their capital.

THE ASHIKAGA SHOGUNATE

Japan now had two rival imperial courts, a northern one at Kyōto and a southern one at Yoshino, but Takauji sought to reunify the country in a feudal fashion by recreating the shogunate. He had himself appointed shogun in 1338, founding a shogunal line that was to last until 1573. His Ashikaga shogunate, or *Bakufu,* however, was far different from that of Yoritomo — so much so, in fact, that it represented a second major stage in the development of Japanese feudalism.

One great difference from the Kamakura shogunate was that the Ashikaga never established effective control over all Japan. Another difference lay in the fact that there was no longer any thought that the bulk of the warriors of Japan were personal retainers of the Ashikaga shogun, as they had been of Yoritomo a century and a half earlier. Instead, it was recognized that the warrior class had divided into a number of separate lord-and-retainer groups. The Ashikaga problem was to achieve some sort of control over these lords, rather than over the warrior class as a whole.

The Organs of Government. The Ashikaga shogunate was outwardly modeled on that of Yoritomo, however different the inner realities might be. Takauji and his heirs occupied the post of shogun, but they made Kyōto, instead of Kamakura, their capital. Unlike the Minamoto, some of them assumed high posts in the civil government. The third shogun, Yoshimitsu (1368–1394), worked his way up from Inner Minister in 1381 to Minister of the Left and finally became the Grand Minister of State when he retired from the shogunate in 1394. Some of his successors followed his example in all but the top position.

A manager (*kanrei*, originally called *shitsuji*) shared the shogun's power in Kyōto, in imitation of the Hōjō regents. This post came to be occupied traditionally by lords from three families of Minamoto descent who had been closely allied to Takauji from the start and who had become powerful in and around the Kyōto area. These families were the Shiba, centered in Echizen north of Kyōto, the Hatakeyama, established both north and south of the capital, and the Hosokawa, who controlled eastern Shikoku and the adjacent parts of Honshū.

The same administrative structure Kamakura had used — an Administrative Board, a Board of Retainers, and a Board of Inquiry — operated under the supervision of the shogun and his manager. Moreover, as early as 1336 Takauji issued a code to supplement the Jōei Code of Kamakura. This was the Kemmu Code (*Kemmu shikimoku*, named for the "year period"), which specified the new seat of government and described the modified organs of administration. It would be a mistake, however, to assume that Japan was effectively ruled by the "laws" and boards which Takauji had set up. At first litigants crowded Kyōto, but the Ashikaga shogunate never achieved a position in most of Japan to enforce what decisions it did make.

The Ashikaga shoguns established a Kantō manager at Kamakura, just as the Hōjō had set up deputies at Kyōto. The post of Kantō manager was extremely important in the early days, because the Ashikaga's own holdings were centered in that region. At first it was filled by members of a local branch of the Ashikaga family, but this branch was destroyed in 1439, when its head attempted to make himself shogun. Subsequently, the post of Kantō manager was assigned to the Uesugi family, which was powerful in the area and had hitherto provided assistants to the Kantō managers. A Kyūshū deputy (*tandai*), in a post first created under the Hōjō in 1275 during the Mongol invasions, was appointed to control West Japan. Another deputy and sometimes two were appointed in the extreme north.

The Shogun and His Vassals. Despite this rather impressive superstructure, the Ashikaga never really ruled all or even much of Japan. They continued the Kamakura system of appointing provincial protectors, but many of these appointments, particularly in the more distant regions, amounted to little more than the recognition that certain lords already exercised effective control over their respective areas. Such appointments were not meaningful rewards for past services which would engender future loyalty, as they had been under Yoritomo.

In an effort to win the full support of his vassals, Takauji decreed that half the income of the estate owners should go to the military class. This great increase of the old "commissariat rice" tax of the Kamakura dealt a serious blow to the owners, but it did little to bolster shogunal finances or power, since most of the new revenue went into the hands of the local lords. In fact, the Ashikaga had to rely for their income largely on their own lands or on such trade taxes as they were able to impose in the vicinity of Kyōto.

The Ashikaga never had more than the nominal loyalty of most of their supposed vassals and usually they were quite unable to control them. Many of the protectors were relatives of the Ashikaga, and the shoguns attempted to extend their control over the protectors through a network of kinship ties. What military power the Ashikaga exercised, however, depended to a large extent on the more or less voluntary support of their supposed vassals, who were in fact little more than allies. For more than two centuries no one challenged the right of the Ashikaga to the title of shogun, but their position, when compared with that of Yoritomo and the Hōjō regents, was often not much more than a legal fiction.

During the Ashikaga period it was not the shoguns but the local lords (later to be known as daimyo) who were the key figures. The development of this group and their areas of supremacy in the course of the fourteenth and fifteenth centuries was a long, slow process, with many local variations. By the time of the overthrow of Kamakura, many local military leaders had already won such domination over neighboring stewards and lesser warriors that they were able to take their followers with them when they switched sides. In fact, this was the fundamental reason for the sudden collapse of the Hōjō. Eventually, through the careful administration of rewards and punishments, some of the local lords were able to convert all the military men in their spheres of power into their direct vassals or into "rear vassals," that is, the vassals of their own leading vassals. But this process took many generations and had not even approached completion until the early sixteenth century.

With the decline of effective central government, local authority came to depend increasingly on sheer power. A lord who relaxed his control over his vassals or suffered some serious military defeat was likely to see his followers desert him or seek to supplant him. As a result, there was a constant reshuffling of allegiances throughout the Ashikaga period, and vassals, often of obscure origin, frequently rose to replace their former lords. The lord-vassal unit thus tended to be quite unstable, despite the absolute loyalty that the vassal supposedly owed his lord.

Under such conditions family solidarity became imperative. A warrior family could no longer afford to divide the patrimony or permit women to share in it. In this strictly military society, women were eventually excluded from the inheritance and relegated to the socially and legally inferior status that they were to retain until the twentieth century. Some form of primogeniture also became necessary to consolidate the property and power of the family over successive generations. In feudal Europe it had become the rule for the eldest son to inherit his father's position and property, but in Japan the father retained the right to choose any one of his sons as heir, or, if lacking one, to adopt a son. Such an adopted heir might be a member of a collateral line or the husband of one of his daughters. But whatever the origin of the heir, it became established during the Ashikaga period that only one son, natural or adopted, should inherit the father's position and the bulk, if not all, of his property.

The Yoshino and Muromachi Periods. The weakness of the Ashikaga shogunate and the instability of the lord-vassal units into which Japan had disintegrated naturally made this time, as in feudal Europe, one of continual warfare. From 1336 until 1392 much of the warfare centered around the two rival imperial lines at Yoshino and Kyōto, and therefore this period has been named the Yoshino period or, in imitation of a phase of Chinese history, the age of the "Southern and Northern dynasties" (*Nambokuchō*).

Most of the participants in these wars probably were not motivated by devotion to either imperial line, but the existence of two rival sources of legitimate authority gave ambitious military men ample opportunity to further their own interests by resorting to arms, supposedly in support of one side or the other. Most were as crassly opportunistic as Takauji had been in 1333, and almost all switched sides at one time or another. Only a few notable exceptions can be cited, such as Kitabatake Chikafusa (1293–1354), who not only gave Go-Daigo loyal military support but wrote a history of Japan, the *Jinnō shōtōki* (*Record of the Legitimate Succession of the Divine Emperors*), to prove that Go-Daigo's line should be acknowledged as the correct one. This work also put forth the nationalistic doctrine of Japan's unique superiority as the result of its divine and unbroken line of rulers.

Go-Daigo died in 1339, but the struggle continued for another half century. Takauji, who lived on until 1358, was never able to stabilize the situation even around the capital. His own brother eventually turned against him, joining the "Southern" cause. The Yoshino partisans even seized Kyōto briefly in 1353 and again in 1355. Takauji's son and successor, Yoshiakira (1358–1367), proved no more successful in subduing his enemies than had his father.

Eventually the vain hope of restoring imperial rule faded, and both sides wearied of the struggle. The third shogun, Yoshimitsu (1368–1394; died 1408), succeeded in establishing his military control over a considerable part of the country, and in 1392 he was finally able to persuade the "Southern" line to return to Kyōto, with the understanding that the throne would again alternate between the two lines, as it had before Go-Daigo had upset the system. But the Ashikaga failed to live up to their bargain. While Go-Daigo's line is considered by Japanese historians to have been the legitimate one between 1336 and 1392, it never again occupied the throne and eventually disappeared into obscurity, even though for the better part of a century occasional military uprisings occurred in its name.

The Ashikaga government following the reunification of the two imperial courts in 1392 is usually called the Muromachi shogunate, from the area in the northwestern part of Kyōto where the shoguns resided at this time. During the next three-quarters of a century, the Ashikaga managed to maintain some degree of peace and order in and around Kyōto. This does not mean that they were able to prevent local wars even in the capital district; in fact, the sixth shogun was killed by an embittered vassal in 1441. Nor did the Ashikaga exercise any real control over their more distant or more powerful vassals. Nevertheless, the years between 1392 and 1467, when large-scale warfare again broke out throughout Japan, was the only period during which the Ashikaga shoguns gave any real appearance of ruling the country.

ECONOMIC GROWTH IN FEUDAL JAPAN

One might assume that the extreme political decentralization and constant warfare of the Ashikaga period would have stopped Japan's economic development or even pushed it backward, but this was, on the contrary, a period of rapid economic growth. The great expansion of the handicraft industries at this time gives evidence both of technological advances and of a rising standard of living. Important technological improvements also took place in agriculture, and production per acre seems to have doubled or even tripled in many parts of the country. Moreover, the developing feudal system actually proved to be a great stimulus, rather than a check, to the economy.

The rising local lords, by bringing under their control a number of hitherto economically independent estates, considerably increased the size of the local economic units and thus encouraged a much wider exchange of goods. Markets, which were usually held once during each ten-day week, flourished under the protection of these local feudal leaders or under the patronage of influential shrines and temples. Such markets naturally fostered the development of a professional commercial class of retailers and wholesalers. These developments, already noticeable in the latter part of the thirteenth century, became much more obvious in the fourteenth and fifteenth centuries, as the new units of local feudal power slowly took shape.

The clearest sign of the development of the economy was the gradual shift, between the twelfth and fifteenth centuries, from barter to the predominant use of money in trade. In the eighth and ninth centuries the government's efforts to popularize the use of money had failed, but now its use grew rapidly and spontaneously. Because the government mint had disappeared back in the tenth century, the Japanese, now that they felt the need for coinage, were forced to rely for the most part on imported Sung and, later, on Ming cash. The currency situation was further confused by the circulation of some earlier Japanese cash and much counterfeit coinage. Gold and silver coins were not minted in Japan before the sixteenth century, but the money economy was already so far advanced a century or two earlier that money orders had come into use for the transfer of large sums.

One of the early signs of the development of a money economy was the growing indebtedness, toward the end of the Kamakura period, of the steward class to usurers. The usurers included some of the more prosperous warriors, and Buddhist temples also played an important role as institutions for moneylending and the deposit of valuables. By the late fourteenth century, however, professional moneylenders were taking the lead in the expanding commercial activity of Kyōto and the other centers of trade. These bankers and pawnshop keepers, who were called "storehouse" men (*dosō*), had often got their start as prosperous sake brewers.

The Za System. Political confusion and warfare naturally did not help the growth of commerce, and still greater restrictions were imposed by the multiplicity of feudal authorities, all eager to erect barriers to tax the trade which passed through their domains. The medieval merchants, however, succeeded in meeting these feudal hazards by forming groups known as *za*, which specialized in the production or transport of certain goods, such as paper, sake, vegetable oils, or salt, or else in certain trades or professions, such as those of carpenters, blacksmiths, or dancers and actors. The *za* could be compared, at least in basic functions, to the medieval guilds of Europe, since their fundamental objective was to establish local monopoly rights in the production or transportation of their wares or the exercise of their professions. Through the payment of fees, a *za* would obtain from the various local authorities in its area of operation not only official recognition and protection but also exemption from the barrier taxes. Protected thus from ruinous tolls and dangerous competition, a group of tradesmen could safely continue and expand its activities.

Although the *za* system may seem extremely restricted by modern standards, it did give handicraft workers, traders and members of the humbler professions much greater freedom and higher status than they had ever enjoyed before. They had been little more than slave workers in government offices under the Nara system, or the domestic servants of noble families during the Fujiwara period. Now they had their own independent organizations which were qualified to enter into contractual relationships with the greatest of feudal authorities. The product of a perceptibly expanding economy, the *za* led to still further economic growth.

The beginnings of the *za* go all the way back to the twelfth century, but they did not become a dominant feature of the economy until the Ashikaga period. Many started under the protection of Shintō shrines and Buddhist temples. In Kyōto, which, despite its many vicissitudes during the feudal period, apparently remained a city of a few hundred thousand and was the chief industrial and commercial center, the *za* often operated under the partronage of remnants of the old civil government, contributing through their fees to the maintenance of the otherwise impoverished court aristocracy.

The Development of Towns. The economic growth of Ashikaga times led to the development in the fifteenth and sixteenth centuries of many towns, some of which, in contrast to Japan's earlier cities, were purely commercial centers and not political capitals. These new trade towns grew up at ports, at post stations on the major roads, at market places, or around major temples, which not only attracted pilgrims but often constituted important centers of economic activity. One example of a "temple town" is the modern city of Nara, which grew up around the great religious establishments, particularly the Tōdaiji and the Kōfukuji, located in the vicinity of the old imperial capital. Towns naturally developed at several of the ports in West Japan which were engaged in trade with the continent. Hakata, today a part of the city of Fukuoka, is an example of such a "port town." By the sixteenth century the most important port town was Sakai, at the eastern end of the Inland Sea. Located in what later became the southern suburbs of the city of Ōsaka, Sakai formed the medieval precursor of that great metropolis.

Another important category was the "castle town." In the early four-teenth century the local military leaders relied heavily on fortresses lo-cated in impregnable spots in the mountains, but, as they consolidated their realms, many of these lords began to erect their major strongholds at strategic points near the center of their domains, either on small hills or on completely flat land. During the sixteenth century towns grew up around the more conveniently located castles, and these naturally became the centers of economic activity in their respective spheres of military dominance. Most of the more important castle towns which appeared at this time have survived to become the middle-sized cities and prefectural capitals of modern Japan.

The townsmen in the castle towns, as well as those in the purely com-mercial centers, often achieved a considerable degree of autonomy in running their local affairs. An extreme case was the port of Sakai, which managed to win for itself virtual independence of all feudal authority, thus occupying for a short time a position comparable to that of the free cities of feudal Europe.

Overseas Trade and Piracy. One of the clearest signs of the rapid development of the economy during the feudal period was the growth of foreign trade, as Japan at last began to take a major part in the great maritime commerce that had been flowing along the coasts of Asia ever since the eighth century. By the late eleventh century Japanese ships had begun to visit the shores of Korea, and they started to go to China in the twelfth. During the period of Taira supremacy, Kiyomori gave impetus to this trade and developed the port facilities at his estate at Fukuhara, in what is now the city of Kōbe.

During the course of the thirteenth century Japanese traders became still more active abroad. The Great Buddha of Kamakura seems to have been financed in part by foreign trade, and Zen monks, many of whom had visited China or were themselves Chinese, actively fostered contact with the continent. For example, the Zen monk Soseki, who is better known as Musō Kokushi (the National Teacher, Musō, 1275–1351), around 1342 persuaded the Ashikaga shogunate to send a trading ship to China. From the profits of the expedition he built the Tenryūji monastery on the edge of the hills west of Kyōto. This venture inspired the dispatch of later "Tenryūji ships" by the monastery for its own profit, and similar trading ventures were organized by other monasteries.

The overseas trading activities of the Japanese frequently shaded off into piracy. This, in a sense, was a sign of the feudalization of the Japa-nese economy. With the exception of the Zen monks, the chief organizers of foreign trading expeditions were the feudal leaders of western Japan, and the men on their ships were usually as much warriors as they were mariners or traders. Consequently, if trade were denied by Korean or

Chinese authorities, or if the expected profits failed to materialize, the Japanese readily resorted to their swords to insure the economic success of their ventures.

Piracy actually proved to be a stimulus to international trade, rather than a hindrance to it. The reason for this was that the Chinese and Korean governments looked upon foreign trade as essentially undesirable. Consequently, it often took the actual or threatened use of Japanese swords to open the continental ports to any significant exchange of goods.

Known as *Wakō*, or "Japanese marauders," the pirate-traders from Japan became active in Korean waters in the thirteenth century, and by the fourteenth their depredations had reached very serious proportions. An armada dispatched by the Koreans in 1419 to suppress the pirates failed completely to achieve this objective. However, piracy in Korean waters gradually declined after the Koreans in 1443 made a treaty with the Kyūshū deputy and the Sō, who were the lords of Tsushima, to permit entry of fifty Japanese trade ships each year. The number was subsequently increased, and the Japanese also won the right to maintain permanent settlements in three ports in South Korea.

The Tally Trade With China. Meanwhile, during the fourteenth century, the Japanese pirate-traders had become active along the whole length of the coast of China. Their depredations (see pages 319 and 331–332) induced the first Ming emperor to attempt to bring Japan under control through the Chinese tributary system, but his efforts produced no concrete results, partly because of the warfare and division of authority in Japan. However, after the reunification of the two imperial lines in 1392, Yung-lo, the third Ming emperor, succeeded in getting Yoshimitsu, the third Ashikaga shogun, to enter into formal tributary relations with China — the first time any Japanese ruler had done this since the ending of the embassies to the T'ang in the ninth century. In 1404 an agreement was made according to which the Japanese would send a mission to China on two ships every ten years. As we have noted, tallies (*kangō*) from stub-books were provided to prove the authenticity of these missions and prevent private traders or pirates from claiming to be Japanese ambassadors.

The Chinese obviously were motivated by the desire to have their suzerainty recognized and by the hope that Japanese piracy could be eliminated through controlled commerce, but the trade itself they regarded as of little value. The Japanese, on the other hand, were motivated exclusively by the prospect of economic profit; the shogunate was only too happy to attempt to monopolize the lucrative trade with China. To do this, Yoshimitsu was ready to call himself the "King of Japan" and "subject" of the Ming, and he and most of his successors adopted a humble tone in their communications with the Chinese court, receiving its envoys with signs of great deference. For this they have been condemned by later Japanese historians, but they themselves obviously did not regard this as too heavy a price to pay for the financial benefits of trade. The strong influence at the Ashikaga court of Zen monks who were in close contact with China had helped to build up a feeling of great respect for Chinese culture. Consequently, the acceptance of China's nominal suzerainty was probably not so distasteful to the Ashikaga as to the political leaders who preceded and followed them.

The tally trade did not meet the expectations of either the Ming or the Ashikaga. Between 1404 and 1410, the Japanese seem to have sent six embassies instead of the one prescribed by the agreement, but the Chinese, anxious to placate them, made no objections. Then suddenly in 1411 Yoshimitsu's son and successor, Yoshimochi, repudiated the agreement on the nationalistic grounds that such relations with China did not meet the pleasure of the gods of Japan. The Ming subsequently liberalized the terms to three ships each ten years, and in 1432 Yoshinori, the sixth shogun, perhaps induced by the declining economic fortunes of the Ashikaga, resumed the missions. Between then and 1549 eleven embassies went to China — the authorized number for this period of 117 years, though some embassies consisted of as many as nine ships instead of the specified three. Moreover, the Chinese authorities often found it difficult to control the unruly Japanese warriors when the terms of trade were not to their liking, and, as the prestige of the Ashikaga withered, private trade flourished increasingly and piracy became worse than ever.

The expeditions after 1432 could not even be termed shogunate embassies, since some of the ships were financed by monasteries, rival feudal families, or even Sakai merchants. The cargoes and tally stub-books of the embassy that returned in 1469 were captured by the Ōuchi family, which had been powerful in West Honshū since the Kamakura period, and the Ōuchi came to monopolize the trade completely in later years. It was actually the overthrow of the Ōuchi by their vassals in 1557, rather than the end of the Ashikaga shortly later, that brought to a close this century and a half of official relations with the Ming.

The records of the embassies to China give some idea of the nature and scope of trade between Ashikaga Japan and Ming China. The chief import was Chinese copper coinage, which, as we have seen, was much in demand in Japan. More than 50,000,000 cash are said to have been brought back by the single mission of 1453. Silk goods probably came second in value to cash, and porcelains, books, paintings and miscellaneous fine handicraft goods also figured prominently among the imports. The Zen monasteries of Japan and some private families still own great collections of early Chinese paintings, porcelains and books dating back to this trade.

The Japanese exports included raw products, such as sulphur, copper and fine tropical woods, the latter obtained by the Japanese through trade with the Ryūkyū Islands. Manufactured goods, however, were more important, the greatest exports being swords and lances. The Chinese government tried to suppress this trade in weapons, but the fine swords of Japan were much in demand in China, selling at times for as much as 10,000 copper cash apiece. The embassy of 1483 alone exported more than 37,000 swords to China. Folding painted fans, which were a Japanese invention, were also exported in large numbers, along with other artistic goods, such as picture scrolls, wine bottles and ink slabs. The exporting of so many fine manufactured articles and art goods suggests that Japan, which in earlier centuries had been a relatively backward area compared to China, was by the late fifteenth century drawing technologically abreast of its great continental neighbor.

THE ZEN CULTURE OF THE ASHIKAGA PERIOD

During the Ashikaga period brilliant cultural developments paralleled the growth of the economy. Despite constant warfare and growing political anarchy, this was one of the richest and most creative periods in Japanese cultural history.

The centering of the shogunate in Kyōto seems to have brought about a complete and highly productive blending of the traditional refinement of the court with the vigor of the more dynamic classes newly risen through feudalism. The increased contact with China also brought new influences from abroad, which had a most stimulating effect on the now thoroughly Japanized civilization. While some aspects of Ashikaga culture were almost purely Chinese, most of the cultural developments of the time were distinctively Japanese, and they remain among the greatest of Japan's contributions to world civilization.

The Zen monks, who dominated contact with the continent, were of course the chief transmitters of the new stimuli from China. In addition, they contributed so much to shape the new cultural developments within Japan itself that the whole Ashikaga period may be characterized as an age of Zen culture. Zen monks were among the leading scholars, writers and artists of the time, and often they served as the arbiters of aesthetic taste at the shogunal court. They even occupied positions of political importance as advisers to the government, organizers of the expeditions to China, and drafters of the shoguns' messages to the Ming emperors. In the latter function, they often demonstrated a complete mastery of the most stilted forms of Chinese composition. Musō Kokushi, who has been mentioned as instrumental in the sending of the first "Tenryūji ship" to China around 1342, typified these Zen statesmen. He exercised great influence over Takauji and in 1339 persuaded him to erect Zen temples, called Ankokuji ("Bring Peace to the Country"), in every province.

Although Zen became dominant at the shogunal and imperial courts, it did not completely supersede the rival sects. The popular faith movement continued its spectacular growth among the common people, and the great monastic establishments of the older sects remained until the sixteenth century both militarily powerful and influential as landowning and moneylending institutions. The Enryakuji, the Tendai center on Mount Hiei, is said to have had 3000 buildings, and its warrior monks still could overawe the imperial court and shogunate in Kyōto. Tendai and the other older sects, however, had grown intellectually moribund and religiously corrupt. Homosexuality, which was common among the feudal warriors of Japan, as in many other military societies, became equally common in monastic life.

In contrast with the inner decay of the older sects, the newly risen Zen monasteries were full of religious and intellectual vigor as well as aesthetic creativeness. Five monasteries each in Kyōto and Kamakura received official recognition under the headship of the great Nanzenji ("Southern Zen Monastery"), the center of the Rinzai sect in the hills at the eastern edge of Kyōto. These Zen monasteries played so important a cultural role that some aspects of Ashikaga culture have been given the label of Gozan, or "Five Monasteries."

The Ashikaga shoguns, who helped bring together the warrior class, the old court culture, and the new stimuli from China, actually played a more significant cultural than political role in Japanese history. This was particularly true of Yoshimitsu (1368–1394; died 1408) and Yoshimasa (1443–1473; died 1490), the third and eighth shoguns. The Zen monks and secular artists, scholars and literary men at their courts produced much that was most distinctive and creative in Ashikaga culture.

After his retirement from the shogunate to Buddhist orders, Yoshimitsu in 1397, built for his residence the Golden Pavilion (Kinkakuji) on the northwestern outskirts of Kyōto. This building has given its name to the culture of the period between 1392 and 1467, a notable era, when the capital area enjoyed relative peace and stability. Similarly, Yoshimasa, a decade after his retirement in 1473, built for himself the Silver Pavilion (Ginkakuji) on Higashiyama, the "Eastern Hills" of Kyōto; and thus the later phase of Ashikaga culture, when it came to and passed its full bloom, is known as the Higashiyama period.

While much of the best in Ashikaga culture was developed in and around Kyōto, the political decentralization of the period helped to spread the culture as a whole throughout Japan. The "five monasteries" of Kamakura, of course, formed a second major center. Moreover, other centers of Zen learning flourished under the patronage of the Uesugi family at the old Ashikaga School, in the northern part of the Kantō

Plain, and, to a lesser extent, at the Kanazawa[1] Library, which had been founded during the Kamakura period by a Hōjō in what is now part of the city of Yokohama. During the latter part of the Ashikaga period feudal lords in all parts of Japan also began to gather Zen and secular scholars and artists around them, in the same fashion as the shoguns.

The Zen culture of the Ashikaga period cannot be described in words any more adequately than can Zen philosophy; it can be understood only by direct aesthetic perception. Something, however, should be said about its origins and tendencies. This culture drew from two distinct sources: one was Zen philosophy and the associated arts as these had been developed in Sung China; the other was the delicate sensibility, impressionism, and love of form and ritual of the native aesthetic tradition. In Ashikaga culture the originally Taoist sense of man's identity with nature and the Zen desire to achieve intuitively an understanding of the basic principles of the universe seem to have merged with the Japanese sensitivity to the beauties of nature; the intuitive indirection of Zen fused with the native tendency toward allusion and suggestion; and Zen and warrior restraint and discipline combined with the older love of form and ritual.

The result was a disciplined tranquillity and sophisticated simplicity which bordered at times on self-conscious aestheticism. Universal truth and beauty were to be perceived and appreciated through some small but most carefully executed expression. The small was preferred to the big, the intimate to the impressive, the simple to the complex, the natural to the artificial, the old and misshapen to the new and perfect. The emphasis was on what might be called "the cultivation of the little," which admirably fitted the restricted economic and social conditions of Japanese life in this and later ages. "The cultivation of the little" might at times degenerate into a sort of snobbish pose — a mock simplicity — but it has remained until today the source of much that is distinguished in Japanese culture and helps account for the extraordinarily high level of aesthetic taste that the Japanese still maintain. The tremendous influence of Japan's sophisticated simplicity on Occidental aesthetic taste, particularly since the Second World War, suggests that the Zen-inspired "cultivation of the little" may also have a significant role in our own freer and more affluent civilization.

The tea ceremony is one of the most distinctive expressions of the Zen culture of the Ashikaga period. It is enjoyed by a small gathering of art lovers in a simple, bare room close to the beauties of nature. The tea is prepared and served in slow, graceful, almost rhythmic motions, and, after it has been ceremoniously sipped from a common vessel, this bowl — by preference a simple, seemingly coarse type of pottery — and the other objects used in making and serving the tea are discussed and admired in quiet leisure.

[1] Pronounced Kanezawa in medieval times.

The tea ceremony was developed at the shogunal court in late Ashikaga times under such men as Sōami and his father and grandfather, Geiami (1431–1485) and Nōami, who were painters, landscape gardeners, poets and the general arbiters of taste in Kyōto. The greatest of the tea masters under whom the ceremony took final shape was Sen no Rikyū (1521–1591). In the late sixteenth century the tea ceremony sometimes became an excuse for ostentatious display, and, as taught today to girls of breeding, it is often merely part of a ritualistic training in good manners; yet its slow, measured pace, disciplined simplicity, and concentration on a few restricted objects of beauty can still convey a great sense of peace and contentment. In its self-imposed limitations, the tea ceremony exemplifies the Japanese "cultivation of the little."

ART, LITERATURE AND THOUGHT

The greatest of the Zen arts was the Sung style of landscape painting (see pages 226–228), in which the artist seeks to convey the essence of nature by eliminating minor detail and accenting with bold brush strokes what he considers to be important. Or, again, he might select some small aspect of nature to serve as a microcosm epitomizing the whole. In these paintings, man and his handiwork — temples, bridges, boats — usually appear only as insignificant details, blending into the great pattern of nature.

The earlier Zen landscape artists produced works that are hardly distinguishable from those of the Sung and yet, instead of being merely imitative, these paintings often equal the best produced in China. Josetsu and Shūbun were two of the leading Zen artists of the early fifteenth century, and Sesshū (1420–1506) was the greatest of all. (See Plate 63.) Kano Masanobu and his son Motonobu (1476–1559) made this style of landscape painting the specialty of the hereditary school of painters which they founded, but in their hands it departed from its Sung prototypes and became distinctively Japanese. The Kano School remained the dominant "official" school of painters until the nineteenth century, rivaled only by the Tosa School, the one hereditary line of painters of the older picture-scroll tradition that survived from the Kamakura period.

Stately, heavy-roofed Zen monasteries in a way typify the architecture of Ashikaga times, but the two most important buildings of the period were the relatively small and seemingly insignificant Golden and Silver Pavilions built, respectively, by Yoshimitsu and Yoshimasa. Unfortunately the Golden Pavilion was burned down in 1952, and the reconstructed building, covered with gold leaf in imitation of what is said to have been its original appearance, gives a garish impression as compared with the building that was standing before the fire.

The mixture of styles and the light, airy construction of these two pavilions illustrate important steps in the development of Japan's modern domestic architecture, which is both so very practical and aesthetically satisfying. By this time the thick rush floor mats called *tatami* were already beginning to be spread to cover the whole floor area of each room instead of just special sitting areas. A pronounced preference had already developed in interior decorating for natural colors instead of paint and for gnarled or twisted tree trunks instead of artificially shaped pieces of lumber.

The *tokonoma* had also made its appearance. It had started as a shrine-like alcove in the main room of a residence, but under the influence of Zen aesthetics it became a part of the room reserved for the display of art objects — a painting, a calligraphic scroll, a Chinese porcelain, a piece of lacquer or an arrangement of flowers. The Japanese limit the display in the *tokonoma* to a single piece or, at most, a few choice items. These are frequently changed so that what is displayed will really be noticed and appreciated. The Japanese realize that a number of objects detract from the enjoyment of the individual work and that familiarity is likely to lead to inattention, as is so frequently the case in the Occident. Thus the *tokonoma* too may be considered an example of the Japanese "cultivation of the little."

Landscape Gardening. An important feature of the Golden and Silver Pavilions consisted in the gardens that surrounded them. The ponds, trees, bushes and stones of these gardens were as inherent a part of the over-all design as the buildings themselves. In fact, the closeness to nature of the Zen artists led them to put almost greater emphasis on the natural setting of a building than on its actual construction. Under their influence, landscape gardening became a fine art in Japan, with aesthetic canons that have had a great influence in the Occident during recent times. In contrast to the geometric regularity that once appealed to Occidental taste, the Japanese felt that gardens should not only be natural but should, ideally, approach small replicas of nature as a whole, suggesting in their restricted compass the broader beauties of mountains and seascapes.

Musō Kokushi (1275–1351), one of the first great landscape gardeners, is given credit for the classic elegance of the garden of the Tenryūji and the cool, shaded beauty of the so-called moss garden at the Saihōji not far away. In later times, larger and more sumptuous gardens became the style. A typical example is the garden dating from the seventeenth century at the Katsura Detached Palace near the Saihōji. (See Plate 67.) These larger gardens usually appeal more readily to uninitiated Western tastes, but the smaller, simpler and more austere gardens of medieval times are both closer to the original Zen spirit and aesthetically more satisfying to those familiar with them. Many feel that the fifteenth-century "rock garden" at the Ryōanji (also pronounced Ryūanji) in

Kyōto should be reckoned the finest of all the Japanese gardens. It is an extreme example, consisting only of a few well selected and carefully placed rocks in a sea of meticulously raked white sand. (See Plate 66.)

The miniscule garden of the modest contemporary Japanese home successfully continues the medieval tradition and offers a good example in landscape gardening of "the cultivation of the little." The minor arts of arranging flowers, growing dwarf trees, and creating tray landscapes in sand or clay, all of which derive from Zen aesthetics, also illustrate the same spirit.

Literary and Intellectual Trends. Although Zen tastes permeated Ashikaga literature, there were also strong survivals of earlier traditions. A famous example of a traditional type of work is the *Tsurezuregusa* (*Grasses of Idleness*), a miscellany of jottings written by a courtier named Yoshida Kenkō (1283–1350), who had retired to a hermitage. In its melancholy tone, it is reminiscent of the *Hōjōki*, composed a little over a century earlier by another retired courtier. Similarly, the *Taiheiki* (*Record of the Great Peace*) tells of the almost incessant warfare of the period between 1318 and 1367 in the manner of the tales of the warrior class of the Kamakura period. The *Otogi-zōshi* ("Companion Booklets"), which were simple popular stories of comic, romantic, or strange and wondrous happenings, seem to have evolved from the brief historical and Buddhist stories of earlier times as well as from the novels of the Fujiwara court.

In Japanese poetry little new inspiration appeared, but a new form was developed. This was the "chain poem" (*renga*), in which two or more poets took turns composing, in almost endless succession, alternating three- and two-line units (the basic elements of a traditional thirty-one-syllable poem). These "chain poems" represented the ultimate development of the Japanese literary tendency toward a subtle and complex associative technique. At the hands of masters such as Sōgi (1421–1502) or Shinkei (1406–1475), the *renga* were sustained poetic efforts of much larger scope than the brief *tanka* could ever be. The composition of "chain poems" was immensely popular, but in the hands of lesser poets the form became almost as much an elaborate game as a literary art.

The more specifically Zen type of writing, known as "Five Monasteries Literature," was composed in pure — and reasonably good — Chinese. Aside from Zen philosophy itself, it consisted, during the early Ashikaga period, primarily of poetry. Later it came to include many writings on the Neo-Confucian philosophy of Sung China and on history.

The Neo-Confucian works included in the "Five Monasteries Literature" prepared the way for a great revival of interest in Confucianism in the seventeenth century, and the historical writings helped cultivate a more realistic awareness of the past than had existed in earlier ages. This growing interest in antiquity, however, was paralleled by a veritable passion for the latest fashions and the latest imports from China. In fact, the Ashikaga Japanese seem to have shown the same paradoxical contrast between a self-conscious interest in the past and an insistence on being up-to-date that characterizes the modern West.

The more sophisticated view of the past actually dated back to the Kamakura period. The *Gukanshō* (*Jottings of a Fool*), written about 1220 by an aristocratic Tendai abbot, Jien, was the first critical and analytical work on Japanese history. Kitabatake Chikafusa's *Jinnō shōtōki* (*Record of the Legitimate Succession of the Divine Emperors*) of the fourteenth century can be regarded as a continuation of this tradition, though with an added nationalistic bias.

During the Ashikaga period there was also a great revival of interest in ancient rituals and customs and in earlier works of literature, which resulted in the composition of many literary commentaries and studies of the court life of the past. This increased interest in the past, combined with the vague stirring of national consciousness reflected in the *Jinnō shōtōki*, may have contributed to the revival of Shintō during the Ashikaga period. The great national shrines, such as the one at Ise, which had lost their earlier income from the now impoverished imperial court, came to rely on the financial support of popular religious associations formed throughout the country. Thus they became the goal of masses of Shintō pilgrims. At Kyōto, Yoshida Kanetomo (1435–1511), a descendant of the ancient priestly family of Urabe, the "Corporation of Diviners," also developed a new syncretic Shintō doctrine, known as Yoshida or Yuiitsu ("Unique") Shintō. This was based on the "five classics" of Shintō, which were actually forgeries of about a century earlier. Yoshida Kanetomo held that Shintō, far from being merely a local manifestation of universal Buddhist truth, was itself the fundamental principle from which both Confucianism and Buddhism had stemmed.

The Nō Drama. The most significant and original literary development of the Ashikaga period was the *Nō* drama. *Nō* had its origins in the symbolic dances which had been performed to music at the imperial court ever since the Nara period and in similar mimetic performances among the common people. By the fourteenth century such dances had evolved into simple dramas and these were then further developed into the *Nō* drama at Yoshimitsu's court. The men chiefly responsible for this achievement were Kan'ami (1333–1384), a Shintō priest by profession, and his son Seami (or Zeami; 1363–1443), who were the founders of one of the hereditary lines of *Nō* performers (the Kanze) that still exist. Kan'ami and Seami composed the dramas in which they acted, and Seami also wrote the *Kadensho* (*Book of the Flowery Tradition*), the chief theoretical and critical discussion of the art of *Nō*.

The *Nō* drama is not unlike that of ancient Greece. It is performed on an almost bare stage by two main actors, the protagonist and an assistant, who are elaborately costumed and wear masks that are themselves fine works of art. In addition, there may be two or three subordinate characters and always there is a chorus which helps fill in the narrative. Both the actors and the chorus chant their lines to the accompaniment of highly rhythmic orchestral music, and the librettos are in large part poetry or at least a poetic type of prose. The actions of the players are supposed to be realistic, but in a highly restrained and stylized manner. In typical Japanese fashion, they suggest emotions rather than display them. The climax of the play always consists of a dramatic dance performed by the protagonist. (See Plate 70.)

In subject, the *Nō* plays usually concern the Shintō gods or famous figures in Buddhist or secular history, and generally they center around some concept of Buddhism, usually the ideas stressed by the popular faith sects rather than by Zen. The protagonist frequently turns out to be the spirit of some historical person, tied to this earth by worldly desires but longing for salvation. Several short plays were performed at a single sitting, and comic pieces, known as *Kyōgen* ("Crazy Words"), which were usually realistic burlesques of contemporary feudal society or of Buddhism, were interspersed between the more serious pieces.

The *Nō* drama, while not specifically Zen in inspiration, offers a good example of the highly refined and disciplined spirit of Zen aesthetics. As one of Japan's most distinctive contributions to world literature, it also illustrates the cultural creativeness of the feudal period.

THE LATE ASHIKAGA PERIOD

The weakness of centralized political authority during the Ashikaga period seems to contrast sharply with the economic growth and cultural brilliance of the age, but actually the foundations were being laid at this time for a more efficient form of centralized government. The growing power of the local lords often reduced the nation as a whole to virtual anarchy, yet the emerging realms of these lords were beginning to produce more effective local government than had ever existed before. By the late Ashikaga period the local units had become the solid building stones with which a more stable political structure could be erected.

The Ōnin War and Its Aftermath. Throughout the Ashikaga period there was a steady evolution of feudal institutions and the society and economy that lay behind them, but change became much more rapid after the final collapse of centralized authority following the outbreak in 1467 of a great conflict named, after the "year period," the Ōnin War. A dispute over the heir selected by the eighth shogun, Yoshimasa (1443–

1473), and long-smoldering succession disputes among the Shiba and Hatakeyama, two of the families from which the shogun's manager was selected, gave an excuse to two powerful military rivals to have it out with each other. These leaders were Hosokawa Katsumoto, who had been manager from 1452 to 1464, and Yamana Mochitoyo (better known by his monkish name of Sōzen), whose family had long controlled much of the north coast of West Honshū. Lords from all over Japan eagerly joined the fray, intent on local gains against their own rivals. The leaders of the two factions both died in 1473, and the war finally subsided into a stalemate of exhaustion in 1477. The capital area, however, had been laid waste and the shogunate ruined as a political force.

The Ōnin War proved to be only the beginning of a century of conflict unequaled in the rest of Japanese history. Local wars raged all over Japan, as the last shreds of centralized control disappeared. Most of these wars had nothing to do with the shogunate, but some struggles in the capital area took place ostensibly over succession disputes in the Ashikaga line, and no less than three of the later shoguns died in exile. This final phase of the Ashikaga shogunate is aptly named, after the period before China's first unification, the age of the "Warring States" (*Sengoku*). After 1467 the shogun's control over the country rapidly dwindled to a myth almost as empty as that of imperial rule. So feeble did the shogunate become that the virtual deposition of the last Ashikaga shogun in 1573 passed almost unnoticed by the rest of the country.

The Daimyo and Their Realms. The drastic decline of shogunal power during the last century of the Ashikaga period reflected the rising power of the local lords, who from this period on can properly be called daimyo. The realms over which these lordly families ruled had already started to emerge early in the fourteenth century and by the sixteenth had taken definite shape. The stronger daimyo by then had, in effect, become absolute rulers within their own domains. These they administered in accordance with their own "house laws," compiled to supplement the old Kamakura and Ashikaga codes. Usually these laws were characterized by both meticulous detail and oppressive severity. The private affairs of a daimyo's vassals, such as marriages and adoptions, were strictly controlled, as were all contacts with other domains. Punishments were barbarous and mercilessly enforced. A daimyo's principal vassals, who commonly held sub-fiefs, and also his lesser hereditary retainers still clearly constituted a feudal class, but the daimyo kept both groups on short leash if he could.

Toward the other classes in his domain, the sixteenth-century daimyo proved even more of a despot. He was supported primarily by the uniform taxes and labor levies he imposed on his peasants, and from them he drew the bulk of the manpower for his armies. If he were a good ruler, he took positive measures to increase the agricultural productivity and tax yield of his domain. He was equally careful to supervise and tax his merchants, and he often encouraged their activity both as a valuable economic asset and as a source of transport in war. Thus his "castle town" became a petty capital and the center of the economic life in its area. Successful daimyo could be termed, for all practical purposes, "petty kings." They were in fact called kings by the Europeans who first reached Japan in the middle of the sixteenth century.

As the daimyo rose in power, the lesser members of the military aristocracy naturally lost both power and prestige. This change reflected the declining role of the mounted knight, who had been the chief bulwark of the Kamakura system. In the course of the fourteenth and fifteenth centuries, large bodies of foot soldiers gradually supplanted the individual knight as the basic military unit; the foot soldier's pike replaced the horseman's sword as the chief weapon of hand-to-hand combat, and the *ashigaru*, or "light foot," came to predominate in the armies of the time. Warfare, which had once been the occupation of a warrior elite, was becoming the serious business of the whole daimyo realm. The captains of the growing daimyo armies were still mounted and armored men, like the knights of the twelfth century, but their function had changed. No matter how great his prowess, the individual warrior had become unimportant compared to the territorial lord who could mobilize large forces of foot soldiers from among his vassals and peasants.

As the daimyo gained absolute control over their respective areas of military dominance, they absorbed into their realms the remnants of the old private estates. In view of the disintegration of centralized control at the time of the fall of Kamakura and the almost incessant warfare of the whole Ashikaga period, it is surprising that the estates had not disappeared much earlier. The incorporation of estates into the territories of the local lords was, in fact, a remarkably slow process. Only by gradual stages did a lord's actual control over the various estates in his area become transformed into outright ownership of the whole territory, which in theory was held as a fief from the shogun. Similarly, the lord's assessment of fees against the estates in his area only slowly became a uniform system of taxation, and a steward's control over the estate he managed and his *shiki* right to income from it were only slowly transformed into a subfief held from the local lord. Vestiges of the old estates, such as their theoretical ownership by court families and even a small flow of income to their Kyōto owners, in a few cases actually survived until the late fifteenth century.

When, after the Ōnin War, the estates finally disappeared and the income to the Kyōto aristocracy from this source stopped completely, the imperial court and the nobility found themselves, of course, reduced to serious straits. During the second half of the fifteenth century and the first half of the sixteenth, their fortunes reached their lowest ebb. The court could no longer afford the luxury of maintaining retired emperors, and therefore emperors remained on the throne until they died. From 1500 to 1521 and from 1526 to 1536 there was not even a properly enthroned emperor, because the court had grown too poor to carry out the necessary ceremonies. The court nobility subsisted largely on fees received from affluent military men in return for court appointments, or on fees from Kyōto *za* which wished to use the protection of the court's prestige. One emperor was even reduced to selling examples of his beautiful calligraphy to eke out a living.

The Fall of Old Families and the Rise of New. As the daimyo domains became more sharply defined and effective political and military units, warfare among them also became more clear-cut. Defeat increasingly led to annihilation, and, as a consequence, feudal houses rapidly rose and fell during the sixteenth century. The Shiba, the Hatakeyama, the Hosokawa, and the Yamana, who had figured prominently in the wars in and around the capital since the early Ashikaga period, all fell or passed into obscurity. The Shiba and the Hatakeyama never regained strength after the end of the Ōnin War in 1477, and both houses had disappeared a century later. The Yamana lost much of their domain along the northern coast of West Honshū in the Ōnin War but survived as minor daimyo in this area until the nineteenth century. The Hosokawa continued until the sixteenth century to be powerful in the region around the eastern end of the Inland Sea, but the main line of the family disappeared about 1588, and only a distantly related branch of daimyo in Kyūshū continued the name into modern times.

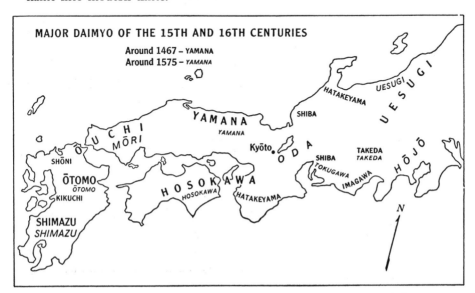

MAJOR DAIMYO OF THE 15TH AND 16TH CENTURIES

Around 1467 – YAMANA
Around 1575 – YAMANA

In East Japan, the Uesugi, who had risen to prominence in the early Ashikaga period and had replaced a branch of the Ashikaga as the main power in the Kantō area in the middle of the fifteenth century, were themselves replaced as overlords of the Kantō around 1546 by one of their vassals, a newly risen family of Hōjō based at Odawara. Uesugi Kenshin (or Terutora; 1530–1578), a great military leader and the daimyo of a collateral line from Echigo on the west coast, conducted protracted campaigns against the Hōjō and the Takeda daimyo of Kai to restore the family's fortunes. His wars with the renowned general Takeda Shingen (1521–1573) became particularly famous but won him no permanent gains. His line, however, survived as prominent daimyo in North Honshū.

In West Japan, the Ōuchi in the extreme western end of Honshū, the Ōtomo[2] in northeastern Kyūshū, the Shōni in northern Kyūshū, the Kikuchi in central Kyūshū, and the Shimazu in Satsuma in the south of Kyūshū had all been locally powerful since late Kamakura days. The Ōuchi, partly because of their monopoly of the official trade with China, had become probably the most powerful lords in all Japan by the middle of the sixteenth century. But they were destroyed by their own vassals and in 1557 were replaced by the Mōri as overlords of West Honshū. The Shōni and the Kikuchi both disappeared around the middle of the sixteenth century, and the Ōtomo had faded into insignificance by 1600. Only the Shimazu survived with undiminished strength in their isolated stronghold in the extreme south. Thus they became the sole feudal line to play a leading role in both medieval and modern times.

The downfall of these various old families was more than offset by the rise of powerful new families, such as the Hōjō and the Mōri. The more successful daimyo domains were growing steadily larger and better organized, and it was merely a matter of time before one of them would become large and efficient enough to reunify Japan and impose on the country a more thoroughly centralized rule than it had ever known before.

SIGNS OF DISINTEGRATION OF THE
FEUDAL SYSTEM

The existence of vestiges of the old civil government and the estate system that derived from it make much of early Japanese feudalism merely "proto-feudal" by European standards. Only during the middle and late Ashikaga period, though probably at somewhat different times in different parts of the country, did Japan pass through the stage most

[2] Not related to the Ōtomo family of antiquity, whose name is written differently in Chinese characters.

like that of high feudalism in the West. In this stage, land ownership and government fell into a clear hierarchical pattern, with the shogun at the top, his theoretically enfeoffed vassals next, followed by their sub-infeudated vassals, and so on down the line to the lowest members of the military aristocracy. This pattern, however, if it ever really existed in full, was at best quite transitory. By the sixteenth century the very foundations of the feudal system had begun to disintegrate. The shoguns had faded into a political fiction; the stronger daimyo had begun to convert their vassals and military retainers into a sort of hired army and bureaucracy; and various newly risen groups, theoretically outside the structure of feudal rule, were attempting to take a share in leadership.

The Fading of Old Class Lines. A fundamental reason for this dis-integration in the feudal system was the disappearance of the once clear functional distinction between the aristocratic warriors and the com-moners. The humble foot soldier had been important in warfare since the beginning of the Ashikaga period; the famed Japanese pirates were as much tradesmen as warriors; the *za* merchants and the townsmen of Sakai possessed arms and knew how to use them; and successful daimyo no longer relied exclusively on aristocratic warrior-retainers but mobilized as large armies as they could from their domains. The common soldiers in such armies could in no sense be called aristocrats. They were simply the more warlike and adventurous members of the lower classes, or even simple peasants, pressed temporarily into military service.

The blurring of the functional line between warriors and commoners was not the only indication of the extent to which the sharp class cleav-ages of earlier society had become outdated by the sixteenth century. The old court aristocracy had all but disappeared, surviving only in impoverished obscurity, and the distinction among the lower classes between the "good people" and the "lowborn" had disappeared entirely.

It should be noted in passing, however, that during the Ashikaga period the "lowborn" came to be replaced at the bottom of society by a small group of *eta,* commonly called "outcasts." Judging from their numbers in modern times, these probably constituted only about one to three per cent of the population. They seem to have been of diverse origins, including criminals and persons vanquished in warfare, but the majority probably came from groups whose professions, such as butchery and leatherwork, violated Buddhist dictates against the taking of animal life and thus brought down on them the opprobrium of society. Regarded as not fully human, they were forced to live in special villages or seg-regated districts of towns. Most of them congregated in the old capital area and in West Japan. Since 1871 the *eta* have enjoyed legal equality with other Japanese, but social prejudice against them still remains strong.

Village Administrative Units. The absorption of the old estates into the emerging realms of the daimyo had a profound effect on rural society. As the estates, with their scattered parcels of land, disappeared, villages took their place as the chief units of local administration and agricultural production. This transition from the estate to the village as the fundamental unit of rural organization occurred earlier in the economically and institutionally more advanced central areas than in peripheral regions, but eventually it came to all Japan.

Both the individual villages, which were principally of early origin, and the groupings of contiguous villages that were formed at this time for administrative purposes constituted much more natural and consolidated units than the estates had been, centering, as they frequently did, around sources of water used in common for irrigation or around the ancient local shrines, which often were survivals left from the early *uji*. The village administrative units which emerged in the Ashikaga period are still a dominant element in the rural scene in Japan.

Since the villages had a considerable degree of local autonomy, the peasants now were much freer than the serf-like cultivators of the estates had been. The formation of consolidated daimyo domains in effect removed the feudal authorities from the intimate daily contact with the peasantry that had been necessary on the estates. For the most part, villagers were allowed to run their own local affairs as long as the village as a whole dutifully provided its share of taxes and labor services to the ruling lord.

Though they maintained their aristocratic, military traditions, the descendants of the old managerial class who remained in the villages became increasingly identified with village interests. They were the biggest local landowners, they normally occupied by hereditary right the post of village headman, and they were commonly regarded as retainers of the local lord. However, a number of factors — the tax responsibilities they shared with the peasants, the agricultural problems they faced in common, and the village-centered religious and social groupings — tended to make these rural aristocrats more an upper crust of peasant society than the bottom stratum of the feudal system, as they had previously been.

The Rising Strength of the Lower Classes. As we have seen, the early feudal system had given the lower classes a more secure and prominent position in society than they had ever enjoyed before. The growing military role of the foot soldier in the fifteenth and sixteenth centuries and the tendency of the village aristocrats to side with their fellow villagers now gave the common man a measure of political power for the first time in Japanese history. One aspect of this development was the rise of individual commoners to leadership — the occasional man of lowly origin who solely through his military and administrative talents managed to work his way up from common soldier to captain to vassal to overlord. Probably many families rose in this way, though the Japanese love for high pedigrees has usually made it seem as though the newly risen lords came from humble offshoots of once noble families.

Still more important was the exercise of political and military power by groups of commoners led by the rural aristocracy. This sort of challenge to the feudal system naturally occurred increasingly as central authority declined. Rioting villagers and townsmen had begun to be a serious menace to the feudal rulers as early as 1428. From then until the end of the Ashikaga period popular uprisings were common in all parts of central Japan. Usually the rioters concentrated their attacks on the storehouses of pawnbrokers and moneylenders, in an effort to force a cancellation of their debts either by the frightened usurers themselves or by the shogunate or some local authority. After 1441 such outbreaks repeatedly induced the shogunate to order the cancellation of debts under the name of *tokusei*, or acts of "virtuous administration." Unlike the *tokusei* of the Kamakura period, these cancellations of debts in the fifteenth and sixteenth centuries were not enacted for the benefit of the shogunate's retainers but simply to placate the common citizenry.

Even more significant than these sporadic popular outbursts was the organization of permanent military and governmental bodies by commoners. The semi-independent town of Sakai provides but one example of this kind of banding together. Most of the popular political units centered around congregations belonging to the popular faith sects. The great monasteries of the old sects still survived from pre-feudal times as rich landowners and military powers, but these new Buddhist communities presented a challenge to feudalism of an entirely different sort.

After being suppressed in Kyōto in the middle of the fifteenth century, the militant followers of Nichiren created various autonomous communities in the provinces. The followers of the True sect (*Shinshū*) built up even larger political bodies. Rennyo (1415–1499), the hereditary head of the Honganji ("Temple of the Original Vow") in Kyōto, wrote in simple Japanese and proved so successful a propagator of the True sect doctrine that the jealous Tendai monks of Mount Hiei burned his temple and drove him out of the city in 1465. He then went to Echizen on the northwest coast and built his following into an effective military organization. For the next century this group and similarly organized congregations of the True sect contended with the feudal lords for local military and political control. Because of their religious fanaticism they came to be known as the Ikkō or "Single-Minded" sect, and their frequent uprisings and wars are called the Ikkō Uprisings.

The community that Rennyo founded in Echizen defeated and killed the lord of the neighboring province of Kaga in 1488 and thereafter ruled that province for almost a century. Similar but smaller self-ruling communities grew up elsewhere. Between 1532 and 1536 the True sect followers in the capital district were involved in a series of many-sided battles with the similarly organized Nichiren adherents, the local feudal authorities and the monasteries of the older sects. The greatest military and political center developed by the True sect was the fortress-like Honganji temple north of Sakai, around which the great city of Ōsaka first formed.

The Centralization of Power. This challenge to feudal authority by the lower classes probably hastened the consolidation by the daimyo of their control over their respective territories. In the face of this challenge, they had to develop a more thorough and efficient control over their realms or they ran the risk of seeing their feudal type of rule supplanted by more popularly based political systems. But the consolidation of power by the daimyo was also in its way destructive of feudalism, since it could be achieved only by subordinating the feudal rights of all classes to the interests of the individual daimyo and by extending the latter's power more uniformly over all within his realm.

Thus by the middle of the sixteenth century political and social realities had moved far beyond the situation usually pictured as high feudalism in Europe. And once again the movement was in the same general direction as that taken by European society — in other words, toward the centralization of political power that characterized Europe in early modern times. In fact, when the Europeans first arrived in Japan, in the sixteenth century, they found political and social conditions which were completely understandable to them in terms of the sixteenth-century Europe they knew.

13

Tokugawa Japan:

A Centralized Feudal State

POLITICAL CENTRALIZATION AND FOREIGN STIMULI

By the middle of the sixteenth century, as we have seen, Japanese feudalism showed many of the same signs of breakdown that had appeared in European feudalism as it gave way to the more centralized monarchies of early modern times. This disintegration could be seen in the expansion of domestic and foreign trade, the rise of commercial towns, the breakdown of the old class structure as the functional distinction between warrior-aristocrats and commoners became blurred, and the appearance of religious and commercial groupings of commoners who could challenge the military power and political authority of the feudal lords. Most important, the feudal privileges and autonomous status of vassals, rear vassals and the lesser feudal elements had begun to be submerged by the growing absolutism of the stronger daimyo.

The Third Phase of Japanese Feudalism. By analogy with the European experience, it might seem that Japanese feudalism was about to be supplanted entirely by one or more unified "kingdoms" comparable to those of early modern Europe. Indeed, the overseas expansion of Europe at this time did have its counterpart in the great activities of the Japanese traders in the sixteenth century. But the political reunification of the islands followed a very different course from that taken by the rising national states of Europe. Japan underwent no radical reshaping of political and social institutions such as Europe experienced in the eventual end of feudalism, the Reformation and the Counter-Reformation, and the rise of mercantilism. The Japanese found a simpler, less revolutionary solution to the problems posed by new stimuli from abroad and the need to bring effective unity to a feudal society. They built upon the older feudal order, instead of sweeping it away, and they eliminated most of the foreign stimuli, instead of continuing their overseas commercial expansion.

Thus Japan, rather than developing into a modern national state in commercial and military competition with the other countries of the world, entered into the third major phase of its feudal development — a phase characterized by political unity and national isolation. The country was reunified and subjected to a central political control that proved in some ways as thorough and efficient as that of any European state before the age of Napoleon, but the basic patterns of social organization and political structure remained entirely feudal. Any comparable stage in European feudalism — if such a stage ever existed — must have been very transitory. In fact, according to European notions the efficiently controlled system of late Japanese feudalism seems almost a contradiction in terms.

By choosing a simple, evolutionary solution to their problems in the sixteenth and early seventeenth centuries, the Japanese were able to attain effective unity and stability much more rapidly than the new national states of Europe. The stability they achieved, however, though an immediate blessing, may have been in the end a calamity for them, because it completely inhibited further development of economic, political and social institutions. During the next two centuries Japan's institutional and technological progress certainly did not keep pace with that of the West. As a result, the social and political order that took shape in Japan about the time of the first settling of the American colonies maintained its essential structure for more than two centuries, until the new nation that evolved from the small American colonies had expanded across a whole continent and, reaching across the broad Pacific, became a prime agent in the ultimate downfall of Japan's late feudal order. Institutional and technological backwardness in comparison with the West — this was the price the Japanese had to pay in the nineteenth century for the peace and political stability their ancestors had been enjoying for many generations.

It is not easy to explain why Japan, whose feudal development had paralleled Europe's in so many ways, took such a different historical turn during the sixteenth century. One reason may have been that feudal Japan maintained stronger traditions of political unity than those of the emerging states of feudal Europe, and therefore effective unity could be created without great revolutionary changes. The clarity of the geographical unit and the strong awareness of a long period of unified government throughout Japan contrasted with the vagueness of many national boundaries in Europe and with the tradition of a universal, polyglot Roman Empire, rather than a single clear-cut state. Because of these differences, the achievement of effective national units had been a much more difficult process in Europe, requiring the destruction of feudalism itself, while in Japan a united state could be achieved simply by building with the elements provided by the feudal system.

Another reason was certainly the greater distance of Japan from rival powers. A great increase in contact with the outside world during the sixteenth century seems to have contributed to the rapid reunification of Japan, but the protective seas and the remoteness of the country permitted the Japanese, when they became fearful of foreign influences at the beginning of the seventeenth century, to reimpose a considerable degree of isolation. Behind this artificially erected barrier, they were spared the sharp military and economic competition that impelled each of the rival states of Europe to forge ahead institutionally and technologically. Once unity had been achieved, the Japanese were able to put a sharp brake even to evolutionary change. They could thus maintain what seems by Western standards an anachronistic survival of feudal institutions within a society which in technology, economic development and effective political controls compared respectably with the most advanced of the European monarchies of the early seventeenth century.

The Coming of Portuguese Traders and Missionaries. While the reunification of Japan resulted mainly from the long process of domestic evolution, the sudden appearance of European traders and missionaries in the sixteenth century was undoubtedly a contributory factor. The military and naval skills of the European powers and the teachings of European missionaries posed a definite threat to Japan that called for a unified response. Moreover, the weapons and possibly other of the technological advances introduced by the Europeans facilitated the necessary centralization of power.

Soon after the Portuguese found their way around Africa and then pushed on to India in 1498, they and other European explorers began to dominate the great maritime trade routes that had existed for some seven or eight centuries along the coasts of Asia. The Portuguese reached Japan only a half century after they rounded the Cape of Good Hope. The first group to arrive landed at Tanegashima, an island off the southern tip of Kyūshū, apparently in 1543. Within a few years, Portuguese vessels were frequenting the ports of Kyūshū. In 1549 the Jesuit missionary Francis Xavier started preaching Christianity in West Japan and also in Kyōto.

Although the Portuguese seem to have had a certain contempt for the other Asians they had met, they respected and liked the Japanese. Evidently they were attracted by the martial skills and strong sense of honor of the feudal warrior class — qualities the Europeans could understand and appreciate because of their own feudal background. The Japanese similarly respected the Jesuit missionaries as men of discipline and learning, comparable to their own Zen priests. In fact, Christianity at first appeared to them as only another variant of the Buddhist doctrines that were so popular in Japan. Both sides too were eager for the profits of trade, and the Japanese, with their old realization that much could be learned from abroad, were receptive to both the religion and the material civilization of the Portuguese.

The daimyo of Kyūshū, who wished to entice the lucrative Portuguese trade to their respective ports, often showered favors on the missionaries, because of the missionaries' influence over their lay compatriots. Some daimyo, motivated more by a desire for economic profit than for spiritual gain, embraced Christianity and forced the people in their realms to follow suit. The small Ōmura daimyo became a Christian as early as 1562. In 1571 he established his town of Nagasaki as the chief port of call for the Portuguese ships and in 1579 he gave the government of this rapidly rising community to the Jesuits. The much greater Ōtomo daimyo was baptized in 1578.

The religious intolerance of the missionaries soon stirred up strong opposition among the Buddhist clergy, who in turn often induced the local political authorities to expel the missionaries or proscribe their religion. Many of those who had become converts for economic reasons, or who had been forced to do so by their lords, later abandoned the faith. There were, however, many sincere believers. Those in the capital district, where trade did not figure among the inducements, were particularly earnest, although the faith remained numerically strongest in Kyūshū.

The Christians in Japan have been estimated to have numbered 150,000 around 1582, about 300,000 by the end of the century, and perhaps as many as 500,000 in 1615. They thus constituted a much larger proportion of the population than they do today. In fact, Japan was the Jesuits' most promising missionary field in Asia. Wholly aside from forced conversions and economic inducements, Christianity seems to have met a greater response in Japan than in neighboring lands. It is hard to say why this was so, but the relative receptivity of the Japanese to foreign influences, the resemblance of certain aspects of Christianity to Japanese Buddhism, the similarity of Japanese feudal ideals to those of Europe, and the mutual respect of the Japanese and Portuguese must all have been factors.

The Influence of European Contact. The trade with the Portuguese and the technological advances they introduced probably had a more immediate effect on Japanese society and government than did Christianity. The coming of the large Portuguese ships had meant a further expansion of foreign trade, which in turn stimulated general economic growth and thus helped intensify the conditions that were leading to the breakdown of the old feudal system. New plants, such as tobacco and potatoes from the Americas, were introduced and in time considerably affected agriculture. The Japanese were much interested in the mechanical wares of the Europeans and found the Portuguese themselves fascinating. There was a veritable craze for everything Portuguese. At times modish Japanese even adopted European dress. Many Portuguese words entered the language, and a few, such as *pan* for "bread," still survive. A number of decorative painted screens of the period accurately portray the Portuguese ships and traders and the tall, forbidding missionaries. Since the Portuguese had arrived in Japan from the south and appeared to the Japanese to be dark-complexioned southerners, these paintings were called "Screens of the Southern Barbarians" (Namban-byōbu). (See Plate 69.)

With their strong military concern, the Japanese were particularly interested in the firearms and the techniques of warfare that the Portuguese brought with them from Europe. In fact, they were so impressed by the arquebuses of the first Portuguese who reached Tanegashima in 1543 that for a long time all firearms went by the name of *tanegashima*. Within a couple of decades of their introduction, guns had become a major weapon in Japanese warfare.

The Europeans may also have introduced improved methods of castle construction. In any case, the century following the arrival of the Portuguese was the greatest period of castle building in Japanese history, and all of Japan's existing castles date from that time. These castles had wide moats and massive earth-backed stone walls that could easily withstand the cannon-fire of the day, but the buildings themselves were flimsy by comparison with European castles, being made of thick, whitewashed mud walls on wooden frameworks. (See Plate 68.)

All this had immediate military repercussions. The richer daimyo, who could afford the new weapons and build the new type of fortress, became all the more dominant over their poorer and less modernized rivals. Thus they employed European innovations to accelerate the centralization of military and political power, which had already been started partly because of the threat posed by the Europeans' arrival.

Nobunaga and Hideyoshi Reunify the Country

The men who managed to reunify Japan were three successive daimyo from the region between the capital district and the Kantō — an area close enough to the capital to permit them to conquer it with relative ease, yet far enough away to escape the chaotic division of power among feudal lords, great monasteries, and religious or commercial associations of commoners that characterized the region around Kyōto. These three great unifiers first built secure bases of power in their home areas, then won domination over the capital district, and finally spread their control throughout the whole country.

The Career of Oda Nobunaga. The first of the great unifiers was Oda Nobunaga (1534–1582), the heir of a newly risen minor daimyo in Owari, where the great city of Nagoya now stands on the largest plain in that part of Japan. Nobunaga started his career of empire building in 1560 by defeating Imagawa, the greatest daimyo in that region. Then, after consolidating his strength locally through conquests and marriages, he marched on Kyōto and captured it in 1568, on the pretext of supporting the candidacy of a claimant to the post of shogun. Nobunaga made his man shogun, but the prestige of the Ashikaga had fallen so low that when his puppet proved difficult to manage he decided, in 1573, to drive this last shogun out of Kyōto and did not bother to select a successor, thus ending the Ashikaga shogunate.

Nobunaga spent the rest of his life consolidating his control over the capital area. In 1576 he built for his headquarters a great castle — the first of the new type — at Azuchi on a spur of hills overlooking the eastern shore of Lake Biwa, and one by one he destroyed the neighboring daimyo or forced them into vassalage.

A great part of Nobunaga's efforts went into eliminating the military power of the Buddhist church — both the great monasteries of the older sects and the more recently risen congregations of the popular faith sects. In 1571 he destroyed the 3000 buildings of the Enryakuji on Mount Hiei above Kyōto and massacred most of its monks. By threat or force he reduced the military strength and holdings of several of the other great monasteries. He also broke the power of the True sect or Ikkō groups in a ten-year war between 1570 and 1580. The temporal power of the True sect community that had ruled Kaga for a century was eliminated in two campaigns, the first led by Uesugi Kenshin, the powerful daimyo of Echigo on the west coast, and the second by Nobunaga himself. Nobunaga also destroyed this sect's communities in Ise and in 1580, after repeated sieges, finally managed to force the Ikkō adherents to abandon their great fortress at the Honganji in Ōsaka. Before the end of the century, the military power of the Buddhist monasteries, which had been a prominent feature of Japanese history for five centuries, had been entirely and permanently eliminated. Nobunaga's bitter opposition to the Buddhists inclined him to favor the Christians, and his interest and patronage help explain the phenomenal success of the missionaries in the capital region.

Nobunaga never made much headway in bringing the great daimyo of East and West Japan under his suzerainty. During his campaigns in the capital area, however, his rear was protected from the daimyo of East Japan by a loyal ally, Tokugawa Ieyasu (1542–1616). A petty vassal of Imagawa, Ieyasu had rebelled against his overlord after Imagawa's defeat by Nobunaga in 1560. Ieyasu had then consolidated his power in his native province of Mikawa by crushing the local True sect adherents and had seized the neighboring province of Tōtōmi from Imagawa. Now a relatively powerful daimyo, he prevented the newly risen Hōjō of Odawara from falling on Nobunaga and bore the brunt of the repeated attacks by the great general Takeda Shingen of Kai. Eventually the pressure exerted by the lords of East Japan on Nobunaga and Ieyasu slackened. Takeda died of wounds in 1573, and by 1582 his domain had been entirely lost by his less able successor. Another great general, Uesugi Kenshin, who had been pressing Nobunaga from the north, died in 1578, and his successor too proved less formidable.

The Rise of Hideyoshi. Nobunaga dispatched his best general, Hideyoshi (1536–1598), to conquer West Honshū in 1577. During the next five years Hideyoshi made slow but steady progress against the newly risen but powerful Mōri family of this region. He personally exemplified the breakdown of strict class lines that was taking place throughout Japan. A foot soldier of humble origin, he rose through sheer ability to become Nobunaga's leading general and an enfeoffed vassal. Since he lacked any distinguished family name, he successively used the names of Hashiba, Taira, and Fujiwara before settling in 1586 on the surname of Toyotomi.

In 1582, while Hideyoshi was still campaigning against the Mōri, Nobunaga was treacherously slain by another of his chief vassals, who, like Hideyoshi, was a self-made man. Hideyoshi returned at once from the west and destroyed the traitor. Four of Nobunaga's leading vassals then made themselves the guardians of Nobunaga's infant grandson, who was named successor, but within less than a year Hideyoshi had crushed his chief rival in the group and had seized mastery of central Japan for himself. Even the remaining members of the Oda family were forced to acknowledge his suzerainty and survived only as minor vassals.

Hideyoshi then proceeded to complete Nobunaga's work of reunifying the country. In 1585 his armies eliminated the military power of several great monasteries south of the capital region and forced the strongest daimyo of Shikoku to submit. After an inconclusive fight with Hideyoshi in 1584, Tokugawa Ieyasu finally accepted his suzerainty two years later, as did also the Mōri of West Honshū and the Uesugi of Echigo.

With all of central Japan firmly under his control, Hideyoshi started on the conquest of the more distant areas. In 1586 he moved with an army of 250,000 men against the Shimazu, who had become the chief power in Kyūshū. By the early part of the next year he had beaten them into submission, but he generously permitted them to keep the greater part of their domains in the extreme south of the island.

Hideyoshi now turned eastward and in 1590 descended on the Hōjō in the Kantō. The chief Hōjō castle, at Odawara, withstood a two-month siege by a force of 300,000 men but finally capitulated, and the Hōjō were reduced to petty vassals. Meanwhile their great domain had been overrun, and the Date of the Sendai area and the other hitherto independent lords of North Honshū had been overawed into acknowledging Hideyoshi's suzerainty. After two and a half centuries of political disunity, all Japan had at last been reunited under the effective control of a single man.

Hideyoshi's Government. It is worth noting that neither Nobunaga nor Hideyoshi attempted to assume the title of shogun. Instead they sought prestige and legitimacy through a close association with the imperial court. They rebuilt the Kyōto palace and provided the emperors, as the ultimate source of all political authority, with adequate, though modest, economic support. The re-establishment of an effective central government thus brought to an end the worst days of poverty for the emperors and the Kyōto nobility. Nobunaga and Hideyoshi contented themselves with high titles in the old civil government. Nobunaga briefly held the posts of Inner Minister and Minister of the Right, and Hideyoshi occupied the topmost position of *kampaku* in 1585. After he relinquished this post to his adopted son Hidetsugu in 1591, he became known as the *taikō*, a title used by retired *kampaku*.

In 1583 Hideyoshi built for himself a great castle-palace on the site of the Honganji fortress of the True sect at Ōsaka. This became the greatest castle of its day, and the huge inner moats and walls still remain as a conspicuous sight in downtown Ōsaka. Hideyoshi also constructed for himself the Jurakudai palace in Kyōto in 1587 and the Momoyama ("Peach Hill") castle a little south of the city in 1594. The Momoyama castle has given its name to the period, for the age of Nobunaga and Hideyoshi is commonly called the Azuchi-Momoyama period, from their respective headquarters.

The castles and palaces of both Nobunaga and Hideyoshi were monumental and sumptuous structures. Their woodwork was elaborately carved or lacquered, and their interior walls and sliding partitions were decorated with gold leaf and large paintings by the leading artists of the official Kano School. In sharp contrast with the Zen aesthetic standards of the Ashikaga shoguns, the taste of these great military men seems to have run to imposing size and splendor. Hideyoshi wanted everything to be on a grand scale. In 1589 he erected a great bronze Buddha, larger than those of Kamakura and Nara, at Kyōto; this Buddha, however, was destroyed in an earthquake in 1596. Even the tea ceremony, as performed by Hideyoshi, turned into a grandiose affair. His so-called Kitano Tea Party held at Kyōto in 1587 was a veritable public art festival, attended by thousands during a ten-day period, and featuring art exhibits and dramatic and dancing performances.

Although Hideyoshi served in theory as the emperor's chief minister and acted in fact like an absolute monarch, he made no effort to revive the ancient organs of civil government and to rule through them. Instead, he controlled the country through the old feudal device of vassalage. The bulk of the country remained in the hands of daimyo, who were the autonomous rulers of their own realms and did not even pay regular taxes to the support of the central government.

Despite these feudal divisions, however, Hideyoshi actually controlled the country with a heavy hand. Although he generously permitted former equals and even rivals to continue as daimyo, he usually reduced their fiefs and sometimes moved them about as he wished. He also interspersed the less reliable daimyo with his own trusted supporters. The Shimazu, for example, had been allowed to remain as the daimyo of southern Kyūshū, but their fief was counterbalanced by the creation of new ones given to safe daimyo, such as the two Christian generals Konishi and Kuroda and the violently anti-Christian Katō Kiyomasa. All three of these men had risen from obscurity to prominence in Hideyoshi's service and therefore were considered entirely reliable. Most of the Kantō Hideyoshi gave in 1590 to Tokugawa Ieyasu, who had proved himself a faithful vassal in the destruction of the Hōjō. However, Hideyoshi's real motive may not have been to reward Ieyasu with a larger realm but to shift this greatest and most dangerous of his vassals from his old established area of rule to a new region, where the people might prove less loyal and thus might undermine his strength.

Although Hideyoshi did not exact taxes as such from his vassals, he clipped their economic wings and forced them to contribute to his government by demanding heavy military services and substantial participation in his many ambitious construction projects. Clearly, he conducted himself as the *de facto* ruler of the whole country. He minted copper, silver and gold coins and put order into the currency system; he established new land measures and taxation rates; he carried out a land survey over all Japan; he controlled foreign relations; and he made his decrees the absolute law of the land. To aid him in ruling, Hideyoshi set up a sort of cabinet, consisting of five commissioners (*bugyō*), who took charge of various aspects of the administration. Usually two or three of them acted jointly on important matters, in the traditional Japanese fashion. These men, who held fiefs of middle size (near the capital district for the most part), could be relied on as entirely trustworthy henchmen, since they were all self-made individuals who had forged ahead in Hideyoshi's service.

It may seem strange that Hideyoshi, who undoubtedly was driven by a megalomaniac desire for power and glory, should have been content with this somewhat paradoxical combination of absolute centralized authority in practice and almost complete local autonomy in theory. Vassalage, however, was the political organization he understood, and his use of the daimyo system permitted him to reunify Japan and restore peace much more rapidly than if he had forced his rivals into bitter-end resistance by giving them no alternative but extinction. The theoretical autonomy of the daimyo probably seemed a small price to pay for the quick subjugation of the country and the resulting peace.

In fact, the desire to bring peace and stability to Japan as rapidly as possible seems to have been one of Hideyoshi's principal objectives, and this helps to explain many of his specific policies, such as his re-establishment of rigid class lines. One of the ways to create stability, he apparently thought, was to halt the swift social changes that had been taking place during his lifetime — the kind of changes that had made possible his own spectacular rise from the bottom to the top of the political heap. As a self-made man himself, Hideyoshi may also have been particularly afraid that other humble men of ability, unless kept severely in their place, might make their fortunes at the expense of his heirs. In any case, he attempted by government fiat to keep warriors, peasants and townsmen separate from one another, thus reinforcing the functional differences that had been disappearing.

Hideyoshi inaugurated his program in 1588 by ordering all peasants to surrender their swords, and he applied the law vigorously throughout the country. Through this so-called "sword hunt," he re-established a clear and visible distinction between the sword-wearing aristocrat and the swordless commoner. He was also responsible for a series of laws — the most famous ones were enacted in 1591 — prohibiting military retainers from leaving their lords' service to become merchants or farmers, and preventing farmers from deserting their fields to become merchants or laborers, as had frequently happened during the recent wars. Thus he helped stabilize the daimyo realms through which he hoped to rule Japan.

The Persecution of Christianity. Hideyoshi's desire for stability also helps explain his attitude toward the Christians. At first he treated the missionaries with the same favor shown by Nobunaga, and he always remained anxious to maintain the profitable trade with the Portuguese. In 1587, however, he suddenly ordered all missionaries banished from Japan, and he subsequently confiscated their "sub-fief" of Nagasaki. He also ordered his vassals to secure his permission before embracing Christianity and to refrain from converting by force the people they ruled, though he placed no restriction on the beliefs of the lower classes.

Hideyoshi appears to have turned against the missionaries because he feared that Christianity was becoming a disturbing factor in society and a potential political menace. The Jesuits were religiously intolerant, and some of their converts, such as the Ōtomo daimyo, were fanatical persecutors of Buddhism. Still worse, the bond of Christianity had become a basis for cooperation among some of the daimyo of Kyūshū. In addition, Christianity was so popular even in Kyōto that conversion had become a stylish fad, and many of Hideyoshi's chief lieutenants were being baptized. It seemed possible that the allegiance of his vassals to this foreign religion, and to the foreign head of their organized church, might stand in the way of their feudal loyalties and thus might endanger Hideyoshi's supreme control. The time had come, he must have thought, to put a check to the growth of this dangerous religion.

For a decade Hideyoshi did not attempt to enforce strictly his ban on the missionaries, remaining content so long as they restricted their activities to their own flock. But he was eventually stirred into taking more drastic action. Most of the Jesuits had stayed on in Kyūshū under the protection of Christian daimyo, and they continued to proselytize secretly, making new converts among the Kyūshū daimyo and even among the officers of Hideyoshi's own court. The Franciscans also started open missionary activity in Kyōto under the protection of the Spanish diplomatic missions from the Philippines, which had first come in 1592. Some Spaniards, eager for a share in the Japanese trade, were ready to calumniate the Portuguese, and the Franciscans fell into quarrels with the Jesuits. Moreover, Hideyoshi had become aware of the role of Christian missionaries in other parts of Asia as the forerunners of colonial conquest. He seems to have been particularly incensed by the boasting innuendoes of a shipwrecked Spanish pilot in 1596. For these various reasons, he suddenly enforced his ban on the missionaries in 1597 (late 1596 according to the Japanese calendar), crucifying six Spanish Franciscans, three Portuguese Jesuits and seventeen Japanese believers.

The Invasions of Korea. Hideyoshi's invasion of Korea in 1592 may also have been inspired in part by his desire for domestic peace. After centuries of almost incessant warfare, Japan was oversupplied with hardened fighting men. A good bloodletting abroad, he evidently thought, would help preserve the peace at home. In addition, a generous distribution of the spoils of war was the time-honored feudal technique for maintaining the loyalty of one's vassals. But a much more fundamental reason for the invasion, no doubt, was Hideyoshi's inordinate ambition. He seems to have lusted for more worlds to conquer. Great China, not little Korea, was his ultimate goal. He even talked of moving the emperor and the capital of Japan to Peking. On the other hand, he seems to have been entirely unaware of the magnitude of the undertaking. He apparently regarded the conquest of Korea and China as comparable to the subjugation of West or North Japan. Actually he assigned much smaller armies to this task than he had marshaled against either the Shimazu or the Hōjō.

The story of Hideyoshi's Korean campaigns has already been told (pages 332–333 and 442–444), and only a few details need be added here. He himself never joined his armies in the field but left them to the command of some of his leading vassals. His original invading force of some 160,000 men was divided into nine armies mobilized from West Japan. The leaders of the first two armies to reach Korea, the ardent Buddhist Katō Kiyomasa and the equally ardent Christian Konishi Yukinaga, who commanded a largely Christian army, reaped most of the glory of the easy early victories. Konishi and Katō again were the leading generals in the second invasion of 1597. This was made with about 140,000 men but met stiffer resistance and was terminated by Hideyoshi's death the next year.

Hideyoshi accomplished none of his objectives in his invasions of the continent. He did not become master of China, which for him meant the world; there were no substantial spoils of war to be divided; and the bloodletting did not prevent his vassals from dispossessing his heir and fighting over the succession. The terrible effects of the war on Korea and the strain it put on the Ming dynasty have already been discussed. Its lasting effects on Japan were slight and they were largely in the field of culture. The Japanese acquired technical knowledge of printing and other matters from their Korean adversaries, and the Korean potters who were brought back to Japan as captives became the founders of the most important traditions of pottery making during the following centuries. For Japan the only important political and military result of the war was perhaps to weaken the participating daimyo, who included some of Hideyoshi's most loyal vassals, to the advantage of less reliable stay-at-homes like Tokugawa Ieyasu.

IEYASU FOUNDS THE TOKUGAWA SHOGUNATE

In 1595 Hideyoshi had done away with his adopted son and heir Hidetsugu in favor of his infant natural son Hideyori, who was still only five years old when Hideyoshi died in 1598. As in the case of Nobunaga's young heir, five of the greatest vassals became joint regents. These regents were Maeda in Kaga north of the capital, Mōri and Ukita (a hero of the Korean campaigns) in West Honshū, Uesugi, who had recently been shifted to North Honshū, and Tokugawa Ieyasu of the Kantō, whose domain was a little greater than that of Hideyoshi himself, and at least twice the size of that of any of his rivals in the regency council.

The joint regency worked no better for Hideyoshi's heir than it had for Nobunaga's. A struggle for power started at once between the strongest member, Ieyasu, and the others, some of whom were determined to thwart his ambitions. Eventually, Uesugi in North Honshū overtly defied Ieyasu's authority and Ieyasu in the early summer of 1600 marched against him. But before Ieyasu's forces had come fully to grips with Uesugi's, a coalition of daimyo organized by Ishida, the most prominent of Hideyoshi's original commissioners, or cabinet members, took the field against him in the capital area. Among Ishida's adherents were Mōri and Ukita of the regency council, and Konishi and Shimazu of Kyūshū. Ieyasu marched back west, and, after preliminary skirmishes and castle sieges, the two main forces met in the early autumn at Sekigahara ("Barrier Field") in the strategic pass between the plain around Lake Biwa and that around Nagoya. Defections of certain key daimyo from Ishida's side threw the victory to Ieyasu, and Mōri's meek surrender of the Ōsaka castle shortly afterward brought a virtual end to the war.

The Tokugawa *bakufu*, or shogunate, was not officially founded until 1603, when Ieyasu had the emperor give him the title of shogun. He had first established a claim to Minamoto descent, since two successive shogunal lines of Minamoto origin had given rise to the idea that the post was limited to this one blood line. The supremacy of the Tokugawa family over all Japan, however, actually started with Ieyasu's victory at Sekigahara in 1600, and he at once set about establishing a system of rule for the country.

The Assignment of Realms to the Vassals. Ieyasu seems to have been essentially a cautious man. He realized that it would take many years of campaigning to destroy the more powerful and remote of his enemies. He also knew that many of his allies still felt strong loyalty toward Hideyoshi's heir. Since he was anxious to stabilize matters and restore peace to the country as quickly as possible, he followed Hideyoshi's policy of ruling indirectly through the familiar daimyo system and treating with generosity not only the daimyo who had stayed neutral in 1600 but also some of his open enemies.

The Ōsaka castle had been surrendered on the understanding that Hideyoshi's heir would be left in possession of it together with a large domain. Ieyasu lived up to this agreement and even betrothed one of his granddaughters to the young Hideyori. Though he executed Ishida and the Christian general, Konishi, banished Ukita to a remote island, and confiscated 91 of the 214 daimyo realms then in existence, he did allow the Uesugi to continue their rule, though in a much smaller fief in North Honshū, and let the Mōri family retain about a quarter of its realm in West Honshū. He treated the relatively inaccessible Shimazu of Satsuma much more generously, and when they made their peace with him in 1602 they suffered no reduction of their holdings in South Kyūshū. Ironically, it was to be the Mōri and Shimazu fiefs which would take

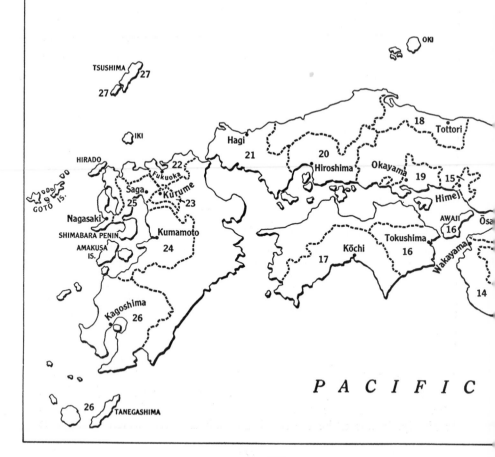

MAJOR DAIMYO DOMAINS

1 – TSUGARU
2 – SATAKE
3 – NAMBU
4 – SAKAI
5 – DATE
6 – UESUGI
7 – HOSHINA (MATSUDAIRA)
8 – TOKUGAWA (MITO)
9 – MAEDA (KAGA)
10 – TOKUGAWA (OWARI)
11 – MATSUDAIRA (ECHIZEN)
12 – II
13 – TŌDŌ
14 – TOKUGAWA (KII)

15 – SAKAKIBARA
16 – HACHISUKA
17 – YAMANOUCHI (TOSA)
18 – IKEDA
19 – IKEDA
20 – ASANO
21 – MŌRI (CHŌSHŪ)
22 – KURODA
23 – ARIMA
24 – HOSOKAWA
25 – NABESHIMA (HIZEN)
26 – SHIMAZU (SATSUMA)
27 – SŌ

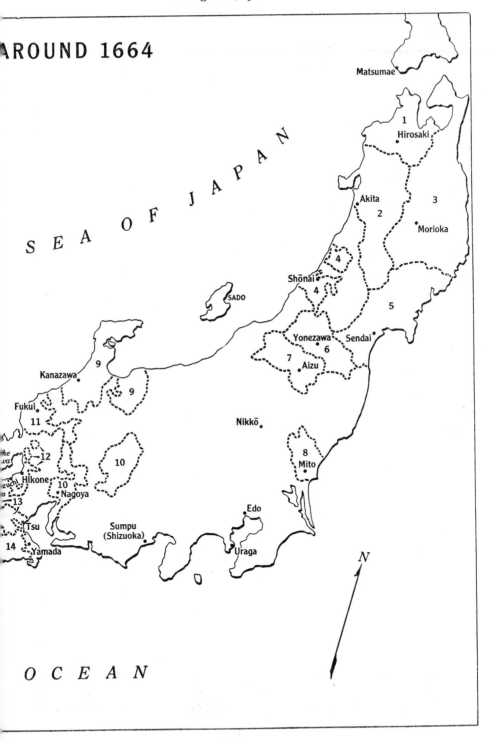

AROUND 1664

Matsumae

1

Hirosaki

SEA OF JAPAN

Akita

2

3

Morioka

4

Shōnai

4

5

SADO

Yonezawa

Sendai

6

9

7

Aizu

Kanazawa

9

Fukui

Nikkō

11

8

10

Mito

12

10

Hikone

10

13

Nagoya

Edo

Tsu

Sumpu
(Shizuoka)

Uraga

14

Yamada

N

OCEAN

the lead in the destruction of the Tokugawa two and a half centuries later.

Like Hideyoshi, Ieyasu took care to see that his allies and old vassals held preponderant power. North Honshū was entrusted largely to the Date of Sendai and others who had aided him against the Uesugi in 1600. Maeda of Kaga, who also had sided with Ieyasu, received new territories, becoming the greatest of his vassals. One of the generals who had played turncoat at Sekigahara was rewarded with a greater fief than that of the Mōri in West Honshū. And in Kyūshū, the continuance of the hostile Shimazu domain was offset by the establishment of two large fiefs, Fukuoka in the north and Kumamoto in central Kyūshū, given respectively to Kuroda and Katō Kiyomasa, who had campaigned locally in Ieyasu's behalf. (Katō's son was deprived of his fief in 1632, and it was then given to the Kyūshū branch of the Hosokawa.)

Most of the central portion of the country, from the Kantō to and including the greater part of the old capital area, Ieyasu reserved for himself, his family and the men who had already been his vassals before his victory in 1600. The daimyo of this inner zone were on the whole relatively small lords, as compared with the greater of the daimyo in more peripheral areas, but together with Ieyasu they constituted a central power bloc that was entirely trustworthy and militarily unchallengeable.

Ieyasu, remembering the success of Yoritomo and the failure of the Ashikaga in creating their respective shogunates, decided to keep his capital in his eastern base of power. When invested with the Kantō by Hideyoshi in 1590, he had established his headquarters on the site of an old fortification at the fishing village of Edo. Here he had set about building a great castle, which, when it was finally completed in 1606, surpassed even that of Hideyoshi at Ōsaka. Like most of the other great castles, this fortress consisted of concentric circles of wide moats and massive stone walls. (The outermost circle was more than two miles in diameter.) Ieyasu made this castle the headquarters of his government, and the period of Tokugawa rule, therefore, is also known as the Edo period. The city of Edo which grew up around the great fortress was the beginning of the modern metropolis of Tōkyō, and the beautiful moats, walls, and grounds of the imperial palace in the heart of Tōkyō today are the remnants of the inner circle of the castle Ieyasu constructed.

The Destruction of Hideyoshi's Heir. Ieyasu, naturally mindful of the failure of both Nobunaga and Hideyoshi to pass on their hard-earned supremacy to their heirs, devoted his remaining years to seeing that the Tokugawa did not suffer the same fate. In 1605 he resigned the position of shogun to his already mature third son, Hidetada, who was chosen more for his steadiness and reliability than for his brilliance. Hidetada followed his father's precedent when he resigned in 1623 in favor of his own mature son, Iemitsu. Thus there could be no succession dispute, nor was the shogunate left in a child's weak hands. Ieyasu, however, remained the real ruler until his death in 1616, administering the country from a castle he built at Sumpu, the modern Shizuoka, while Hidetada carried on the outward forms of shogunal rule at Edo.

Ieyasu realized that his victory in 1600 had not been complete. Although he exacted written oaths of fealty from his vassals, he knew that many of them still felt only slight loyalty to him and that Hideyoshi's heir at Ōsaka might well serve as a symbol around which opposition to the Tokugawa could form. He was already fifty-seven years old in 1600, but, cautious man that he was, he bided his time until he had so consolidated his rule that he felt safe in forcing a showdown with Hideyori. Finally, in 1614, Ieyasu professed to take umbrage at the wording of an inscription on a large bronze bell in a monastery Hideyori had built in connection with the restoration of the Great Buddha that his father had had cast in Kyōto. Ieyasu stopped the dedication of the image and monastery and soon forced Hideyori into war.

So thoroughly had Ieyasu done his work that no important daimyo dared come to Hideyori's support, although some 90,000 fighting men, mostly dispossessed daimyo and masterless warriors (known as *rōnin*), flocked to Hideyori's standard. The greatly superior Tokugawa forces proved unable to take the Ōsaka castle by assault or cannon-fire in the early winter of 1614–15, but, after more than a month of siege, the wily Ieyasu persuaded the defenders to sign a compromise peace, permitting Hideyori to continue in possession of his domain and castle but allowing the Edo forces to fill in the outermost ring of moats and level the outer battlements. Ieyasu's men actually went on to fill in some of the inner moats as well. When Ieyasu treacherously renewed the attack early the next summer, the defenders, forced to sally forth from their shrunken castle, were destroyed in a few days of hard fighting. Thus the potential menace of Hideyoshi's heir had been entirely removed when Ieyasu died in 1616 at the age of seventy-three.

THE RETURN TO ISOLATION

The intense determination of Ieyasu and his successors to insure the continuance of Tokugawa rule probably explains their attitude toward the outside world. They followed Hideyoshi's lead in regarding Christianity as a menace to social stability and a possible threat to their rule, even though at first they too desired the profits of trade with the Europeans.

Ieyasu actually was eager for foreign trade. Although he never rescinded Hideyoshi's orders expelling the missionaries, he treated them at first not just tolerantly but with respect and friendliness. Persecutions continued in some daimyo realms, for even the Christian daimyo had largely turned against the religion, now that it was in official disfavor. Ieyasu, however, allowed the Jesuits to renew their activities in the Kyōto area. Moreover, in his desire to persuade the Spanish to establish a trade station in his own area in the Kantō, he permitted Spanish Franciscans to establish a mission at Edo.

However, when Ieyasu discovered that he could have trade without the nuisance of Christian missionaries, his attitude toward Christianity gradually changed. In 1609 a Dutch ship reached Hirado (an island off the northwest coast of Kyūshū which had figured prominently from the start in the Portuguese trade), and in 1613 it was followed by an English ship. Both the Dutch and the English established regular trading missions at Hirado, but neither of these Protestant nations had the slightest interest in missionary activities at this time. Ieyasu was also helped to realize that trade could be divorced from religion by the counsel of Will Adams, the English pilot of a Dutch vessel stranded in Japan in 1600. Adams, who had found favor with the shogun by building European-type ships for him and had become a petty retainer and trusted adviser on foreign trade, pointed out to Ieyasu that in Europe religious tolerance was not considered a prerequisite for diplomatic or trade relations.

The Stamping Out of Christianity. Ieyasu, like Hideyoshi before him, had meanwhile become increasingly suspicious of the Christians. The Spaniards had sent few ships and seemed less interested in trade than in missionary work, in charting the coasts of Japan, and in expelling the Dutch; the Protestants and Catholics denounced each other in violent terms; and the Jesuits and Franciscans kept up their bickering. Ieyasu's various European informants and some Japanese who had been assigned to infiltrate the Christian movement also told him of the religious persecutions and wars of Europe and the close association of the cross and the sword in the Spanish and Portuguese conquests in Asia and the Americas. Moreover, Christianity was particularly strong among Hideyori's adherents at Ōsaka, and Ieyasu discovered a case of connivance and even a small plot against himself among some of his own Christian retainers. For these various reasons, he finally came to the same conclusion Hideyoshi had reached a quarter of a century earlier — that Christianity should be checked for the safety of the regime. Now that Ieyasu had consolidated his control over the country, the destruction of the Christians apparently seemed a lesser menace to the peace he had established than their continuance as a possible future threat to Tokugawa rule.

As early as 1606 Ieyasu started to issue anti-Christian edicts, and in 1609 he showed a further hardening of his attitude. Angered by the treatment of the Japanese participants in a fight with some Portuguese in Macao near Canton, he ordered the small lord of Arima in Kyūshū, the one remaining Christian daimyo, to seize the great Portuguese trade ship at Nagasaki. The lord of Arima complied, forcing the Portuguese captain to blow up his vessel in desperation (January, 1610, in the Western calendar). But this faithful act did not spare the Christian daimyo from being replaced soon by his apostate son.

In 1612 Ieyasu began to enforce his anti-Christian edicts in earnest. He ordered all his Christian retainers to give up their religion, executing some who would not comply. He also started to close down the churches and other Christian institutions. Finally, in 1614, he attempted to round up and deport all the missionaries, together with a number of prominent Japanese converts.

Although he stood firm in his resolve to suppress Christianity, Ieyasu killed no foreign missionaries; but under his successor, Hidetada, the persecution mounted in intensity. This was partly because of the tenacity which the missionaries displayed under persecution. No fewer than 47 of the 156 who were in Japan in 1614 managed to evade or escape from Ieyasu's net, and many others — Dominicans and Augustinians as well as Franciscans and Jesuits — slipped back into Japan on trading ships. But a more fundamental reason for the ferocity of Hidetada's persecution of the Christians was his own fear. He seems to have been truly frightened by the possibility of conquest by the Spanish in cooperation with the Japanese Christians and was determined to enforce his father's anti-Christian edicts to the letter. Four missionaries were executed in 1617 and 120 missionaries and Japanese believers in 1622. Those of Hidetada's vassals who for one reason or another had hitherto shielded the Christians in their realms were now forced to join in the persecution. Even Date Masamune, the powerful lord of Sendai in North Honshū, who in 1613 had dispatched a large embassy to the papacy by way of Mexico, in 1620 was induced to turn on the Christians in his realm.

The persecution grew steadily more severe. Fiendish tortures were instituted which forced thousands of Japanese converts and even a few missionaries to apostatize. In time a simple system was devised for sorting out believers from unbelievers. Suspect persons were led to some Christian devotional object, such as a bronze plaque bearing a figure of Christ or of Mary, and those who refused to step on this image, called a *fumie* or "treading picture," were dealt with accordingly. The Catholic church recognizes a total of 3125 martyrdoms in Japan between 1597 and 1660.

Christianity lingered on longest in Nagasaki and its environs, where most of the population had been converted. Finally, in 1637, the still partially Christianized peasantry of the Shimabara Peninsula (the old Arima domain) and the near-by islands of Amakusa, together with some *rōnin,* or masterless warriors, rose in revolt against the local feudal authorities. The uprising started over oppressive taxation and misgovernment but soon developed into a great Christian rebellion. The rebels, said to have numbered some 20,000 fighting men in addition to their women and children, took refuge in an old castle on the Shimabara Peninsula. It required an army of 100,000 men, supported by the fire-power of a Dutch ship, to reduce this fortress in the spring of 1638. The defenders were all but annihilated, and with this slaughter the Christian movement came to a virtual end in Japan. The few missionaries who subsequently slipped into the islands were all caught and executed. Although a few small isolated communities of crypto-Christians kept alive some vague notions of their faith, Christianity ceased to be significant as either a political or a religious force.

The Restriction of Trade. Hideyoshi and Ieyasu, despite their determination to restrict the growth of Christianity, had never let the Christian problem seriously interfere with foreign trade, but Hidetada and his successor, Iemitsu, definitely subordinated trade to their anti-Christian policies. This was partly due to their greater timidity, but it also probably reflected the hardening of the feudal political system, which was based economically on agriculture. As Tokugawa rule became firmly established, foreign trade seemed less necessary or desirable. The government became increasingly determined to monopolize what foreign trade there was and to deny its profits to rival daimyo or other groups. Therefore there was a steady increase in the restrictions placed on foreign trade, and these combined with the persecution of Christianity to limit contact with the outside world so severely that Japan eventually withdrew into a state of almost complete isolation.

The Portuguese had been only one element in the great expansion of foreign trade during the second half of the sixteenth century. Chinese traders, not only from China itself, but also from the Chinese communities in Southeast Asia, were frequenting Japanese ports in larger numbers than ever before. So many Japanese merchant-adventurers went abroad that in time they established permanent quarters for themselves in various towns in the Philippines, South Vietnam, Cambodia and Siam. In Siam the Japanese group even exercised military influence in domestic politics. A single Japanese community in the Philippines is said to have numbered 3000 inhabitants in the early seventeenth century. There were also the mixed Sino-Japanese pirate communities that centered on Formosa (see pages 332 and 355–356).

The trade of the Japanese in Southeast Asia, as well as that of the Chinese in the ports of Japan, consisted mainly of an exchange of Japanese silver for Chinese raw silk and silk textiles. The Portuguese, Spanish and Dutch too found themselves dealing primarily in Chinese silk, since

European goods were not enough in demand to figure prominently in East Asian trade. Because of the mercantilist theories of the age, the Europeans preferred to buy Chinese silk with Japanese silver rather than with precious metals from Europe or the Americas. The Japanese trade thus became very important to them.

After Hideyoshi had established his mastery over Japan, he attempted to bring the Japanese who were trading abroad under his control by instituting a system of accrediting ships with documents bearing his "red seal." Ieyasu followed him in this practice, and during the next few decades the whole silk trade in Japanese ports was also made a carefully controlled monopoly of a group of officially appointed merchants.

After Ieyasu's death, the measures designed to control trade as well as those aimed at the elimination of the Christians became increasingly restrictive. In 1616 European ships were limited to Nagasaki and Hirado, and in 1624 Hidetada's fears caused him to sever all relations with the Spanish. In the previous year the English had abandoned their trade mission at Hirado as unprofitable.

The most important limitations on foreign contact were imposed in a series of laws issued between 1633 and 1639. The Chinese merchants were restricted to Nagasaki; as a means of preventing Christians and their ideas from entering the country, all Japanese were prohibited on pain of death from going abroad or from returning to Japan if they had already gone overseas; and a prohibition was placed on the building of ships of more than 500 *koku* (about 2500 bushels) capacity, thus limiting Japanese shipping to coastal vessels. Because of these measures Japan's tremendous overseas activities suddenly ended, and those Japanese already abroad were left to be absorbed by the native populations.

In 1639 the Portuguese, whose share in Japan's trade by then was much smaller than that of the Chinese or the Dutch, were expelled because of suspected complicity in the Shimabara Revolt. The meaning of this order became unmistakably clear with the execution of the members of a Portuguese mission which came in 1640 to reopen relations. Finally, in 1641, the Dutch were moved from Hirado to Nagasaki, where they were kept almost like prisoners on Deshima (or Dejima), a small artificial island in the harbor. By these successive steps Japan succeeded in blocking off most of the channels of foreign contact.

It should be noted, however, that this self-imposed isolation was by no means complete. The Chinese and Dutch were still permitted to reside at Nagasaki, and, though the trade was strictly controlled, a considerable exchange of goods continued. In fact, the trade grew so large and so seriously drained Japan of metals that limitations had to be placed on it in the late seventeenth century. Even then, the annual export quota allowed the Chinese as late as 1715 was about 25,000 pounds of silver and 4,000,000 pounds of copper, and the Dutch were allowed half as much.

When these quotas were subsequently reduced still further, dried sea products, largely from Hokkaidō, were developed as an important export item to supplement metals.

Actually Japanese commercial relations with the outside world were not limited to the Chinese and Dutch. Trade continued with Korea through the Sō, the daimyo of Tsushima, and with China and other areas through the Ryūkyū (in Chinese, Liu-ch'iu) Islands. The Ryūkyūs, which are inhabited by a people who culturally and linguistically represent merely a variant of the Japanese, had played a large role in Japanese foreign trade in the fifteenth century. At that time the Shimazu realm of South Kyūshū had already established special relations with these islands and also some control over them, and in 1609 the Shimazu conquered the Ryūkyūs, annexing the northern islands of the chain and making the kings, whose capital was on Okinawa, their vassals. But they did not interrupt the Ryūkyūs' tributary relations with China, since these relations afforded a profitable avenue of trade for the Shimazu with the outside world.

Through these various commercial contacts, the Japanese continued to learn about developments in the outside world. In particular, the annual trips to Edo of representatives of the Dutch mission at Nagasaki kept the Tokugawa rulers informed of Europe and its civilization. Conversely, the reports of some of the Dutch representatives constituted the chief source of knowledge about Japan in the West.

The Results of Isolation. The isolation imposed on Japan by the Tokugawa thus remained far from absolute, but it was sufficient to have a considerable influence on Japanese history and culture — perhaps as great an influence as Japan's original isolation, which had been a natural result of geography. The isolation policy of the Tokugawa succeeded in keeping out not only all military and political threats and various upsetting ideas, but also a good deal of the economic stimulation that more liberal trade would have produced. At any rate, during the two centuries after its adoption Japan was certainly far freer of external pressures and influences than it had been during the preceding century.

The most obvious result of isolation was the creation of the stability that Hideyoshi and Ieyasu had worked for. They had sought to bring peace and order by freezing the social system and maintaining the status quo between themselves and their vassals, but actually during their lifetimes there had been a tremendous development in the centralization of the state and in the economy and culture. If Japan had remained open to foreign trade and other foreign influences, the rapid evolutionary development of the economy, society and government, which had long characterized Japanese history, would undoubtedly have continued, and a more thoroughly centralized form of government, accompanied by a more modernized economy and society, would probably have emerged. But the closing of the door to foreign trade and other influences made it possible for Ieyasu's successors to achieve a degree of stability that would have been impossible under his own more dynamic foreign policies. The somewhat anachronistic combination of feudal vassalage and strict centralized control that had been established in the time of Hideyoshi and Ieyasu hardened, and then gradually fossilized. Even economic and social changes, though never fully stopped, were appreciably slowed. Japan, settling into two centuries of unbroken peace, slackened to a hardly perceptible rate of internal evolutionary change.

Another major result of isolation was that Japan, because of this slowed rate of change, inevitably fell behind Europe in economic, political and social development. In Ieyasu's time Japan was almost abreast of Europe technologically and militarily, and perhaps considerably ahead in effective political and social integration — as even European observers of the time freely admitted. The seventeenth and eighteenth centuries, however, were a period of very rapid growth in the Occident. When the Japanese were again thrown into close contact with the Europeans in the nineteenth century, they found that their slower pace of progress had left them far behind. The European menace that Hidetada and Iemitsu had feared with little justification in the seventeenth century was transformed by their policy of isolation into a very real menace indeed by the nineteenth century. The Tokugawa isolation thus was a major tragedy for the Japanese, because it placed them under extremely heavy pressures in the nineteenth and twentieth centuries to catch up again with the West.

On the other hand, the isolation of the Tokugawa, by turning the Japanese inward on their own resources, gave them a chance to develop their own culture more fully. During this long peaceful period they developed distinctive aesthetic and literary tendencies and ways of living that still remain strong. Despite the limits imposed by isolation, this proved to be culturally a most creative period.

THE SAMURAI AND DAIMYO SYSTEM

The Tokugawa political and social system, which was to last almost unchanged for two and a half centuries, was put together under Hideyoshi and Ieyasu, and it hardened into shape under Hidetada (1605–1623; died 1632) and Iemitsu (1623–1651). Even in the early seventeenth century it was a conservative system, and in some ways reactionary. The chief object of the Tokugawa was to stop all political change. Thus they maintained during a period of prolonged peace the methods of military rule developed in a period of incessant warfare. In other words, they retained most of the feudal forms of rule that had survived the decline which feudalism underwent during the sixteenth century. They even followed Hideyoshi's lead in checking social mobility, reimposing by law the strict class lines that had started to fade.

Social Classes. Although Hideyoshi and Ieyasu, as well as the majority of their henchmen, were themselves mainly self-made men, they put an effective stop to such social climbing. They adopted in theory the ancient Confucian division of society into four classes: first, the samurai [1] or warrior-administrators, from the daimyo down to foot soldiers; next, the peasants, since these were the primary producers; third, the artisans, as secondary producers; and lowest, the merchants, whose usefulness to society was considered doubtful.

In practice there was little attempt to prevent the lower three classes from mixing or to force the relatively wealthy merchant class into an unnatural position at the bottom of society. The Tokugawa, however, did do their best to keep the samurai distinct from and superior to the other classes. This one social line was made as sharp as possible. There was to be no intermarriage; a clear badge of distinction was provided by the two swords, one long and the other short, which a samurai was entitled to wear but which were denied to others; political authority was to be solely in the hands of the military; and a samurai, however humble, was considered so far above the lower classes that his privileges included, at least in theory, the right of *kirisute* ("to cut down and leave"), that is, the right to kill a disrespectful commoner on the spot.

One reason why so clear a line could be drawn at this time between the military and the other classes was that the shifting about of their vassals by Hideyoshi and Ieyasu had brought many daimyo and their military retainers into control of populations with whom they had had no previous contact. An outstanding example of this had occurred when Hideyoshi moved Ieyasu away from his original base in Mikawa and Tōtōmi to the Kantō. Such a shift cut the old bonds woven from common local interests and long-existing relations between the retainer class and the farming community. After such a move the interests of the military retainers naturally tended to become more exclusively identified with those of their lord. Thus an effective class distinction could be drawn.

This isolation of the samurai from the rest of society created serious problems for borderline groups. *Rōnin,* or masterless samurai whose lords had been dispossessed or who, as extra sons or for some other reason, had failed to find employment with their fathers' lords, formed a floating and sometimes troublesome group. Though they belonged to the samurai class by heritage, they found no place in it.

Similarly, the old class of aristocratic rural military men had the choice

[1] The term samurai, or "retainer," was originally descriptive of a specific category of the military class (*bushi*) but has come to be used generically for the whole class.

either of being considered peasants or of leaving their farms to become their lords' close retainers and residing at the lords' capitals. Only in certain restricted areas of Japan did the rural aristocracy manage to survive as "village samurai" (*gōshi*). In Tosa on Shikoku, for example, retainers of the former local lord (Chōsokabe) were allowed to continue in this capacity when, as a result of the Battle of Sekigahara, a new lord (Yamanouchi) was assigned there as daimyo, bringing with him his own hereditary retainers. Again, in Satsuma in Kyūshū, Hideyoshi's reduction of the size of the domain resulted in a relatively high percentage of retainers among the total population, consequently forcing some of the samurai to continue as self-supporting farmers. In most of Japan, however, the old rural aristocracy lost its military status and was relegated to the lower classes, though it usually retained its wealth and traditions of local leadership.

The Agrarian Basis of Government. Another reactionary step under the early Tokugawa was to base government almost exclusively upon agricultural income. For some time the daimyo of western Japan had profited from foreign trade, which had also been an important source of income for Hideyoshi and Ieyasu. But Ieyasu's successors changed all this. Fear of Christianity was probably only one of the reasons for this change. A more fundamental reason may have been the agrarian mentality of the military men from the broad agricultural lands of East Japan, who had once again established their mastery over the country. In any case, foreign trade was strictly controlled and limited, and there was little effort to tax domestic trade. Instead, the government became more fully dependent on agricultural taxes than it had been for some centuries past. A comparison could be made with the Chinese dynasties, which so frequently in their early years put little stress on revenue from any source but agriculture. Such a restricted financial basis was to prove one of the greatest weaknesses of the whole Tokugawa regime.

Careful land surveys allowed the Tokugawa and the individual daimyo to impose uniform taxes on all their agricultural lands. The rate of taxation, however, varied from realm to realm. In the early Tokugawa period, it usually came to around 40 or 50 per cent of the yield of rice lands. When the daimyo began to experience serious economic difficulties during the eighteenth century, the tax rate began to creep up, largely through the imposition of supplementary taxes.

The Han System. The utilization of the somewhat antiquated daimyo system of vassalage was itself a highly conservative, if not reactionary, step in the early seventeenth century. This curious compromise between actual centralized control and theoretical local autonomy had proved under Hideyoshi and Ieyasu a useful expedient for stabilizing the political situation, at least temporarily; but under their successors it became rigidly frozen, and was maintained without significant change thereafter.

The daimyo realms, called *han*, numbered as many as 295 in the early Tokugawa period but were later reduced to about 265. These covered more than three-quarters of the land and thus provided most of the local administration and also the bulk of the army. In fact, each *han* was an autonomous unit of local government supporting an autonomous force in the Tokugawa military establishment, even though its autonomy in both fields was in fact carefully supervised by a powerful central government.

The daimyo were ranked according to several different systems of classification. The most meaningful system graded the lords according to the productive capacity of each *han*, which was measured in terms of taxable rice yield. This system, like so much else under the Tokugawa, dated back to Hideyoshi. Only lords whose lands were estimated to produce upwards of 10,000 *koku* (a *koku* equals 4.96 bushels) ranked as daimyo. Since the estimates were made only at rare intervals, they often became quite inaccurate, and *han* located in originally less heavily populated peripheral areas sometimes actually produced much larger yields than they were given credit for. The estimates, however, provided a reasonably accurate indication of relative prestige. According to this system, the *han* ran all the way from 1,022,700 *koku* for the Maeda of Kaga down to a large number of minimal 10,000-*koku* realms.

The daimyo were divided into three major political categories. The collateral descendants of the Tokugawa shoguns who did not themselves become shoguns were called *shimpan* ("related *han*").[2] In the second category of daimyo came the *fudai* or "hereditary" daimyo, who, with only a few exceptions, comprised the descendants of those men who had recognized Ieyasu as their overlord before 1600. The third category comprised the *tozama* or "outer" daimyo, the descendants of the daimyo who theoretically had been equals of Ieyasu in 1600. Allies, neutrals and enemies of the Tokugawa at the time of the Battle of Sekigahara thus fell into the single *tozama* category; but in reality there were great and lasting differences in their relationships with the Tokugawa. For example, the Maeda of Kaga, as befitted old allies, maintained a tradition of friendly feelings, and the Yamanouchi of Tosa, whom Ieyasu had made major daimyo, always felt a debt of gratitude toward his descendants. On the other hand, former open enemies, such as the Mōri of Chōshū in western Honshū and the Shimazu of Satsuma in southern Kyūshū, carefully nurtured a tradition of hostility which was to have important repercussions in the nineteenth century.

The greatest lords were for the most part *tozama*, but the *fudai* gradually became the most numerous, because the *tozama*, as outsiders, were dealt with more severely in the seventeenth century and many of their

[2] These, together with collateral branches dating from before Ieyasu's time, were also known as *kamon*.

fiefs were confiscated for infractions of the Tokugawa laws. Whereas the *tozama* outnumbered the *fudai* 119 to 72 in 1602, by the middle of the nineteenth century they were themselves outnumbered 97 to 145. As we have seen, the *fudai*, together with the shogun and the collateral branches of the Tokugawa, occupied almost the whole of the strategic central part of the country from the Kantō to the old capital area. Small *fudai* daimyo also were eventually scattered throughout the country at strategic points on the flanks of the more dangerous *tozama*.

MAJOR HAN AROUND 1865
(including all of 200,000 *koku* or more)

Daimyo	Status	Capital City (and Province)	Officially estimated rice yield (in koku)
(Tokugawa	shogun	Edo	7,000,000)
Maeda	*tozama*	Kanazawa (Kaga)	1,022,700
Shimazu	*tozama*	Kagoshima (Satsuma)	770,800
Date	*tozama*	Sendai	625,600
Tokugawa	*shimpan*	Nagoya (Owari)	619,500
Tokugawa	*shimpan*	Wakayama (Kii)	555,000
Hosokawa	*tozama*	Kumamoto	540,000
Kuroda	*tozama*	Fukuoka	520,000
Asano	*tozama*	Hiroshima	426,000
Mōri	*tozama*	Hagi (Chōshū)	369,000
Nabeshima	*tozama*	Saga (Hizen)	357,000
Tokugawa	*shimpan*	Mito	350,000
Ikeda	*tozama*	Tottori	325,000
Tōdō	*tozama*	Tsu	323,900
Matsudaira	*shimpan*	Fukui (Echizen)	320,000
Ikeda	*tozama*	Okayama	315,200
Hoshina (or Matsudaira)	*shimpan*	Aizu	280,000*
Hachisuka	*tozama*	Tokushima	257,900
Ii	*fudai*	Hikone	250,000**
Yamanouchi	*tozama*	Kōchi (Tosa)	242,000
Arima	*tozama*	Kurume	210,000
Satake	*tozama*	Akita	205,800
Nambu	*tozama*	Morioka	200,000
Sakai	*fudai*	Shōnai	170,000***
Uesugi	*tozama*	Yonezawa	150,000
Sakakibara	*fudai*	Himeji	150,000
Tsugaru	*tozama*	Hirosaki	100,000
Sō	*tozama*	Tsushima	100,000

Grand total for all Japan: 26,000,000
Total of *han* above 200,000 *koku*: 9,085,400

* Previously 230,000 ** Previously 350,000 *** Previously 140,000

Each daimyo remained an autocrat within his *han* so long as he did not transgress any shogunal laws, and he had his own vassals and lesser retainers. The vassals had their own retainers and their own sub-fiefs, which in the case of a great daimyo *han* might be larger than a fief assigned to a 10,000-*koku* daimyo. None of these rear vassals, however, could rank with the daimyo, since they were not the direct vassals of the shogun. The great majority of a daimyo's retainers possessed no fiefs but received hereditary stipends, usually figured in bags of rice (*hyō*), each of which theoretically amounted to the equivalent of the tax yield from one *koku* of produce. It was roughly estimated that five *hyō* of stipend (or five *koku* of a fief) were sufficient to provide for all the needs of one person for a year.

A daimyo's vassals and lesser retainers usually held hereditary positions in his army and government, ranking from hereditary councilors down to simple gate guards. Most of these, including the enfeoffed vassals but not the vassals' retainers, lived in the daimyo's capital town or, in the case of a large *han*, at other assigned posts. Thus they tended to lose the character of feudal local rulers and landholders and to become a group of salaried bureaucrats and soldiers.

The military class as a whole, from the daimyo families down to the lowest gate guards or "village samurai" and their families, is estimated to have numbered about five or six per cent of the population in the middle of the nineteenth century. The percentage was probably not very different in the seventeenth century. However, considerable differences existed between *han*. Some daimyo, having lost much of their territory or having been assigned to smaller fiefs in the early years of Tokugawa rule, consequently had a comparatively high proportion of samurai in the populations they controlled, while others, particularly *fudai* daimyo and collateral members of the Tokugawa family, who possessed relatively few hereditary retainers but had been rewarded with large fiefs, counted a much lower percentage of samurai in their *han*.

The *han* governments were usually miniature replicas of the shogun's government. They were organized according to each daimyo's own "house laws," but these, by shogunal decree, were usually patterned after laws enacted by the Edo government, and many of the shogunal laws applied directly to all the *han* as well as to the shogun's own domain.

While the *han* paid no taxes to the shogun's government, they helped support it in other ways. The presents given on a variety of occasions were practically compulsory and were carefully specified, but in essence they remained only a form of ritual tribute, rather than taxes. On the other hand, the *han* relieved the shogunate of most of the burdens of local government and local defense. They also had to provide soldiers for guard duty at Edo and various other strategic places and could be called upon for other military services at any time. Moreover, the *han* were required to perform various special services, such as aiding in the building of the Edo castle and the construction and repair of dikes. The assignment of such duties, of course, reduced the costs of the Edo government and could also be used as punishments or as routine measures to keep the daimyo from amassing excessive wealth.

Controls Over the Han. The independent military strength of the daimyo and their local autonomy naturally posed a serious problem. A coalition of daimyo could, at least in theory, outweigh the shogunate in both economic and military strength. The Tokugawa, however, saw to it that this would not happen by instituting an elaborate system of controls.

The shoguns bound the major daimyo families to the Tokugawa through marriages and forbade the daimyo families to contract marriages among themselves or, for that matter, to have any direct mutual contact without the explicit permission of Edo. Moreover, the daimyo were not free to expand their military establishments, build fortifications, or even repair their castles without the express permission of the central government. Although autonomous in theory, they were forced, as we have seen, to pattern their governments and laws on those of Edo, and they were strictly accountable for the administration of their *han* and the suppression of subversive activities within them. They were ordered to report any signs of disloyalty in neighboring *han*, and the shogunate maintained a system of *metsuke* (a term which might be translated as either "censors" or "spies"), who kept close check on activities in each *han* and sometimes even acted as *agents provocateurs* in order to trap dissident elements.

Gross maladministration, the slightest hint of disloyalty, or even the lack of an heir might lead to the confiscation of a daimyo's whole realm or, more commonly, to its reduction in size or the assignment of the daimyo and his retainers to a smaller *han*. With the exception of the greater *tozama* lords, who had to be handled with special care, the majority of the daimyo families were moved at least once in the course of the Tokugawa period, as either a promotion or a demotion.

The most important mechanisms developed to control the daimyo were the system of hostages and the system of alternate attendance of the daimyo on the shogun at Edo. The holding of hostages had long been used by feudal lords to insure the loyalty of their vassals, and all the daimyo were already in the habit of leaving their wives and children at Edo, on an ostensibly voluntary basis, before this practice was made mandatory in 1634. At the barriers on the roads leading into Edo a special watch was kept for women leaving the city and guns entering, for either might signify a plot against the regime.

The Sankin Kōtai System. The occasional attendance of a vassal on his lord to pay homage and render him service had been a feature of Japanese feudalism from the start, but the Tokugawa made this hitherto somewhat haphazard practice a key feature of their governmental structure. It was already in effective operation — also on an ostensibly voluntary basis — before Ieyasu's death, and legislation in 1635 and again in 1642 established it as a rigid and elaborate institution under the name of *sankin kōtai* ("attendance by turn").

Basically, the system divided each of the various categories of daimyo into two groups, which would alternate annually with each other in attendance on the shogun at Edo. The two groups of *fudai* daimyo with *han* in the Kantō, however, alternated semi-annually, a few peripheral daimyo who were assigned special local defense duties came for briefer periods, and some other permanent or temporary irregularities in the system were permitted. The ceremonial and practical duties of the daimyo while they were in attendance on the shogun were prescribed in great detail, as were also their military establishments in Edo, the size and equipment of their retinues on the journey between Edo and their *han*, and the routes they should follow. The constant movement of these great daimyo trains, usually consisting of several hundred persons, along the main highways — particularly along the Tōkaidō, the great coastal road between Edo and Kyōto — was one of the most colorful features of life in the Tokugawa period.

The *sankin kōtai* system proved entirely effective in keeping the vassals of the Tokugawa in line. By placing half of the daimyo at any given time at the mercy of the shogunate, it re-enforced the hostage system, and it further reduced the possibilities of rebellion by converting the daimyo into shogunal courtiers, who often looked upon their stay in their own *han* as a form of temporary exile from their families and the pleasures of life at Edo.

The *sankin kōtai* system also placed an extremely heavy economic burden on the daimyo, thus reducing their capacity to stand up against the shogunate. Each daimyo had to undertake a costly annual expedition to reach Edo or to return thence to his *han;* moreover, each had to maintain, in addition to his *han* government, a mansion with a permanent staff in Edo. In fact, the greater daimyo maintained several such establishments at the capital. By the middle of the seventeenth century, Maeda, the greatest of the daimyo, kept about 10,000 people permanently in his four large mansions in Edo, and when he himself was there several thousand more retainers poured in. A *han* usually spent well over half its tax income to maintain its Edo personnel and establishments, and another five to ten per cent might go into the costs of the journey to and from the shogunal capital.

Clearly, the *sankin kōtai* system helped to insure the complete sub-

元旦諸侯登城圖

藩邸玉帛此宗朝
關陰何須百戰勞
四海中原一致
道含直容
人發秀有美容
城川原時露宮
地第秦公叔景
郎望搆蒼佳桓
車回擲意龍
如第雲番如
流元馬

DAIMYO PROCESSION IN EDO

*A two-page wood-block print of a daimyo (in a palanquin) and his en-
tourage passing the gate of a daimyo mansion in Edo on the way to the
shogun's castle to pay his respects on New Year's Day. In the foreground
is the head of a second procession. The traditional pine and bamboo decorations in front of the gate are still displayed on New Year's Day. The
text at the top is a poem in good Chinese describing the scene. The illustration is from the* Edo meisho zue *(Illustrations of Famous Places in
Edo),* a work in twenty volumes jointly produced by Saitō Yukio and his
son and grandson, whose lives spanned the years 1737 to 1878. The work
was printed in 1834 and 1836.*

servience of the daimyo to the shogun, but it did much more than this.
It helped to develop a good network of roads between Edo and all other
parts of the country; it brought the samurai leaders from all over Japan
into close and stimulating contact at the capital; and, as we shall see, it
greatly furthered the commercialization of the economy by making
each daimyo convert a large proportion of his rice income into currency
for use in travel and at Edo. Thus, while the *sankin kōtai* helped insure
the political success of the Tokugawa system, in the long run it contributed to the system's ultimate collapse by undermining the whole
feudal economy.

TOKUGAWA GOVERNMENT

Despite the large degree of autonomy permitted the daimyo, the shogun in fact operated as a despot, against whose decisions even the daimyo had no real recourse. He ruled through a complicated governmental structure, which had a dual nature. His shogunal administration, or *bakufu*, was, on the one hand, the government of the "super-daimyo" realm possessed personally by the shogun and, on the other, the national government of Japan, ruling the rest of the country indirectly through its control over the individual daimyo.

The Domains of the Shogun and the Shimpan. By the latter part of the seventeenth century the shogun's personal domain had an agricultural productive capacity of about 7,000,000 *koku*, which was roughly seven times that of the Maeda, the greatest of the daimyo. Known as the *tenryō*, or "heavenly domain," it was scattered throughout much of Japan but was concentrated most heavily around Edo. It included many of the major mines, such as the gold and silver mines of the island of Sado, and all the greatest and most strategic cities and towns, such as Edo, Kyōto, Ōsaka, Nagasaki, Sakai (which had lost its previous autonomy), and Yamada (where the Ise shrines were located). Therefore it included a high proportion of the total population of Japan, perhaps as much as a third.

The shogun, like the daimyo, maintained a large number of personal retainers of less than daimyo rank. Those with the right of audience with the shogun were called "bannermen" (*hatamoto*), while those lacking this right, and usually with less than 100 *koku* of annual stipend, were called "honorable house men" (*gokenin*). During much of the period, the bannermen totaled around 5000 and the "honorable house men" three or four times that number. The more important of the direct shogunal retainers had their own fiefs, though only the greatest actually resided on them. These small fiefs together accounted for a little less than 3,000,000 *koku* of the Shogun's 7,000,000-*koku* personal domain.

The shogun's position was bolstered by the major collateral daimyo lines called *shimpan*. The greatest of these were the daimyo of three *han* established in strategically important areas between the years 1609 and 1619. These *han* were located at Mito northeast of Edo, at Nagoya (Owari) between Edo and Kyōto, and at Wakayama (Kii) south of Ōsaka. The three lines of daimyo, who were known as the "Three Houses" (*Sanke*), were descended from the seventh, eighth and ninth sons of Ieyasu, and one of their duties was to provide a shogun if the ruling shogun had no heir. The Wakayama line actually did provide the able eighth shogun and also the fourteenth, and the Mito line gave the fifteenth, who was the last. In the middle of the eighteenth century three sons of the eighth and ninth shoguns were selected to form three new collateral lines, known as the "Three Lords" (*Sankyō*), which also had the same function. The "Three Lords," unlike the "Three Houses," bore their own distinctive surnames but lacked autonomous *han*, receiving handsome stipends instead.

THE TOKUGAWA SHOGUNS

1. Ieyasu	1603–05; d. 1616
2. Hidetada	1605–23; d. 1632
3. Iemitsu	1623–51
4. Ietsuna	1651–80
5. Tsunayoshi	1680–1709
6. Ienobu	1709–12
7. Ietsugu	1713–16
8. Yoshimune	1716–45; d. 1751
9. Ieshige	1745–60; d. 1761
10. Ieharu	1760–86
11. Ienari	1787–1837; d. 1841
12. Ieyoshi	1837–53
13. Iesada	1853–58
14. Iemochi	1858–66
15. Yoshinobu or Keiki	1866–67; d. 1913

The rest of the collateral lines of Tokugawa daimyo, eighteen in number at the end of the period, were given Ieyasu's original family name of Matsudaira, as were a number of *fudai* daimyo and even some of the great *tozama*, as a special honor, though the latter two groups usually did not use this name except ceremonially.

The Central Government. The Tokugawa shoguns, like their predecessors in previous shogunates, in theory derived their authority from the emperors, but on the whole they held themselves and their government aloof from the Kyōto court. Actually, Ieyasu and Hidetada did occupy the post of Grand Minister of State, and one of Hidetada's daughters was made an empress, while her daughter in turn ascended the throne as the first female sovereign in nine centuries; but these precedents were not followed by later shoguns.

The shoguns, while not involving themselves in the Kyōto court, provided rather generously for its support and also kept it under close surveillance and control. The stipend which they gave the emperor was raised from 10,000 *koku* at first to 30,000 by 1705. In addition, they granted stipends to the major families of court nobles — as much as 2865 *koku* in one case. Ieyasu in 1615 issued a set of laws to regulate the imperial court. His Kyōto deputy (*shoshidai*) acted as the military governor of the city, in addition to supervising the daimyo of West Japan, and a group of shogunal officers known as Masters of Court Ceremony (*Kōke*) kept strict control over all the court ceremonies and activities. Court ranks and posts in the old civil government were used among the military aristocracy as a means of indicating prestige, but these were actually assigned by the shogun, not the emperor; in most cases they were considered to be hereditary honors.

The officials of the shogun's government, who were drawn almost exclusively from among the *fudai* daimyo, bannermen and "honorable house men," gave their services as part of their feudal duties. Most posts were occupied by two or more men who alternated each month in assuming responsibility. Although the officials were chosen for their ability, they could only be assigned posts commensurate with their status in the feudal system. Some mobility was introduced in the early eighteenth century by a system of temporary augmentation of stipends or fiefs, to allow able administrators to serve in higher posts than those to which they would otherwise have been entitled. All but the highest posts in time came to carry specific salaries granted the incumbent in addition to his fief or hereditary stipend. It was also possible, in truly exceptional cases, for particularly outstanding men to receive permanent promotion in the feudal system, in order to permit them to advance further in the bureaucracy. Thus there was selection according to talent, and even a little promotion; but hereditary feudal status remained the chief determinant of bureaucratic position.

The shogunal administration grew in haphazard fashion from the old family government of the Tokugawa. A group of eleven leading *fudai* and collateral Tokugawa daimyo (but excluding the "Three Houses") acted as a top advisory body. The supreme administrative body, which formed a sort of cabinet, consisted usually of from three to six *fudai* daimyo, although at times in the early seventeenth century there were as many as eleven. These men, who were known as elders (*rōjū*, originally called *toshiyori*), wielded wide authority over matters of national policy and supervised the activities of a great variety of administrative offices. Between 1638 and 1684 one or two Great Elders (*Tairō*) were placed over the other elders, being thus, in a sense, prime ministers, but thereafter this post was only sporadically and briefly revived, usually during some specific crisis. Posts as elders or Great Elders came to be limited for the most part to a very few *fudai* families. For example, most of the later Great Elders came from the most important *fudai* daimyo family, the Ii of Hikone. (See table, page 605.)

A second or little cabinet was made up of a group of usually three to five *fudai* daimyo called the Junior Elders (*Wakadoshiyori*), who often were subsequently promoted to elders. These men supervised another diverse group of administrative offices having to do mainly with the services to the shogun of his direct retainers, that is, the bannermen and "honorable house men." In addition, the six or seven chamberlains (*sobashū*) and the Grand Chamberlain (*Sobayōnin*), when one was appointed, exercised considerable influence over government decisions, particularly in later years, because of their close association with the shogun.

There were also a number of important administrative posts and boards operating either directly under the shogun or under one of the two cabinet councils. Of these, the most important were the Commissioners of Temples and Shrines (*Jisha Bugyō*), who supervised the secular affairs of all the religious institutions in the country, and the Commissioners of Finance (*Kanjō Bugyō*, usually four in number), who managed what amounted to a Ministry of Economics and supervised the forty-odd local magistrates (*daikan*) of the shogunal domain. The local magistrates administered that part of the shogun's domain which was not parceled out to bannermen. Two Town Commissioners (*Machi Bugyō*) were assigned to administer each of the major cities — Edo, Ōsaka and Kyōto. Other commissioners controlled Nagasaki and its foreign trade, a number of other shogunal towns, and, after 1720, Uraga, which commanded the sea approaches to Edo. In addition, there were the various censors or spies (*metsuke*) and a Supreme Court of Justice (*Hyōjōsho*), made up of several of the high administrative officers.

The Legal System. The shogunal government operated under a conglomeration of laws and regulations. The most basic collection was the *Laws for the Military Houses* (*Buke shohatto*), put out by Ieyasu in 1615. These consisted of thirteen general maxims and prohibitions designed to regulate the activities of the daimyo and the whole military class. Almost all of Ieyasu's successors in turn issued their own *Laws for the Military Houses*, modifying and amplifying Ieyasu's code.

There were in addition innumerable lesser regulations and edicts establishing the details of administrative procedure, along with a harsh code of penal punishments, which treated commoners much more severely than samurai. However, the peasants usually regulated their own village affairs on the basis of local customary law, without running the risk of the intervention of government authorities. Certain important admonitions and regulations, such as the prohibition of Christianity, were displayed on boards erected at places where passers-by would see them. Some slight degree of order was provided the jumble of laws by occasional codifications, which had become necessary by the middle of the eighteenth century. Local administrators and judges, however, were always allowed wide latitude in application of the law, since the Japanese followed Chinese legal concepts in feeling that universal ethical principles should take precedence over the letter of the law.

THE ETHICAL SYSTEM

The Tokugawa authorities faced the special problem of attempting to rule, during a period of prolonged peace, through a military caste and through what had originally been locally based armies. Military morale and martial virtues had to be maintained, or the ruling class would collapse; but an excess of fighting spirit or a return of the soldier to the actual practice of his profession might upset the peace. For a generation or two the turbulence of the *rōnin* — that is, the members of the warrior class who had not found a satisfactory place for themselves in the new system — did pose serious difficulties. On the whole, however, the Tokugawa solved the problem successfully by encouraging a strict ethic for the military class. Thus a moral code of conduct, and the philosophy on which this code was based, not only became fundamental elements in the Tokugawa system but were consciously recognized as such by its shapers.

The Military Arts and Bushidō. The first of Ieyasu's *Laws for the Military Houses* encouraged learning and the military arts. It is interesting that learning was put first, but it is not surprising in view of the literary bent given by the Chinese to all of East Asian civilization. The cultivation of the military arts, however, was taken seriously. This became especially necessary as warfare became increasingly a matter of theory and as the generation that had had practical experience of warfare gradually passed from the scene.

Schools were founded in the various *han* to teach martial skills, but since these skills were taught more as arts, rather than as actual fighting techniques, they tended to become formalized. For example, little was done in gunnery, which had become so important in Japanese warfare even before the end of the sixteenth century. Instead, the military skills associated with medieval warfare, such as archery and fencing, were stressed. The whole emphasis tended to fall on the creation of warrior-like character rather than practical military ability. In other words, the martial arts came to be regarded as morally uplifting, like sports. *Jūjitsu*, the wrestling-fighting technique now popularized in the West under the more modern name of *jūdō*, might be included in this category of military sports, in contrast to *sumō*, the popular style of wrestling, in which human behemoths attempt to throw each other out of a ring.

The cultivation of the military arts represented only a part of the samurai code of conduct. Other elements, such as personal loyalty, obedience, sobriety, frugality and the acceptance of class distinctions were also spelled out in Ieyasu's *Laws for the Military Houses*, and further virtues were added by later shoguns until a detailed and firm body of ethical precepts had been established. In time this code came to be known as *Bushidō*, the "Way of the Warrior." The "learning" that the Tokugawa shoguns constantly recommended was usually directed toward the inculcation of this ethical system.

Bushidō, despite its careful elaboration, suffered from inherent weaknesses and contradictions. It was suited primarily to the social system and ethical needs of a period of constant warfare, and though it came to be modified somewhat to meet conditions in a time of peace and order, still it was ill adapted to the increasingly bureaucratic structure of government or to the rapidly expanding commercial economy. *Bushidō* thus did not really satisfy the demands of the times, as the authentically feudal ethics of the Kamakura and Ashikaga warriors had succeeded in doing, and the Tokugawa rulers were forced to seek philosophical props for *Bushidō* from outside the area of feudal ethics.

The Decline of Buddhism and the Rise of Confucianism. It is significant that no effort was made to find these supports in Buddhism, the religion which had dominated Japanese thought for a millennium. Buddhism, in fact, was falling into obvious decline. It had been unable to withstand the military pressures of the great unifiers of the late sixteenth century and had proved an intellectually ineffective bulwark against Christianity. Worse still, warrior-scholars and sophisticated townsmen alike had begun to show a disdain, almost a contempt, not only for its clergy but also for some of its basic ideas, just as the intellectual classes in China and Korea had turned away from Buddhism some centuries earlier.

This does not mean that Buddhism in Japan fell into such serious decay as it had in China and Korea. Actually, the great majority of Japanese remained Buddhist believers — many of them devoutly so. Buddhism also developed important new functions in society. Iemitsu ordered all Japanese to be registered as parishioners of some temple, as a means of checking on Christians. Moreover, temple schools (*terakoya*), which had already developed in the Ashikaga period, now became the chief institutions for primary education among the common people. But Buddhism had lost much of its spiritual vigor and the position of intellectual eminence it had previously enjoyed.

For a philosophical foundation for their system the Tokugawa rulers turned not to Buddhism but to Confucian rationalism and its ideal of a secular social order. This was perhaps natural, because the chief focus in Confucianism was precisely on the problem that most concerned the founders of the Tokugawa shogunate — namely, the creation and maintenance of a stable political and social order on the basis of a firm ethical code. However, one cannot but be struck by the parallel between the secularization of Japanese thought at the close of the true feudal period and the secularization of Western thought during the Renaissance, at somewhat comparable stages of development. The reasons for this parallel deserve study, for they may throw further light on the relationship in both areas between the changing attitudes toward religion and the fading of feudal social and political institutions.

Confucianism had of course been known and honored in Japan ever since the seventh century. The Tokugawa political system, however, despite its formal feudal structure, was in certain ways much closer to Chinese political norms than anything Japan had ever experienced. Consequently, Confucian thought now fitted the Japanese situation better than ever before, and the Tokugawa period thus became much more of a Confucian age than any previous period had been. The Confucian concept of a human order established in harmony with immutable natural principles seemed to justify the rigid social cleavages and political absolutism of the Tokugawa system. The Confucian emphasis on loyalty, on the ethical basis of government, and on intellectual orthodoxy and the Chinese ideal of bureaucratic civil rule were all extremely useful to the Tokugawa rulers. Such ideas gave their system a firm philosophical base, made doubly secure by the authority of antiquity and the traditional prestige of anything Chinese.

Neo-Confucianism in Japan. The type of Confucianism that flourished under official patronage in Tokugawa Japan was the orthodox school stemming primarily from the twelfth-century philosopher Chu Hsi, who is known in Japan as Shushi (see pages 238–239). The Japanese accepted the whole metaphysics of this so-called Neo-Confucianism, including its theory that the fundamental goodness of man's nature grows out of the basic order of the universe. Chu Hsi's emphasis on the "investigation of things" became less strictly a matter of textual research in Japan than in China. Many of the Tokugawa Confucianists actually were physicians or botanists and they showed a definitely scientific interest in natural phenomena. The Japanese thinkers, however, like the later Chinese, were most concerned with the practical ethics of Confucianism. What particularly appealed to them was the Confucian emphasis on the moral basis of political legitimacy, on loyalty, on a hierarchical family and social order, on a moderate, middle-of-the-road point of view, and on all the conservative virtues. These were the ideas that were needed to keep dissatisfied daimyo and unruly samurai in line and prevent upsetting social changes.

Neo-Confucianism had been introduced into Japan by the Zen scholars of the Ashikaga period. The man who brought this thinking to Ieyasu's attention was a monk named Seika (1561–1619), a humble scion of the once great Fujiwara. Seika forsook Buddhist orders to become Japan's first lay philosopher. His disciple, Hayashi Razan (or Dōshun, 1583–1657), was made a councilor by Ieyasu in 1608 and played a large role as the drafter of laws and a developer of the Tokugawa political and ethical system. He established Chu Hsi's school as a rigid Tokugawa orthodoxy. His grandson in 1691 became the first hereditary President of the Confucian University at Edo, which had been established on a modest scale in 1630. This university, like similar institutions in China, maintained a semi-religious cult of Confucius, but it, of course, lacked the broad political function of the official educational institutions in China, since in Tokugawa Japan the top bureaucratic posts remained the preserve of certain feudal aristocrats.

Ieyasu valued Seika and Razan as men whose knowledge proved useful not only in giving a philosophical foundation to his political system but also in setting up his administration and conducting foreign relations with other East Asian countries. But the influence of Confucianism went far beyond this. Its "culturalism" (see pages 290–294) may have contributed to the willingness of Ieyasu's immediate successors to cut themselves off from the "barbarian" Europeans, and unquestionably it became a factor in the growing xenophobia of late Tokugawa times. Confucian economic theory also confirmed the feudal rulers in their emphasis on agriculture as the sole economic basis for government and encouraged them to disregard both foreign and domestic trade.

Confucianism also helped turn Japanese interests back to ancient history, since history, as the source of knowledge about human society, constituted an important part of Confucian scholarship. Razan himself, on the model of Chu Hsi's *Outline and Details of the Comprehensive Mirror (T'ung-chien kang-mu)*, started the compilation of *The Comprehensive Mirror of Our State (Honchō tsugan)*, which was completed by his successors around 1670 in 310 chapters. Razan's Sinophile attitude in this work is illustrated by his suggestion that the Japanese imperial line was descended from a Chinese princeling.

Confucianism also helped develop broad scholarly interests among the samurai and in time produced an outburst of intellectual activity that quite overshadowed their traditional military prowess. Thus it helped turn warrior-aristocrats into the scholar-bureaucrats that were needed to operate the Tokugawa system. Confucianism also encouraged the study and use of the Chinese language. In other words, the "learning" advocated by the Tokugawa shoguns was primarily scholarship in the Chinese language. Thus, despite Japan's self-imposed isolation, this was a period when large numbers of scholars studied deeply and were much influenced by a great variety of Chinese writings and once again wrote many of their books in classical Chinese, often with a high degree of grammatical accuracy and even with elegance.

Tokugawa Ethics. The most important influence of Confucianism, however, can be seen in the field of ethics and social relations. From Confucianism came the theory of the four classes and the identification of the samurai with the scholar-administrator of China. Even *Bushidō*, though it was based on the concepts of feudal society, actually came to be more Confucian than feudal both in content and in terminology. Instead of talking about the relationship between lord and vassal, Tokugawa moralists stressed the five Confucian relationships, which start with that between ruler and minister.

Japanese ethical standards thus more closely approximated those of China than they had ever done before; yet the strict ethical code that resulted from this combination of Neo-Confucian philosophy and the ideals and social system of feudal Japan remained quite distinct from that of China. For one thing, loyalty to one's lord, that is, to the political unit, always took clear precedence in Japan over loyalty to one's family. Moreover, Confucian morality in general, as applied within the strict class lines of Japanese society, built up tensions that were less apparent in the freer, more egalitarian society of China. There seem to have been more artificialities in Japanese society, and these in turn apparently necessitated a greater effort at conformity and, consequently, stronger social pressure on the individual.

Each member of the samurai class was taught to feel a tremendous sense of duty to his family, to his lord, and to society — to feel that he must live up to his status and the specific obligations which it imposed upon him. He became deeply imbued with such concepts as *giri*, "duty," and *on*, the debt of gratitude owed one's superior for his "benevolence." Above all, he developed a sense of discipline, for discipline was essential if he were to play his assigned role in society and live up to his duty, honor, and obligations. Though lacking the compulsions of the Occidental sense of sin, the individual Japanese developed an almost equal internal driving force from his sense of duty. It impelled him to strive hard to avoid the shame of failing in his specific obligations and to win the honor of accomplishing as much as, if not more than, society expected of him.

These attitudes spread from the samurai to the other classes. In part this was the result of strict regulations and harsh punishments. The old Chinese device of collective responsibility, which had been used in Japan for many centuries, was now uniformly applied as the "five-man unit" (*gonin gumi*) system, and it carried a sense of strict obligation and discipline down to the lowest social levels. There was also an element of conscious imitation. The lower classes often tried to act and think like their social and political superiors. As a result, discipline and a keen sense of duty and honor became major characteristics of the Tokugawa Japanese as a whole, probably accounting as much as the elaborate political structure for the enduring qualities of the Tokugawa regime.

Tokugawa ethics, however, had its weaknesses as well as its virtues. Based as it was on a foreign philosophical orthodoxy and a somewhat outmoded domestic social system, it was by no means perfectly suited to the society that developed during Tokugawa times. Perhaps just because of its artificiality, it became all the more rigid and inflexible. A greater effort of will power and discipline was required to apply the ethical system than would have been necessary if it had been well adapted to economic and social conditions. Any modifications whatsoever in ethical concepts, it was feared, might open the way for the rejection of the whole order. The less naturally the ethical code applied to society, the more meticulous had to be the observance of each formal detail. The more unrealistic the social relations or attitudes this code demanded, the greater had to be the discipline and driving sense of duty of those attempting to apply it. Thus the Tokugawa ethical system, which started as a solid framework for the political and social order, proved somewhat restrictive from the start and became increasingly a rigid shell, impeding the growth of Tokugawa society.

The Tokugawa ethical system has left its legacy, both good and bad, to the modern Japanese. Its sense of duty and honor and the discipline and drive which it engendered must be counted among the greatest assets the Japanese have had in their turbulent recent history. On the other hand, the rigidity and formalism of Tokugawa ethics may be responsible for a tendency to sacrifice moral principles and true courtesy to a punctilious observance of form and etiquette. The burdensome sense of obligation in the Tokugawa code of ethics and its strict limitations on the freedom of the individual also seem to have produced a certain tenseness of personality among the Japanese.

THE DYNASTIC CYCLE IN TOKUGAWA JAPAN

Although the Tokugawa system had its inner contradictions, tensions and other flaws, it proved extremely effective in maintaining both the peace of the country and the supremacy of the Tokugawa family for two and a half centuries. The Shimabara Revolt of 1637–38, the last real military disturbance before the middle of the nineteenth century, was in fact the last time that the lower classes posed any sort of military or political threat to the supremacy of the feudal aristocracy. For two centuries they had been doing this with considerable local success, but under the Tokugawa, centralized military and political power had become so effective that private groups could no longer hope to challenge it. Peasant riots occurred with increasing frequency in the latter half of the Tokugawa period, but these were merely desperate efforts to escape crushing indebtedness, win tax rebates, or eliminate specific types of misgovernment. They did not represent any organized attempt to throw off the military and political control of the military class, as had the popular uprisings of the fifteenth and sixteenth centuries.

The Tokugawa Peace. The few incidents and natural catastrophes that did disturb the routine of government under the Tokugawa actually served to show how complete was their peace and how absolute their rule. This may be indicated by a brief recital of the major disturbances. In 1651, when Ietsuna became shogun as a child of ten, Yui Shōsetsu, a popular military teacher at Edo, organized an attempted *coup d'état* of dissatisfied *rōnin*, but the plot was discovered and the leaders executed. A second *rōnin* plot was foiled the next year. These *rōnin* disturbances occurred largely as the result of the plight of many samurai who had been made masterless by the destruction of their lords in earlier years. After 1652 the *rōnin* problem subsided, and it did not again become troublesome until the closing years of the Tokugawa period.

The suicide of some of Iemitsu's chief officials on his death in 1651 led to the prohibition in 1663 of this old custom, which was known as "following in death" (*junshi*). A revolt of Ainu in Hokkaidō in 1669 was suppressed by the daimyo of Matsumae, established at the southern tip of the island. In 1684 the able but arbitrary Great Elder Hotta Masatoshi was assassinated by one of the Junior Elders. A great deal of adverse comment was stirred up when Yanagizawa Yoshiyasu, a talented man but only a 150-*koku* samurai in origin, rose, under the patronage of Tsunayoshi, the fifth shogun, to become a 150,000-*koku* daimyo and the Great Elder (1706–1709). Both criticism and inconvenience were caused by Tsunayoshi's dog decrees, which earned him the sobriquet of the Dog Shogun. Influenced by Buddhist doctrines he attempted to protect animals and, because of his own birth in the zodiacal year of the dog, severely punished any mistreatment of dogs and took elaborate measures to care for strays.

Natural disasters probably did more to disrupt Tokugawa rule than any of these human incidents. In 1657 much of the city of Edo was destroyed by fire, the first and greatest of many conflagrations that ravaged the city during Tokugawa times. In 1703 a great earthquake killed tens of thousands of people in the Kantō, and in 1707 Mount Fuji erupted disastrously, though for the last time. In 1783 occurred a still more destructive eruption of Mount Asama, which is still a very active volcano in Central Honshū. There were particularly serious famines for several years following this eruption, as there had been earlier in the 1730's.

The event that stirred the country more than any other during the Tokugawa period, though it posed no threat to the government, was the so-called Incident of the Forty-Seven *Rōnin*, which occurred in 1702 (1703 by the Western calendar). This affords a good illustration of both the ideals and the working of the Tokugawa system. Almost two years earlier the small daimyo of Akō in West Honshū had drawn his sword under severe provocation, and had wounded a shogunal official in the

Edo castle. Since merely to draw one's sword within the castle grounds meant the death penalty, the daimyo was forced to commit suicide, and his *han* was confiscated. However, forty-seven of his samurai, who were now reduced to the status of *rōnin*, vowed vengeance on the official who had caused their lord's downfall. Knowing that the official and the other shogunal authorities would suspect as much, they scattered and in some cases abandoned their own families by sinking ostensibly into lives of debauchery. Then, when they felt that they were no longer under surveillance, they stormed the official's Edo residence one snowy night and killed him. Public opinion was strongly in their favor, but eventually they were forced to commit suicide to atone for their crime. The conduct of these forty-seven *rōnin*, often cited to exemplify the height of feudal virtue, has remained one of the favorite themes of Japanese playwrights ever since.

The Decline of Government Finances and Morale. One can see how great was the Tokugawa peace if the Incident of the Forty-Seven *Rōnin* was the most renowned event during a period of two centuries. But the currents of historical change flowed on in deeper channels, eroding the less visible foundations of the Tokugawa system. In fact, certain elements of the dynastic administrative cycle, familiar from Chinese history, reappear clearly and in a comparable time span in Tokugawa history (see pages 114–123).

Under the first three shoguns, the Tokugawa regime was extremely affluent, but by the latter part of the seventeenth century it began to experience serious financial difficulties. The soaring expenditures of the *bakufu* and the individual daimyo began to exceed their income, which for the most part was tied to the less rapidly expanding agricultural yield. Many daimyo, under the guise of forced loans, reduced the stipends paid their retainers, sometimes by as much as 50 per cent. This hurt the morale of the warrior class, which was already being undermined by the inevitable relaxing of the martial spirit during a prolonged period of peace. Moreover, as might be expected from the Chinese dynastic cycle, the later shoguns on the whole provided less forceful, or at least somewhat erratic, leadership. The government, though it had increased in complexity, was in some ways becoming less efficient. Laxity and corruption grew more common among officials. Unsound policies, such as currency debasement, were employed to fill empty treasuries. River dikes, roads, and other public works were sometimes allowed to fall into disrepair, increasing the likelihood of natural disasters.

Another aspect of the dynastic cycle can be seen in the growth of the population. Before the end of the seventeenth century, the natural population increase during a time of peace had brought considerable pressure on the limited food resources of an isolated country. As a result, famines became more common, and natural disasters produced greater suffering than if there had been a wider margin of safety. These conditions, combined with the government's demands for higher tax yields, led in turn to an increase in peasant unrest and rioting. This whole story of weakening leadership in the shogunate, administrative laxness and inefficiency, financial difficulties and popular unrest, which had become so typical of the Chinese dynastic cycle, was mirrored in most of the daimyo *han* — on a smaller scale, of course, but often in accentuated form.

The latter part of the Tokugawa period falls into an alternating series of rallies against the "dynastic" decline and open routs. The rallies usually witnessed a return of the elders to control of the central government, after a period of supremacy by the chamberlains, who usually represented a slightly lower-ranking stratum of feudal society. The rallies were also characterized by a return to traditional economic and ethical policies: a greater emphasis on traditional feudal virtues, strict political morality in place of open corruption, a more purely agrarian basis for government finances, lower limits on foreign trade, sound money in place of debased coinage, and stronger controls over commercial enterprises. Such orthodox economic notions naturally brought with them monetary deflation and a general depression of the economy.

The first rally was started by the Confucian scholar Arai Hakuseki (1657–1725), who from 1709 to 1716 was the chief shaper of government policy under two shoguns. Following a period of growing luxury, administrative laxity, and misrule under Tsunayoshi, the Dog Shogun, and his Grand Chamberlain and later Great Elder (Yanagizawa), Hakuseki attempted to bring back order and discipline. It was his policy to make the laws more practical, to restore a sound currency by eliminating the debased coinage, to cut down the export of silver and copper, to inaugurate a sort of budgeting system in shogunal finances, and to tighten up morality by a stronger emphasis on Confucian ritual.

Yoshimune's Reforms. Hakuseki's efforts at reform were soon superseded by those of Yoshimune, the eighth shogun, who was brought in from the collateral Wakayama line in 1716. Dismissing Hakuseki at once, Yoshimune injected a strongly reactionary element into the reform program. His basic plan was to return to the martial spirit, frugal ways and administrative efficiency of the early Tokugawa, or, rather, to the rigid, idealized picture of that age as it appeared to men of a century later. Since he was at least partially successful in his effort, he has appeared to Japanese historians to correspond to those strong Chinese emperors who, coming midway in a dynasty, sometimes gave it a second start.

Much of what Yoshimune attempted was sound. He sought to increase agricultural production through reclamation projects and the popularization of new crops, such as sweet potatoes and sugar cane. He cut governmental expenses and between 1722 and 1730 even reduced the period of attendance of the daimyo in Edo. He tried to restore sound money. He also tried to improve administration and morale by inculcating in the samurai class, through education, a revived martial spirit, greater literary skill, and a higher sense of responsible leadership. He himself led the way by a strict example of simplicity and uprightness, and also by a plethora of exhortations. He insisted on high standards among his subordinates. For example, Ōoka Tadasuke, an able and incorruptible official whom Yoshimune appointed to be a commissioner of Edo and later made a 10,000-*koku* daimyo, won the reputation of being the wisest judge and best administrator of the whole Tokugawa period.

Many of Yoshimune's efforts, however, though well intentioned, produced results that tended to nullify his aims. To aid shogunal finances, he increased tax pressures on the peasants, thus stimulating further peasant unrest. His effort to restore the more strictly feudal conditions of an earlier age led to a type of formalism that actually proved injurious both to administrative efficiency and to morale. His emphasis on financial solvency undermined his efforts to restore the old feudal virtue of disdain for the profit motive, and his licensing of commercial monopolies and attempts to regulate rice prices, all in the interests of the finances of the shogunate and the military class, helped to commercialize the economy and thus to destroy the financial foundations of feudal rule. His further limitations on the Nagasaki trade had a depressing effect on the economy, as did also his efforts at currency reform and his insistence on extreme frugality. Such policies reduced production in the non-agricultural sectors of the economy, while some of his other policies increased the agricultural yield. As a result, the price of rice fell much more sharply than the prices of non-agricultural goods and services. This situation hurt the military men, for they received their now somewhat reduced stipends largely in fixed amounts of rice, part of which they had to sell to obtain money for their many necessary expenditures, especially those incurred in connection with service in Edo.

Thus Yoshimune's reforms, which have been much praised by traditional historians, did little to stem the tide, and even before his retirement in 1745, they were recognized as being largely a failure. These reforms were followed by a period in which Yoshimune's concern for money matters survived, but not his reformist zeal. The morale and finances of the military class further deteriorated, and the efficiency of government was again reduced by corruption and economic difficulties.

The Policies of Tanuma. According to traditional historians, the evil genius of this period was Tanuma Okitsugu, a samurai who, despite having inherited only a small fief (600 *koku*), rose under shogunal patronage to become first the Grand Chamberlain and later one of the elders (1769–

1786), being elevated in the process to the rank of a 57,000-*koku* daimyo. Under the tenth shogun, Ieharu (1760–1786), Tanuma exercised great power, but his son, a Junior Elder, was assassinated in 1784, and upon Ieharu's death, two years later, Tanuma himself was stripped of his offices and holdings, while his heir was reduced to 10,000 *koku*, the minimal level for a daimyo.

Tanuma has been condemned for having allowed the practice of giving presents to superiors to develop into open bribery and corruption, even though the underlying cause of this situation was the growing impoverishment of the Edo bureaucracy. He has also been criticized for having made no effort to curb the luxurious living of both the military class and the townsmen or to restore the military vigor and feudal virtues of earlier times. However, as we have seen, even Yoshimune's efforts along these lines had had no lasting effect. The increase in the number of famines and destructive riots by peasants and city mobs at this time has also been laid at Tanuma's door; yet this actually resulted more from the general "dynastic" decline than from misgovernment on his part. Traditional historians have even blamed Tanuma for the great natural disasters of the period, such as the Asama eruption of 1783 and the great famines that followed it, since according to Confucian theory the ruler must take moral responsibility for all phenomena.

Actually, Tanuma was an energetic and liberal-minded administrator. Since he made no effort to fight against the economic and social currents of his day, as Yoshimune had done, his policies often had more constructive and lasting effects. Tanuma harbored none of the typical feudal prejudice in favor of an agrarian economy. He did follow Yoshimune's lead in developing agriculture, through reclamation projects and riparian works, but he also realistically attempted to enlarge the base of shogunal finances to include the non-agricultural areas of the economy. He encouraged foreign trade, which by this time depended on exports of dried sea products from Hokkaidō as well as on the old staple, copper. He planned an extensive program of colonization and development in Hokkaidō. He tightened up such traditional shogunal monopolies as those on gold, silver and copper, and he made a vigorous effort to expand mining. He added new monopolies, particularly in items imported from abroad, such as alum, camphor, and the supposedly medicinal root, ginseng. He even attempted to establish monopolies in lime and lamp oil. He sought to secure government profits by licensing the large merchant associations under government charters. He taxed both trade and transportation, albeit in a piecemeal and largely ineffective fashion. He even attempted to make the government the chief moneylending agency to needy daimyo, though the capital for this project was to be derived largely from the wealthy merchants. His monetary policies, like those of many other Tokugawa administrators, were aimed primarily at making profits for the government through debasement of the currency, but he did add a useful set of silver coins to the existing coinage.

Reaction Under Matsudaira Sadanobu. Tanuma's downfall was followed by a period of energetic conservative reforms. Under the slogan of "Back to Yoshimune," every effort was made to restore earlier feudal institutions and virtues and to eradicate the freer economic doctrines and unorthodox ideas of Tanuma's period.

Matsudaira Sadanobu, one of the elders between 1787 and 1793, was the leader in this period of backward-looking reform. As the son of one of the "Three Lords," he himself had been a candidate for shogun but instead had been made the daimyo of a collateral line, in which position he established the reputation of being a fine administrator by rehabilitating the *han's* finances. Under the new shogun, Ienari, Sadanobu immediately dismissed Tanuma's henchmen from office and reversed all of Tanuma's policies. He set up a famine storehouse system and encouraged all types of production. He also embarked on a program of rigorous governmental economy and strict limitation of consumption by all classes, issuing exhortations and many extremely detailed sumptuary laws. He again reduced foreign trade and contact and insisted on a return to orthodox economic and philosophical ideas. To save the impoverished bannermen and "honorable house men" of the shogunate, he canceled their indebtedness to usurers incurred before 1785 and reduced to a meaningless level the interest on their later debts. This, no doubt, came as a temporary boon to his retainers, but he did them lasting economic harm by prohibiting further loans.

Sadanobu's policies, known from the year period as the "Kansei Reforms," helped alleviate famine conditions in the country, temporarily bolstered the shogunal finances, and restored feudal prestige and authority. However, they also disrupted the nation's developing commercial economy and stirred up strong opposition. In the long run, his efforts proved even less successful than those of Yoshimune. In fact, his repairing of the superstructure of government was more than offset by his removal of the new financial underpinnings that Tanuma had been developing. The government appeared strengthened but actually it was more seriously undermined than before, since once again it was forced to rely largely on the restricted agricultural sector of the economy.

Mizuno's Tempō Reforms. After Sadanobu's retirement, the old conditions of social and economic decline soon reappeared. Then, following a decade of serious famines, a final desperate attempt at reform was made between 1841 and 1843. Under the leadership of Mizuno Tadakuni, one of the elders (1834–1845), a determined effort was put forth, in conscious imitation of Yoshimune and Sadanobu, to turn back the clock of historical change.

Mizuno insisted once more on personal frugality and governmental economy; he intervened forcibly again in behalf of the debt-ridden bannermen; he attempted to regulate prices and to abolish the merchant associations that his predecessors had licensed; he tried to consolidate the shogun's personal domain more conveniently, around the two major cities, Edo and Ōsaka; and he prohibited peasants from leaving their farms and ordered those who had migrated to the cities to return to their villages. This last policy had been a basic feature of the early Tokugawa system, but it had proved increasingly unworkable despite occasional legislation. Though strenuous, the effort in 1843 hardly slowed the stream of people moving to the city. The population of Edo was reduced slightly for a few months, but by the next spring it had risen to new heights.

Mizuno's whole effort, known as the "Tempō Reforms," proved entirely unrealistic under the social and economic conditions that had now developed. While economy and frugality helped, the only real palliatives to dynastic decline would have been innovations of the type Tanuma had advocated, that is, better organized government monopolies and more income from the non-agricultural sector of the economy through new types of taxes and closer government cooperation with merchant associations. Both the shogunate itself and many of the *han* were moving in this direction, but their efforts were perhaps too little and certainly they were too late, for the reappearance of the Westerners in force in Japanese waters had begun to put unprecedented new pressures on the Tokugawa system. The downward spiral picked up speed, ending during the 1860's in a complete "dynastic" collapse.

ECONOMIC GROWTH:
AGRICULTURE AND THE PEASANTRY

The financial decline of the shogunate and of the whole military class gives the superficial impression of general economic decline, but the Tokugawa period was actually a time of steady growth and development in the economy as a whole. In fact, the ebbing fortunes of the ruling military class were a sign not of over-all decay but of the failure of the Tokugawa system to adjust rapidly enough to changing economic conditions. The relative position of the samurai and the daimyo was deteriorating, but not the general economy. While the feudal political structure and the agrarian basis of government finances reflected little change, the economy of Japan as a whole became commercialized, and some features of an incipient capitalism made their appearance, in somewhat the same way as capitalism had emerged from the breakdown of European feudalism.

Economic growth was naturally hampered by the isolation forced on the country at the beginning of Tokugawa rule. However, as we have seen, this isolation was far from complete in the economic field. Also, the new crops and technological advances previously introduced by the Europeans had a stimulating effect on the economy long after the exclusion policy had gone into effect, and a trickle of new technological advances continued to seep in through the Dutch and Chinese.

Foreign stimulus, however, proved much less of a spur to economic growth than the Tokugawa system itself. The peace and stability which the Tokugawa provided for two and a half centuries permitted much greater production and a tremendous increase in accumulated wealth. The Ōsaka campaigns and the Shimabara Revolt were only localized wars, and after 1638 no man-made disturbances, besides an occasional riot, destroyed property or disrupted economic activity. It would be hard to find a parallel for such a prolonged period of peace anywhere else at any time in world history.

Under these conditions there was a great expansion of agriculture. During the first half of the Tokugawa period the land under cultivation seems to have doubled as a result of reclamation efforts. There was a parallel development in the water control and irrigation projects necessary for rice cultivation. Even during the second half of the period substantial increases were registered in irrigation projects and lands under cultivation. Technological advances in farming were also made throughout the Tokugawa period and naturally these helped to increase the yield. Labor-saving farm tools came into use, and there was a tremendous improvement in the number and the quality of plant types, as well as a great growth in the use of commercial fertilizers, such as dried fish, oil cakes and night soil from the towns, which, while they cost money, increased yields and reduced labor needs for collecting fertilizers. Improved seed strains and better winter drainage of the fields also permitted a great expansion of double cropping.

The Commercialization of the Rural Economy. The gradual unification and commercialization of the economy during the Tokugawa period also brought a slow shift from subsistence farming to commercial farming, in which a significant part of the acreage was devoted to specialized cash crops. This specialization of crops naturally increased total production a great deal. Despite the efforts of the authorities everywhere to maximize the rice yields, there was a marked increase after the late seventeenth century in regional industrial crops, such as cotton, sesame seeds for oil, mulberry leaves for silkworms, indigo, tobacco and sugar cane. All in all, Japanese agriculture made such advances during the Tokugawa period that by the nineteenth century Japan seems to have been well ahead of any other country in Asia in agricultural technology.

Local specialty crops and the resulting commercialization of the whole economy stimulated the development of locally based village industries, such as silk production and weaving, cotton spinning and weaving, dyeing and sake brewing. Such local industries, as well as those of the expanding cities, which we shall consider later, increased the demand for labor. As a result, there was a drop in seasonal underemployment, which had characterized the earlier economy of agricultural Japan, and rural labor wages rose rapidly during the eighteenth and nineteenth centuries.

The growing demand for labor, together with the advancing agricultural technology, had a profound effect upon traditional farming patterns. On the one hand, poor families now had alternate means of support outside of farming. On the other, the owners of large farming units now found it difficult to retain or to hire the necessary number of farm hands. They also discovered that indentured or hired help did not provide the high level of skills that farming increasingly required. As a result, there was a steady trend away from large farming units toward smaller farms that could be efficiently run by a small family nucleus (father, mother and children) without much outside help.

The Shrinking Family Unit. This change in turn tended to break up the large, extended families which had previously characterized the more prosperous farming communities. These extended families had included hereditary servants as well as collateral branches of the family. Such lesser members of the group frequently farmed their own tiny portions of the total holding, but their miniscule farms were never adequate for support, and therefore the sub-branches of an extended family had to depend on the main holding, supplying it with free labor in return for the economic security of membership in the larger group. According to the new system, the large holding tended to become broken up into a series of farms of nuclear family size. The owner would naturally retain one of these farms for the main family, but the others would be assigned through tenancy to the former branch families, or even to the families of hereditary servants. In the process, the lesser families became independent social and economic units, and the bond between them and the owners gradually changed from a matter of social obligation to a more openly economic one.

Such changes, of course, occurred very slowly and through hardly perceptible individual steps. In the seventeenth century the process was already well along in the old capital area around Kyōto and Ōsaka, because this was then economically the most advanced and most urbanized part of the country. By the early nineteenth century, however, changes of this sort were far advanced in most of Japan and had appeared to some degree even in remote and backward rural areas. One result was a considerable increase in social mobility in farming communities.

These economic and social changes in rural Japan became extremely significant in Japan's subsequent development. The breakup of the old extended family pattern produced, at one end of the scale, well-to-do landowning families, who, being freed from the direct administration of all their lands and from providing economic support for their collateral branches and hereditary servants, could now devote their energies increasingly to village industries. Thus they developed entrepreneurial attitudes and skills which, as we shall see, became important in late Tokugawa times and grew still more so in Japan's subsequent modernization. At the other end of the scale, the tenant families, in their spare time, and the growing group of landless villagers became accustomed to working for wages as laborers in the village industries. The transition from this type of employment to work in the cities could be made with relative ease, and the tenant farmers and landless villagers thus formed the reservoir from which the Tokugawa cities drew their expanding populations and the modern industries of Japan their great labor force.

Population Growth. These changes in rural Japan may also have influenced the growth of population. During the seventeenth century a rapid rise in numbers paralleled the increasing production rate. National censuses were started in 1721 and they were usually made every six years thereafter, but they generally excluded samurai and several other categories. These censuses indicate that the population was approaching 30,000,000 by 1721. This probably represented an increase of about 50 per cent in little more than a century — giving Japan at the time a population which far exceeded that of such European countries as France, Italy, Germany or England. For more than a century after 1721, however, the population total seems to have remained almost stationary, although agricultural production and the other sectors of the economy continued to expand steadily.

The reasons for this anomalous situation are not entirely clear. One explanation might be the slowing down of the rate at which new lands were being brought under cultivation; but this fails to take into account the increasing productivity of the lands already under cultivation. Another factor may have been the breakup of the farming community into economically independent nuclear family units. In the earlier, extended-family system, the richer and poorer nuclear families together formed a cooperative farming group, and the total population of a village thus tended to keep pace with the general level of village production. In the new system, the richer and poorer families were economically independent of each other. The advantages of technological improvements and commercialized farming accrued largely to the rich, who had the capital to finance such changes, and the tax system further benefited them. Since there were relatively few new land surveys and consequent reassessments of taxes after 1700, the improved lands of the rich tended to be undertaxed and the less improved lands of the poor proportionately overtaxed. This situation may explain one of the apparent contradictions of Tokugawa society — the increase of peasant unrest despite the expansion of agricultural production during a period of stable population. It also may help to explain the failure of the population to grow after 1721. Despite the rapidly growing wealth of a small segment of village society, the bulk of rural families remained too poor to be able to feed more mouths; thus village populations remained stable even though the over-all productivity of the village increased.

Poverty and a limited food supply forced a large proportion of the peasants and, for that matter, the poorer of the samurai and townsmen as well, to limit their families by artificial means. Both abortion and infanticide became common. Infanticide went by the matter-of-fact name of *mabiki,* an agricultural term for the "thinning" of a row of plants.

Peasant Unrest and Riots. Curiously enough, the pressures of a limited food supply were most severe on the farmers who produced it, because the financial burden of maintaining the feudal superstructure fell with disproportionate weight on the agrarian sector of the economy. The very importance of agriculture to the *han* and to the shogunal finances produced an odd contrast between the high respect paid agriculture and the abominable treatment meted out to agriculturalists. All the rulers and theorists agreed that farming was the foundation of the state, and in theory they ranked farmers next to the samurai; but in practice the Tokugawa authorities squeezed the peasant unmercifully for every penny of revenue they could extract from him. He was also subjected to detailed sumptuary laws designed to minimize his consumption and thus maximize the amount of taxes he could pay. As we have noted, these burdens fell much more heavily on the many poor peasants than on the few rich ones.

The more desperate the financial situation of the feudal rulers, the worse were the exactions they made on their peasants. In fact, the effort to squeeze more from the agricultural groups sometimes led to a decrease of both produce and taxes, because the peasants in desperation abandoned their fields for the easier life of the cities and the overtaxed agricultural lands then lay fallow. Naturally, feudal rulers did their best to prevent their peasants from deserting, but, as we have seen, it became increasingly difficult to enforce these restrictions in the latter half of the period.

The breakup of the larger farming units tended to free the poorer peasants from their former direct dependence on the rich, but as tenants or independent small holders they had even less economic security than before. Moreover, the commercialization of the economy increased their vulnerability. Specialization in crops made them dependent on purchasing with money many essential goods, and the feudal rulers increasingly demanded their taxes in money instead of in kind. This double need for money often led the poorer peasants into debt, both in times of bad crops and when too bountiful harvests brought down the price of rice. Debts were covered by mortgages, and, through the foreclosure of these mortgages, much of the agricultural land which the poorer peasants had held in their own names passed into the hands of rich peasants or sometimes even into the hands of city usurers. Thus the tenancy deriving from the breakup of earlier large holdings was augmented by tenancy resulting from foreclosed mortgages. Tenancy disputes had become common by the first half of the eighteenth century. By the middle of the nineteenth century more than a quarter of the agricultural land was tenant-operated — in some villages as much as 60 per cent.

The peasant had no recourse against his oppressors except flight or riots. This may be the reason for the prevalence of organized demonstrations and destructive rioting by the peasantry, directed sometimes against the rich landowners and usurers and sometimes against the feudal authorities. Such outbursts became more frequent during Yoshimune's rule in the early eighteenth century and still more numerous during the repeated famines after 1780. For example, under Tanuma in the 1780's, again during the famine period of the 1830's, and also in the last decade of the shogunate, there were single years in which more than twenty such uprisings occurred in various parts of Japan. Since many tens of thousands of angry peasants participated in the larger disturbances, the authorities not infrequently were forced to make concessions. Yet the peasants, being all but weaponless, never presented a serious military challenge to the Tokugawa system, and in most cases the authorities soon reasserted their control by executing the ringleaders. Peasant riots, however, did contribute to the economic and political disruption of the Tokugawa system in its later years.

Peasant Society. The great number of peasant riots in the second half of the Tokugawa period has given rise to the assumption that the peasants all existed in unrelieved misery. Actually the Japanese farmers were probably no worse off in respect to food supply, taxes and rent than most other peasants of the time in Asia. In many ways they were far ahead of the average. The very unrest in rural areas perhaps indicated a rising standard of living, or at least higher economic expectations. Much of what had earlier been thought of as luxurious city living had by the nineteenth century become commonplace in rural Japan.

The peasants, moreover, were permitted considerable autonomy in running their own local affairs, so long as they remained politically docile and paid their taxes. The joint development and use of water resources for irrigation gave rise to many cooperative enterprises. In fact, during the Tokugawa period the peasant villages developed into the highly integrated social and economic communities they still remain today.

In particular, the upper levels of the peasantry, despite the scorn of the samurai, could scarcely be termed a suppressed class. Descendants in large part of the old rural aristocracy, they provided the villages with a self-respecting and capable leadership. Their surprisingly high degree of literacy and their substantial, prosperous-looking farmhouses indicated a relatively high standard of living and explain how rural Japan was able to produce a considerable share of Japan's leadership after the collapse of the Tokugawa.

ECONOMIC GROWTH:
URBANIZATION AND A MONEY ECONOMY

The non-agricultural sectors of the economy — industry, trade and other services — expanded even more rapidly during the Tokugawa period than did agriculture. This was partly because they faced less rigid natural limits than those imposed on farming by Japan's geography. But the Tokugawa system itself was also an important factor. Its agrarian orientation and disdain for trade tended, paradoxically, to benefit trade and industry more than agriculture. In contrast to the crushing tax load of the peasant, the city dweller had only to pay for the public services in his home town and to meet certain relatively light taxes imposed by his lord on his home and business undertaking. In other words, the official esteem for agriculture, which resulted in its heavy tax burden, meant that commerce and industry carried a disproportionately light load, permitting their greater expansion.

Naturally, the centralization of the Tokugawa system gave the non-agricultural sectors of the economy a tremendous impetus for growth. The samurai and their families, as we have seen, constituted about five or six per cent of the total population at the end of the Tokugawa period. In each *han* this quite sizable administrative and military class was gathered largely in the daimyo's capital town, and the *sankin kōtai* system made it necessary for about half the daimyo and a considerable percentage of the total samurai population to be concentrated in Edo at any given time. Naturally trade and services had to be developed on a large scale to supply the needs of the daimyo and samurai both at their *han* capitals and at Edo. Coastal transport, chiefly in the hands of private merchants, grew to large proportions to meet these needs. A great tonnage, though in small vessels, annually entered port at Ōsaka and Edo. The constant movement of the daimyo and many thousands of the samurai between their *han* and Edo also necessitated extensive transport and hotel services along the major highways. Thus the effectiveness of the feudal system of the Tokugawa greatly stimulated the growth of the non-agricultural — and therefore non-feudal — aspects of the economy.

The Development of Towns and Cities. The disproportionate growth of industry, trade and other services can be clearly seen in several phenomena. One was the urbanization of society during this period. The capitals of the more than 260 *han* developed into towns commensurate with the size of the realms administered from them. A minimal 10,000-*koku* daimyo might have a capital town of about 3000 inhabitants, while Kanazawa, the capital of the 1,022,700-*koku* Maeda, grew to about 60,000. Innumerable post-station towns also appeared along the highways, and great cities grew up in the area directly administered by the shogun. Kyōto remained a major center of handicraft production, with a population of around 400,000. Edo, which grew from the fishing villiage it had been in 1590 into a city of more than a half a million in the early seventeenth century, may have been the largest city in the world in the eighteenth century, when its population approached the million mark. Ōsaka, which had become the major commercial center for all West Japan, had a population of around 400,000 in the late eighteenth century. Thus, there was a disproportionate increase in urban population during the seventeenth century, and city populations continued to increase even during the subsequent period when the total population appears to have been relatively stable. In short, the current tendency in Japan for population growth to occur largely in the cities dates back at least to the eighteenth century.

Another sign of economic expansion was the clear rise in living standards, and still more in economic expectations, among the urban dwellers. Pictorial evidence, in addition to various items remaining from the Tokugawa period, show the increasing opulence of city life — which the frantic sumptuary legislation of the period also illustrates. What had been strict but realistic control of consumption in the early seventeenth century, including limitations on such matters as the colors and fabrics to be worn by city people and the types of food they could eat, were entirely unrealistic and absurdly reactionary two centuries later. In fact, before the end of the Tokugawa period Japan seems to have established the clear lead in living standards over most of the rest of Asia that she has maintained ever since.

Of course, not all city people were prosperous merchants. Much of the population was made up of recent migrants who had fled the economic pressures of rural life. These newcomers became servants, day laborers and petty storekeepers, living close to the economic margin. In hard times they, like the peasants, sometimes resorted to destructive rioting because of the soaring price of rice. Large-scale riots of this sort first occurred in Edo in 1732 in the time of Yoshimune. Between 1783 and 1787, during Tanuma's supremacy, particularly severe riots broke out in Ōsaka, Edo and many other towns. Other series of wide urban rioting came in 1836–37 and again in 1866.

The rioting in Ōsaka in 1837 even took a slightly revolutionary turn — the first military defiance of the authorities since the Shimabara Revolt two centuries earlier. Ōshio, a former police official turned scholar, was so distressed by the plight of the poor, the corruption of the authorities and the greed of the rich that he led a small band of followers in an attempt to seize the city, but the uprising was crushed within a day, and Ōshio was forced to commit suicide.

Much of the urban way of life proved destructive to feudal society, just as the mercantile economy of the cities was injurious to the agrarian basis of feudal rule. Class lines inevitably became blurred in the topsy-turvy economy of the great cities of the shogunal domain. Runaway peasants became the city proletariat; impoverished samurai and *rōnin* sank to the status of mere townsmen; and rich commoners began to acquire samurai status, sometimes by purchasing the privilege from a needy daimyo but more commonly through their official association with a *han* or with the shogunate as bankers, managers of monopolies, or financial or business agents.

The Need of the Daimyo and the Samurai for Money. Still another sign of economic advance was the much wider use of currency and credit than ever before. Even when the daimyo and samurai were in their own *han*, they were town residents and so had a greater need of money than if they had constituted a truly feudal class living on their own estates; and the *sankin kōtai* system, as we have seen, further increased their money needs. For these reasons, and on account of the general economic growth, rice and other commodities virtually dropped out of use as mediums of exchange. The only major exceptions were the payment of agricultural taxes and samurai stipends; and in the latter part of the Tokugawa period even agricultural taxes were often paid in money.

The shogunate minted gold, silver and copper currency through special monopolies set up for this purpose. (The monopoly for silver coins, the Ginza, has given its name to modern Tōkyō's main shopping street.) Many of the daimyo also issued paper money, but most of it was inadequately backed and, in any case, could only be used locally. Commercial credit was much more important than paper currency. Pawnshops and mutual credit associations flourished, and the large money exchangers, particularly those in Ōsaka and Edo, developed modern banking functions. Their services were much in demand because of the many types of coinage in use, but they also became depositories for money and the providers of capital for the shogunate, the daimyo, and a great variety of commercial and manufacturing activities throughout the country. Interest usually ran at 1 per cent a month or a little more. Commercial notes and money orders came into use for major financial transactions and for the transport of large sums of money. The tremendous expansion of the monetary resources of the country through credit of this type, together with the repeated debasement of the coinage by the shogunate, had a generally inflationary influence which may have helped to spur economic growth.

Most of the *han* of western Japan maintained commercial offices and warehouses in Ōsaka to dispose of their excess rice produce and to acquire commodities needed at home. The financial officers stationed at Ōsaka, who naturally occupied an extremely important place in the economic life of the *han*, were at first only trusted samurai, but in time their group came to include men of merchant origin. Because of these *han* warehouses and its strategic location at the head of the Inland Sea, Ōsaka grew into the great rice market for all West Japan, as did Edo for all East Japan. By the end of the seventeenth century trade in rice had developed to the point where there were dealings in futures, and any fluctuation in either the Ōsaka or the Edo price of rice, or in the various elements of the confused monetary system, was immediately reflected in adjustments in prices at the other city. In this respect the economy of feudal Japan kept pace with the developing grain and money markets of such European centers as London and Amsterdam.

Most of the daimyo and samurai were at a disadvantage when they tried to convert their feudal agricultural incomes into money. In so far as they remained true to the feudal virtue of disdaining financial matters, they became the victims of astute businessmen. They were also as vulnerable as the peasantry to fluctuations in rice production and prices. A bad year might cut into tax yields and stipends, and bumper crops could bring a disastrous fall in prices.

The reasons for the steadily worsening position of the daimyo and the samurai, however, went deeper than this. Most of them simply lived beyond their means. The *sankin kōtai* system absorbed a large part of the income of the daimyo, and residence half the time in Edo pervaded their lives with an element of competitive display and conspicuous consumption that might not have been present if they had remained on their respective fiefs.

Despite all sumptuary legislation, the economic expectations of the daimyo and the samurai rose steadily in this period of generally rising living standards, but their incomes did not. For the most part, the latter remained tied to rice production, which accounted for a shrinking portion of the total economy. Since the members of the military class had increased along with the rest of the population in the seventeenth century, they came to press almost as hard as the peasantry on the limited food resources available to them. In fact, the bitterness of samurai-peasant relations and the obvious feeling of frustration in both groups during the second half of the Tokugawa period might be traced to their desperate competition over an agricultural yield that did not keep pace with the other sectors of the economy or with the living standards of the merchant class.

In these circumstances, it is not surprising that both the daimyo and the samurai fell heavily in debt to the city merchants. The chief way in which the shogunate and the individual *han* attempted to prevent this was by various belt-tightening attempts, such as economy drives and sumptuary laws. The samurai should chew his toothpick in feigned contentment even though his stomach was empty. Efforts were also made to exact more from the peasants; or, again, the debts of the military class were sometimes canceled or reduced by law. The shogunate could pass the squeeze along to its direct retainers and to the daimyo by making special assessments on them, and, as we have noted, the daimyo in turn usually cut samurai stipends in the guise of forced loans to the *han* treasury. Such measures, however, dealt only with the symptoms, not the basic malady.

Efforts to Save the Finances of the Ruling Class. The only effective solution to this problem of recouping government finances and the personal finances of the members of the military class was for the shogunate and the individual *han* to find other sources of wealth besides rice or to tax or otherwise participate more heavily in the non-agricultural sector of the economy. It is for this reason that Tanuma's innovations were so significant. On the whole, however, the taxation of trade and industry by the shogunate and the *han* remained piecemeal, and not very effective. The most important type of commercial taxation, if such it can be called, was the occasional exaction from rich merchants of forced (and usually unrepaid) loans called *goyōkin* ("money for the lord's needs"). Tanuma started this practice in 1761. Also, all of a merchant's wealth could be confiscated for gross disregard of sumptuary laws or some other offense. The most spectacular example of this occurred in 1705, when the shogunate confiscated all the wealth of Yodoya, the richest of the Ōsaka merchants, on the charge of unbefitting ostentation.

Both the shogunate and the *han* proved comparatively successful in participating directly in trade and developing new sources of agricultural income besides rice. From the start, foreign trade had been of much financial help to the Sō of Tsushima and the Shimazu of South Kyūshū. In time the Matsumae of Hokkaidō, an area too cold to grow much rice, developed as their chief source of income the local sea products that were much in demand for foreign trade. The Shimazu were likewise successful in developing sugar cane as a major cash crop, since it did not grow so well in the rest of Japan. Similarly, the small *han* located in the agriculturally poor mountain areas sometimes lived primarily off the paper their forests produced. Other daimyo developed other special cash crops or, with merchant capital or advice, transformed the part-time handicraft industries of their peasantry into *han* monopolies. The licensing of monopolistic merchant associations also became a popular way to derive income from trade.

The samurai had less room for economic maneuver than their lords.

Those in responsible posts, however, sometimes commercialized their positions by taking fees from merchants with whom they had dealings on *han* business. In the latter part of the Tokugawa period, some saved themselves economically by adopting merchant boys as heirs or marrying their children to the children of their merchant creditors — all, of course, in direct violation of a basic principle of the Tokugawa system. Poorer samurai practiced infanticide to reduce their economic liabilities. Some simply abandoned their feudal duties, giving up their reduced stipends in return for a better living as commoners. A large number of the poorer samurai families, like the poorer peasants, were forced into supplementary occupations, eking out their inadequate stipends by cottage industries, such as the making of straw sandals.

ECONOMIC GROWTH: TRADE AND INDUSTRY

The economic misery of the poorer peasants and the growing indebtedness of the military class were more than offset by the rapid economic rise of the mercantile and manufacturing classes. The "townsmen" (*chōnin*), as they were called, grew much more rapidly in numbers than any other class. Although they were theoretically relegated to the bottom of society, they came to control a disproportionate amount of the wealth. Despite forced loans, occasional confiscations and sumptuary laws supposedly limiting their consumption, the wealthier merchants lived in a luxurious and elegant manner. And they conducted their business on a large scale. They controlled fleets of coastal vessels; their loans to a daimyo often far exceeded his annual revenue; and they sometimes held lesser samurai in such helpless indebtedness that they might keep their proud debtors virtually on allowance. Some merchants not only acquired extreme wealth but also gained a little political influence. The rice brokers of Edo, for instance, by boycotting the shogunate in 1776 forced it to back down in its efforts to lower interest rates and stop manipulation of the rice market.

The Unified National Market. Because of the rapid commercial growth in the late sixteenth century, the Japanese economy by the beginning of the Tokugawa period had already outgrown the old restrictive medieval guilds (*za*). The development of the consolidated daimyo realm had resulted in the elimination of the innumerable barriers used in medieval times to tax trade. Nobunaga and Hideyoshi had led the way in eliminating such taxes from the broad territories they controlled and in abolishing the medieval guilds. They also concentrated merchants in their respective capitals of Azuchi and Ōsaka and encouraged them to expand their commercial activities. During the Tokugawa period, the need for money on the part of the daimyo unified the whole country, to a large extent, into

WHOLESALE SAKE FIRMS IN EDO

From the Edo meisho zue *of 1834 and 1836.*

a single national market. Within this larger area, the extensive shogunal domain constituted a still more completely unified economic unit, restrained by none of the many local restrictions on private trade that the individual *han* still maintained.

Actually, a disproportionate development of commerce and industry took place within the shogun's direct area of rule. His was geographically the key, central part of Japan, including the great cities of Edo, Ōsaka and Kyōto as well as a large proportion of the economically most advanced parts of the country. The shogun's area also had certain other advantages. Excluding the retinues and representatives of the daimyo in Edo and Ōsaka, the population of this territory counted a low percentage of members of the military class — perhaps as little as two per cent, in contrast to the national average of five or six per cent. This was because the Tokugawa rulers, as the victors in 1600, had taken for themselves a broad domain in comparison with the number of their hereditary retainers, while some of their rivals had been forced to squeeze large followings into shrunken fiefs. As a result, the townsmen of Ōsaka and Kyōto and the peasants of much of the shogun's territory were free of the supervision and oppression of a locally entrenched feudal class.

Another advantage of the shogun's territory to businessmen and bankers consisted in the tacit protection the shogun afforded them in their dealings with impecunious daimyo. Merchants and bankers at the *han* capitals were almost entirely at the mercy of their respective lords. Those in the shogun's domain, of course, stood equally powerless before the shogunate itself, but as the shogun's "subjects" they could deal with the daimyo on almost equal business terms. Thus the shogun's territory played a very special role in Japan's commercial development, in some ways similar to that of the royal charter cities in the economic development of Europe.

The Development of Commercial Firms. Large-scale wholesale merchants dominated the city trade of the Tokugawa period. At first the government prevented such merchants from banding together in restrictive associations, but in the second half of the seventeenth century this prohibition was gradually relaxed, and in 1721 Yoshimune removed it entirely. Thereafter the merchant associations usually enjoyed official sanction and were commonly taxed through a government licensing system. These associations, commonly called *kabu-nakama*, sought to stabilize prices, fix interest rates and establish monopolistic controls within certain areas in the commodities in which they dealt. Similar associations were also formed among manufacturers, such as the weavers of fine textiles in Kyōto and the flourishing pottery makers of North Kyūshū, and by the providers of services, such as building contractors and carpenters. Edo and Ōsaka each came to have more than a hundred associations of these various types.

Many family firms gradually grew to large proportions in the production of sake and other commodities, in the retailing of tea, cloth and other goods, or in banking operations. The great house of Mitsui is a good example of such a family business. The founder of the firm started as a sake brewer in Ise around 1620 but added a pawnshop and began to deal in rice. His son founded a drygoods store in Edo in 1673 with great financial success. Soon the firm had branch stores in Kyōto and Ōsaka. In 1691 it became official banker to the shogunate and to the imperial court as well. It continued to prosper throughout the Tokugawa period and survived the turmoil of the shogunate's collapse to become the leading company of modern Japan and for a while perhaps the largest private economic enterprise in the world.

The development of the cities and of urban commerce probably occurred most rapidly during the seventeenth century, a period which saw too the greatest agricultural expansion and population growth. This was also the time when most of the large urban merchant firms, like that of

MITSUI DRYGOODS STORE IN EDO

From the Edo meisho zue. *The Mitsui trademark, the character for "three"* (mitsu) *inside the character for "well"* (i), *which is still in use by the great Mitsui industrial combine, appears on the curtains and shop signs on both sides of the street. Samurai (with flattish, conical hats and two swords) and two wandering Buddhist priests (with baskets over their heads and flutes in their hands) are portrayed in the street together with townsmen and a group of geisha. At the top of the picture is a caption followed by a seventeen-syllable* haiku *on Mount Fuji by Sōkan (1465?– 1553?), a famous master of chain poems.*

the Mitsui, were founded. The Genroku era, from 1688 to 1704, is usually regarded as the culmination of this period of rapid commercial development.

Thereafter the pace of urban commerce and population increase definitely slackened — one reason being the periodic government retrenchments aimed at restoring the agrarian basis of the economy and the financial solvency of the shogunate, because these so-called reforms inevitably resulted in periods of economic depression. Perhaps a more basic reason was the inability of the shogunate and the *han* to continue to grow in financial strength. The great city merchants depended in large part on the shogunate and the *han* as their chief customers, borrowers of money, or providers of rice and other commodities. Hence their business to some degree stagnated along with government finances. Still another factor could be found in the growing restrictions on the freedom of trade in the cities. After 1721 the merchant associations freely permitted by Yoshimune gave economic protection to their members but obviously restricted the further development of trade.

This slowing of commercial development in the cities should not be interpreted as applying to the whole country. During the eighteenth century, in fact, the commercialization of agriculture and of the whole rural economy began to accelerate. Peddlers had begun to penetrate to even the remotest areas, and shops were appearing in hitherto purely farming communities. Village industries were being developed by wealthy landholders and, in areas close to the cities, by rich townsmen as well. The breakup of the large farming unit and the extended family that had lived on it freed the more prosperous peasants to invest their excess wealth and energy in fields other than agriculture. Men of this type were starting sake breweries, small textile works or plants for making *miso*, a fermented bean paste, or some other food product. Such developments became particularly common in the heavily urbanized area of the old capital district and in the silk-producing areas of central Honshū. The silk-weaving town of Kiryū on the northern edge of the Kantō Plain provides an extreme case. In the eighteenth century it had already built dormitories for the textile workers, and by 1846 it had some 267 small weaving establishments, which together operated more than 5000 looms.

The new commercial and industrial enterprises of the rural areas were less dependent on the shogunate and the *han* and less restricted by merchant associations than were urban commercial enterprises. As a consequence, they remained on the whole more flexible and aggressive. In the first half of the nineteenth century, village entrepreneurs even began to invade the big cities, which had long been the preserves of the urban merchants, and in this were greatly aided by the shogunate's frontal attack on the merchant associations during the Tempō Reforms of 1841–43. Occasionally provincial businessmen became big operators, like Zeniya (1773–1852), a man from the Maeda *han* in Kaga, who came to possess a fleet of some 123 ships trading all the way from the Kurile Islands in the north to the Ryūkyū Islands in the south. Most provincial businessmen, however, continued to operate on a small scale; but, as a group, they probably contributed more to the subsequent modernization of the Japanese economy than did the wealthy but more cautious big merchants of the cities.

The Relationship of Economic Growth to Feudalism. The spectacular expansion of trade and industry and the appearance of incipient capitalism in a still largely feudal Japan paralleled remarkably the economic growth of Europe in late feudal and early modern times; and the contrast to conditions throughout the rest of Asia suggests a definite causal relationship between feudalism and these developments in both Japan and Europe.

For example, this economic growth may have been stimulated by the exclusion of the lower classes from political leadership in the feudal systems of both Japan and Europe and the parallel exclusion of the ruling feudal aristocracy from the economic activities of the lower classes. Thus, in the case of Japan, a merchant family like the Mitsui never dissipated its energies in seeking high social status and political power, since there were insurmountable barriers in these directions. Instead, it concentrated on developing its commercial interests. And all businessmen and manufacturers in Japan knew that members of the military class would not deign to displace them in their own fields of activity.

Despite government monopolies, forced loans and confiscations, economic entrepreneurs seem to have had greater security in feudal Japan, as in feudal Europe, than they had in the non-feudal societies of China and the other Asian lands. In the non-feudal countries excess wealth tended to go into land, the safest investment, or into short-term trade ventures and usury. In Japan, wealthy commoners felt sufficiently protected by the class distinctions and prejudices of feudalism to venture into long-range investments in manufacturing and trade. The differences from China were sufficient to give Japan in the nineteenth century a much better running start toward the modernized economic system of the West.

THE NEW URBAN CULTURE

The townsmen of the Tokugawa period cannot be equated with the bourgeoisie of early modern Europe, because they were politically much more subordinated to their feudal rulers and socially and psychologically much more severely oppressed. Their economic role, however, was comparable, and culturally they proved to be the most dynamic group in Tokugawa society. Most of the new trends in literature and art originated with men of the merchant class or with persons of samurai or peasant descent who had adopted the bourgeois way of life. The citizens of the *han* capitals, which remained under the strong control of the daimyo, played only a minor part in these developments, but the townsmen of the great cities — Edo, Ōsaka and Kyōto — dominated the new culture of the Tokugawa period as completely as the Zen monasteries and the shogunal court had dominated Ashikaga culture, or the imperial court that of earlier ages.

This does not mean that the military men had no cultural role. They kept alive the old feudal ethics and dominated scholarship and most intellectual activities. They also helped preserve various aspects of the old culture, such as the *Nō* drama, the tea ceremony and the art of flower

PLATE 66. The fifteenth-century "rock garden" of the Ryōanji in Kyōto, suggestive of islets in the sea.

PLATE 68. Outer walls and gate (lower left) and inner walls and central tower (upper right) of Himeji Castle, west of Kōbe, dating from the late sixteenth century.

PLATE 67. Garden and tea house on the grounds of the Katsura Detached Palace near Kyōto, dating from the early seventeenth century.

PLATE 69. Four panels of a six-panel "Screen of the Southern Barbarians" (Namban-byōbu), showing Portuguese grandees (left) arriving at a missionary establishment (upper right) and a Japanese street scene (lower right).

PLATE 70. Photograph of a masked *Nō* actor performing a dance, with musicians in back and the traditional pine tree painted on the back wall.

PLATE 71. Multicolored woodblock print by Utamaro (1753–1806), depicting the "chrysanthemum festival" on the ninth day of the ninth month. A description of the festival is at the right and the artist's signature at the left.

PLATE 72. Wood-block print of 1740 by Okamura Masanobu showing a Kabuki theater in Edo. Note on the left the runway through the audience to the stage.

PLATE 73. Wood-block print of a scene near the post station at Ui, one of the "Fifty-three Post Stations on the Tōkaidō" by Hiroshige (1797–1858).

PLATE 74. Wood-block print of Mount Fuji seen from Tagonoura on the Tōkaidō, one of the "Thirty-six Views of Mount Fuji" by Hokusai (1760–1849).

arrangement. Except for painting, however, most of the traditional artistic and literary forms that they favored became somewhat stereotyped.

The townsmen, too, had received a strong cultural heritage from medieval times. They cultivated the same keen sense of discipline, obligation and honor as the samurai and maintained their own elaborate codes of ethics and etiquette. This was not mere imitation of the socially superior samurai. Confucian ethical concepts proved as valuable to an ambitious merchant family as to a conscientious samurai family, and the virtues which they instilled contributed to success in business as well as in government. Therefore a family like the Mitsui developed a family code of conduct as strict as that of any daimyo. The ethical aspects of the Tokugawa system became very much a part of the culture of the townsmen, and it was they as much as the samurai who passed on to the modern Japanese the old standards of duty and discipline and a feeling for the punctilious observance of the rules of etiquette.

The Urban Spirit. Rapid commercial expansion and wealth gave the bourgeois society ample opportunity for innovation and cultural growth, and both the life and the arts of the Tokugawa townsmen overflowed with vitality and originality. Naturally their departures from the norms set by the feudal military class are the most interesting features of their culture.

The cities offered a social freedom undreamed of in samurai or village life. The merchants became extremely money-conscious and fond of luxury. Many city people were frivolous, even dissolute, and it was of course these aspects of urban life that caught the attention of artists and writers. Fashion loomed important, and the latest feminine styles in hair arrangement, sleeve lengths in kimonos, and width of sashes (*obi*) were as assiduously followed as comparable fashions in the Occident today. Masculine styles were set by leading actors or recognized dandies, the richest, most elegant "men about town." Ceremonies became steadily more elaborate; novelty was highly esteemed, whether in entertainment or in restaurant dishes; and the quick-witted, joke-loving, cocky city man developed contempt for the stolid peasant and even a degree of disdain for the pompously serious aristocrat.

There was a decided flamboyance to the culture of the townsmen which contrasted sharply with Zen aesthetic ideals. But this flamboyance was always tempered by the Zen heritage — and also by the sumptuary laws, which at times made it hazardous to put on too obvious a show of wealth. For all their love of luxury, the townsmen acquired a very sophisticated taste. They aimed at restrained elegance, not ostentatious display, and their inclinations were toward refined sophistication, not garish vulgarity. The Tokugawa bourgeois taste skillfully combined a love of daring colors and bold design with the Zen feeling for restraint and discipline. It is this cultivated taste, rather than the original Zen tradition alone, which became the dominant Japanese aesthetic sense — an aesthetic sense which in recent years has also had a strong influence in the West.

The Amusement Quarters. The centers of social and artistic life in the cities were the various types of amusement quarters, including houses of prostitution, bathhouses (which in early Tokugawa times had much the same function), restaurants, theaters, and a great variety of amusement booths. The most famous of the amusement quarters were the Yoshiwara in Edo, the Shimabara in Kyōto and the Shimmachi in Ōsaka, but these great cities also had other amusement districts, and lesser ones were to be found in the other towns throughout the country.

Because of the strictness of Japanese society, the amusement quarters played a large role in the development of Tokugawa culture. The commercial activities of the bourgeoisie were not in themselves conducive to brilliant cultural innovation. With their own rigid codes and their devotion to their family enterprises, the merchants, as businessmen, could become almost as sober and conservative as the samurai. As a class, they frowned on any demonstrativeness or display of emotion, either at home or at work. It was only when they sought relaxation and diversion from the heavy pressures of duty and the restraints of etiquette that they created a stimulating new atmosphere. Theaters, restaurants and brothels provided an escape from the often stifling restrictions of the Tokugawa system.

The special place of the houses of prostitution within the amusement quarters was a natural outcome of the position of women and the nature of marriage in Tokugawa society. The warrior-dominated feudal age had left women in a position entirely subordinate to men. No self-respecting merchant family, any more than a samurai family, would think of allowing its womenfolk any social freedom. In other words, there was no polite mixed society. Moreover, marriages among merchant families, as among those of the military class, were arranged not by the two principals but by the families, solely for the serious business of strengthening family fortunes and continuing the family line. Romantic love and individual preferences simply did not merit consideration. The young couple, usually meeting for the first time at their marriage ceremony, might subsequently develop respect and love for each other, but their important function as a couple was to bear children and train family heirs. Consequently, romance and a social mixing of the sexes could be found only outside the family — in short, in the amusement quarters.

Thus brothels and the more refined institutions that grew from them did not exist merely to provide for illicit sex relations, which in themselves presented no great problem in a society devoid of puritanical notions. Their more important function was to provide amusing social intercourse between men and women and, if possible, a sense of romance. The women in these institutions were usually indentured servants, sold by their impoverished parents to the owners of the houses of prostitution. In their relations with their patrons, however, they were made to appear talented, glamorous and even respectable. Those capable of the training became accomplished dancers or musicians and, above all, amusing conversationalists.

The prostitutes fell into many grades, according to their polite accomplishments as well as their beauty, and each category acquired its own strict prerogatives and code of etiquette. The higher grades met patrons only by appointment, in houses of assignation, and they demanded solicitous courting before they would deign to bestow their favors. The leading courtesans were regarded as people of note and the determiners of style. Wealthy merchants not infrequently purchased the freedom of their favorite courtesans and set them up as their recognized mistresses or even made them their legal wives. It was in this way that the tradition of the modern geisha, or "accomplished person," developed.

The gay, stimulating life of the city amusement quarters was not limited to the merchant class, for the samurai, themselves now confirmed city dwellers, came to frequent these areas in increasing numbers. The amusement districts, however, were in a sense "off limits" to the samurai, who went there always in theory incognito and sometimes even masked their faces. Naturally, in these circumstances they could insist on none of their normal feudal prerogatives. In such places all classes met as equals, and only money determined prestige.

The freedom and licentiousness of the amusement quarters contrasted sharply with the discipline of Tokugawa society as a whole. Dissolute *rōnin*, profligate sons of wealthy merchants, and dissipated young apprentices by no means constituted the Tokugawa ideal. On the other hand, the amusement areas seem to have provided a culturally creative antidote to the sober, rigidly controlled and ethically self-conscious Tokugawa system. They gave the balancing *yin* to officialdom's stuffy *yang*. Thus the amusement quarters too formed an integral part of Tokugawa society, though many strains and stresses naturally existed between life in them and the official order.

Tokugawa literature is full of the clash between duty (*giri*) and "human feelings" (*ninjō*), or passion. In a typical case, a rich young man's hopeless love for a courtesan runs counter to his duty to family and society. Neither love nor duty wins a clear-cut victory, and the only solution is for the ill-fated lovers to commit double suicide (*shinjū*). This romantic view of love suicide combined with the samurai tradition of honorable suicide to give the modern Japanese a feeling that suicide offers a reasonable and respectable escape from a difficult situation.

The Literate City Dweller. It took several decades after the founding of the Tokugawa shogunate for these social phenomena and the arts and literature associated with them to develop. Then, in the latter part of the seventeenth century, there was a sudden flowering of bourgeois culture. The name Genroku, which belongs specifically to the year period from 1688 to 1704 but is applied loosely to the last two decades of the seventeenth century and the early decades of the eighteenth, is used for this first great period of townsman culture.

The center of bourgeois life during the Genroku period was Ōsaka, for Kyōto, a less vital community, had lost its lead, and Edo was still a raw, new city, dominated by a heavy concentration of daimyo and samurai. By the latter part of the eighteenth century, however, Edo had become the cultural as well as the political capital. In fact, during the last century of Tokugawa rule this city of samurai and townsmen became so much the center of all artistic, literary and intellectual activity, as well as of political life, that it quite naturally remained the capital of Japan even after the fall of the Tokugawa.

Although the key figures in Tokugawa bourgeois culture were the affluent merchants on whose wealth it depended, a much wider group, including denizens of the amusement quarters, large numbers of samurai and *rōnin*, and many humbler city dwellers, of course participated. It is hard to say how far down the economic scale the new culture penetrated, but it was obviously quite far. One measure of its spread was the literacy enjoyed by the urban population. Naturally the city samurai could read, but so also could the whole business class — not just the great merchants themselves, but also their wives and clerks. An ability to read was assumed necessary for almost any sort of business activity. In fact, except for recent arrivals from the farm and other servants and laborers, the city people seem to have enjoyed a high degree of literacy.

One result of widespread literacy was a phenomenal development of printing in response to public demand for reading matter. There had been some printing activity in Japan ever since the eighth century, but in the main this, as in China and Korea, had only served the purpose of establishing correct texts of important books or disseminating weighty works of learning. At the end of the sixteenth century the Japanese printing industry received new stimulation both from the Korean printers brought back by Hideyoshi's armies and from the Jesuits, who operated a press to print Christian literature. But public demand was the real reason for the spectacular growth of printing during the next few decades.

Numerous publishing houses flourished during the Tokugawa period, and these issued a flood of popular works, from inspirational essays down to open pornography. Throughout much of the period there was a running fight between the publishers pandering to the lowest tastes and the authorities, who were determined to suppress salacious literature. At first movable type was used for some of the popular works, but it was soon abandoned in favor of wood-block printing, which permitted the inclusion of illustrations that helped attract readers. The texts were usually written in the *kana* syllabaries or, when Chinese characters were used, included *kana* readings of the characters for the benefit of less educated readers.

TOKUGAWA LITERATURE

Such printing activity, in addition to all the influences in the whole dynamic new society of the Tokugawa cities, helped produce new currents in literature. These innovations appeared first in the theater. *Nō*, even after it was dropped by the shogunal court in 1711 at the insistence of the Confucian philosopher Arai Hakuseki, was kept alive in other circles and by four hereditary families of performers. However, the new type of drama, called *Kabuki*, was not a direct outgrowth of the *Nō* drama, but instead was a new welling up from the lower classes of the urge for dramatic expression.

Kabuki and the Puppet Theater. A renegade Shintō priestess who led a troupe of dancers and actors in Kyōto at the beginning of the seventeenth century is usually given credit for founding *Kabuki*. In the early years, however, the interest of acting groups such as the one she led seems to have been more in sex than in serious dramatic performance, since both female and male actors usually engaged in prostitution on the side. The authorities, alarmed by the immorality of the theater, soon banned women from the stage. As a result, the theater became limited to men for the remainder of the Tokugawa period, and the portrayal of feminine parts by men became a curious convention that Japanese actors, like their Chinese counterparts, developed into a high dramatic art.

The low tone of the early *Kabuki* gave a rival dramatic form, the puppet theater, a chance to develop. The puppets were associated with *Jōruri*, a style of reciting old tales to the accompaniment, not of the classical four-stringed lute, but of a new banjo-like instrument, the three-stringed *samisen*, recently introduced from the Ryūkyū Islands. In the late seventeenth century puppet performances illustrating *Jōruri* recitations became extremely popular and also developed into a great art. The two men chiefly responsible for this development were Takemoto Gidayū (1651–1714), who founded a very successful puppet theater at Ōsaka, and Chikamatsu Monzaemon (1653–1724), a man of samurai origin who served as Takemoto's chief writer of *Jōruri* texts. The keen competition of other theaters and playwrights helped stimulate these men to their best endeavors.

Chikamatsu, living a century after Shakespeare, was in a sense the creator of the modern Japanese theater. His early *Jōruri* texts amount to little more than popularizations of *Nō* librettos, and he never departed from a conventional poetic meter and highly ornamented style for his narrative passages. However, he gradually developed the structure of his plots, expanded the realistic dialogue element, and turned his attention to the portrayal of character and the analysis of psychological attitudes, giving to the Japanese stage a force and richness it had never had before.

Chikamatsu's *Jōruri* fall into two basic types, historical dramas and contemporary domestic plays. The first are loosely constructed, episodic reworkings of incidents from classical novels, early medieval warrior tales, and *Nō* plays. Though generally weak in plot and peopled only by stock characters, they abound in dramatic incidents, which the Tokugawa audiences loved, and in time they did become somewhat more realistic. Indeed, Chikamatsu began to choose for his subject matter recent political events, only thinly disguised as earlier history in order to circumvent a ban on using Tokugawa feudal society as a subject for the theater. The most popular of all his works, *The Battles of Koxinga* (*Kokusen'ya kassen*), which ran for seventeen consecutive months when it was first produced, dealt with the swashbuckling career of the famous Chinese-Japanese pirate, who had died only a few years earlier (see pages 355–356).

Chikamatsu's twenty-four contemporary domestic plays, which all date from his last two decades, are well constructed and highly realistic. They were not only written for bourgeois audiences but concern the life of the townsmen. Most of them treat emotional problems, such as the clash of love and duty; thus, they frequently end in double suicide. Many were based on recent incidents familiar to the Ōsaka audiences, and the characters were always realistic types clearly identifiable in urban society.

The puppets used in the *Jōruri* theater at first were small enough to be operated by manipulators who remained out of sight, but in time the dolls came to be about two-thirds life-size and each was operated by three men, all on stage but supposedly rendered unnoticeable by black shrouds. These large puppets gave an extremely realistic appearance, and they were made to act in close imitation of the *Kabuki* actors, just as the latter tended to imitate the slight, arresting jerkiness of the puppets. Though the puppets eventually lost out in popular appeal to the live actors, the art has been maintained until today by the Bunrakuza, an Ōsaka theater.

The *Kabuki* of the eighteenth and nineteenth centuries owed much to the puppet theater, not only in acting style but also in repertoire. Its librettos usually evolved through practical stage experience by the hereditary lines of actors, but the *Jōruri* of Chikamatsu were frequently used as a basis for the plays. Many other librettos were developed from *Nō* plays, from the medieval warrior tales, or directly from historical incidents. The most popular of all the *Kabuki* plays, *The Treasury of Loyal Retainers* (*Chūshin-gura*), dramatized the Incident of the Forty-Seven *Rōnin*, placed for safety's sake in an earlier age.

The *Kabuki* often employed an on-stage chorus, as in the *Nō*, to chant the narrative portions of the play. Instrumental accompaniments were used, especially for these narrative portions and for background music to set the emotional tone. Stage settings became extraordinarily realistic, and

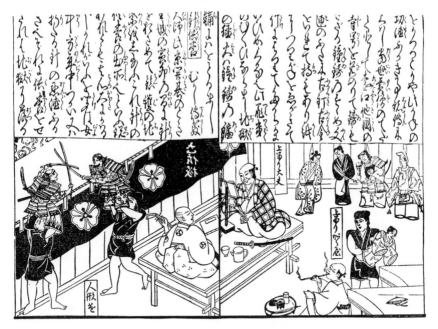

B<small>ACKSTAGE AT A</small> P<small>UPPET</small> T<small>HEATER</small>

A two-page illustration from the Jinrin kimmō zui *(Collection of Illustrations for the Cultivation of Morality), a work printed in 1690. On the left appear the manipulators of the puppets, in the center the musician and reciter, and on the right extra puppets hanging up. The texts above the illustrations in this work contain materials of an encyclopedic nature.*

the revolving stage facilitated dramatic transitions from one setting to another. The approach to the stage from one side, first used in the *Nō*, was developed into a runway down through the audience, permitting "roadway" scenes and a heightened sense of intimacy between the actors and the spectators. (See Plate 72.) The influence of the *Nō* was clear in the dances which highlighted some of the performances, and in the tendency to strike tableaux. The influence of the puppets survived in a love for scenes of violence and a tendency toward exaggerated gesture. On the whole, however, the acting could be described as realistic, and the audiences particularly appreciated scenes of seeming calm that vibrated with taut emotion.

The *Kabuki* stage is still very much alive today, being ably maintained by hereditary lines of great actors at the Kabukiza in Tōkyō and elsewhere. In the first half of the nineteenth century, however, it was supplanted in popularity among the city masses by the small vaudeville house, know as *yose*, where variety shows of storytelling, jokes and singing were presented.

Prose Writers. New forms of prose writing, as well as of drama, flourished in Tokugawa merchant society, growing out of the flood of booklets printed during the seventeenth century to meet the increased demand for reading matter. At first these works, usually called "*kana* booklets" (*kana-zōshi*), consisted mainly of uplifting tracts on religion and ethics, moralistic tales, and popular history. The fictional element, which was slight, was limited for the most part to adaptations of Chinese stories or imitations of outmoded ancient romances and medieval wonder tales.

Out of these "*kana* booklets," however, evolved writings closer in content and spirit to Tokugawa urban society, with greater appeal to bourgeois tastes. These included practical guidebooks, especially to the famous amusement quarters, with information about prominent courtesans or popular actors. Amusing anecdotes and realistic touches were added to enliven the traditional tracts and cautionary tales. Such more up-to-date works were called *ukiyo-zōshi*, or "fleeting-world booklets," for the term "fleeting world" (*ukiyo*), which reflected the Buddhist emphasis on the transience and vanity of life, had acquired the connotations of "modern" and "stylish."

From such beginnings, Ihara (or Ibara) Saikaku (1642–1693), an Ōsaka townsman, developed character portrayals of amusing bourgeois types that transformed the "fleeting-world booklets" into a major new literary genre. His first important work, *An Amorous Man (Kōshoku ichidai*

WOOD-BLOCK ILLUSTRATION FROM *An Amorous Woman*

This illustration, by Yoshida Hambei, first appeared in a 1686 edition of the work. It shows the heroine consulting an oculist, whose graphic sign appears on the outside of his house at the extreme right.

otoko, sometimes translated as *The Man Who Spent His Life in Love*), published in 1682, set an entirely new style. This he followed with a series of comparable books, such as *An Amorous Woman* (*Kōshoku ichidai onna*); *Five Amorous Women* (*Kōshoku gonin onna*, translated into English as *Five Women Who Loved Love*); *The Everlasting Storehouses of Japan* (*Nihon eitai-gura*); and *Twenty Examples of Unfilial Conduct in This Land* (*Honchō nijū fukō*).

Saikaku proved himself a master of allusive and poetic diction and of the plays on words that are so much loved by the Japanese, but his writings were all extremely realistic, and for subject matter he concentrated chiefly on the merchant families and amusement quarters of Ōsaka. He might parody old classics and ancient attitudes, but his real interest lay in the money-grubbing self-made man and such an individual's less disciplined heirs. His cynicism came as a refreshing departure from the heavy moralizing of earlier writers. "Money," he wrote, "is the townsman's pedigree. ...No matter how splendid a man's ancestors, if he lacks money he is worse off than a monkey-showman." [3] He portrayed the guile and hedonism of the city man with amused admiration. Wealth seemed to him a fitting reward for cleverness. His realism was detailed and explicit, bordering at times on the pornographic, though he maintained at least a guise of moralistic censure, perhaps for the benefit of the official censors, who frowned on his efforts. The urban public, however, was delighted by his comic portrayals of its more flamboyant members and his penetrating analysis of the foibles of bourgeois society.

Saikaku's lead was followed by another author of merchant background, Ejima Kiseki (1667–1736). Kiseki's first literary success, published in 1699, was a critique of actors which raised this type of work to a new level of artistic writing and professional competence. He followed this with a series of extremely popular criticisms of famous courtesans, but after breaking with his Kyōto publishers, the Hachimonjiya ("Figure-of-Eight Store"), he turned to character sketches of bourgeois types. In 1715 he published *Characters of Modern Sons* (*Seken musuko katagi*), which consists of the stories of twelve young rakes, and he followed this with comparable works on daughters, old men and shop clerks. His own succinct summary of his view of bourgeois society is that "Parents toil, their children idle, and the grandchildren beg."

The later Tokugawa writers may not have equaled Saikaku and Kiseki, but a few are worth mentioning. Ueda Akinari (1734–1809), the son of an Ōsaka prostitute, at first followed Kiseki's lead in character sketches but later, under Chinese influence, shifted to imaginative wonder stories. Takizawa Bakin (1767–1848), the son of a *rōnin*, became a prolific and popular Edo author, with more than 300 works to his credit. He wrote long,

---

[3] This and the following quotation from Kiseki are from Howard Hibbett, *The Floating World in Japanese Fiction*, New York: Oxford University Press, 1959.

learned, didactic novels, much influenced by Chinese models and exemplifying the traditional ethics of the military class. A more interesting product of late Tokugawa society was Jippensha Ikku (1766–1831), a samurai by origin, whose *Shanks' Mare Travels* (*Hizakurige*) became so popular that it appeared serially. This work is a picaresque novel about the wanderings of two rogues, in which the samurai and their pretensions are freely satirized.

Haiku. Poetry had always been the most tradition-bound type of literature in Japan, but Tokugawa bourgeois society produced its own new poetic form — the seventeen-syllable *haiku*, which was developed in the sixteenth and seventeenth centuries from a type of chain poem known as *haikai.* Since the *haikai* permitted much greater freedom in vocabulary and ideas than the more aristocratic forms of poetry, they enjoyed a wide vogue among the common people. The three-line, seventeen-syllable initial element (*hokku*, meaning "initial phrase") in the *haikai* chain poems gradually became established as an independent poetic genre, now know as *haiku*. The terms *haikai*, *hokku* and *haiku*, however, are often used interchangeably for these seventeen-syllable poems.

The *haiku* pleased bourgeois society because it recognized no limitations set by poetic tradition and its brevity demanded the sharp wit so much admired by the townsmen. To be good, a *haiku* in a mere seventeen syllables had to set a scene or mood and then by some sudden verbal twist bring a flash of intuitive perception. Composing *haiku* required no classical education or long literary preparation, but it did demand the sort of mental and verbal dexterity that urban life fostered. It was up-to-date both in its vocabulary and its ideas, and its gay, irreverent spirit appealed to those who chafed under the restrictions of feudal society and ethics. Before the end of the seventeenth century the composition of *haiku* had become a veritable craze for men of wit from all levels of society, and as a form *haiku* has retained its great popularity until today.

Perhaps some idea of the nature of *haiku* can be gained from the following three examples, which have been chosen as particularly adaptable to literal translation, though in the process they necessarily lose much in idiom and even more in connotation:

Tsuki ni e o 　sashitaraba yoki 　　uchiwa kana	To the moon, a handle 　add — a good 　　fan indeed.
Aozara ni 　matsu o kaitari 　　kyō no tsuki	In the blue sky 　it has drawn a pine 　　— tonight's moon.
Asagao ni 　kyō wa miyuran 　　waga yo kana	In a morning-glory 　today I seem to see 　　— my life, alas.

One of the earliest of the important *haiku* poets was also the greatest. This was Matsuo Bashō (1644–1694), a former samurai who established himself as a professional *haiku* master at Edo. His most famous work is *The Narrow Road of Oku (Oku no hosomichi)*, a poetic account of a trip to North Honshū. While Bashō remained much interested in chain poems, the later masters, such as Yosa Buson (1716–1783) and Kobayashi Issa (1763–1827), both of peasant origin, were more exclusively *haiku* poets. Issa reflected his humble origin both by his homely diction and by his sympathy for the downtrodden.

Tokugawa Art

In the main, Tokugawa art reflected bourgeois society as much as did the literature. Yet in the early decades of the seventeenth century, before the townsmen had become numerous and rich, the need and interests of the military class still set the tone in most fields of art. The palaces and castles of the daimyo and the screens and wall paintings which decorated them dominated both architecture and painting.

The mausoleums erected for Ieyasu and his grandson Iemitsu at Nikkō in the mountains north of the Kantō Plain illustrate the grandiose architectural style inherited from the late sixteenth century. The fussy details and profusion of colors and carvings used to decorate these buildings might have made them tawdry were it not for their magnificent setting in a towering forest of cryptomeria. It is significant that the later palaces, temples, and mausoleums of the Tokugawa period added nothing important to Japanese architecture. All the developments of interest occurred in domestic architecture, as the medieval residence and rustic teahouse gradually evolved into the simple but refined domestic style of modern Japan.

Because of the declining interest in Buddhism, sculpture all but disappeared, just as the sculpture of China and Korea had deteriorated along with the falling fortunes of Buddhism in those countries some centuries earlier. All that remained of the once great tradition of the sculptor were such minor efforts as ornamental architectural details and the small ivory carvings (*netsuke*) used in the fastenings on tobacco pouches, pillboxes and the like.

Early Tokugawa painting, which followed the established traditions, is well illustrated by the sumptuous wall and screen paintings of the Nijō castle in Kyōto. The official Kano School of painters continued to flourish under such masters as Tannyū (1602–1674), who frequently used traditional Chinese subjects. This strong Chinese influence gave rise in the eighteenth century to the so-called Southern (*Nanga*) or Literati (*Bunjinga*; in Chinese, *Wen-jen-hua*) School of painters, who followed in name as well as in subject matter and techniques their Chinese prototypes of the Ming and Ch'ing periods.

New Trends in Painting. The side currents of Tokugawa painting proved, on the whole, more interesting than the main stream of academic art. For example, Hanabusa Itchō (1652–1724), a *haiku* poet, combined the early feudal *Yamato-e* style with the strong influence of contemporary bourgeois realism. So also did Itō Jakuchū (died 1800) and Maruyama Ōkyo (1733–1795), the founder of a school which bears his surname. Ōkyo borrowed Occidental principles of perspective in his search for realism. Shiba Kōkan (1738–1818) went further in the Western style, experimenting with copperplate etchings and oil paints.

Another significant development appeared in the growth of a school of decorative painters who freely manipulated the traditional elements of landscape painting purely for a bold, striking design effect. Their favorite mediums were lacquer ware and large folding screens. The originator of this style was Hon'ami Kōetsu (1558–1637), and it reached its apogee under Ogata Kōrin (1658–1716).

The influence of the developing bourgeois society on the more traditional artistic trends was only indirect, except in an economic way. The rich merchants helped create a large market for paintings and other art objects which supported a great number of professional artists. During these centuries urban commercial wealth also fostered the industrial arts, making the Tokugawa period the golden age for fine textiles, lacquer ware and pottery.

Moreover, bourgeois society became the direct stimulus and setting for the most significant of all the artistic developments of Tokugawa times — the so-called *ukiyo-e*, or "pictures of the fleeting world." In this usage the term "fleeting world" had, as in literature, the connotations of "modern" and "stylish." *Ukiyo-e*, reflecting the interests of the townsmen, portrayed domestic scenes, everyday city life and, later in the period, well-known scenes and places. But the most common subjects of *ukiyo-e* artists were the famous actors and the beauties of the amusement quarters, who so interested all bourgeois society.

Wood-Block Prints. At first, most *ukiyo-e* were paintings, but by the late seventeenth century wood-block prints in this style were also becoming popular. Wood blocks had long been widely employed in China to make inexpensive religious pictures and illustrations for serious works such as art catalogues or books on botany. In Japan they had also been much used since the early seventeenth century to illustrate popular books. Now, however, they were put to a new use — to produce independent works of art for the general public.

The early prints were simply black-and-white line cuts, but in time artists began to add some color to these by hand. Then they began to print a few simple colors, and finally they devised intricate printing processes to produce delicately shaded, multicolored prints. With metic-

SHARAKU DRAWING OF WANDERING ENTERTAINERS

ulous accuracy a wood carver would make from the artist's original
drawing a large number of different blocks — sometimes several dozen
for a single picture — to reproduce each of the colors and shadings that
was to appear in the finished work. These were then printed over one
another, with the greatest care in exact superimposition, until all the
colors and shadings had been added to the picture. Wood-block prints
of this type thus represented a triumph of technical skill as well as
of art.

Hishikawa Moronobu (died 1694) was one of the greatest *ukiyo-e*
painters and the first of the important wood-block artists. (See page 579.)
He was followed by Nishikawa Sukenobu (1671–1751), who illustrated
Kiseki's books for the Hachimonjiya, and by a group of artists, known
by the name of Kaigetsudō, who specialized in the portrayal of beauties
in strong, sweeping lines. Suzuki Harunobu (1724–1770) became the
first master of the multicolored-print technique. Sharaku, who apparently was active as an artist only briefly, in 1794 and 1795, produced an
amazing series of caricatures of actors; Utagawa Toyokuni (1769–1825)
made more realistic prints of actors in action. Kitagawa Utamaro (1753–
1806) is considered the greatest portrayer of beautiful women. (See
Plate 71.) The last great wood-block artists turned more to famous scenes
and landscapes. Katsushika Hokusai (1760–1849), who came under the

influence of Occidental art, is particularly famous for his "Thirty-six Views of Mount Fuji" (see Plate 74), while Andō Hiroshige (1797–1858) is best known for his "Fifty-three Post Stations on the Tōkaidō" (see Plate 73).

In Tokugawa times wood-block prints were considered somewhat vulgar or plebeian, but they have since been recognized as works of great art. Whether portraying beauties, actors, or landscapes, they were not simply attempts at exact reproduction; rather, the aim was to produce a satisfying composition, in which conscious distortion and great selectivity of detail served to bring out what seemed to the artist the essence of his subject. Closer on the whole to Occidental styles than most of the earlier paintings of East Asia, these prints aroused great interest in the West in the nineteenth century and had considerable influence on the French Impressionists. It is indicative of the high aesthetic standards of Tokugawa bourgeois society that it was Japan, among all the countries of the world, that pioneered in the development of art of high quality available at popular prices.

CONFUCIAN PHILOSOPHY

The intellectual accomplishments of the Tokugawa period were more the product of samurai society than of the townsmen. Thus they gave only an imperfect reflection of the economic and social changes of the urban sector of Japanese life, and often as a reverse image, showing the samurai interests that stood in opposition to those of the townsmen. Except for a few unusual individuals late in the period, none of the leading thinkers questioned the basic class structure or economic organization of Tokugawa society or the class morality of the samurai. They failed to see any need for fundamental social and economic changes. Their main efforts were directed toward correcting the obvious dislocations of the society and the economy by treating them as ethical problems which could be cured by the correct application of Confucian ethics or the principles of *Bushidō*. Consequently, intellectual and economic currents tended to flow in different channels, albeit in the same historical terrain.

The channels of Tokugawa thought, however, were not wholly limited to the narrow Confucian orthodoxy and *Bushidō* of the founders of the system, because the shoguns' encouragement of "learning" and Confucian philosophy helped transform a significant proportion of the samurai from stolid warriors into inquiring intellectuals and so made possible a rich proliferation of new ideas. Some of these ideas came directly from heterodox Chinese thinkers; others evolved from contemporary conditions in Japan itself. One of the main reasons for the diversity of thought during the Tokugawa period was the multiplicity of autonomous political units. Unorthodox schools could always find patronage in one or more of the *han*, even when they were frowned on by the shogunate. On the whole, heterodox thought displayed more vitality than Neo-Confucian orthodoxy, and it produced many concepts which in the long run proved as subversive to the Tokugawa system as the life and economy of the bourgeoisie. Thus, despite the fact that they were working from quite different directions, the samurai intellectuals and the urban merchants unwittingly cooperated in undermining the Tokugawa system.

Orthodox Neo-Confucianism. During the seventeenth century Hayashi Razan, together with his son and his grandson, firmly established the Chu Hsi School of Neo-Confucianism at Edo (see pages 616–617). They were particularly aided in this by the ardent patronage of Tsunayoshi, the fifth shogun (1680–1709). Others of Ieyasu's descendants, as leading daimyo, helped to spread orthodox Confucianism to the samurai class throughout Japan. Ieyasu's grandson Hoshina (or Matsudaira) Masayuki (1611–1672), the powerful lord of Aizu in North Honshū, proved an outstanding champion of orthodox Confucianism, as did another grandson, Tokugawa Mitsukuni (1628–1700), the daimyo of Mito.

Mitsukuni's special interest was history, an important area of Confucian scholarship. In 1657 he started the compilation in Chinese of a *History of Great Japan* (*Dai Nihon shi*) on the model of Ssu-ma Ch'ien's *Historical Records* (see pages 111–113). In 1665 he put this work under the supervision of Chu Shun-shui (1600–1682), a Ming loyalist who had fled from the Manchus to Japan. The great undertaking, however, was not even partially completed until 1720, and it did not reach its final form of 397 chapters until 1906.

Various independent philosophers and writers also helped spread the Confucian ethical code. Kinoshita Jun'an (1621–1698) was an important teacher of orthodox Confucian philosophers at Edo. Kaibara Ekken (1630–1714), from the Kuroda *han* in North Kyūshū, wrote in simple Japanese instead of classical Chinese and thus helped transmit Chu Hsi's ideas to the lower classes as well as to the samurai. *The Great Learning for Women* (*Onna daigaku*), which is sometimes attributed to Kaibara and his devoted wife and is certainly based on his ideas, became the most important ethical text for women. The bourgeois playwrights and novelists also helped popularize Confucian morality among the non-samurai classes.

The Wang Yang-ming School. Even the orthodox philosophers manifested diverse tendencies. Kaibara, for instance, showed his original training as a physician by his special interest in natural phenomena, which led him to compile catalogues of vegetables, medicinal herbs and other flora. From the very beginning there were also philosophers who rebelled against Chu Hsi's brand of orthodoxy. Some looked instead to the Idealist School of the Ming Confucianist Wang Yang-ming (Ōyōmei in Japanese); others, under the name of the "Ancient Learning" (*Kogaku*) School, followed the lead of the contemporary Ch'ing scholars in attempting to get back of the Sung philosophers to the "Han Learning" of earlier Confucianism (see pages 308–309 and pages 378–379).

The emphasis in Wang Yang-ming's thinking on an intuitive moral sense, on personal discipline and on action rather than words appealed to many Japanese thinkers because of their background in Zen, which stressed similar elements. These views were also more suited to the warrior mentality than the intellectual rationalism and bookishness of Chu Hsi's orthodoxy. The shogunate, however, opposed the followers of Wang Yang-ming, partly on account of its own blind conservatism but also, perhaps, with a vague realization of the implications of Wang Yang-ming's thought. His inner source of intuition and his stress on self-discipline naturally encouraged independence of mind, and his teachings put more stress than did orthodox Japanese Confucianism on the Chinese ideal of individual merit, rather than hereditary privilege, as the criterion of a man's worth and status. The Wang Yang-ming philosophy, though by no means opposed to the Tokugawa system, fostered attitudes that could easily lead to subversive thought.

The first important follower of Wang Yang-ming in Japan was Nakae Tōju (1608–1648), who retired from the service of a daimyo in Shikoku to care for his mother in a rural area near Lake Biwa. Thus he demonstrated through action his belief in filial piety as the fundamental virtue. On the other hand, he departed decidedly from Chinese philosophical norms in his emphasis on a supreme personal deity.

The greatest of Nakae's many disciples was Kumazawa Banzan (1619–1691), a *rōnin* by origin, who became so much the model samurai that he rose to be the chief minister of the great Ikeda daimyo of Okayama, where he instituted a vigorous reform program. As a practical statesman, he advocated realistic philosophical ideas and showed his original turn of mind by writing in *kana* rather than in classical Chinese. His ideas on the whole could scarcely be termed revolutionary, and his advocacy of a return to a more complete rice economy was actually reactionary; but his mild unorthodoxy eventually led to his expulsion from office. During the last four years of his life the shogunate, because of certain reform proposals he had presented to it, kept him either in custody or under surveillance.

Despite official disapproval, the Wang Yang-ming school of thought remained strong throughout the Tokugawa period. It is significant that Ōshio, the leader of the almost revolutionary uprising in Ōsaka in 1837, was a member of this school, and it is probably no mere accident that several of the openly revolutionary thinkers of the last years of Tokugawa rule, as well as some of the young men who eventually overthrew the shogunate and formed a new government, were influenced by Wang Yang-ming's theories.

The "Ancient Learning" School. Whatever the later revolutionary role of Wang Yang-ming's followers may have been, it was the members of the "Ancient Learning" School who stood in more direct opposition to the orthodoxy of Chu Hsi in the seventeenth century. One of these, Yamaga Sokō (1622–1685), a *rōnin* by origin, was a master of military science who even evinced interest in the weapons and tactics introduced by the Europeans. In attempting to build up a suitable ethic for a true warrior class, he wished to return directly to Confucius, who had lived in a society somewhat closer to that of Japanese feudalism than the bureaucratic society of the Sung Neo-Confucianists. Yamaga contributed more than any other man to making *Bushidō* a comprehensive code of samurai behavior. Because of his unorthodox views, he was sent into virtual exile in Akō in West Honshū. There he became the teacher of the man who later distinguished himself as the leader of the Forty-Seven *Rōnin* and thus brought posthumous credit to his mentor because of his own exemplary conduct.

Another advocate of the "Ancient Learning" was Itō Jinsai (1627–1705), the son of a Kyōto lumber dealer, who became an extremely popular Confucian teacher at the old capital. He specifically rejected the later reinterpretations of Confucius and returned instead to the *Analects* and the *Mencius* for the underlying truths of Confucian thought (see pages 69–71 and 80–81). Unlike Yamaga Sokō, he appeared little interested in the military arts, stressing in their place the old Confucian virtue of "benevolence" or "love" (*jen*). His son Tōgai (1670–1736) continued his work, editing and amplifying his writings.

A third member of the "Ancient Learning" School, Ogyū Sorai (1666–1728), the son of a doctor in the shogun's service, rejected both the Neo-Confucianists and Itō Jinsai's approach by going back beyond Confucius himself to the Six Classics — a category which included, along with the Five Classics, a lost *Classic of Music* (see pages 64–66). Ogyū prided himself on his Chinese scholarship and was a thorough-going Sinophile in all things. This Sinophile tendency, incidentally, reached even greater extremes in the writings of his most famous disciple, Dazai Shundai (1680–1747). On the other hand, Ogyū was no mere textual scholar. In complete defiance of most Confucian thought of the previous millennium, he agreed more with Hsün-tzu than with Mencius in feeling that man's basically evil nature necessitates control by strict legal institutions (see pages 81–82). He was also a confirmed utilitarian, believing that the rites or etiquette so stressed in Confucianism could be justified only by their social usefulness. While not challenging hereditary feudal authority, he argued for a greater role in government for men of talent. Despite such glaringly unorthodox views, Ogyū was well thought of even by an arch-conservative like Yoshimune.

The Diversity of Tokugawa Thought. In view of the non-intellectual heritage of the samurai class and the fact that Confucianism was a borrowed philosophy, one cannot but be impressed by the diversity and independence of Japanese thought already in the seventeenth century. Subsequently it was to grow even broader and to free itself further from its Chinese prototypes There was a marked tendency toward cosmopolitan interests and a rationalistic openness of mind. A good example is provided by the orthodox philosopher-statesman Arai Hakuseki (1657–1725), whom we have already met as the chief determiner of shogunal policy from 1709 to 1716. After his retirement from political life, he devoted himself to a great variety of studies: geography, even including that of Europe; language studies, including Dutch; legal institutions; social organization; and history. Similarly, Miura Baien (1723–1789), who was the son of a non-samurai village physician in Kyūshū and himself refused to accept samurai status, groped his way toward what might be called a modern scientific point of view. Rejecting all scholarly authority and the traditional East Asian concepts of the natural order, his inquiring mind demanded that everything be verified by empirical evidence.

By the eighteenth century most thinkers, whether orthodox or not, were devoting a great deal of attention to practical economic problems — usually with the hope of bolstering the traditional Tokugawa system. Most manifested the typical feudal bias in favor of the agrarian side of the economy, but a few developed iconoclastic doctrines. For example, Kaiho Seiryō (1755–1817), a man of well-to-do samurai background who forsook his feudal duties for the life of a scholar, ridiculed the disdain of the military class for the profit motive, pointing out that a samurai's service to his lord actually amounted to a business transaction in which the retainer obtained rice by trading his ability to his lord.

The shogunal authorities, particularly during the periods of so-called reform, sought to discourage or even suppress unorthodox views. Yoshimune, for example, replaced Arai Hakuseki in the shogunal councils by a physician's son, Muro Kyūsō (1658–1734), who was an ardent defender of Chu Hsi and a champion of the shogunate against the innuendoes of heterodox thinkers. Matsudaira Sadanobu in 1790 went further, ordering the suppression of heterodox views first in the shogunal university and subsequently in the official *han* schools.

In spite of such measures, however, unorthodox philosophers continued to thrive and the scope of Tokugawa thought to broaden. Although many of the heterodox thinkers were frankly critical of specific shogunal policies, they were not consciously anti-Tokugawa. However, Confucian thought and scholarship in Japan did send out offshoots that in time became openly subversive.

OTHER INTELLECTUAL TRENDS

The Lower Classes. One significant development of the Tokugawa period was the growing intellectual activity among the lower classes, which came as both a sign and a product of the relatively high educational standards among the townsmen and the peasants. It also indicated the growing freedom of society. By the eighteenth century many townsmen and peasants felt free to think for themselves, however subserviently their social status might require them to behave. Different aspects of this burgeoning of intellectual freedom among the lower classes can be seen in the rich urban literature of the period, the appearance of a series of excellent scientific treatises on farming, and the development of philosophies specifically designed for the non-military classes. These philosophies helped spread to the townsmen and peasants some of the dominant Confucian concepts of the samurai; but, on the other hand, they were also subversive to the established social and ethical code in that they gave the lower classes an increased sense of dignity and importance in society.

Ishida Baigan (1685–1744), a peasant by origin who worked his way up in a Kyōto merchant house, turned first to the study of Shintō and then to Confucianism, but finally, after a sort of personal religious awakening, he founded his own religion, to which he applied the Chinese term "Learning of the Mind," or *Shingaku* (in Chinese, *Hsin-hsüeh*). He taught conformity with the natural moral order through a selfless spirit of service, applying his doctrine specifically to the merchant class. He urged merchants to conduct their business with honesty, diligence and charity and argued that they, as the stewards of the nation's wealth, were performing a function in society comparable to that of the samurai. Thus he gave a moral justification to commercial activity and helped transmit to the townsmen the high ethical standards and sense of mission that the samurai had assumed for themselves. There was nothing directly subversive about Ishida's ideas, but they contributed to an entirely non-feudal concept of economic activity. In this sense they helped prepare the Japanese, in the same way that the Protestant ethic had prepared Europeans, for a more modern economy and society.

Another peasant, Ninomiya Sontoku (1787–1856), a very successful farmer from near Edo, helped institute practical agrarian improvements in several areas in the Kantō and became a sort of peasant sage. There was, of course, nothing revolutionary in his advocacy of mutual aid and cooperation in farm communities and his insistence on careful, long-term planning and budgeting. However, his emphasis on the dignity of manual work and on labor as the source of all the virtues carried overtones of a much more egalitarian social order than existed under the Tokugawa.

Shintō and Nationalism. A resurgence of interest in Shintō and a rising tide of nationalistic sentiment were two other important and closely related trends in Tokugawa thought. The Confucian philosophers in their distaste for Buddhism were inclined to regard Shintō with tolerance or even with favor. Their emphasis on historical studies, which constituted an essential part of Confucianism, also whetted their interest in Shintō as it had flourished in early times, and these historical studies in turn drew general attention to the ancient role of the emperors both as actual rulers and as the divinely descended heads of the Shintō cult.

The rising interest in Shintō, by stressing Japan's differences from China, contributed in turn to the development of a nationalistic spirit expressed through Shintō symbolism. This was not entirely new, for in the thirteenth and fourteenth centuries signs of this sort of national consciousness had appeared in the reaction to the Mongol invasions and in Kitabatake Chikafusa's writings in defense of Go-Daigo's imperial line. Such concepts, however, had been quiescent for some time until they were stirred up again by the early Tokugawa Confucianists.

The rise of nationalism during the Tokugawa period cannot be dismissed as just an accidental by-product of Confucianism. The recent contact with the nations of Europe and the resulting policy of isolation, which so emphasized Japan's cultural and political distinctiveness, were unquestionably contributing factors. So also, no doubt, was the traditional realization of the Japanese that, although much of their higher civilization had been borrowed from China, they themselves were in no sense Chinese. This realization may have created a sense of inferiority, which in turn demanded a compensatory assertion of uniqueness and superiority expressed in terms of irrational nationalistic doctrines. Such seems to have been the origin of at least some of the expressions of national consciousness in early medieval times, which may have some analogy to the early expressions of nationalistic feeling in North Europe — an area which, as a cultural offshoot of Mediterranean civilization, stood in somewhat the same cultural and historical relationship to the Mediterranean region as Japan did to China.

The rapid rise of nationalistic sentiment in Japan after the seventeenth century was also associated with the broad economic and social changes then taking place, just as the rise of nationalism in Europe was associated with the political and social changes that were taking place there. The striking parallels in the development of strong nationalistic currents in post-feudal Europe and in Tokugawa Japan, which was also in many ways a post-feudal society, deserve careful comparative study. It is probably no mere accident that Japan, the one Asian country to go through a feudal experience comparable to that of Europe, was the only non-Western country which developed a strong national consciousness before the late nineteenth century.

Nationalism in itself was not subversive to the Tokugawa, but the nationalistic use of the imperial line as a symbol was definitely so. Even orthodox Confucianism, through its historical orientation, contributed directly to this subversive aspect of nationalism, by calling attention to the imperial traditions of Confucianist China and also to the former power of the Japanese emperors. This historical interest made people aware that loyalty, the great Confucian and feudal virtue, was ultimately due the emperor, not his theoretical delegate, the shogun. In time such ideas naturally stirred up doubts as to the right of the Tokugawa to rule at all.

Even Hayashi Razan, the chief founder of the orthodox Confucian school, became sufficiently interested in Shintō to write a book about the Shintō shrines. In the *History of Great Japan*, Tokugawa Mitsukuni's great historical undertaking, Chu Shun-shui, the Ming loyalist, placed chief emphasis on the concept of loyalty to the throne. And the Mito historians, despite their Confucian background, followed Kitabatake Chikafusa's lead in ascribing Japan's greatness to the divinely descended, unbroken line of emperors. Yamazaki Ansai (1618–1682), one of the most important of the early orthodox Confucianists, in his later years turned increasingly to Shintō, equating Japanese foundation myths with Chinese cosmology. Indeed, his thinking developed such a nationalistic twist that he stated that if Confucius and Mencius were to lead the Chinese in attacking Japan he could best follow their teachings by fighting and capturing them in defense of his country.

Yamaga Sokō, the "Ancient Learning" master of military science and *Bushidō*, was convinced of the superiority of Japan to China and attributed this superiority less to the martial valor he so much admired than to the divine and unbroken line of emperors, who, he felt, should be the focus of all loyalties. Arai Hakuseki, who was very conscious of foreign relations, felt that the shogun's position as *de facto* ruler but not sovereign ought to be made clear to other nations. He also attempted to bring the Kyōto court and the Edo government closer together by intermarriage between the imperial and Tokugawa families and by making shogunal ceremonies conform to those of Kyōto.

"National Learning" (*Kokugaku*). Under this sort of stimulation from the Confucianists, there arose a group of anti-Confucian, nationalistic Shintō thinkers, known as the "National Learning" (*Kokugaku*) School, who sought in Japan's early traditions and culture the true expression of the national spirit, unsullied by continental influences. A forerunner of this movement was the monk Keichū (1640–1701), who, under the patronage of Tokugawa Mitsukuni, wrote commentaries on

the ancient poetical anthology, the *Man'yōshū*, as well as on other literary works. Subsequently, Kada Azumamaro (1699–1736), a Shintō priest at a Kyōto shrine, appealed to Yoshimune for a general revival of the study of early Japanese literature. Kamo Mabuchi (1697–1769), another Shintō priest, arguing that the poems of the *Man'yōshū* represented the pure, unspoiled Japanese spirit, fostered a revival of this poetic style.

Kamo's disciple, Motoori Norinaga (1730–1801), the son of a cotton goods dealer and himself a physician, devoted more than thirty years to producing a great *Commentary on the Kojiki (Kojiki den)*, in order to make this first mythological account of Japan's national beginnings more generally understandable. He also turned his attention to the eleventh-century *Tale of Genji* and the thirteenth-century poetical compilation, the *Shin kokinshū*, as expressions of the true Japanese spirit. His selection of these works as the virtual scriptures of "National Learning" constituted a rejection of Confucian rationalism and ethics in favor of emotional expression. The latter was exemplified in the simple feeling of awe in primitive Shintō, the supra-human mythology of the *Kojiki*, and the concentration on the emotional side of life in *The Tale of Genji* and in Japanese poetry. Motoori argued that the Japanese foundation myths were the origin of the "True Way," which had been transmitted to Japan through the divinely descended imperial line but was only imperfectly reflected in other countries.

Hirata Atsutane (1776–1843), a physician of samurai origin, was even more specific in his assertion of Japan's national superiority as the land of the gods and much more violent in his rejection of almost everything he recognized as being of foreign origin. At the same time he was unconsciously eclectic in his borrowings from Confucianism, Taoism and Buddhism. He was also much interested in Western science and medicine, and his emphasis on a "Creator" may have reflected the influence of Christianity, with which he was quite familiar.

The "National Learning" School naturally produced a nationalistic fervor in some circles and a revived interest in the imperial line which was to prove highly subversive to the Tokugawa in their last years of rule. A foretaste of this occurred a century earlier, when Takenouchi Shikibu, a *rōnin* teacher at the imperial court, became so outspoken an advocate of the primacy of loyalty to the throne that he had to be expelled from Kyōto in 1758 and seventeen of his noble pupils punished. In 1767 Yamagata Daini and Fujii Umon, two similar "loyalist" teachers in Edo, were executed, allegedly for hatching a plot against the shogunate.

Subversion, however, was not the main fruit of the school of "National Learning." Its leaders were learned students of ancient texts, and their philological research gave impetus to a great growth in literary and historical scholarship. An extraordinary example of this is provided by the blind scholar, Hanawa Hokiichi (1746–1821), who in 1819 completed, under the title of *An Assortment of Writings* (*Gunsho ruijū*), a huge collection of 1270 Japanese literary and historical texts in 660 volumes. He then started on a second collection of 2103 works, which his son subsequently brought out as *An Assortment of Writings Continued* (*Zoku gunsho ruijū*).

Popular Shintō Sects. "National Learning" also may have contributed to the sudden appearance in the early nineteenth century of several popular religious movements with strong Shintō leanings. These should be clearly distinguished from the traditional Shintō cults and the nationalistic doctrines that centered around Shintō mythology. These new religions were all definitely eclectic; but their identification as offshoots of Shintō, rather than of Buddhism or Confucianism, shows how much the prestige of the ancient Japanese cults had been restored.

The new religions, which spread largely among the peasants, were usually theistic, commonly prophesied great changes to be brought about by the new doctrines, and sometimes included faith healing. Several of them have continued to prosper and grow until today. The Kurozumi sect, founded by a peasant of this name, centers on the worship of the Sun Goddess. Tenrikyō, the "Teaching of Heavenly Truth," founded by a woman in 1838, remains at present the strongest numerically and the most affluent, with a great religious center at the birthplace of its founder, a town (renamed Tenri), a few miles south of the ancient capital of Nara.

"Dutch Learning." One branch of Tokugawa scholarship which was not itself subversive but inevitably produced upsetting new ideas was the study of the Occident and its sciences. Despite the isolation policy, the Japanese, as we have seen, continued to acquire knowledge about the West through the Dutch trading post at Nagasaki. Since Dutch was the language through which this knowledge had to be obtained, the study of the West came to be known as "Dutch Learning" (*Rangaku*).

By the eighteenth century, the fear of Christianity, which had inspired the isolation policy, had so far receded into the background of general thinking that a freer attitude toward the Europeans and their knowledge became possible. For example, when the shogunate assigned the great Confucian scholar Arai Hakuseki to examine an Italian priest who had attempted to smuggle himself into Japan in 1708, his questioning of the priest resulted in a book called *A Report on the Occident* (*Seiyō kibun*) in which Hakuseki showed a frank admiration for Western scientific knowledge. In 1720 Yoshimune, for all his conservatism, relaxed the ban on foreign books, except those dealing with Christianity. He also encouraged some of his officials to take up Dutch studies, and one of them in 1745 produced a Dutch-Japanese dictionary.

Interested private scholars joined the official interpreters at Nagasaki in studying the Dutch language, and Western scientific knowledge began to spread throughout Japan. This was particularly true during Tanuma's period of liberal policies, between 1769 and 1786, when the Swedish physician Thunberg and the Dutchman Titsingh provided valuable scientific information at the Dutch trading post in Nagasaki. A few of the daimyo, notably Shimazu Shigehide (1745–1833) of South Kyūshū, became personally interested in Western science, and other daimyo patronized specialists in such studies. Shigehide founded a medical school in 1774 and subsequently institutes of astronomy and mathematics. Among the many scholarly undertakings he supported was an encyclopedia of agricultural plants and medicinal herbs, completed in 1804. In 1808 the shogunate itself founded an office for the translation of Western books which engaged in translating most of a Dutch encyclopedia and many other works.

The relative freedom of medical studies from the oppression of Tokugawa Confucian orthodoxy may account for the prominent role of physicians and sons of physicians in Tokugawa thought. Medicine naturally became a major interest of the scholars of "Dutch Learning."

DUTCH DINNER PARTY

A wood-block print by Hayashi Shihei, based on a sketch made while he was being entertained by the Dutch on the islet of Deshima in Nagasaki Harbor. The empty chair is the one he vacated to make the sketch.

One of the first important undertakings in this field was the translation in 1774 by Sugita Gempaku (1733–1817) of a Dutch medical work. This was followed in 1783 by *An Introduction to Dutch Learning (Rangaku kaitei)*, by another physician, Ōtsuki Gentaku (1757–1827), which greatly aided Japanese scholars in their study of the Dutch language.

Among the many other scholars of Western learning at this time, Hiraga Gennai (1728?–1779) stands out for the breadth of his interests, which led him to study botany, experiment with electricity, asbestos and balloons, write plays and satirical novels, and join the other artists who were trying out Occidental techniques of painting and etching. The spirit of Western science also spread to individuals who were not themselves experts in "Dutch Learning," leading to such accomplishments as the surveying and mapping of all Japan by the cartographer Inō Chūkei (or Tadataka; 1745–1818).

Knowledge of the scientific progress and military strength of the West — especially when it was combined with the new nationalistic spirit — often led to criticism of shogunate policies, and even to more fundamentally subversive thinking. Hayashi (or Rin) Shihei (1738–1793) in 1786 wrote a work called *A Discussion of the Military Problems of a Maritime Country (Kaikoku hei dan)*, in which he so sharply criticized the government for the weakness of its defenses against the growing menace of the Russians in the north that he was imprisoned in 1792 and his work confiscated.

Honda Toshiaki (1744–1821), who had himself voyaged as a ship's captain to Hokkaidō in 1801, also advocated improved defenses but went on to develop more broadly revolutionary doctrines. For instance, he favored the use of the Western alphabet in place of the cumbersome Chinese characters. He also advocated the complete end of isolation, and felt that Japan should become the "England of the East." Above all, he believed in imperialist expansion, particularly northward, to make Japan a prosperous world power. In the next generation Satō Nobuhiro (1769–1850) advocated a comprehensive and highly revolutionary plan for a completely centralized and authoritarian form of government, based on Occidental science and Western administrative institutions.

Thus the learning which the shoguns themselves had encouraged led eventually to the appearance of thinkers who hoped either for a drastic reform of the long-established Tokugawa system or for its complete abolition. In short, the intellectual props of the Tokugawa system had themselves started to give way at the same time that its economic and social foundations were crumbling.

These signs of change, however, are more obvious to us today than they were to the contemporary Japanese. The Tokugawa shogunate entered the nineteenth century beset by many problems but still rigidly firm and apparently beyond challenge. Its political shell was unchanged and seemed almost unchangeable. For most people, the old ethics and the old institutions remained entirely valid. The great majority of the Japanese could scarcely imagine any other system, and subversive thoughts were limited to a peripheral fringe of society. It took a strong blow from outside Japan to shake its political structure and reveal how weak its economic and social foundations had become, and how unreliable its ideological supports.

14

East Asia on the
Eve of Modernization

In this volume we have been concerned with the growth and development of East Asian civilization from its beginnings in North China until the first half of the nineteenth century. The story up to this point has been a diverse one, covering as it does a span of more than three millenniums and such very different geographical areas and peoples as those of China, Japan, Korea and Central Asia. But despite the great diversity of institutions and cultures, we have labeled the whole of this earlier phase of East Asian civilization "traditional," because, until the nineteenth century, changes tended to be slow and evolutionary, stemming largely from within the area itself and usually remaining within a framework inherited from earlier times.

Changes of a much more radical sort, which originated largely in pressures and influences from outside East Asia, began in the middle of the nineteenth century and have continued ever since. These naturally have not swept aside all that was traditional in East Asia, but they have altered life so much that the great tradition inherited from the past has become only one element in the modern scene.

The chief reason for these sudden changes was the overwhelming military, economic and political impact of the technologically more advanced countries of the West. The story of this impact and of the resulting modification of East Asian civilization we have reserved for the next volume; but before closing this one we might glance forward at this phase of history from the vantage point of traditional East Asian civilization as it had developed by the first half of the nineteenth century.

One cannot but be struck by the great differences among the various countries of East Asia in the speed and nature of their responses to the West during the past century. Manifold changes have brought a considerable degree of modernization to all these countries, but at decidedly different rates and in strikingly different ways.

These variations in response must be attributed mainly to the differences in the traditional societies of the countries of East Asia. Only such differences can explain why a basically similar impact could have brought such varied initial results in China, Korea and Japan — why relatively small Japan, for example, soon became a world power, while China sank to the status of an international problem, and Korea disappeared temporarily into the Japanese Empire. Such differences in tradition and, consequently, in response to the West must be understood if one is to bring any perspective to the study of the modern century of East Asian history. Without such perspective, one could easily fall into the erroneous assumption of some "old China hands" that the disorganized, chaotic China of the past century represented the normal or even the inevitable China, or assume that the ascendancy achieved by Japan in East Asia by the beginning of the twentieth century might have continued indefinitely, despite China's overwhelming advantage in geographical size and population. Some of the sharp contrasts between China, Japan and Korea are now diminishing, as Korea re-establishes its independence and China continues to modernize and succeeds in reasserting its position as a great power in the world. And yet other contrasts remain as sharp as ever.

The weakness of the Chinese state during the century of treaty relations from 1842 to 1943 (the period of the "unequal treaties") gave Western observers the misconception that Chinese political life was, by its own nature and habit, normally disorganized. Since the Chinese Communists' rise to power in 1949, however, attitudes have shifted. The Chinese people seem now all too susceptible to tight organization under a despotic central authority. By looking back at earlier periods we can see that this Chinese capacity for authoritarian organization is nothing new, even though communism exploits it more intensively and drastically than has ever been done before.

In this perspective, the modern century of weakness up to 1949 becomes the exception, not the norm, a temporary interregnum between periods of unity and central power. Yet it would be a great mistake to conclude that the Chinese Communist regime is merely a new dynasty, an example of history repeating itself in an old pattern. China today is probably more new than old, more modernized than traditional in many of its ideas, attitudes and institutions. Nevertheless, one set of features, that of a strong central leadership indoctrinating a bureaucracy, organizing the populace, and superintending their labor and livelihood, is strongly reminiscent of earlier ages when new dynasties came to power.

We are left with this question: Why was the Chinese state so weak in its first century of modern contact with the West? Part of the answer undoubtedly lies in the complex fact of dynastic decline, which had set in again by 1800 and gradually increased in severity. Perhaps this alone might have been enough to make the Chinese state disorderly and ineffective in the early twentieth century. The domestic collapse, however, was reinforced by a set of influences from abroad, the impact of Western ways that often proved wholly at variance with traditional Chinese ways. This Western impact provides what is usually regarded as the other part of the explanation of China's recent political weakness.

There is still much dispute as to which set of factors, internal or external, was the more important in China's failure to respond effectively at first to the Western challenge. Classical Chinese notions support the explanation that internal political decline preceded and invited foreign aggression; "barbarian" invasion was considered a sign that Confucian government had temporarily failed. Marxism-Leninism, on the other hand, sets forth the opposite view: that, although it made use of the decadent forces of domestic "feudalism," "imperialism" nevertheless became the primary and dominant factor, penetrating and destroying the old economic order, exploiting and impoverishing a China which it had made "semi-colonial."

Of course, dynastic decline and Western imperialism both have played important roles in China's history during the past century; but when we compare China with Japan we see that this whole argument over the precedence of dynastic decline or imperialist pressure, as posed by traditional Chinese scholars and Marxist historians, deals with what really is only a secondary issue. Japan, which in the same period was undergoing comparable dynastic decline and suffering from similar imperialist pressures, reacted entirely differently, and with spectacular success. The contrast between the Chinese and Japanese responses lay not in the dynastic cycle or in foreign stimuli but in the basic institutional and cultural differences between these two different members of East Asian civilization. In Japan there were many stimulating factors, absent or weak in China, that facilitated a quick and successful response to the new problems of the nineteenth century. In China there were certain inhibiting factors which Japan either lacked or experienced to a lesser degree.

Perhaps the greatest difference between China and Japan during the early nineteenth century lay in the rate of internal evolutionary change. Probably many more changes were taking place in China than has been generally recognized. Nevertheless, the rate of internal change seems to have been much greater in Japan. Despite all the efforts of the political power-holders and orthodox intellectual leaders, rapid changes were occurring in almost everything except the formal structure of government and the official ideology. Japan, with an already mobile society, could easily be diverted into new directions of motion by the external impact, whereas China was characterized by inertia, which had first to be overcome. Or, to shift metaphors, the structure of society and government in Japan had already been seriously undermined, and therefore it crumbled rapidly under foreign pressures, making way for a largely new edifice. But in China the social and political structure was so solidly based that it took many decades of heavy external blows before the old structure was sufficiently demolished to permit significant structural modification.

This second figure suggests that, ironically enough, it may have been the basic solidity, rather than the weakness, of the Chinese order that made it unprepared to meet the Western challenge in the nineteenth century. Certainly the Chinese social, political and ideological systems had achieved under the Ch'ing a stability unparalleled at any time in Japan or, for that matter, in any country of the Occident. And this was not a mere stability of stagnation. The Chinese people were more or less adequately sustained in their livelihood; their cultural life was vigorous; they had achieved a considerable degree of equilibrium within the limits of their institutions and way of life. The Japanese, on the other hand, despite all the efforts of the Tokugawa, had failed to stabilize their system. Many of them were restless and dissatisfied — much like the peoples of Europe in modern times — and herein lay a great advantage over the Chinese in facing the problems of the restless modern world.

Another great difference between the nineteenth century Chinese and Japanese lay in their contrasting views of the outside world. To the Chinese, the world consisted of one central civilized land, with peripheral "barbarians" capable of participating in civilization only to the extent of their adoption of Chinese culture and their recognition of the suzerainty of the Middle Kingdom. This attitude made it extremely difficult for the Chinese to understand the international, multi-state system of the Occident. It was even harder for them to appreciate the possibility that the Europeans might have things the Chinese could usefully adopt, or that China could profit from trade relations, which were traditionally felt to be unimportant.

The Japanese, on the other hand, despite a keen awareness of having derived much of their own higher culture from China, felt a strong national distinctiveness from the Chinese. Therefore they could grasp much more quickly the European concept of equal but independent political units and also see with greater clarity that there was much to be learned from the West. While the Chinese struggled for decades with the intellectual question of what if anything was to be adopted from the "barbarians," the Japanese were already learning and applying Western knowledge and experience.

Still another contrast was that of size and centralization. China, the world's largest country, was politically so centralized that no one but the men at the capital could make significant innovations. These officials, however, were too busy running the ponderous machine of government and too isolated from external realities by the red tape of a complex administrative system to be able to think of basic changes. Moreover, the vastness of the Chinese sub-continent and the size of its governmental structure kept foreign stimuli at a distance. For a long while Western influences penetrated no farther than the cities on the coast or on the major inland waterways, while the small body of officials and scholars who had direct contact with the West remained for many decades only a tiny leaven in the great mass of the bureaucracy.

Although Japan was geographically so much smaller than China, her potential leadership, because of feudal political institutions, was much more widespread, not only among the 265 "autonomous" *han* but even among the various social groups with their differing functions in society. If one geographical area or sector of Japanese society failed to respond adequately to the crisis created by Western pressures, another one would; in fact, this is what happened.

Korea in the nineteenth century resembled China more than Japan in its failure to respond with success to the external challenge. Actually, the Western impact was less severe there than in either of the other countries, but dynastic decline, because of the extraordinary length of Yi rule, had become more pronounced. Other important factors may be found in Korea's social, cultural and intellectual conditions, which, on the whole, were similar to those of China. The Koreans had achieved a degree of cultural stability comparable to that of China but perhaps more stultifying, because it had as its central focus a set of ideas of foreign origin and a source of ultimate authority outside Korea itself. The Yi dynasty did not face the same problem of size as did the Ch'ing, but the concentration of all political initiative at a court no longer capable of taking decisive action had the same inhibiting effect. And the acceptance by the Koreans of the Chinese view of the world made it as difficult for them as for the Chinese — perhaps more so — to understand the Western international order or accept the possibility that they might learn from the Occident. In any case, Korea's initial response to the Western challenge was to prove largely ineffective. Lacking the protection of great size that China had, Korea was swallowed whole into the Japanese Empire.

In addition to the points already mentioned, Japan possessed one other important advantage over China and Korea in facing the problems brought by the West in the nineteenth century. Japanese society was not only already in motion; it seems to have been moving in the same general direction in which the Western pressures impelled it. Perhaps because Japan's feudal experience had been similar to that of Europe, the nation was already evolving along a course not far different from the one Europe had taken as it moved from feudalism toward what we now call "modern society." A class structure rather like that of feudal Europe was breaking down in somewhat the same way as it had broken down in the West. The feudal economy also was crumbling, much as it had done in Europe, and this economy was giving place to rudimentary forms of the capitalist system. The Japanese also were developing a much keener appreciation than either the Chinese or Koreans of the place of trade, both domestic and foreign, in the national economy. Most important of all, the Japanese already had a strong national consciousness and therefore reacted as a national unit to the foreign challenge, easily adopting the techniques of national organization already developed by the West.

In all these ways the Japanese had, as it were, a running start in some of the specific directions of development that were to prove necessary for national survival in the nineteenth and twentieth centuries. This, of course, does not mean that Japanese society would have developed in the way or at the speed it has during the past century if there had been no Western impact. But the motion within traditional Japanese society was a decided help to its subsequent modernization, not a hindrance. The Chinese and Koreans, on the other hand, were standing relatively immobile; indeed, they were facing in a different direction entirely from that in which the Western impact pushed them. It was not until after they had been bowled off their feet and had dazedly found their bearings that they could consciously join the race. It is not surprising that the much greater speed of Japan's start proved a decisive factor during the first century of modernization in East Asia.

The Pronunciation
of Chinese, Korean and Japanese

The Romanization systems used in this book are those generally considered standard in the English-speaking world: Wade-Giles for Chinese (with the omission of a few unnecessary diacritical marks); McCune-Reischauer for Korean; and Hepburn for Japanese. There is one major exception to this rule, however. Common Chinese geographical names are normally given according to the Chinese Post Office system, which often follows southern Chinese pronunciations and not the Peking pronunciation of standard Northern Chinese (Mandarin or *kuan-hua*). For example, the city that has been the capital of China for most of the past five and a half centuries is generally Romanized Peking and pronounced accordingly, but the Wade-Giles Romanization of the name would be Pei-ching, pronounced something like Bay-jing.

The three standard systems of Romanization have points of similarity and therefore can be considered together. The following guide to pronunciation is a non-technical presentation which ignores many finer points but will be adequate for the general reader.

Vowels. The basic vowels, *a*, *e*, *i*, *o* and *u*, in Chinese, Korean and Japanese transcriptions are pronounced as in Italian, German and Spanish.

   a as in f*a*ther
   e as in *e*nd
   i as the first *e* in *e*ve
   o as in *o*ld (but with less of the *ou* sound of English)
   u as in r*u*de
There are, however, some exceptions in CHINESE:
   e (except when following *i* or *y*) is pronounced like the *u* in *u*p
   ih is pronounced something like the *ir* in st*ir*
   o is often pronounced more like the *o* of s*o*ft
   u when it follows *ss* or *tz* is sometimes hardly pronounced (and in Japanese too it is often barely audible; e.g., *desu* = *des'*)
Diphthongs and long vowels:
   In CHINESE two vowels coming together are pronounced always as diphthongs, that is, run together (*ai* as the *i* in *i*ce; *ou* as the *o* in *o*bey; *ao* as the *ow* in c*ow*).

675

In JAPANESE only *ai* and *ei* (like the *a* in *a*le) are diphthongs; other vowels coming together are pronounced as separate syllables. Long vowels (*ō* and *ū*) are formed like the corresponding short vowels (*o* and *u*) but are held much longer. This distinction between long and short vowels is very important in Japanese.

In KOREAN *ae* is like the *a* in *a*dd; *oe* like the *ö* of German; and *ŭi* like the *uee* in q*uee*r.

Other vowels:

    ŏ in Korean is like the *u* of b*u*t

    ŭ in Korean is something like the *oo* in f*oo*t

    ü in Chinese is like the *ü* of German or *u* of French

Consonants. The consonants and the semi-vowels *w* and *y* in Chinese, Korean and Japanese transcriptions are generally pronounced as they are in English. The following are the chief exceptions:

In the paired aspirated consonants (*ch'*, *k'*, *p'*, *t'*, *ts'*, *tz'*) and unaspirated consonants (*ch*, *k*, *p*, *t*, *ts*, *tz*) of CHINESE and KOREAN (the last two in each listing do not occur in Korean), the aspirated forms are more like the corresponding English consonants, which are usually aspirated, that is, are accompanied by a marked exhalation of air, and the unaspirated forms are closer to the corresponding consonants in French.[1] To the ears of English-speaking persons, however, the unaspirated consonants of Chinese often sound like the corresponding voiced consonants and are usually so pronounced by all but expert speakers of Chinese. Thus, in Chinese *ch* is pronounced as *j*, *k* as *g*, *p* as *b*, *t* as *d*, *ts* and *tz* as *dz*.

In CHINESE:

    hs (which occurs only before *i* and *ü*) is pronounced rather like *sh* (which occurs before *a*, *e* and *u*)

    j is pronounced something like *r* (*jen* sounds like *run*)

    ss (which occurs only before the lightly pronounced *u*) is not to be distinguished from *s*

Correspondence in Pronunciation. Words and names of Chinese origin, as used in Korean and Japanese, are pronounced somewhat differently from Chinese. Actually, the Korean forms are sometimes closer to ancient Chinese than are the modern Chinese. Both Korean and Japanese preserve certain consonantal finals to syllables that have been lost in standard modern Chinese (though they are retained in the southern coastal "dialects"). The general nature of the correspondence in pronunciation for words and names of Chinese origin in the three languages can be seen

---

[1] The use of ' in Japanese transcriptions has nothing to do with aspiration. It follows *n* when the *n* is part of the preceding syllable and not the initial consonant for the vowel which follows.

in the following chart of the cardinal points, which are much used in place names in all three countries and also appear in the names of the Korean political factions. (There are also native Japanese words for the cardinal points, which have no relationship to these Chinese-derived words.) The names are given below in their traditional East Asian order:

	CHINESE	KOREAN	JAPANESE
EAST	*tung*	*tong*	*tō*
WEST	*hsi*	*sŏ*	*sai*
SOUTH	*nan*	*nam*	*nan*
NORTH	*pei*	*puk*	*hoku*

Bibliography

Most of the primary record of East Asian civilization is in writings in Chinese, Japanese or other East Asian languages, as is also the greater part of the scholarly knowledge derived from the study of such records. Works in European languages thus form only a reflection of the whole body of written materials, and books in English only a segment of this reflection.

The following list of books is not meant to be an exhaustive bibliography but simply a guide to further reading and an aid to those who may wish to build up a modest library on East Asian history and culture. Therefore, only books in English have been included and, for the most part, only those which are not out of print but are readily available. Special note has been taken of economical paper-back editions.

Much more extensive bibliographies can be found in several of the books listed below. In addition, useful bibliographical guides are provided by L. C. Goodrich, *A Syllabus of the History of Chinese Civilization and Culture* (New York: China Society of America, sixth edition, revised, 1958); Hershel Webb, *An Introduction to Japan* (New York: Columbia University Press, second edition, 1957); Hugh Borton, Serge Elisséeff, William W. Lockwood, John C. Pelzel, *A Selected List of Books and Articles on Japan in English, French, and German* (Cambridge: Harvard University Press, 1954); and the *Korean Studies Guide* (Berkeley and Los Angeles: University of California Press, 1954).

The *Journal of Asian Studies,* a quarterly published in Ann Arbor, Michigan, carries current bibliographies as well as articles of general interest. The *Harvard Journal of Asiatic Studies* is devoted exclusively to scholarly articles on East Asian history and culture. The most useful chronology, really an historical epitome, is in W. L. Langer, *An Encyclopedia of World History* (Boston: Houghton Mifflin, 1940, revised edition, 1948); the China sections are mainly by Charles S. Gardner, the Japan sections by Edwin O. Reischauer. The best survey of East Asian geography as a whole is to be found in George B. Cressey, *Asia's Lands and Peoples; A Geography of One-Third the Earth and Two-thirds Its People* (New York: McGraw-Hill, second edition, 1951).

China. The best account of Chinese geography is George B. Cressey, *Land of the 500 Million* (New York: McGraw-Hill, 1955). A few general histories of China should be noted. One reliable general source (with an extensive bibliography) is Kenneth Scott Latourette, *The Chinese: Their History and Culture* (New York: Macmillan, third edition, revised, 2 volumes, 1946). A briefer, though in some ways more detailed, survey is by Professor L. Carrington Goodrich of Columbia University, *A Short History of the Chinese People* (New York: Harper and Brothers, third edition, revised, 1959), which stresses the origins and development of China's material culture and its early contacts with foreign peoples. C. P. Fitzgerald, *China: A Short Cultural History* (London: Cresset Press, revised edition, 1950), though not a carefully balanced account, contains some excellent essays on aspects of Chinese history. A readable but rather superficial survey is a translation from the French, René Grousset, *The Rise and Splendour of the Chinese Empire* (Berkeley and Los Angeles: University of California Press, 1953).

For an authoritative brief survey of archaeological origins, with a bibliography, see Li Chi, *The Beginnings of Chinese Civilization: Three Lectures Illustrated with Finds at Anyang* (Seattle: University of Washington Press, 1957). The best general work on archaeology is Cheng Te-k'un, *Archaeology in China* (Cambridge, England: Heffer, vol. 1, 1959). Herrlee G. Creel, *The Birth of China* (New York: Frederick Ungar, 1954), has an excellent general account of the Shang and early Chou periods.

China's early social structure is dealt with by Derk Bodde in a chapter, "Feudalism in China," on pages 49–92 of Rushton Coulborn, ed., *Feudalism in History* (Princeton: Princeton University Press, 1956). The chapter on Japanese feudalism in this book (pp. 24–48) is by Edwin O. Reischauer. Marcel Granet, *Chinese Civilization* (reprinted in Meridian Books), a translation from the French, is an analysis of early Chinese society. The most thorough statistical research on the "gentry" class, in the sense of degree-holders and officials, is Chung-li Chang, *The Chinese Gentry; Studies in their Role in Nineteenth-Century Chinese Society* (Seattle: University of Washington Press, 1955). Work in this field has been stimulated by the systematic writings early in this century of Max Weber, recently made available in English — for example, *The Religion of China: Confucianism and Taoism*, translated by H. H. Gerth (Glencoe, Illinois: Free Press, 1951).

Arthur Waley, the best known of all translators, has contributed a number of very attractive translations of classical Chinese literature — *The Book of Songs* (London: G. Allen and Unwin, 1937); *The Analects of Confucius* (London: G. Allen and Unwin, 1938); *The Way and Its Power* (London: G. Allen and Unwin, 1934; Evergreen Books), which is a translation of the *Tao te ching*; and *Three Ways of Thought in Ancient China* (London: G. Allen and Unwin, 1939; New York: Doubleday Anchor Books, 1956), which includes extensive quotations from the *Chuang-tzu*, the *Mencius*, and the legalist philosophers. James R. Ware has published a new translation of the *Analects* under the title of *The Sayings of Confucius* (New York: Mentor Books, 1955). A collection of passages from the classics is also to be found in Lin Yutang, *The Wisdom of China and India* (New York: Random House, 1942).

On Chinese philosophy the leading general work is the translation by Derk Bodde of Fung, Yu-lan, *A History of Chinese Philosophy* (vol. 1, Peiping: H. Vetch, 1937; reissued together with the publication of vol. 2, Princeton: Princeton University Press, 1952). Fung, Yu-lan, *A Short History of Chinese Philosophy* (New York: Macmillan, 1948), edited by Professor Bodde, is a separate study. The greatest of the sages is re-studied in detail by H. G. Creel, *Confucius: The Man and the Myth* (New York: John Day, 1949). Professor Creel has also done a readable non-technical survey, *Chinese Thought from Confucius to Mao Tse-tung* (Chicago: University of Chicago Press, 1953). A fresh account of Taoism is presented in Holmes Welch, *The Parting of the Way: Lao Tzu and the Taoist Movement* (Boston: Beacon Press, 1957).

On the Han, a valuable study of the work of the great historian Ssu-ma Ch'ien is to be found in Burton Watson, *Ssu-ma Ch'ien; Grand Historian of China* (New York: Columbia University Press, 1958). Homer H. Dubs has also translated the annals section of the official history, *The History of the Former Han Dynasty by Pan Ku* (Baltimore: Waverly Press, vol. 1, 1938; vol. 2, 1944; vol. 3, 1955). There are also A. F. P. Hulsewe, *Remnants of Han Law* (Leiden: Brill, 1955) and C. Martin Wilbur, *Slavery in China during the Former Han Dynasty* (Chicago: Field Museum of Natural History, 1943).

Relatively few studies for the general reader have as yet appeared on the long period from 220 to 1644 A.D. Edwin O. Reischauer, *Ennin's Diary: The Record of a Pilgrimage to China in Search of the Law* (New York: Ronald Press, 1955) translates a unique first-person account of T'ang China. The companion volume, *Ennin's Travels in T'ang China* (New York: Ronald Press, 1955), rounds out this ninth-century Marco Polo's picture of China at the apex of world civilization. Other recent monographs include Edwin G. Pulleyblank, *The Background of the Rebellion of An Lu-shan* (New York: Oxford University Press, 1955); E. A. Kracke, Jr., *Civil Service in Early Sung China, 960–1067* (Cambridge: Harvard University Press, 1953); and James T. C. Liu, *Reform in Sung China* (Cambridge: Harvard University Press, 1959).

Among topical surveys the largest is Joseph Needham's projected seven-volume *Science and Civilization in China* (vol. 1, *Introductory Orientations*, Cambridge, England: Cambridge University Press, 1954; vol. 2, *History of Scientific Thought*, 1956). Lien-sheng Yang, *Money and Credit in China, A Short History* (Cambridge: Harvard University Press, 1952) describes these important institutions over two millenniums. James Robert Hightower, *Topics in Chinese Literature: Outlines and*

Bibliographies (Cambridge: Harvard University Press, 1950) provides a guide to this undeveloped field. Another important topical monograph is T. F. Carter, *The Invention of Printing in China and Its Spread Westward*, as revised and brought up to date by Professor L. C. Goodrich (New York: Ronald Press, second edition, 1955 [1925]).

Chinese intellectual history, including Buddhism and Neo-Confucianism, may be pursued in vol. 2 of Bodde's translation of Fung, already noted, and in symposia representing a score of authors — Arthur F. Wright, ed., *Studies in Chinese Thought* (New York: American Anthropological Association, Memoir No. 75; and Chicago: University of Chicago Press, 1953); John K. Fairbank, ed., *Chinese Thought and Institutions* (Chicago: University of Chicago Press, 1957); David Nivison and A. F. Wright, eds., *Confucianism in Action* (Stanford: Stanford University Press, 1959); and A. F. Wright, ed., *The Confucian Persuasion* (Stanford: Stanford University Press, 1960). A. F. Wright, *Buddhism in Chinese History* (Stanford: Stanford University Press, 1959) provides an excellent brief survey. W. T. de Bary with others has compiled a valuable volume of readings which includes some new translations, *Sources of the Chinese Tradition* (New York: Columbia University Press, 1960).

Study of Chinese border relations with Manchuria, Mongolia, and Turkestan has been illumined and greatly stimulated by Owen Lattimore, *Inner Asian Frontiers of China* (New York: American Geographical Society, 1940, second edition, 1951). The most thorough account of any of the "barbarian" dynasties is Karl August Wittfogel and Chiasheng Feng, *History of Chinese Society: Liao 907-1125* (Philadelphia: American Philosophical Society, 1949). Much work on the history of the Mongols has been done in Europe, particularly in France. A readable account, even though somewhat out of date, is Harold Lamb, *Genghis Khan: Emperor of All Men* (New York: McBride, 1930; Bantam Books). A detailed study of the Mongols' trans-Asian imperial structure is given in George Vernadsky, *The Mongols and Russia* (New Haven: Yale University Press, 1953).

Marco Polo is a field in himself. One of the most available of many editions is the translation of William Marsden in the Everyman's Library (Dutton). There are others by Benedetto and Ricci, by Moule and Pelliot, Manuel Komroff and in the Penguin Classics. Henry H. Hart, *Venetian Adventurer* (Palo Alto: Stanford University Press, 1942) describes the Polos' great adventure in its medieval setting.

The chief milestone in our knowledge of the Ch'ing dynasty is A. W. Hummel, ed., *Eminent Chinese of the Ch'ing Period (1644-1912)* (Washington, D.C.: Government Printing Office, 2 volumes, 1943-44), a biographical dictionary recounting the official careers and achievements of some 800 Chinese of note. This is the main reference work for serious students of the Ch'ing period. No similar work is available for other dynasties. Among monographic works are Franz Michael, *The Origin of Manchu Rule in China* (Baltimore: Johns Hopkins Press, 1942) and L. C. Goodrich, *The Literary Inquisition of Ch'ien-lung* (Baltimore: Waverly Press, 1935).

Chinese art, as something to look at as well as read about, is beautifully and critically represented in a popular volume, Laurence Sickman and Alexander Soper, *The Art and Architecture of China* (Penguin Books, 1956), with excellent plates and references also to the larger works of Osvald Siren and others. An interesting popular survey of fine arts and crafts is by William Willetts, *Chinese Art* (Pelican Books, 2 volumes, 1958).

One neglected short-cut to understanding China lies in the numerous excellent translations of literature now available. Standard translations of the famous pre-modern novels should now be in all libraries, particularly Arthur Waley, trans., *Monkey* (New York: John Day, 1943; Grove Press); Pearl Buck, trans., *All Men Are Brothers* (New York: John Day, 1933; Grove Press); Wang Chi-chen, trans., *Dream of the Red Chamber* (New York: Twayne, revised edition, 1958 [1929]); Clement Egerton, trans., *The Golden Lotus* (London: G. Routledge, 4 volumes, 1939), or a somewhat expurgated edition with an introduction by Arthur Waley, *Chin P'ing Mei* (New York: G. P. Putnam's Sons, 1940); and Wang Chi-chen, *Traditional Chinese Tales* (New York: Columbia University Press, 1943). Lin Yutang, *Famous Chinese Short Stories* (New York: John Day, 1952; Pocket Books) is also available.

In the field of Chinese poetry, a timeless subject, Arthur Waley's many volumes include *Chinese Poems* (London: G. Allen and Unwin, 1946), *Translations from the Chinese* (New York: Alfred A. Knopf, 1941), *The Life and Times of Po Chu-i, 772–846 A.D.* (New York: Macmillan, 1949), and *Yuan Mei, Eighteenth-Century Chinese Poet* (London: G. Allen and Unwin, 1956; Grove Press). Among other useful books are Robert Payne, *The White Pony* (New York: John Day, 1947), William Hung, *Tu Fu, China's Greatest Poet* (Cambridge: Harvard University Press, 1952), L. Cranmer Byng, *A Lute of Jade* (New York: Dutton, 1923; Grove Press), and Soame Jenyns, *T'ang Dynasty Poems* (London: J. Murray, 1940; Grove Press, 2 volumes). Another recent addition on ancient Chinese poetry is David Hawkes, *Ch'u Tz'u: the Songs of the South* (Oxford: Clarendon Press, 1959).

Korea. Relatively few books in English on Korea can be recommended. Shannon McCune, *Korea's Heritage; A Regional and Social Geography* (Rutland, Vermont, and Tokyo: Charles E. Tuttle Co., 1956) provides a good geographical survey. Cornelius Osgood, *The Koreans and Their Culture* (New York: Ronald Press, 1951) includes a sociological study together with a brief history, based on traditional but not very accurate sources. There is also In-sob Zong, *Folk Tales from Korea* (London: Routledge and Kegan Paul, 1952).

Japan. The best geographical survey of Japan is Glenn Thomas Trewartha, *Japan; A Physical, Cultural and Regional Geography* (Madison: University of Wisconsin Press, 1945). The small booklets of the *Japanese Tourist Library* (Tokyo: Japan Tourist Bureau) form handy introductions to many aspects of Japanese culture.

Pre-modern Japanese history is admirably covered in essay style by G. B. Sansom, *Japan; A Short Cultural History* (New York: Appleton-Century, revised edition, 1944). A more detailed account of early Japanese history is provided by the same author in *A History of Japan to 1334* (Stanford: Stanford University Press, 1958). This volume is to be followed shortly by two others, carrying the story up to 1615 and to 1854. Edwin O. Reischauer, *Japan Past and Present* (New York: Alfred A. Knopf, revised edition, 1953) furnishes a very brief survey of the whole of Japanese history.

Several more specific historical studies should also be mentioned. C. R. Boxer, *The Christian Century in Japan 1549–1650* (Berkeley: University of California Press, 1951) is a very readable account of that fascinating phase of Japanese history. Some of the same story together with an illuminating discussion of foreign intellectual influences in the decades preceding and following the opening of Japan in the nineteenth century is told in G. B. Sansom, *The Western World and Japan* (New York: Alfred A. Knopf, 1950). John W. Hall, *Tanuma Okitsugu, 1719–1788; Forerunner of Modern Japan* (Cambridge: Harvard University Press, 1955) provides an excellent study of an important phase of Tokugawa history, and two significant aspects of economic developments in that period are presented in Thomas C. Smith, *The Agrarian Origins of Modern Japan* (Stanford: Stanford University Press, 1959) and Charles David Sheldon, *The Rise of the Merchant Class in Tokugawa Japan 1600–1868* (Locust Valley, N.Y.: J. I. Augustin, 1958).

For intellectual history, philosophy and religion, the most important work is Ryusaku Tsunoda, William Theodore de Bary, and Donald Keene, *Sources of the Japanese Tradition* (New York: Columbia University Press, 1958). This substantial volume includes translations from a large number of representative religious leaders and thinkers together with helpful introductory comments. Masaharu Anesaki, *History of Japanese Religion* (London: Kegan Paul, 1930) is a good general survey. D. T. Suzuki, *Zen Buddhism* (Anchor Books) is a general presentation of this subject by a recognized authority. An interesting analysis of Japanese character and ethics, meant to apply to the contemporary Japanese, but actually applying better to the Tokugawa period, is to be found in Ruth Benedict, *The Chrysanthemum and the Sword* (Boston: Houghton Mifflin, 1946). Other valuable monographs on Tokugawa thought are Robert Bellah, *Tokugawa Religion; The Values of Pre-Industrial Japan* (Glencoe, Ill.: Free Press, 1957) and Donald Keene, *The Japanese Discovery of Europe: Honda Toshiaki and Other Discoverers, 1720–1798* (London: Routledge and Kegan Paul, 1952).

For literature, there is Donald Keene, *Japanese Literature; An Introduction for Western Readers* (Grove Press) and an excellent anthology by the same author: *Anthology of Japanese Literature from the Earliest Era to the Mid-nineteenth Century* (Grove Press).

For translations of earlier literature, there are two outstanding works by Arthur Waley: *The Tale of Genji* (London: G. Allen and Unwin; and New York: Literary Guild, 1935; the first section is now available also in Anchor Books), and *Japanese Poetry, the "Uta"* (Oxford: Clarendon Press, 1919; and London: Lund Humphries, 1945). For *haiku* poetry there is Harold G. Henderson, *An Introduction to Haiku* (New York: Doubleday, 1958). In addition, there are Helen Craig McCullough, *The Taiheiki; A Chronicle of Medieval Japan* (New York: Columbia University Press, 1959) and Edwin O. Reischauer and Joseph K. Yamagiwa, *Translations from Early Japanese Literature* (Cambridge: Harvard University Press, 1951), which includes background studies as well as translations of several works of the eleventh to thirteenth centuries.

For Tokugawa fiction, Howard Hibbett, *The Floating World in Japanese Fiction* (London and New York: Oxford University Press, 1959) offers an excellent background study and translations; G. W. Sargent, *The Japanese Family Storehouse* (Cambridge, England: Cambridge University Press, 1959), and William Theodore de Bary, *Five Women Who Loved Love* (Rutland, Vermont, and Tokyo: Charles E. Tuttle Co., 1956) are fine translations and studies of two outstanding works by Saikaku, *Nippon eitaigura* and *Kōshoku godai onna*.

In the field of theater, Arthur Waley, *No Plays of Japan* (Evergreen Books) is a paper-back edition of a famous earlier work (New York: Alfred A. Knopf, 1922). For Tokugawa drama and its background, there are Donald Shively, *The Love Suicide at Amijima; A Study of a Japanese Domestic Tragedy by Chikamatsu Monzaemon* (Cambridge: Harvard University Press, 1953) and Donald Keene, *The Battles of Coxinga: Chikamatsu's Puppet Play, Its Background and Importance* (London: Taylor's Foreign Press, 1951). A more general work on Kabuki is Earle Ernst, *The Kabuki Theatre* (New York: Oxford University Press, 1956; Evergreen Books).

In the field of art, a standard work with good illustrations is Robert Treat Paine and Alexander Soper, *The Art and Architecture of Japan* (Penguin Books, 1955). Langdon Warner, *The Enduring Art of Japan* (Grove Press, Evergreen Books) is a paper-back edition of a well-known earlier work (Cambridge: Harvard University Press, 1952). James Michener, *The Floating World* (New York: Random House, 1954) is an excellent general introduction to the wood-block print artists. The Charles E. Tuttle Co. (Rutland, Vermont, and Tokyo) has an excellently illustrated series of paper-back booklets on Japanese painters (Sesshū and Sōtatsu) and wood-block artists (Harunobu, Hiroshige, Hokusai, Kaigetsudō, Kiyonaga, Sharaku and Utamaro).

Illustration Acknowledgments

The map and chart on the end papers of this book and the text maps were drawn by Lilli Mautner in collaboration with the authors.

Following are acknowledgments or explanations of illustrations not included elsewhere in the text.

Title page: The character for "east" is from a manuscript in the hand of Chao Meng-fu (1254–1322), a famous calligrapher and painter, who, though living under the Mongol dynasty, was a descendant of the founder of the Sung dynasty. This is combined with a stamped tile design probably from about the third century B.C.

Page 3 Farmers in a rice field. Detail from the late Ming work on technology, *T'ien-kung k'ai-wu* (1637).

Page 20 After G. B. Cressey, *China's Geographic Foundations.*

Page 32 Drawing of a *t'ao-t'ieh* or animal mask design with ram-like horns, from an early Chinese bronze in the William Rockhill Nelson Gallery of Art at Kansas City.

Page 34 Redrawn from the original in the Museum of Far Eastern Antiquities, Stockholm.

Page 53 Redrawing of the traditional *yin-yang* symbol surrounded by the eight trigrams.

Page 56 From W. C. White, *Tomb Tile Pictures of Ancient China,* Plate LXXII.

Page 85 Stamped tile design probably from about the third century B.C. From W. C. White, *op. cit.,* Plate CVII.

Page 109 From a slide in the Fogg Art Museum, Harvard University.

Page 134 A stone figure in low relief of an *arhat* or Buddhist saint, from T'ien-lung-shan in Shansi and dating from the Northern Ch'i Dynasty (550–577). The original is in the Fogg Art Museum of Harvard University.

Page 169 Adapted from Adachi Kiroku: *Chōan Shiseki no Kenkyū,* 1933.

Page 180 From *The Art and Architecture of China* by Laurence Sickman and Alexander Soper, Penguin Books, 1936.

Page 183 Drawing after a painting on a round fan by the famous Southern Sung artist Ma Yüan and dating from the late twelfth or early thirteenth century. The original is in the Museum of Fine Arts in Boston.

Page 243 A bearded "barbarian" horseman with his felt boots and compound bow, half held in its case on his left, and quiver of arrows on his right. Horse is branded. Horseman wears a cloth cap. Redrawn from the Sung painting, "Lady Wen-chi Returning from Exile," in Museum of Fine Arts, Boston.

Page 290 "Model for four men seated and drinking." From the seventeenth-century *Mustard Seed Garden Painting Manual* (*Chieh-tzu yüan hua-chuan*).

Page 345 Developed from photographs, illustration shows the strongly fortified construction of a Peking city gate, with the outer entrance and gate tower giving access to an enclosed area, still outside the main entrance and gate tower.

Page 394 Rubbing of a design in low relief on a great bronze bell cast in the eighth century and now at the Kyŏngju Museum at the site of the old Silla capital. The central figure is a Buddhist angel.

Page 450 The *torii*, in front of the Itsukushima Shrine at Miyajima, an island in the Inland Sea, near the modern city of Hiroshima. This was the chief family shrine of the Ise Taira, a great family of the twelfth century. Since this *torii* stands in the sea, the main uprights are each buttressed by two smaller uprights.

Page 510 Tokyo National Museum.

Page 519 A mounted imperial guard as depicted in a scroll painting dated 1247. The original is in the Ōkura Collection in Tōkyō.

Page 579 Three dancers as portrayed in a woodblock print by Moronobu in *Wakoku hyakujo* ("One Hundred Women of Our Land") first published in 1698.

Page 655 Courtesy, Museum of Fine Arts, Boston.

Page 666 From Nagami Tokutarō, *Nagasaki no bijutsu shi*.

Page 669 From a woodblock entitled in Dutch "Hollandisch Groot Schip" by Isono Bunsai, who was active as an artist in Nagasaki from the 1830's through the 1850's.

CREDITS FOR PLATES

Plate 1. Photo, Air Photographic and Charting Service (MATS), U.S. Air Force.

Plate 2. J. L. Buck, *Land Utilization in China*, (University of Nanking, 1937), Atlas volume, p. 142, plate 5.

Plate 3. Detail from stone engravings on walls of Wu family shrines, Chia-hsiang, Shantung. Second century A.D. Restored by Wilma Fairbank from a rubbing.

Plate 4. From *Chao Tzu-ku erh-shih-ssu hsiao shu-hua ho-pi.*

Plate 5. From *Erh-shih-ssu hsiao t'u-shuo* (Shanghai, 1873).

Plates 6–7. Courtesy, Museum of Fine Arts, Boston.

Plate 8. Nelson Gallery — Atkins Museum, Kansas City, Missouri (Nelson Fund).

Plate 9. *Life* photo by Dmitri Kessel. Courtesy *Life* Magazine. Copr. 1955 Time Inc.

Plate 10. Restored by Wilma Fairbank from a rubbing.

Plate 11. National Museum of Korea, Seoul.

Plate 12. Hsi-ch'eng Museum, Ch'eng-tu, Szechwan.

Plates 13–14. Restored by Wilma Fairbank from rubbings.

Plate 15. Courtesy, Benjamin Rowland.

Plate 16. Courtesy, Osvald Siren.

Plate 17. Photo: Asuka-en, Nara.

Plate 18. Rowland Collection, Cambridge, Massachusetts. Courtesy, Benjamin Rowland.

Plate 19. Courtesy, Museum of Fine Arts, Boston.

Plate 20. Courtesy, Fogg Museum, Harvard, University.

Plate 21. Nelson Gallery — Atkins Museum, Kansas City, Missouri (Nelson Fund).

Plate 22. Courtesy, Laurence Sickman.

Plate 23. Photo by Paul Pelliot.

Plate 24. Courtesy, Laurence Sickman.

Plate 25. Photo: Courtesy of the American Museum of Natural History.

Plate 26. Nelson Gallery — Atkins Museum, Kansas City, Missouri (Nelson Fund).

Plate 27. The University Museum, Philadelphia.

Plates 28–31. Courtesy, Museum of Fine Arts, Boston.

Plate 32. *Ch'ing-ming shang-ho t'u-chuan*, Peking, 1958.

Plate 33. Courtesy, Museum of Fine Arts, Boston.

Plate 34. Fogg Art Museum, Harvard University.

Plate 35. Nelson Gallery — Atkins Museum, Kansas City, Missouri (Nelson Fund).

Plates 36–38. From *Ch'ing-tai ti-hou hsiang*, Palace Museum publication, Peiping, 1934.

Plate 39. Charles S. Cutting.

Plate 40. From a slide in authors' collection.

Plate 41. Chinese Association for Cultural Relations.

Plate 42. From T. Sekino, *Chōsen koseki zufu.* Korean Government Library, 1915.

Plate 43. From Plate X, Vol. II, *T'ung-kou* by H. Ikeuchi and A. Umehara, Tokyo, 1940.

Plate 44. National Museum of Korea, Seoul.

Plate 45. U.S. Army photograph

Plate 46. National Museum of Korea, Seoul.

Plate 47. Photo: Bureau of International Relations, Korean Ministry of Foreign Affairs.

Plate 48. National Museum of Korea, Seoul.

Plates 49–50. Photos: Norman F. Carver, Jr., Kalamazoo, Michigan.

Plates 51–58. Photos: Asuka-en, Nara.

Plate 59. Tokyo National Museum.

Plates 60–62. Courtesy, Museum of Fine Arts, Boston.

Plates 63–65. Tokyo National Museum.

Plate 66. Photo: Information Office, Consulate General of Japan, New York.

Plates 67–68. Photos: Japan Tourist Association.

Plate 69. Tokyo National Museum.

Plate 70. Photo: Information Office, Consulate General of Japan, New York.

Plate 71. Courtesy, Museum of Fine Arts, Boston.

Plate 72. The Art Institute of Chicago.

Plates 73–74. Courtesy, Museum of Fine Arts, Boston.

Index

(*Since practice varies widely in the use of hyphens and word divisions in non-Western names and words, hyphens and word divisions have been ignored in the listing of the non-Western names and words in this Index. Page numbers given in italics refer to maps.*)

71; recluses mentioned in, 73; and the *Mencius*, 80; quoted, 306; Itō Jinsai and, 659

Ancestor worship, in traditional Chinese society, 28, 29; in ancient China, 37, 46–47, 50; in the early Han period, 102; Chen-yen and, 171; Khitan Yeh-lü clan and, 251; in Koguryŏ, 408

Ancient civilizations, 9, *10–11*, 12

"Ancient Learning" (*Kogaku*), 658–659

Ancient and Modern Collection (Kokinshū), 516

Andaman Islands, 14

Andō Hiroshige, 656

Anesthetics, discovered by Chinese, 139

Anglo-French expedition of 1860, 381

An-hsi ("Pacify the West"), 155, *156*

Anhwei, 280, 367, *368*

Animal mask (*t'ao-t'ieh*), 45

Animism, in China, 37

Ankokuji, 564

An Lu-shan, 191–192, 204

Annam, 155, *195*, 198, *199*, *210*, 300, 317

An-nan ("Pacify the South"), 155, *156*

An-pei ("Pacify the North"), 155, *156*

Anping, 355, *368*

An Shih-kao, 146

Anti-foreignism, in late T'ang and Sung China, 235–237

Antiquarianism, in late T'ang and Sung times, 228; in Ming and Ch'ing times, 383; in Ashikaga Japan, 569

Antoku, 525, 528, 529, 531

An-tun (Marcus Aurelius Antoninus), 108

An-tung ("Pacify the East"), 155, *156*

An-yang, 35–36, 39, 44–45

A-pao-chi, 251

Aquinas, Thomas, 238

Arabs, and late T'ang and Sung China, 157, 191, 215; and Chinese foreign trade, 216; and rise of Mongol power, 261; obstruct Sino-Western trade, 280, 281; and Mongol Empire, 285; sea routes of, 321; missions to China from, 322

Arai Hakuseki, 622, 647, 660, 663, 665

Aramaic, 257

Archaeology, of China, 13–14, 32–36; of Korea, 401, 403–405, 408; of Japan, 456–462

Architecture, of the Shang, 47–48; of the Han, 110–111; of Chinese pagodas, 146; of Six Dynasties and early T'ang China, 179–180; of the late T'ang and Sung, 226; of the Khitan, 254; of the Ming and Ch'ing periods, 389; early Japanese, 489, 510; of the Kamakura period, 548, 549; of the Ashikaga period, 566–567;

of the Azuchi-Momoyama period, 586; of the Tokugawa period, 653

Arima, *592*, 597, 605

Aristocracy, Shang, 47; Chou, 51; Earlier Han, 97; merges into the "gentry," 186; fading of, in T'ang and Sung times, 220–221; of early Japan, 471, 486, 498–499; and central government, 501; of the court, 503, 505; local leadership and, 521–522; and feudalism, 544–545, 572, 575; and Hideyoshi, 588; rural, 602–603

Aristotle, 71

Armenia, *268*, 270

Armor, early Japanese, 460, 523

Army of the Green Standard, 365

Arquebuses, 583

Art, of the Shang period, 45; of the Chou period, 56; of the Han period, 109–110; Chinese Buddhist, 171, 178–179; of the late T'ang and Sung, 226–228; of Korea, 408, 413, 421, 436; of early Japan, 488–490; of Fujiwara Japan, 510–511; of the Kamakura period, 549; of the Ashikaga period, 566; of the Tokugawa period, 653–656

Asama, Mount, 620, 624

Asano, *592*, 605

Ashigaru ("light foot"), 572

Ashikaga family, 554

Ashikaga School, *530*, 564

Ashikaga shogunate, relations of, with Korea, 442; founding of, 553; government of, 554–557; growth of domestic economy during, 557–560; foreign trade and diplomatic relations during, 560–563; Zen culture during, 563–566; art, literature and thought during, 566–570; latter period of, 570–574; decline of feudal system of, 574–578; end of, 584

Ashikaga shoguns. *See* specific shoguns listed according to their given names.

Asoka, 143

Assembled Essentials on the T'ang (T'ang hui yao), 232

Assortment of Writings (Gunsho ruijū), 665

Assortment of Writings Continued (Zoku gunsho ruijū), 665

Astronomy, of the Chou period, 39; of the Han period, 109, 110; of the Six Dynasties and early T'ang, 178; study of, in Tokugawa Japan, 666

Asuka period, 489n.

"Attendance by turn." *See* sankin kōtai system.

Audit Officers (*Kageyushi*), 501–502

Auguries. *See* divination.

Index

Borneo, 317, *318*
Bow, 252, 266, 523; *see also* compound bow; crossbow.
Brahmaputra River, *358*, 360
"Branch monastery" (*kokubunji*), 491
Breathing exercises, 102, 139
Brick tea, 329
Bronze, in early China, 33; tripods, 33, 45; in Shang culture, 35–36, 48; mirrors of, 111, 179; introduced to Korea, 402; in Yayoi culture, 458; 459
Bronzes, Shang, 44–45, 185; Chou, 49; Sung interest in, 228
Brothels, 224, 644–645
Buddha, 62, 140; teachings of the, 142–143, 144; of the Future, 294
Buddhism, coming of, to China, 135, 137, 145–147; influence of, on popular Taoism, 139–141; origin and spread of, 141–145; age of, in China, 147–148, 170; decline of, in Asia, 148; in the Six Dynasties period, 158; development of Chinese sects of, 170–172; degeneration of, in China, 172, 175, 185; role of, in Chinese society, 172–174; persecuted by the Northern Wei, Northern Chou and the T'ang, 174–175; cultural influence of, 175–176; persecuted by the Later Chou, 197; and late T'ang and Sung arts, 226; persecuted in late T'ang and Sung China, 236; influence of, on Neo-Confucianism, 237, 239; and Khitan Liao, 253; in the Hsi Hsia kingdom, 255; adopted by Mongol rulers of China, 271, 278; introduced into Tibet, 277; in Koguryŏ, 406, 408; in Paekche, 408; in Silla, 410, 412–414; in Koryŏ, 420; decline of, in Yi-dynasty Korea, 434; spread of, to Japan, 474–475; in early Japan, 488–494; assimilated in Fujiwara Japan, 507–510; revival of, in Kamakura period, 544–549; persecution of Pure Land sect of, 545–546; in the Ashikaga period, 577–578; and early Christianity in Japan, 582; decline of, in Japan, 615
Buddhist art, in China, 178–179, 226, 227; in Korea, 413, 421; in early Japan, 488–491, 492, 510
Buddhist "law," 143
Buddhist missionaries, early, 145–146; in Six Dynasties China, 176; to Japan, 490
Buddhist monasteries, in China, 158, 173–175, 180; in Silla, 413; in P'o-hai, 414; in Koryŏ, 420; in early Japan, 480, 491–493, 504; military ventures of, 510, 526, 529; in the Kamakura period, 538, 549, 552; in the Ashikaga period, 577; subjugated by Oda Nobunaga, 584

Buddhist scriptures, 143–144, 146, 147, 171; printed in T'ang and Sung China, 229; printed in Koryŏ, 420
Bugyō (commissioners), 587
Buke shohatto (*Laws for the Military Houses*), 613, 614
Bunjinga (Literati School), 653
Bunrakuza, 648
Bureau of Archivists (*Kurōdo-dokoro*), 502
Bureau of Military Affairs (*Shu-mi-yüan*), 199, 200, 274
Bureau of Policy Criticism (*Chien-yüan*), 201
Bureau of Yin and Yang (*Ommyō-ryō*), 495
Bureaucracy, in "Oriental" society, 48; appearance of, in Eastern Chou period, 58, 72; in Earlier Han period, 96–98, 107; in factional struggles, 116–117; and the dynastic cycle, 118; and Wang Mang, 121; in Later Han period, 124–126; in Sui and T'ang empires, 163–166; under the T'ang, 168, 186, 190, 192; under the Sung, 197, 200–203, 205–206; of the Northern Sung, 207–208; of the Southern Sung, 211, under the Mongols, 273, 277, 278; under the Ming, 298, 299, 316–317; developed by the Manchus, 353; under the Ch'ing, 373; of Koryŏ, 417; in Yi-dynasty Korea, 426, 431–432; and factionalism in the Yi government, 437–442; in Tokugawa Japan, 612; *see also* civil service; examination system.
Burials, of the Shang, 47–48; of the Chou, 49; handled by Buddhist monasteries, 173; in Silla, 409; *see also* tombs; tumuli.
Burma, 98; languages of, 15, *16*, 17; Buddhism in, 144; invaded by Mongols, 273; Ch'ing expeditions against, 390
Burmese language, *16*, 17
"Burning of the Books," 88
"Burning of the Sanjō Palace," 544
Bushi, 525, 541, 602n.
Bushidō, 541, 615, 656, 659
Byōdōin, 510
Byzantium, 133, 148–149

Calendar, Chinese, in Chou times, 77; lunar, 117; adopted by Prince Shōtoku, 476
Calligraphy, 43, 88, 179, 228–229
"Calons," 363
Cambaluc, 279, 283
Cambodia, Khmer language of, *16*, 18; Buddhism in, 144; relations of, with Ming China, 317; Japanese in, 598

Index

Chou, Duke of, 38, 50, 57, 70, 121

Chou dynasty, 38–39, 113

Chou dynasty of Empress Wu, 157

Chou, Later, 196–197

Chou, Northern, 153, 155, 167, 169, 175

Chou period, early, 49–50; individual states during, 50–51; society of, 51–52; growth of economy and culture during, 53–57; growth of political and cultural unit during, 57–60; political instability during, 60–62; philosophers of, 62–64; classics produced during, 64–69; schools of thought during, 69–84; and Toynbee's theory of civilization, 128–129; social change during, 135

Chou, state of, 38, 57, *59*, 60–62, 86

Chou, Western, 53–54; and Korean foundation myths, 403

Chou-k'ou-tien, 13–14

Chou Kung. *See* Chou, Duke of.

Chou li (Rituals of Chou), 67–68, 121, 206

Chou Tun-i, 238

Christianity, under the Yüan, 277; reaches the Philippines, 395; comes to Korea, 447; comes to Japan, 581–582; persecuted by Hideyoshi, 588–589; in Hideyoshi's army, 590; persecuted by the Tokugawa, 595–599; in eighteenth-century Japan, 665

Christians, employed by Mongols, 276; at Yüan court, 281

Chu (prefecture), 417n.

Ch'u dynasty (Ten Kingdoms), *195*, 196

Ch'u, King of (Later Han), 146

Ch'u state (Eastern Chou period), *59*; rise of, 59–62; Ch'ü Yüan and, 69; and early Taoism, 73–74; one of the "Six States," 86; fall of, 86; Hsiang Yu and royal family of, 91–92

Ch'uan-ch'i, 386

Ch'üan-chou, *199*, *210*, *269*, 323; trade to, 215–216, 285

Chuang, King of Ch'u, 61

Chuang-tzu, 74, 75, 102, 138

Chu Hsi, purged from office, 209; and the *T'ung-chien kang-mu*, 231; philosophy of, 238–241; and Wang Yang-ming, 308–309; complete works of, 371; *chia* system of, 374; attacked by Ch'ing scholars, 377, 379; teachings of, in Japan, 616, 657–659

Chü-jen ("recommended man"), 305

Chu-ko Liang, 130

Chumbi, *358*, 360

Chün. See commanderies.

Chün-chi-ch'u ("Military Plans Office"), 372

Ch'un ch'iu. *See Spring and Autumn Annals.*

Ch'un ch'iu fan lu (Luxuriant Dew of the Spring and Autumn Annals), 106

Chung (conscientiousness toward others; loyalty), 71

Ch'ungch'ŏng, *430*, 431

Chungin ("middle people"), 428, 436

Chungjong of the Yi dynasty. *See* Yi Chungjong.

Chungking, 344

Chung-kuo, 37

Chung-shu Men-hsia (Secretariat-Chancellery), 200

Chung-shu-sheng (Imperial Secretariat), 168; (Central Chancellery) 274, 299, 315

Chung yung. See Doctrine of the Mean.

Chün-t'ien system. *See* "equal field" system.

Chün-tzu (gentleman), 71

Chün-wei (Military Governor), 87

Chün-yao ("equal service"), 303, 338

Chusan Island, and piracy, 331–332, 356

Chūshin-gura (The Treasury of Loyal Retainers), 648

Chu-shu chi-nien (Bamboo Annals), 69

Chu Shun-shui, 657, 663

Chūsonji, 520, 536

Chu Ti. *See* Yung-lo.

Ch'u tz'u (Elegies of Ch'u), 69

Chu Wen (Chu Ch'üan-chung), 194, 196

Ch'ü Yüan, 69, 111

Chu Yüan-chang. *See* Hung-wu.

Cinnabar, 102, 138, 139

"Cinnabar fields," 139

"Circuits" (*tao*), 167, 201, 203, 301; (*lu*), 201; (*dō*), 482

"Circulating *nembutsu*," 508

Civil Affairs, Ministry of, 485

Civil Governor (*shou*), 87

Civil service, under the Sung, 201–203, 205; local "permanent," 313

Civil service examinations. *See* examination system.

Clan system, Chinese, 37, 251

Classes, the four traditional, 30, 602; in Shang times, 48; in Chou times, 51, 55; in Earlier Han period, 96–97; in Koryŏ society, 417–418, 425; under the Yi dynasty, 427–428, 430; in Ashikaga Japan, 575–578; of Tokugawa society, 602–603, 634, 661–662

Classic of Changes (I ching), 65–66, 68, 105, 138, 238

Classic of Documents (Shu ching or *Shang shu)*, 65, 67–68, 88, 103, 121, 378

Index

Li T'ai-po. *See* Li Po.
Literacy, in East Asia, 43; in Eastern Chou China, 58; in Tokugawa Japan, 646
Literary criticism, 181
Literary inquisition of the Ch'ien-lung emperor, 382
Literary Selections (Wen hsüan), 181
Literati *(ju)*, 72, 105, 304–305
"Literati-painting" *(wen-jen-hua)*, 385, 653
Literature, essay on by Pan Ku, 114; of Six Dynasties and early T'ang China, 180–182; of T'ang and Sung times, 228–229, 232–235; of the Ming period, 308; popular, 386–388; of Fujiwara Japan, 515–518; of feudal Japan, 542, 568–570; of Tokugawa period, 647–653
Li Tzu-ch'eng, 343, 354–355, 366
Liu family (Han dynasty), 122
Liu Chih-chi, 231
Liu-ch'iu Islands, 317; *see also* Ryūkyū Islands.
Liu Hsiang, 114
Liu Hsieh, 181
Liu Hsin, 114, 121
Liu Hsiu. *See* Han Kuang Wu Ti.
Liu Pang (or Liu Chi). *See* Han Kao Tsu.
Liu Pei, 127, 128, 130
Liu-pu. See Six Ministries.
Liu Sung, 132, 134, 464
Liu Yen, 192
Liu Yü, 132
Liu Yüan, 150
"Living Buddha," 361
Li Yü, 234
Li Yüan, 155
Li Yüan-hao, 255
Local magistrates *(daikan)*, 613
Loess, 22–23
Lo Kuan-chung, 387
Lo-lang (Nangnang), *100*, 101, 111, 403–406
Longevity, search for, 102
Lotus sect. *See* Nichiren sect.
Lotus Sutra, 144, 171, 490, 546
Louis IX of France, 283
Louis XIV of France, 282
"Lowborn" *(ch'ŏnmin)*, 419, 422, 425, 428, 446; *(semmin)*, 487, 521, 575
Lo-yang, *3*r, *100*, *152*; capital of the Eastern Chou, 53; capital of the Later Han, 123, *127*; capital of Wei, 130; capital of the Western Chin, 132; An Shih-kao at, 146; Northern Wei capital, 147, *153*; and the canal system, *162*; captured by An Lu-shan, 191; during the Five Dynasties, 196

Loyalty, in China, 71; in Japan, 540–541, 618
Lu ("circuits"), 201
Lü, Empress, 94, 117
Lü (penal law), 167
Lu state (Eastern Chou period), 50, 57, 59, 62; events of recorded in *Spring and Autumn Annals*, 66; native state of Confucius, 69–70
Lu Chiu-yüan (Hsiang-shan), 238, 309
Lung-men, 147, *152*, 178
Lung-shan culture. *See* Black Pottery culture.
Lun heng (Disquisitions), 105
Lun yü. See Analects.
Lü Pu-wei, 86–87, 105
Lü-shih ch'un ch'iu (The Spring and Autumn Annals of Mr. Lü), 105
Lute *(p'i-pa)*, 109
Lu-Wang School. *See* Idealism.
Luxuriant Dew of the Spring and Autumn Annals (Ch'un ch'iu fan lu), 106

Mabiki, 630
Macao, 597
Machi Bugyō (Town Commissioners), 613
Ma Chih-yüan, 234
Madagascar, 18
Maeda, 590, *592–593*, 594, 604, 605, 610, 633
Magadha, 142
Magatama, 409, 460, 467, 472
Magistrate. *See* district magistrates; local magistrates *(daikan)*.
Ma-han people, 405–406, 408
Mahayana, 144–145, 148, 171, 412–414
Maitreya, 294
Maize, 393
Makura no sōshi (Pillow Book), 516
Malacca, 322, 336
Malay languages, *16*, 18
Malay Peninsula, 9, 14, 108, *318*; tributary to China, 273, 317; and Chinese junk trade, 336
Malaya, Chinese-speaking people in, 15–17; Malay languages of, 18; spread of Islam to, 395
Man Who Spent His Life in Love, The (Kōshaku ichidai otoko), 650–651
Manager *(kanrei)*, 554
Managers, of estates, 521
Man-chou (Manchu), 352
Manchu script, 257, 352, 369
Manchuria, languages of, 15–18; Jürched in, 208–209; part of Chinese Empire under "barbarian" dynasties, 243; Khitan control over, 249; and the Yüan,

Metals, in early China, 33; in early Korea, 402; in early Japan, 458

Metropolitan degree-holder. *See chin-shih.*

Metsuke, 607, 613

Mexico, 597

Miao-Yao languages, *16,* 17, *358*

Michinaga, 504, 516, 518, 526

Middle East, Han silk found in, 109; weakness of, against Mongols, 261; reached by Ming maritime expeditions, 322, *368–369; see also* Near East, West Asia.

"Middle Kingdom," 37

"Middle people" (*chungin*), 428, 436

"Middle Way," 142

Mi Fu (Mi Fei), 228

Miidera, 509

Mikawa, *530,* 585

Milfoil plant, 65

Military Affairs, Bureau of (*Shu-mi-yüan*), 199, 200, 274

Military colonies (*t'un-tien*), 159

Military Governor (*chün-wei*), 87

"Military Plans Office" (*Chün-chi-ch'u*), 372

Military system, during the Six Dynasties, 159; of the T'ang, 160, 189–190; of the Sui, 164; of the Sung, 197–198, 205–206; of the Khitan Liao, 251–252; of the Jürched Chin, 258; of the Mongols, 265–266; of the Ming, 301; of the Manchus, 364–365; of early Japan, 485–486, 522–524; in feudal Japan, 533; of Tokugawa Japan, 604

"Militia" (*fu-ping*) system, 159, 189–190

Milk, Chinese abhorrence for, 24, 47

Millet, 50, 161, 250

"Millet Ruler" (Hou Chi), 50

Mimana. *See* Kaya.

Min, *195,* 196

Min "dialect," *16,* 17

Minamoto family, 522, 525–531, 534, 550–551, 591

Minamoto (individuals). *See* under given names.

Ming *Collected Statutes,* 329, 352

Ming dynasty, stability during, 290–291; ethnocentrism during, 291–293, 306; founding of, 294–295; Peking under, 296–297; administration of, 297–304, *300;* law of, 302–304; land and taxes under, 302–303; examination system under, 304–306; educational system of, 306–308; literary production during, 308; philosophy of, 308–309; gentry under, 309–313; despotism of, 314–317; foreign relations and tribute system of, 317ff.,

330–333; empire of, *318;* maritime expeditions of, 321–323; anti-commercialism of, 323–325, 331; and the Mongol problem, 325–330; troubles of, with Japan, 330–333; aids Korea against the Japanese, 332–333, 443; economic growth during, 333–340; collapse of, 340–344; and Liao-tung, 346; commanderies of, 348–349; control of, over Manchuria, 349–350; and Nurhachi, 351–354; and Koryŏ, 425; and the Manchu subjugation of Korea, 444

Ming History (Ming shih), 344, 371

Ming loyalist scholars, 375–378, 657, 663

Ming chia. See Dialecticians.

Ming Huang. *See* T'ang Ming Huang.

Ming-i tai-fang lu (A Plan for the Prince), 376

Ming-ju hsüeh-an, 376

Ming shih. See Ming History.

Ming Ti. *See* Han Ming Ti.

Ming T'ai Tsu. *See* Hung-wu.

Mining, in China, 212, 216, 218

Minister of the Left (*Sadaijin*), 485, 554

Minister of the Right (*Udaijin*), 485, 486, 504, 544, 586

Ministries (*shō*), 485

Ministry, of Civil Affairs, 485; of the Imperial Household, 485; of Justice, 168, 485; of Personnel, 165, 168, 305; of Popular Affairs, 485; of Public Works, 168; of Revenue, 168; of Rites, 164, 168, 305

Minor Merit Subjects, 427

Mirror of the Eastland (Azuma kagami), 544

Mirrors, bronze, of Han times, 111; of the T'ang period, 179; in the Yayoi culture, 458; Japanese sacred mirror, 467, 468; in Shintō, 472

Miso, 641

Missionaries, Christian, in China, 307, 357, 370; and Korea, 447; in Japan, 581–582, 588–589, 596–598; *see also* Buddhist missionaries.

Mito, *592–593,* 605, 610; historians of, 663

Mitsui, 639–640, 642

Miura family, 539

Miura Baien, 660

Miya ("palace; shrine"), 471

Miyajima. *See* Itsukushima.

Mizuno Tadakuni, 625–626

Moluccas, *318,* 336

Mo-tzu (also Mo-tzu), 78–79, 80

Momoyama ("Peach Hill"), *481,* 586

Mon, *16,* 18

Monasteries. *See* Buddhist monasteries; Taoist monasteries; Zen monasteries.

Index

Stoicism, 73
Stone tablets, 107, 130
Stone tools, 33, 47, 456
"Storehouse" men *(dosō)*, 558
Straits of Malacca, *318*, 336
Strange Stories from a Chinese Studio (Liao-chai chih-i), 386
Strategic and Economic Advantages and Disadvantages of the Districts and States of the Empire (T'ien-hsia chün-kuo li-ping-shu), 377
"Street committee" system. *See pao-chia* system.
Students, Japanese, in T'ang China, 477–478
Stupas, 146
Subprefects, 301, 367
Subprefectures, under the T'ang *(hsien)*, 167; under the Sung, 201; under the Jürched Chin, 258; under the Ming and Ch'ing *(chou)*, 299–300; in Korea *(kun* or *gun)*, 411, 417
Succession, in ancient China, 37; among Shang rulers, 38; in the Chou period, 49; in the Yamato state, 469
Sugar cane, 622, 636
Sugawara no Michizane, 504, 506
Sugita Gempaku, 667
Sui dynasty, conquests of, 133, 154; reunifies China, 153–154; collapse of, 154–155, 161; "equal field" system of, 159–161; revives examination and school system, 164; local government under, 167; fails to conquer Koguryŏ, 410; diplomatic relations of, with Japan, 476–477
Suicide, 541, 645
Suiko, 475
Sui Wen Ti, 153–154, 164, 167, 410
Sui Yang Ti, 154, 162, 410
Sumatra, *318;* visited by I-ching, 146–147; tributary to the Sui, 154; tributary to the Yüan, 273; visited by Friar Odoric, 282–283; relations of, with the Ming, 317; Ch'eng Ho's fighting in, 322
Sumitomo (Fujiwara), 525
Summer palace, 362, 370
"Summer Tax," 302, 339
Sumō, 614
Sumptuary laws, 551, 625, 633, 636
Sumpu, *593*, 595
Sun Goddess, 463, 465, 468, 472, 508, 665
"Sun Princess," 463
Sun Ch'üan, 127
Sung History. See Sung shu.
"Sung Learning," 377–378

Sung, Northern, a period of Chinese history, 183–185; government of, 197–198; military weakness of, 198; imperial power of, 198–200; empire of, *199;* government of, 200–202; decline and reform in, 203–207; financial difficulties of, 204; bureaucratic factionalism under, 205–206; and Wang An-shih's reforms, 206–208; and the Jürched Chin, 208; compared to the Southern Sung, 211; maritime trade under, 215; and "barbarian" empires, 244; and the Khitan Liao, 254; and the Hsi Hsia, 255
Sung period, "commercial revolution" in, 211–214; trade during, 212–217; expansion of currency system during, 217–219; early modern society of, 220–224; fading of aristocracy during, 220–221; urbanization of society during, 222–224; decline in status of women during, 224–225; development of arts during, 225–228; literature of, 232–235; statesman-literatus ideal of, 235; Neo-Confucianism in, 235–241; cultural stability achieved during, 241
Sung, Southern, *210, 262;* establishment of, 208ff.; and the Jürched Chin, 209, 258–259; maritime trade under, 215–216; conquered by the Mongols, 271–273
Sung state (Eastern Chou), 50, 57, 59, 62
Sungari River, 208, *210*, 255, 349
Sungars. *See* Dzungars.
Sung Chiang, 386
Sung Hui Tsung, 208, 228
Sŭngjŏngwŏn. See Royal Secretariat.
Sung Kao Tsung, 209
Sungkiang region, 336
Sung Shen Tsung, 206, 208
Sung shu (Sung History), 464, 468–470, 476
Sung T'ai Tsu (Chao K'uang-yin), 197–198, 203, 205
Sung T'ai Tsung, 197
Sung Ying-hsing, 308
Sung Yüan hsüeh-an, 376
Sunspots, 110
Sun-tzu, 79
Superintendencies of Merchant Shipping *(Shih-po-ssu)*, 215, 285, 320
Superintendency of Dependencies. *See* Mongolian Superintendency.
"Superior Capital." *See* Shang-tu.
Supreme Capital of the Liao, 253, 256
Supreme Court of Justice *(Hyōjōsho)*, 613
Supreme Ti, 46

Index

Index

HIJ—R—73210/698765